RADIO PROGRAMS, 1924–1984

ALSO BY VINCENT TERRACE

Experimental Television, Test Films, Pilots and Trial Series, 1925 through 1995: Seven Decades of Small Screen Almosts
(McFarland, 1997)

Television Specials: 3,201 Entertainment Spectaculars, 1939 through 1993
(McFarland, 1995)

Television Character and Story Facts: Over 110,000 Details from 1,008 Shows, 1945–1992
(McFarland, 1993)

Radio Programs, 1924–1984

A Catalog of Over 1800 Shows

by VINCENT TERRACE

McFarland & Company, Inc., Publishers
Jefferson, North Carolina, and London

Index prepared with the help of Jennifer Santarsiero.

British Library Cataloguing-in-Publication data are available

Library of Congress Cataloguing-in-Publication Data

Terrace, Vincent, 1948–
Radio programs, 1924–1984 : a catalog of over 1800 shows / by Vincent Terrace.
p. cm.
Includes index.
ISBN 0-7864-0351-9 (library binding : 50# alkaline paper) ∞
1. Radio programs—United States—Catalogs. I. Title.
PN1991.9.T47 1999
016.79144'75'0973—dc21 98-26269
CIP

Manufactured in the United States of America

McFarland & Company, Inc., Publishers
Box 611, Jefferson, North Carolina 28640

Contents

Preface

This book is the largest and most detailed description of radio series ever published—an alphabetical listing of 1,835 entertainment programs broadcast from 1924 through 1984.

A considerable amount of information has been culled from the actual programs. The listings provide casts (performers and their characters), information about character relationships, storylines, announcers, musicians, producers, hosts, variety and dramatic show regulars, dates, networks, running times, and miscellaneous interesting facts.

There is also information regarding the radio series that became television series, including those programs that were adapted to television during the experimental years of the small screen.

The book includes 517 actual radio program openings and 243 closings. It is completely indexed and cross-referenced.

Much of the information in this book cannot be found in any other reference work to date.

Photographs used in this book are courtesy of Howard Frank of Personality Photos, Inc., Post Office Box 50, Midwood Station, Brooklyn, New York 11230.

Most of the tapes of programs used in researching this book came from Andy Blatt of Vintage Broadcasts, Post Office Box 50065, Staten Island, New York 10305 (1-800-418-1445).

A Note on Radio Networks

ABC is the American Broadcasting Company. It was formed in 1944 (see NBC for further information).

CBS is the Columbia Broadcasting System. It was formed in 1927 when United Independent Broadcasters merged with the Columbia Phonograph Broadcasting Company.

"Mutual" is the Mutual Broadcasting System. It was formed in 1934 and is also known as MBS.

NBC is the National Broadcasting Company. The first American network, it was formed in 1926 by General Electric, RCA and Westinghouse under the leadership of David Sarnoff. From 1926 to late 1944, NBC owned two separate networks: NBC Red and NBC Blue. When the Federal Communications Commission began its investigation of chain broadcasting and monopolies, NBC sold the Blue Network to Life Savers candy company owner Edward J. Noble, who transformed it into ABC. The Red Network became simply NBC. In the text, NBC Blue is listed as NBC Blue and NBC Red as simply NBC; however, when a show aired on both NBC Red and NBC Blue, "Red" has been added to prevent confusion.

THE PROGRAMS

1. The A&P Gypsies. Variety, 60 min., NBC, 1924–1936.

A program of music sponsored by the Great Atlantic and Pacific Tea Company (the supermarket chain known as A&P). The series, which began in 1923 over a local New York radio station (WEAF), originally featured Russian, gypsy and Hungarian music.

Host: Harry Horlick. ***Vocalist:*** Frank Parker. ***Announcers:*** Phil Carlin, Milton Cross, Ed Thorgersen. ***Orchestra:*** Harry Horlick.

2. The Abbott and Costello Kids' Show. Children, 30 min., ABC, 1947–1949.

A Saturday morning program of comedy routines, songs, awards, quizzes and performances by guest stars (child and adult). The series featured a nine-year-old vocalist and a young boy as the announcer. The two featured segments were:

The Lou Costello, Jr., Youth Foundation Award. This segment recognized outstanding children under the age of 16 (for example, William Robinson, Jr., who braved a fierce snowstorm to find help for his sick father). Recipients were selected by letters submitted by listeners. Merchandise prizes and a gold trophy were awarded to the selected child.

Bubble or Nothing. A quiz segment wherein four boys and four girls competed. Each was given a piece of chewing gum and at the sound of a bell had to blow a bubble. The first boy and the first girl to blow a bubble won a prize. The remaining six players also won a prize if they could correctly answer a silly question (for example, "In what state do we find the Ohio River?").

Hosts: Bud Abbott and Lou Costello. ***Vocalist:*** Anna Mae Slaughter. ***Announcer:*** Johnny McGovern.

OPENING

ANNOUNCER: The American Broadcasting Company presents *The Abbott and Costello Kids' Show*, transcribed in Hollywood, with our guest star, Norma Jean Nilsson, Cookie on the *Blondie* show, and featuring the Lou Costello, Jr., Youth Foundation Award. Every Saturday morning on this program, some lucky boy or girl will receive hundreds of dollars in valuable gifts and the Lou Costello, Jr., Youth Foundation gold trophy for good citizenship. We'll tell you how to win it later in the program, but first let's have some laughs with our stars, Bud Abbott and Lou Costello.

LOU: H-e-y, A-b-b-o-t-t!

CLOSING

BUD: Well, boys and girls, that's all for today.

LOU: Hey, kids, be sure to listen next Saturday when we will have two guests, really two guest stars, that great cowboy star Tim Holt and his dad, Jack Holt. Well, so long kids, till next Saturday.

ANNOUNCER: Listen to next week's award winner and remember you can nominate a winner by writing a letter to Abbott and Costello, Hollywood, California. And don't miss the regular *Abbott and Costello Show* on Wednesday nights. *The Abbott and Costello Kids' Show* is transcribed in Hollywood.

3. The Abbott and Costello Show. Comedy, 30 min., NBC, summer of 1940; NBC, 1942–1947; ABC, 1947–1949.

A weekly series of sketches highlighting the comedic talents of motion picture stars Bud Abbott and Lou Costello. Many of the skits revolved around Bud and Lou's efforts to succeed in some sort of business venture (for example, starting their own exterminating company) or with Lou's efforts to achieve a goal (for example, becoming a famous singer). Guests assisted in the sketches and songs, and musical numbers were performed between

Bud Abbott (bottom) and Lou Costello starred in *The Abbott and Costello Show*.

acts. A recurring skit on the ABC version of the program was "Sam Shovel, Private Detective," a spoof of radio detective series with Lou as the dauntless Sam Shovel and Bud as Lt. Abbott of the police department. *Other regular characters:* Sebastian, Lou's troublesome nephew (later called Lou's kid brother); Ketsel, the Jewish foil; and various members of the Melonhead family (for example, Judge Melonhead, Officer Melonhead, Lawyer Melonhead)—people who became involved with Bud and Lou's antics.

Cast: Bud Abbott (*Bud Abbott*); Lou Costello (*Lou Costello/Sebastian*); Sid Fields (*The Melonheads*); Artie Auerbrook (*Ketsel*). ***Regulars:*** Elvia Allman, Iris Adrian, Mel Blanc, Wally Brown, Sharon Douglas, Verna Felton, Lou Krogman, Pat McGeehan, Frank Nelson, Martha Wentworth, Benay Venuta. ***Vocalists:*** Amy Arnell, Connie Haines, Marilyn Maxwell, Susan Miller, Marilyn Williams, The Delta Rhythm Boys, The Les Baxter Singers. ***Announcers:*** Frank Bingman, Jim Doyle, Ken Niles, Michael Roy. ***Orchestra:*** Skinnay Ennis, Charles Hoff, Matty Matlock, Jack Meakin, Will Osborne, Freddie Rich, Leith Stevens, Peter Van Steeden.

EARLY OPENING (1943)

ANNOUNCER: *The Abbott and Costello Program.* Listen to the music of Freddie Rich and his orchestra and the songs of Connie Haines and tonight's special guest, Bert Gordon, the Mad Russian of radio, and starring Abbott and Costello.

CLOSING (1943)

BUD: Good night folks, good night neighbors.

LOU: Good night to everybody in Paterson, New Jersey.

ANNOUNCER: Tune in next week for another great *Abbott and Costello Show* with our special guest Edward Arnold. This is Ken Niles wishing you all a very pleasant good night from Hollywood.

LATER OPENING (1948)

LOU: H-e-y, A-b-b-o-t-t! What time is it?

BUD: Why, it's time for *The Abbott and Costello Show.* We're on the air for ABC here in Hollywood.

LOU: Well, what are we waiting for? Let's go with *The Abbott and Costello Show.*

ANNOUNCER: Yes, it's *The Abbott and Costello Show*, produced and transcribed in Hollywood for your listening and laughing pleasure. Chuckles by the carload and music by Matty Matlock. So hold on to your chairs, folks, they're here, Bud Abbott and Lou Costello.

CLOSING (1948)

ANNOUNCER: Listen each Wednesday night at this time for the great *Abbott and Costello Show*, produced and transcribed in Hollywood by Charles Vanda, featuring Marilyn Williams and Matty Matlock and his orchestra. Be sure to stay tuned for the outstanding enjoyment that follows throughout the evening on these ABC stations.

THE ABBOTT MYSTERIES *see* **THE ADVENTURES OF THE ABBOTTS**

4. THE ABE BURROWS SHOW. Comedy, 15 min., CBS, 1947–1948.

Humorist Abe Burrows in an adult-oriented program of monologues, songs and celebrity interviews. When the program left the air in 1948, a revamped early morning version ("Breakfast with Burrows") appeared on CBS during the summer of 1949.

Host: Abe Burrows. ***Announcer:*** Michael Fitzmaurice. ***Music:*** The Milton DeLugg Quartet.

5. ABIE'S IRISH ROSE. Comedy-Drama, 30 min., NBC, 1942–1944.

Ethnic differences as seen through the marriage of a Jewish boy (Abraham "Abie" Levy) and an Irish Catholic girl (Rosemary Murphy) in New York City in 1942. Based on the Broadway play by Anne Nichols. *Other regular characters:* Pat Murphy (a widower), Rosemary's father; Solomon "Sol" Levy (a widower), Abie's father; Isaac Cohen, Sol's friend, a lawyer; Marmala Cohen, Sol's wife. Sol owns the Solomon Levy Department Store in the Bronx. While Abie worked for his father, he took a second job as the Security Manager of the Flanagan and Robinson Department Store (in New Jersey) when Rosemary gave birth to twins.

Cast: Richard Bond, Sydney Smith, Richard Coogan, Clayton "Bud" Collyer (*Abie Levy*); Betty Winkler, Mercedes McCambridge, Julie Stevens, Marion Shockley (*Rosemary Levy*); Walter Kinsella (*Pat Murphy*); Alfred White, Charlie Cantor, Alan Reed (*Solomon Levy*); Menasha Skulnik (*Isaac Cohen*); Anna Appel (*Marmala Cohen*); Dolores Gillen (*The twins*). ***Announcer:*** Howard Petrie. ***Music:*** Joe Stopak.

OPENING

ANNOUNCER: Yes folks, Drene, America's largest-selling shampoo, once again brings you that lovable, laughable show, Anne Nichols' *Abie's Irish Rose*. And now for tonight's visit with the Murphys and the Levys.

CLOSING

ANNOUNCER: Now, be sure to listen again next Saturday night at this same time for another episode of the Murphys, the Levys and their friends. *Abie's Irish Rose* is dedicated to the spirit of freedom and equality which gives to this nation its greatness. It is America. *Abie's Irish Rose* is written by Anne Nichols and brought to you by Procter and Gamble, the makers of Drene, America's largest-selling shampoo. This is Howard Petrie. Good night.

6. ACADEMY AWARD THEATER. Anthology, 30 min., CBS, 3/30/46 to 12/18/46.

Condensed versions of Academy Award–winning motion pictures that used as many of the original film casts as possible. Adaptations included the following:

Suspicion. Cary Grant and Ann Todd in a story about a woman's efforts to prove that her husband is planning to murder her.

The Maltese Falcon. Humphrey Bogart, Sydney Greenstreet and Mary Astor in Dashiell Hammett's tale of detective Sam Spade's efforts to recover the Maltese Falcon, a priceless statue stolen by Casper Gutman, "The Fat Man."

Portrait of Jennie. Joan Fontaine and John Lund in the story of an impoverished New York artist who believes he has found the ideal model—beautiful and captivating—until she begins to mature with incredible speed.

The Front Page. Pat O'Brien and Adolphe Menjou in the Hecht-MacArthur play about a newspaper reporter's attempts to cover one last story—that of a convicted murderer who has escaped.

Music: Leith Stevens. ***Producer:*** Dee Engelbach. ***Adaptations:*** Frank Wilson.

7. ACTION. Audition (Anthology), 30 min., produced on 1/15/45.

A proposed series of high action stories with William Gargan as the host and star (to take on various roles). The audition episode, "High Explosive," starred Jane Wyatt and Robert Lowery in a story about men who risk their lives transporting dangerous cargo.

OPENING

ANNOUNCER: From Hollywood, Radio Creators present *Action*. Tonight, "High Explosive." In exactly 60 seconds, *Action* raises the curtain on Act One, but first, your weekly Man of Action, screen, stage and radio star, William Gargan.

GARGAN: Good evening, ladies and gentlemen, welcome to *Action*. Tonight's play about the men who live dangerously stars Jane Wyatt, who is currently featured with Cary Grant in the movie *None but the Lonely Heart*, and Robert Lowery, soon to be seen in Paramount's *Dangerous Passage*.

ANNOUNCER: And now Maxwell Shane's radio adaptation of his Paramount picture *High Explosive*, starring Jane Wyatt and Robert Lowery. William Gargan as Mike Douglas begins tonight's drama of *Action*.

8. ADD A LINE. Game, 30 min., ABC, 7/4/49 to 9/26/49.

A daily game show that called for players to add the final line to a rhyme given them by the host. The player who scored the most correct answers won the game. John Nelson served as the host.

9. THE ADELE CLARK SHOW. Variety, 30 min., ABC, 8/10/45 to 9/21/46.

A weekly program of music and songs with singer Adele Clark as the host. Gene Kirby did the announcing and Jack Kelly and his orchestra provided the music.

10. ADVENTURE PARADE. Anthology, 15 min., Mutual, 1946–1949.

Dramatizations of classic children's stories. Adaptations ran one week (Monday through Friday), with a new story beginning the following Monday.

Host–Story Teller: John Griggs (as "Roger Elliott" for the first six weeks; after that, Griggs used his own name). ***Announcer:*** George Hogan.

OPENING

ANNOUNCER: Adventurers atten-shun! Fall in for *Adventure Parade*. The Mutual Broadcasting Company cordially invites all adventurers from six to 60 to join in a parade of the world's most famous stories. Stories of action, mystery, and adventure on *Adventure Parade.*

11. ADVENTURES BY MORSE. Adventure, 30 min., Syndicated, 1944.

The global exploits of Bart Friday, a daring ship's captain, and his ever-faithful first mate, Skip Turner. The title refers to the show's creator, Carlton E. Morse.

Cast: Elliott Lewis, David Ellis, Russell Thorson (*Bart Friday*); Barton Yarborough (*Skip Turner*). ***Producer-Writer:*** Carlton E. Morse.

OPENING

MORSE: If you like high adventure, come with me. If you like the stealth of intrigue, come with me. If you like blood and thunder, come with me.

12. THE ADVENTURES OF BILL LANCE. Crime Drama, 30 min., ABC, 6/14/47 to 1/4/48.

Gerald Mohr as Bill Lance, a tough private detective working out of Los Angeles. Owen James did the announcing.

Note: The program appeared locally in Los Angeles from 1944 to 1945 with John McIntire as Bill Lance.

THE ADVENTURES OF BULLDOG DRUMMOND *see* **BULLDOG DRUMMOND**

THE ADVENTURES OF CAPTAIN DIAMOND *see* **CAPTAIN DIAMOND**

THE ADVENTURES OF CASANOVA *see* **THE MODERN ADVENTURES OF CASANOVA**

13. THE ADVENTURES OF CHAMPION. Adventure, 15 min., Mutual, 1949–1950.

Serialized stories that focused on Champion, the wonder horse of Western film star Gene Autry. Guests appeared in the stories.

THE ADVENTURES OF CHARLIE CHAN *see* **CHARLIE CHAN**

THE ADVENTURES OF CHRISTOPHER LONDON *see* **CHRISTOPHER LONDON**

14. THE ADVENTURES OF CHRISTOPHER WELLS. Crime Drama, 30 min., CBS, 9/28/47 to 6/22/48.

Christopher Wells is a New York newspaper reporter with a knack for finding trouble and taking a beating from thugs for trying to expose them. Stories follow Wells as he and his assistant Stacy McGill seek the front page stories.

Cast: Myron McCormick, Les Damon (*Christopher Wells*), Charlotte Lawrence, Vicki Vola (*Stacy McGill*). ***Orchestra:*** Peter Van Steeden.

15. THE ADVENTURES OF DICK COLE. Adventure, 30 min., Syndicated, 1942.

Incidents in the life of Dick Cole, a cadet at the Farr Military Academy, who always manages to find excitement and help good defeat evil. Based on characters appearing in Bluebolt and Foremost Comics.

Cast: Leon Janney (*Dick Cole*). ***Announcer:*** Paul Luther. ***Music:*** Lew White.

16. THE ADVENTURES OF FATHER BROWN. Crime Drama. 30 min., Mutual, 6/10/45 to 7/29/45.

A crime is established as the program begins. Either a person close to the crime or the police will seek the help of Father Brown, a Catholic parish priest and amateur sleuth with a sharp mind for solving mysteries. "Understanding the human mind is essential," says Father Brown. "To understand how a criminal acts as he does, one must, so to speak, get inside of him, understand his every thought. When I've done this, when I've reached the point of committing the crime myself, then I know who the criminal is." Stories follow Father Brown as he helps the police (especially Detective Flambeau) bring the guilty to justice. *Other regular characters:* Nora, the rectory housekeeper.

Cast: Karl Swenson (*Father Brown*); Bill Griffis (*Detective Flambeau*); Gretchen Davidson (*Nora*). ***Announcer:*** John Stanley. ***Music:*** Bill Worgen. ***Producer:*** Frances Shirley Oliver.

OPENING

ANNOUNCER: The Mutual Broadcasting System presents *The Adventures of Father Brown.* From the exciting pages of G.K. Chesterton comes the best-loved detective of them all, Father Brown, played by Karl Swenson.

Now, for tonight's adventure, "The Mystified Mind."

CLOSING

ANNOUNCER: Next week, "Prophecy of Doom," an exciting adventure in which a world-famous mind reader prophesizes the death of a famous inventor—at a moment to be decided by a watch that cannot tell time. *The Adventures of Father Brown* is based on stories by G.K. Chesterton. This is the Mutual Broadcasting System.

17. THE ADVENTURES OF FRANK MERRIWELL. Adventure, 30 min., NBC, 1946–1949.

A turn-of-the-century adventure about the exploits of Frank Merriwell, a student at Yale University who excelled in athletics and fought for the rights of people threatened by evildoers. *Other regular characters:* Inza Burrage, Frank's girlfriend; Bart Hodge, Frank's friend; and Elsie Bellwood, Bart's girlfriend.

Cast: Lawson Zerbe (*Frank Merriwell*); Jean Gillespie, Elaine Rost (*Inza Burrage*); Harold Studer (*Bart Hodge*); Patricia Hosley (*Elsie Bellwood*). ***Announcer:*** Harlow Wilcox. ***Orchestra:*** Paul Taubman.

OPENING

ANNOUNCER (over hoofbeats): There it is, an echo of the past; an exciting past, a romantic past; the era of the horse and carriage, gaslit streets and free-for-all football games. The era of one of the most beloved heroes in American fiction, Frank Merriwell, the character created by Burt L. Standish. Merriwell is loved as much today as he ever was. And so, the National Broadcasting Company brings him to radio in a brand new series of stories. Today, "The Riddle of the Wrong Answer" or "Gambling Is the Devil's Pastime."

18. THE ADVENTURES OF FRANK RACE. Adventure, 30 min., Syndicated, 1949–1950.

Prior to World War II, Frank Race was a dedicated criminal attorney. When the U.S. became involved in the conflict in 1941, Frank became a counter espionage agent for the government. When the war ended, Frank continued in his capacity as a spy, and stories follow his efforts as he and his assistant Mark Donovan help defeat evil.

Cast: Tom Collins, Paul Dubov (*Frank Race*); Tony Barrett (*Mark Donovan*). ***Announcer:*** Art Gilmore. ***Music:*** Ivan Ditmars.

OPENING

ANNOUNCER: *The Adventures of Frank Race* starring Tom Collins. Many things were changed during the war. The face of the Earth was altered and the people of the Earth changed. Before the war, Frank Race was an attorney, but he traded his law books for the cloak and dagger of the O.S.S.; and when it was over, his former life was over, too. Adventure had become his business—*The Adventures of Frank Race.*

19. THE ADVENTURES OF GRACIE. Comedy, 30 min., CBS, 9/19/34 to 9/25/35.

The program, sponsored by White Owl Cigars, followed the travels of Gracie Allen, a scatterbrained woman who involves her friend and traveling companion George Burns in various comical adventures. Also known as "The Vintage White Owl Program." Music and songs were presented between acts.

Hosts-Stars: George Burns and Gracie Allen. ***Vocalists:*** The Picken Sisters, The White Owl Buccaneers. ***Announcer:*** Bill Goodwin. ***Orchestra:*** Robert Emmett Dolan.

20. THE ADVENTURES OF HELEN AND MARY. Children, 30 min., CBS, 1929–1934.

Fairy tale adventures with two children (Helen and Mary) as they wander through a storybook world of make believe. In 1934, the title changed to *Let's Pretend* (see for further information).

Cast: Estelle Levy (*Helen*); Patricia Ryan (*Mary*). ***Music:*** Maurice Brown.

21. THE ADVENTURES OF LEONIDAS WITHERALL. Mystery, 30 min., Mutual, 6/4/44 to 5/6/45.

Leonidas Witherall, a British criminology professor, teaches at the Meredith School for Boys in the town of Dalton. He is said to look like William Shakespeare ("Yeah, but if I could only write like him") and is intensely interested in crime. He lives on Birch Hill with his housekeeper, Mrs. Mollet, a woman who is head of the Ladies' Literary Group and as curious as Leonidas when it comes to crime. She is easily excited, very nosy and loves to meddle in other people's business (so much that she often stumbles upon and involves Leonidas in crimes). If something happens in town, Mrs. Mollet knows about it (if she says, "I didn't know that," Leonidas responds, "How did that get by you?"). People in trouble seek Leonidas's help and stories follow his and Mrs. Mollet's efforts to solve baffling mysteries. When Mrs. Mollet learns that Leonidas is going to investigate a murder, she says, "We're going to investigate a murder. Let me get my coat." Leonidas quotes from the Bard and also relates aspects of his work to the cases on which he is working.

Cast: Walter Hampden (*Leonidas Witherall*); Agnes Moorehead, Ethel Remey (*Mrs. Mollet*); Jack MacBryde (*Police Sgt. McCloud*). ***Announcer:*** Carl Caruso. ***Music:*** Milton Kane. ***Producer:*** Roger Bower.

OPENING

ANNOUNCER: WOR/Mutual presents the distinguished American actor Walter Hampden in *The Adventures of Leonidas Witherall*. Tonight's adventure, "The Corpse Meets a Deadline." Leonidas Witherall is the New England schoolmaster who looks like Shakespeare and is always getting mixed up in murders.

CLOSING

ANNOUNCER: WOR/Mutual has presented the distinguished American actor Mr. Walter Hampden in *The Adventures of Leonidas Witherall*. The character of Leonidas Witherall is from the mystery novel by Alice Tilden. Next week, Leonidas meets a very interesting hitchhiker, doesn't he, Mr. Hampden?

HAMPDEN: Yes. Leonidas is driving along the highway when he meets a young lady who asks him for a hitch... Soon Leonidas is receiving a very practical lesson in how to win friends and influence homicidal maniacs. We hope you'll be listening next Sunday at seven. And until then, good night.

ANNOUNCER: Listen again next Sunday evening at seven P.M., Eastern War Time, for *The Adventures of Leonidas Witherall*. This program came to you from the studios of WOR in New York. This is the Mutual Broadcasting System.

Note: The audition episode (with Walter Hampden and Agnes Moorehead) dealt with the duo's efforts to find a killer at a mountain resort. It aired on CBS on 9/7/43.

22. THE ADVENTURES OF MAISIE. Comedy, 30 min., Mutual, 1945–1948.

Mary Ann Anastasia O'Connor is named after her mother's favorite sister and is better known by her stage name, Maisie Revere. She is a glamorous blonde, born in Brooklyn, New York, who sees the world as a bevy of opportunity but always winds up with the short end of the stick. She is an entertainer ("I've been Little Eva to the Hunchback of Notre Dame"), has served with the USO and has "a wanderlust in my blood like the show business." Stories follow her world adventures as she seeks work. Maisie lives from paycheck to paycheck, is prone to sneaking out of hotel rooms by fire escapes and seems to always become involved in the problems of others. Her efforts to help those in trouble while seeking to strike it rich is the focal point of each episode. "Show business is in my blood and I guess it always will be," she says. Based on the motion picture *Maisie*. (See also the following entry.)

Cast: Ann Sothern (*Maisie Revere*). ***Supporting Cast*** (various roles): Hy Averback, Arthur Q. Bryan, Hans Conried, Virginia Gregg, Peter Leeds, Johnny McGovern, Sidney Miller. ***Announcer:*** John Easton. ***Music:*** Harry Zimmerman. ***Producer:*** John L. Greene.

OPENING

EFFECT: Sound of a lady walking followed by a man whistling (the wolf call).

MAN: Hiya, babe, say how about a—

EFFECT: Man getting his face slapped.

MAN: Ouch!

MAISIE: Does that answer your question, buddy?

ANNOUNCER: *The Adventures of Maisie* starring Ann Sothern. You all remember Metro-Goldwyn-Mayer's famous Maisie pictures. In just a moment, you'll hear Maisie on radio starring the same glamorous star you all went to see and loved on the screen, Ann Sothern. And now, here's Ann Sothern as Maisie.

MAISIE: Yes, I'm Maisie like the man said, Maisie Revere of Brooklyn. They say all roads lead to Brooklyn and I believe it because I personally walked all over them. I'm in show business; it seems I'm either walking to a job that is ready to fold or walking back from one that has...

CLOSING

ANNOUNCER: You have just heard *The Adventures of Maisie* starring Ann Sothern. And now again, here is Maisie.

MAISIE: Well, feet, you got a new job dancing in a night club, so let's get there and get going.

ANNOUNCER: Maisie was written by John L. Greene. Original music was composed and conducted by Harry Zimmerman. Supporting cast included Hans Conried, Johnny McGovern, Virginia Gregg, Sidney Miller and Peter Leeds. John Easton speaking.

23. THE ADVENTURES OF MAISIE. Comedy, 30 min., Syndicated, 1949–1952.

A revised version of the prior title that places Maisie Revere, the gorgeous girl who traveled around the world seeking show business jobs, back in Brooklyn, where she resides at Mrs. Kennedy's Boarding House (1325 East 12th Street) and where she has a steady boyfriend, Eddie Jordan. Maisie takes what show business jobs she can get while Eddie can't seem to keep a steady job. Maisie loves Eddie and wants him to make money so they can get married. Since Eddie has a difficult time finding work on his own, Maisie has taken it upon herself to find Eddie work. He dreads to hear the words "Eddie, I just got you another job" as the new job might be similar to ones Maisie found him in the past (for example, sock salesman at Bixel's Department Store; cabin boy on a garbage barge; parachute tester; boys' camp counselor). Eddie is always several months behind on the rent at Mrs. Kennedy's and is very reluctant to get married (he uses the excuse of having to get a steady job before taking the step). Men are always whistling at Maisie; she can have her choice of any man, but she wants Eddie. "The things I do so we can get married and have a home one day" comprise the basis for each story.

Cast: Ann Sothern (*Maisie Revere*); Pat McGeehan (*Eddie Jordan*); Bea Benaderet, Elvia Allman (*Mrs. Kennedy*). ***Supporting Cast*** (various roles): Hy Averback, Sandra Gould, Peter Leeds, Johnny McGovern, Jeffrey Silver. ***Announcers:*** John Easton, Jack McCoy. ***Music:*** Harry Zimmerman.

OPENING

ANNOUNCER: *The Adventures of Maisie* starring Ann Sothern.

MAISIE: Yes, I'm Maisie like the man said, Maisie Revere. For a while I thought maybe, perhaps there was a chance it would be changed to Maisie Jordan, but my boyfriend, Eddie... well, ever since he's been old enough to hold a steady job, he hasn't. It's not that Eddie is lazy, but, you see, he went to college and studied stuff like 14th century Flemish poetry, the art of rug weaving and all that stuff there ain't a buck in. Eddie barely makes enough money to pay his room rent...

CLOSING

ANNOUNCER: And now once again, here's Maisie.

MAISIE: Come on, feet, get movin'. See if you can find little old Maisie a good job for a change.

ANNOUNCER: You just heard *The Adventures of Maisie* starring Ann Sothern. Maisie is presented by arrangement with Metro-Goldwyn-Mayer. Maisie was written by John L. Greene. John Easton speaking.

24. THE ADVENTURES OF MICHAEL SHAYNE. Crime Drama, 30 min., ABC, 1952–1953.

A third series based on the characters created by Brett Halliday in his book *Dividend on Death* (see also *Michael Shayne* and *The New Adventures of Michael Shayne*). Shayne is a tough private detective based in New York City. He is assisted by his secretary and girlfriend Phyllis Knight, and stories relate their adventures as they risk their lives to help their clients.

Cast: Robert Sterling (*Michael Shayne*); Judith Parrish (*Phyllis Knight*). ***Music:*** John Duffy.

OPENING

ANNOUNCER: The American Broadcasting Company takes great pride in presenting a new series based on Michael Shayne, the fictional detective created by Brett Halliday and starring Robert Sterling as Michael Shayne in *The Adventures of Michael Shayne*.

THE ADVENTURES OF MR. MEEK *see* **MEET MR. MEEK**

25. THE ADVENTURES OF NERO WOLFE. Mystery, 30 min., NBC Blue/ABC, 1943–1944; Mutual, 1945–1946.

At 601 West 35th Street in New York City stands the residence of Nero Wolfe, gourmet, horticulturalist and master detective who solves difficult crimes for his clients—all for a steep fee ($1,000 plus a $500 retainer). Nero, however, rarely leaves his home and relies on the legwork of his investigator Archie Goodwin to gather the clues he needs to solve a case. When he feels he has sufficient evidence to resolve a case, he gathers all the suspects at his home and proceeds to expose the guilty party (and eventually turn them over to the police). Based on the characters created by Rex Stout and also titled *The Amazing Nero Wolfe*. See also *The New Adventures of Nero Wolfe*.

Cast: J.B. Williams, Santos Ortega, Luis Van Rooten, Francis X. Bushman (*Nero Wolfe*); Joseph Julian, Louis Vittes, Elliott Lewis (*Archie Goodwin*). ***Announcers:*** Jim Bannon, Carl Eastman. ***Music:*** Lew White. ***Producer:*** Travis Wells.

OPENING (from 12/15/46)

ANNOUNCER: For soft, smooth, romantic hands, Jergens Lotion. Jergens, the makers of Jergens Lotion for soft, smooth, romantic hands, presents *The Amazing Nero Wolfe* starring Francis X. Bushman as Nero Wolfe, the celebrated criminologist, and Elliott Lewis as Archie.

CLOSING

ANNOUNCER: Tonight's program concludes the current series of *The Amazing Nero Wolfe* starring Francis X. Bushman as Nero Wolfe and Elliott Lewis as Archie, brought to you by Jergens Lotion. The characters of Nero Wolfe and Archie Goodwin were created by Rex Stout. This is Jim Bannon saying good night for Jergens Lotion, the lotion for soft, smooth, romantic hands. This is the Mutual–Don Lee Broadcasting System.

26. The Adventures of Ozzie and Harriet. Comedy, 30 min., CBS, 1944–1948; NBC, 1948–1949; CBS, 1949; ABC, 1949–1954.

Humorous incidents in the lives of the Nelson family: parents Ozzie and Harriet and their children, David and Ricky, who live at 1847 Rogers Road (an address originally given as 845 Rogers Road). This became the basis for the television series of the same title (and originally titled "The Ozzie Nelson–Harriet Hilliard Show"). *Other regular characters:* Syd "Thorny" Thornberry, their neighbor; Harriet's mother; Gloria, the Nelson's maid; their son's friends Emmy Lou and Roger; and the Nelson family dog, Nick.

Cast: Ozzie Nelson (*Himself*); Harriet Hilliard Nelson (*Herself*); Tommy Bernard, Joel Davis, David Nelson (*David Nelson*); Henry Blair, Ricky Nelson (*Ricky Nelson*); John Brown (*Syd "Thorny" Thornberry*); Lurene Tuttle (*Harriet's mother*); Bea Benaderet (*Gloria*); Janet Waldo (*Emmy Lou*); Dink Trout (*Roger*).

Vocalists: Harriet Hilliard, The King Sisters, Ozzie Nelson. ***Announcers:*** Jack Bailey, Verne Smith. ***Music:*** Billy May, Ozzie Nelson. ***Producers:*** Dave Elton, Ozzie Nelson.

OPENING

ANNOUNCER: The solid silver with beauty that lives forever is International Sterling. From Hollywood, International Silver Company, creator of International Sterling, present *The Adventures of Ozzie and Harriet*, starring America's favorite young couple, Ozzie Nelson and Harriet Hilliard.

CLOSING (typical of the war years, when pleas were given)

OZZIE: Harriet and I have been asked to remind you that even though the war is over, the government still needs tin to send food to our soldiers in Europe; it needs tin to pack medical supplies for our wounded soldiers; it needs tin to put civilian goods back on the market. The need is great and the supply is limited.

HARRIET: And it will take some time before we can get normal shipments from such places as the Dutch East Indies and Malaya. So, for the time being, our most valuable tin mine is the American kitchen.

OZZIE: Let's make sure that the tin cans are… washed thoroughly and prepared in accordance with local salvage requirements. Thanks a lot, folks, and good night.

HARRIET: Good night folks.

ANNOUNCER: You have been listening to *The Adventures of Ozzie and Harriet*, presented by International Silver Company, creators of International Silver. This is Verne Smith inviting you to be with us next week, same time, same station for *The Adventures of Ozzie and Harriet*.

27. The Adventures of Philip Marlowe. Crime Drama, 30 min., NBC, 1947; CBS, 1948–1951.

The sign on his office door (Room 41) reads simply "Philip Marlowe—Private Investigator." But Marlowe is anything but simple; he's a hard-hitting, two-fisted Los Angeles–based detective who gives clients their money's worth

Ozzie Nelson and Harriet Hilliard of *The Adventures of Ozzie and Harriet.*

and will go to any lengths to solve a crime. Marlowe lives on Franklin Square, doesn't offer his clients a drink of liquor like the high-priced investigators ("I can't afford it") and has a simple philosophy: "Crime is a sucker's road and those who travel it wind up in jail." Stories, based on the character created by Raymond Chandler, chart Marlowe's various cases.

Cast: Van Heflin, Gerald Mohr (*Philip Marlowe*); Jeff Corey (*Lt. Abar*); Larry Dobkin (*Lt. Matthews*). ***Announcers:*** Wendell Niles, Roy Rowan. ***Music:*** Richard Aurandt, Lyn Murray. ***Producer:*** Norman MacDonnell.

OPENING

ANNOUNCER: From the pen of Raymond Chandler, outstanding author of crime fiction, comes his most famous character and crime's most deadly enemy, as CBS presents *The Adventures of Philip Marlowe*. Now, with Gerald Mohr starring as Philip Marlowe, we bring you tonight's unusual story, "The Grim Echo."

28. The Adventures of Rin Tin Tin. Adventure, 30 min., Mutual, 1/2/55 to 12/25/55.

While on patrol, Rip Masters, a lieutenant with the Fighting Blue Devils of the 101st Cavalry, discovers two survivors of an Apache raid: a young boy named Rusty and his dog Rinty, better known as Rin Tin Tin. Rip, who is stationed at Fort Apache in Arizona, unofficially adopts the boy and his dog. Stories (set in the 1880s) relate Honorary Cpl. Rusty's (and Rinty's) efforts to help the cavalry maintain the peace. Based on the television series of the same title. The radio cast is not identified. *Other regular characters:* Sgt. Biff O'Hara and Major Swanson. See also *Rin Tin Tin*.

Announcer: Don Morrow.

OPENING

Announcer: The National Biscuit Company presents *The Adventures of Rin Tin Tin*.

Rusty: Yo, Rinty!

Chorus: Rin Tin Tin, Rin Tin Tin, Rinty, Rinty, Rin Tin Tin. *Rin Tin Tin* is brought to you by Shredded Wheat and Milkbone too. Rinty and Rusty, side by side; loyal heroics, the regiment's pride. You'll find them in the thrilling *Adventures of Rin Tin Tin*.

Announcer: The National Biscuit Company presents this week's *Adventures of Rin Tin Tin*.

CLOSING

Announcer: Don't forget next Sunday at this time over this same station for another exciting chapter in *The Adventures of Rin Tin Tin*, presented by the National Biscuit Company, makers of Milkbone dog biscuits, and Nabisco, the original Shredded Wheat. For *The Adventures of Rin Tin Tin* on television, consult your local newspaper for time and station. This program came to you transcribed from New York.

29. The Adventures of Sam Spade. Crime Drama, 30 min., ABC, summer of 1946; CBS, 1946–1950; NBC, 1950–1951.

Sam Spade is a tall, broad-shouldered private detective working out of Los Angeles. He doesn't have much money, considers his job a living and is happy doing it. He is what the criminals call "the bloodhound type"—the type they despise because he accomplishes things—"things they don't like." Sam has an office in a drafty building and dictates his cases to his faithful secretary Effie Perrine, a bubbly, man-hungry adult version of radio's *Corliss Archer*. Stories follow Sam as he takes whatever cases he can get to make money. Sam's license is 137596 and he refers to his cases as "capers." Effie ends each episode with "Period. End of report." Based on the characters created by Dashiell Hammett.

Cast: Howard Duff, Stephen Dunne (*Sam Spade*); Lurene Tuttle (*Effie Perrine*); William Conrad (*Lt. Kelsey*). ***Announcer:*** Dick Joy. ***Music:*** Lud Gluskin. ***Producer:*** William Spier.

OPENING (Howard Duff episodes)

Announcer: Dashiell Hammett, America's leading detective fiction writer, and William Spier, radio's outstanding producer-director of mystery and crime drama, join their talents to make your hair stand on end with *The Adventures of Sam Spade*, presented by the makers of Wild Root Creme Oil for the hair. And now, with Howard Duff starring as Sam Spade, Wild Root brings to the air the greatest private detective of them all in *The Adventures of Sam Spade*.

Sound: Telephone rings.

Effie: (after picking up the receiver): Sam Spade Detective Agency.

Sam: Hello, sweetheart, it's only me.

Effie: Oh, Sam, why so modest?

Sam: If you will only contain your feminine curiosity for a few moments, I'll be right over to dictate my report of "The Bow Window Case."

CLOSING

Announcer: *The Adventures of Sam Spade*, Dashiell Hammett's famous private detective, are produced and directed by William Spier. Sam Spade is played by Howard Duff; Lurene Tuttle is Effie. Join us next Sunday when author Dashiell Hammett and producer William Spier join forces for another adventure with Sam Spade, brought to you by Wild Root Creme Oil. Again and again, the choice for men who put good grooming first.

OPENING (Stephen Dunne episodes)

Announcer: In response to requests representing millions of listening friends, the National

Broadcasting Company is pleased to bring you again *The Adventures of Sam Spade*. William Spier, radio's outstanding producer-director of mystery and crime drama, brings you the greatest crime adventure of them all in *The Adventures of Sam Spade*.

30. THE ADVENTURES OF SUPERMAN. Adventure Serial, 15 and 30 min. versions, Syndicated, 1938–1939; Mutual, 1940–1949; ABC, 1949–1951.

Far away in the outer regions of space there existed the planet Krypton which, inhabited by super-intelligent beings, was being drawn closer to its sun and destruction. When Jor-El, a scientist, discovered this but failed to convince anyone of its reality, he began preparations to save his wife Lara and their infant son Kal-El. With only time enough to complete a miniature experimental rocket when the planet began to explode, Jor-El and Lara placed Kal-El in it and set its controls for the planet Earth. Shortly after the rocket took off, Krypton exploded and scattered billions of particles of Kryptonite, the only substance that can destroy Kal-El, into the universe. During the long journey of the rocket ship to Earth, the infant became a man. The ship landed in a desert where a strange being, dressed in a blue and red costume, emerged. While exploring his new surroundings, the being, "a Superman in our world," rescued a boy and his father from a runaway trolley. With their help and their promise to keep his secret, the being became Clark Kent and, seeking to use his great abilities to benefit mankind, he acquired a job as a reporter for the *Daily Planet*, a crusading newspaper in Metropolis. Stories follow Clark's endless battle against crime as the mysterious Superman. *Other regular characters:* Perry White, the editor; reporters Lois Lane and Jimmy Olsen; Beanie, the office boy; and Batman and Robin, the crusaders who help Superman.

Cast: Bud Collyer, Michael Fitzmaurice (*Clark Kent/Superman*); Joan Alexander (*Lois Lane*); Jackie Kelk (*Jimmy Olsen*); Julian Noa (*Perry White*); Stacy Harris, Gary Merrill, Matt Crowley (*Batman*); Ronald Liss (*Robin*). ***Announcers-Narrators:*** Jackson Beck, Frank Knight, George Lowther, Dan McCullough. ***Music:*** John Gart.

OPENING

ANNOUNCER: Boys and girls, your attention please. Presenting a new, exciting radio program featuring the thrilling adventures of that amazing and incredible personality. Faster than a speeding bullet, more powerful than a locomotive, impervious to bullets.

VOICES: Up in the sky, look! It's a giant bird! It's a plane! It's Superman!

ANNOUNCER: And now, Superman, a being no larger than an ordinary man but possessed of powers and abilities never before realized on Earth. Able to leap into the air an eighth of a mile at a single bound, hurtle a 20-story building with ease, race a high-powered bullet to its target, lift tremendous weights and bend solid steel in his bare hands as though it were paper. Superman, the strange visitor from a distant planet, champion of the oppressed, physical marvel extraordinary who has sworn to devote his existence on Earth to helping those in need.

CLOSING

ANNOUNCER: Fellows and girls, follow *The Adventures of Superman*, brought to you every day, Monday through Friday, same time, same station, by the makers of that super delicious cereal, Kellogg's Pep. *Superman* is a copyrighted feature appearing in Superman-D.C. Publications. This is Mutual.

31. THE ADVENTURES OF THE ABBOTTS. Crime Drama, 30 min., Mutual, 1945–1947; NBC, 1954–1955.

Pat and Jean Abbott are newlyweds fascinated by murder and mayhem. Their efforts to help the police solve baffling crimes—from robbery to murder—is the focal point of the series. Adapted from the "Pat Abbott" stories by Frances Crane. Also known as *The Abbott Mysteries*.

Cast: Charles Webster, Les Tremayne, Don Briggs, Les Damon (*Pat Abbott*); Julie Stevens, Alice Reinheart, Claudia Morgan (*Jean Abbott*). ***Announcer:*** Frank Gallop, Cy Harrice. ***Music:*** Albert Buhrmann, Hank Sylvern.

OPENING

ANNOUNCER: The National Broadcasting Company presents *The Adventures of the Abbotts* starring Claudia Morgan and Les Damon as Jean and Pat Abbott, those popular characters of detective fiction created by Frances Crane. NBC invites you to join Pat and Jean each week at this time for another exciting, recorded adventure in romance and crime.

Tonight's story, "The Canary Yellow Sack." And here is Claudia Morgan as Jean Abbott to set the stage for tonight's puzzle in murder.

JEAN: Good evening. (She would then begin the story.)

THE ADVENTURES OF THE FALCON *see* **THE FALCON**

THE ADVENTURES OF THE SAINT *see* **THE SAINT**

THE ADVENTURES OF THE SCARLET PIMPERNEL *see* **THE SCARLET PIMPERNEL**

32. THE ADVENTURES OF THE THIN MAN. Crime Drama, 30 min., NBC, 1941–1942; CBS, 1943–1947; NBC, 1948; Mutual, 1948–1949; ABC, 1950.

Nick Charles is a former private detective turned mystery editor for a New York City publishing house. He is married to Nora, a beautiful but trouble-prone woman who has an uncanny knack for stumbling upon crimes. Stories relate the adventures that occur when Nick becomes involved in Nora's efforts to solve crimes (the situations are complicated by Nora, who feels that her feminine instinct is keener than Nick's training as a detective). Based on the characters created by Dashiell Hammett. Also titled *The New Adventures of the Thin Man*.

Cast: Les Damon, Les Tremayne, Joseph Curtin, David Gothard, Bill Smith (*Nick Charles*); Claudia Morgan (*Nora Charles*). ***Announcer:*** Ed Herlihy, Ron Rawson, Tom Shirley. ***Music:*** Fred Fradkin. ***Producer:*** Himan Brown.

OPENING

SCENE: Nick attempting to play the sponsor's theme on the piano.

NORA: No, Nicky, darling, that's not it.

NICK: It isn't, Nora?

NORA: No, it goes like this. (She takes over the piano and sings.) Thirty-three fine brews, blended into one great beer.

ANNOUNCER: Pabst Blue Ribbon Beer presents *The New Adventures of the Thin Man* with Nick and Nora Charles, the happiest married couple in radio. Claudia Morgan as Nora and Les Tremayne as Nick in tonight's adventure of the Thin Man entitled "The Adventures of the Passionate Palooka."

33. THE ADVENTURES OF TOPPER. Comedy, 30 min., NBC, 6/7/45 to 9/13/45.

George and Marian Kerby are a reckless young couple who meet an untimely end when they crash their car into a tree. They are laid to rest in the Pleasantville Cemetery, but until they can make up for their past misgivings, they are not permitted to enter Heaven. They are proclaimed Low Plain Spirits and decide to begin their mission by haunting their old residence to brighten up the dreary life of its new owner, Cosmo Topper. Topper is a middle-aged, henpecked businessman whose life suddenly changes when George and Marian, who appear and speak only to him, turn his life upside down. Malvena, Cosmo's wife, tries to understand, but attributes the strange things she sees (Cosmo talking to no one, calling George and Marian's names) to his imagination. George and Marian turn Cosmo's simplest problems into major disasters. Based on the characters created by Thorne Smith. *Other regular characters:* Heliatrope, the Topper's maid, and Mr. Borris, Topper's boss.

Cast: Roland Young (*Cosmo Topper*); Hope Emerson (*Malvena Topper*); Paul Mann (*George Kerby*); Frances Chaney (*Marian Kerby*); Bob Corley (*Heliatrope*); Ed Latimer (*Mr. Borris*). ***Announcer:*** Richard Kollmar.

OPENING

GEORGE: Hey, Topper.

MARIAN: Topper, darling, we're back.

COSMO: Here we go again.

ANNOUNCER: *The Adventures of Topper* is a new comedy series based on Thorne Smith's hilarious best-seller and is brought to you by the makers of those bubbly light, crisper corn flakes, Post Toasties.

SONG: We toast 'em crisp, we toast 'em light; you can tell by the taste we toast 'em. They're a tasty treat, so good to eat, delicious and light, Post Toasties.

ANNOUNCER: And now let's meet Topper.

TOPPER: Hello, my name is Cosmo Topper. I suppose some of you have a couple of friends who are considered nobody. Well, I have a couple of friends who have no bodies; a pair of ghosts named George and Marian Kerby. The trouble they've caused me. If things continue as they are, they'll be the death of me yet.

CLOSING

ANNOUNCER: Be sure to listen to *Topper* starring Roland Young next Thursday when Mr. Topper intercepts a present meant for Marian. Remember, *Topper*, next Thursday, same time, same station. This is Richard Kollmar saying good night from the makers of those bubbly light, crisper corn flakes, Post Toasties. This program has come to you from our Radio City studios in New York. This is the National Broadcasting Company.

34. THE AFFAIRS OF ANN SCOTLAND. Crime Drama, 30 min., ABC, 10/30/46 to 10/22/47.

A light-hearted look at crime solving as seen through the cases of Ann Scotland, a charming private detective who uses her wits to solve crimes.

Cast: Arlene Francis (*Ann Scotland*). ***Announcer:*** Ken Niles. ***Music:*** Del Castillo.

35. THE AFFAIRS OF PETER SALEM. Crime Drama, 30 min., Mutual, 1949–1953.

Peter Salem is a suave and sophisticated private detective who believes in a non-violent approach to solving crimes. Stories follow Peter as he and his assistant Marty strive to solve baffling crimes through deductive reasoning.

Cast: Santos Ortega (*Peter Salem*); Jack Grimes (*Marty*).

36. THE AFFAIRS OF TOM, DICK AND HARRY. Variety, 30 min., Mutual, 1937–1949.

Music, songs and comedy vignettes with a male vocal group known as Tom, Dick and Harry.

Cast: Bud Vandover (*Tom*), Marlin Hurt (*Dick*), Gordon Vandover (*Harry*). ***Vocalist:*** Edna O'Dell. ***Announcer:*** Jack Brickhouse. ***Music:*** Robert Trendler.

37. AFRICAN TREK. Variety, 30 min., NBC Blue, 1939–1944.

Josef Marais as the host of a weekly program of African music, songs and stories. Juano Hernandez and the Burford Hampden Chorus were the regulars. Burford Hampden and his orchestra supplied the music.

38. AGAINST THE STORM. Serial, 15 min., NBC, 1939–1942; Mutual, 1949; ABC, 1951–1952.

Originally, this told the story of Christy Allen, a refugee from Central Europe struggling to adjust to a new life in the United States. Later, following Christy's marriage to Philip Cameron, stories charted incidents in the lives of the Camerons, a wealthy New England family.

Cast: Gertrude Warner, Claudia Morgan (*Christy Allen*); Arnold Moss, Alexander Scourby, Elliott Reid (*Philip Cameron*); Roger DeKoven (*Jason Allen*); May Seymour, Florence Malone, Katharine Raht (*Margaret Allen*); Dolores Gillian, Joan Tompkins, Ethel Owen (*Siri Allen*); Chester Stratton, Eddie Mayehoff (*Mark Scott*); Ruth Mattheson (*Nicole Scott*); Charlotte Holland (*Kathy Reimer*); Jane Erskine (*Lucretia Hale*); Leslie Bingham (*Penny*); James Meighan, Walter Vaughn (*Reid Wilson*); Philip Clarke (*Dr. Reimer*); Lawson Zerbe (*Pascal Tyler*); Mary Hunter (*Kip Tyler*); Sarah Burton (Lisa); Lenore Kingston (*Ebba*); Ian Martin (*Nathan*); Michael Ingram (*Manuel*). ***Announcers:*** Nelson Case, Ralph Edwards, Richard Stark. ***Sponsor:*** Ivory Soap.

OPENING

ANNOUNCER: For Philip Cameron in Hawthorne and Pascal Tyler in Arizona, a letter from Lucretia Hale has found importance today. Today we bring you another chapter of *Against the Storm*, written by Sandra Michael and presented by the makers of Ivory Soap.

39. THE AIR ADVENTURES OF JIMMY ALLEN. Children, 15 min., Syndicated, 1933–1936.

Serialized stories about Jimmy Allen, a 17-year-old messenger for the Kansas City Airport during the early years of aviation, as he and his friend, veteran pilot Speed Robertson, tackle dangerous air missions around the world. In 1933 episodes, Jimmy was an apprentice pilot for National Airways (Speed was his instructor); his plane, in later episodes, was the *Blue Bird Special*.

Cast: Murray MacLean (*Jimmy Allen*); Robert Fiske (*Speed Robertson*).

OPENING

VOICE (over hum of an airplane): *The Air Adventures of Jimmy Allen!*

ANNOUNCER: You have just heard the inspirational identification tag known in radio as the signature of *The Air Adventures of Jimmy Allen*. And now to episode 948.

40. AL GOODMAN'S MUSICAL ALBUM. Variety, 30 min., NBC, 1951–1953.

Bandleader Al Goodman as the host of a weekly program of music and songs. Felix Knight and Elaine Malbin were the regulars and the Al Goodman Orchestra provided the music.

THE AL JOLSON SHOW *see* **THE LIFEBUOY PROGRAM**

41. AL PEARCE AND HIS GANG. Comedy, 15 and 30 min. versions, NBC Blue, 1933–1939; CBS, 1939–1945.

Outlandish sketches featuring an array of buffoons, most notably Elmer Blurt, the shy door-to-door salesman; the Laughing Lady; and Arlene, the Human Chatterbox (her telephone conversations were with a never-heard character named Mazie). Songs and musicals numbers were featured between skits.

Cast: Al Pearce (*Host/Elmer Blurt*); Arlene Harris (*Human Chatterbox*); Kitty O'Neil (*Laughing Lady*); Bill Comstock (*Tizzie Lish*); Jennison Parker (*Yahbut*); Monroe Upton (*Lord Bilgewater*); Harry Stewart (*Yogi Yorgeson*). ***Regulars:*** Morey Amsterdam, Andy Andrews, Orville Andrews, Gary Brechner, Harry Foster, Earl Hodgins, Billy House, Martha Mears, Cal Pearce, Don Reid, Tony Romano, Mabel Todd, Hazel Warner. ***Vocalists:*** Marie Green and Her Merry Men, Nick Lucas, the Sportsmen, the Three Cheers. ***Announcer:*** Ken Roberts. ***Music:*** Ivan Ditmars, Carl Hoff, Larry Marsh, Harry Sosnik.

42. THE ALAN YOUNG SHOW. Comedy, 30 min., NBC, 1944–1947; ABC, 1949.

Events in the everyday life of Alan Young, a likeable young man with a knack for finding misadventure. Stories focus in particular on his romance with Betty Dittenfeffer; his efforts to impress her father (Papa), who feels that he is not good enough for his daughter; and his encounters with millionaire Hubert Updike.

Cast: Alan Young (*Himself*); Doris Singleton (*Betty Dittenfeffer*); Jim Backus (*Hubert Updike*); Ed Begley (*Papa Dittenfeffer*). ***Regulars:*** Charlie Cantor, Ken Christy, Ruth Perrott. ***Vocalists:*** The Smart Set. ***Announcers:*** Larry Elliott, Michael Roy, Jimmy Wallington. ***Music:*** George Wyle.

43. ALBUM OF MANHATTAN. Gossip, 15 min., Mutual, 1940–1941.

Louis Sobol as the host of a program reporting on the people and events in New York City.

44. THE ALDRICH FAMILY. Comedy, 30 min., NBC Red, 1939; NBC Blue, 1939–1940; NBC Red, 1940–1944; NBC, 1946–1953.

Mythical Centerville, U.S.A., was the setting for a weekly series that explored comical incidents in the life of Henry Aldrich, an overeager teenage boy with a penchant for getting into trouble. Henry lives at 117 Elm Street with his father Sam (a private practice attorney), his mother Alice and sister Mary. Henry attends Central High School and most often finds misadventure with his best friend Homer Brown. *Other regular characters:* Kathleen Anderson, Henry's girlfriend; Homer's mother and father (Will); Kathleen's mother; Willie Marshall, the pesty little boy; and Dizzy and Toby, Henry and Homer's friends. Kathleen has a dog named Daisy (she hates Homer "because she resents me for eating one of her dog biscuits"). Henry's address was also given as 303 Elm Street; his phone number was Elm-431; and Homer's phone number was Elm-232. Based on the Broadway play *What a Life* by Clifford Goldsmith.

Cast: Ezra Stone, Norman Tokar, Raymond Ives, Dick Jones, Bobby Ellis (*Henry Aldrich*); Clyde Fillmore, House Jameson, Tom Shirley (*Sam Aldrich*); Lea Penman, Katharine Raht, Regina Wallace (*Alice Aldrich*); Betty Field, Jone Allison, Mary Mason, Charita Bauer, Mary Shipp, Mary Rolfe, Ann Lincoln (*Mary Aldrich*); Jackie Kelk, Jack Grimes (*Homer Brown*); Mary Shipp, Ann Lincoln, Ethel Blume, Jean Gillespie (*Kathleen Anderson*); Eddie Bracken (*Dizzy Stevens*); Ed Begley (*Will Brown*); Agnes Moorehead, Leona Powers (*Homer's mother*); Dick Van Patten (*Toby Smith*); Alice Yourman (*Kathleen's mother*); Norman Tokar (*Willie Marshall*). ***Announcers:*** George Bryan, Dick Dudley, Ralph Paul, Dan Seymour, Harry Von Zell, Dwight Weist. ***Music:*** Jack Miller.

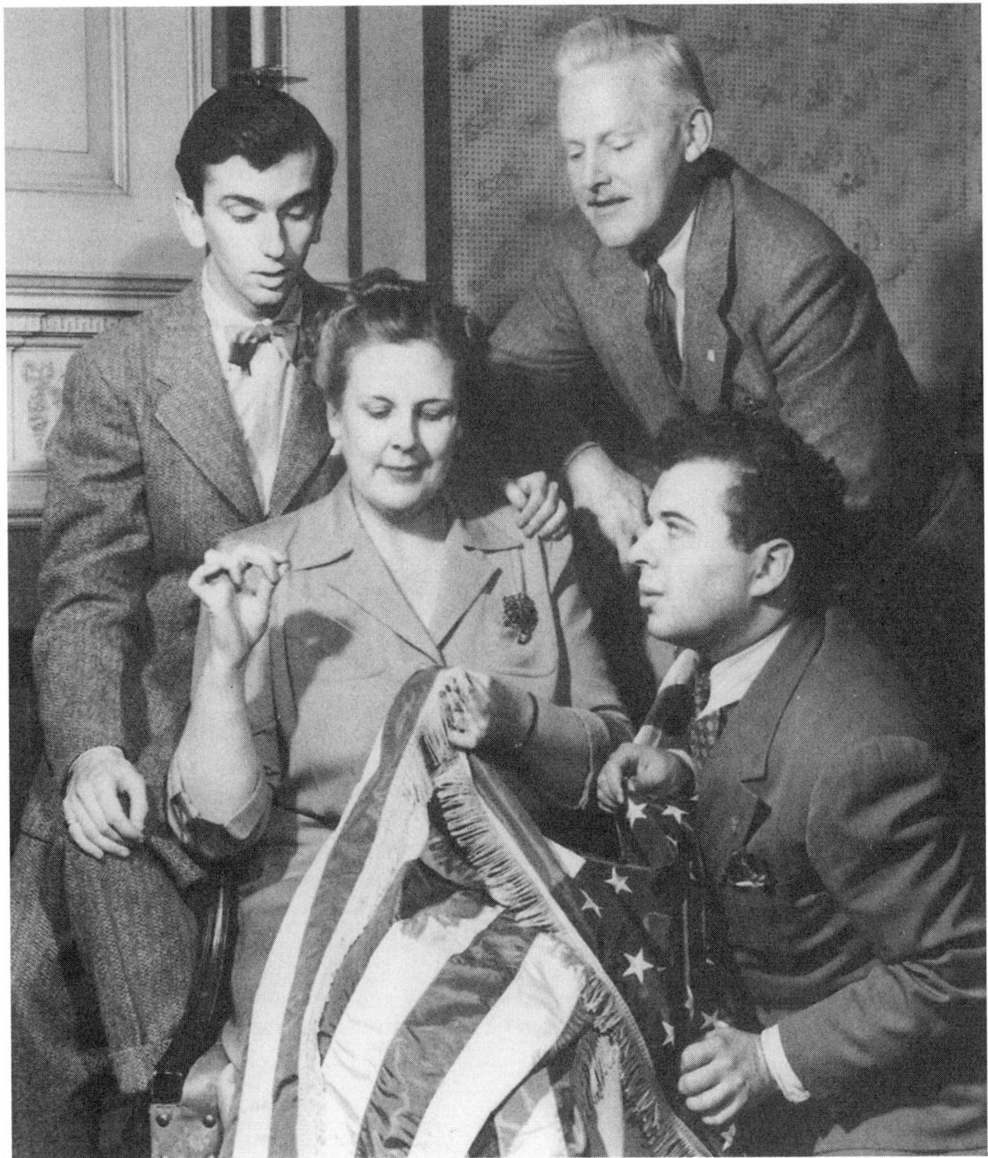

The players on *The Aldrich Family* were (clockwise from top left) Jackie Kelk, House Jameson, Ezra Stone and Katherine Raht.

OPENING

ANNOUNCER: And now the Jell-O family presents—

MRS. ALDRICH (in shrill voice): Henry, Henry Aldrich!

HENRY (voice cracking): Coming, Mother.

ANNOUNCER: Yes, it's *The Aldrich Family*, based on characters created by Clifford Goldsmith, and starring Ezra Stone as Henry and Jackie Kelk as Homer. And, yes, it's the Jell-O family—

HENRY AND HOMER (singing): Oh, the big red letters stand for the Jell-O family... That's Jell-O, yum, yum, yum. Jell-O puddings, yum, yum, yum. Jell-O tap-i-o-ca pudding, yes sir-ree.

45. ALEC TEMPLETON TIME. Variety, 30 min., NBC, 1939–1941; 1943–1944; 1947–1948.

A weekly series of music and songs with Alec Templeton, a blind pianist.

Host: Alec Templeton. ***Regulars:*** Billy Mills, Edna O'Dell, Pat O'Malley, the William Miller Chorus. ***Announcer:*** Fort Pearson. ***Orchestra:*** Ray Noble, Daniel Sardenber, Alec Templeton.

46. The Alfredo Antonini Orchestra. Music, 30 min., Mutual, 1939.

A weekly program that mixed classical music with popular songs of the era.

Host: Alfredo Antonini. ***Regulars:*** Harry Kramer, Arthur Whiteside. ***Orchestra:*** Alfredo Antonini.

47. Alias Jane Doe. Drama, 30 min., NBC, 4/7/51 to 9/22/51.

Stories follow the adventures of a beautiful and adventurous female magazine reporter who dons various disguises to acquire story material. She writes of those experiences under the alias Jane Doe.

Cast: Kay Phillips (*Jane Doe*); Tudor Owen (*Her editor*). ***Also*** (various roles): Lamont Johnson, Eric Sinclair. ***Announcer:*** Frank Martin.

48. Alias Jimmy Valentine. Drama, 15 min., NBC Blue, 1938–1939.

Events in the life of Jimmy Valentine, a famous safecracker who used his talents to help people in trouble. Based on the character created by O. Henry.

Cast: Bert Lytell, James Meighan (*Jimmy Valentine*).

49. Alka-Seltzer Time. Comedy, 15 min., CBS, 1948–1949.

The program, also known as *Herb Shriner Time*, and sponsored by Alka-Seltzer, featured the rural (Indiana) comedy of its host, Herb Shriner. Durward Kirby did the announcing and the Raymond Scott Quintet supplied the music.

50. Allen Prescott Presents. Variety, 30 min., NBC, 1941.

Allen Prescott as the host of a weekly program of music and songs. Vocals were by Diane Courtney and the group Hi, Lo, Jack and a Dame. Jimmy Lytell and his orchestra provided the music.

51. Amanda of Honeymoon Hill. Serial, 15 min., NBC Blue, 1940–1942; CBS, 1942–1946.

The conflicts and tensions that exist between two families: the Dykes and the Leightons. The feud began when Amanda Dyke, daughter of a blue-collar family, married Edward Leighton, an artist and son of a Southern blue blood family. The title refers to Edward's mansion on Honeymoon Hill.

Cast: Joy Hathaway (*Amanda Dyke*); Boyd Crawford, George Lambert, Staats Cotsworth (*Edward Leighton*); John MacBryde (*Joseph Dyke*); John Connery (*Col. Leighton*); Florence Edney, Cecil Roy (*Aunt Mazie*); Elizabeth Love (*Mrs. Leighton*); Jay Meredith (*Marion Leighton*); Irene Hubbard, Muriel Starr (*Susan Leighton*); Ruth Yorke (*Olive Courtleigh*); George Lambert (*Walter Courtleigh*); Helen Shields (*Sylvia Meadows*); John Raby (*Roy Calvert*); Patricia Wheel (*Claire Treman*); Chester Stratton (*Tom Ames*); Lamont Johnson (*Bruce Douglas*); Rod Hendrickson (*Martin Douglas*). ***Announcer:*** Howard Claney, Hugh Conover, Frank Gallop. ***Producers:*** Anne Hummert, Frank Hummert.

OPENING (from 6/6/44)

ANNOUNCER: Now the makers of Phillips Milk of Magnesia Tablets presents *Amanda of Honeymoon Hill*, radio's drama of love and life in wartime in the romantic South; the story of a beautiful valley girl, Amanda Dyke, who married the son of the aristocratic family up on the hill, Edward Leighton. And now for our drama, *Amanda of Honeymoon Hill*.

CLOSING

ANNOUNCER: Today we make an urgent appeal to the women of America to join the WAVES. As you know, our American Navy has now become the biggest in the world... This rapid growth of the Navy has made it necessary now, today, to call upon the women of America for one of the most important jobs women have been asked to do in this war—to enlist by the thousands as WAVES. You're needed to put on the glorious blue uniform of the Navy, to step in and free a sailor from a shore job so he can take his place on one of the hundreds of new Navy ships and planes which now go forward to fight in one of the fiercest battles of the war... For further details, go to your nearest Navy recruiting station today. Do this at once, today. Our American Navy needs you as a WAVE in order to use its mighty strength most effectively in the days just ahead. *Amanda of Honeymoon Hill* is presented each day at this time by the makers of Phillips Milk of Magnesia Tablets. Don't miss our broadcast tomorrow. And please stay tuned for *Second Husband*, which follows immediately. This is CBS, the Columbia Broadcasting System.

52. The Amazing Adventures of Flash Gordon. Science Fiction, 15 min., Mutual, 4/27/35 to 2/6/36.

A radio adaptation of the comic strip by Alex Raymond. Flash Gordon, the son of a famous scientist, Dale Arden, his beautiful and resourceful girlfriend, and Dr. Zarkoff, the brilliant scientist, are citizens of the undersea kingdom of Atlantis, where Flash has become its emperor. Serialized stories follow Flash as he risks his life to protect Atlantis from the sinister forces threatening to conquer it. See also *The Amazing Interplanetary Adventures of Flash Gordon*.

Cast: James Meighan (*Flash Gordon*); Irene Watson (*Dale Arden*); Owen Jordan (*Dr. Zarkoff*).

OPENING

Announcer: *The Amazing Adventures of Flash Gordon*. Groves Emulsified Nose Drops bring to your radio the further interplanetary adventures of Flash Gordon. It is the same daring and resourceful Flash Gordon whose exploits have held you spellbound in the newspapers. Now through your loudspeakers, every Monday, Tuesday, Wednesday and Thursday at this same time, travel with Flash Gordon, Dale Arden and Dr. Zarkoff to the lost continent of Atlantis on the ocean floor.

CLOSING

Announcer: Come with us every Monday, Tuesday, Wednesday and Thursday at this same time for further interplanetary adventures with Flash Gordon.

53. The Amazing American. Game, 30 min., NBC, 1940.

Contestants were asked to associate the travel services of the Greyhound Bus Lines with facts about America. A lecture, reconstructed to resemble a parlor game and containing facts about an unknown American locale, was read to the studio audience. A player chosen from the audience was then asked several questions concerning the lecture. He was permitted to receive two clues per question, but each clue diminished the point value of the questions. If a player failed to answer a question within the allotted time limit, he received no points for that particular question. The player with the highest score was crowned "The Amazing American" and received Greyhound bus tickets to the city of his choice.

Host: Bob Brown. ***Vocalists:*** The Ranch Boys. ***Orchestra:*** Roy Shields.

54. The Amazing Interplanetary Adventures of Flash Gordon. Science Fiction, 15 min., Syndicated, 1939.

A revised version of *The Amazing Adventures of Flash Gordon* (see entry) that takes Flash away from Atlantis and propels him and his friends Dale Arden and Dr. Zarkoff to distant planets to battle evildoers, in particular Ming, the merciless leader of the warring planet Mongo. Based on the comic strip by Alex Raymond.

Cast: Gale Gordon (*Flash Gordon*); Franc Hale (*Dale Arden*); Maurice Franklin (*Dr. Zarkoff*); Bruno Wick (*Ming*).

OPENING

Announcer: Presenting *The Amazing Interplanetary Adventures of Flash Gordon*. These thrilling adventures come to you as they are pictured each Sunday in the big, full-page *Comic Weekly*, the world's greatest pictorial supplement of humor and adventure. The full-page *Comic Weekly* is distributed everywhere as an integral part of your Hearst Sunday newspaper.

CLOSING

Announcer: These amazing adventures are graphically portrayed in full color action pictures in the *Comic Weekly*, the big, full-page picture supplement distributed each Sunday with your Hearst newspaper. Don't miss the *Comic Weekly* next Sunday. And don't forget our date next week for the next chapter in *The Amazing Interplanetary Adventures of Flash Gordon*.

55. The Amazing Mr. Malone. Crime Drama, 30 min., ABC, 1949–1950; NBC, 1950–1951.

A revised version of *Murder and Mr. Malone*

(see entry). Following the opening theme, the suspects in a murder are established by John J. Malone, a noted criminal attorney based in Chicago (at the Prescott Building—but, as his clients say, "You're never there"). "For my money, you're the best mouthpiece in town," say the people who hire him not only as their legal counsel, but as a detective who will go to any non-violent confrontation to get results—"It's time I was amazing." The program concludes with Malone recapping a case and stating the facts that led him to resolve it.

Cast: Gene Raymond, George Petrie (*John J. Malone*); Larry Haines (*Lt. Brooks*). ***Announcers:*** Arthur Gary, Art Gilmore, Dick Tufeld. ***Producer:*** Bernard L. Schubert.

OPENING

ANNOUNCER: The National Broadcasting Company presents *The Amazing Mr. Malone*, an exciting half-hour of mystery starring George Petrie as the lawyer whose practice before every type of bar has become a legend. Our locale is the city of Chicago; the time is the present and the hero of these weekly adventures is the amazing Mr. Malone.

MALONE: Malone's the name, John J. Malone, attorney and counselor at law. My hobby is collecting clichés. Tonight I would like to try out for your inspection a little number that goes "A Strong Offense Is the Best Defense."

CLOSING

MALONE: Ever hear the story of "The Incurable Gambler"? This boy would take a chance on anything. He found out murder was a bad bet. I'll tell you all about it next week, so why not pick me up at my office at this same time. I'll be waiting for you. Good night.

ANNOUNCER: George Petrie was starred as John J. Malone. *The Amazing Mr. Malone* has come to you from New York. Three chimes mean good times on NBC. This Sunday, you're invited to meet one of your favorite families here on NBC, the Blandings. Cary Grant and Betsy Drake star every Sunday. This is NBC, the National Broadcasting Company.

56. The Amazing Mr. Smith. Comical Mystery, 30 min., Mutual, 4/7/41 to 6/30/41.

Geoffrey Smith is a man with a knack for attracting trouble. He is independently wealthy and has recently been discharged from the Army. He has "inherited" Herbie, his former sergeant, who now works as his valet, chauffeur and butler. Geoffrey has the ability to go anywhere and become involved with murder and mayhem. Stories follow Geoffrey's lighthearted adventures as he helps people in trouble. (See also the following entry.)

Cast: Keenan Wynn (*Geoffrey Smith*); Charlie Cantor (*Herbie*). ***Announcer:*** Harry Von Zell. ***Music:*** Harry Salter.

57. The Amazing Mr. Smith. Comical Mystery, 30 min., CBS, 1946–1947.

A revised version of the prior title that continues to relate events in the life of Geoffrey Smith, the wealthy amateur sleuth who possesses an uncanny knack for finding trouble anywhere. Geoffrey (still assisted by Herbie) claims that he acquired his sleuthing skills by watching *Thin Man* movies but also admits, "I should have watched William Powell, not Myrna Loy."

Cast: Alan Johnston (*Geoffrey Smith*); Ed Brophy (*Herbie*). ***Announcer:*** Ken Niles. ***Music:*** Lud Gluskin. ***Producers:*** Martin Gosch, Howard Harris.

OPENING

ANNOUNCER: *The Amazing Mr. Smith* starring Alan Johnston as Geoffrey Smith and Ed Brophy as Herbie. Geoffrey Smith, so you all will know, is a young man about Hollywood who has the amazing faculty for attracting trouble in various and unexpected forms. From his family, Geoff Smith has inherited a comfortable income; while from his Army career, he has inherited his ex-sergeant, Herbie, who has since become a devoted valet, chauffeur and bodyguard. Our story for today starts late Friday evening as we find Geoff and Herbie speeding up the coast highway toward Loon Point. They are to spend the weekend as invited house guests of Patricia Gilmore, and so begins "The Story of the Hooting Owl."

58. The Amazing Mr. Tutt. Comedy-Drama, 30 min., CBS, summer of 1948.

An adaptation of the *Saturday Evening Post* stories (by Arthur Train) about Ephriam Tutt, an uncanny and cantankerous New England attorney who often encounters misadventure while defending clients. He is assisted by Bonnie Doon.

Cast: Willard Wright (*Ephriam Tutt*); John Beal (*Bonnie Doon*). ***Announcer:*** Roy Rowan. ***Music:*** Lud Gluskin.

59. The Amazing Mrs. Danbury. Comedy, 30 min., CBS, 4/21/46 to 6/16/46.

The chaotic day-to-day activities of Mrs. Jonathan Danbury, a sharp-tongued old woman and the owner of a department store, as she struggles to cope with life at home and at work.

Cast: Agnes Moorehead (*Mrs. Jonathan Danbury*); Cathy Lewis (*Her daughter*); Dan Wolfe (*Her son*). ***Announcer:*** Ken Niles.

The Amazing Nero Wolfe *see* **The Adventures of Nero Wolfe**

60. America Calling. Variety, 30 min., CBS, 1952–1953.

A series devoted to playing the record requests of servicemen overseas. A highlight of the program was its efforts to help wives and girlfriends talk to servicemen via on-the-air telephone conversations.

Host: Rebel Randall. ***Announcer:*** George Walsh.

61. The American Album of Familiar Music. Variety, 30 min., NBC, 1931–1950; ABC, 1950–1951.

A long-running Sunday evening program of music and songs featuring performances by a cast of regulars and weekly guest stars.

Regulars: Vivian Della Chiesa, Donald Dame, Jean Dickenson, Margaret Down, Gustave Haenschen, Betrand Hersch, Daniel Lieberfeld, Evelyn MacGregor, Frank Munn. ***Announcers:*** Andre Baruch, Howard Claney, Roger Krupp. ***Orchestra:*** Abe Lyman. ***Producers:*** Anne Hummert, Frank Hummert.

OPENING

Announcer: *The American Album of Familiar Music* offers for your enjoyment a program of supremely lovely songs and melodies that capture all hearts... (The cast of regulars was then introduced.)

62. An American in England. Anthology, 30 min., CBS, 12/1/42 to 12/15/42.

Dramas that depict the horror of war as seen through the eyes of American soldiers stationed in England. Joseph Julian served as host and narrator. Music was by Benjamin Britten, Lyn Murray and the Orchestra of the Royal Air Force. Edward R. Murrow was the producer and Norman Corwin wrote and directed.

63. American Melody Hour. Variety, 30 min., NBC Blue, 1941–1942; CBS, 1942–1948.

Vivian Della Chiesa as the host of a program featuring popular songs and musical selections. Frank Black, Frank Munn and Conrad Thibault were regulars; Frank Hummert produced.

64. American Musical Festival. Variety, 30 min., CBS, 1941.

A weekly program of classical music featuring the Howard Barlow Orchestra and the hosting and commentary of Nicolai Berzowski.

American Radio Warblers *see* **The Canary Pet Show**

65. The American School of the Air. Anthology, 30 min., CBS, 1930–1948.

A daily educational series that dramatized current events, historical happenings and great moments in literature. A regular feature of the program was "The Hamilton Family," a short segment wherein geography lessons were presented as the family visited various locales.

Cast ("Hamilton Family"): Gene Leonard (*Father*); Betty Garde (*Mother*); Ruth Russell (*Their daughter*); Albert Aley, John Monks, Walter Tetley (*Their sons*). ***Regulars:*** Lyman Bryson, Ray Collins, Mitzi Gould, Parker Fennelly, Chester Stratton. ***Announcer:*** Robert Trout. ***Music:*** Channon Collinge, Dorothy Gordon.

66. American Women. Anthology, 15 min., CBS, 1943–1944.

The program, broadcast during the height of the Second World War, presented stories designed to recruit women for the war effort.

Host-Narrators: Eloise Kummer, Charlotte Manson. ***Producers:*** Bob Brown, Ted Robertson.

The Amident Toothpaste Show *see* **The George Burns and Gracie Allen Show**

Freeman Gosden (left) and Charles Correll starred in *The Amos 'n' Andy Show*.

67. THE AMOS 'N' ANDY SHOW. Comedy, 15 and 30 min. versions, NBC, 1929–1939; CBS, 1939–1943; NBC, 1943–1948; CBS, 1948–1954.

Andrew Halt Brown, Amos Jones and George "Kingfish" Stevens are three friends who reside on Lenox Avenue in New York City. Amos is married to Ruby, the father of Arbadella, and partners with Andy in a one-taxi business called the Fresh Air Taxi Cab Company of America, Inc. (The cab has no windshield, hence the company name.) Amos, the level-headed one, has taken on the job of driver while the rather dimwitted Andy has proclaimed himself the company president. Andy is single, considers himself a ladies' man and is forever getting into trouble as he attempts to find a wife. George is the schemer of the group, a henpecked con artist who devises elaborate business ventures (that rarely work) to acquire money. George is married to—and always arguing with—Sapphire over his prospect of finding a legitimate job. The three are also members of a lodge called the Mystic Knights of the Sea (of which George is the "Kingfish") and stories follow their ups and downs as they struggle to make ends meet. *Other regular characters:* Madame Queen, Andy's on-and-off romantic interest; Lightnin', the cab company janitor; Mama, Sapphire's mother; Algoquin J. Calhoune, the inept lawyer; Shorty, the barber; Henry Van Porter, a friend; Genevieve Blue, the cab company secretary.

Cast: Freeman Gosden (*Amos Jones, George Stevens and Lightnin'*); Charles Correll (*Andrew H. Brown and Henry Van Porter*); Elinor Harriot (*Ruby Jones*); Terry Howard (*Arbadella Jones*); Harriette Widmer (*Madame Queen*); Ernestine Wade (*Sapphire Stevens*); Lillian Randolph (*Mama*); Johnny Lee (*Algoquin J. Calhoune*); Lou Lubin (*Shorty*); Madaline Lee (*Miss Genevieve Blue*); Millie Bruce (*Various roles*). ***Announcers:*** Jim Ameche, Art Gilmore, Bill Hay, John Lake, Ned LeFevre, Del Sharbutt, Olan Soule, Burrett Wheeler, Harlow Wilcox. ***Vocalists:*** The Four Knights, The Jeff Alexander Chorus, The Jubalaires. ***Organist:*** Gaylord Carter. ***Orchestra:*** Jeff Alexander, Lud Gluskin.

OPENING

AMOS: Andy, listen, the man is just about to say it.

ANDY: Yeah, let's everybody listen.

ANNOUNCER: Rinso, the new Rinso with Solium, brings you *The Amos 'n' Andy Show*. Yes, sir, Rinso, the soap that contains Solium, the sunlight ingredient, brings you a full half-hour of entertainment with the Jubalaires, Jeff Alexander's orchestra and chorus, and radio's all-time favorites, Amos and Andy. And now Lever Brothers Company, the makers of Rinso, invite you to sit back, relax and enjoy Amos and Andy.

NOTE: In 1926, over station WGN in Chicago, Freeman Gosden and Charles Correll brought two blackface characters to radio in a series called *Sam and Henry*. In 1928, over station WMAQ, it became *The Amos 'n' Andy Show* and one year later began its network run over NBC. In 1954, Gosden and Correll became the stars of *The Amos 'n' Andy Music Hall*, a 25-minute CBS series of chatter and songs, which originated from the mythical Grand Ballroom of the Mystic Knights of the Sea Lodge.

68. THE ANDREWS SISTERS EIGHT-TO-THE-BAR RANCH. Variety, 30 min., NBC Blue, 1944; ABC, 1945–1946.

Nineteen forties recording artists and motion picture performers, the Andrews Sisters starred in this country-western variety outing that was set at a ranch called Eight-to-the-Bar (where Gabby Hayes was the foreman). In 1946, when Nash-Kelvinator Appliances became the sole sponsor, the title became *The N-K Musical Showroom* and added a weekly guest star to the format.

Hosts: The Andrews Sisters (Patty, Maxene and LaVerne). ***Regulars:*** Jane Froman, George "Gabby" Hayes, Curt Massey, the Riders of the Purple Sage (singers). ***Announcers:*** Andre Baruch, Marvin Miller. ***Orchestra:*** Vic Schoen. ***Producer:*** Lou Levy.

69. THE ANSWER MAN. Information, 15 min., Mutual, 1936–1952; Syndicated, 1954.

The Answer Man, as the host was called, provided answers to questions submitted by listeners. From 1954 to 1956 the program's format was syndicated with each market supplying their own host as "the Answer Man." The network version was sponsored over the years by Colgate Toothpaste, Frommer's Beer, Post Grape Nuts Flakes and Rayve Shampoo.

Host: Albert Mitchell as "the Answer Man." ***Producer:*** Bruce Chapman.

OPENING

ANNOUNCER: Frommer's White Label, the premium beer that is two ways light, presents Albert Mitchell's program *The Answer Man*. And here he is, the Answer Man.

ANSWER MAN: Good evening, ladies and gentlemen. Now, if you're ready, the first question is...

70. APPOINTMENT WITH MUSIC. Variety, 30 min., NBC, 1948.

Snooky Lansen as the host of a weekly program of music and songs. Dorothy Dillard, the Dixie Doms and the Varieteers were the regulars. Ernie Kelly did the announcing and

Beasley Smith and his orchestra provided the music.

71. ARCH OBOLER PLAYS. Anthology, 30 min., NBC, 1939–1940; Mutual, 1945.

Dramatizations of stories written by Arch Oboler. The program, also known as *Arch Oboler Presents*, was hosted by Oboler, with music by Jack Meakin and his orchestra.

OPENING

ANNOUNCER: *Arch Oboler Plays*. Stories of the unusual.

ARCH: This is Arch Oboler. To live forever, to never die; to live forever through the troubles to come, the joys to be. I've thought of that; you've thought of that. So, tonight's play, "The Immortal Gentleman," should be, in many ways, as close to you as your own blood. The play begins after a short message.

ANNOUNCER (after commercial): And now to Arch Oboler's play, "The Immortal Gentleman."

72. ARCHIE ANDREWS. Comedy, 30 min., NBC Blue, 5/31/43 to 1/7/44; Mutual, 1/17/44 to 6/2/44; NBC, 6/2/45 to 9/12/53.

The mythical town of Riverdale was the setting for a weekly series about the comic adventures of a group of close-knit teenagers: Archie Andrews, Jughead Jones, Veronica Lodge, Betty Cooper and Reggie Mantle. Based on the comic strip by Bob Montana. *Other regulars:* Fred and Mary Andrews, Archie's parents; Mr. Weatherbee, the principal of Riverdale High School; and Mr. Lodge, Veronica's father. Veronica's phone number was given as Riverdale 318.

Cast: Jack Grimes, Charles Mullen, Burt Boyer, Bob Hastings (*Archie Andrews*); Harlan Stone, Jr., Cameron Andrews (*Jughead Jones*); Rosemary Rice, Vivian Smolen (*Veronica Lodge*); Doris Grundy, Joy Geffen, Yvonne Mann (*Betty Cooper*); Paul Gordon (*Reggie Mantle*); Vinton Haworth, Arthur Kohl, Reese Taylor (*Fred Andrews*); Alice Yourman, Peggy Allenby (*Mary Andrews*); Arthur Maitland (*Mr. Weatherbee*); Bill Griffis (*Mr. Lodge*). ***Announcers:*** Ken Banghart, Dick Dudley, Bob Sherry. ***Organist:*** George Wright. ***Producer:*** Kenneth MacGregor.

OPENING

ANNOUNCER: Yes, here he is again, the youngster millions of readers of *Archie Comics* and magazines know and love so well, Archie Andrews and all his gang. And now for our weekly visit to Riverdale.

CLOSING

ANNOUNCER: You've been listening to another chapter in the adventures of Archie Andrews, based on the copyrighted feature in *Archie Comics* magazine. In tonight's cast were Bob Hastings as Archie, Harlan Stone as Jughead, Rosemary Rice as Veronica and Yvonne Mann as Betty. Tune in next Saturday for more merry adventures with *Archie Andrews*. This is Bob Sherry wishing you a great weekend. So long. This is NBC, the National Broadcasting Company.

73. ARMCHAIR ADVENTURES. Anthology, 15 min., CBS, 1952.

Original plays and adaptations of stories with Marvin Miller as the host, announcer and voices for all the characters.

74. ARMSTRONG OF THE SBI. Adventure, 30 min., ABC, 9/5/50 to 6/28/51.

A spinoff from *Jack Armstrong, the All-American Boy* about Jack Armstrong, the former high school boy, who was now the chief investigator for the Scientific Bureau of Investigation, and his assistants Betty and Billy Fairfield. *Other regulars:* Vic Hardy, the head of the SBI.

Cast: Charles Flynn (*Jack Armstrong*); Patricia Dunlap (*Betty Fairfield*); Dick York (*Billy Fairfield*); Ken Griffin, Carlton KaDell (*Vic Hardy*). ***Announcers:*** Ken Nordine, Ed Prentiss. ***Producer:*** James Jewell.

OPENING

ANNOUNCER: *Armstrong of the SBI*. Tonight hear a dramatic mystery of suspense and intrigue as Armstrong, chief investigator of the SBI, brings us another thrilling adventure on *Armstrong of the SBI*.

75. THE ARMSTRONG THEATER OF TODAY. Anthology, 30 min., CBS, 1941–1954.

Varying presentations, both dramatic and comedic, sponsored by the Armstrong Cork Company, and featuring radio's top talent.

Commercial pitchgirl ("The Armstrong Girl"): Julie Conway, Elizabeth Reller. ***Announcers:*** George Bryan, Tom Shirley.

Janette Davis and Arthur Godfrey were featured in *Arthur Godfrey Time*.

76. THE ART VAN DAMME QUINTET. Variety, 15 min., Syndicated, 1945.

A weekly series of music and songs with Art Van Damme, leader of a popular instrumental musical group of the 1940s.

Host: Art Van Damme. ***Regulars:*** Louise Carlyle, Chuck Calzoetta, Max Marlash, Lew Skalinder, Benny Week. ***Announcer:*** George Stone. ***Music:*** The Art Van Damme Quintet.

77. ARTHUR GODFREY TIME. Variety, 30 min., CBS, 1945–1972.

A long-running early morning program of music, songs and homespun chatter with humorist Arthur Godfrey. Selected episodes were rebroadcast as *Arthur Godfrey's Digest* on CBS in 1950.

Host: Arthur Godfrey. ***Substitute Host:*** Robert Q. Lewis. ***Regulars:*** Pat Boone, Patti Clayton, Janette Davis, Julius LaRosa, Bill Lawrence, Frank Parker, Lu Ann Simms, Marshal Young, the Chordettes, the Four Clubmen, the Jubalaires, the McGuire Sisters, the Mariners, the Polka Dots, the Symphonettes. ***Announcer:*** Tony Marvin. ***Orchestra:*** Archie Bleyer, Hank Sylvern. ***Producer:*** Will Roland.

ARTHUR GODFREY'S DIGEST *see* **ARTHUR GODFREY TIME**

78. ARTHUR GODFREY'S TALENT SCOUTS. Variety, 30 min., CBS, 1946–1958.

Performances by talented but undiscovered performers. Winners were determined by a studio audience vote. The program, sponsored by Lipton Tea, became the basis for the TV series of the same title.

Host: Arthur Godfrey. ***Vocalists:*** Peggy Marshall and the Holidays. ***Announcer:*** George Bryan. ***Orchestra:*** Archie Bleyer. ***Producer:*** Irving Mansfield.

OPENING

SONG (by the Holidays): Here comes Arthur Godfrey, your talent scout M.C. Brought to you by Lipton's Brisk Lipton Tea... Now here comes Arthur Godfrey, the talent's on its way.

79. ARTHUR'S PLACE. Comedy-Variety, 30 min., CBS, 1947.

Comical events in the life of Arthur Moore, the misadventure-prone owner of Arthur's Place, a Midwestern diner.

Cast: Arthur Moore (*Himself*); Sara Berner (*His girlfriend*). ***Music:*** Jeff Alexander.

80. ARTHUR TRACY, YOUR STREET SINGER. Variety, 15 min., CBS, then Mutual, 1931–1935; NBC Blue, 1940–1942.

A popular program of songs with Arthur Tracy, a vocalist who was known as the Street Singer.

81. AS THE TWIG IS BENT. Serial, 15 min., CBS, 1941–1942.

The struggles of Andrea Reynolds, a young schoolteacher, as she attempts to establish a new life in Beachmont, a small rural community. *We Love and Learn* becomes the title in 1942. In 1955, the spinoff series *The Story of Ruby Valentine* aired (see entry).

Cast: Barbara Terrell, Joan Banks, Betty Worth (*Andrea Reynolds*); George Coulouris, Horace Braham (*Frank Harrison*); Effie Palmer (*Principal Blakely*); Karl Swenson (*Music teacher*); Henry M. Neely (*Janitor*); Frank Lovejoy (*Bill Peters*); Mitzi Gould (*Taffy Grahame*); Don MacLaughlin (*Kit Collins*); Grace Keddy (*Mrs. Van Cleave*); Bill Podmore (*Van Cleave's butler*); Ann Thomas (*Dixie*); Sybil Trent (*Thelma*); Lesley Woods (*Mickey*); Ethel Everett (*Mrs. Wickes*); Sarah Burton (*Laura*); Norman Rose (*Peter*); Barbara Weeks, Lilli Darvas (*Madame Sophie*); Charme Allen (*Mrs. Carlton*); Juano Hernandez (*Abraham Watts*); Carlo DeAngelo (*Carlo*); Jose Ferrer (*Minister*). ***Also:*** Jackie Grimes, Ethel Owen, Larry Robinson, Betty Jane Taylor. ***Announcers:*** Dick Dunham, Adele Ronson, Tom Shirley, Fred Uttal. ***Organists:*** Herschel Leucke, Charles Paul. ***Producer:*** Don Becker.

82. ASK ELEANOR NASH. Women, 15 min., NBC Blue, 1941–1942.

A program of beauty tips and fashion advice for women with host Eleanor Nash.

83. THE ASK-IT-BASKET. Game, 30 min., CBS, 1938–1941.

Four contestants, chosen from the studio audience, compete. A general knowledge type of question is read by the host. The first player to identify himself through a buzzer signal receives a chance to answer. A correct response scores the player one point. The player with the highest point score is the winner and receives $25; $10 is awarded to the second highest scorer; and $5 is the prize for a third-place finish.

Hosts: Jim McWilliams, Ed East. ***Announcer:*** Del Sharbutt. ***Sponsor:*** The Colgate Palmolive Company.

84. ASK ME ANOTHER. Game, 30 min., NBC, 6/16/46 to 9/22/46.

A player, chosen from the studio audience, is asked a general knowledge type of question. An incorrect response disqualifies the player, but a correct response earns the player $10 and the opportunity to remain as long as he can correctly answer succeeding questions. A player's winnings are determined by the number of questions he answers correctly in a row.

Host: Happy Felton. ***Announcer:*** Jay Sims. ***Orchestra:*** Vincent Peters.

85. At Home with Faye and Elliott. Variety, 15 min., Syndicated, 1946.

Celebrity interviews, husband-and-wife chatter with the hosts, household tips and other items of interest to women.

Hosts: Faye Emerson, Elliott Roosevelt. ***Announcer:*** Jim Ameche.

86. Attorney-at-Law. Serial, 15 min., NBC Blue, 1937–1938.

The program, also known as *Terry Regan, Attorney-at-Law*, relates dramatic incidents in the life of a young attorney (Terry Regan).

Cast: Jim Ameche, Henry Hunter (*Terry Regan*); Fran Carlon, Betty Winkler (*Sally Dunlap, his secretary*); Grace Lockwood (*Terry's mother*); Lucy Gilman (*Terry's sister*); Fred Sullivan (*Terry's father*).

87. Attorney for the Defense. Crime Drama, 30 min., Mutual, 1946.

The cases of Roger Allen, a crusading young San Francisco attorney who specializes in helping people with problems far beyond the norm. Shortly after the premiere, the leading character became Jonathan Brixton.

Cast: Michael Raffetto, Al Hodge (*Roger Allen/Jonathan Brixton*); Barton Yarborough (*His assistant*).

88. The Atwater Kent Auditions. Variety, 30 min., NBC, 1927–1932.

A showcase for amateur talent sponsored by Atwater Kent Radios. Like *Arthur Godfrey's Talent Scouts* and *Major Bowes' Original Amateur Hour*, this pioneering program brought talented amateurs from all 48 states to New York to be judged by both celebrities and studio audience members. Here ten finalists were chosen each year and competed in a grand championship face-off for a $5,000 first prize.

Host-Announcer-Vocalist: Graham McNamee.

89. Auction Gallery. Human Interest, 30 min., Mutual, 1945–1946.

Each week, various items were described, then put up for bid. The studio audience as well as home listeners (who had two weeks to respond by mail) were permitted to bid. The player with the highest bid acquired the item.

Host: Dave Elman.

90. Auction Quiz. Game, 30 min., NBC Blue, 1941–1942.

The studio audience is divided into seven sections with each section representing a different subject category. A question, submitted by a listener, was offered for auction to members of the appropriate section. Players now bid for a chance to answer the question. The high bid becomes the prize for that question. If the player answers correctly, he shares the prize money with the listener who submitted the question; if not, the listener receives a consolation prize.

Host-Quizmaster: Chuck Acree. ***Auctioneer:*** Bob Brown. ***Announcer:*** Dan Donaldson.

91. Audition Shows.

Radio, like television, produced test programs (called "audition programs") for possible series. Several such programs have been included to give you an idea of what might have been if the audition episodes sold. For information on these programs, see the following titles: *Action, Daisy Discovers America, Johnny Nighthawk, June's My Girl, Mulligan's Travels, The Smiths of San Fernando, Special Assignment, United States Postal Inspector* and *What's with Herbert?*

92. Aunt Jemima. Variety, 15 min., CBS, 1929; NBC Blue, 1929–1930; CBS, 1932–1944; ABC, 1944–1945; CBS, 1952–1953.

A long-running program of music and songs of the Old South under the sponsorship of Aunt Jemima Pancake Mix.

Cast: Tess Gardell, Amanda Randolph, Harriette Widmer (*Aunt Jemima*). ***Host-Announcer:*** Marvin Miller. ***Vocalists:*** Vera Lane, Mary Ann Mercer, Bill Miller, William Mueller, the Mixed Chorus, the Old Plantation Sextet. ***Orchestra:*** Harry Walsh.

93. Aunt Jenny's Thrilling Real Life Stories. Drama, 15 min., CBS, 1937–1956.

The program opened in the kitchen of a woman known only as Aunt Jenny, who lived in the town of Littleton. Here, she welcomed friends who found comfort in telling her their troubles. Listeners shared the stories via short dramatizations based on Aunt Jenny's real life experiences. Following the story, Aunt Jenny gave a cooking tip making use of the sponsor's product, Spry (a cooking grease). Also known as *Aunt Jenny's Real Life Stories*.

Cast: Edith Spencer, Agnes Young (*Aunt Jenny*). ***Announcer:*** Dan Seymour (as Danny, her assistant). ***Organist:*** Elsie Thompson.

OPENING

ANNOUNCER: Time now for Spry's double-feature treat of the day: *Aunt Jenny's Thrilling Real Life Stories* and—

AUNT JENNY: A luscious strawberry cream pie that needn't take a bit of sugar.

ANNOUNCER: Welcome, folks, it's Spry time here at Aunt Jenny's cheery kitchen. And it's Maytime all over America. That means strawberries now and loads of luscious fruits to come. Aunt Jenny, I would say there is no better time than now to tell the folks about Spry Perfect Pastry Magic.

AUNT JENNY: You're right, Danny. Fresh, ripe fruit in a tender, mouthwatering pie crust is a treat no one can resist.

ANNOUNCER: All you need is Spry and the new Spry Perfect Pastry method.

AUNT JENNY: And ladies, be listening for a tip on making a luscious strawberry cream pie that doesn't take a grain of your precious sugar.

DANNY: You remember, ladies... (Danny recaps the prior episode and introduces the next story.)

CLOSING

DANNY: And now here's Aunt Jenny with a golden thought for today.

AUNT JENNY: Ladies, the secret of happiness and success in whatever we do is to keep going on. Quitters never win and winners never quit.

DANNY: Well, that's a thought we need every day, Aunt Jenny. Now, folks, be sure to be on hand Monday for Spry's double feature–treat of the day: the continuation of Aunt Jenny's Thrilling Real Life Story—

AUNT JENNY: And tender Spry oatmeal muffins.

DANNY: This is Dan Seymour again inviting you to join us Monday for *Aunt Jenny's Thrilling Real Life Stories*, brought to you by Spry, sensational new Spry with cake improver. Rely on Spry. This is CBS, the Columbia Broadcasting System.

94. AUTHOR, AUTHOR. Game, 30 min., Mutual, 1939.

The format called for well-known authors to match wits with the fictional detective Ellery Queen (created by Frederic Dannay and Manfred B. Lee). A short dramatic or humorous sequence was read to Ellery and his guests. Each had to design a complete plot around it. Shortly after the premiere, the format changed and found famous authors supplying endings to stories sent in by listeners.

Host: S.J. Perelman, Ogden Nash. ***Ellery Queen Portrayed By:*** Frederic Dannay, Manfred B. Lee. ***Announcers:*** Frank Knight, Robert L. Slayon.

95. AUTHOR'S PLAYHOUSE. Anthology, 30 min., Mutual, 1940–1941; CBS, 1941; NBC, 1941–1944.

Adaptations of various works of literature—from popular short stories to the works of famous playwrights. Wynn Wright created the program and Roy Shields and his orchestra provided the music.

OPENING (from 1/11/42)

ANNOUNCER: *Author's Playhouse*. Presenting Howard Grigsby's delightful comedy of a sculptress, a husband and a 12-foot statue of New England granite, "Second Fiddle." *Author's Playhouse*, NBC's popular Sunday night dramatic series, brings you radio adaptations of short stories, representative selections by contemporary authors as well as from the works of the great masters of the past. Tonight's drama is from the pen of Howard Grigsby and amply illustrates this young author's flair for comedy situations and dialogue. And now, "Second Fiddle."

96. AUTUMN IN NEW YORK. Variety, 30 min., CBS, 1952.

Jimmy Carroll and Frances Green as the cohosts of a weekly program of music and songs. Alfredo Antonini and his orchestra provided the music.

97. AVALON TIME. Variety, 30 min., NBC, 10/1/38 to 5/1/40.

The program, sponsored by Avalon Cigarettes, features music, songs and comedy, set against the background of a sophisticated hillbilly barn dance.

Host: Red Foley. ***Regulars:*** Janette Davis, Del King, Kitty O'Neil, Red Skelton, the Neighbors Boys. ***Orchestra:*** Phil Davis.

98. The Avenger. Crime Drama, 30 min., Syndicated, 1945–1946.

Seeking a way to battle crime, a famous biochemist (Jim Brandon) invents the Telepathic Indicator (which enables him to pick up thought flashes) and the Secret Diffusion Capsule (which renders him invisible). With his newly developed weapons and the help of his assistant Fern Collier, Brandon becomes the Avenger, a mysterious figure who battles criminal elements.

Cast: James Monks (*Jim Brandon*); Helen Adamson (*Fern Collier*). ***Music:*** Doc Whipple.

OPENING

Announcer: *The Avenger*! The road to crime ends in a trap that justice sets. Crime does not pay! The Avenger, sworn enemy of evil, is actually Jim Brandon, a famous biochemist. Through his numerous scientific experiments, Brandon has perfected two inventions to aid him in his crusade against crime as the Avenger. The Telepathic Indicator, by which he is able to pick up thought flashes, and the Secret Diffusion Capsule, which cloaks him in a black light of invisibility. Brandon's assistant, the beautiful Fern Collier, is the only person who shares his secret and knows that he is the man the underworld fears as the Avenger!

99. The Baby Snooks Show. Comedy, 30 min., CBS, 1944–1949; NBC, 1949–1951.

A weekly visit to the home of the Higgins family on Sycamore Terrace. Here lives Baby Snooks, the mischievous and unpredictable seven-year-old daughter of Lancelot and Vera Higgins, and her brother, Robespierre. Stories relate to the chaos that results (especially to "Daddy") as Baby Snooks, a child far beyond her years, tries to help people she believes are in trouble. The character of Baby Snooks, created by Fanny Brice, first appeared on *The Ziegfeld Follies of the Air* on CBS in 1936. Here Jack Arthur played "Daddy." From 1937 to 1944, Baby Snooks and Daddy appeared as a 15-minute segment of *Maxwell House Coffee Time* with Fanny Brice as Baby Snooks and Jack Arthur, Alan Reed and Hanley Stafford as "Daddy."

Cast: Fanny Brice (*Baby Snooks Higgins*); Hanley Stafford (*Lancelot "Daddy" Higgins*); Lalive Brownwell, Lois Corbett, Arlene Harris (*Vera "Mommy" Higgins*); Leone Ledoux (*Robespierre Higgins*). ***Regulars:*** Elvia Allman, Sara Berner, Georgia Ellis, Stan Farr, Celeste Rush, Martha Wentworth. ***Vocalist:*** Bob Graham. ***Announcers:*** Ken Roberts, Harlow Wilcox, Don Wilson. ***Orchestra:*** Carmen Dragon.

OPENING

Announcer: Sanka is the coffee that lets you sleep; but now wake up, it's time for Baby Snooks! Yes, it's *The Baby Snooks Show* starring Fanny Brice as Baby Snooks, with Hanley Stafford as Daddy … and brought to you by Sanka Coffee … the coffee that's 97 percent caffeine free, so it will never interfere with your sleep. And now, Baby Snooks.

100. Bachelor's Children. Serial, 15 min., CBS, 1936–1946.

The dramatic story of Dr. Robert Graham, a World War I veteran who becomes the guardian of two young women (Ruth Ann and Janet) following the death of their father, a former comrade of Robert's. As the story progressed, Dr. Graham married the elder sister, Ruth Ann, while Janet married Robert's best friend, Sam Ryder. From this point on, stories followed events in the lives of the two couples.

Cast: Hugh Studebaker (*Dr. Robert Graham*); Marjorie Hannan, Laurette Fillbrandt (*Ruth Ann Graham*); Patricia Dunlap (*Janet Ryder*); Olan Soule (*Sam Ryder*); Beryl Vaughn (*Norma Starr*); Arthur Peterson (*Wilton Comstock*); Peg Hallias (*Allison Radcliffe*); Raymond Edward Johnson (*Dr. Bruce Porter*); Janice Gilbert (*Kathleen Carney*); Marie Nelson, Helen Van Tuyl (*Ellen Collins*); Frank Dane (*Lawrence Mitchell*); Charles Flynn (*Michael Kent*); Ginger Jones (*Marjorie Carroll*); John Hodiak (*Davey Lane*); Muriel Bremner (*Susan Grant*). ***Announcers:*** Don Gordon, Russ Young.

OPENING (from 6/6/44)

Announcer: Wonder Bread, the bread that's doubly fresh; fresh when you buy it and fresh when you eat it, presents *Bachelor's Children. Bachelor's Children*, radio's most beloved serial, is brought to you by the makers of Wonder Bread and Hostess Cakes and is dedicated to the grocers of America. And now *Bachelor's Children*, written by Bess Flynn.

CLOSING

Announcer: Helen had a most uncomfortable

day and this evening she decides to have a talk with Janet. Please try to hear *Bachelor's Children* tomorrow when this conversation takes place. Meanwhile, in the interest of your family's appetite and health, get new Wonder Bread, made with Vitamin B-1, the bread that's doubly fresh; fresh when you buy it, fresh when you eat it. This program has come to you from our Chicago studios in the Wrigley Building. This is CBS, the Columbia Broadcasting System.

101. BACKSTAGE WIFE. Serial, 15 min., Mutual, 1935–1936; NBC Blue, 1936; NBC Red, 1936–1955; CBS, 1956–1959.

The dramatic story of a pretty Iowa stenographer (Mary) who meets, falls in love with and marries Larry Noble, a handsome Broadway star, and her struggles to adjust to a new life as she becomes involved in the world of show business. Also known as *Mary Noble, Backstage Wife*.

Cast: Vivian Fridell, Claire Niesen (*Mary Noble*); Ken Griffin, James Meighan, Guy Sorel (*Larry Noble*); Ethel Own (*Clara Noble; Larry's mother*); Wilda Hinkel (*Larry Noble, Jr.; Larry and Mary's son*); Eileen Palmer (*Goldie*); Alan MacAteer (*Pop*); John M. James (*Arnold Carey*); Charlotte Keane (*Bea*); Bartlett Robinson (*Rupert*); Susan Douglas (*Jean Baker*); Dorothy Sands (*Margot*); George Petrie (*Marty*); Anne Burr (*Regina Rawlings*); Eloise Kummer (*Marcia Mannering*); Patricia Dunlap (*Betty Burns*); Dorothy Francis (*Sylvia King*); Sherman Marks (*Joseph Binney*); Elmira Roessler (*Jenny Davis*); Charles Webster, Frank Dane, Mendel Kramer (*Tom Byron*); Ginger Jones, Vicki Vola (*Kitty Marshall*); Malcolm Meecham (*Gerald Marshall*); Henrietta Tedro, Ethel Wilson (*Maude Marlowe*); Joyce Hayward (*Vi Waters*); Charme Allen (*Mercy*); Charlotte Manson (*Marcelle Betrand*); Helen Claire (*Virginia Lansing*); Phil Truex (*Cliff Caldwell*); Donna Creade (*Judith Merritt*); Luise Barclay (*Sandra Carey*); Leo Curley (*Ed Jackson*); John Larkin (*Peter Darnell*). ***Announcers:*** Sandy Becker, Ford Bond, Harry Clark, Roger Krupp. ***Organist:*** Chet Kingsbury. ***Producers:*** Anne and Frank Hummert.

OPENING

ANNOUNCER: We present again today *Backstage Wife*, the story of Mary Noble, an Iowa girl who marries Larry Noble, handsome matinee idol, dream sweetheart of a million other women, and her struggles to keep his love in the complicated atmosphere of backstage life.

102. THE BAKER'S BROADCAST. Comedy-Variety, 30 min., CBS, 1933–1935; NBC, 1935–1938.

Fleischmann's Yeast was the sponsor of this program that featured two different formats. From 1933 to 1935, comedian Joe Penner was the host and the program is also known as *The Joe Penner Show* (see this title for information). After Penner quit in 1935, the format became that of a variety series featuring music, songs, performances by guest stars and cooking tips using the sponsor's product.

Host: Robert Ripley. ***Vocalists:*** Harriet Hilliard, Shirley Lloyd, Martha Mears, Ozzie Nelson. ***Orchestra:*** Ozzie Nelson. ***Producer:*** Ed Gardner.

103. THE BARON AND THE BEE. Quiz, 30 min., NBC, 7/1/53 to 9/8/53.

The format had two two-member teams compete in a spelling bee in return for prizes. The "Baron" of the title was derived from Baron Munchausen, the teller of tall tales character created by Jack Pearl in 1933. See also *The Jack Pearl Show*.

Host: Jack Pearl. ***Co-Host:*** Cliff Hall (as Sharlie, Jack's straight man). ***Organist:*** Paul Taubman.

104. BARRY CAMERON. Serial, 15 min., NBC, 1945–1946.

Dramatic incidents in the lives of Barry and Anna Cameron, a young couple struggling to survive the difficult first years of marriage.

Cast: Spencer Bentley (*Barry Cameron*); Florence Williams (*Anna Cameron*); Doris Rich (*Vinnie*); Dorothy Sands (*Mary Ann Clark*); Scott McKay (*John Nelson*); Elsie Hitz (*Josephine*); King Calder (*Will Stevenson*); Coleen Ward (*Frances*); Mary Hunter (*Martha Stevenson*). ***Announcer:*** Larry Elliott.

105. BARRY CRAIG, CONFIDENTIAL INVESTIGATOR. Crime Drama, 30 min., NBC, 1951–1955.

Barry Craig is a New York–based private detective who guarantees to keep his clients' business confidential. Stories relate his efforts to help the people who are unable to turn to the police for help. Originally titled *Barry Crane, Confidential Investigator*.

Cast: William Gargan (*Barry Craig*).

OPENING

ANNOUNCER: The National Broadcasting Company presents William Gargan in another transcribed drama of mystery and adventure with America's number one detective, *Barry Craig, Confidential Investigator*.

THE BARTON FAMILY *see* **THE STORY OF BUD BARTON**

106. THE BATTLE OF THE SEXES. Game, 30 min., NBC Red, 1938–1943; NBC Blue, 1943–1944.

The original format found two four-member teams, men vs. women, competing in a general knowledge question-and-answer session. Each correct response scored points and members of the highest scoring team each received a wristwatch as a prize. In 1942, the program altered its format to accommodate servicemen. Soldiers were pitted against female canteen workers in a spelling bee that awarded war bonds and cash prizes for correct answers.

1938–1942 Hosts: Frank Crumit (Male Team Captain); Julia Sanderson (Female Team Captain). ***1942–1944 Hosts:*** Jay C. Flippen, Walter O'Keefe. ***Announcer:*** Ben Grauer.

107. THE BAXTERS. Drama, 15 min., NBC, 1943–1947.

A series of light dramatic incidents faced by an average American family—parents Bill and Marge and their children Janie, Sara and Bud—during wartime. The program, geared to a family audience, was sponsored by the PTA and titled after World War II *The Baxters Carry On*.

Cast: Arthur Peterson (*Bill Baxter*); Fern Parsons (*Marge Baxter*); Jane Webb (*Janie Baxter*); Eva Grant (*Sara Baxter*); Arthur Young (*Bud Baxter*). ***Announcer*** (Voice of the PTA): Eva Grant.

108. BEAT THE BAND. Game, 30 min., NBC, 1940–1941; 1943–1944.

A music-oriented question, submitted by a home listener (who received $10), was read to the studio orchestra. If an orchestra member failed to identify the song to which the question referred, the listener won an additional $10 and 50 cents was placed in the kitty (bass drum) by the orchestra. The orchestra member who identified the most songs won the money in the kitty. In a later format, the listener received $25 for each question that stumped the band and a pack of Raleigh Cigarettes (the show's sponsor, 1943–44) was tossed into the kitty. At the end of the show, the cigarettes were donated to the Armed services.

Host: Garry Moore (1940–1941); Hildegarde Loretta Sell (1943–1944). ***Vocalists:*** Perry Como, Marilyn (Marvel) Maxwell, Elmo Tanner, Marilyn Thorne. ***Announcers:*** Marvin Miller, Tom Shirley. ***Orchestra:*** Ted Weems, Harry Sosnik.

109. BEAT THE CLOCK. Game, 30 min., CBS, 1/5/49 to 5/4/49.

A game show, suited more for television than radio, that found selected members of the studio audience attempting to perform stunts before the time on a ticking clock ran out. Prizes were awarded to players who were able to beat the clock and successfully perform stunts. While a failure on radio, a successful television version appeared on CBS (1950–1958) and ABC (1958–1962).

Host: Bud Collyer. ***Announcer:*** Johnny Olsen. ***Organist:*** Ivan Ditmars.

110. THE BEATRICE KAY SHOW. Variety, 30 min., Mutual, 1946.

A weekly program of music, songs and light comedy.

Host: Beatrice Kay. ***Regulars:*** Lon Clark, the Elm City Four, Peter Lind Hayes. ***Announcer:*** Jay Jackson. ***Orchestra:*** Henry Levine, Hank Sylvern.

111. BEHIND THE FRONT PAGE. Anthology, 30 min., Mutual, 1948.

Dramatizations based on front-page newspaper stories and featuring weekly guest stars. Gabriel Heatter was the host-announcer-narrator.

112. BEHIND THE MIKE. Anthology, 15 min., NBC Blue, 1940–1942.

Graham McNamee as the host of a weekly series that dramatized behind-the-scenes stories of radio broadcasting. Harry Von Zell did the announcing.

113. Behind the Story. Anthology, 15 min., Mutual, 1949–1957.

Dramatizations of little-known incidents in the lives of famous people. Stories were factual and were presented as yarns with direct quotes once used by the subjects. Marvin Miller, who served as the host and narrator, also performed all the character roles.

114. Believe It or Not. Anthology, 15 and 30 min. versions, NBC Red, 1930–1931; NBC Blue, 1931–1932; NBC Red, 1934; NBC Blue, 1935–1937; NBC Red, 1937–1938; CBS, 1939–1940; NBC Blue, 1942; Mutual, 1944; CBS, 1945; NBC Red, 1947–1948.

Variety (songs and music) coupled with dramatizations based on the unusual happenings that appeared in the *Ripley's Believe It or Not* newspaper column (which featured oddities of every kind).

Host: Robert L. Ripley. ***Substitute Hosts:*** George Abbott, Gregory Adams. ***Regulars:*** Harriet Hilliard, Linda Lee, the Men About Town. ***Announcers:*** Bill Griffis, Don Hancock. ***Orchestra:*** Ozzie Nelson, Frank Novak, B.A. Rolfe.

OPENING

Announcer: Believe It or Not! Yes, *Believe It or Not*, pages from the sketchbook of Robert L. Ripley, and here speaking for Bob Ripley is the dean of newsreel commentators, Gregory Adams.

Adams: Thanks you, Bill Griffis, and welcome, everyone, to Bob Ripley's radio auditorium, a collection of amazing facts documented by Bob Ripley in his never-ending search for the truth—the truth which is always more unbelievable than fiction.

115. The Bell Telephone Hour. Music, 30 min., NBC, 1940–1958.

A long-running program of concert music that featured performances by a cast of regulars as well as weekly guest stars.

Host: James Melton. ***Regulars:*** Francia White, the Ken Christy Chorus. ***Orchestra:*** The Bell Symphony Orchestra; Donald Voorhees.

116. The Ben Bernie Show. Variety, 30 min., CBS, 1931–1938; NBC, 1940–1943.

Music, songs, and comedy with Ben Bernie, a popular orchestra leader of the era who was called "The Old Maestro." Also known as *The Pabst Blue Ribbon Show* (from 1931–1935, when the beer company sponsored the program).

Host: Ben Bernie. ***Regulars:*** Buddy Clark, Jackie Heller, Pat Kennedy, Lew Lehr, Jane Pickens, Manny Prager, Frank Price, Mary Small, Dick Stabile, Bill Wilgus. ***Announcers:*** Bob Brown, Harry Von Zell, Harlow Wilcox. ***Orchestra:*** Bob Gibson.

117. Ben Bernie's Musical Quiz. Game. 30 min., CBS, 1938–1940.

Two teams, men vs. women, competed in a series of music-oriented question-and-answer rounds in return for merchandise prizes.

Host: Ben Bernie. ***Regulars:*** Carol Bruce, the Bailey Sisters. ***Announcer:*** Dan Seymour. ***Orchestra:*** Bob Gibson.

118. The Benny Goodman Show. Variety, 30 min., CBS, then Mutual, 1939–1946.

A continuation of *Benny Goodman's Swing School* (see next title) that provided a forum for popular songs. Bert Parks served as the host and Peter Donald, Art Lund and Martha Tilton were the regulars. Clayton "Bud" Collyer did the announcing and the Benny Goodman Orchestra provided the music.

119. Benny Goodman's Swing School. Variety, 30 min., NBC, 1936–1939.

A Tuesday evening program of swing music sponsored by Camel cigarettes and featuring the music of the Benny Goodman Orchestra. Benny Goodman served as the host; Meyer Alexander was the musical director; and the regulars were the Camel Swing Chorus and the Goodman Instrumental Trio and Quartet. See also the prior title.

OPENING

Announcer: Camel cigarettes presents *Benny Goodman's Swing School*, the Tuesday evening rally of everybody who gets a lift from the new pulsating music of youth, swing. Tonight, the King of Swing presents the world's greatest swing band, the Goodman Instrumental Trio and Quartet, and the Camel Swing Chorus under the direction of

Meyer Alexander and all brought to you by the makers of Camel cigarettes.

120. The Benny Rubin Show. Variety, 30 min., NBC, 1949–1950; ABC, 1950–1951.

Comedian Benny Rubin as the host of a program that combined comedy with talk, music and songs. Lillian Bernard, Lou Bernard, Jackie Coogan, Edith Fellows, Vinnie Monte and the Andrews Twins were the regulars. Don Ward did the announcing; Rex Maupin and his orchestra provided the music.

121. Bert Lytell Dramas. Anthology, 15 min., Mutual, 1938–1939.

Dramas that depict the crucial moments that affect the lives of ordinary people. Also known as *Bert Lytell's Adventures*. Bert Lytell served as the host and Helen Choate and Jay Jostyn were regular performers.

122. Best of All. Variety, 60 min., NBC, 1954–1955.

Robert Merrill as the host of a weekly program that featured Broadway show tunes and guests from the Great White Way. Vocalist Elizabeth Doubleday was the regular; Kenneth Banghart did the announcing; and Skitch Henderson and his orchestra provided the music.

123. Best Seller. Anthology, 15 min., CBS, 1960.

A daily program that dramatized popular novels in five 15-minute segments. One of the last of radio's anthology programs.

Host-Narrator: Bret Morrison. ***Leading Roles:*** Jim Boles.

124. The Better Half. Game, 30 min., Mutual, 1942–1946.

The format pitted husbands against their wives in a series of stunts to determine the better half. Cash prizes were awarded to the players who successfully completed their stunts.

Hosts: Tom Slater, Tiny Ruffner.

125. Betty and Bob. Serial, 15 min., NBC Blue, 1932–1936; CBS, 1936–1938; NBC Red, 1938–1940.

The story of a young married couple (Bob and Betty Drake) and their efforts to run a small town newspaper (the *Trumpet*). Betty was a poor secretary who married the wealthy Bob Drake. Bob's family disapproved of him marrying beneath his social status and cut off his funds, thus opening the door for him and Betty to succeed on their own.

Cast: Don Ameche, Les Tremayne, Spencer Bentley, Carl Frank, J. Anthony Hughes, Van Heflin (*Bob Drake*); Elizabeth Reller, Betty Churchill, Alice Hill, Arlene Francis, Edith Davis, Mercedes McCambridge (*Betty Drake*); Frankie Pacelli (*Bobby Drake, Jr.*); Edith Davis, Dorothy Shideler (*Mae Drake*); Herbert Nelson (*Carl Grainger*); Eleanor Dowling (*Ethel Grainger*); Ned Wever (*Al Bishop*); Francis X. Bushman (*Peter Standish*); Betty Winkler (*Marcia*); Eliose Kummer (*Kathy Stone*); Don Briggs (*Tony Harker*). ***Producers:*** Anne Hummert, Frank Hummert.

126. Betty Boop Fables. Children, 15 min., NBC Blue, 1932–1933.

Betty Boop, the scantily clad 1920s flapper and Depression-era symbol of enthusiasm created by Max Fleischer, in a weekly series of misadventures as she struggles to cope with life.

Cast: Mae Questel (*Betty Boop*); Red Pepper Sam, William Costello (*Freddie Frog*). ***Music:*** Victor Erwin.

127. Betty Clarke Sings. Variety, 15 min., ABC, 1/16/49 to 1/15/50.

Vocalist Betty Clarke as the host of a program of music and songs. Don Lowe did the announcing; music was by Frank Bantor (novachord) La La Porta (guitar) and Veryle Mills (harp).

128. The Betty Crocker Magazine of the Air. Women, 15 min., NBC, then CBS, 1926–1947; ABC, 1947–1952.

Cooking tips, recipes, fashion ideas, household hints and related information for housewives, sponsored by General Mills (Betty Crocker is the company's homemaking expert).

Host: Zella Layne (as Betty Crocker). ***Announcer:*** Win Elliot.

129. Betty Moore's Triangle Club. Women, 15 min., NBC Blue, then CBS, 1931–1943.

Decorating ideas, household hints, cooking

and related topics of interest for housewives sponsored by Moore Paints (Betty Moore is the company's spokesperson).

Host: Margaret MacDonald (as Betty Moore). ***Regulars:*** George Gann, Johnny Thompson. ***Music:*** Dahl Gable.

130. BEULAH. Comedy, 30 min., ABC, 1947; CBS, 1947–1952.

A revamped version of *The Marlin Hurt and Beulah Show* (see for original concept). On radio, Beulah was originally played by a man (Marlin Hurt) and was the black maid to the McGees on *Fibber McGee and Molly*. In 1945, Hurt was given his own series as Beulah, but died a year later and the program was canceled. In 1947, ABC revised the concept with Beulah (first played by a man) as the black maid to the Hendersons, a white middle-class American family. Like the television version this series spawned, Beulah's efforts to solve domestic problems was the focal point of the program. *Other regular characters:* Harry and Alice Henderson (who lived at 213 Lake Street); Donnie, their son; Oriole, Beulah's friend; and Bill Brown, Beulah's boyfriend.

Cast: Bob Corley, Hattie McDaniel, Louise Beavers, Lillian Randolph (*Beulah*); Hugh Studebaker, Jess Kirkpatrick (*Harry Henderson*); Mary Jane Croft, Lois Corbett (*Alice Henderson*); Henry Blair, Sammy Ogg (*Donnie Henderson*); Ruby Dandridge, Amanda Randolph, Butterfly McQueen (*Oriole*); Ernest Whitman (*Bill Brown*). ***Announcers:*** Johnny Jacobs, Marvin Miller, Hank Weaver. ***Music:*** Buzz Adlam, Gordon Kibbee.

131. BEYOND TOMORROW. Anthology, 30 min., CBS, 2/23/50 to 4/13/50.

A weekly series of chilling science fiction dramas with Mitchell Grayson as the producer. The program premiered in February of 1950 as *Beyond This World* and changed its title to *Beyond Tomorrow* in April 1950.

OPENING

ANNOUNCER: And now for tonight's story, let's go *Beyond Tomorrow*. Are you afraid to face tomorrow, or whatever may be beyond tomorrow? Do you think you're up to spending a weekend on the moon or entertaining a house guest from Mars? Can you and your children adjust to the strange, new, wonderful world that is being wrought in the test tubes and cyclotrons of science beyond tomorrow? *Beyond Tomorrow*, a new program of probabilities, drawn from the vast library of science fiction where anything is possible and possibly may happen to you.

132. THE BICKERSONS. Comedy, 30 min., NBC, 1946–1947; CBS, 1947–1948; CBS, summer of 1951.

Incidents in the lives of John and Blanche Bickerson, a quarrelsome husband and wife. Their never-ending verbal battle as Blanche struggled to correct John's shortcomings was the focal point of each episode. The program began as a skit on *The Charlie McCarthy Show*; it is also known as *Drene Time* (when sponsored by Drene Shampoo) and *The Old Gold Show* (when Old Gold cigarettes handled the show). On *The Charlie McCarthy Show*, John worked as a bowling ball salesman and traveled 80 miles each way to work. In the actual series, John is a vacuum cleaner salesman for Eagle Appliances.

Cast: Don Ameche, Lew Parker (*John Bickerson*); Frances Langford, Marsha Hunt (*Blanche Bickerson*); Danny Thomas (*Amos Jacobs, Blanche's brother*). ***Also:*** John Brown, Pinky Lee, Lou Lubin, Benny Rubin, Lurene Tuttle. ***Announcers:*** John Holbrook, Marvin Miller. ***Orchestra:*** Carmen Dragon, Tony Romano.

OPENING

ANNOUNCER: Now here are Don Ameche and Frances Langford as John and Blanche Bickerson in [title of episode]. Now, the story begins.

133. THE BIG BREAK. Variety, 30 min., NBC, 1947.

A showcase for amateur talent that gave promising performers a chance for that big break.

Host: Eddie Dowling. ***Announcer:*** David Ross. ***Orchestra:*** Ray Bloch.

134. BIG CITY SERENADE. Variety, 30 min., NBC, 1951–1953.

Vocalist Skip Farrell as the host of a weekly program of music and songs featuring Henry Cooke. Joseph Gallichio and his orchestra provided the music.

135. THE BIG GUY. Crime Drama, 30 min., NBC, 5/21/50 to 11/5/50.

Joshua Sharp is a widower, the father of two children (Debbie and Joshua, Jr.) and he works as a private detective on a strictly cash basis. Josh not only cares for his children but also for his clients; when he is on a case, he will do what it takes to help them; he will not break the law—"There are some things that even the biggest of big guys can't do." Stories follow Sharp as he uses a non-violent approach to solving crimes—deductive reasoning.

Cast: Henry Calvin (*Joshua Sharp*); Denise Alexander (*Debbie Sharp*); David Alexander (*Joshua Sharp, Jr.*). ***Announcer:*** Fred Collins. ***Music:*** George Wright.

OPENING

JOSH: [Laughing.]

DEBBIE: How tall are you, Papa? Tell me how tall.

JOSH: I'm twenty-foot-five in my stocking feet.

JOSH, JR.: How big are your shoes?

DEBBIE: What size do you wear?

JOSH: Size 902 in a triple Z.

DEBBIE: That's our Papa, *The Big Guy*.

ANNOUNCER: NBC presents *The Big Guy*, the first of a new series of adventures of a very unusual detective, Joshua Sharp. Joshua Sharp works for his clients on a strictly cash basis to provide for the needs of his nearest and dearest; his nearest and dearest are two in number—Josh, Jr., and his daughter Debbie. To these two, Sharp is both father and mother; to his clients he is a good detective; to Josh and Debbie, he is the friendly magician, the fabulous hero, the giant among giants—*The Big Guy*. Tonight's adventure with *The Big Guy*, "The Unheard Voice."

CLOSING

ANNOUNCER: The National Broadcasting Company has presented the adventures of *The Big Guy*, played by Henry Calvin. This is Fred Collins speaking for NBC, the National Broadcasting Company.

136. THE BIG HAND. Anthology, 30 min., ABC, 1951.

Weekly guests appeared in dramatizations of adventure stories in which the hand of fate played a crucial part. Rex Maupin and his orchestra provided the music.

137. BIG JON AND SPARKIE. Children, 60 and 15 min. versions, ABC, 1950–1958.

Music, songs and sketches set against the background of the Pumkin Crossing General Store. Arthur Fields served as the host (Big Jon) and did the voices for the characters, most notably Sparkie, the mischievous Elf from the Land of Make Believe who wanted to become a real boy. (Sparkie spoke in a high-pitched voice—a tape of Fields played at a fast speed.) Other characters included Mayor Plumpfront and Ukey Betcha. Ireene Wicker appeared to tell stories and sing; and William J. Mahoney, Jr., played Gil Hooley (of Gil Hooley and His Leprechaun Marching Band). This daily program was complemented with a two-hour (later 90-minute) Saturday morning edition called *No School Today* that used the same format but added an assistant (Fred Hall) and Jolly Bill the Newsman (played by Bill Steinke). *No School Today* ran from 1950 to 1956 and both versions were produced by Arthur Fields.

OPENING

SPARKIE: Hey, hey, ho there. Hi, boys and girls, hi, kids; hey, come in here right now 'cause it's time for—

JON: Big Jon—

SPARKIE: —and Sparkie!

JON: Well, hello again and we go again with another hour of stories and songs for the younger generation and the young at heart. Hi, this is Big Jon. And Sparkie, the little Elf from the Land of Make Believe who more than anything else in the world wants to become a real boy, is right here with me. Yes, sir, once again from San Francisco, California, within sight of the Golden Gate, it's time for the biggest party in the world because it goes all away around the world. Time for *Big Jon and Sparkie* and *No School Today*.

138. THE BIG 'N' LITTLE CLUB. Children, 30 min., ABC, 1949.

Songs, stories and varied entertainment for the small fry with host Dick Collier and his assistant Phil Cramer.

139. THE BIG SHOW. Variety, 90 min., NBC, 11/5/50 to 4/20/52.

Radio's last attempt at a big-budget variety show that featured performances by top name guest stars from around the world. Each guest talked and chuckled with the host and the program concluded with a segment called "The Actor's Company," wherein scenes from Broadway plays were performed. After a two-

George Sanders, Peggy Lee, Portland Hoffa, Groucho Marx, Fred Allen and host Tallulah Bankhead during a broadcast of *The Big Show*.

year struggle with poor ratings (but good reviews), *The Big Show* lost its battle to the growing popularity of television.

Host: Tallulah Bankhead. ***Announcers:*** Ed Herlihy, Jimmy Wallington. ***Orchestra/Chorus:*** Meredith Willson.

OPENING

HOST: For the next hour and 30 minutes, this program will present in person such bright stars as—

STARS (each in their own voice): Louis Armstrong, Bob Hope, Deborah Kerr, Frankie Laine, Jerry Lewis, Dean Martin, Dorothy McGuire, Jimmy Wallington, Meredith Willson.

HOST: And my name, dahling, is Tallulah Bankhead.

ANNOUNCER: The National Broadcasting Company presents *The Big Show.*

SONG (chorus): So listen, America, don't turn us off, America; we're going to fill your pot of gold up high.

ANNOUNCER: *The Big Show*, 90 minutes with the most scintillating personalities in the entertainment world, brought to you this Sunday and every Sunday at this same time as the Sunday feature of NBC's all-star festival. And here's your hostess, the glamorous, unpredictable Tallulah Bankhead.

TALLULAH: Well, dahlings, here we are with *The Big Show*, this week in Los Angeles, the City of Angels; or is it Los Angel-is, the City of the Angels? Well, to be safe, I'll call it L.A., lousy with actors. [Her monologue would continue and lead into the show.]

CLOSING

TALLULAH: Well, dahlings, that's our show for this week. We're off for New York again, where we'll bring you next Sunday, Christmas Eve, a load of presents to distribute—Jimmy Durante, Bert Lahr, Robert Merrill, Margaret O'Brien, Edith Piaf, Ed Wynn and Meredith Willson and the Big Show Orchestra and Chorus. We'll be dedicating our Christmas Eve show to all our men in uniform all over the world. Until then, dahlings,

may the good Lord bless and keep you, whether near or far away.

ANNOUNCER: *The Big Show*, the Sunday night feature of NBC's all-star festival, has been brought to you by your local Ford dealer, who's proud to say the new 1951 Ford is the car that's built for the years ahead; by RCA Victor, world leader in radio, first in recorded music and first in television; by Chesterfield, the only cigarette that combines mildness with no unpleasant aftertaste; and by Anacin, for the fast relief of headache pain. This is NBC, the National Broadcasting Company.

140. BIG SISTER. Serial, 15 min., CBS, 1936–1952.

The series, set in the town of Glen Falls, relates dramatic incidents in the lives of two married sisters, Ruth Evans Wayne and Sue Evans Miller. Also known as *Rinso's Big Sister* (when sponsored by Rinso soap powder).

Cast: Ruth Chatterton, Nancy Marshall, Alice Frost, Marjorie Anderson, Mercedes McCambridge, Grace Matthews (*Ruth Evans Wayne*); Helen Lewis, Haila Stoddard, Dorothy McGuire, Peggy Conklin, Fran Carden (*Sue Evans Miller*); Martin Gabel, Paul McGrath, Staats Cotsworth (*Dr. John Wayne; Ruth's husband*); Ned Wever, Richard Kollmar, Joseph Julian (*Jerry Miller, Sue's husband*); Berry Kroeger, Ian Martin, Arnold Moss, David Gothard (*Dr. Reed Bannister*); Elspeth Eric (*Diane Ramsey*); Ann Shepherd, Teri Keane (*Hope Melton Evans*); Ed Begley, Horace Braham (*Waldo Briggs*); Jim Ameche, Jr. (*Richard Wayne*); Richard Widmark (*Eric Ramsey*); Arlene Francis (*Lola Mitchell*); Joseph Julian (*Peter Kirkwood*); Charlotte Holland (*Addie Price*); Vera Allen (*Nurse Burton*); Michael O'Day (*Neddie Evans*); Santos Ortega (*Dr. Duncan Carvell*); Eric Dressler (*Frank Wayne*); Evelyn Varden (*Mrs. Carvell*); Carl Benton Reid (*Roger Allen*); Chester Stratton (*Samson*); Elizabeth Love (*Harriet Durant*); Louise Fitch (*Margo Kirkwood*); Patsy Campbell (*Ginny Price*); Helene Dumas (*Vera Wayne*). ***Announcers:*** Jim Ameche, Hugh Conover, Fred Uttal. ***Organist:*** Richard Leibert. ***Orchestra:*** William Meeder.

OPENING

ANNOUNCER (over clock chimes): Rinso presents *Big Sister*. Yes, there's the clock in Glen Falls Town Hall telling us it's time for Rinso's story of *Big Sister*, brought to you by the new soapy rich Rinso; R...I...N...S...O.

141. THE BIG STORY. Anthology, 30 min., NBC, 1947–1955.

Dramatizations based on headline-making newspaper stories. The reporter whose story was chosen for broadcast appeared on the program for an interview and to receive a check for $500.

Host-Narrator: Robert Sloane. ***Regular Cast:*** Robert Dryden, Alice Frost, Betty Garde, Bernard Grant, Bill Quinn. ***Announcer:*** Ernest Chappell. ***Music:*** Vladimir Selinsky.

OPENING

ANNOUNCER: Pall Mall, famous big cigarette, presents *The Big Story*, another in a thrilling series based on true experiences of newspaper reporters. Tonight, to Russ Wilson of the Des Moines *Tribune* goes the Pall Mall award for *The Big Story*. Now, the authentic and exciting story of "The Case of the Ambitious Hobo."

142. THE BIG TALENT HUNT. Variety, 30 min., Mutual, 1948.

A parody of the normal programs that showcase promising amateur talent with a look at people who possess unusual skills (for example, jugglers, one-man bands and yodelers).

Host: Jim Backus. ***Announcer:*** Ted Brown. ***Orchestra:*** Emerson Buckley.

143. BIG TOWN. Crime Drama, 30 min., CBS, 1937–1948; NBC, 1948–1951; CBS, 1951–1952.

Big Town is a fictional city beset by crime. Through the pages of his newspaper *The Illustrated Press*, editor Steve Wilson seeks to expose the criminals and their rackets. Stories, based on actual newspaper files, relate Steve's exploits as well as those of Lorelei Kilbourne, the society editor who assists Steve and often becomes involved with shady characters. *Other regular characters:* Dusty Miller, the photographer; Police Inspector Callahan; District Attorney Miller; Miss Foster, Steve's secretary; the newsboy who shouts "Get Your *Illustrated Press*"; and Eddie, the cab driver. This show served as the basis for the television series of the same title.

Cast: Edward G. Robinson, Edward Pawley,

Ona Munson and Regs, an "extra" for the January 1, 1941, episode of *Big Town*.

Walter Greaza (*Steve Wilson*); Claire Trevor, Ona Munson, Fran Carlon (*Lorelei Kilbourne*); Lawson Zerbe, Casey Allen (*Dusty Miller*); Dwight Weist (*Inspector Callahan*); Gale Gordon (*D.A. Miller*); Helen Brown (*Miss Foster*); Ted de Corsia (*Eddie*); Bobby Winkler, Michael O'Day (*Newsboy*). ***Narrator:*** Dwight Weist. ***Announcer:*** Ken Niles. ***Organist:*** John Gart. ***Orchestra:*** Leith Stevens. ***Producers:*** Phil Cohen, Jerry McGill.

OPENING

NEWSPAPER BOY: Extra, extra, get your *Illustrated Press*. Read all about the new 1940 Rinso that washes clothes whiter and brighter. Read all about it!

ANNOUNCER: The new 1940 top-speed Rinso with its marvelous new suds booster that licks hard water and gives you much richer suds, Rinso brings you Edward G. Robinson in an exciting story from *Big Town*, a story of life and death on the highways of America. Ona Munson heads the supporting cast. Now let's see what's going on in *Big Town*. In tonight's presentation, Mr. Robinson is heard as Steve Wilson, managing editor of the *Illustrated Press*. He is aided and abetted by Lorelei, the girl reporter played by Ona Munson.

144. THE BILL GOODWIN SHOW. Variety, 30 min., CBS, 1947.

A weekly program of music, songs and light comedy hosted by Bill Goodwin. Elvia Allman, Jim Backus, Mary Jane Croft, Norene Gamel, Peggy Knudsen, Shirley Mitchell and the Girlfriends were the regulars. Jeff Alexander and his orchestra provided the music.

145. THE BILLIE BURKE SHOW. Comedy, 30 min., CBS, 1944–1946.

The little white house on Sunnyview Drive is the residence of Billie Burke, a well-meaning young woman with her head in the clouds; her unemployed brother, Julius, and their maid, Daisy. Julius has a terrible temper and flies off the handle at the drop of a pin. Billie feels his temper costs him prospective jobs and hopes to help him curtail it and become more dignified. But Billie's meddling always places Julius in embarrassing situations and his efforts to undo Billie's good intentions are the focal point of stories. Julius often exclaims, "Of all the people in the world, why did I have to get you for a sister?" Billie's response is quite simple—"I don't know Julius, I guess you're just lucky." Julius claims to have a law degree; Billie is a member of the Saturday Night Ladies Club and Daisy calls Billie "Miss Billie." In July 1946, Julius acquires a job as an attorney for the Baby Buggy Bumper Company. *Other regular characters:* Banker Guthrie and Col. Fitts, rivals for Billie's hand.

Cast: Billie Burke (*Billie Burke*); Earle Ross (*Julius Burke*); Lillian Randolph (*Daisy*); Marvin Miller (*Banker Guthrie and Col. Fitts*). ***Announcers:*** Tom Dickson, Marvin Miller. ***Music:*** Carl Bonowitz. ***Producer:*** Axel Gruenberg.

OPENING

ANNOUNCER: Listerine toothpaste presents *The Billie Burke Show*. Get two or more women together and chances are sooner or later they'll start talking about nylon stockings. Well, if you're tired of just talking about nylons and think it's time you got some, why not enter the weekly Listerine toothpaste contest? First prize is 12 pairs of exquisite Nylons of Note by Holproff, the famous quality stockings which feature a choice of three different leg lengths in each size… All you have to do is complete this sentence: "I like Listerine toothpaste because…" I'll give you the rules later, so have a pencil and paper ready to take them down. And here she is, that bright, smiling morning star, our Miss Leading Lady, Miss Billie Burke.

BILLIE: Good morning, everybody, good morning [she would then begin the show].

CLOSING

BILLIE: Goodbye, Mr. Miller, goodbye, everybody, till next Saturday. And remember [singing], Look for the silver lining and try to find the sunny side of life.

ANNOUNCER: Tune in again next Saturday when the makers of Listerine toothpaste again present *The Billie Burke Show*. Your announcer is Marvin Miller. This is CBS, the Columbia Broadcasting System.

146. BILLY AND BETTY. Children, 15 min., NBC, then CBS, 1935–1940.

Exciting stories for children about a brother and sister (Billy and Betty White) and their friend (Melvin Castlebury) who find adventure in everything they do.

Cast: Jimmy McCallion (*Billy White*); Audrey Egan (*Betty White*); Elliott Reid (*Melvin Castleberry*). ***Announcer:*** Kelvin Keech.

147. BILLY BACHELOR. Serial, 15 min., NBC, 1932–1935.

A daily children's drama that followed the adventures of Billy Bachelor, the editor of a newspaper founded by his uncle, in the town of Wheatenaville (named after the sponsor, Wheatena cereal). *Other regular characters:* Peter and Pan, the twins who were his wards;

and Janet, his assistant. Also known as *Wheatenaville Sketches*.

Cast: Ray Knight (*Billy Bachelor*); Janet Freeman (*Janet*); Vivian Block (*Pan*); Bobby Jordan (*Peter*).

148. The Bing Crosby Show. Variety, 30 min., CBS, then NBC, 1931–1946.

A weekly program of music, songs and performances by top-name guest stars. See also *Philco Radio Time*.

Host: Bing Crosby. ***Regulars:*** Connee Boswell, Bob Burns, Rosemary Clooney, Skitch Henderson, Peggy Lee, the Buddy Cole Trio, Jud Conlon's Rhythmaires, the Red Nichols Combo. ***Announcers:*** Ken Carpenter, Glenn Riggs. ***Orchestra:*** John Scott Trotter.

Bing Crosby hosted *The Bing Crosby Show* from 1931 to 1946.

149. Biographies in Sound. Anthology, 60 min., NBC, 1955–1958.

Biographical profiles of famous people presented in a series of sketches, followed by interviews with people associated with the subject. Leith Stevens and his orchestra provided the music; Joseph Meyers was the producer.

150. Birds Eye Open House. Variety, 30 min., NBC, 1945–1946.

A weekly program of music and songs sponsored by Birds Eye frozen vegetables and Gaines dog food. Dinah Shore served as the host; Harry Von Zell did the announcing and Robert Emmett Dolan and his orchestra supplied the music.

151. The Bishop and the Gargoyle. Crime Drama, 30 min., NBC Blue, 1936–1942.

Retiring from his duties as a servant of God and interested in crime, a bishop joins the parole board of Sing Sing State Prison. There he meets the Gargoyle, a convict he befriends and later reforms (Gargoyle takes an interest in the bishop's cause). After completing his sentence, the Gargoyle joins forces with the bishop and stories relate their efforts to bring criminals to justice.

Cast: Richard Gordon (*The Bishop*); Milton Herman, Ken Lynch (*The Gargoyle*). ***Note:*** On November 29, 1941, NBC adapted an episode of the radio series to television in an experiment titled "The Item of the Scarlet Ace," wherein the Bishop (Richard Gordon) and the Gargoyle (Ken Lynch) sought to capture an elusive criminal known as the Scarlet Ace.

152. The Black Book. Anthology, 15 min., CBS, 1952.

A series of mystery and suspense presentations with Paul Frees as the host and narrator. John Dehner appeared as a regular performer in stories. Clarence Cassill did the announcing; Leith Stevens and his orchestra provided the music.

153. The Black Castle. Anthology, 15 min., Mutual, 1943–1944.

Chilling dramatizations of people trapped in unexpected and dangerous situations. The host, the Wizard of the Black Castle, was assisted by his raven, Diablo.

Starring: Don Douglas (as all characters, including the host and announcer).

OPENING

ANNOUNCER (over eerie sound effects); Now, up these steps to the iron-studded oaken door which yawns wide on rusted hinges, bidding us enter. [Over music:] Music, do you hear it? Wait. It is well to stop, for here is the Wizard of the Black Castle.

WIZARD: There you are, back again, I see. Well, welcome, come in, come in. You'll be overjoyed at the tale I have for you tonight.

154. THE BLACK HOOD. Crime Drama, 15 min., Mutual, 1943–1945.

Kip Burland is a rookie police officer who is secretly the mysterious figure for justice, the Black Hood. Kip, who acquires magical powers from a specially developed black hood, is assisted by Barbara Sutton, a newspaper reporter who is the only other person aware of his dual identity. Together they battle the criminal elements.

Cast: Scott Douglas (*Kip Burland*); Marjorie Cramer (*Barbara Sutton*).

OPENING

ANNOUNCER: *The Black Hood.*

VOICE: Criminals beware! The Black Hood is everywhere.

BLACK HOOD: I, the Black Hood, do solemnly swear that neither threats nor bribes nor bullets nor death itself shall keep me from fulfilling my vow to erase crime from the face of the Earth!

155. THE BLACK MUSEUM. Anthology, 30 min., Mutual, 1951–1952.

A revised version of *Whitehall 1212* (see entry). Dramatizations based on Scotland Yard's Black Museum, which houses a collection of murder weapons associated with England's most bizarre and baffling crimes. Each drama centered on one of the weapons and how it was used to commit a crime. Produced in England.

Host: Orson Welles.

OPENING

ORSON: This is Orson Welles speaking from London.

SOUND: The chimes of Big Ben.

ORSON: From *The Black Museum*, a repository of death. Yes, here in a grim stone structure on the Thames, which houses Scotland Yard, is a warehouse of homicide. Here, everyday objects, a silk scarf, a length of twine, a child's toy, are all touched by murder.

ANNOUNCER: From the annuls of the Criminal Investigation Department of the London Police, we bring you the dramatic stories of the crimes recorded by the objects in Scotland Yard's Gallery of Death, *The Black Museum*.

CLOSING

ORSON: And now until we meet next time in this same place and I tell you another story in *The Black Museum*, I remain, as always, obediently yours.

156. BLACK NIGHT. Variety, 30 min., ABC, 1950–1951.

A weekly program that featured nocturnal visits to Chicago's points of interest. Music, songs and narration were used to highlight each visit.

Host: Don Dowd. ***Vocalists:*** Carolyn Gilbert, Loretta Poynton. ***Orchestra:*** Rex Maupin.

157. BLACKSTONE PLANTATION. Variety, 30 min., CBS, then NBC, 1929–1933.

The program, sponsored by Blackstone Cigars, presented a mixture of talk, songs and music.

Host: Frank Crumit, Julia Sanderson. ***Regulars:*** Ted de Corsia, Don Escondido, Santos Ortega, Don Rodrigo.

158. BLACKSTONE, THE MAGIC DETECTIVE. Adventure, 15 min., Mutual, 1948–1949; 1952.

Fictionalized events based on the life of Harry Blackstone, a former stage magician who uses his abilities to help people in trouble. Each program opened with Blackstone telling his friends John and Rhonda about an incident from his life (which was dramatized for listeners) and concluded with him explaining how certain magic tricks were performed.

Cast: Ed Jerome (*Harry Blackstone*); Ted Osborne (*John*); Fran Carlon (*Rhonda*). ***Announcer:*** Alan Kent. ***Music:*** William Meader.

OPENING

ANNOUNCER: *The Magic Detective*, starring the world's greatest living magician, Blackstone. Tonight, he recalls the story of "The Locked Book." Right after the story, Blackstone will explain tricks that you yourself can perform and reveal the guarded secrets of the world's greatest living magician.

159. BLIND DATE. Game, 30 min., NBC, 1942–1943.

Soldiers and/or sailors, chosen from the studio audience, vie for a date with a glamorous film actress (a guest). A dramatic sketch is performed by members of the regular cast and stopped prior to its conclusion. Each of the servicemen, previously supplied with a comedy blackout line, reads it to complete the sketch. Each reading is judged by the studio audience (applause) and the serviceman who scores

Arthur Lake and Penny Singleton were Dagwood and Blondie Bumstead on *Blondie*.

highest receives the date. In the closing segment of this World War II series, a mother's letter to her serviceman son is read and relayed via shortwave. See also the following title.

Host: Frances Scully. ***Dramatic Cast:*** Connie Haines, Mercedes McCambridge, Lizzie Tish (a comic female impersonator). ***Vocalists:*** The Bryant Sisters. ***Music:*** The Melodates Orchestra.

160. Blind Date. Game, 30 min., ABC, 1943–1946.

A revamped version of the prior title that now has servicemen attempting to persuade glamourous girls to accept dates with them. Six servicemen appear but compete two at a time. Two men are seated on stage opposite a girl whose image is obstructed by a large screen. Each male had to telephone the girl and, within a two-minute, ten-second time limit, convince her to go out with him. The girl chooses the one she feels is the most romantic and the couple receives a sponsored evening at a New York supper club. Three such rounds are played and the men who are not chosen receive a consolation prize. Served as the basis for the television series of the same title.

Host: Arlene Francis. ***Announcer:*** Tiny Ruffner. ***Music:*** Arnold Johnson.

161. Bloch Party. Variety, 60 min., CBS, 1951.

A weekly program of music and songs with orchestra leader Ray Bloch as the host. Judy Lynn and the Russ Emery Chorus were the regulars. Martin Sweeney did the announcing and Ray Bloch's orchestra provided the music.

162. Blondie. Comedy, 30 min., CBS, 1939–1948; NBC, 1948–1949; ABC, 1949–1950.

Humorous events in the lives of the Bumstead family: Dagwood, a bumbling architect/bookkeeper for the J.C. Dithers Construction Company; Blondie, his attractive, seemingly scatterbrained but logical wife; and their children, Alexander (nicknamed "Baby Dumpling") and Cookie. A recurring aspect of the series was J.C.'s constant firing of Dagwood and

Blondie's efforts to get Dagwood back his job. ("Mr. Dithers needs you," says Blondie. "Yea, but he doesn't know he needs me," says Dagwood.) *Other regular characters:* Julius C. "J.C." Dithers, Dagwood's boss; Cora Dithers, J.C.'s wife; Herb Woodley, Dagwood's neighbor; Harriet, Blondie's friend; Alvin Fuddle, Alexander's friend; and Mr. Fuddle, Alvin's father. Based on the comic strip by Chic Young.

Cast: Penny Singleton, Alice White, Patricia Van Cleve, Ann Rutherford (*Blondie Bumstead*); Arthur Lake (*Dagwood Bumstead*); Leone Ledoux, Larry Sims, Jeffrey Silver, Tommy Cook (*Alexander Bumstead*); Marlene Ames, Joan Rae, Norma Jean Nilsson (*Cookie Bumstead*); Hanley Stafford, Arthur Q. Bryan (*J.C. Dithers*); Elvia Allman (*Cora Dithers*); Hal Peary, Frank Nelson (*Herb Woodley*); Dix Davis (*Alvin Fuddle*); Mary Jane Croft (*Harriet*); Arthur Q. Bryan, Harry Lang (*Mr. Fuddle*). ***Announcers:*** Bill Goodwin, Howard Petrie. ***Orchestra:*** Billy Artzt, Harry Lubin.

OPENING

ANNOUNCER: Uh-uh-uh, don't touch that dial, listen to—

DAGWOOD: B-l-o-n-d-i-e!

ANNOUNCER: Yes, folks, it's another half-hour of fun with Blondie and Dagwood, brought to you by the great new 1947 Super Suds and Lustre Creme Shampoo for true hair loveliness.

CLOSING

ANNOUNCER: Remember, folks, every Sunday over these same CBS stations, a half-hour of fun with all the Bumsteads, brought to you by Lustre Creme Shampoo, the creme shampoo for true hair loveliness, and the great new 1947 Super Suds.

SONG: Super Suds, great new suds, 1947 suds.

ANNOUNCER: Tell all your friends to tune in next Sunday at this same time for—

DAGWOOD: B-l-o-n-d-i-e!

ANNOUNCER: This is Howard Petrie saying good night from Hollywood. This is CBS, the Columbia Broadcasting System.

163. THE BLUE BEETLE. Crime Drama, 15 min., Mutual, 1938.

While investigating a case involving the selling of marijuana cigarettes, rookie patrolman Dan Garrett is machine-gunned down. He is near death when the mysterious Dr. Franz comes to his aid and gives him a secret formula (2-X) he developed. Dan recovers immediately and also acquires superhuman vitality and incredible strength. Now, with super powers and a specially developed suit of blue chain armor, Dan wages a war against the underworld in York City—striking at a moment's notice and always leaving behind his trademark—little blue beetles. Dr. Franz is the only other person who knows of Dan's dual identity (he also supplies Dan with an array of devices; for example, Formula X-4 to melt locks; invisibility fluid; a poison detector ring).

Cast: Frank Lovejoy (*Dan Garrett*); Paul Ford (*Police Commissioner*).

OPENING

SOUND: Police whistles, then a voice saying *The Blue Beetle*.

ANNOUNCER: Leaping down upon the underworld to smash gangland comes the friend of the unfortunate, enemy of criminals, a mysterious, all-powerful character. A problem to the police, but a crusader for law; in reality Dan Garrett, a rookie patrolman. Loved by everyone but suspected by none of being the *Blue Beetle*. As the Blue Beetle, he hides behind a strange mask and suit of impenetrable blue chain armor, flexible as silk but stronger than steel. Giving the Green Hornet a run for his money, Dan Garrett's father was killed by a gangster's bullet. Dr. Franz, an apothecary on a side street, is the only person who knows the secret identity of the Blue Beetle. Today's episode: "Smashing the Dope Ring."

164. BLUE RIBBON MUSIC TIME. Variety, 30 min., NBC, 1947.

Vocalist Georgia Gibbs as the host of a weekly program of music and songs sponsored by Pabst Blue Ribbon Beer. Jimmy Wallington did the announcing and David Rose and his orchestra provided the music.

165. BLUE RIBBON TIME. Variety, 30 min., CBS, 1944–1947.

The program, also known as *Pabst Blue Ribbon Time*, featured music and songs under the sponsorship of Pabst Blue Ribbon Beer. Kenny Baker was the host. The Robert Armbruster Chorale provided songs and backup vocals for guests; Ken Niles did the announcing and Robert Armbruster and his orchestra provided the music.

166. Blue Ribbon Town. Variety, 30 min., CBS, 1943–1944.

A weekly program of music, comedy and songs sponsored by Pabst Blue Ribbon Beer. Comedian Groucho Marx served as the host with Leo Gorcey as his foil. Kenny Baker, Donald Dickson and Virginia O'Brien were the regulars; Dick Joy and Ken Niles did the announcing; and Robert Armbruster and his orchestra furnished the music. Dick Mack was the producer.

167. Bluegrass Brevities. Variety, 15 min., CBS, 1939.

Chuck Hurton as the host of a program of country and western music and songs. Also featured were announcer Alan Jackson and Robert Hutsell and his orchestra.

168. The Bob and Ray Show. Comedy, 15, 30 and 60 min. versions, 1946–1951 (local); NBC, 1951–1953; Mutual, 1955–1957; CBS, 1959–1960; National Public Radio, 1960–1984.

Offbeat satirical skits featuring an array of characters created by Bob Elliott and Ray Goulding. These include: Wally (Bob), the remote location interviewer; Steve Bosco (Bob), the sportscaster (who always seemed a bit tipsy); Tex Blaisdell (Bob), the country and western entertainer; Mary McGoon (Ray), the recipe lady; Natalie Attired (Ray), the singer who said songs; and Eddie (Bob), Natalie's drummer. The program also featured spoofs of radio programs (for example, "Mary Backstage, Noble Wife," "One Feller's Family," "Jack Headstrong," the All American American," "Mr. Trace, Keener Than Most Persons" and "The Bob and Ray Gourmet Club"). Also known as *Matinee with Bob and Ray*. See also *Pick and Play with Bob and Ray*.

Stars: Bob Elliott, Ray Goulding. ***Announcer:*** Jack Costello. ***Organist:*** Rosa Rio. ***Music:*** The Paul Taubman Trio.

OPENING

Bob: It's Bob and Ray time.

CLOSING

Ray: Well, I guess that should do it for today. So until next time, this is Ray Goulding reminding you to write if you get work.

Bob: Bob Elliott reminding you to hang by your thumbs.

169. The Bob Burns Show. Comedy, 30 min., CBS, 1941–1944; NBC, 1944–1947.

Comic tales of a man called the Arkansas Traveler (a character created by Bob Burns), who roamed across the country doing good deeds. Also known as *The Arkansas Traveler*.

Cast: Bob Burns (*The Arkansas Traveler*). ***Regulars:*** Carry Allen, Doug Gourlay, Shirley Ross, Ann Thomas. ***Orchestra:*** Billy Artzt, Gordon Jenkins.

170. The Bob Crosby Show. Variety, 15 min., CBS, 1935–1936; 30 min., NBC, 1943–1946.

A weekly program of music and songs with Bob Crosby (Bing's brother), a vocalist and orchestra leader (of the Bob Cats).

Star: Bob Crosby. ***Host:*** Johnny Mercer. ***Vocalists:*** Bob Haggart, The Pied Pipers, Jo Stafford, Kay Starr, Eileen Wilson. ***Announcers:*** John Lund, Les Tremayne. ***Orchestra:*** The Bob Cats.

171. The Bob Hawk Show. Game, 30 min., CBS, 1945–1947; NBC, 1947–1953.

Comedy bits by quizmaster Bob Hawk were interspersed with a game show that found selected studio audience members competing in a question-and-answer quiz round for prizes. The program was sponsored by Camel cigarettes and winners were called a "lemac" (camel spelled backward).

Host: Bob Hawk. ***Regulars:*** Art Carney, Charles Stark. ***Announcer:*** Dennis James. ***Orchestra:*** Peter Van Steeden.

Bob Hawk's Quixie Doodle Quiz *see* **Quixie Doodle**

172. The Bob Hope Show. Variety, 30 min., CBS, 1941–1942; NBC, 1943–1955.

A weekly program of music, songs, monologues and comedy sketches sponsored by Pepsodent Tooth Paste. Bob appeared as himself with a recurring cast of regular players: Prof. Colonna; Vera Vague, the man-chasing girl; Brenda and Cobina, the society girls; Miriam, the sponsor's pitchgirl; and Honey Chile, the Southern Belle. The program is also known as *The Bob Hope Pepsodent Show*.

Cast: Bob Hope (*Himself*); Jerry Colonna (*Prof. Colonna*); Barbara Jo Allen (*Vera Vague*); Blanche Stewart (*Brenda*); Elvia Allman (*Cobina*); Trudy Erwin (*Miriam*); Patricia

Wilder, Claire Hazel (*Honey Chile*). ***Regulars:*** Frank Fontaine, Irene Ryan. ***Vocalists:*** Doris Day, Bill Farrell, Judy Garland, Gloria Jean, Frances Langford, the Six Hits and a Miss Vocal Group. ***Announcers:*** Hy Averback, Art Baker, Bill Goodwin, Larry Keating, Wendell Niles. ***Orchestra:*** Les Brown, Skinnay Ennis, Al Goodman, Red Nichols.

OPENING

ANNOUNCER: Tonight, from the home of Ken Murray's blackouts, the El Capitan Theater in Hollywood, Lever Brothers Company presents *The Pepsodent Show* starring Bob Hope and his special guest, Al Jolson. (Audience applause would then be heard, followed by Bob's theme song, "Thanks for the Memory" and Bob himself opening the program with his monologue).

Bob Hope hosted the weekly variety program *The Bob Hope Show.*

173. THE BOB SMITH SHOW. Variety, 30 min., NBC, 1954.

Music and songs coupled with a quiz format that found selected members of the studio audience having to determine a mystery year through a series of indirect clues. Merchandise prizes were awarded to successful players.

Host: Bob Smith. ***Regulars:*** Clark Dennis, the Honeydreamers. ***Orchestra:*** Bobbie Nicholson.

174. BOBBY BENSON AND THE B-BAR-B RIDERS. Western, 30 min., CBS, 1932–1936; Mutual, 1949–1955.

Bobby Benson is a 12-year-old boy who, after the death of his parents, inherits the B-Bar-B Ranch in Big Bend, Texas. Stories follow his adventures as he and his foreman and guardian, Tex Mason, struggle to protect their ranch from desperados. Between 1932 and 1936, when the program was sponsored by Heckers H-O Oats cereal, the ranch was called the H-Bar-O Ranch. Bobby rides a horse named Amigo. Also known as *Bobby Benson's Adventures*, *The B-Bar-B Ranch* and *Songs of the B-Bar-B*. *Other regular characters:* Windy Wales, the handyman and teller of tall tales; Harka, the Indian; Bobby's Aunt Lilly; Polly, Bobby's friend; and the Chinese cook.

Cast: Richard Wanamaker, Ivan Curry, Billy Halop (*Bobby Benson*); Herb Rice, Neil O'Malley, Charles Irving, Al Hodge, Tex Ritter (*Tex Mason*); Don Knotts (*Windy Wales*); Florence Halop (*Polly Armstead*); Craig McDonnell (*Harka*); Larraine Pankow (*Aunt Lilly*); Herb Rice (*Chinese cook*). ***Announcers:*** Andre Baruch, Carl Caruso, Bob Emerick, Dan Seymour, Carl Warren.

OPENING

ANNOUNCER: Here they come. They're riding fast and they're riding hard. It's time for excitement and adventure in the modern West

Billy Halop played the title character in *Bobby Benson and the B-Bar-B Riders.*

with *Bobby Benson and the B-Bar-B Riders*. And out in front, astride his golden palomino Amigo, it's the cowboy kid himself, Bobby Benson.

BOBBY: B-Bar-Beeeeeeeeee.

175. THE BOBBY DOYLE SHOW. Variety, 15 min., NBC, 1947.

Vocalist Bobby Doyle as the host of a program of music and songs that featured the Honeydreamers Quintet. Jack Lester announced; Harry Kogen and his orchestra provided the music.

176. BOLD VENTURE. Adventure, 30 min., Syndicated, 1951–1952.

Slate Shannon is an adventurer who, after the death of a friend, becomes the guardian of his beautiful daughter, Sailor Duval. Not content with life in the United States, Slate and Sailor move to Havana, where they become owners of a rundown hotel (Shannon's Place) and a boat called the *Bold Venture*. Stories relate their efforts to run a hotel and charter boat service while at the same time helping people in trouble.

Cast: Humphrey Bogart (*Slate Shannon*); Lauren Bacall (*Sailor Duval*). ***Announcer:*** Marvin Miller. ***Music:*** David Rose.

OPENING

ANNOUNCER: *Bold Venture*! Adventure, intrigue, mystery, romance; starring Humphrey Bogart and Lauren Bacall—together in the salty setting of tropical Havana and the mysterious islands of the Caribbean. *Bold Venture*.

CLOSING

ANNOUNCER: And so our two stars, Humphrey Bogart and Lauren Bacall, have brought to a close our latest *Bold Venture* story. May we invite you to listen again next week at this same time for another exciting adventure starring Humphrey Bogart and Lauren Bacall together in *Bold Venture*.

177. BOSTON BLACKIE. Crime Drama, 30 min., NBC, Summer of 1944; NBC, 1945–1948.

Boston Blackie is a master thief who decided to go straight and use his skills to bust crime as a private detective. He has knowledge of the underworld to fight crime and claims, "I can open any vault in the world with these fingers." Now, based in New York City, Blackie uses his skills as a criminal to help Inspector Faraday of the N.Y.P.D. Homicide Department capture lawbreakers. *Other regular characters:* Mary Wesley, Blackie's girlfriend, a nurse; and Shorty, Blackie's friend, an ex-con who assists Blackie (and hopes by doing so he doesn't wind up back in the slammer). Shorty, a short man with no other name, calls Blackie "Boss." Based on the character created by Jack Boyle.

Cast: Chester Morris, Richard Kollmar (*Boston Blackie*); Lesley Woods, Jan Miner (*Mary Wesley*); Richard Lane, Maurice Tarplin, Frank Orth (*Inspector Faraday*); Tony Barrett (*Shorty*). ***Announcers:*** Larry Elliott, Harlow Wilcox. ***Organist:*** Hank Sylvern. ***Producer:*** Jeanne Harrison.

OPENING

ANNOUNCER: And now meet Richard Kollmar as Boston Blackie, enemy to those who make him an enemy, friend to those who have no friends.

178. THE BOSTON POPS ORCHESTRA. Variety, 60 min., NBC, 1951.

Arthur Fiedler hosted and conducted the world-famous Boston Pops Orchestra in a weekly program combining popular standards with light classical music. Ben Grauer was the announcer.

179. THE BOTANY SONG SHOP. Variety, 15 min., ABC, 1950–1951.

Vocalist Ginny Simms as the host of a program of music and songs sponsored by Botany Mills. Harry Von Zell did the announcing; the Buddy Cole Trio provided the music.

180. BOUQUET FOR YOU. Variety, 30 min., CBS, 1946.

Vocalist Patti Clayton as the host of a weekly program of music and songs. Louise King, Bill Leach and Billy Williams were the regulars. Franklyn MacCormack and Lee Vines did the announcing; and the Caesar Petrillo and Howard Smith orchestras provided the music.

181. BOX 13. Crime Drama, 30 min., Syndicated, 1948–1949.

Dissatisfied with his job as a newspaper columnist for the *Star Times*, Dan Holiday quits to become a mystery novelist. To acquire material for his books, Dan places a personalized ad in the *Star Times* ("Adventure wanted. Will go anywhere, do anything. Box 13") and responds to the offers that arrive. *Other regular characters:* Suzy, Dan's secretary (she brings Dan the mail from Box 13 and "rescues me from the nut house at the *Star Times*." Suzy was originally the receptionist at the paper's personal ad department who quit to become Dan's secretary).

Cast: Alan Ladd (Dan Holiday); Sylvia Picker (*Suzy*).

OPENING (typical; Dan's comments would vary from episode to episode)

ANNOUNCER: *Box 13*, with the star of Paramount Pictures, Alan Ladd, as Dan Holiday.

GIRL'S VOICE: Box 13, Box 13, Box 13, Box 13.

DAN (walking to Box 13): Well, this is great. Rain, rain, rain. Bet even the ducks wouldn't come out in weather like this. But me, I'm an idiot. I gotta go and take up a profession like being a writer ... so I can be out on a cold wet night beating my brains out looking for an idea... What a way to make a living. I could have stayed a reporter at the *Star Times* with nice assignments like listening to political speeches or covering the opening of a manhole. Oh, no, not me. I have to write fiction, do it the hard way. [He now arrives at the paper.] Well, I might as well open the usual door, go to the usual place and hear the usual comments. [At this point, Suzy would greet him and the story would begin as Dan picked up his mail.]

182. BRAVE TOMORROW. Serial, 15 min., NBC, 1943–1944.

The dramatic story of the Lambert family (Hal, the father; his wife Louise; their children Jean and Marty). Their story of love and courage is designed to show that "from today's defeats we build our brave tomorrows."

Cast: Raymond Edward Johnson, Roger DeKoven (*Hal Lambert*); Jeanette Dowling (*Louise Lambert*); Nancy Douglass, Flora Campbell (*Jean Lambert*); Jone Allison, Andree Wallace (*Marty Lambert*); Frank Lovejoy (*Brad Forbes*); House Jameson (*Whit Davis*). ***Also:*** Ginger Jones, Carl Eastman, Myra McCormick, Margaret MacDonald, Paul Stewart. ***Announcer:*** Ed Herlihy. ***Music:*** William Meader.

OPENING

ANNOUNCER: *Brave Tomorrow* is the story of love and courage written by Ruth Adams and brought to you by Ivory Soap.

183. BREAK THE BANK. Game, 30 min., Mutual, 1945–1946; ABC, 1946–1949; NBC, 1950–1951; ABC, 1951–1953; NBC, 1953–1954; Mutual, 1954–1955.

Selected members of the studio audience compete in a series of question-and-answer rounds. Each correct response earns a player five dollars; players continue until defeated by two incorrect responses or until they break the bank by answering eight straight questions for the top prize of $500 (later increased to $1,000). Players who are defeated forfeit their earnings (which are placed into the bank to build the jackpot). Served as the basis for the television series of the same title (1948–1956).

Hosts: Clayton "Bud" Collyer, John Reed King, Johnny Olsen, Bert Parks. ***Announcers:*** Clayton "Bud" Collyer, Win Elliot. ***Organist:*** Lew White. ***Orchestra:*** Hank Sylvern, Peter Van Steeden.

184. BREAKFAST AT SARDI'S/BREAKFAST IN HOLLYWOOD. Variety, 30 min., NBC Blue, 1942–1943; ABC, 1943–1950.

A morning program of chatter, music, songs and interviews (with patrons of Sardi's restaurant in Hollywood). When host Tom Breneman purchased his own restaurant, he moved the locale and changed the title to *Breakfast in Hollywood*.

Hosts: Tom Breneman, Jack McElroy, Garry Moore, Arch Presby. ***Hostess:*** Nell Olson. ***Regulars:*** Jack Coy, Johnny Montgall. ***Announcers:*** John Nelson, Carl Pierce. ***Orchestra:*** Gaylord Carter. ***Producers:*** Charles Harrell, Ralph Hunter.

185. THE BREAKFAST CLUB. Variety, 60 min., NBC Red, 1933–1941; NBC Blue, 1941–1943, ABC, 1943–1968.

A very popular, live, early morning program of chatter, songs, skits and music broadcast from Chicago at nine A.M. each morning. The program featured the morning prayer, the walk around the breakfast table and such characters as Aunt Fanny (who dispensed gossip), Sam, "The Fact and Fiction Man" (who cited tidbits from "Sam's Almanac"), and Toots and Chickie, a wacky married couple played by Jim and Marian Jordan (who would later become famous as "Fibber McGee and Molly"). Also known as *Don McNeill's Breakfast Club*. The program was also simulcast on television in the early 1950s.

Cast: Don McNeill (*Host*); Fran Allison (*Aunt Fanny*); Sam Cowling (*Sam*). ***Regulars:***

Host Tom Breneman helps *Breakfast in Hollywood* celebrate the beginning of its seventh year on the air.

Eugene Baird, Jack Baker, Anita Bryant, Janette Davis, Clark Dennis, Johnny Desmond, Johnny Johnston, Jim and Marian Jordan, Annette King, Patsy Lee, Marion Mann, Nancy Martin, Edna O'Dell, Jack Owens, Gale Page, Patti Page, Russell Pratt, Mildred Stanley, Johnny Thompson, Ilene Woods. ***Vocal Groups:*** The Cadets, The Merry Macs, The Three Romeos, The Vagabonds. ***Announcers:*** Bob Brown, Don Dowd, Charles Irving, Fred Kasper, Durward Kirby, Bob McKee, Robert Murphy, Ken Nordine, Louis Roen. ***Orchestra:*** Eddie Ballantine, Walter Blaufuss, Joseph Gallichio, Harry Kogen, Rex Maupin.

186. Breezing Along. Variety, 30 min., NBC Blue, 1939–1940.

The program, sponsored by Philip Morris cigarettes, couples music and songs with a quiz segment called "Swing Go" (wherein a contestant had to supply the last line of a rhyme sent in by a listener with a song title). The program concluded with a short segment relating stories called "Pipe Dreams."

Host: Davis Ross. ***Pipe Dreams Host:*** Alan Reed. ***Vocalists:*** Jack Smith, The Bel-Airs. ***Orchestra:*** Johnny Green.

187. Brenda Curtis. Serial, 15 min., CBS, 1939–1940.

Brenda is a brilliant actress who relinquishes her career to devote time to her husband Jim, a lawyer, and to establish a home in New York City. Stories relate the problems that befall the newlywed couple as Brenda struggles to begin a new life.

Cast: Vicki Vola (*Brenda Curtis*); Michael Fitzmaurice, Hugh Marlowe (*Jim Curtis*); Helen Choate (*Myra Belden*); Agnes Moorehead (*Brenda's mother*).

188. Brenthouse. Serial, 30 min., NBC Blue, 1938–1940.

Following the death of her husband, Portia Brent inherits his business, a book publishing company called Brenthouse. Stories follow Portia as she struggles to run the company and raise her three children (Jane, Nancy and Peter).

Cast: Hedda Hopper, Georgia Backus, Kathleen Fitz (*Portia Brent*); Florence Baker (*Jane Brent*); Lurene Tuttle (*Nancy Brent*); Ernest Carlson, Larry Nunn (*Peter Brent*); Margaret Brayton (*Martha Dudley*); Wally Maher (*Lance Dudley*); Ben Alexander (*Philip West*); Al Cameron (*Steve*); Anne Stone (*Gabrielle*); Jane Morgan (*Nora Lawson*); Naomi Stevens (*Daphne Royce*); Gavin Gordon (*Dr. Norfolk*).

189. BRIDE AND GROOM. Human Interest, 30 min., ABC, 1945–1950.

Couples about to marry submitted stories about themselves to the program. A panel of judges reviewed the letters and selected couples to appear on the broadcast. Prior to the broadcast, a couple was married in a small chapel just off the ABC radio studios. Following the ceremony, the couple was brought on stage and interviewed. After sharing elements of their meeting and courtship, they were showered with wedding gifts. This served as the basis for the television series of the same title.

Host: John Nelson. ***Announcer:*** Jack McElroy.

190. BRIGHT HORIZON. Serial, 15 min., CBS, 1941–1945.

A spinoff from *Big Sister* that focuses on the life of Michael West, a restaurant singer who is outwardly soft-hearted and idealistic but inwardly a man filled with hard, bitter disillusionment. Alice Frost, who plays the leading character of Ruth Wayne on *Big Sister*, appeared in early episodes to establish the series.

Cast: Richard Kollmar, Joseph Julian (*Michael West*); Sammie Hill, Joan Alexander (*Carol West*); Frank Lovejoy (*Larry*); Lesley Woods (*Margaret McCarey*); Ronald Liss (*Bobby*); Renee Terry (*Barbara*); Lon Clark (*Keith Richards*); Alice Goodkin (*Lily*); Audrey Totter (*Bonnie*); Richard Keith (*Charles McCarey*). ***Also:*** Will Geer, Jackie Grimes, Santos Ortega, Chester Stratton. ***Announcer:*** Marjorie Anderson. ***Organist:*** John Gart.

191. BRIGHT STAR. Comedy-Drama, 30 min., NBC, 1952–1953.

Susan Armstrong is the editor of the *Morning Star*, a newspaper in the town of Hillsdale. George Harvey is her star reporter, a man who will go to any lengths to get a story. Susan and George are also in love with each other, but neither will admit it ("Miss Armstrong is only interested in me as a reporter," exclaims George). Despite what George says or believes, Susan does love him and he does love Susan. Their various schemes to get the other to break down and propose is the subplot of stories which focus on Susan as she struggles to run the newspaper she inherited from her father. *Other regular characters* (but credit is not given): Patience, Susan's cook; and Sammy, the paper's janitor. Also known as *The Irene Dunne–Fred MacMurray Show*.

Cast: Irene Dunne (*Susan Armstrong*); Fred MacMurray (*George Harvey*). ***Announcer:*** Harry Von Zell.

OPENING

ANNOUNCER: *The Irene Dunne–Fred MacMurray Show* starring Irene Dunne as Susan and Fred MacMurray as George, together in the gay, new exciting comedy adventure, *Bright Star*.

GIRL: Have you heard what happened at the *Star*?

MAN: Did you hear what he said to her?

GIRL: Do you know what she told him?

ANNOUNCER: Yes, the whole town is talking. The "star" they're talking about is the *Morning Star*, a newspaper. The "her" they're talking about is Susan, lovely attractive headstrong Susan. And the "him," well, you can see him now, walking down the street over there. He's George... [the story would then begin.]

CLOSING

ANNOUNCER: Irene Dunne and Fred MacMurray will be back next week in another exciting comedy adventure in the gay new series, *Bright Star*. This is Harry Von Zell inviting you to join us then.

192. THE BRIGHTER DAY. Serial, 15 min., NBC, 1948–1949; CBS, 1949–1956.

The small town of Three Rivers is the setting for a dramatic series about a widowed reverend (Richard Dennis) and his attempts to raise his four children (Liz, Althea, Barbara and Grayling).

Cast: Bill Smith (*Richard Dennis*); Margaret Draper, Grace Matthews (*Liz Dennis*); Jay Meredith (*Althea Dennis*); Lorna Lynn (*Barbara Dennis*); Billy Redfield (*Grayling Dennis*); Pat Hosley (*Patsy*); Ann Hilary (*Sandra Talbot*); John Larkin (*Cliff*). ***Narrator:*** Ron Rawson. ***Announcers:*** Bill Rogers, Len Sterling. ***Organist:*** William Meeder. ***Producer:*** David Lesan.

OPENING

ANNOUNCER: *The Brighter Day*. Our years are as the falling leaves. We live, we love, we dream, and then we go. But somehow we keep hoping, don't we, that our dreams will come true on that Brighter Day.

BRING 'EM BACK ALIVE *see* **THE JUNGLE ADVENTURES OF FRANK BUCK**

193. BRINGING UP FATHER. Comedy, 15, min., NBC, 1941–1942.

"The man who invented marriage must have been a bachelor or he never would have invented it," says Jiggs, the henpecked husband of the iron-willed Maggie, a woman who keeps a tight rein on him. Jiggs hasn't the nerve to stand up to Maggie and has to concoct stories just to get out of the house (especially to his favorite hangout, Dinty Moore's, for his weekly card game). Maggie is famous for throwing things at Jiggs when she gets mad at him (which is often). The Jiggs family is wealthy and Maggie is a society matron who is always planning some sort of function for a lord or a lady. Jiggs wants no part of the society scene; he wants a simple life, and his efforts to live that easy life is the focal point of stories. *Other regular characters:* Nora, their daughter; Dinty Moore, the bar owner. Based on the comic strip by George McManus.

Cast: Mark Smith, Neil O'Malley (*Jiggs*); Agnes Moorehead (*Maggie*); Helen Shields (*Nora*); Craig McDonnell (*Dinty Moore*). ***Music:*** Merle Kendrick.

OPENING

SONG (Chorus): Wish Jiggs, stand up to be a man; don't let Maggie go and get right under your collar.

JIGGS (singing): I don't want to be in society, I'm just a simple guy. I'm going down to Dinty's where you're supposed to waste your time.

CHORUS: Wish, Jiggs, it's time you took your stand; it's sure not to make you quit this singing of *Bringing Up Faaaa-ther*.

ANNOUNCER: We now have the pleasure of bringing before our microphones some old friends of yours. You've met them hundreds of times before in the pages of your newspaper, the popular brainchildren of George McManus in that most famous of all comic strips called *Bringing Up Father*. The trials and tribulations of the lovable Jiggs, the iron rule of Maggie, his wife, and the love affairs of the beautiful Nora, their daughter. All these old acquaintances are coming into your home for the first time in real life.

CLOSING

ANNOUNCER: We'll all be wiser after the next episode of *Bringing Up Father*, which we'll be pleased to broadcast over this station next week. Till then, Jiggs and Maggie and *Bringing Up Father* bid the top of the day to you. This King Features Syndicate program, supervised by William Morris, was produced at Cameo Broadcasting and Recording Studios in New York.

194. BROADWAY IS MY BEAT. Crime Drama, 30 min., CBS, 1949–1954.

The crime, the criminals and the difficulties of living in a large city as seen through the eyes of Danny Clover (later named Anthony Ross), a detective with the N.Y.P.D. whose beat is Broadway from Times Square to Columbus Circle. *Other regular characters:* Detective Gino Tartaglia, Danny's assistant; Mugowen, the coroner.

Cast: Larry Thor (*Danny Clover*); Charles Calvert (*Gino Tartaglia*); Jack Kruschen (*Mugowen*). ***Music:*** Alexander Courage, Wilbur Hatch, Robert Stringer. ***Producer:*** Elliott Lewis.

OPENING

DANNY: Broadway is my beat, from Times Square to Columbus Circle, the gaudiest, the most violent, the lonesomest mile in the world.

ANNOUNCER: *Broadway Is My Beat* with Larry Thor as Detective Danny Clover.

CLOSING

DANNY: Broadway leaps against the night; the sound it makes is the crash of life deep inside the earth; the hiss of neon; the laughter and screams. They meet together. The sound you hear is shock. There's another sound—the teardrop—but no one listens, no one hears; it's Broadway, the gaudiest, the most violent, the lonesomest mile in the world. Broadway, my beat.

ANNOUNCER: *Broadway Is My Beat* stars Larry Thor as Detective Danny Clover with Charles Calvert as Tartaglia and Jack Kruschen as Mugowen. The program is produced and directed by Elliott Lewis with musical score composed and conducted by Alexander Courage. This is CBS, the Columbia Broadcasting System.

195. Broadway Matinee. Variety, 30 min., CBS, 1944.

A program of music and songs from the Great White Way coupled with interviews with Broadway performers.

Host: Jim Ameche. ***Regulars:*** Patsy Garrett, Ronald Graham. ***Orchestra:*** Allen Roth.

196. Brownstone Theater. Anthology, 30 min., Mutual, 1945–1946.

Adaptations of plays and stories that were popular at the turn of the century. Each story is enacted by a regular cast of players.

Host-Narrator: Clayton Hamilton. ***Performers:*** Jackson Beck, Neil Hamilton, Gertrude Warner. ***Music:*** Sylvan Levin.

197. Buck Private and His Girl. Serial, 15 min., NBC Blue, 1941.

The story of a young draftee (Steve), his girlfriend (Anne) and their romance—which is shattered by the outbreak of World War II.

Cast: Myron McCormick (*Private Steve Mason*); Anne Seymour (*Anne*). ***Also:*** Joan Banks, Alexander Kirkland, Don McLaughlin, Tom Powers.

198. Buck Rogers in the 25th Century. Science Fiction, 15 min., CBS, 1932–1936; 30 min., Mutual, 1939–1947.

It is Pittsburgh in the year 1919 when Buck Rogers, a young Air Corps veteran, begins surveying the lower levels of an abandoned mine. Behind him, crumbling timber supports give way and the roof caves in. After an unsuccessful attempt to escape, Buck is rendered unconscious by a peculiar gas that places him in a state of suspended animation.

As the years pass, the earth shifts and fresh air enters the mine and awakens Buck. Buck emerges from the mine to find himself standing in the midst of a vast forest. He then meets Wilma Deering, a lieutenant on the Space General's staff, and learns that it is the year 2430 and the place is no longer Pittsburgh, but Niagara, America's new capital. Buck eventually becomes a member of the Space General's staff and stories relate Buck's efforts to help Wilma and the scientific genius Dr. Huer battle evil, particularly Killer Kane, a madman bent on controlling the universe. Based on the comic strip by Dick Calkins and Phil Nowlan. *Other regular characters:* George "Buddy" Wade, Buck's ward; Ardala, the villainous alien ruler (Kane's cohort); Black Barney, a friendly but dense Martian who gave up his evil ways (as a space pirate) to help Buck and Wilma; Willie, Buck's child protégé.

Cast: Curtis Arnall, Carl Frank, Matt Crowley, John Larkin (*Buck Rogers*); Adele Ronson, Virginia Vass (*Wilma Deering*); Edgar Stehli (*Dr. Huer*); Ronald Liss (*Buddy Wade*); Bill Shelley, Arthur Vinton, Dan Ocko (*Killer Kane*); Elaine Melchoir (*Ardala*); Jack Roseleigh, Joe Granby (*Black Barney*); Junius Matthews, Walter Tetley (*Willie*). ***Announcers:*** Paul Douglas, Jack Johnstone, Kenny Williams, Fred Uttal.

OPENING (1932)

Announcer: *Buck Rogers in the 25th Century*—and the shower of silver dollars from Popsicle Pete's money box. Buck Rogers, who was held in suspended animation for 500 years, is now adventuring in the amazing world of the 25th century. By turning a little dial to project us ahead in time, we are able to be with Buck and his friends in the wonderful world of the future, a world that sees a lot of our scientific and mechanical dreams come true. You know, there is nothing supernatural or mystic about Buck; he's just an ordinary human being who keeps his wits about him. And now, *Buck Rogers in the 25th Century.*

OPENING (1946)

Announcer: *Buck Rogers in the 25th Century.* Buck Rogers is back on the air. Buck and Wilma and all their fascinating friends and mysterious enemies in the super-scientific 25th century. This program is brought to you by the makers of Popsicle, Fudgesicle, and Cremesicles, those delicious frozen confections on a stick; the biggest five cents worth anywhere. And now for Buck Rogers and his thrilling adventures 500 years in the future.

Bud Barton *see* **The Barton Family**

199. The Buddy Clark Show. Variety, 30 min., CBS, 1938; 15 min., Mutual, 1939.

Vocalist Buddy Clark as the host of a weekly program of music and songs. Ted de Corsia, Anne Elstner and Nan Wynn were the regulars; the orchestras of Frank Novak and Leith Stevens provided the music.

Matthew Crowley starred as *Buck Rogers in the 25th Century* in 1936.

200. BUDDY CLARK'S SUMMER COLONY. Variety, 30 min., CBS, 1939.

A summer series of music and songs coupled with light comedy. Vocalist Buddy Clark served as the host. Hildegarde Loretta Sell and the comedy team of Fray and Braggrate were the regulars. Leith Stevens and his orchestra provided the music.

201. BULLDOG DRUMMOND. Mystery, 30 min., Mutual, 1941–1947; 1953–1954.

A whodunit series dealing with the exploits of Capt. Hugh Drummond, a dashing British police sleuth working in the United States. Drummond is nicknamed "Bulldog" for his tiresome pursuit of lawbreakers. Based on the books by H.C. McNeile. Also known as *The Adventures of Bulldog Drummond*.

Cast: George Coulouris, Santos Ortega, Ned Wever, Sir Cedric Hardwicke (*Hugh "Bulldog" Drummond*); Everett Sloane, Luis Van Rooten, Rod Hendrickson (*Denny, his assistant*). ***Announcers:*** Ted Browne, Henry Morgan. ***Organist:*** Lew White. ***Producer:*** Himan Brown.

Burl Ives and "Aunt Fanny" entertain during a broadcast of the *Burl Ives Coffee Club*.

OPENING

ANNOUNCER (over the echo of footsteps and a foghorn): Out of the fog, out of the night, and into his American adventures comes *Bulldog Drummond*. Yes, it's time for mystery with Santos Ortega as Bulldog Drummond in [title of episode would be given, followed by Bulldog establishing the evening's story].

202. BURL IVES COFFEE CLUB. Variety, 30 min., CBS, 1941–1946; 15 min., Mutual, 1946–1948.

An informal session of chatter, music and folk songs with folk singer Burl Ives. Early CBS episodes (1941–1942) are also known as *The Wayfaring Stranger*.

Host: Burl Ives. ***Regulars:*** Juan Arvizi, the Deltha Rhythm Boys, Genevieve Rowe. ***Announcer:*** Hugh Brundige. ***Orchestra:*** Walter Gross.

BURNS AND ALLEN *see* **THE GEORGE BURNS AND GRACIE ALLEN SHOW**

THE BUSTER BROWN GANG *see* **THE SMILIN' ED McCONNELL SHOW**

203. THE BUSY MR. BINGLE. Comedy, 30 min., Mutual, 3/18/43 to 6/10/43.

J.B. Bingle is a somewhat scatterbrained businessman who owns the Bingle Pin Company. He is married to an absent-minded woman and is assisted by Miss Pepper, the only employee with brains. Stories focus on J.B. as he struggles to run his company despite the problems caused by the shortages of World War II. *Other regular characters:* Wizer, the jovial company salesman; Clarence, the henpecked inventor (he responds with "Yes I will," "Yes I am," or "Yes I can" when asked something); Tommy, the lovesick office boy.

Cast: John Brown (*J.B. Bingle*); Ethel Owen (*Miss Pepper*); Jackson Beck (*Wizer/Clarence/Tommy*); Elizabeth Moran (*Mrs. Bingle*).

OPENING

MISS PEPPER: Mr. Bingle, what are you doing?

BINGLE: I'm not sure, Miss Pepper, but I'm so busy.

ANNOUNCER: WOR/Mutual presents *The Busy Mr. Bingle*, a new kind of radio pleasure for the whole family. Mr. Bingle is really J.B. Bingle, head of the Bingle Pin Company, and he keeps busy getting the firm into and out of trouble. Now you're about to meet the happy Bingle office family: Miss Pepper, the secretary; Wizer, the master salesman; Clarence, the inventor; Tommy, the office boy; and J.B. Bingle himself, who is just entering the office. (The show would then begin.)

CLOSING

ANNOUNCER: You have been listening to WOR/Mutual's presentation of *The Busy Mr. Bingle. The Busy Mr. Bingle* is heard each Thursday evening at 8:30 P.M. Eastern War Time over most of these stations. This program was an international exchange feature heard over the coast-to-coast network of the Canadian Broadcasting System. If you live in or around New York and would like to see a broadcast of *The Busy Mr. Bingle*, you may secure tickets by writing "Mr. Bingle" in care of WOR, New York City. We hope you'll join us next Thursday when *The Busy Mr. Bingle* will be busier than ever.

TOMMY: Good night, J.B.

J.B.: Good night.

MISS PEPPER: Good night, J.B.

J.B.: Good night.

WIZER: Good night, J.B.

J.B.: Good night.

CLARENCE: I hope you sleep well, J.B.

J.B.: Oh, that Clarence, he's wonderful!

ANNOUNCER: *The Busy Mr. Bingle* is played by John Brown. This is Mutual.

204. BY KATHLEEN NORRIS. Anthology, 15 min., CBS, 1939–1940; NBC, 1940–1941.

A daily series of short dramatizations based on stories written by author Kathleen Norris.

Host-Narrator: Ethel Everett (as Kathleen Norris). ***Performers:*** Mildred Baker, Arlene Blackburn, Mary Cecil, Betty Garde, House Jameson, Florence Malone, Santos Ortega, Effie Palmer, Lawson Zerbe. ***Announcer:*** Dwight Weist. ***Producer:*** May Bolhower, Phillips H. Lord.

205. BY POPULAR DEMAND. Variety, 30 min., Mutual, 1945–1946.

A weekly program that featured music and songs requested by listeners. Clayton "Bud" Collyer served as the host and announcer; Harry Babbitt and Mary Small were the regulars; and Ray Bloch and his orchestra provided the music.

206. CABIN B-13. Anthology, 30 min., CBS, 1948–1949.

A luxury liner called the *Moravania* sits in waiting at the docks of Southampton. Aboard the virtually deserted ship, in Cabin B-13, resides the vessel's physician, Dr. Fabian, a man who has traveled many thousands of miles and has seen many things. He writes his experiences in a journal and in weekly stories he relates to listeners his memories of the passengers he has known.

Cast: Arnold Moss (*Dr. Fabian*). ***Music:*** Merle Kendrick.

OPENING

ANNOUNCER: *Cabin B-13.*

DR. FABIAN: My name is Fabian, ship's surgeon of the luxury liner *Moravania*. Tonight, as we lay alongside the great docks of the port of Southampton, the ship is ghostly deserted; our passengers on this world cruise have gone to London, and as I sit here in my cabin, B-13, I'm reminded how the tides and storms of a thousand voyages have brought nothing more strange, more sinister than man's desire for adventure in the strange ports and lands we touch. [He would then begin a story; for example, "I remember Bill and Brenda Leslie. It was years ago, before the war..."]

207. CAFE ISTANBUL. Adventure, 30 min., ABC, 1952–1953.

The Cafe Istanbul is a cabaret in the Far East where sultry songstress Mademoiselle Madou performs. The cafe is also a hangout for spies, criminals and the Secret Police. Stories follow Madou's adventures as she becomes involved with the various clientele. Shortly after its premiere, the format changed somewhat to take on the appearance of an anthology with Mademoiselle Madou relocating to San Francisco (and becoming the owner of a nightclub) who told dramatic tales of love, adventure and intrigue.

Cast: Marlene Dietrich (*Mademoiselle Madou*); Ken Lynch (*American*); Arnold Moss (*Cop*). ***Music:*** Ralph Norman.

208. CALAMITY JANE. Drama, 30 min., CBS, 1946.

A tongue-in-cheek portrayal of a conniving newspaper reporter (Jane) and her sometimes fumbling attempts to expose racketeers. The program ran for only three episodes in March 1946.

Cast: Agnes Moorehead (*Jane*); Dan Wolfe (*Her Grandfather, the publisher*). ***Also:*** Bill Johnstone, Cathy Lewis. ***Announcer:*** Ken Niles.

209. CALIFORNIA CARAVAN. Anthology, 30 min., Mutual, 1947–1950.

Dramatizations based on the legends stemming from the gold rush days of 1849.

Performers: Paul Frees, Virginia Gregg, Michael Hayes, John McGovern, Bob Purcell, Bob Shennon, Herb Vigran. ***Announcer:*** Fort Pearson.

210. CALL FOR MUSIC. Variety, 30 min., NBC, 1948.

A weekly program of music and songs hosted by Dinah Shore (who was assisted by a weekly guest star). Jack Rourke was the announcer and Johnny Mercer and his orchestra provided the music. See also *Birds Eye Open House* and *The Dinah Shore Show*.

211. CALL ME FREEDOM. Anthology, 30 min., ABC, 1953.

Dramatizations based on the ideals and principles of America's heritage. Produced in cooperation with the Freedom Foundation at Valley Forge. Nelson Olmsted was the host and narrator.

212. CALL THE POLICE. Crime Drama, 30 min., NBC, 1947–1948; CBS, 1949.

A look at the work of law enforcement officers across the country as seen through the investigations of Bill Grant, a police commissioner, and Libby Tyler, a criminal psychologist. The stories are hard-hitting recreations of gruesome crimes, the step-by-step actions of the criminals and the police efforts to apprehend the culprits. At the end of each broadcast, deserving real-life police officers are awarded the "Call the Police Plaque of Valor" and a cash award.

Cast: Joseph Julian, George Petrie (*Commissioner Bill Grant*); Amzie Strickland (*Libby Tyler*); Robert Dryden (*Sgt. Maggio*). ***Announcers:*** Hugh James, Jay Sims. ***Music:*** Ben Ludlow. ***Producer:*** John Cole.

OPENING

ANNOUNCER: Rinso, the new Rinso with Solieum, presents *Call the Police*.

VOICE: Attention homicide section, crime squad detail. Murder suspect in your zone.

VOICE: Between you and the evil outside the law stands the policemen of your community. He gives up his safety so you may be safe and sometimes he gives up his life to protect yours.

ANNOUNCER: New Rinso, the soap that contains Solieum, the scientific sunlight ingredient, brings you *Call the Police*, a new series of realistic radio dramas inspired by the courageous work of police departments all over America.

CLOSING

ANNOUNCER: This is Hugh James reminding you to be with us again next week when Lever Brothers, the makers of Rinso with Solieum, bring you another exciting police case. Be sure to listen next week for *Call the Police*. This is NBC, the National Broadcasting Company.

213. THE CALLAHANS. Variety, 30 min., Syndicated, 1944.

Music and comedy set against the background of a Broadway theatrical house owned by the Callahan family (Ma and Pa and their daughter, Penelope).

Cast: Elsie Mae Gordon (*Ma Callahan*), Arthur Hill (*Pa Callahan*), Florence Halop (*Penelope Callahan*). ***Regulars:*** Jack Arthur, Donald Bain, Joe Latham, Ed Latimer, Ethel

Owen, Betty Winkler. ***Announcer:*** Ted Campbell. ***Orchestra:*** Van Alexander, Jerry Sears.

214. Calling All Cars. Anthology, 30 min., CBS, 1933–1939.

Dramatizations based on cases from the Los Angeles Police Department. The facts of a specific crime are related to the listener. An introduction to the people involved in the case follows. The story is then dramatized (using in some instances, actual names and places) followed by the method of apprehension, the court trial (if any) and the fate of the criminal.

Host: Chief James E. Davis, L.A.P.D. ***Announcer-Narrator:*** Frederick Lindsley.

OPENING

Announcer: *Calling All Cars*, a presentation of the Rio Grande Oil Company.

Voice: Los Angeles Police calling all cars, attention all cars. Broadcast 69, a holdup. Defendant is described as five feet, 11 inches, weight about 190 pounds. Escaped in a maroon-colored coupe; license unknown. This suspect held up and robbed Mae West, motion picture actress, of more than $15,000 in jewelry and cash. Go get him, boys. That's all. Rosenquist.

Announcer (over sirens and music): Many listeners tonight have already read the story of "The Mae West Diamond Robbery" in the March issue of "Calling All Cars News." Over 3,000,000 motorists have already driven into the Rio Grande service stations and asked for their free copy of this unique publication. During 1935, it will be the policy of *Calling All Cars* to bring you from time to time rebroadcasts of outstanding cases we have dramatized in the past. Thousands of you have written to us and expressed your desire to hear the Mae West jewel robbery dramatized again. So it is with pleasure that *Calling All Cars* tonight brings you "The Mae West Jewel Robbery" with Miss Martha Wentworth playing her now famous impersonation of Miss West. What other past cases of *Calling All Cars* would you like to hear again? Write to *Calling All Cars*, care of the station to which you are now listening and tell us what preceding case you would like to hear. And now we turn the microphone over to Chief James E. Davis of the Los Angeles Police Department, who has a message for you. [He would then relate the details of the evening's story.]

CLOSING

Announcer: Ladies and gentlemen, if you want further information on the Mae West diamond robbery, you can get the story illustrated in the March issue of the "Calling All Cars News." Just drive into any Rio Grande service station and ask for your free copy. You are under no obligation to buy anything.

Voice: Los Angeles calling all cars. Attention all cars. Cancellation of broadcast 69 regarding a holdup. Suspect described in this broadcast is now in custody. That's all. Rosenquist.

Narrator: This is your narrator, Frederick Lindsley, bidding you good night for the Rio Grande Oil Company.

215. Calling All Detectives. Game, 30 min., Mutual, 1945.

The program begins with a dramatization of a whodunit with Robin, the crime guide, giving listeners specific clues. When the story reached its climax, it was interrupted and five minutes of air time relinquished to the local stations carrying the program. Local announcers then telephoned listeners (selected from postcard entries). The listener had to identify the culprit based on Robin's clues. Once the five minutes elapsed, the local stations rejoined the network and the story concluded. Listeners who correctly uncovered the culprit received war bonds as a prize. The amount varied with the local station; at WGN in Chicago, for example, a $100 bond was awarded for a correct response and a $25 bond for an incorrect answer.

Host: Vincent Pelletier (as Robin). ***Organist:*** Dick Platt.

216. Calling America. Variety, 30 min., Mutual, 1939.

A weekly program of talk, music, songs and short dramatizations with Arthur Hale as the host and commentator. Robert Allen, Grace Barrie, Drew Pearson and the Tune Twisters were the regulars. Erno Rapee and his orchestra provided the music.

217. The Camel Caravan.

The overall title for several variety programs sponsored by Camel cigarettes that used its name in the title.

The Camel Caravan, 30 min, CBS, 1933–1936. *Host:* Walter O'Keefe. *Orchestra:* Glen Gray.

The Camel Comedy Caravan, 30 min, CBS, 1942–1943. *Host:* Jack Carson. *Regulars:* Mel Blanc, Connie Haines, Herb Shriner. *Announcer:* Ken Niles. *Orchestra:* Freddie Rich.

The Camel Comedy Caravan, 30 min., NBC, 1943–1945. *Hosts:* Jimmy Durante, Garry Moore. *Vocalist:* Ginny Simms. *Announcer:* Howard Petrie. *Orchestra:* Xavier Cugat. See also *The Jimmy Durante–Garry Moore Show*.

Camel Presents Harry Savoy, 30 min., NBC, 1944. *Host:* Harry Savoy. *Regulars:* Paula Kelly and the Modernaires, Benay Venuta. *Orchestra:* Peter Van Steeden.

The Camel Caravan, 30 min., CBS, 1951. *Host:* Vaughn Monroe. *Vocalist:* Sally Sweetland. *Announcer:* Joe King, Wayne Nelson. *Orchestra:* Vaughn Monroe, Sauter-Finnegan.

218. Campana Serenade. Variety, 30 min., NBC, 1943–1944.

Actor Dick Powell as the host of a weekly program of music and songs sponsored by Campana Cosmetics. Martha Tilton and the Music Maids were the regulars. Henry Chorles did the announcing; and the orchestras of Lud Gluskin and Matty Malneck provided the music.

OPENING

Dick (singing); Lovely to look at, delightful to know, and heaven to kiss; a combination like this is my most impossible scheme come true; imagine finding a dream like you.

Announcer: *Campana Serenade*, coast to coast from Hollywood, starring Dick Powell, with Martha Tilton and Lud Gluskin's orchestra. Presented by Campana, the makers of Solitaire, the new cake makeup.

219. The Campbell Playhouse. Anthology, 60 min., CBS, 1939–1940; 30 min., CBS, 1940–1941.

A continuation of *The Mercury Theater on the Air* under the sole sponsorship of the Campbell Soup Company. The program continued to present quality dramatizations of books, plays and movies with Orson Welles at the helm. The program was cut to 30 minutes and aired as *The Orson Welles Theater* on CBS from 1941–1943.

Host-Star: Orson Welles. ***Dramatic Cast:*** William Alland, Edgar Barrier, Ray Collins, Joseph Cotten, John Houseman, Burgess Meredith, Agnes Moorehead, Frank Readick, Everett Sloane, Richard Wilson. ***Announcer:*** Ernest Chappell. ***Music:*** Bernard Herrmann. ***Producer:*** Orson Welles.

OPENING

Announcer: The makers of Campbell soups presents *The Campbell Playhouse*, Orson Welles, producer.

Orson: Good evening, this is Orson Welles. Tonight's story, which is about a hurricane, is called "The Hurricane," and the aim is to show you what a cyclone of a diameter of from 50 to 100 miles can do to a South Seas island paradise and the lives of the people who are still alive after it blows over. But the hurricane isn't the star of "The Hurricane." Mary Astor is, as she was in the picture. Now, just a minute before we set sail for the lands of soft music, sweet breezes, big blows and Miss Astor, Ernest Chappell hurries up our armchair gangplank with an interesting mealtime reminder for us all. Ladies and gentlemen, Mr. Chappell.

Ernest: Thank you Orson Welles. [He then delivers a Campbell soup commercial.] And now we bring you "The Hurricane" with Orson Welles and our guest of the evening, Miss Mary Astor.

CLOSING

Announcer: This concludes our *Campbell Playhouse* presentation of "The Hurricane." And now, Mr. Welles, if you please, a word about next week's story.

Orson: Certainly, Mr. Chappell. Next Sunday, ladies and gentlemen, we'll offer you that most celebrated of latter-day murder mysteries, "The Murder of Roger Ackroyd." For our guest star we have an actress who's known and loved by you all, Edna Mae Oliver. So until then, until next Sunday and "The Murder of Roger Ackroyd" and my sponsors, the makers of Campbell's soups, and all of us in *The Campbell Playhouse*, I remain obediently yours.

Announcer: The makers of Campbell's soups join Orson Welles in inviting you to be with us in *The Campbell Playhouse* again next Sunday evening when we bring you the celebrated mystery, "The Murder of Roger Ackroyd" with Edna Mae Oliver as our guest. This is Ernest Chappell saying thank you and good night.

220. Campbell's Tomato Juice Program. Comedy, 30 min., CBS, 10/2/35 to 3/24/37.

Humorous skits that revolve around a scatterbrained woman (Gracie Allen) and her level-headed friend, the recipient of her antics, George Burns. The skits are interspersed with songs and musical numbers and the program also features parodies of plays (for example, "Lucretia Borgia," "The Private Life of Mrs. Jesse James," "A Christmas Carol," "College Holiday"). Sponsored by Campbell's.

Stars: George Burns and Gracie Allen. ***Regulars:*** Tony Martin, Milton Watson. ***Announcers:*** Ted Husing, Ken Niles. ***Orchestra:*** Jacques Renard.

221. Campbell's Tomato Juice Program. Variety, 30 min., CBS, 1937.

A revamped version of the prior title that drops the comedy of George Burns and Gracie Allen (who switched to NBC to do *The Grape Nuts Program*; see entry) to become a weekly program of music, songs and light comedy.

Host: Ken Murray. ***Vocalist:*** Shirley Ross. ***Announcer:*** Ken Niles. ***Orchestra:*** Lud Gluskin.

222. Can You Top This? Game, 30 min., Mutual, 1940–1945; NBC, 1942–1948; Mutual, 1948–1950; ABC, 1951; NBC, 1953–1954.

A joke, sent in by a listener (who received $10), was told to the studio audience by the Joke Teller. The audience reaction (applause) was registered on a large laugh meter (from one to a thousand) that was displayed on stage. Three regular panelists appear and each has to relate a joke in the same category with the object being to beat the listener's score. Each time a panelist failed to do so, five dollars was added to the listener's amount (to a total limit of $25). The program became so popular that it aired on both NBC and Mutual for several years. Served as the basis for the television series of the same title.

Host: Ward Wilson. ***Joke Teller:*** Peter Donald. ***Panelists:*** Senator Edward Ford, Harry Hershfield, Joe Laurie, Jr. ***Announcers:*** Peter Donald, Charles Stark.

OPENING

Host: *Can You Top This?* Why does a chicken cross the road?

Peter: That was no chicken, that was my wife.

Host: Can you top that, Harry Hershfield?

Harry: Sure.

Host: Can you, Senator Ford?

Ford: I might.

Host: And you, Joe Laurie, Jr.?

Joe: Maybe.

Announcer: Those expedient exclamations introduce the pint-size author-comedian, Joe Laurie, Jr., the popular after-dinner speaker and current topic humorist, Senator Ford, and well-known cartoonist and after-dinner speaker, Harry Hershfield. These effervescent entertainers bring you another session of *Can You Top This?* with the best wishes of Kirkman's Soap Flakes. And now, here's your master of ceremonies, Ward Wilson.

CLOSING

Announcer: And thus ends another laugh session of *Can You Top This?*, originated by Senator Ford. Join us again next week, same time, same station, same gang, other jokes, some new, some old. Until then, we remain yours for bigger and better laughs. This is Mutual.

223. The Canary Pet Show. Variety, 15 min., Mutual, 1937–1952.

A novelty program (sponsored by Hartz Mountain Pet Foods) that featured songs by trained canaries (in particular Frankie, "the Canary Crooner," who sang to organ and violin accompaniment). Also titled *American Radio Warblers*, *Hartz Mountain Canaries* and *Master Radio Canaries*.

Host: Jess Kirkpatrick.

OPENING

Announcer (over birds chirping and dogs barking): Just listen to our pets. They're calling your pets from coast to coast. Hello, everyone, this is Jess Kirkpatrick speaking for Hartz Mountain pet foods and welcoming you to *The Canary Pet Show*.

224. Candid Microphone. Comedy, 30 min., ABC, 1947–1948; CBS, 1950.

"No one ever knows when he's talking to the Candid Microphone," said the announcer for a show that used hidden microphones to record the unsuspecting reactions of people to prearranged comical situations. Served as the basis for the television series *Candid Camera*.

Narrators: Allen Funt, Don Hollenbeck.

Cast: Joe Graham, Glen Houser, John Larkin, Al Smith. ***Announcers:*** Les Griffith, Ken Roberts. ***Music:*** Bernie Green.

OPENING

ANNOUNCER: The *Candid Microphone*. The American Broadcasting Company presents the *Candid Microphone*, the program that brings you the secretly recorded conversations of all kinds of people as they react in real life to all kinds of situations. No one ever knows when he's talking to the Candid Microphone.

CLOSING

ANNOUNCER: So until next week, *Candid Microphone* goes back into hiding, the better to catch you in our act. Nothing is off the record when the man with the hidden mike crosses your path with the mike that hears without being seen, the *Candid Microphone*. The *Candid Microphone* is tailored for your enjoyment, so we're always glad to hear your candid comments about it. If there is someone you'd like to hear us catch off guard, tell it to Candid Mike. Write to Candid Microphone, in care of the American Broadcasting Company, New York 20, New York. But whether or not you write, we invite you to please drop in again next Thursday when we'll be heard over most of these ABC stations. *Candid Microphone* is a copyrighted Allen A. Funt Production. *Candid Microphone* was transcribed. This is ABC, the American Broadcasting Company.

225. CANDY MATSON, YUKON 2-8209. Crime Drama, 30 min., NBC, 6/49 to 5/51.

"My name is Matson, Candy Matson. I'm a private investigator," says Candy when she introduces herself to suspects. She is extremely feminine and shows no signs of being squeamish. She has a sweet voice, but is not sweet on criminals. Stories follow her exploits as she uses both brains and beauty to solve cases. Candy is assisted by Rembrandt Watson and she is in love with Ray Mallard, a police lieutenant with an office in San Francisco's Hall of Justice Building. Ray, who often found himself involved with Candy's cases, claims, "She is a cute little snoop who snoops her way into my case investigations." Ray rarely drives a squad car and does so only when it is absolutely necessary. Ray calls Candy "Cupcake"; Candy calls Rembrandt "Ducky." Candy, whose phone number is reflected in the title (she works out of her apartment), carries a .32 caliber revolver. The Hall of Justice Building is on Montgomery Street. In the last episode (5/21/51), Ray is promoted to captain and proposes to Candy. *Other regular characters:* Montgomery the Mole, Candy's snitch.

Cast: Natalie Masters (*Candy Matson*); Henry Lemp (*Ray Mallard*); Jack Thomas (*Rembrandt Watson*); Jerry Walter (*Montgomery the Mole*). ***Announcer:*** Bud Heidi. ***Organist:*** Eloise Rowan. ***Producer:*** Monte Masters.

OPENING

SOUND: Phone rings.

CANDY (picking up receiver): Hello, YUkon 2-8209. Yes, this is Candy Matson.

ANNOUNCER: From San Francisco, the National Broadcasting Company presents another yarn in the adventures of that attractive private eye, *Candy Matson, YUkon 2-8209*.

CLOSING

ANNOUNCER: For excitement and adventure and romance, just dial—

CANDY: Candy Matson, YUkon 2-8209.

ANNOUNCER: The program stars Natalie Masters and is written and directed by Monte Masters. The program came to you from San Francisco and this is NBC, the National Broadcasting Company.

226. CANTEEN GIRL. Variety, 15 min., NBC, 8/28/42 to 12/29/42.

Sentimental ballads, dramatic monologues and music set against the background of the Stage Door Canteen, a New York nightclub.

Host: Phyllis Jean Creare.

227. CAPTAIN DIAMOND'S ADVENTURES. Anthology, 30 min., NBC Blue, 1932–1937.

Capt. Diamond is an old salt and lighthouse keeper with many stories to tell. Each week, he and his wife would spin a tale to their young visitor, Tiny Ruffner. As the captain spoke, the story was dramatized for the listening audience. The program, sponsored by Diamond Salt, is also known as *The Adventures of Captain Diamond*.

Cast: Al Swenson (*Capt. Diamond*); Florence Malone (*Mrs. Diamond*); Edmund "Tiny" Ruffner (*Tiny Ruffner*).

228. Captain Flagg and Sergeant Quirt. Comedy, 30 min., NBC, 1941–1942.

A radio adaptation of Maxwell Anderson's Broadway play *What Price Glory*, relating the mishaps of two bickering Marines (Capt. Flagg and Sgt. Quirt).

Cast: Victor McLaglen, William Gargan (*Captain Flagg*); Edmund Lowe (*Sgt. Quirt*); John Smith (*Major General*); Gloria Jones (*General's wife*). ***Music:*** Lou Kosloff.

229. Captain Midnight. Adventure, 15 min., Mutual, 1940–1949.

The story of a private citizen (Jim Albright, called "Red" by his friends) who devotes his life to fighting crime. Named "Captain Midnight" for his daring World War I air tactics, Albright now commands the Secret Squadron, a government organization designed to combat evil. Assisted by Chuck Ramsey, Ichabod Mudd and Joyce Ryan, serialized stories relate his endless battle against criminal elements, especially the sinister Ivan Shark and his lovely but lethal daughter Fury. Each member of the Secret Squadron had the code name "SS" and a number (for example, Chuck and Joyce were SS-2 and SS-3). Listeners could join the Secret Squadron by sending a seal from the sponsor's product (Ovaltine) and a dime. They would receive a Secret Squadron decoder and membership in the Captain Midnight society. Served as the basis for the television series of the same title (1954–1956).

Cast: Ed Prentiss, Bill Bouchey, Paul Barnes (*Captain Midnight*); Bill Rose, Jack Bivins, Johnny Coons (*Chuck Ramsey*); Hugh Studebaker, Art Hearn, Sherman Marks (*Ichabod "Ichy" Mudd*); Angeline Orr, Marilou Neumayer (*Joyce Ryan*); Boris Aplon (*Ivan Shark*); Rene Rodier, Sharon Grainger (*Fury Shark*). ***Announcers:*** Pierre Andre, Don Gordon, Tom Moore.

OPENING

Announcer: The makers of Ovaltine present *Captain Midnight. Captain Midnight*, brought to you every day, Monday through Friday, at this same time by the makers of Ovaltine. *Captain Midnight* is written for red-blooded young Americans, both boys and girls; yes, for mother and dad, too; for everyone who's young in spirit. *Captain Midnight* will bring you plenty of excitement, mystery and suspense; thrills galore. It lets you live a story of real adventure in the air and on the ground. You'll never want to miss a single broadcast of *Captain Midnight* and you'll want all your friends to enjoy it too. So be sure to tell them to listen in every day. This program is brought to you by the makers of Ovaltine, the famous food drink that is a favorite with millions of Americans, young and old … and now to *Captain Midnight*.

CLOSING

Announcer: Be sure to tune in tomorrow, same time, same station, to *Captain Midnight*. Now just a word about you … if you like the way this program begins, keep on spreading the news to all the fellows and girls you know, will ya? And don't forget to try Ovaltine this very night … and then be sure to tune in tomorrow, same time, same station for another stirring adventure with *Captain Midnight*, brought to you every day, Monday through Friday, by the makers of Ovaltine. See you tomorrow. And until then, this is Pierre Andre, your Ovaltine announcer, saying good-bye and happy landing. This is the Mutual Broadcasting System.

230. Captain Stubby and the Buccaneers. Variety, 15 min., Syndicated, 1946–1948.

A program of music and songs spotlighting a pirate motif with the novelty orchestra Captain Stubby and the Buccaneers.

Host: Tom Foute (as Captain Stubby). ***Regulars:*** Sonny Fleming, Jerry Richards, Tiny Stokes, Tony Walberg. ***Announcer:*** John Dalton. ***Orchestra:*** Phil Davis.

231. The Career of Alice Blair. Serial, 15 min., Mutual, 1939–1940.

A daily drama about the struggles of a young career woman in New York City. Martha Scott (1939) and Betty Moran (1940) played the role of Alice Blair.

232. The Carefree Carnival. Variety, 30 min., NBC, 1933–1935.

A program of country and western music, songs and comedy with hosts Gene Arnold and Ray Tollinger. The regulars were Barbara Jo Allen (as Vera Vague), Charlie Marshall and the comedy team of Nuts and Bolts. Meredith Willson and his orchestra provided the music.

Marilou Neumayer portrayed Joyce Ryan on *Captain Midnight*.

233. Caricatures in Rhythm. Variety, 30 min., NBC, 1938.

Orchestra leader Harry Reser as the host of a program of music and songs. Barry McKinley, Dorothy Rochelle and the Tune Twisters were the regulars. Also with Harry Reser's orchestra.

234. Carl Hohengarten's Orchestra. Variety, 25 min., CBS, 1939.

A program of big band music with the orchestra of Carl Hohengarten (who also served as the host). Tommy Bartlett, Todd Hunter and David McCall were regulars.

235. Carle Comes Calling. Variety, 30 min., CBS, 1948.

Orchestra leader (and program host) Frankie Carle in a program of music and songs with regulars Marjorie Hughes, Greg Lawrence and the Starlighters. Frankie Carle's orchestra provided the music.

236. The Carmen Miranda Show. Variety, 60 min., NBC, 1939.

Singer-actress Carmen Miranda as the host of a weekly program of music, songs and light comedy that featured top name guest stars. Judy Ellington and the Rodgers Sisters were the regulars. LeRoy Miller did the announcing and music was supplied by the Charles Barnet and Nat Shilkret orchestras.

Singer-actress Carmen Miranda hosted the weekly *Carmen Miranda Show*.

237. The Carnation Contented Hour. Variety, 30 and 60 min. versions, NBC, 1931–1950; CBS, 1950–1951.

A popular, long-running program of music and songs sponsored by the Carnation Milk Company that featured performances by top name guests who often acted as the host for that particular broadcast. (There was no actual host.) On other occasions, the announcer provided introductions for listeners.

Announcers: Vincent Pelletier, Jimmy Wallington. ***Regulars:*** Buddy Clark, Jo Stafford, the Ken Lane Singers. ***Orchestra:*** Percy Faith, Victor Young. ***Producers:*** C.H. Cottingham, Harry K. Gilman.

238. The Carnation Family Party. Interview, 30 min., CBS, 1950–1951.

The program, sponsored by Carnation Milk, featured interviews with people who had to prove or disprove certain facts about them. Participants received prizes for sharing various aspects of their personal lives with listeners.

Host: Jay Stewart. ***Announcer:*** Larry Thor.

239. Carnival with Bernie West. Variety, 30 min., NBC, 1946.

Bernie West as the host of a weekly program of music, songs and comedy. The regulars were Lynn Collier, Billy Greene, Pat Hosley, Art Kahl, Flora MacMichael, Johnny Morgan and Grace Valentine. Bob Sherry did the announcing; Henry Levine and his orchestra furnished the music.

240. Carolina Calling. Variety, 30 min., CBS, 1946–1951.

A revised version of *Carolina Hayride* (see next entry) that continued to present a weekly showcase for the best in country and western music, songs and comedy.

Host: Grady Cole. ***Regulars:*** Harry Blair, Claude Casey, Fred Kirby, Howard Turner, the Briarhoppers, the Johnson Family, the Shawnee River Boys, Whitey and Hogan.

241. Carolina Hayride. Variety, 30 min., CBS, 1944–1945.

A weekly program of country and western music, songs and comedy. See *Carolina Calling* for information on the revised version of this program.

Host: Arthur Smith. ***Regulars:*** Claude Casey, Larry Walker, the Briarhoppers, Ma Johnson's Family, the Southland Jubilee Singers, the Tennessee Ramblers, Whitey and Hogan.

242. Caroline's Golden Store. Comedy, 15 min., NBC, 1939–1940; CBS, 1940.

Humorous incidents in the lives of Caroline, the proprietor of a small-town general store, and the people who frequent it (usually to discuss their problems and the day's activities with Caroline).

Cast: Caroline Ellis (*Caroline*). ***Regulars*** (Customers): Guila Adams, Frank Behrens, Jack Brinkley, Cliff Carl, Ginger Jones, Joan Kay, Harriette Widmer. ***Announcer:*** Franklyn MacCormack.

243. Carson Robison's Buckaroos. Variety, 15 min., NBC Blue, 1932–1933; 30 min., Mutual, 1939–1940; Syndicated, 1949–1950.

A weekly program of country and western music with Carson Robison, head singer of the Buckaroos, as the host. Jack Costello did the announcing; Bill, John and Pearl Mitchell comprised the Buckaroos.

244. The Carters of Elm Street. Serial, 15 min., NBC, 1939–1940; CBS, 1945–1946.

Dramatic incidents in the lives of the Carters: Jeff, his second wife Mara and their children Mildred (married), Bunny and Jess. *Other regular characters:* Sidney Randolph, Mildred's husband; Mattie Belle, the Carters' housekeeper. The Carters live on Elm Street in the small town of Galesville.

Cast: Vic Smith (*Jeff Carter*); Virginia Payne (*Mara Carter*); Virginia "Ginger" Jones (*Mildred Carter Randolph*); Ann Russell (*Bunny Carter*); William Rose (*Jess Carter*); Herbert Nelson (*Sidney Randolph*); Harriette Widmer (*Mattie Belle*). ***Producers:*** Anne Hummert, Frank Hummert.

OPENING

Announcer: Ovaltine presents *The Carters of Elm Street*, the story of a second wife and her fight for happiness.

Carton of Smiles *see* **Appendix**

Casa Cugat *see* **The Xavier Cugat Show**

245. The Case Book of Gregory Hood. Crime Drama, 30 min., Mutual, 1946–1949; ABC, 1950–1951.

In a luxurious apartment overlooking San Francisco's Golden Gate Bridge lives Gregory Hood, an amateur composer and notorious lady killer who runs an import business dealing in rare items. Hood travels the world seeking items for his business. Each item he manages to find has an intriguing history associated with it—usually a link to a modern-day mystery. Stories begin with Gregory discussing an object with his friend Harry, then telling him (and listeners) the mystery he became involved with as he and his assistant, Sandor "Sandy" Taylor, sought the object.

Cast: Gale Gordon, Elliott Lewis, Jackson Beck, Paul McGrath, Martin Gabel, George Petrie (*Gregory Hood*); Carl Harper, Bill Johnstone (*Sandor "Sandy" Taylor*); Harry Bartlett (*Harry*). ***Announcer:*** Harry Bartlett. ***Music:*** Dean Fossler. ***Producer:*** Frank Cooper.

OPENING

Announcer: Petri Wine brings you *The Case Book of Gregory Hood*. Tonight, the Petri family, the family that took good time to bring you good wine, invites you to listen to the story of "South of the Border," another exciting adventure from *The Case Book of Gregory Hood*. And I would like to ask you if you know one sure way to turn a simple meal into a regular feast? Just serve that meal with a good Petri dinner wine... Remember those five letters P-E-T-R-I. They spell the product name in the long history of fine wines.

Announcer: Well, it's Monday night in San Francisco and we have a date with Gregory Hood and his friend, Sandor Taylor...

CLOSING

Harry: Well, Greg, what story out of your case book are you going to tell us next week?

Gregory: Next week, Harry, I'm going to tell you of the strange adventure Sandy and I had last fall when we flew up to Yosemite on a fishing trip. It concerns some brook trout I cooked under the starlight, an uninvited guest and a sudden tragedy. See you next week, Harry.

Announcer: The Petri Wine Company of San Francisco, California, invites you to tune in again next week, same time, same station. *The Case Book of Gregory Hood* comes to you from our Hollywood studios. This is Harry Bartell saying good night for the Petri family. For a solid hour of exciting mystery drama, listen every Monday on most of these same stations at eight for *Michael Shayne*, followed immediately by *The Case Book of Gregory Hood*. This is the Mutual Broadcasting System.

246. The Cases of Mr. Ace. Crime Drama, 30 min., ABC, 1947.

Edward Ace is a Manhattan-based private investigator with offices on Sixth Avenue. He is tough, prefers handling homicide cases and hates working in the dark—"I prefer to know my clients' intentions." Stories relate his case investigations.

Cast: George Raft (*Edward Ace*). ***Announcer:*** Carlton KaDell. ***Music:*** Del Castillo.

OPENING

Announcer: *The Cases of Mr. Ace* starring George Raft and produced and directed by Mason James.

247. Casey, Crime Photographer. Crime Drama, 30 min., CBS, 1943–1955.

The Blue Note Cafe, a cozy little bar, is the hangout for the reporters of a crusading newspaper called the *Morning Express*. One such patron is Jack Casey, a top-notch photojournalist who covers the crime news of a great city (he lives on Mulberry Street). Stories follow Casey's exploits as he and his girlfriend, fellow reporter Anne Williams, become personally involved in the stories they cover. *Other regular characters:* Ethelbert, the Blue Note Cafe bartender; Bill Logan, the police captain. Also titled *Flashgun Casey*, *Casey, Press Photographer* and *Crime Photographer*. Served as the basis for the television series *Crime Photographer* (1951–1952).

Cast: Matt Crowley, Staats Costworth (*Jack Casey*); Jone Allison, Alice Reinheart, Betty Furness, Lesley Woods, Jan Miner (*Anne Williams*); John Gibson (*Ethelbert*); Jackson Beck, Bernard Lenrow (*Capt. Bill Logan*). ***Announcers:*** Bill Cullen, Bob Hite, Tony Marvin, Ken Roberts. ***Blue Note Pianists:*** Herman Chittison, Juan Fernandez, Teddy Wilson. ***Organist:*** Lew White. ***Orchestra:*** Archie Bleyer.

OPENING

Announcer: The Anchor Hocking Glass Corporation brings you *Crime Photographer*. Good evening, ladies and gentlemen, this is Tony Marvin. Every week at this time, the Anchor Hocking Glass Corporation and its more than 10,000 employees bring you another adventure of *Casey, Crime Photographer*, ace cameraman who covers the crime news of a great city. Written by Alonzo Dean Cole, our adventure for tonight: "Death in Lover's Lane."

248. The Cass Daley Show. Comedy, 30 min., CBS, 1950.

Cass Daley is a likable small-town girl who believes in helping people—whether they want her help or not. Comic situations develop as Cass goes about minding other people's business.

Cast: Cass Daley (*Herself*); Fred Howard (*Her father*); Lurene Tuttle (*Her mother*). ***Announcer:*** Arch Presby. ***Orchestra:*** Robert Armbruster.

249. Catch Me If You Can. Game, 30 min., CBS, 5/9/48 to 6/13/48.

Two contestants compete: the Climber and the Challenger. A question is read by the host and the Climber receives the first chance to answer. If the opponent believes the wrong answer was given, he challenges by attempting to give the correct response. If his challenge is successful, he defeats the Climber and moves to the first rung of a ladder. He then becomes the Climber and a new Challenger is brought on. If, however, the Climber gives a correct response, he moves up one rung on the ladder and a new player becomes the Challenger. The first player to reach the top rung (the Golden Door) receives the opportunity to unravel a mystery sentence for merchandise prizes.

Host: Bill Cullen. ***Announcer:*** George Bryan.

250. Cavalcade of America. Anthology, 30 min., CBS, 1935–1939; NBC Blue, 1940; NBC Red, 1941–1953.

Stories of American history featuring the famous and the obscure; people who risked their lives to help shape our country. Top name guests appeared on the DuPont-sponsored program; it was so authentic that a board of historical advisors was established to choose material and authenticate each facet of the broadcast.

Announcer-Narrators: Clayton "Bud" Collyer, James Famin, Gabriel Heatter. ***Organist:*** Rosa Rio. ***Orchestra:*** Robert Armbruster, Donald Voorhees.

OPENING (from 11/2/42)

Announcer: Starring Madeleine Carroll as Amelia Earhart on the *Cavalcade of America*, sponsored by DuPont, makers of better things for better living through chemistry. As these words are spoken, 22,000 women

(From left): Tony Roberts, Lois Nettleton, Norman Rose, Terri Keane and host E.G. Marshall line up to record a program for *The CBS Radio Mystery Theater*.

are now piloting civil air patrol planes; others are ferrying bombers to distant places. Thousands of American women are pouring through the gates of factories, shipyards and airplane plants after a hard day's work. Today we know that there is hardly a job a woman cannot do; and if there is one woman who proved that fact once and forever, it is America's greatest woman flyer, whose thrilling story we tell this evening. For her courage, skill and persistent efforts to prove a woman's place in aviation, *Cavalcade* salutes Amelia Earhart.

CLOSING

ANNOUNCER: Thank you Madeleine Carroll. Ladies and gentlemen, next week *Cavalcade* will be proud to honor the men of our Merchant Marine in a new radio play called "Torpedo Run," a story based on the actual experiences of the heroic men who carry the goods over the seven seas fighting submarines beneath and bombers overhead. Our star will be the popular stage and screen star, Dean Jagger. This is Clayton Collyer sending best wishes from DuPont. This program came to you from New York. This is NBC, the National Broadcasting Company.

251. The CBS Radio Mystery Theater. Anthology, 60 min., CBS, 1/4/74 to 12/31/84.

Mystery presentations that attempted to revive the lost art of radio drama. Five hour-long programs were produced each week (for a total of 1600) and featured top name guests as well as performers from the golden age of radio. Stories included:

Ghost in the Well. The story of an artist who, after painting the portrait of a girl he envisions, suddenly finds himself face to face with her spirit and involved in her plight as she attempts to prove who murdered her in 1799. *Stars:* Court Benson, Patricia Elliott, William Griffis, Tony Roberts.

The Impossible Is True. The story of a girl who fears that there is a horrible curse of death on her and her family. *Stars:* Earl Hammond, Ann Williams.

Wise Child. While on vacation, a married couple finds an abandoned baby which they keep and raise as their own. The story focuses on the changes that occur in the couple's lives when the baby, seemingly possessed by an unknown force, takes over their minds. *Stars:* Ralph Bell, Jackson Beck, Ann Williams.

Crossfire. A cabbie suddenly finds himself involved in a crossfire between two rival gangs when his fare, a jeweler, becomes involved in a murder. *Stars:* Court Benson, Earl Hammond, Russell Horton, Ann Williams.

Host-Narrator: E.G. Marshall (1974–1984); Tammy Grimes (1984). ***Creator-Producers:*** Himan Brown, Norman Corwin.

OPENING

HOST: *The CBS Radio Mystery Theater* presents [over a squeaking door] "Ghost in the Well." Come in, welcome, I'm E.G. Marshall. [He would then introduce the evening's presentation.]

CLOSING

HOST: This is E.G. Marshall inviting you to return to our *Mystery Theater* for another adventure in the macabre. Until next time, pleasant dreams [the squeaking door closes].

252. CEILING UNLIMITED. Anthology, 15 and 30 min. versions, CBS, 1942–1944.

Dramatic presentations coupled with music and songs, *Ceiling Unlimited* explored the history of aviation during wartime.

Host: Joseph Cotten, Orson Welles. ***Vocalist:*** Nan Wynn. ***Announcer:*** Pat McGeehan. ***Orchestra:*** Wilbur Hatch.

253. CENTRAL CITY. Serial, 15 min., NBC, 1938–1941.

Central City, an industrial complex of 50,000 people, is the setting for a daily look at the problems faced by a typical American family.

Cast: Tom Powers (*Commentator*); Frank Wilcox (*Father*); Selena Royle (*Mother*); Eleanor Phelps (*Daughter*); Van Heflin (*Daughter's fiancé*); Myron McCormick (*Daughter's ex-fiancé*). ***Also:*** Harry Bellaver, Elspeth Eric, John McBryde, Everett Sloane. ***Producers:*** Anne Hummert, Frank Hummert.

254. CHALLENGE OF THE YUKON. Adventure, 15 and 30 min. versions, Local Detroit, 1939–1947; ABC, 1947–1951.

The original title for what would eventually become *Sergeant Preston of the Yukon* (see for additional information). Just as William Preston completes his U.S. college education, he receives word from Canada that his father has been killed in the Yukon by an evil criminal named Spike Wilson. The time is 1898, and to have the legal authority to capture Wilson, Preston joins the Royal Canadian Mounted Police (where he is made a constable and assigned to capture Wilson). After much difficulty, Preston apprehends Wilson, who is sentenced to life imprisonment.

Shortly after, while on duty, Constable Preston intervenes in a lynx attack and rescues a husky puppy that had been raised by a female wolf. He adopts the dog, names him Yukon King and teaches him to lead a sled team, respect good men and hate evil ones. Months later, when Spike escapes from prison, Preston is again assigned to capture him. When he does, Preston is promoted to sergeant and Spike is sentenced to death. Stories, set in the early 1900s, relate Sgt. Preston's efforts to maintain law and order in the early gold rush days of the Yukon. Also assisting Preston is his horse, Rex.

Cast: Paul Sutton (Sgt. William Preston). ***Announcers:*** Fred Foy, Jay Michael (network); Bill Morgan (local).

OPENING

ANNOUNCER: King, the swiftest and strongest of Eskimo lead dogs, blazes the trail through storm and snow for Sgt. Preston and meets the *Challenge of the Yukon*. Sgt. Preston was typical of the small band of Northwest Mounted Police who preserved law and order in the Yukon during the gold rush of '98. That was the year that brought over 50,000 men swarming into the Klondike region and the greed for gold led to frequent violence and bloodshed. But in spite of the odds against them, the force preserved a splendid record in maintaining the right. The challenge of the Northwest was answered and justice ruled triumphant!

CLOSING

ANNOUNCER: *Challenge of the Yukon*, a copyrighted feature of the Challenge of the Yukon, Inc., is brought to you every Saturday at this time and originated in the transcription studios of WXYZ, Detroit. The characters and events in tonight's drama were fictitious. Bill Morgan speaking, this is the Michigan Radio Network.

255. THE CHAMBER MUSIC SOCIETY OF LOWER BASIN STREET. Variety, 30 min., NBC Blue/ABC, 1940–1944; NBC, 1950–1952.

A Sunday afternoon program of blues and jazz music. ***Hosts:*** Orson Bean, Milton Cross, Gene Hamilton, Jane Pickens. ***Regulars:*** Diane Courtney, Lena Horne, Henry Levine, Jack McCarthy, Dinah Shore, Zero Mostel. ***Orchestra:*** Henry Levine, Paul LaValle.

OPENING

ANNOUNCER: Four-thirty Sunday afternoon in New York and the R.C.A. building now stands up straight and respectfully removes its hat as we tune in on another concert by the no-doubt world-renowned *Chamber Music Society of Lower Basin Street*, whose members have gathered here to read from the classics of the three Bs—Barrelhouse, Boogie Woogie and the Blues. [The host would then be introduced and the music would begin.]

256. CHANCE OF A LIFETIME. Game, 30 min., ABC, 1949–1952.

Four players compete. As a series of letters appears on an electronic board (related by the announcer), players are each permitted to choose three. If a bell sounds, the player in the process of selecting his letters receives a luxury gift; if a buzzer is heard, a less expensive gift is awarded. Following this segment, players are given a last opportunity to increase their winnings by pitting everything in a ten-second race against time. If, within that time, a player is able to choose a bell-associated letter from the board, he wins; if not, he loses everything.

Hosts: John Reed King, Don Wilson. ***Assistant:*** Janice Ford. ***Announcer:*** Ken Roberts.

257. CHANDU, THE MAGICIAN. Adventure, 15 min., Mutual, 1932–1936; 30 min., Mutual, 1948–1949; ABC, 1949–1950.

After living in India for a number of years, American secret agent Frank Chandler returns to the United States to begin a quest: to battle evil wherever it exists as the mysterious Chandu the Magician (as he is known in the secret places of the Far East). While in India, Frank acquired supernatural powers from an old Hindu yogi he called "My Teacher." Before Chandler left India to live with his widowed sister Dorothy in San Francisco, the yogi gave him the Emerald Casket of Three Times Three—which endows him with unique powers. The drowning death of Dorothy's husband on the high seas (the ship on which he was traveling sank) prompted Frank to return home. Serialized stories follow Frank's relentless efforts to battle evildoers, the most notorious of which is his greatest enemy, Roxor. *Other regular characters:* Bob and Betty, Dorothy's children; Princess Nadji, Frank's romantic interest.

Cast: Gayne Whitman, Tom Collins (*Frank Chandler/Chandu*); Margaret MacDonald, Irene Tedrow (*Dorothy Regent*); Bob Bixby, Lee Miller (*Bob Regent*); Betty Webb, Joy Terry (*Betty Regent*); Veola Vonn (*Princess Nadji*); Louis Van Rooten (*Roxor*). ***Announcer:*** Howard Culver. ***Producer:*** Sara Armbruster, Raymond P. Morgan.

OPENING

SOUND EFFECT: A large gong sounding.

ANNOUNCER (over music): *Chandu the Magician*. Good evening, ladies and gentlemen. The makers of White King Granulated Soap present for your enjoyment tonight and every weekday evening at this time *Chandu, the Magician*. Listen and you will travel to strange lands, you will thrill to high adventure, romance and mystery... There are many tales told on radio, but only one Chandu; there are many soaps on your grocer's counter, but none like White King... Now let the play begin.

CLOSING

ANNOUNCER: We pause before we say good evening to suggest that you and your family listen to *Chandu* every weekday evening at this time. Travel with us to strange places and faraway lands, into the mystery and intrigue of Egypt and the Near East. And of course we like to have you use the soap we make, White King Granulated Soap... So, on your radio, remember *Chandu, the Magician* ... and at your grocer's, remember White King Granulated Soap. Good night.

258. CHAPLAIN JIM. Drama, 30 min., NBC Blue, 1942; Mutual, 1945–1946.

Serial-like stories of a young American chaplain's experiences with various outfits on the battlefields during World War II. The program, based on actual incidents, was sponsored by the War Department and was actually a means by which to relate patriotic messages to the radio audience.

Cast: John Lund, Don MacLaughlin (*Chaplain Jim*). ***Announcers:*** George Ansbro, Vin-

Fibber McGee and Molly (Jim and Marian Jordan, left) with Charlie McCarthy and Edgar Bergen in *The Charlie McCarthy Show.*

ton Hayworth. ***Organist:*** Rosa Rio. ***Producers:*** Anne Hummert, Frank Hummert.

259. THE CHARLES BOYER SHOW. Anthology, 30 min., NBC, 1950–1951.

A weekly series of dramatic stories in which host Charles Boyer played a night-clubbing Parisian who earned his keep by spinning yarns to visiting novelists. Also known as *Presenting Charles Boyer*.

260. CHARLIE AND JESSIE. Comedy, 15 min., CBS, 1941.

A daily domestic series about the mishaps that plague a young married couple: Charlie, a salesman for Bissell, Cartwright, Emerson and Spillwork, and his wife Jessie.

Cast: Donald Cook (*Charlie*); Diane Bourbon, Florence Lake (*Jessie*). ***Announcer:*** Nelson Case.

261. CHARLIE CHAN. Mystery, 15 and 30 min. versions, NBC Blue, 1932–1933; Mutual, 1936–1938; NBC Red, 1944; ABC, 1944–1945; Mutual, 1947–1948.

Serialized adventures of the famed Oriental detective Charlie Chan, a master investigator with the Honolulu Police Department, who incorporates scientific knowledge and deductive reasoning to solve baffling crimes. He is assisted by his number one son, Lee. Based on the characters created by Earl Derr Biggers. Also known as *The Adventures of Charlie Chan*.

Cast: Walter Connolly, Ed Begley, Santos Ortega, William Rees (*Charlie Chan*); Leon Janney, Rodney Jacobs (*Lee Chan*). ***Announcer:*** Dorian St. George. ***Organist:*** Lew White. ***Producers:*** Alfred Bester, Chick Vincent.

OPENING

ANNOUNCER: Right now, sit back, relax and listen to the greatest Oriental detective of them all, the incomparable Charlie Chan, in a new and exciting series. Join this famous detective of fiction, films and radio as he combines the wisdom of the East with the science of the West in a dramatic chapter from the adventures of *Charlie Chan*.

262. The Charlie McCarthy Show. Variety, 60 and 30 min. versions, NBC, 1937–1948; CBS, 1949–1955.

A weekly series of music, songs and comedy skits that revolve around Charlie McCarthy, the elegantly dressed wooden dummy of ventriloquist Edgar Bergen. Charlie's antics, especially those with the weekly guest star, were the focal point of the program. Edgar's other dummies: Mortimer Snerd and Effie Klinker (Mortimer was the less than intelligent country bumpkin; Effie, who came on late in the series, was an old maid). A regular segment of the series was "The Bickersons" with Don Ameche and Marsha Hunt (later Frances Langford) as the quarrelsome married couple, John and Blanche Bickerson (see *The Bickersons* for information). The program was originally titled *The Chase and Sanborn Hour* and is also known as *The Edgar Bergen and Charlie McCarthy Show*. See also *The Edgar Bergen Hour*.

Cast: Edgar Bergen (*Edgar Bergen/Charlie McCarthy/Mortimer Snerd/Effie Klinker*); Barbara Jo Allen (*Vera Vague, the vocalist*); Norman Field (*Charlie's school principal*); Pat Patrick (*Ersel Twing*); Richard Haydn (*Prof. Carp*). Mentioned but never heard was Charlie's good friend Skinny Dugan. ***Regulars:*** Don Ameche, Jim Backus, Gary Crosby, W.C. Fields, Marsha Hunt, Frances Langford, June Kilgore, Jack Kirkwood, Dorothy Lamour, Eddie Mayehoff, Bill Rapp, Carol Richards, Bill Thompson. ***Vocalists:*** Donald Dixon, Anita Ellis, Dale Evans, Anita Gordon, the King Sisters, the Sportsmen, the Stroud Twins. ***Announcers:*** Ben Alexander, Bill Baldwin, Ken Carpenter, Nelson Case, Bill Goodwin, Howard Petrie. ***Orchestra:*** Robert Armbruster, Ray Noble.

OPENING

Announcer: The makers of instant Chase and Sanborn Coffee present *The Charlie McCarthy Show*. This is Ken Carpenter, ladies and gentlemen, greeting you from Hollywood, California, on behalf of Edgar Bergen, Charlie McCarthy, Mortimer Snerd, Don Ameche, Marsha Hunt of *The Bickersons* by Bill Rapp; Ray Noble and his orchestra and Pat Patrick as Ersel Twing.

263. The Charlie Ruggles Show. Variety, 30 min., Syndicated, 1943–1945.

A weekly program of comedy skits, songs and music with film star Charlie Ruggles as the host. Linda Ware provided the vocals; Tony Marvin did the announcing; Archie Bleyer and his orchestra provided the music.

264. Charlie Wild, Private Detective. Crime Drama, 30 min., NBC, 1950–1951; CBS, 1951.

Charlie Wild is a New York–based private investigator. He is very curious-minded and tough when he has to be, although he would prefer to devise a way to apprehend a killer through trickery rather than a face-to-face confrontation. Stories relate his exploits as he and his sidekick McCoy investigate crimes. Served as the basis for the television series of the same title.

Cast: George Petrie, Kevin O'Morrison, John McQuade (*Charlie Wild*); Peter Hobbs (*McCoy*). ***Announcer:*** Bill Rogers.

265. The Charlotte Greenwood Show. Comedy, 30 min., NBC Blue, 1944.

Charlotte Greenwood is a struggling actress who, while waiting for her big break, works as a reporter for the *Post Dispatch*, a small paper in the town of Lake View. Charlotte, who was born on Long Island (New York), can sing, dance and act, but Roger, her agent, can only get her minor parts. While she waits, she reports and her efforts to get the scoops for the paper are the focal point of stories (which feature vocals between acts). *Other regular characters:* Mr. Anderson, the editor; Tommy Brooks, the copy boy. Also known as *The Hallmark Charlotte Greenwood Show*. See also the following title.

Cast: Charlotte Greenwood (*Charlotte Greenwood*); John Brown (*Mr. Anderson*); Harry Bartell (*Tommy Brooks*); Ed McDonald (*Roger*). ***Vocalists:*** The Hallmark Chorus. ***Announcer:*** Wendell Niles. ***Orchestra:*** Charles Hathaway.

OPENING

Announcer: A Hallmark card will best express your perfect tastes, your thoughtfulness.

Chorus: Welcome now to our show; here's a friend you all know, Charlotte Greenwood, she's with us again.

Announcer: *The Hallmark Charlotte Greenwood Show*, brought to you every Sunday at this time by the makers of Hallmark greeting cards. And here is our star, that lovable lady of stage and screen, Charlotte Greenwood.

CLOSING

CHARLOTTE: Friends, it's been fun visiting with you again. It's always a pleasure for all of us to visit with our friends, dropping in at their house to chat for a moment, to laugh together and to bring back memories of good times. And now, until Sunday at this very same time, this is Charlotte Greenwood saying—

CHARLOTTE (singing): So long, friends, until we meet again, so long, neighbors, until next Sunday, time to say so long.

ANNOUNCER: *The Charlotte Greenwood Show* has been brought to you by Hallmark cards. Wendell Niles speaking. This is the Blue Network.

266. THE CHARLOTTE GREENWOOD SHOW. Comedy, 30 min., ABC, 1945–1946.

Following the death of her sister and brother-in-law in a car accident, actress Charlotte Greenwood becomes the legal guardian of their children, Barbara, Jack and Robert Barton. The children inherited the Barton estate as an investment in their future; unfortunately, the estate's securities pay small dividends, the house is heavily mortgaged, the farm they own is not being worked and the lunchroom owned by the family is barely paying its own way. Stories follow Charlotte's adventures as she struggles to raise the children and find ways to make the estate pay to provide for Barbara, Jack and Robert's future. *Other regular characters:* Sylvester, the butler; Jonathan P. Reynolds, the attorney for the Barton estate. Also known as *The Hallmark Charlotte Greenwood Show.*

Cast: Charlotte Greenwood (*Charlotte Greenwood*); Janet Waldo (*Barbara Barton*); Cliff Carpenter (*Jack Barton*); Dix Davis (*Robert Barton*); Parker Fennelly (*Sylvester*); Edward Arnold (*Jonathan P. Reynolds*). ***Announcer:*** Wendell Niles. ***Orchestra:*** Charles Hathaway.

OPENING

ANNOUNCER: *The Charlotte Greenwood Show.* And here she is, that lovable lady of stage, screen and radio, Charlotte Greenwood.

CHARLOTTE: Hello, friends and thank you, Wendell. I know that you are all familiar with the story of the turkey that turned into a Thanksgiving dinner, but our story today has to do with a Thanksgiving Day that turned into a turkey.

ANNOUNCER: Yes, ladies and gentlemen, Charlotte Greenwood is brought to you this Sunday and every Sunday at this time by the makers of Hallmark greeting cards to remind you that whenever you want to remember someone, you'll find a Hallmark card that says just what you want to say the way you want to say it. And now to Lake View and the Barton home, where Charlotte is bringing up the Barton children. [The story would then begin.]

CLOSING

CHARLOTTE: And now, until next Sunday at this very same time, this is Charlotte Greenwood (now singing): So long until we meet again, so long, neighbor, till next Sunday, so until then, so long.

ANNOUNCER: This program came to you from Hollywood. This is the American Broadcasting Company.

267. THE CHASE. Anthology, 30 min., NBC, 1952–1953.

Dramatizations based on the theory that at one time or another every person is either the hunter or the hunted—physically or mentally. Varying stories and casts.

THE CHASE AND SANBORN HOUR *see* **THE CHARLIE MCCARTHY SHOW**

268. THE CHESTERFIELD PROGRAM. Comedy, 30 min., CBS, 9/30/38 to 6/23/39.

Skits featuring the antics of Gracie Allen, a scatterbrained young woman, and her level-headed friend George Burns. The program, which also featured songs, music and parodies of famous plays (for example, "When a Prince of a Fella Meets a Cinderella," "Three Loves Has Gracie and Two to Go," "Jitterbugs of the Jungle"), was sponsored by Chesterfield cigarettes.

Stars: George Burns and Gracie Allen. ***Vocalist:*** Frank Parker. ***Announcer:*** Paul Douglas. ***Orchestra:*** Ray Noble.

269. THE CHESTERFIELD SUPPER CLUB.

The overall title for three musical variety series sponsored by Chesterfield cigarettes.

The Chesterfield Supper Club, 15 min.,

NBC, 1944–1947. *Host:* Martin Block. *Vocalists:* Mary Ashworth, Perry Como, the Satisfiers. *Orchestra:* Ted Steele.

The Chesterfield Supper Club, 15 min., NBC, 1947–1948. *Host:* Tex Beneke. *Vocalists:* Eddie Hubbard, Garry Stevens. *Orchestra:* Glenn Miller.

The Chesterfield Supper Club, 15 min., NBC, 1948–1949; 30 min., NBC, 1949–1950. *Host* (Monday, Wednesday, Friday): Perry Como. *Vocalists:* The Fontaine Sisters. *Announcer:* Tom Reddy. *Orchestra:* Mitchell Ayres. *Host* (Tuesday): Jo Stafford. *Announcer:* Tom Reddy. *Orchestra:* Paul Weston. *Host* (Thursday): Peggy Lee. *Featured:* The King Cole Trio. *Announcer:* Tom Reddy. *Orchestra:* Dave Barbour.

CHESTERFIELD TIME (with Fred Waring) *see* **THE FRED WARING SHOW**

270. CHESTERFIELD TIME. Variety, 15 min., CBS, 1943–1944.

A weekly program of music and songs that, sponsored by Chesterfield cigarettes, became *The Chesterfield Supper Club* (see prior title) when it switched networks.

Host: Martin Block. ***Vocalists:*** Johnny Johnston, Monica Lewis. ***Orchestra:*** Paul Baron.

271. THE CHICAGO THEATER OF THE AIR. Variety, 60 min., Mutual, 1940–1954.

A live, weekly Saturday evening program that presented abridged versions of grand operas and dramatic operettas (actors doubled for singers in speaking parts). Broadcast from WGN in Chicago.

Host: Lee Bennett. ***Baritones:*** Bruce Foote, Thomas L. Thomas, Earl Willkis. ***Sopranos:*** Nancy Carr, Marian Claire. ***Tenor:*** Attilio Baggiore. ***Contralto:*** Ruth Slater. ***Regulars:*** Donald Graham, Lawrence Lane, Cal McCormick, the WGN Chorus. ***Dramatic Cast:*** Rita Ascott, Bob Bailey, Luise Barclay, Muriel Bremner, Fran Carlon, Everett Clarke, Patricia Dunlap, Laurette Fillbrandt, Betty Lou Gerson, Norman Gottschalk, Alice Hill, Bob Jellison, John Larkin, Barbara Luddy, Marvin Miller, Bret Morrison, Donna Reade, Olan Soule, Les Tremayne, Willard Waterman, Kay Westfall, Betty Winkler. ***Announcers:*** Marvin Miller, John Weigle. ***Music:*** The WGN Orchestra. ***Choral Director:*** Robert Trendler.

272. CHICK CARTER, BOY DETECTIVE. Crime Drama, 15 min., Mutual, 1943–1945.

In July 1943, just three months after the premiere of *Nick Carter, Master Detective*, Nick's adopted son Chick was spun off into this series of his own, portraying a juvenile detective who battled a variety of criminals, the most notorious of which was the Rattler. *Other regular characters:* Sue, Chick's assistant; Tex, their friend.

Cast: Bill Lipton, Leon Janney (*Chick Carter*); Jean McCoy, Joanne McCoy (*Sue*); Gilbert Mack (*Tex*); Stefan Schnabel (*The Rattler*). ***Announcer:*** Ken Powell.

OPENING

ANNOUNCER (over telegraph sounds): Mutual to Y...O...U. Sending. Are you ready?

VOICE: Y...O...U to Mutual, go ahead.

ANNOUNCER: Then listen to the adventures of *Chick Carter, Boy Detective*.

273. CHICKEN EVERY SUNDAY. Comedy, 30 min., NBC, 7/6/49 to 8/24/49.

Jim and Emily Hefferen are a married couple who own a boarding house in Tucson, Arizona. Jim constantly attempts get-rich-quick schemes that eventually fail; Emily is patient and practical and opposes Jim's mindless ventures. Stories relate the comic incidents that befall Jim and Emily as they attempt to run the boarding house. Based on the Broadway play by Julius and Philip G. Epstein.

Cast: Harry Von Zell (*Jim Hefferen*); Billie Burke (*Emily Hefferen*). ***Music:*** David Baskerville.

274. CHIP DAVIS, COMMANDO. Adventure, 30 min., CBS, 1942–1943.

A World War II series about America's battle against Nazism as seen through the assignments of Chip Davis, a daring American who was a member of the London-based Commandos, an organization of the Allied Nations' best fighters united in an all-out effort to defeat the Third Reich. Chip introduces himself: "My name is Davis. My friends call me Chip." A cast is not identified. ***Music:*** Charles Paul. ***Producer:*** Robert Louis Shallot.

OPENING

ANNOUNCER: Out of the night, grim shadows rise; the steel of vengeance finds its mark. The Commandos have struck again! Columbia presents *Chip Davis, Commando*, the story of an American and his exciting adventures in Britain's famous fighting unit. Tonight's adventure, "Anniversary in Holland."

CLOSING

ANNOUNCER: You have been listening to *Chip Davis, Commando*, Columbia's weekly series about an American in Britain's famous fighting unit. Join us again next Sunday at seven P.M. Eastern War Time for another story with Chip Davis and the men of the United Nations who share his adventures in the Commandos. The adventure: "Convoy to America," in which Chip sees action in the Atlantic while en route to the United States. This is the Columbia Broadcasting System.

275. CHOOSE A SONG PARTNER. Variety, 15 min., ABC, 1948.

A weekly program of music and songs with Don Moreland as the host. Beryl Vaughn was the featured vocalist; music was by organist Adele Scott.

276. CHOOSE UP SIDES. Game, 30 min., CBS, 1940.

Two teams of experts answer questions submitted by listeners, who receive $10 if theirs is chosen. The team with the most correct answers wins and receives $50. Henry McLemore served as the host.

277. THE CHORALIERS. Variety, 30 min., CBS, 1950.

Eugene Powell and his vocal group, the Choraliers, in a weekly program of music and songs. Frank Knight did the announcing.

278. CHRISTOPHER LONDON. Crime Drama, 30 min., NBC, 1/22/50 to 4/30/50.

Christopher London is a troubleshooter, a man who solves the most difficult problems of others. Women find him attractive, but he is a loner and prefers not to talk about himself. His clients treat him well and some spare no expense—"If you don't come back, I'd like to think you died in luxury." Stories, based on the character created by Erle Stanley Gardner, relate London's efforts to solve his clients' problems. Also known as *The Adventures of Christopher London*.

Cast: Glenn Ford (*Christopher London*). ***Music:*** Lyn Murray. ***Producer:*** William N. Robson.

OPENING

LONDON: A knife in his back, a nameless Filipino in San Francisco. With a bullet in her back, a girl in the mid–Pacific. But there were others, 8,000 of them on an island in the Philippines.

ANNOUNCER: The National Broadcasting Company presents *Christopher London*, created especially for radio by the world's foremost mystery writer, Erle Stanley Gardner. Produced and directed by William N. Robson and starring Mr. Glenn Ford.

LONDON: I'm Christopher London. The whole thing started with a vague conversation about the murder of an unknown Filipino. Mr. Adams, president of the San Francisco Sugar Company, either could not or would not say what, if anything, he suspected...

CLOSING

ANNOUNCER: That was *Christopher London* starring Glenn Ford and created especially for radio by the world's most widely read mystery writer, Erle Stanley Gardner. Mystery fans, you'll find two other great pulse-packed adventure programs on most of these NBC stations every Monday night. Listen tomorrow night for *Night Beat* and *Dangerous Assignment* in one hour of intrigue and adventure on NBC. And be with us again next week at this same time when *Christopher London* returns with another exciting excursion against crime. Stay tuned for the Phil Harrises, then *Sam Spade* on NBC.

279. THE CHRISTOPHER LYNCH SHOW. Variety, 10 min., Mutual, 1953.

A brief and short-lived program of music with Christopher Lynch and the Emerson Buckley Orchestra.

CHRISTOPHER WELLS *see* **THE ADVENTURES OF CHRISTOPHER WELLS**

280. CIMARRON TAVERN. Western, 15 min., CBS, 1945–1946.

Incidents in the lives of the people who frequent the Grand Hotelish, a tavern in Cimarron, Oklahoma, during the 1800s. Stories focus in particular on the adventures of Star Travis, a Federal Scout, and his young companion

Randy Martin, an orphan whose parents were killed after they established the hotel.

Cast: Paul Conrad (*Star Travis*); Ronald Liss (*Randy Martin*); Chester Stratton (*Joe Barton*). ***Also:*** Stephen Courtleigh, Tony Burger, Carl Emory, Ethel Everett, Neil O'Malley. ***Announcer:*** Bob Hite.

281. CINDERELLA, INC. Human Interest, 30 min., CBS, 1940.

Four housewives, selected from areas around the country, were brought to New York City, housed in lavish quarters, served breakfast in bed, escorted to a night club, attired in expensive clothes—in short, pampered from head to toe. After their experiences, each housewife related her impressions, feelings and thoughts to listeners.

Host: Bob Dixon. ***Announcer:*** Tony Marvin.

282. THE CINNAMON BEAR. Children, 15 min., Syndicated, 1937.

Each Christmas, a young brother and sister (Jimmy and Judy Barton) look forward to placing a large silver star ornament on top of their tree. One Christmas, while searching for the star in the attic, they find an old trunk. When they open the trunk, a stuffed bear comes to life as Paddy O'Cinnamon. He speaks with an Irish accent, wears a green scarf and is 14 inches tall. Paddy tells the children that the Crazy Quilt Dragon, who likes shiny things, has taken the star. The 26-episode serial follows Paddy as he and Jimmy and Judy embark on a dangerous quest through magical Maybe Land to retrieve the silver star. The program, broadcast weekdays between Thanksgiving and Christmas, was first heard in 1937 and as current as 1997. Although all 26 episodes exist, not all roles are identified and some still remain a mystery.

Cast: Buddy Duncan (*Paddy O'Cinnamon*); Barbara Jean Wong (*Judy Barton*); Verna Felton (*Judy's mother*); Joseph Kearns (*Crazy Quilt Dragon*); Lou Merrill (*Santa Claus*); Elvia Allman (*Melissa, Queen of Maybe Land*). ***Also:*** Gale Gordon, Frank Nelson, Slim Pickens, Hanley Stafford, Martha Wentworth. ***Narrator:*** Bud Heistand. ***Songs:*** The Paul Taylor Quartet. ***Music:*** Felix Mills.

OPENING (from Chapter 1)

VOICE: And here's *The Cinnamon Bear.*

ANNOUNCER: This is the story of *The Cinnamon Bear* and his very marvelous adventures with Judy and Jimmy Barton.

CLOSING (from Chapter 26)

ANNOUNCER: And so ends the story of *The Cinnamon Bear*. Whether Judy and Jimmy dreamed these adventures or whether they really happened doesn't matter. They were truly wonderful and certainly most magical. And now that the Silver Star is shining brightly on the very top of Judy and Jimmy's tree, we can smile our brightest holiday smile and say a merry Christmas to you all. We hope you'll always remember little Paddy O'Cinnamon, the Cinnamon Bear; that's the one thing that will make him very happy. And I can tell you on his behalf, he'll be much obliged to you.

283. THE CIRCLE. Variety, 60 min., NBC, 1939.

A weekly program of variety performances coupled with discussions of current events, literature and drama. The high-budgeted program became one of the most famous flops in radio when host Ronald Colman quit five weeks into the series.

Host: Ronald Colman. ***Regulars:*** Madeleine Carroll, Cary Grant, Carole Lombard, Chico Marx, Groucho Marx, Basil Rathbone, Lawrence Tibbett. ***Producer:*** Carl Kuhl.

284. THE CISCO KID. Western, 30 min., Mutual, 1942–1943; Syndicated, 1946–1954.

The Robin Hood–like adventures of the Cisco Kid and his dimwitted partner Pan Pancho as they roam throughout the Old West helping people victimized by evildoers. Cisco, who was quick with his gun but never shot to kill, was never paid for his services (his reward was a kiss by a beautiful girl). Cisco's horse is named Diablo; Pancho calls his horse Loco. Served as the basis for the 1951 television series of the same title.

Cast: Jackson Beck, Jack Mather (*The Cisco Kid*); Louis Sorin, Harry Lang, Mel Blanc (*Pan Pancho*). ***Also*** (various roles): Bryna Raeburn, Jean Ellyn, Mark Smith, Vicki Vola. ***Announcers:*** Marvin Miller, Michael Rye.

OPENING (same as the television version)

ANNOUNCER: Here's adventure. Here's romance. Here's the famous Robin Hood of the Old West, the Cisco Kid.

285. The Cities Service Concert. Variety, 60 min., NBC, 1927–1940; 30 min., NBC, 1940–1957.

A long-running program of music, songs and concert performances featuring top name entertainers. Also titled *Highways in Melody* (1944–1948) and *The Cities Service Band of America* (1948–1957).

Vocalists: Jessica Dragonette, Ross Graham, Dorothy Kristen, Lucille Manners, the Cavaliers Quartet, the Ken Christy Chorus, the Revelers Quartet. ***Pianists:*** Frank Banta, Milton Rittenberg. ***Orchestra:*** Frank Black, Rosario Bourdon, Edwin Goldman, Paul LaValle. ***Announcer:*** Ford Bond.

286. City Hospital. Drama, 30 min., CBS, 10/6/51 to 11/8/58.

Incidents in the lives of the patients at City Hospital as seen through the eyes of Dr. Barton Crane, the medical director, and his nurse, Kate Morrow. Served as the basis for the television series of the same title.

Cast: Santos Ortega, Melvin Ruick (*Dr. Barton Crane*); Anne Burr (*Kate Morrow*). ***Announcer:*** John Cannon. ***Producer:*** Ira Ashley.

OPENING

Announcer: *City Hospital.* City Hospital, where life begins and ends, where around the clock, 24 hours a day, men and women are dedicated to the war against suffering and pain.

287. Clara, Lu and Em. Serial, 15 min., Local Chicago (WGN), 1930–1931; NBC Blue, 1931–1934; NBC Red, 1934–1936; NBC Blue, 1936; CBS, 1942–1945.

A gossip session wherein three housewives, who lived in the same apartment building, got together in the kitchen or backyard to exchange talk. The original format, which aired in 1930, dealt with the gossip of three spinsters; the housewives format was first incorporated in 1942. Clara was the compulsive housewife; Lu was a widow; and Em was married and the mother of five children (none of whom was heard).

Cast: Louise Starkey, Fran Harris (*Clara*); Isabel Carothers, Harriet Allyn (*Lulu "Lu" Casey*); Helen King, Dorothy Day (*Emma "Em" Krueger*). ***Announcer:*** Don David. ***Music:*** Lou Webb.

288. Claudia and David. Drama, 30 min., CBS, 1941.

Serial-like stories about incidents in the lives of architect David Naughton and his naive 18-year-old wife Claudia, who is struggling to cut the apron strings that bind her to her mother and adjust to marriage. Also known as *Claudia*.

Cast: Patricia Ryan, Katherine Bard (*Claudia Naughton*); Richard Kollmar, Paul Crabtree (*David Naughton*); Jane Seymour, Peggy Allenby (*Mrs. Brown, Claudia's mother*); Irene Hubbard (*David's mother*). ***Announcers:*** Joe King, Charles Stark. ***Music:*** Peter Van Steeden.

289. The Cliche Club. Game, 30 min., ABC, 1950.

The object calls for a panel to unscramble and correct a phrase submitted by a listener (who received a cash prize if the panel failed to do so).

Host: Walter Kiernan. ***Panelists:*** Frederick Lewis Allen, Carol Lynn Gilmer, Edward Hill, Agnes Rogers. ***Announcer:*** Les Griffith.

290. The Cliquot Club Eskimos. Variety, 30 min., NBC, 1926–1936.

A program of music and songs sponsored by Cliquot Club Beverages (whose logo featured an Eskimo, hence the title).

Host: Harry Reser. ***Regulars:*** Jimmy Brierly, Everett Clarke, Virginia Hauer, Merle Johnson, Raymond Knight. ***Announcer:*** Phil Carlin. ***Orchestra:*** Harry Reser.

291. Cloak and Dagger. Anthology, 30 min., NBC, 5/7/50 to 10/22/50.

Dramatizations based on the files of the Office of Strategic Services (O.S.S.) during World War II. Col. Corey Ford, co-author of the book *Cloak and Dagger*, served as the host.

OPENING

Host: Are you willing to undertake a dangerous mission for the United States knowing in advance you may never return alive?

Announcer: What you have just heard is the question asked during the war of agents to the O.S.S. ordinary citizens who to this question answered yes. We have the honor at this time to present a former O.S.S. officer, co-author of the book *Cloak and Dagger*, on which this series is based, Col. Corey Ford.

FORD: Thank you. The O.S.S., the Office of Strategic Services, was America's top secret intelligence agency during the war. It was this country's first all-out effort in black warfare; dropping undercover operatives behind enemy lines, organizing local partisans to blow bridges and dynamite tunnels, outwitting the best spy systems of Europe and Asia. The success of the O.S.S. is known, but the story behind that success, the story of the everyday, average Americans of every race, creed and color, who risked their lives knowing all too well that if they were caught they would face torture and probably death, is what Alistair McBain and I have tried to tell in *Cloak and Dagger*. We feel it is a story in which every American can take deep pride.

ANNOUNCER: The National Broadcasting Company takes you behind the scenes of a war that nobody knew. This is—

VOICE: *Cloak and Dagger*.

292. THE CLOCK. Anthology, 30 min., ABC, 11/3/46 to 5/23/48.

Dramas based on the central theme of man vs. time. The narrator, posing as Father Time, introduced the story, then commented about the effects time had on the people involved.

Narrator: Gene Kirby as Father Time. ***Announcer:*** Bill Cargo. ***Music:*** Bernard Herrmann.

OPENING

SOUND: A clock chiming, then ticking.

FATHER TIME: It's nice to have friends and I count quite a few of my own. Most people consider me to be a very good fellow to know well. If you pardon a bit of boasting on my part, they find that their time is enjoyable; the minutes and hours of their lives are valuable things indeed. To these people, working towards an end for themselves and their families, time provided them with the opportunity to relax, to do a job and to build for the future. Yes, I count myself lucky to have so many friends. But I also have some enemies. Who are my enemies? I'll tell you who they are. [They are different for each episode; for example:] They are the inmates of prisons throughout the world, the misfits and socially outcast. Many of them can be reclaimed, many of them serve out their terms, pay their debt to society and begin anew. But there are a few, a very few who will never change. These are the hardened types, the killers ... these are the ones who watch my hands as they slowly turn year after year, who watch my face, knowing for them, time has no rewards. These are the ones, my friends, who hate me and who despise the world...

293. CLUB 15.

A daily variety series that was distinguished by three versions (each taking its name based on the program's length):

Club 15, 15 min., CBS, 1947–1950. *Host:* Bob Crosby. *Regulars:* The Andrews Sisters, Patti Clayton, the Modernaires, Margaret Whiting. *Announcer:* Del Sharbutt. *Orchestra:* Jerry Gray.

Club 15, 15 min., CBS, 1950–1951. *Host* (Monday, Wednesday, Friday): Bob Crosby. *Regulars:* The Andrews Sisters. *Announcer:* Del Sharbutt. *Orchestra:* Jerry Gray. *Host* (Tuesday, Thursday): Jo Stafford. *Regulars:* The Modernaires. *Announcer:* Del Sharbutt. *Orchestra:* Jerry Gray.

Club 15, 15 min., CBS, 1951–1953. *Hosts:* Bob Crosby, Dick Haymes. *Regulars:* Giselle MacKenzie, the Modernaires, Jo Stafford. *Announcer:* Del Sharbutt. *Orchestra:* Jerry Gray.

294. CLUB MATINEE. Variety, 60 min., NBC Blue, 1937–1942; 30 min., ABC, 1945–1946.

A daily program of music, songs and comedy that also featured performances by promising talent.

Hosts: Garry Moore, Durward Kirby, Ransom Sherman. ***Vocalists:*** Clark Dennis, Johnny Johnston, Evelyn Lynne, Phil Shukin, the Escorts and Betty, the Three Romeos. ***Also:*** Bill Short (bass player). ***Announcer:*** Durward Kirby. ***Orchestra:*** Rex Maupin.

295. THE CLYDE BEATTY SHOW. Adventure, 30 min., Mutual, 1950–1952.

Life in the circus world as seen through the eyes of Clyde Beatty, a wild animal trainer and owner of the Clyde Beatty Circus. He is assisted in his adventures by Harriet Evans Beatty, his wife, a former cabaret dancer, who is now a circus performer. (When the Depression hit the dancing field, Harriet applied for a job at the circus. She and Clyde soon fell in love and married. Not content with just being a housewife, she was taught how to tame lions and given her own act—parading Anna Mae the elephant in the center ring with a lion riding the elephant's back and a tiger running alongside her.) *Other regular characters* (not credited): Grant Williamson, the circus manager; Hugo, the cage boy (assists Clyde in shows); Red Baxter, the clown.

Cast: Clyde Beatty (*Clyde Beatty*); Harriet Beatty (*Harriet Beatty*). ***Announcers:*** Jackson Beck, Larry Thor. ***Producer:*** Shirley Thomas.

OPENING

ANNOUNCER: *The Clyde Beatty Show.* The world's greatest wild animal trainer, Clyde Beatty, with an exciting adventure from his brilliant career. The circus means thrills, excitement, snarling jungle beasts. The circus means fun for young folks and old. But under the big top you see only a part of the story; the real drama comes from behind the scenes, where 500 people live as one family, where Clyde Beatty constantly risks death in the world's most dangerous act on Earth. This master of the big top has journeyed to Africa and India, hunting down his beasts in their native jungle. All this is part of the Clyde Beatty story. [The show would then begin with Clyde beginning a story.]

CLOSING

ANNOUNCER: All stories are based upon incidents in the career of the world famous Clyde Beatty of the Clyde Beatty Circus. This is a Commodore production.

296. COAST-TO-COAST ON A BUS. Children, 60 min., NBC Blue, 1927–1944; ABC, 1945–1948.

Each Sunday morning, a busload of children rode the White Rabbit Line to some locale. While en route, the talented cast of juveniles sang, danced and acted in skits. The slogan of the White Rabbit Line was "Jump anywhere, any time." The series began in 1924 (to 1927) as a local New York program called *The Children's Hour.*

Cast: Milton Cross (*Conductor*); Madge Tucker (*Lady Next Door*); Audrey Egan (*Mumsey Pig*). ***Regulars*** (Kids): Ann Blyth, Edwin Bruce, Gwen Davies, Jeanne Elkins, Jean Harris, Bob Hastings, Helen Holt, Tommy Hughes, Jackie Kelk, Bill Lipton, Ronald Liss, Billy Mauch, Bobby Mauch, Michael O'Day, Pamela Prescott, Billy Redfield, Lawrence Robinson, Niels Robinson, Susan Robinson, Joy Terry, Renee Terry. ***Music:*** Walter Fleischer. ***Creator-Producer-Writer-Director:*** Madge Tucker.

OPENING

CONDUCTOR (over bus horn): *Coast-to-Coast on a Bus.* The White Rabbit Line jumps anywhere, any time.

SONG (kids singing): Oh, we just roll along, taking her up, taking her down ... all day long, we just roll along...

CONDUCTOR: Good morning, little and big folks, children and grownups, passengers on the White Rabbit Bus. Today... [The conductor would then begin the show by relating the destination of the imaginary bus.]

297. THE COCA-COLA SUMMER SHOW. Variety, 30 min., CBS, summer of 1948.

Roger Pryor as the host of a program of music and songs sponsored by Coca-Cola beverages. Nestor Charles and Los Ponchos were the regulars and Charles Lichter and his orchestra provided the music.

298. THE COKE CLUB. Variety, 15 min., Mutual, 1943–1951.

A daily series of music and songs sponsored by Coca-Cola beverages and featuring popular vocalists. Leah Ray served as the host; Morton Downey and the Coke Club Quartet were the regulars. David Ross did the announcing; Jimmy Lytell and his orchestra provided music.

OPENING

ANNOUNCER: Yes, friends, it's time for another transcribed session of *The Coke Club,* which brings you the romantic voice of Morton Downey, with Leah Ray as your hostess, Jimmy Lytell and his orchestra, the Coke Club Quartet, and yours truly, David Ross. And now, your hostess, Leah Ray...

299. THE COLGATE SPORTS NEWSREEL. Anthology, 15 min., NBC, 9/39 to 6/51.

The program, also known as *Bill Stern's Colgate Sports Newsreel* and *The Colgate Shave Creme Sports Newsreel,* features dramatizations based on events in the lives of sports figures or people somehow related to sports.

Host: Bill Stern. ***Announcer:*** Arthur Gary. ***Organist:*** Murray Ross.

OPENING

CHORUS: C-O-L-G-A-T-E, Colgate presents Bill Stern.

ANNOUNCER: With *The Colgate Shave Creme Sports Newsreel.*

CHORUS: Bill Stern, the Colgate Shave Creme man, is on the air. Bill Stern, the Colgate Shave Creme man with stories rare. Take his advice and you'll look keen; you'll get a shave that's smooth and clean; you'll be a Colgate brushless fan.

BILL: Good evening, ladies and gentlemen, this is Bill Stern bringing you the 352nd edition of *The Colgate Shave Creme Sports Newsreel* featuring strange and fantastic stories, some legends, others mere hearsay, but all so interesting we'd like to pass them on to you. Our guest tonight is the famous singing star of radio, Miss Joan Edwards, but first Reel One, portrait of August the second. Tonight is August the second. Because it is, I'd like to tell you one of the greatest fight stories of all time—a story that reputedly begins and ends on another August second, a story of the great John L. Sullivan...

CLOSING

BILL: And that's the "Three-O-Mark" for tonight. Next Friday night we'll be back, same time, same station, with another edition of *The Colgate Shave Creme Sports Newsreel.* This is Bill Stern for Colgate Shave Creme wishing you all a good, good night.

CHORUS: Bill Stern, the Colgate Shave Creme man, is on his way; Bill Stern, the Colgate Shave Creme man, has lots to say. He told you tales of sports heroes; the inside dope he really knows. So listen in next Friday night, C-O-L-G-A-T-E.

ANNOUNCER: *The Bill Stern Show* tonight came from New York City.

300. THE COLGATE SPOTLIGHT. Variety, 30 min., CBS, 1941.

Ed East as the host of a program, sponsored by Colgate, that featured performances by undiscovered talent. Jeff Spartin did the announcing and Charles Hathaway and his orchestra provided the music.

301. COLLEGE BOWL QUIZ. Quiz, 30 min., NBC, 1953–1955.

The forerunner of television's *G.E. College Bowl.* Two teams of college students competed in a question and answer session. Winning teams received a $500 college grant; losers were awarded various individual prizes.

Host: Allen Ludden. ***Announcer:*** Roger Tuttle.

302. COLLEGE PROM. Variety, 30 min., NBC Blue, 1935–1936.

Music, songs and interviews set against the background of a college campus where each week listeners were invited to attend a mythical prom.

Host-Announcer: Ford Bond. ***Vocalist:*** Ruth Etting. ***Orchestra:*** Red Nichols.

303. THE COLLIER HOUR. Anthology, 60 min., NBC Blue, 1927–1932.

Dramatizations based on stories appearing in *Collier's* magazine (also the sponsor). Also featured were musical numbers and discussions of current events. The most popular segments were serialized versions of the "Fu Manchu" stories by Sax Rohmer.

Cast: John B. Kennedy, Jack Arthur, Phil Barrison (*Editor*); John Greig (*Prof. Lucifer Butts*); Arthur Hughes (*Fu Manchu*). ***Announcer:*** John B. Kennedy. ***Orchestra:*** Ernest La Prade. ***Producer:*** Malcolm La Prade.

304. COLONEL HUMPHREY FLACK. Comedy, 30 min., NBC, 1947.

Retired Col. Humphrey J. Flack and his companion Uthas P. (Patsy) Garvey believe they are modern-day Robin Hoods. With larceny in their minds and charity in their hearts, they travel throughout the world and, through imaginative deceptions, outwit confidence men in their attempts to assist the needy.

Cast: Wendell Holmes (*Humphrey J. Flack*); Frank Maxwell (*Uthas P. Garvey*). ***Announcer:*** Dick Dudley.

COLONEL STOOPNAGLE AND BUDD *see* **STOOPNAGLE AND BUDD**

305. COLUMBIA PRESENTS CORWIN. Anthology, 30 min., CBS, 1944–1945.

Dramatizations based on stories written by Norman Corwin and featuring a different cast each week. Stories included:

Movie Primer. Frank Gallop, Minerva Pious

and Everett Sloane in a story that satirizes the movie industry.

You Can Dream, Inc. John Griggs, Minerva Pious and Robert Trout in a fantasy about a company that sells daydreams to people in need of a change of life.

Dorie Got a Medal. Josh White, Mary Lou Williams and the Golden Gate Quartet in a jazz and jive opera about a black Navy messboy who became a hero at Pearl Harbor.

Tel Aviv. The audition episode for the series "Passport for Adams" with Myron McCormick, Joseph Julian and June Alexander in the story of an American newspaper editor and his photographer (here meeting the people of Tel Aviv).

El Capitan and the Colonel. Burl Ives, Joseph Julian and Katherine Locke in a story about a soldier who meets a beautiful girl on a cross-country train trip.

Host: Norman Corwin. ***Narrators:*** Martin Gabel, Earl Wrightson. ***Announcers:*** Harry Marble, Roy Rowan. ***Music:*** Bernard Herrmann, Lyn Murray, Earl Robins, Alexander Semmler. ***Producer-Writer-Director:*** Norman Corwin.

306. THE COLUMBIA WORKSHOP. Anthology, 30 min., CBS, 1936–1947.

A showcase for aspiring actors, writers, producers and directors. During its first year, the program dramatized scripts of unknown writers and featured equally unknown actors, producers and directors. Beginning in 1937, the works of established writers gradually replaced those of unknowns. Prominent radio performers were also brought in to act with promising talent. Stories include:

The Red Badge of Courage. Chester Stratton in an adaptation of the novel about the battles of the Civil War as seen through the eyes of a young Union soldier.

John Brown's Body. Ray Collins and Luis Van Rooten in a story about the attack at Harper's Ferry and John Brown's predictions of the future. Based on the poem by Stephen Vincent Benet.

The Plot to Overthrow Christmas. Ray Collins, Martin Gabel, Karl Swenson and Luis Van Rooten in a holiday tale about the devil's fiendish plot to kill Santa Claus and end the celebration of Christmas.

This Is from David. Agnes Moorehead as a mother who puts work ahead of her young son.

A Crop of Beans. Ted de Corsia and Agnes Moorehead in a tragic story about the struggles of a farm couple during the Depression.

307. COMEDY BY—. Comedy, 30 min., Mutual, 1940.

George Byron as the host of a weekly program that spotlighted the performances of guest comedians. Comics Howard and Shelton and the Eaton Boys were the regulars. Bob Stanley and his orchestra provided the music.

COMEDY CARAVAN *see* THE JIMMY DURANTE–GARRY MOORE SHOW

308. COMEDY OF ERRORS. Game, 25 min., Mutual, 1949–1952.

A short skit, which contains an error, was read to selected members of the studio audience. The first player to spot and correct the error won the round and $5. The highest scoring cash player was the winner.

Host: Jack Bailey. ***Announcer:*** Fort Pearson. ***Organist:*** Eddie Dunstedter.

309. COMMUNITY SING. Variety, 30 and 45 min. versions, CBS, 1936–1937.

A Sunday evening program of songs in which the studio audience is led in a community sing. The program was broadcast from two locations: Milton Berle and Wendell Hall hosted from New York City; Billy Jones and Erne Hare ("The Happiness Boys") were in charge of the festivities from Philadelphia. Paul Douglas did the announcing.

310. CONFESSION. Anthology, 30 min., NBC, 1953–1954.

Dramatizations based on the files of various corrections departments throughout the country. The program was presented in cooperation with the California State Department of Corrections.

Cast: Paul Frees (*Richard A. McGee, Director of the California State Department of Corrections*). ***Music:*** J. Frederick Albech.

OPENING

VOICE: The confession you are about to hear is an actual recording. All right, read the statement please.

MAN: I make this confession of my own free will

Elsa Maxwell (left) visits Constance Bennett on *The Constance Bennett Show.*

because it is true. There wasn't any force or violence used upon my person to induce me to make these statements. Without promise of immunity or gratuity, I confess.

VOICE: You understand, of course, your statements will be made public to the radio program *Confession*.

MAN: I do.

ANNOUNCER: You are listening to *Confession*. This confession is a matter of documented record. You will hear the story of this crime experience told in the person's own words. This is *Confession*.

311. CONFIDENTIALLY YOURS. Anthology, 30 min., NBC, 1950.

Dramatizations based on the crime cases of Jack Lait, a reporter for the now-defunct New York *Daily Mirror*. Jack Lait appeared as the host and narrator. Bob Warren did the announcing and Jack Miller and his orchestra provided the music.

312. CONNEE BOSWELL PRESENTS. Variety, 30 min., NBC Blue, 1943–1944; ABC, 1944.

Vocalist Connee Boswell, a member of the 1930s singing trio the Boswell Sisters, as the host of a program of music and songs. Louis Jourdan, Jack Pepper and the Tympany Five were the regulars. Jack McCarthy did the announcing; Paul Whiteman and his orchestra provided the music.

313. THE CONSTANCE BENNETT SHOW. Talk, 15 min., ABC, 1945–1946.

Topics of conversation of interest to women. The program used topics submitted by listeners; it is also known as *Constance Bennett Calls on You*. Constance Bennett was the host; George Ansbro and Robert Latting did the announcing.

314. CONSUMER QUIZ. Game, 30 min., CBS, 1946.

Five female contestants, chosen from the studio audience, were involved. Each player had to answer questions based on shopping. The program's resident expert judged the women based on their responses. The player who was best at responding to the questions won a cash prize.

Host: Fred Uttal. ***Shopping Expert:*** Joan Barton. ***Producer:*** Cledge Roberts. ***Note:*** On June 30, 1946, CBS adapted the program to television in a live test program that failed to generate a series.

315. CORONET ON THE AIR. Anthology, 30 min., NBC Blue, 1937.

Deems Taylor as the host of a weekly program that dramatized various features from the pages of *Coronet* magazine. Robert Armbruster and his orchestra provided the music.

316. CORONET QUICK QUIZ. Game, 5 min., NBC Blue, 1944.

The host asked eight questions in rapid-fire succession, followed immediately by the answers. The purpose was for listeners to test their mental powers and ability to answer questions rapidly. Sponsored by *Coronet* magazine. Charles Irving was the host and Don David announced.

317. CORONET STORY THEATER. Anthology, 5 min., NBC Blue, 1944; ABC, 1944–1947.

A daily five-minute program of dramatizations from the pages of *Coronet* magazine. Marvin Miller, who served as the host and narrator, also provided voices for all the characters. Vic Perrin did the announcing.

318. CORRECTION PLEASE. Game, 30 min., CBS, 1943–1945; NBC, 1945.

Selected members of the studio audience received $10 bidding money. A multiple choice question was read and three answers appeared on a board, one of which was wrong. Contestants then bid for the opportunity to correct the error. If the highest bidding player corrected the statement, he won ten times the bet amount. If he was incorrect, the bet amount was deducted from his total.

Hosts: Jim McWilliams, Jay C. Flippen. ***Orchestra:*** Jerry Fears, Jack Shilkret.

319. COSMO TUNE TIME. Variety, 30 min., Mutual, 1945.

A weekly program of music and songs featuring the material available on the sponsor's product, Cosmopolitan Records.

Host: Alan Kent. ***Vocalists:*** The Four Chicks and a Chuck. ***Orchestra:*** Henry Busse, Ernie Madriguera, Bernie Weissman.

320. THE COTY PLAYGIRL. Variety, 15 min., NBC, 1931.

A program of music and songs sponsored by Coty Cosmetics. Irene Bordoni and Adele Ronson served as hosts. The orchestras of Eugene Ormandy and Ray Noble provided the music.

321. COULD BE. Game, 30 min., NBC, 1939.

Couples celebrating various occasions (for example, a wedding anniversary) were the contestants. Players were interviewed, then competed in a quiz segment. A sound effect, which could be one of three things, was played. A musical clue was then supplied by the orchestra. If the couple could identify the sound effect, they won a cash prize—what could be gotten by dipping one hand into a treasure chest of money.

Host: Tony Marvin. ***Orchestra:*** Horace Heidt.

322. THE COUNT OF MONTE CRISTO. Adventure, 30 min., Mutual, 1946–1947.

Falsely accused of bearing treasonable information, Edmond Dantes is convicted and sentenced to life imprisonment in the Château d'If. Learning of a buried treasure from his cellmate, he digs his way out, escapes and retreats to the island of Monte Carlo. Uncovering the treasure, he establishes himself as a mysterious and powerful figure for justice. Stories relate his battle against the forces of corruption in 18th-century France. Based on the story by Alexandre Dumas. *Other regular characters:* Marie Duchene, Edmond's fellow conspirator and romantic interest; René Michon, Edmond's manservant.

Cast: Carleton Young (*Edmond Dantes*); Anne Stone (*Marie Duchene*); Parley Baer (*René Michon*). ***Announcer:*** Charles Arlington. ***Music:*** Dean Fassler.

323. COUNTERSPY. Adventure, 30 min., NBC Blue, 1942–1944; ABC, 1945–1950; NBC, 1950–1953; Mutual, 1954–1957.

The exploits of David Harding, a U.S. government counterspy. During World War II, David's adventures battling the Gestapo and Black Dragon were depicted. After the war, David and his assistant Harry Peters fought the enemies of America at home and abroad. Also known as *David Harding, Counterspy*.

Cast: House Jameson (*David Harding* [first episode]); Don MacLaughlin (*David Harding*); Mandel Kramer (*Harry Peters*). ***Announcers:*** Roger Krupp, Bob Shepherd. ***Producer:*** Phillips H. Lord.

OPENING

ANNOUNCER (over Morse Code): Washington calling counterspy.

DAVID (over Morse Code): Harding, counterspy, calling Washington.

ANNOUNCER: The Blue Network presents *Counterspy*. Germany has its Gestapo, Italy its Zobra, and Japan its Black Dragon. But matched against all of these secret enemy agents are Uncle Sam's highly trained counterspies. Visualize ace counterspy of them all as David Harding.

324. COUNTY FAIR. Game, 30 min., CBS, 1945–1950.

The program is set in a fairground and has contestants competing in various stunt contests in return for prizes.

Hosts: Win Elliot, Jack Bailey, Jack Barry. ***Assistant:*** Larry Keating. ***Announcers:*** Larry Keating, Lee Vines. ***Orchestra:*** Bill Gale. ***Producer:*** Bill Gannett.

325. COUNTY SEAT. Serial, 15 min., CBS, 1938–1939.

Events in the lives of the people of the small town of Northbury as seen through the eyes of Doc Hackett, kindly proprietor of a corner drugstore. *Other regular characters:* Sarah Whipple, Doc's sister; Jerry Whipple, Sarah's son, a high school student.

Cast: Ray Collins (*Doc Hackett*); Charme Allen (*Sarah Whipple*); Cliff Carpenter (*Jerry Whipple*); Jackie Jordan (*Billy Moorehead*); Lucille Meredith (*Laura Paige*); Luis Van Rooten (*Dr. Priestly*).

326. THE COUPLE NEXT DOOR. Comedy, 15 min., CBS, 1957–1960.

The couple next door are an unnamed husband and wife with a six-and-a-half-year-old daughter named Betsy. Their exchange of conversation about everyday life is the basis for each story.

Cast: Peg Lynch (*Mother*); Alan Bunce (*Father*); Madeleine Pierce (*Betsy*). ***Announcer:*** Warren Sweeney. ***Producer:*** Walter Hart.

OPENING

ANNOUNCER: *The Couple Next Door*, written by Peg Lynch and starring Peg Lynch and Alan Bunce.

CLOSING

ANNOUNCER: *The Couple Next Door* is written by Peg Lynch and stars Peg Lynch and Alan Bunce with Madeleine Pierce as Betsy and is produced by Walter Hart. This is Warren Sweeney inviting you to listen tomorrow to *The Couple Next Door*.

Note: An earlier version appeared on CBS in 1937 with Olan Soule and Elinor Harriot as *The Couple Next Door*. When production switched from Chicago to New York, Harold Vermilyea and Lillian Gish became the new couple.

327. THE COURT OF MISSING HEIRS. Human Interest, 30 min., CBS, 12/19/39 to 9/29/42; ABC, 3/31/46 to 4/6/47.

A weekly program that attempted to find real-life heirs by dramatizing the closed files of people with unclaimed inheritances. Also titled (1941) *Are You a Missing Heir?*

Host: James Waters. ***Organist:*** Rosa Rio. ***Producer:*** John W. Loveton.

328. COUSIN WILLIE. Comedy, 30 min., NBC, 7/7/53 to 9/29/53.

Marvin and Fran Sample are a happily married couple who reside at 2164 Mariposa Avenue in Glendale, California. They have two children, Susan and Sandy, and a relative—Willard O. Knott, "Cousin Willie" for short, who lives with them (he came from Milwaukee for a short visit and has decided to stay). Cousin Willie is a well-meaning 23-year-old who can't seem to find his place in society. He is gentle, a bit naive and works as a door-to-door salesman for the P.D. Rocky Reconditioned Vacuum Cleaner Company. Stories relate the simple pleasures and trying times Willie faces as he tackles life head on. *Other regular characters:* Freckles Burke, the receptionist at the vacuum cleaner company (and Willie's girlfriend).

Cast: Billy Idelson (*Cousin Willie*); Marvin

Miller (*Marvin Sample*); Patricia Dunlap (*Fran Sample*); Dawn Bender, Bridget DeCarl (*Susan Sample*); Stuffy Singer, Tony Kaye (*Sandy Sample*); Patte Chapman (*Freckles Burke*). ***Announcer:*** Jimmy Wallington. ***Music:*** Robert Armbruster.

OPENING

ANNOUNCER: This is the one about *Cousin Willie*. Billy Idelson is Cousin Willie. Frank and Doris Hursley write it; and it's produced and transcribed by Homer Canfield. Believe it or not, our Cousin Willie came to California from Milwaukee, Wisconsin, and is staying, temporarily, with his cousins, the Marvin Sample family. So far, he has been with them, temporarily, for seven weeks. Cousin Willie sleeps, temporarily, on the davenport in Marvin's den… [The announcer would mention another thing that Willie temporarily does and the story would begin.]

329. THE CRACRAFT ELECTRIC ORCHESTRA. Variety, 30 min., NBC, 1939.

Andre Monici as the host of a weekly program that features the music of the Thomas Adrian Cracraft Orchestra. Connie Crandell, Don Lamont and Arthur Tubertine were the vocalists.

330. CREEPS BY NIGHT. Anthology, 30 min., ABC, 2/15/44 to 6/20/44.

A weekly series of mystery and suspense presentations enacted by a regular cast. After six episodes, the original host was replaced by a character identified only as "Doctor X."

Original Host-Narrator-Performer: Boris Karloff. ***Cast:*** Edmund Green, Abby Lewis, Gregory Morton, Everett Sloane. ***Music:*** Jeff Crawford. ***Producer:*** Robert Maxwell.

OPENING

ANNOUNCER: We bring you *Creeps by Night*.

HOST: Good evening, this is your Master of Mystery, Doctor X. I'd like to present the sixteenth in a series of dramatic explorations into the vast and unknown labyrinth of the human mind. Tonight, our guest, the internationally known dramatic star, Miss Florence Reed. The story I have chosen is a somewhat weird and spine-chilling narrative of a woman who unwisely looked beyond the shadows of the grave. *Creeps by Night* through your Master of Mystery presents Florence Reed in "The Three Sisters."

331. THE CREIGHTONS. Comedy, 30 min., NBC, 1942.

Events in the lives of the Creighton family: Christopher, a sculptor; his wife Serena, a mystery novelist; and their children, Victor and Crottie.

Cast: John Griggs (*Christopher Creighton*); Ethel Owen (*Serena Creighton*); Norman Tokar (*Victor Creighton*); Sammie Hill (*Crottie Creighton*). ***Music:*** Joseph Stopak.

332. CRESTA BLANCA CARNIVAL. Variety, 45 min., Mutual, 1943–1944.

A weekly program of music and songs sponsored by Cresta Blanca Wines. Frank Gallop served as the host and Morton Gould and Alec Templeton were the regulars. Morton Gould and his orchestra supplied the music.

333. CRIME AND PETER CHAMBERS. Crime Drama, 30 min., NBC, 1954.

"You're a private eye; that's your business. Anything else, that's for laughs," says Peter Chambers. He calls himself "a private Richard": "It doesn't matter what you call it—private eye, confidential investigator—it all adds up to the same thing, a patsy." Chambers is based in New York City and, no matter how innocently a case starts out (for example, delivering a letter for a client), it inevitably ends in murder. And when that happens, Peter's best friend, police detective Louis "Louie" Parker is on the case—"and without you, my case wouldn't be complete," says Louie of Peter. Stories follow both Peter and Louie's efforts to solve crimes—usually as a team, but sometimes independently when Peter's hunches lead him into a different direction. Peter charges $500 for his services.

Cast: Dane Clark (*Peter Chambers*); Bill Zuckert (*Lt. Louis Parker*). ***Announcer:*** Fred Collins.

OPENING

ANNOUNCER: *Crime and Peter Chambers*, created by Henry Kane, transcribed and starring as Peter Chambers, Dane Clark.

CLOSING

ANNOUNCER: And there you've had *Crime and Peter Chambers*. Dane Clark was starred as Peter Chambers. *Crime and Peter Chambers*, transcribed, was created and written by Henry Kane. This is Fred Collins inviting you to tune in next week, same time, same station, for Dane Clark and *Crime and Peter Chambers*. This is NBC, the National Broadcasting Company.

334. The Crime Cases of Warden Lawes. Anthology, 15 min., Mutual, 10/26/46 to 9/23/47.

Dramatizations based on the files of Lewis E. Lawes, warden of Sing Sing Prison. Lawes appeared as himself (the host and narrator) and Cy Harrice did the announcing. Burt Buhrmann supplied the music.

335. Crime Classics. Anthology, 30 min., CBS, 6/15/53 to 6/30/54.

Dramas of true stories from "the records of newspapers of every land and every time." Cases range from a seventeenth-century murder to the assassination of Abraham Lincoln. Each program was hosted by Thomas Hyland, a mythical connoisseur of crime, student of violence and teller of murders.

Cast: Lou Merrill (*Thomas Hyland*). ***Regular Cast:*** Herb Butterfield, Mary Jane Croft, Sam Edwards, Georgia Ellis, Bill Johnstone, Tudor Owen, Ben Wright. ***Announcer:*** Bob Lemond. ***Music:*** Bernard Herrmann. ***Producer:*** Elliott Lewis.

OPENING

Host: Good evening, this is *Crime Classics*. I am Thomas Hyland with another true story of crime. Listen.

Sound: Gun shots.

Host: Six shots from a Colt .44. For no reason other than to get your ear attuned to what you are going to hear. Our hero's name is William Bonny, a lad who was a product of his time and whose time may be described as a blot. So tonight my report to you is on "Billy Bonny, Blood Letter," also known as "The Kid" (Billy the Kid).

Announcer: *Crime Classics*, a series of true crime stories from the records and newspapers of every land from every time. Your host each week, Mr. Thomas Hyland, connoisseur of crime, student of violence and teller of murders. Now, once again, Mr. Thomas Hyland... [The story would then begin.]

CLOSING

Announcer: Here again is Thomas Hyland.

Host: Next week, England in the year 1705 and the lovely young lady whose maiden name was Katharine Hayes and whose ambition was to be a widow. My report to you will be on John Hayes—his head and how they were parted. Thank you. Good night. This is CBS, the Columbia Broadcasting System.

336. Crime Club. Anthology, 30 min., Mutual, 1946–1947.

Dramatizations based on stories appearing in *Crime Club* books.

Host (Librarian): Raymond Edward Johnson.

OPENING

Sound: Telephone ringing; receiver being picked up.

Host: Hello, I hope I haven't kept you waiting. Yes, this is the Crime Club. I'm the librarian. "Dead Men Control"? Yes, we have that Crime Club story for you. Come right over.

Sound: Doorbell rings; door opens.

Host: Ah, you're here, good. Take the easy chair by the window. Comfortable? The book is on the shelf, here it is ... let's look at it under the reading lamp... [At this point, the story would begin.]

337. Crime Doctor. Crime Drama, 30 min., CBS, 1940–1947.

During a caper, master criminal Benjamin Ordway suffers a head injury that produces amnesia. During his illness, Ordway is rehabilitated. Seeking to begin a new life, he attends medical school and specializes in criminal psychology. Later, when his memory returns, he decides to use his skills as a criminal with his knowledge of medicine to help good defeat evil. Stories follow Dr. Ordway as he helps police Inspector Ross and District Attorney Miller solve baffling crimes.

Cast: John McIntire, Hugh Marlowe, Ray Collins, House Jameson, Everett Sloane (*Dr. Benjamin Ordway*); Walter Greaza (*Inspector Ross*); Edgar Stehli (*D.A. Miller*). ***Also:*** Jeanette Nolan, Edith Arnold, Vicki Vola (various good and bad girls). ***Announcer:*** Charles O'Connor. ***Music:*** Ray Bloch.

338. Crime Does Not Pay. Anthology, 30 min., Syndicated, 1949–1951; Mutual, 1952.

Dramatizations of actual crimes. Stories profile the various criminals and try to explain the circumstances that put individuals on the path to destruction.

Vicki Vola had a supporting role on *Crime Doctor*.

Host-Narrator: Donald Buka.

OPENING

ANNOUNCER: *Crime Does Not Pay*. In the interest of good citizenship and law enforcement, we present *Crime Does Not Pay*, based on the famous Metro-Goldwyn-Mayer series of short subjects. In just a moment you will hear "The Kid with a Gun" featuring Donald Buka.

339. THE CRIME FILES OF FLAMOND. Crime Drama, 30 min., Mutual, 1952–1957.

Flamond (no other name given) is a private detective with unique credentials—he is a psychologist and character analyst. He is assisted by Sandra Lake, a secretary with an interest in crime, and stories follow their efforts to solve crimes by discovering the reasons they were committed. Each episode contains "The Basic Clue" that enables listeners to solve the case along with Flamond (the clue is very obvious and can easily be overlooked by listeners). At the end of the episode, Flamond explains "The Basic Clue" that enabled him to solve the case and Sandra, who keeps a card file on each case, titles it (as shown in the opening and closing segments that follow).

Cast: Everett Clarke (*Flamond*); Muriel Bremner (*Sandra Lake*). ***Announcer:*** Bob Cunningham.

OPENING (from File 239, "The Chick That Killed")

ANNOUNCER: Card number 239 from *The Crime Files of Flamond.*

FLAMOND: A new file card please, Miss Lake. Popular nightclub piano player fears flop to wreck his career. Seeks confidential investigation.

ANNOUNCER: Flamond, the most unusual detective in criminal history. Flamond, famous psychiatrist and character analyst. Flamond, who looks beyond laughter and tears, jealousy and greed in order to discover the reason why. And Card Number 239, from *The Crime Files of Flamond.*

CLOSING

ANNOUNCER: And now "The Basic Clue" in File Number 239 of *The Crime Files of Flamond.*

SANDRA (at typewriter): You know, Flamond, there's one thing about this case that I don't dig ... you seemed so darn sure Marie Hale was the killer...

FLAMOND: Marie did Willy a favor when she slashed his hand ... it was Willy's right hand.

SANDRA: Honey, I get it ... with his hand all cut up, Willy could have never fired a revolver.

FLAMOND: Now you dig me, Chick, now you dig me. I gather you've got a title for the file card.

SANDRA: Ah ha, you gather right, boss, I'm calling it "The Case of the Chick That Killed."

340. CRIME IS MY PASTIME. Anthology, 15 min., Mutual, 1945.

Varied mystery presentations wherein a crime and its solution are presented. All stories feature performances by Gerald Mohr and Rod O'Connor (in various roles) and the music of the Len Salvo Orchestra.

341. A CRIME LETTER FROM DAN DODGE. Crime Drama, 30 min., ABC, 1952–1953.

The program, which details the investigations of private detective Dan Dodge, unfolds through a series of flashbacks as Dodge dictates a crime letter to his secretary relating the facts of a recent case.

Cast: Myron McCormick (*Dan Dodge*); Shirley Eggleston (*Secretary*).

342. Crime on the Waterfront. Crime Drama, 30 min., NBC, 1949.

Lou Kagel is a lieutenant with the New York City Police Department. His beat is the waterfront and its associated crime (usually involving incidents aboard ships). Lou is a charmer—the ladies love him but the criminals hate him and some say he's "too smart for his own good." *Other regular characters:* June Sherman, Lou's girlfriend, a newspaper reporter who tags along and assists Lou in his investigations.

Cast: Myron Wallace (*Lou Kagel*); Muriel Bremner (*June Sherman*). ***Announcer:*** George Stone.

OPENING

Sound: Phone ringing, then being picked up.

Voice: Waterfront. Kagel calling.

Announcer: The National Broadcasting Company presents Lou Kagel, ace New York detective, fighter of *Crime on the Waterfront.*

Lou: I'm Lou Kagel. I've been around the waterfront on and off for eight years now; guess I'll never get enough. I don't know, just standing here at the pier, even at six-thirty in the morning, watching those little tugs bring another liner in through all this north river traffic; lights blinking through the fog, boat whistles. The long, low blast of a big babe coming in the Narrows gets me every time. [He would then talk about the evening's episode.]

343. Criminal Case Book. Crime Drama, 30 min., NBC, 1948.

Dramatizations that recount the lives of criminals. Episodes begin with a rough sketch of the crime, then trace the facts that brought about and concluded it. Stories are enacted by a regular cast.

Cast: Jimmy Blaine, Betty Garde, Mitzi Gould, Don Hastings, Bill Keene, Frances Rafferty, Santos Ortega, John Sylvester. ***Announcer:*** Nelson Case. ***Music:*** John Gart.

344. Crooked Square. Anthology, 15 min., Mutual, 1945.

Mystery and suspense presentations enacted by a regular cast (Roger DeKoven, Larry Haines, Ethel Owen, Eddie Nugent, Santos Ortega, Peggy Stanley). Also featured were announcer Tiny Ruffner and the music of Henry Sylvern.

345. The Cuckoo Hour. Comedy, 15 min., NBC Blue, 1930–1936.

A weekly quarter-hour visit to a radio station where the staff is as wacky as its call letters—KUKU. Station manager Ambrose J. Weems appears as the master of ceremonies and Mrs. George T. Pennyfeather gives advice—whether you want it or not—on a show called "Mrs. Pennyfeather's Service for Perturbed People" (where she talks about the home and what to do with it). Various other comedy bits and musical numbers and songs were also a part of the program.

Cast: Raymond Knight (*Ambrose J. Weems*); Adelina Thompson (*Mrs. George T. Pennyfeather*). ***Vocalists:*** Jack Arthur, Mary McCoy. ***Regulars:*** Sallie Belle Cox, Mary Hopple, Carl Matthews. ***Announcer:*** Ward Wilson. ***Orchestra:*** Robert Armbruster. ***Producer:*** Raymond Knight.

OPENING

Announcer: Good evening friends... The next 15 minutes are devoted to ... *The Cuckoo Hour*, radio's oldest network comedy program—and if you don't think that's something, well, maybe you're right. We now turn you over to station KUKU...

346. The Curley Bradley Show. Variety, 15 min., Mutual, 1949.

A program of country and western music with singer/actor Curley Bradley and the music and songs of the T-M-B Bar Ranch Boys. Franklyn MacCormack did the announcing. See also the following title.

347. Curley Bradley—the Singing Marshal. Western, 30 min., Mutual, 1950–1951.

A revamped version of the prior title that drops most of the variety element to focus on Curley Bradley, a law enforcer known as "The Singing Marshal," as he relates tales of the Old West. Stories, which focus on Marshal Curley Bradley's long battle against outlaws, stress more story and less gunplay. Bradley played himself and Don Gordon was the announcer.

348. Curt Massey Time. Variety, 15 min., CBS, 1943.

An Alka-Seltzer–sponsored program of light music and songs with Curt Massey, a singer and violinist.

Host: Curt Massey. ***Vocalists:*** Marian Morgan, Martha Tilton, the Cheerleaders, the Dinning Sisters. ***Announcers:*** Charles Lyon, Jack Narz. ***Orchestra:*** Jack Fascinato, Billy Liebert.

349. CURTAIN TIME. Anthology, 30 min., Mutual, 1938–1939; ABC, 1945–1946; NBC, 1946–1950.

A series of dramatizations enacted first by a regular cast, then by weekly guest stars. The program borrowed elements from *The Mercury Theater* (using the same players each week) and *The First Nighter* (setting the program against the backdrop of a theater where listeners were invited to attend the evening's performance).

Cast: Harry Elders (*Leading man*); Beverly Younger (*Leading lady*). ***Supporting Players:*** Raymond Edward Johnson, Betty Winkler. ***Announcer:*** Don Gordon. ***Music:*** Joseph Gallichio, Henry Weber. ***Producer-Director:*** Norman Felton.

OPENING

ANNOUNCER: Kellogg's Kix brings you *Curtain Time*. Once again, it's *Curtain Time*. Tonight we present the powerful drama of a mother who fought against blind justice. The play, "Beautiful Lady."

ANNOUNCER: Again a gay and fashionable audience crowds every seat for that thrilling moment in the theater, *Curtain Time*. Remember, this play is presented for your enjoyment by General Mills, makers of America's brand new cereal sensation corn K-I-X, Kix. In just a moment, the house lights will dim, but first let's look through our playbill for tonight. "Beautiful Lady" was written for *Curtain Time* by one of radio's best authors, Arch Oboler, and stars two outstanding actors, Margaret Hillias and Hugh Studebaker. The orchestra is under the baton of Henry Weber and the entire production is directed by Blair Wallacer. Now Mr. Weber steps to the stand and the show is on.

350. DADDY AND ROLLO. Comedy, 15 min., Mutual, 1932–1942.

A humorous dialogue between an inquisitive ten-year-old boy (Rollo) and his often bewildered father (Daddy). Craig McDonnell played the part of Daddy; Georgie Ward, then Donald Hughes portrayed Rollo.

351. DAILY DILEMMAS. Game, 30 min., Mutual, 1947–1948.

A dilemma, as faced by nearly everyone in everyday life, was enacted. A selected member of the studio audience was brought on stage, placed opposite a jury of studio audience members, and asked to identify the object of the dramatized dilemma. The jury's decision—whether they approve or disapprove of the answer—determined the player's prize.

Host: Jack Barry. ***Enacting Dilemmas:*** Cecil Roy.

352. DAISY DISCOVERS AMERICA. Audition (Comedy), 30 min., NBC, 5/26/50.

Daisy McLennon was born in Dunsermlime, Scotland. She is 27 years old (although she says she is 26 as she hears Americans like younger women), stands five-feet-two, weighs 105 pounds and has blue eyes. Daisy has come to America to begin a new life and the proposed series was to follow her adventures as she struggles to adjust to a new homeland (New York) and become a citizen. In the audition episode, Daisy causes a traffic nightmare when she gets out of a cab in the middle of the George Washington Bridge so she can admire the view.

Cast: Ella Logan (*Daisy McLennon*); Sheldon Leonard (*Cab driver*); Ed Max (*Cop*); Herb Vigran (*Truck driver*); Dick Ryan (*Judge*). ***Announcer:*** Tyler McVey. ***Orchestra:*** Lou Bring. ***Producer-Writer-Director:*** Charles Isaacs.

OPENING

ANNOUNCER: *Daisy Discovers America* starring Ella Logan as Daisy and featuring Sheldon Leonard, Larry Dobkin, Ed Max, Dick Ryan and Lou Bring's orchestra. In the days that Columbus first discovered America, people have steamed in from Europe to help build this great nation. Partisans from Italy, railroad builders from Ireland, steel workers from the Baltics, painters from France, inventors from England and Scotland. All have joined together in this great melting pot. They are no longer steel workers or painters, they are Americans.

353. THE DAMON RUNYON THEATER. Anthology, 30 min., Syndicated, 1949–1950.

Dramatizations based on Damon Runyon's stories of the characters of old New York's underworld. Each story is seen through the eyes of Broadway, a hood with a heart of gold who hangs out at a respectable joint called Mindy's Bar.

Cast: John Brown (*Broadway*). ***Performers*** (Various Roles): William Conrad, Frank Lovejoy, Sheldon Leonard, Herb Vigran, Peggy Webber, Luis Van Rooten.

OPENING

ANNOUNCER: *The Damon Runyon Theater.* Once again *The Damon Runyon Theater* brings you another story by the master story teller Damon Runyon, and this one, "Broadway Complex." And to tell it to you, here is Broadway (who begins by introducing the characters).

CLOSING

ANNOUNCER: And so ends the famous Damon Runyon story, "Broadway Complex." Listen in again next week for *The Damon Runyon Theater.*

354. DAN HARDING'S WIFE. Serial, 15 min., NBC, 1936–1939.

Rhoda Harding is a widow and the mother of twins (Donna and Dean). Rhoda's husband Dan, a miner, was killed in a job-related accident in Iraq. The twins are young adults and their activities are a part of the daily proceedings as Rhoda struggles to cope with life without Dan.

Cast: Isabel Randolph (*Rhoda Harding*); Loretta Poynton (*Donna Harding*); Merrill Fugit (*Dean Harding*); Carl Hanson (*Arnie Topper*); Alice Goodkin (*Peggy Latham*); Herbert Nelson (*Ralph Fraser*); Tommye Birch (*Eva Foster*); Judith Lowry (*Mrs. Graham*); Willard Farnum (*Jack Garland*); Hugh Rowlands (*Stooge Lewis*); Templeton Fox (*Margot Graham*); Herb Butterfield (*Rex Kramer*). ***Announcers:*** Norman Barry, Les Griffith.

355. DANGER DR. DANFIELD. Crime Drama, 30 min., ABC, 1946–1951.

Stories begin with Dr. Daniel Danfield, a brilliant criminal psychologist, dictating the results of a recent case to his secretary, Rusty Fairfax. As Rusty types, a flashback is used to relate aspects of the case he is dictating. When the crime has been established, Dr. Danfield begins his investigation (he is usually called in by the police because the crime didn't follow a particular pattern). Daniel is deeply interested in the criminal mind and looks for every opportunity to further his knowledge by meeting with the criminals themselves—preferably from behind bars or by going undercover to meet them on their own turf. This is fine with Daniel, but not with Rusty, who fears for his life—"Don't, you can't, I know you'll be murdered, I know you will." "Nonsense, Miss Fairfax, I must go, a man's life is at stake." Rusty is not so easily convinced and vows to help, often complicating cases and giving Daniel something extra to worry about: Rusty's safety. Following the successful conclusion of the case, the program returns to Daniel's office, where he dictates his thoughts about the case to Rusty.

Cast: Michael Dunn (*Dr. Daniel Danfield*); JoAnne Johnson (*Rusty Fairfax*).

OPENING

VOICE: *Danger, Dr. Danfield.*

DANFIELD: The human mind is like a cave. Beyond the light, there are dark passages and mysterious recesses. I, Dr. Daniel Danfield, have explored those unknown retreats and know their secrets.

ANNOUNCER: Dr. Daniel Danfield, authority on crime psychology, has an unhappy facility for getting himself mixed up in hazardous predicaments because of his astounding revelations regarding the workings of the criminal mind. As our story opens, we find Dr. Danfield in his office dictating to his pretty secretary, Rusty Fairfax...

356. DANGER IS MY BUSINESS. Interview, 15 min., Mutual, 1941.

Jay Sims as the host and announcer for a program of one-on-one interviews with people involved in hazardous occupations.

357. DANGER WITH GRANGER. Crime Drama, 30 min., Mutual, 1956–1957.

Steve Granger is a private detective who has to look behind him quite often. The people he has put away have a chip on their shoulder and getting even with Granger would be the first step in removing it. Granger has a knack for ruffling the wrong feathers and murder and mayhem seem to follow him wherever he goes. Stories follow Steve as he defies danger to investigate various cases. While most radio detectives are quite respectful to women, even the bad ones, Steve has been known to be a little rough—"Granger, you hit a lady!" "Quite the contrary, Lieutenant, I defended myself against a wildcat." Granger also insures his female clients of their safety—"I'm Steve Granger, private detective. We'll see that you're safe. Then you can tell me the whole story. If it holds together, I'll take the case." A cast is not identified, and credits are not given.

OPENING

ANNOUNCER: *Danger with Granger.*

GRANGER: This is Steve Granger, private detective, with a story about a rainy night which was the setting for violent death and which just, incidentally, almost had me labeled by my friends in the police department as nuts. In just a moment I'll take you back to one of my most interesting cases. [After a commercial break, Steve would begin the story:] I took a good look at the young woman who bumped into me in the rain and found a blonde youngster in her early twenties, dressed in nothing but a drenched summer dress which clung to her skin like a label to a perfume bottle…

CLOSING

GRANGER: Steve Granger again. You have just heard one of the most interesting cases in my files and I'll have another for you, so be around next time.

358. DANGEROUS ASSIGNMENT. Adventure, 30 min., NBC, 1950–1953; Syndicated, 1953–1954.

Episodes begin with Steve Mitchell, a handsome international troubleshooter for the U.S. government, receiving an assignment to an exotic locale. Steve is hired to resolve situations that could discredit the United States, and operates without the technical involvement of the government. The story then follows Steve's adventures (which he narrates) as he encounters beautiful women, dangerous criminals and international intrigue. Served as the basis for the 1952 television series of the same title with Brian Donlevy as Steve Mitchell.

Cast: Brian Donlevy, Lloyd Burrell (*Steve Mitchell*).

OPENING

ANNOUNCER: Baghdad! Martinique! Singapore! And all the places of the world where danger and intrigue walk hand in hand, there you will find Steve Mitchell on another *Dangerous Assignment.*

359. DANGEROUSLY YOURS. Anthology, 30 min., CBS, 1944.

A weekly series of adventure stories geared to women (although there is more romance and less action) as told by a man known as "The Voice of Adventure."

Cast: Martin Gabel (*The Voice of Adventure*). ***Regular Performers:*** Victor Jory, Gertrude Warner. ***Music:*** Mark Warnow.

360. THE DANNY KAYE SHOW. Variety, 30 min., CBS, 1945–1946.

A weekly series of music, songs and comedy (various sketches) with comedian Danny Kaye. Sponsored by Pabst Blue Ribbon Beer.

Host: Danny Kaye. ***Regulars:*** Goodman Ace, Eve Arden, Jim Backus, Everett Clarke, Kenny Delmar, Joan Edwards, Butterfly McQueen, Lionel Stander, Everett Sloane, the Four Clubmen. ***Announcers:*** Dick Joy, Ken Niles. ***Orchestra:*** Harry James, Lyn Murray, Harry Sosnik, David Terry. ***Producer:*** Goodman Ace.

361. DANNY O'NEIL AND HIS GUESTS. Variety, 25 min., CBS, 1946–1947.

An expanded (by ten minutes) version of the next title that continues to feature the vocal talents of Danny O'Neil, now accompanied by a different guest star each week. Janette Davis, George Guest, Archie Robbins and the Song Spinners were the regulars. Bill Cullen did the announcing and Archie Bleyer and his orchestra provided the music.

362. THE DANNY O'NEIL SHOW. Variety, 15 min., CBS, 1945–1946.

Singer Danny O'Neil as the host of a program of music and songs. Lorna Lynn was the featured vocalist; Bill Cullen did the announcing; and Ruby Newman and his orchestra provided the music. See also the prior title.

363. THE DANNY THOMAS SHOW. Variety, 30 min., NBC Blue, 1942–1943; CBS, 1947–1948.

Comedian Danny Thomas as the host of a program of music, songs and comedy sketches. The regulars were Kathryn Card, Hans Conried, Donelda Curry, Sid Ellstrom, Art Kahl, Marvin Miller and the Four Escorts and Betty. Ben Gage did the announcing; music was by Elliot Daniel and His All-Girl Orchestra and Rex Maupin and his orchestra.

364. Dark Fantasy. Anthology, 30 min., NBC, 11/14/41 to 6/19/42.

Dramas that depict the plight of people who encounter the world of the unknown. Stories were written by the series host, Scott Bishop. Tom Paxton and Keith Paynton were the announcers.

OPENING

ANNOUNCER: *Dark Fantasy.*

HOST: I am Scott Bishop, I create fantasies for radio. I write weird stories for magazines. I write books on strange subjects. Authors who do these things sometimes attract odd happenings. I don't ask listeners to believe my stories. I don't expect you to believe what I am going to tell you now... [The story would then begin.]

CLOSING

ANNOUNCER: Next Friday night at this time, the National Broadcasting Company will bring you another unusual and fantastic adventure thriller, "Men Call Me Mad," the story of another world and the people who inhabit it. An exciting and weird tale of *Dark Fantasy*, created by Scott Bishop. *Dark Fantasy* originates in the studios of WKY, Oklahoma City. Keith Paynton speaking. This is the National Broadcasting Company.

365. Dark Venture. Anthology, 30 min., ABC, 1945–1948.

Stories of people who are suddenly propelled into unexpected situations and their efforts to overcome adverse circumstances.

Host-Announcer: John Laing. ***Commercial Spokesman:*** Harry Walstrom. ***Music:*** Dean Fossler.

OPENING

ANNOUNCER: *Dark Venture*, presented by Wild Root Creme Oil for the hair. Over the minds of mortals come many shadows. Shadows of greed and hate, jealousy and fear, darkness, the absence of light. Throw in the sudden shadows that spark the minds of men and women; or to be bound with strange impulses which urge them into the unknown. *Dark Venture*. Tonight's venture into the dark features William Tracy in "The Expert," the story of a man who did everything right and then found it was wrong.

SPOKESMAN: *Dark Venture* is brought to you by the Wildroot Company, makers of Wildroot Creme Oil for the hair.

ANNOUNCER: And now tonight's *Dark Venture*, "The Expert."

CLOSING

ANNOUNCER: Next week at this same time the Wildroot Company, makers of Wildroot Creme Oil for the hair, will bring you another original *Dark Venture* story. And now a word to the men. If you want the girls to make you their choice, better make Wildroot Creme Oil your choice... Smart girls use Wildroot Creme Oil too for great grooming and to relieve dryness between permanents... William Tracy will soon be seen in the Hal Roach production *Here Comes Trouble*. This is ABC, the American Broadcasting Company.

366. A Date with Judy. Comedy, 30 min., NBC, 1941–1948; ABC, 1948–1950.

Sixteen-year-old Judy Foster is a pretty high school sophomore "and the cutest date in town." She has an uncanny knack for finding misadventure, receives an allowance of two dollars a week and says things like, "Oh, caterpillars" and "Oh, butterflies" when something goes wrong. She also believes that her family doesn't understand her: "I think the people who are related to me are unsympathetic and full of a lack of understanding. Every time I offer something constructive and valuable in the way of something concrete, I get stepped on before the germ of my idea ever gets a chance to bud into blossom."

Oogie Pringle is Judy's boyfriend and the object of her endless efforts to improve him and make him the man of her dreams. Oogie has a band called the High School Hot Licks and he first met Judy when she ran over him with her tricycle. Melvyn and Dora Foster are Judy's parents. Melvyn owns the Foster Canning Company and met Dora while they were in college. Rounding out the Foster household is Randolph, Judy's twelve-year-old brother. He has an allowance of 75 cents a week and is not as mischievous as Judy (but he's more wise-cracking).

Stories follow events in Judy's life as her unpredictable antics keep her father on the verge of a nervous breakdown. Judy lives at 123 State Street and the afterschool hangouts are the Coke Parlor and Pop Scully's Soda Fountain. *Other regular characters:* Gloria and Mitzi, Judy's friends; Mr. Pringle, Oogie's father. This became the basis for the television series of the same title.

Cast: Dellie Ellis, Louise Erickson, Ann Gillis (*Judy Foster*); Paul McGrath, Stanley Farrar, John Brown (*Melvyn Foster*); Margaret Brayton, Lois Corbett, Myra Marsh (*Dora Foster*); Dix Davis, Johnny McGovern (*Randolph Foster*); Harry Harvey, Richard Crenna (*Oogie Pringle*); Ann Gillis, Sandra Gould (*Gloria*); Mercedes McCambridge, Louise Erickson, Georgia Backus (*Mitzi Hoffman*); Fred Howard (*Mr. Pringle*). ***Announcers:*** Bill Goodwin, Ralph Langley, Marvin Miller, Ken Niles. ***Music:*** Buzz Adlam, Charles Cornell, Hal Gould, Thomas Peluse. ***Producer:*** Helen Mack.

OPENING (1941)

ANNOUNCER: Tums, famous quick relief for acid indigestion, presents *A Date with Judy*, Judy Foster, the cutest date in town. Your date with her each Tuesday at this time is arranged by the makers of Tums, famous quick relief for acid indigestion.

OPENING (1948)

ANNOUNCER: By Transcription.

SONG (Sung by Oogie): I've got a date with Judy, a big date with Judy, oh jeepers and gee, I've got a date with Judy and Judy's got one with me.

ANNOUNCER: The American Broadcasting Company presents *A Date with Judy* starring Louise Erickson as Judy with John Brown as Father.

CLOSING (1948)

ANNOUNCER: This is Ralph Langley inviting you to be with us next week at this same time to keep your date with Judy. This is ABC, the American Broadcasting Company.

367. A DATE WITH MUSIC.

Variety, 15 min., Syndicated, 1946.

A weekly program of music and songs with host Sammy Liver, the announcing of Allyn Edwards and the music of Doc Whipple and his orchestra.

368. DAUGHTERS OF UNCLE SAM.

Variety, 30 min., NBC, 2/22/42 to 4/26/42.

A wartime series of music and songs with Arlene Francis as the host. Fannie Hurst, the Swing Patrol and the Three Saluters were the regulars. B.A. Rolfe and his orchestra provided the music.

369. DAVE ELMAN'S AUCTION GALLERY.

Auction, 30 min., Mutual, 1945.

An over-the-air auction that began with an art object or historical item being described, then offered up for bid. Members of the studio audience bid—as did listeners via the telephone. Though a bit confusing (coordinating bids from the studio and home audiences), the highest bidder received the item. Dave Elman was the host-auctioneer.

370. THE DAVE GARROWAY SHOW.

Variety, 15 min., NBC, 11/12/49 to 10/30/53; 90 min., NBC, 4/18/54 to 6/17/55.

A program of music, songs, light comedy and chatter with humorist Dave Garroway (the format was identical to his 1949 television series *Garroway at Large*). The daily 15-minute version is also known as *Dial Dave Garroway*, *Next, Dave Garroway* and *Reserved for Garroway*. The 90-minute series began as "Sunday with Garroway" and ended as "Friday with Garroway."

Host: Dave Garroway. ***Regulars:*** Charlie Andrews, June Christie, Jim Fleming, Jack Haskell, Vivian Martin, Constance (Connie) Russell. ***Announcer:*** Jack Haskell. ***Music:*** The Joseph Gallichio Orchestra; the Art Van Damme Quintet.

OPENING (from 6/19/51)

ANNOUNCER: And now Dial, the soap that stops odor before it starts, presents *Dial Dave Garroway*.

DAVE (over theme of "Sentimental Journey"): Hello, we've got one of the best-sounding little gangs you ever heard: Constance Russell, Jack Haskell and Art Van Damme. Dial soap, the famous deodorant soap, brings you confidence on these warm June days, any day throughout the year. Just get some Dial soap and feel fresh and clean all over.

SONG: Dial, that's D.I.A.L., Dial soap, the newest, nicest way to stay free and odor safe all day.

DAVE: I have some important advice for you ladies this morning. Advice not of my own, but of a famous psychologist as how to get along with your husband. This expert on family relations says ladies never shout at a man, don't holler or raise your voice ... you can do so much more with just a low, nerve-wrecking whine...

CLOSING

DAVE: We'll be talking to you again tomorrow. Until then, love and peace.

ANNOUNCER: Tomorrow and each weekday at this time, Armour and Company invites you to *Dial Dave Garroway*. This is NBC.

371. DAVID HARUM. Serial, 15 min., NBC, then CBS, 1936–1950.

Life in the small town of Homeville as seen through the eyes of David Harum, the town banker and country philosopher who helps people in trouble.

Cast: Wilmer Walter, Craig McDonnell, Cameron Prud'Homme (*David Harum*); Peggy Allenby, Gertrude Warner, Joan Tompkins (*Susan Wells*); Charme Allen, Eva Condon (*"Aunt" Polly Benson*); Bennett Kilpack (*James Benson*); Ethel Everett (*Elsie Anderson*); Joseph Curtin (*John Lennox*); Marjorie Davies, Claudia Morgan (*Clarissa Oakley*); Paul Stewart (*Charlie*); Philip Reed, Donald Briggs (*Brian Wells*); Billy Redfield (*Willy*); Paul Ford (*Mark Carter*); Florence Lake (*Tess Terwilliger*); Richard McKay (*Henry Longacre*). ***Announcer:*** Ford Bond. ***Music:*** Stanley Davis. ***Producers:*** Anne Hummert, Frank Hummert.

OPENING

ANNOUNCER: We bring you the story that has thrilled America for generations: the true-to-life story of *David Harum*, the kindly little country philosopher who makes life worth living by helping those who need help and by outwitting those who are too clever and scheming in helping themselves.

372. THE DAVID ROSE SHOW. Variety, 30 min., CBS, 1950.

A weekly program of music and songs with orchestra leader David Rose as host and featuring vocalist Lee Simpkins and the announcing of Fort Pearson.

373. A DAY IN THE LIFE OF DENNIS DAY. Comedy, 30 min., NBC, 1946–1951.

The Anderson Boarding House at 324 Elm Street in the town of Weaverville is home to Dennis Day, a soda jerk at the Willoughby Drug Store. Dennis works for Homer Willoughby and is in love with Millie Anderson, a young lady whose parents (Herbert and Clara) own the boarding house and who have a hard time understanding why their daughter is in love with the hapless Dennis. Stories focus in particular on Dennis as he tries to improve his life (to impress Millie's father) and make more money, and the consequences when his efforts fail and he has to settle for his job at Willoughby's. Programs open and close with a song by Dennis Day. Also known as *The Dennis Day Show*; a spinoff from *The Jack Benny Program*.

Cast: Dennis Day (*Dennis Day*); Betty Miles, Barbara Eiler, Sharon Douglas (*Millie Anderson*); Francis "Dink" Trout (*Herbert Anderson*); Bea Benaderet (*Clara Anderson*); John Brown (*Homer Willoughby*). ***Announcers:*** Frank Barton, Verne Smith, Jimmy Wallington. ***Sponsor's Vocalist:*** Ken Carson. ***Music:*** Robert Armbruster, Charles Dant. ***Producer:*** Bill Harding.

OPENING

ANNOUNCER: Ladies and gentlemen, Dennis Day.

DENNIS (Singing): Oh, what makes life seem worthwhile, dwells in your heart and the spell of your smile...

ANNOUNCER: Dennis Day is brought to you by Colgate Lustre Creme Shampoo for soft, glamorous dream girl hair. *The Dennis Day Show* with Barbara Eiler, Bea Benaderet, Dink Trout, John Brown, Charles Dant and His Orchestra and yours truly, Verne Smith, is written by Frank Galen and stars our popular young singer in *A Day in the Life of Dennis Day*.

CLOSING

ANNOUNCER: Dennis Day is brought to you every Wednesday by the Colgate Palmolive Company.

SONG: Dream girl, dream girl, beautiful Lustre Creme girl; hair that gleams and glitters from a Lustre Creme Shampoo.

ANNOUNCER: Yes, Lustre Creme Shampoo leaves hair with new three-way loveliness. One, fragrantly clean; two, glistening with sheen; three, soft, easy to manage... The four-ounce jar only one dollar at all cosmetic counters. Be a dream girl, a lovely Lustre Creme girl.

SONG: Dream girl, dream girl, beautiful Lustre Creme girl, you owe your crowning glory to Lustre Creme Shampoo.

ANNOUNCER: This is Verne Smith reminding you to join us again next week for another Dennis Day show brought to you by Lustre Creme Shampoo for soft, glamorous dream girl hair. Good night. This is NBC, the National Broadcasting Company.

374. Deadline Drama. Anthology, 30 min., NBC Blue, 1944–1945.

A 20-word situation, submitted by a listener, is read to a cast of regular performers, who are given two minutes to construct a seven-minute vignette based on what they had just heard. After the playlet is performed, the listener receives a savings bond for his story.

Cast: Joan Banks, Elsie Mae Gordon, Frank Lovejoy, Ireene Wicker. ***Organist:*** Rosa Rio. ***Producer:*** Charles Martin.

375. Deadline Mystery. Crime Drama, 30 min., ABC, 4/20/47 to 8/31/47.

"Deadline" is a syndicated newspaper column written by crime reporter Lucky Larson. Lucky is tough but also has a soft heart, a situation that always gets him into trouble. He often hits the streets looking for stories, but sometimes stories come looking for him (people in trouble seeking help). The series follows Lucky as he investigates crimes for stories, often helping his good friend, Lt. Tom Burns of the N.Y.P.D. Lucky also has a girlfriend, Lucia—"a classy dame who followed me to Italy a few months ago to kill me because she thought I killed a guy she thought she loved." And, by the way Lucky talks, he loves Lucia's pizza as much as he loves her. Lucky's column appears in over 250 newspapers and he lives at 350 Park Avenue.

Cast: Steve Dunne (*Lucky Larson*); June Whitley (*Lucia*); Byron Kane (*Tom Burns*). ***Announcer:*** Frank Hemingway. ***Music:*** Len Selder.

OPENING

Announcer: From Hollywood, the Knox Company, worldwide distributors of scientifically compounded pharmaceutical products, presents Steve Dunne, star of Columbia Pictures, in *Deadline Mystery*.

CLOSING

Lucky: That's 30.

Announcer: Listen next week at this same time when the Knox Company ... presents another exciting adventure of Lucky Larson starring Steve Dunne through arrangement with Columbia Pictures, producers of *Down to Earth*. The events and characters depicted in this story were entirely fictional and any resemblance to places or people, living or dead, is entirely coincidental. This program came to you from Hollywood. This is ABC, the American Broadcasting Company.

The Dean Martin and Jerry Lewis Show *see* **The Martin and Lewis Show**

376. Dear Margie, It's Murder. Crime Drama, 25 min., Mutual, 1/11/53 to 10/4/53.

Stories revolve around an American studying in England under the G.I. Bill and his efforts to help his Scotland Yard inspector-friend solve crimes. The title is derived from letters sent home by the vet to his girlfriend Margie, in which he relates his experiences. Mason Adams plays the vet and Ian Martin is the inspector.

377. Dear Mom. Comedy, 25 min., CBS, 2/9/41 to 12/14/41.

A comical view of life in an Army boot camp just prior to World War II as seen through the experiences of Homer Stubbs, a not-too-well coordinated private, and his friends, Private Ulysses Hink and Cpl. Red Foster, and their superior, Sgt. Mike Monahan. Stories unfold as Homer writes of his experiences to his mother (hence the title).

Cast: John Walsh (*Homer Stubbs*); Lou Krugman (*Ulysses Hink*); Marvin Miller (*Mike Monahan*); Dolph Nelson (*Red Foster*). ***Announcer:*** Tom Moore.

378. Dearest Mother. Serial, 15 min., Syndicated, 1940–1941.

Following a misunderstanding between a young woman (Rita) and her father, the woman impulsively decides to leave home. She promises, however, that no matter where she is or what her position, she will write to her mother. Stories follow Rita's experiences as she struggles to begin a new life on her own.

Cast: Judith March (*Rita Morgan*); Melba Lee (*Mrs. Morgan*); Fred Howard (*Mr. Morgan*). ***Also:*** Chris Ford, Harriet Linehan, Kay Miller, Frank Mills.

379. Death Valley Days. Anthology, 30 min., NBC Red, 1930–1931; NBC Blue, 1931–1932; NBC Red, 1932–1936; NBC Blue, 1936–1939; NBC Red, 1940–1941; CBS, 1944–1945.

California's Death Valley served as the backdrop for true tales of the Old West: stories of

(From left) Dolph Nelson (*Red Foster*), Marvin Miller (*Sergeant Monahan*) and John Walsh (*Homer Stubbs*) starred in *Dear Mom*.

the pioneers' struggles; of lawlessness; of heartbreak; and of the great men and women who helped shape our country. Stories, which often involve Sheriff Mark Chase, are told by a kindly narrator called the Old Ranger (who was introduced with a trumpet call); programs originally opened to a rendition of "The Lonesome Cowboy." *Other regular characters:* Cassandra "Cousin Cassie" Drinkwater, Mark's housekeeper; the Old Prospector. The program became a television series in 1952 and was revised as *Death Valley Sheriff* (see next entry).

Cast: Tim Frawley, George Rand, Harry Humphrey, Jack MacBryde (*The Old Ranger*); Robert Haag (*Sheriff Mark Chase*); Harvey Hayes (*The Old Prospector*); Olyn Landick (*Cassandra Drinkwater*); John White (*The Lonesome Cowboy*). ***Announcer:*** George Hicks. ***Music:*** Joseph Bonime.

OPENING

MUSIC: Bugle call.

ANNOUNCER: As the old morning bugle call of the covered wagon train dies away among the echoes, another true story of *Death Valley Days* is brought to you by the Pacific Coast Borax Company, who give you the miracle of Borax in three convenient forms—Twenty Mule Team Borax for household use; Twenty Mule Team Soap Chips for washing clothes and dishes; and the new Boraxo for bathroom use. Before you become absorbed in the Old Ranger's story for tonight, we would like to take just a moment of your time to tell you something about Boraxo. Boraxo was created in response to the insistent demands from women for a product that would cleanse the skin as safely as Twenty Mule Team Borax cleanses painted woodwork... Well, the letters we receive every day praising Boraxo tells us that we have succeeded in meeting this demand. For, say our new customers who have discovered Boraxo, and thank you too for *Death Valley Days*, which all of us love. And now here is the Old Ranger [who would then begin the story].

380. Death Valley Sheriff. Adventure, 30 min., CBS, 1944–1945 (*Death Valley Sheriff*); 1945–1951 (*The Sheriff*).

A revised version of *Death Valley Days* (see prior entry) that is set in modern times and relates the exploits of Mark Chase, sheriff of Canyon County, California, as he maintains the peace. *Other regular characters:* Cassandra "Cousin Cassie" Drinkwater, Mark's housekeeper. Also known as *The Sheriff* (its 1945–1951 title).

Cast: Robert Haag, Bob Warren (*Mark Chase*); Olyn Landick (*Cassandra Drinkwater*).

381. December Bride. Comedy, 30 min., CBS, 1952–1953.

At 728 Elm Street in Westwood, California, lives Lily Ruskin, an attractive, 60-years-young widow; her married daughter, Ruth Henshaw; and Ruth's husband Matt. Lily writes the advice column "Tips for Housewives" for the Los Angeles *Gazette*; Matt is an architect for Coricon Company and Associates. Stories follow comical events in the lives of the two families. Served as the basis for the 1954–1959 television series of the same title.

Cast: Spring Byington (*Lily Ruskin*); Doris Singleton (*Ruth Henshaw*); Hal March (*Matt Henshaw*). ***Announcer:*** Johnny Jacobs. ***Music:*** Wilbur Hatch.

OPENING

Announcer: And now *December Bride*, the story of a guy who likes his mother-in-law. Created and transcribed by Parke Levy, featuring Hal March and Doris Singleton, and starring the beloved lady of the screen, Spring Byington.

382. Defense Attorney. Crime Drama, 30 min., ABC, 1951–1952.

Martha Ellis Bryan is a respected attorney who has a reputation for integrity; people trust her and she is famous for proving people innocent. Although she contends "that conducting an investigation is out of my line, I'm an attorney, not a private detective," she turns to sleuthing when complications set in (for example, her client is murdered). Martha doesn't work alone, however; she joins her boyfriend Judson "Jud" Barnes, a reporter for the *Dispatch*, when he is assigned to cover the story. Martha, called "Marty" by Jud, is an excellent judge of character and if she believes a client is innocent, she will defend him. Stories follow Martha as she goes about gathering the evidence she needs to defend her clients.

Cast: Mercedes McCambridge (*Martha Ellis Bryan*); Howard Culver (*Judson Barnes*); Tony Barrett (*Detective Lt. Ed Ledis*). ***Announcer:*** Orville Anderson. ***Music:*** Rex Koury.

OPENING

Announcer: The makers of Kix, tasty, crispy corn puffs, food for action; and the makers of Clorets, the new chlorophyll chewing gum that makes your breath kissing sweet, presents *Defense Attorney*.

Mercedes: Ladies and gentlemen, to depend upon your judgment and to fulfill my obligation, I submit the facts, fully aware of my responsibility to my client and to you as defense attorney.

Announcer: And now we proudly present Miss Mercedes McCambridge as *Defense Attorney*. When Martha Ellis Bryan chose law as a career, she accepted the challenge of defending the defenseless. And now let's listen to a man who sings the blues because he doesn't take time to eat breakfast.

Sad Song: It's a shame to be a Nixee like me; I suffer from a lack of energy.

Announcer: People who are always weary and always dreary are Nixees, so different from cheery, active Kixees. Kixees are men of action who eat Kix.

Happy Song: Oh, it's good to be a Kixee like me, full of pep and energy. Every morning I eat Kix, so I'm never in a fix, it's grand to be a Kixee like me.

Announcer: And now the curtain rises on act one of tonight's *Defense Attorney* story.

CLOSING

Announcer: You have just heard *Defense Attorney* starring Mercedes McCambridge. Next week, another exciting adventure with Mercedes McCambridge, *Defense Attorney*—be sure to listen. *Defense Attorney* is presented by the makers of Kix, tasty, crispy corn puffs, food for action, and by Clorets, the new chlorophyll chewing gum that makes your breath kissing sweet.

Mercedes: This is Mercedes McCambridge reminding you to stay tuned to your ABC station for that entertaining program, *The Original Amateur Hour*, emceed by that great showman and grand person, Ted Mack.

ANNOUNCER: This program came to you from Hollywood. America is sold on the American Broadcasting Company.

THE DENNIS DAY SHOW *see* **A DAY IN THE LIFE OF DENNIS DAY**

383. DESTINY'S TRAILS. Anthology, 15 min., Syndicated, 1945.

A 39-week series that dramatized two of James Fenimore Cooper's *Leatherstocking Tales*: "Deerslayer" and "The Last of the Mohicans."

Cast: Joe Boland, Jean Gillespie, Stacy Harris, Frank Lovejoy, Joseph Julian, Kay Loring, Craig McDonnell, Jerry Macy, Ogden Miles, Alfred Shirley, Gertrude Warner, Lesley Woods.

384. DETECT AND COLLECT. Game, 30 min., CBS, 6/13/45 to 9/4/45.

Selected members of the studio audience compete. Contestants are read a clue (worth $25) that relates to an article concealed on stage behind a curtain. If a player could identify the object, he won the money; if not, a second clue, worth $20, is given. The game continues until the article is identified or until the five clues run out (prizes are determined based on the level at which the identification was made; the fifth and last clue is worth $5). See also the following title.

Host: Wendy Barrie. ***Assistant:*** Lew Lehr. ***Announcer:*** Fred Uttal. ***Orchestra:*** Ted Rapf.

385. DETECT AND COLLECT. Game, 30 min., CBS, 10/4/45 to 9/28/46.

This revised version of the prior title involved home listeners. A musical selection is played, followed immediately by several other tunes. Between each of the tunes, snatches of the first song are inserted. A post card is selected and a home listener is called. If the listener could detect the number of times the original song was played, he won a war bond.

Host: Vincent Lopez. ***Regulars:*** Terry Allen, Judy Lang. ***Announcer:*** Norman Brokenshire. ***Orchestra:*** Robert Stanley.

386. THE DEVIL AND MR. O. Anthology, 30 min., Syndicated, 1971–1972.

Updated versions of stories written by Arch Oboler and originally broadcast on *Lights Out*. Arch Oboler served as the host.

OPENING (from "Alone in New York City")

ANNOUNCER: It's long ago, it's also now. Like a vintage brew that gets tastier by the years, the radio mysteries of the thirties, forties and fifties, although resting in the dusty archives, are still fresh and vibrant. Let's sit back now as the listener did so many yesterdays ago and try to figure out whodunit.

VOICE: Lights out for *The Devil and Mr. O.*

MR. O: Turn out your lights now. We bring you stories of the supernatural and the super-normal, dramatizing the fantasies and the mysteries of the unknown. We tell you this, frankly, so if you wish to avoid the excitement and tension of these imaginative plays, we urge you calmly but sincerely to turn off your radio now. This is Mr. O, Arch Oboler. Once, a long time ago in New York City on top of the Empire State Building, I met a pair of very young and very much in love honeymooners. I remembered those two when I wrote this play you're about to hear. It's not a horror story, yet there is terror in it. I give you now a story about one of the strangest days since our planet began to circle the sun...

CLOSING

MR. O: This is Arch Oboler. Our play has ended and may it always continue to be just that, a play.

ANNOUNCER: Every week we'll reach into the dusty files, brush it off and present a still up-to-date replica of a whodunit of yesterday.

387. DIARY OF FATE. Anthology, 30 min., Syndicated, 1948.

Intriguing tales of how fate affects the lives of people. A different cast appears each week.

Music: Ivan Ditmars. ***Producer:*** Larry Finley.

OPENING (from 4/6/48)

ANNOUNCER: *The Diary of Fate.*

FATE: Book 93, page 861.

ANNOUNCER: In the *Diary of Fate*.

FATE: Yes, here it is, the name Tyler White; occupation, confidence man. Yes, Tyler, yours is the infamous profession of swindling people of wealth and social position by first getting their attention, then their admiration and finally their confidence. And you are well suited for your work. You have been a success but you have always been dishonest. And now, I, Fate, move, and because of two little things—a stray dog and a forgotten cigarette lighter—you will, Tyler White, be executed for a murder you did not commit. But only you and I know that. Take heed, all of you who listen lest you think Fate is unjust, unmindful of mortal rights. In a moment I will make a further entry under the name Tyler White. And what I have written, I read from his record, the *Diary of Fate*.

CLOSING

FATE: And now it is time to close the book; another entry has been carefully noted on the pages of eternity. In the case of Tyler White, as in the cases of all mortals, I, Fate, am but an instrument of the plan and the little things at my command are the tools with which I work. Understand well the moral all you who listen, and remember there is a page for you in the *Diary of Fate*.

ANNOUNCER: The cast included Herbert Lipton, Ruth Perrott, Bob Lowery and Hal Sawyer. *Diary of Fate* is a Larry Finley transcription, brought to you from Hollywood.

DICK DARING'S ADVENTURES *see* **APPENDIX**

DICK COLE *see* **THE ADVENTURES OF DICK COLE**

388. THE DICK HAYMES SHOW. Variety, 30 min., CBS, 1944–1947.

Singer Dick Haymes as the host of a weekly program of music and songs. Cliff Arquette (as "Mrs. Wilson," the comic relief character), Helen Forrest, Martha Tilton and the vocal group Six Hits and a Miss were the regulars. Gordon Jenkins and his orchestra provided the music.

THE DICK ROBERTSON SHOW *see* **APPENDIX**

DICK STEELE, BOY REPORTER *see* **APPENDIX**

389. DICK TRACY. Crime Drama, 15 min., Mutual, 1935–1937; NBC Red, 1938–1939; NBC Blue, 1943–1944; ABC, 1944–1948.

Richard "Dick" Tracy is a master police detective in a large, crime-ridden city. He is fair and honest and will never shoot to kill. He is married to Tess Trueheart and is the father of Dick Tracy, Jr., better known as "Junior Tracy." Stories, which are serial-like in presentation, relate Dick's relentless pursuit of lawbreakers. Based on the comic strip by Chester Gould. *Other regular characters:* Patrick "Pat" Patton, Dick's assistant; Police Chief Brandon. In 1945 and 1946, a half-hour version ran alongside the daily 15-minute episodes.

Cast: Ned Wever, Matt Crowley, Barry Thompson (*Dick Tracy*); Helen Lewis (*Tess Trueheart*); Andy Donnelly, Walter Kinsella, Jackie Kelk (*Junior Tracy*); Howard Smith (*Police Chief Brandon*); Walter Kinsella (*Pat Patton*). ***Narrator:*** Don Gardiner. ***Announcers:*** Don Gardiner, George Gunn, Ed Herlihy, Dan Seymour. ***Music:*** Ray Carter.

OPENING

ANNOUNCER: Boys and girls, here's *Dick Tracy*.

TRACY: Dick Tracy calling headquarters. I am on my way to question Junior about Tess Trueheart's disappearance. That is all.

ANNOUNCER: Presenting Detective Inspector Dick Tracy, protector of law and order.

CLOSING

ANNOUNCER: What is Dick going to do? You'll know tomorrow, so tune in same time, same station for the adventures of *Dick Tracy*, directed by Frank Shinn. This is George Gunn speaking. Any tough detective lives the life of danger. He must be on the alert at all times because tough characters know that the best way of keeping out of his clutches is to get him first. Well, Tracy fans, I guess you know that goes double for Dick Tracy because he's so very tough. That's one of the reasons you can be sure that the adventures of Dick Tracy will keep you on the edge of your seats. *Dick Tracy* is on the air Monday through Friday over more than 100 radio stations throughout the country. Listen to another chapter as Dick Tracy tangles with the underworld tomorrow at this same time over this same station. This is ABC, the American Broadcasting Company.

390. DIMENSION X. Anthology, 30 min., NBC, 4/8/50 to 9/29/51.

Dramatizations based on the works of well-known science fiction writers (for example, Ray Bradbury and Robert Bloch) and performed by top name radio artists. See also *X Minus One*, the revised version of this series.

Narrator: Norman Rose. ***Announcers:*** Fred Collins, Bob Warren. ***Music:*** Albert Buhrmann. ***Producer:*** Van Woodward.

OPENING

ANNOUNCER: Adventures in time and space told in future tense.

VOICE: *Dimension X.*

ANNOUNCER: The National Broadcasting Company in cooperation with Street and Smith, publishers of *Astounding Science Fiction*, bring you *Dimension X.*

CLOSING

ANNOUNCER: You have just heard another adventure into the unknown world of the future, the world of *Dimension X.* Be sure to be with us next week for another *Dimension X.* This is NBC, the National Broadcasting Company.

391. THE DINAH SHORE SHOW. Variety, 15 min., NBC Blue, 1939–1943; CBS, 1943–1946; NBC, 1946–1948; CBS, 1948.

A weekly program of music and songs hosted by Dinah Shore (who was assisted by a guest). Harry Von Zell did the announcing and music was by the orchestras of Robert Emmett Dolan, Gordon Jenkins and Paul LaValle. See also *Birds Eye Open House*, *Call for Music* and the following title.

392. THE DINAH SHORE SHOW. Variety, 60 min., NBC, 1953–1955.

A twice-weekly program of music, songs and performances by guests that was actually a rebroadcast of Dinah Shore's television series soundtrack.

Host: Dinah Shore. ***Regulars:*** The Notables, The Skylarks. ***Announcer:*** Art Baker. ***Orchestra:*** Vic Schoen, Harry Zimmerman. ***Producer:*** Bob Henry.

393. DOC BARCLAY'S DAUGHTERS. Serial, 15 min., CBS, 1938–1940.

The dramatic story of Doc Barclay, a widowed druggist in the small town of Brookdale, as he struggles to raise his three daughters: Connie (recently separated from her husband), Marge (single and performing household duties for her father) and Mimi (married to Tom Clark, a hardware store clerk).

Cast: Bennett Kilpack (*Doc Barclay*); Elizabeth Reller (*Connie*); Vivian Smolen (*Marge Barclay*); Mildred Robin (*Mimi Clark*); Albert Hayes (*Tom Clark*). ***Announcer:*** Tom Shirley. ***Organist:*** Rosa Rio.

394. DOC, DUKE AND THE COLONEL. Comedy, 15 min., NBC, 1945.

An exchange of dialogue between Doc, a retired veterinarian, his friend Duke and a Southern colonel. Jess Pugh played Doc; Clarence Hartzell was Duke; and Cliff Soubier played the Colonel.

395. DOC HOPKINS AND HIS COUNTRY BOYS. Variety, 15 min., Syndicated, 1945.

A weekly program of country and western music with host Doc Hopkins and His Country Boys (his orchestra).

396. DR. CHRISTIAN. Drama, 30 min., CBS, 1937–1954.

The story of Paul Christian and the infinite problems faced by a physician in the small town of River's Bend, Minnesota. Paul, a family doctor forever involved in someone's life, lived in the white house on State Street and was a member of the Bachelor's Club. In 1941, listeners were asked to submit scripts and the program boasted "the only show in radio where the audience writes the scripts" ($500 was awarded for each script that was used, with an annual competition for the best script which awarded the listener $2000). *Other regular characters:* Judy Price, Paul's nurse; Mrs. Hastings, Paul's housekeeper. Also known as *The Vaseline Program* (when sponsored by Vaseline petroleum jelly). Served as the basis for the television series of the same title.

Cast: Jean Hersholt (*Dr. Paul Christian*); Lurene Tuttle, Dorothy Lowell, Rosemary DeCamp, Helen Claire (*Judy Price*); Maide Eburne (*Mrs. Hastings*). ***Announcer:*** Art Gilmore.

OPENING

EFFECT: Phone ringing.

JUDY (answering): Dr. Christian's office.

ANNOUNCER: *The Vaseline Program*, the only show in radio where the audience writes the scripts. Our tenth annual competition for the $2000 Dr. Christian Award is drawing to a close; all scripts must be in the mail by midnight next Wednesday. Now, Jean Hersholt as *Dr. Christian.*

397. THE DOCTOR FIGHTS. Anthology, 30 min., CBS, 6/6/44 to 9/11/45.

Dramatizations based on the actual experiences of doctors assigned to the battlefront during World War II. In 1944, Raymond Massey played the various doctors whose experiences were dramatized. Episodes broadcast during 1945 featured major stars portraying the doctors.

OPENING

ANNOUNCER: Shindley Laboratories presents *The Doctor Fights* starring Lt. Commander Robert Montgomery, United States Naval Reserve, in a thrilling but true story of a doctor in World War II—*The Doctor Fights* starring Robert Montgomery.

VOICE: The eternal providence has appointed me to watch over the life and death of all thy creatures. That I may always serve the patient, a fellow creature in pain, grant me strength and opportunity always to extend the domain of my craft.

ANNOUNCER: This is the prayer of every doctor. It is ages old and yet today it is as new as the heroism of tomorrow's battles. This is a doctor at war.

398. DR. GINO'S MUSICALE. Variety, 30 min., ABC, 1950.

Gene Hamilton as the host of a weekly program of Dixieland music and songs. Henry Levine and his orchestra provided the music.

399. DR. I.Q. Game, 30 min., NBC, 1939–1949; ABC, 1950.

Members of the studio audience, chosen by roving announcers with microphones, were asked questions by Dr. I.Q., the mental banker, in return for silver dollars (varying with the difficulty of the question, usually beginning at $10). Players who failed to correctly answer a question received a box of the sponsor's product (Mars candies) and tickets to the following week's show.

Host (Dr. I.Q.): Lew Valentine, Jimmy McClain, Stanley Vainrib. ***Program Announcer:*** Allan C. Anthony. ***Roving Announcers:*** Robert Enoch, Bert Igou, Gene Kemper, Garry Moore, Bob Richardson.

OPENING

ANNOUNCER: Presenting *Dr. I.Q.* Mars, Incorporated, makers of America's most enjoyable candy bars, brings you another half-hour of fun with your genial master of wit and information, Dr. I.Q., the mental banker. And now, here's the wise man with the friendly smile and the cash for your correct answers, Dr. I.Q.

400. DR. I.Q., JR. Game, 30 min., NBC, 1948–1949.

A children's version of the above title where contestants, chosen by an announcer with a hand-held microphone, won money (in dimes) by answering questions asked of them by Dr. I.Q., the mental banker.

Host (Dr. I.Q.): Lew Valentine. ***Announcer:*** Allan C. Anthony.

DR. KILDARE *see* **THE STORY OF DR. KILDARE**

401. DR. PAUL. Serial, 15 min., NBC, 1949–1954.

Stories of love and service to humanity as seen through the eyes of a small-town doctor. Subplot of the program is the efforts of the doctor's wife to convince her husband to leave town and establish a fancy practice in New York City. Russell Thorson played Dr. Paul and Peggy Webber was his wife. Others in the cast were Henry Blair, Sam Edwards, Gloria Gordon, Bob Holton, Janet Logan, Jean Olivet, Vic Perrin and Willard Waterman.

402. DR. SIX GUN. Western, 30 min., NBC, 1954–1955.

Tales of the Old West as told by a gypsy peddler named Pablo, a man who is proud to tell of the exploits of his good friend Dr. Ray Matson, alias Dr. Six Gun. He is the only doctor to pack a six gun on his hip, but a man who puts healing before killing. Ray is based in the town of Frenchman's Fork, carries a stub-nose derringer in his medical bag and rides a horse named Sage. Pablo has a pet raven named Midnight.

Cast: Karl Weber (*Dr. Ray Matson*); Bill Griffis (*Pablo*).

OPENING

ANNOUNCER: *Dr. Six Gun*. Across the rugged Indian territory rides a tall young man on a mission of mercy. His medical bag strapped on one hip; his six shooter on the other. This is Dr. Six Gun, the first episode in the exciting adventures of *Dr. Six Gun*. Ray Matson, M.D., was the gun-toting frontier doctor who roamed the length and breadth of the old Indian territory. Friend and physician to white man and Indian alike; the symbol of justice and mercy in the lawless West of the 1870s; this legendary figure was known to all as Dr. Six Gun.

PABLO: Dr. Six Gun was my friend. Me? They call me Pablo. It's as good a name as any for a gypsy. I am a peddler and I have many things in my pack. There is not much of which I am proud; but there is one thing—I can call Doc Six Gun my friend. [At this point, Pablo would begin to tell a story and the flashback sequence was used to relate it to the audience.]

403. DR. STANDISH, MEDICAL EXAMINER. Mystery, 30 min., CBS, 1948.

Gary Merrill as Dr. Peter Standish, a medical examiner who uses his knowledge of medicine to help the police solve baffling crimes. Audrey Christie played his assistant and Eric Dressler was the homicide inspector. Lee Vines announced.

404. THE DOCTOR'S WIFE. Serial, 15 min., ABC, 1952.

The drama of a doctor's life as seen through the eyes of his wife. The doctor conducted his practice from an office on Elm Street in a suburban New York town.

Cast: Dan Curtis (*The Doctor*); Patricia Wheel (*His wife*); Margaret Hamilton (*Their maid*); George Hill (*Doctor's brother*).

405. DOLLAR A MINUTE. Audience Participation, 30 min., CBS, 1950–1951.

An unusual concept wherein anyone with a gripe or with a desire to display their talent paid for air time at the rate of one dollar per minute.

Host: Bill Goodwin. ***Music:*** The Elliot Daniel Trio.

406. THE DON AMECHE SHOW. Variety, 30 min., NBC, 1946–1947.

A weekly program of music, songs and dramatic skits featuring the talents of actor Don Ameche. Sponsored by Drene Shampoo.

Host: Don Ameche. ***Regulars:*** Joanell James, Pinky Lee. ***Announcers:*** Truman Bradley, Marvin Miller. ***Orchestra:*** Joe Lilley.

407. DON WINSLOW OF THE NAVY. Adventure, 15 min., NBC Blue, 1937–1944; ABC, 1944.

The serialized adventures of Don Winslow, a commander in the U.S. Navy, his sidekick Red Pennington and Don's girlfriend Mercedes Colby as they battled evil (most notably, a master criminal called the Scorpion).

Cast: Bob Guilbert, Raymond Edward Johnson (*Don Winslow*); Edward Davison, John Gibson (*Red Pennington*); Lenore Kingston, Betty Lou Gerson, Gertrude Warner (*Mercedes Colby*). ***Also:*** Jone Allison, Ted de Corsia, William Pringle.

408. THE DORIS DAY SHOW. Variety, 25 min., CBS, 1/11/52 to 5/26/53.

A weekly program of music and songs with actress-singer Doris Day and the music and Les Brown and his orchestra. Johnny Jacobs and Roy Rowan were the announcers.

409. DOROTHY DIX ON THE AIR. Advice, 15 min., ABC, 1948–1949.

A program of advice based on the newspaper column by Dorothy Dix. Barbara Winthrop portrayed Dorothy Dix; Nancy Prescott assisted; and Joe Ripley did the announcing.

410. THE DOROTHY GORDON SHOW. Children, 15 min., CBS, 1937–1938; Mutual, 1938–1939.

A weekly program of songs, music and stories for children. Actress Dorothy Gordon sang and portrayed all the characters in stories. Henry Morgan did the announcing.

411. THE DOROTHY LAMOUR SHOW. Variety, 30 min., NBC, 1948–1949.

A program of music, songs and comedy sponsored by Sealtest products. The series, which is also known as *The Sealtest Variety Show*, featured top name guests appearing in songs and skits with host Dorothy Lamour. The Crew Chiefs Quartet supplied vocal backing and Henry Russell and his orchestra provided the music.

412. DORSEY DRIVE. Variety, 30 min., NBC, 1946.

Big Band music with host Tommy Dorsey, the music of his orchestra and regulars Ziggy Elman, Stuart Foster and Freddy Martin.

413. Dot and Will. Serial, 15 min., NBC Blue, 1935–1937.

A daily drama that revolved around the activities of a young married couple (Dot and Will Horton), their mothers, their friends and neighbors.

Cast: Florence Freeman (*Dot Horton*); James Meighan (*Will Horton*); Irene Hubbard (*Will's mother*); Effie Palmer (*Mrs. Aldridge, Dot's mother*); Agnes Moorehead (*Rosie*); Peggy Allenby (*Julia*); Helene Dumas (*Dulcy*); Rosemary DeCamp (*Madge*). ***Announcer:*** Franklyn MacCormack.

414. Double or Nothing. Game, 30 min., Mutual, 1940–1947; CBS, 1947–1948; NBC, 1948–1953; ABC, 1953–1954.

A contestant, chosen from the studio audience, selects a category of questions on which he is then quizzed. Each correct response earns him money. When $10 is earned, the player can either quit or risk it on another question in an attempt to double it. Forty dollars is the maximum a player can earn; however, if an incorrect response should be given, the player forfeits his earnings. In later episodes, the maximum prize money was increased to $100.

Hosts: Walter Compton, Todd Russell, Walter O'Keefe, John Reed King. ***Announcers:*** Fred Cole, Murray Wagner. ***Producer:*** Diana Bourbon.

OPENING

Announcer: Feenamint presents *Double or Nothing*. Yes, just three little words, *Double or Nothing*, the thrilling quiz show with the $100 question, presented by Feenamint, the modern chewing gum laxative. And here is the man on the asking end of the $100 question, your paymaster of ceremonies, John Reed King.

415. Dough Re Mi. Game, 30 min., NBC, 1942–1943.

Members of the studio audience compete in a game designed to test their musical knowledge. The first player to correctly identify a mystery song receives a cash prize.

Host: Hope Emerson. ***Announcer:*** Radcliffe Hall. ***Orchestra:*** *Paul LaValle.*

416. Down You Go. Game, 30 min., Mutual, 1952–1953.

Four regular panelists compete. The host presents a cryptic clue that represents a popular slogan, quotation or phrase, indicated by a line of dashes (one per letter) on a large board. Players each receive one free guess. If the phrase is not identified, each player suggests a letter of the alphabet. If an incorrect letter is given, that player is disqualified from the round and forfeits $5 to the listener who sent in the phrase. Based on the television series of the same title.

Host: Dr. Bergen Evans. ***Panelists:*** Robert Breen, Fran Coughlin, Toni Gilman, Carmelita Pope. ***Vocalist:*** Katie Carnes. ***Music:*** The Starnotes.

417. Dragnet. Crime Drama, 30 min., NBC, 6/3/49 to 2/26/57.

Realistic dramatizations based on the files of the Los Angeles Police Department as seen through the grueling investigations of Joe Friday, a sergeant with the homicide division. Cases are followed from the crime to the conclusion (the verdict). The program introduced two terms into the general language: M.O. (method of operation) and R.I. (records and identification). Joe lived in Apartment 12 at 4646 Cooper Street. Seven fourteen was his badge number. Address of headquarters: 1335 Georgia Street. *Other regular characters:* Officer Ben Romero, Joe's first partner (1949–51); Officer Frank Smith, Joe's second partner (1951–56). Served as the basis for the television series of the same title.

Cast: Jack Webb (*Sgt. Joe Friday*); Barton Yarborough (*Officer Ben Romero*); Ben Alexander (*Officer Frank Smith*). ***Announcer:*** George Fenneman, Hal Gibney. ***Music:*** Walter Schumann.

OPENING

Announcer: The story you are about to hear is true; the names have been changed to protect the innocent. Fatima cigarettes, best of all king size cigarettes, brings you *Dragnet* on both radio and television. You're a detective sergeant, you're assigned to the homicide detail. You receive a complaint about the owner of an apartment building; he signs leases for the apartments, then threatens to kill the tenants if they move in. Your job—investigate.

Music: Dum-de-dum-dum.

Announcer: Ladies and gentlemen, the story you are about to hear is true; the names have been changed to protect the innocent. *Drag-*

Jack Webb played Detective Sgt. Joe Friday in *Dragnet*.

net, the documented drama of an actual crime. For the next 30 minutes, in cooperation with the Los Angeles Police Department, we will travel step by step on the side of the law through an actual case transcribed from official police files. From beginning to end, from crime to punishment, *Dragnet* is the story of your police force in action.

FRIDAY: It was Wednesday, May 9th, it was hot in Los Angeles. We were working the night watch out of homicide detail. My partner is Ben Romero; the boss is Capt. Norman, my name is Friday...

CLOSING

ANNOUNCER: The story you have just heard is true; the names were changed to protect the innocent. You have just heard *Dragnet*, a series of authentic cases from official files. Technical advice came from the office of Chief of Police W.H. Parker, Los Angeles Police Department.

418. A DREAM COMES TRUE. Variety, 30 min., Syndicated, 1948–1949.

A weekly series of music, comedy and skits and songs with Bob Hope as the host. Abe Burrows, Dorothy Shay and Frank Sinatra were the regulars; Ralph Edwards did the announcing; and Les Brown and his orchestra provided the music.

419. DREAMBOAT. Variety, 30 min., ABC, 1951.

Vocalist Doris Drew as the host of a weekly program of romantic music and songs with regulars Tom Casey, Jack Lester and Bill Snary. Johnny Jacobs did the announcing and Rex Maupin and his orchestra supplied the music.

420. DREFT STAR PLAYHOUSE. Anthology, 15 min., NBC, 1943–1945.

A daily series that dramatized famous movie scripts in five to ten installments. Top name guest stars appeared on the program. Marvin Miller and Terry O'Sullivan were the announcers.

DRENE TIME *see* **THE BICKERSONS**

421. DUDE RANCH. Variety, 30 min., NBC Blue, 1936–1937.

A weekly program of country and western music, sponsored by Log Cabin syrup, and hosted by singer Louise Massey. Also featuring vocalist Curt Massey and the music of the Westerners.

422. DUFFY'S TAVERN. Comedy, 30 min., CBS, 1941–1942; NBC Blue, 1943–1944; NBC, 1944–1951.

Duffy's Tavern is a rundown bar located in a seedy section of New York's Third Avenue. It has lousy food and horrible service; with a beer, the free lunch costs 15 cents. Patrick J. Duffy, the tavern's owner, has hired and entrusted a Brooklyn-born mug named Archie to manage it. Archie makes $15 a week but sees the bar as a means of conducting various schemes to make money (Duffy is never heard; he telephones at the beginning of each episode to check on his investment). Episodes focus on Archie's activities as he attempts to run the bar. *Other regular characters:* Miss Duffy, Patrick's man-crazy daughter (Archie calls her "Mother Nature's revenge on Peeping Toms"); Clifton Finnegan, Archie's dimwitted friend (whom he calls "a subnormal chowderhead; a dope; a low grade moron"); Eddie, the waiter (he was replaced by another waiter called Fats); Clancy, the Irish cop who frequents the bar; Wilfred Finnegan, Clifton's brother. Served as the basis for the television series of the same title.

Cast: Ed Gardner (*Archie*); Shirley Booth, Florence Halop, Gloria Erlanger, Florence Robinson, Sandra Gould, Hazel Shermet (*Miss

Ed Gardner was Archie on *Duffy's Tavern.*

Duffy); Charlie Cantor (*Clifton Finnegan*); Eddie Green (*Eddie*); Ed Pichon (*Fats*); Alan Reed (*Officer Clancy*); Dick Van Patten (*Wilfred Finnegan*). ***Vocalists:*** Bob Graham, Tito Guizar, Johnny Johnston, Benay Venuta, the Jack Kirby Chorus. ***Announcers:*** Marvin Miller, Rod O'Connor, Alan Reed, Tiny Ruffner, Jay Stewart, Jimmy Wallington, Perry Ward. ***Orchestra:*** Jack Kirby, Matty Malneck, Reet Veet Reeves, Joe Venuti.

OPENING

ANNOUNCER: It's Wednesday night so we take you now to *Duffy's Tavern*, with our guest for tonight, Garry Moore, and starring Archie himself, Ed Gardner. *Duffy's Tavern* is brought to you by Bristol Myers, makers of Trushay for softer, lovelier hands, and Vitalis for well-groomed hair.

EFFECT: Phone rings.

ARCHIE (Answering): Hello, Duffy's Tavern, where the elite meet to eat, Archie the manager speaking, Duffy's ain't here. Oh. Hello, Duffy... [From this point, Archie would set the stage for the evening's episode by explaining to Duffy what is happening.]

CLOSING

ANNOUNCER: It's time now to leave *Duffy's Tavern* for this evening. So let's meet here again at this same time next Wednesday when our guest will be Miss Olga San Juan. Until next Wednesday then, this is Rod O'Connor reminding you that for well-groomed hair, remember Vitalis, and for softer, lovelier hands, remember Trushay. Each Wednesday Bristol Myers brings you *Duffy's Tavern* and *Mr. District Attorney*, which follows immediately over most of these stations. This is NBC, the National Broadcasting Company.

423. THE DUKE OF PADUCAH AND OPRY SONGS. Variety, 30 min., NBC, 1952.

A weekly program of country and western music with Whitey Ford (as the host, the Duke of Paducah), singers Annie Lou and George Morgan, the announcing of Jud Collins and the music of the Moon Mullian Band.

424. THE DUNNINGER SHOW. Variety, 30 min., NBC Blue/ABC, 9/12/43 to 12/27/44; NBC, 6/8/45 to 9/28/45; 6/4/46 to 6/25/46.

An unusual program that mixed music and songs with segments devoted to Joseph Dunninger, a mentalist who performed feats of mind reading on members of the studio audience. Also known as *Dunninger, the Mentalist*. A reward of $10,000 was offered to any person who could prove Dunninger was a fake. The reward was never claimed.

Host: Joseph Dunninger. ***Assistant:*** George Weist. ***Regulars:*** Marilyn Day, Bill Slater, the Andy Love Vocal Group. ***Announcer:*** Don Lowe, Roger Krupp, Bill Neil. ***Orchestra:*** Mitchell Ayres. ***Producer:*** George Weist.

OPENING (from 10/23/44)

ANNOUNCER: Kem Tone, the miracle wall finish, brings you from Memphis, Tennessee, the Master Mentalist.

GIRL'S VOICE: The Mental Marvel.

ANNOUNCER: The newest star in radio, Dunninger... [who would then begin the program with, "Who among you is thinking of a name or a word...?" Kem Tone was a paint product of the Sherwin Williams company.]

425. THE EARL WILSON SHOW. Gossip, 15 min., Mutual, 1944–1945.

A transformation of Earl Wilson's New York *Post* Broadway column from the newspapers to the airwaves. Earl Wilson hosted and Paul Douglas served as his announcer and assistant.

426. Earn Your Vacation. Game, 30 min., CBS, 1949–1950.

A question, "Where on earth would you like to go and why?" is posed to the studio audience. Those with the best responses become contestants and receive the opportunity to win an all-expenses-paid vacation to their desired destination. Each player selects a subject from a group of categories and has to answer questions of ascending difficulty within four plateaus. Each plateau represents a segment of the vacation and each question must be answered correctly to win. An incorrect answer defeated a player. Served as the basis for the television series of the same title.

Hosts: Jay C. Flippen, Steve Allen. ***Announcer:*** Johnny Jacobs.

427. Easy Aces. Comedy, 15 and 30 min. versions, CBS, 1932–1935; NBC Blue, 1935–1942; CBS, 1942–1945; Syndicated, 1945–1946.

Events in the daily lives of the Aces: Jane, a scatterbrained housewife, and her husband Goodman, the recipient of her unpredictable antics. *Other regular characters:* Marge Hall, Jane's friend (who rents a room in their home); Laura, their maid; Johnny Sherwood, Jane's unemployed brother; Betty, Jane's friend. Became the basis for the 1949 television series of the same title. See also *Mr. Ace and Jane.*

Cast: Goodman Ace (*Goodman Ace*); Jane Ace (*Jane Ace*); Mary Hunter (*Marge Hall*); Helene Dumas (*Laura*); Paul Stewart (*Johnny Sherwood*); Ethel Blume (*Betty*). ***Also:*** Frank Butler, Eric Dressler, Leon Janney, Florence Robinson, Everett Sloane. ***Vocalists:*** The Ken Christy Chorus. ***Announcers:*** Ford Bond, Ken Roberts. ***Orchestra:*** Ken Christy, Morris Surdin. ***Producers:*** Anne Hummert, Frank Hummert. ***Writer:*** Goodman Ace.

OPENING

Announcer (over theme music): Once again the strains of "Manhattan Serenade" introduce *Easy Aces*, radio's distinctive laugh novelty.

428. Easy Does It. Variety, 15 min., Mutual, 1946–1947.

A daily daytime program of music and songs. Ted Steele was the host; also featured were songs by Kenny Gardner and Betty Randall and the music of the Ted Steele Orchestra.

429. Easy Money. Mystery, 30 min., NBC, 1946.

A weekly crime series wherein a famous magician turned private detective uses illusion to apprehend criminals. Willard Waterman portrayed the magician; George Stone did the announcing; Lou Webb provided the music.

430. Ed East and Polly. Variety, 30 min., NBC Blue/ABC, 1943–1944.

A daily program of chatter, audience participation (game contests), interviews and sketches with marrieds Ed and Polly East as hosts. They were assisted by Doug Browning, Bob Hamilton and Lee Sullivan. The program began on NBC's Blue Network right before it became ABC.

431. The Ed Sullivan Show. Variety, 30 min., CBS, 1941–1944.

A program of music, songs and comedy featuring both performances by a regular cast as well as those by top name entertainers. Served as the basis for newspaper columnist Ed Sullivan's *Toast of the Town* television series.

Host: Ed Sullivan. ***Regulars:*** Terry Allen, Lynne Gardner, Adele Gerard. ***Announcers:*** David Ross, Harry Von Zell. ***Orchestra:*** Will Bradley.

The Ed Wynn Show *see* **The Fire Chief**

432. The Eddie Albert Show. Variety, 30 min., ABC, 1947; NBC, 1949–1950.

Actor Eddie Albert as the host of a program of music, songs and light comedy. Connie Crowder, Joe Crambly, Barbara Eiler and Earle Ross were the regulars; Basil Adlam and his orchestra provided the music.

433. The Eddie Bracken Show. Comedy, 30 min., NBC, 1945–1946; CBS, 1946–1947.

Eddie Bracken is a well-intentioned young man with one serious drawback: He is calamity prone and his efforts to undo the chaotic situations he creates by trying to help others is the focal point of the stories. *Other regular characters:* Connie Pringle, Eddie's girlfriend; Sheriff Pringle, Connie's father (who can't figure out what Connie sees in Eddie).

Cast: Eddie Bracken (*Eddie Bracken*); Ann Rutherford (*Connie Pringle*); William Demarest (*Sheriff Pringle*). ***Also:*** Shirley Booth, Ruth Perrott, Janet Waldo. ***Announcers:*** John Wald, Jimmy Wallington. ***Music:*** Lee Harlin. ***Producer:*** Mann Holiner.

434. THE EDDIE CANTOR SHOW. Variety, 60 min., NBC, 1931–1935; 30 min., CBS, 1935–1939; NBC, 1940–1949.

A mixture of music, songs and comedy sketches featuring the talents of comedian Eddie Cantor. Also known as *The Chase and Sanborn Hour*, *The Eddie Cantor Pabst Blue Ribbon Show* and *Time to Smile*.

Cast: Eddie Cantor (*Host*); Bert Gordon (*The Mad Russian*); Veola Vonn (*Mademoiselle Fifi*); Harry Einstein (*Parkyskarkas*); Sidney Fields (*Mr. Guffy*). ***Regulars:*** John Brown, Maude Davis, Shirley Dinsdale (a ventriloquist and her dummy, Judy Splinters), Frank Nelson, Nan Rae, Alan Reed, Lionel Stander, the Sportsmen Quartet. ***Vocalists:*** Bobby Breen, Deanna Durbin, Nora Martin, Dinah Shore, Margaret Whiting. ***Announcers:*** Walter Woolf King, Jimmy Wallington, Harry Von Zell. ***Orchestra:*** Cookie Fairchild, Louis Gress, Jacques Renard, Bobby Sherwood, George Stoll. ***Sponsors:*** Chase and Sanborn Coffee, Ipana Toothpaste, Pabst Blue Ribbon Beer.

OPENING

ANNOUNCER: Pabst Blue Ribbon Beer, the finest beer served anywhere, presents—

CHORUS: *The Eddie Cantor Pabst Blue Ribbon Show.*

ANNOUNCER: With our guest star Dan Dailey, our weekly guest Dinah Shore, the Sportsmen, Cookie Fairchild's Orchestra, Alan Reed, Frank Nelson, yours truly Harry Von Zell, and starring your man Friday, Eddie Cantor.

435. EDDIE CONDON'S JAZZ CONCERT. Music, 30 min., NBC, 1944.

A weekly program of jazz music with guitarist–orchestra leader Eddie Condon.

Host: Eddie Condon. ***Regulars:*** Billy Butterfield, Bob Casey, Sonny Greer, Joe Grasso, Bobby Hackett, James P. Johnson, Jonah Jones, Max Kominsky, Gene Krupa, Joe Marsala, Miff Mole, Liza Morrow, Tony Mottola, Hot Lips Paige, Pee Wee Russell, Gene Schroeder, Willie Smith, Muggsy Spanier, Rex Stuart. ***Orchestra:*** Eddie Condon.

436. THE EDDY ARNOLD SHOW. Variety, 30 min., CBS, 1956.

Country and western music and songs with singer Eddy Arnold. Bill Allen did the announcing and the regulars were Dorothy Dillars, Joan Hager, Marvin Hughes and Anita Kerr.

437. THE EDDY DUCHIN SHOW. Variety, 30 min., NBC, 1938; 15 min., ABC, 1947.

A weekly program of music and songs with orchestra leader Eddy Duchin.

Host: Eddy Duchin. ***Regulars:*** Durelle Alexander, Tony Russell, Jimmy Shields, Nan Wynn, the Mullin Sisters, the Tune Twisters. ***Announcer:*** Frank Waldecker. ***Orchestra:*** Eddy Duchin.

THE EDGAR BERGEN AND CHARLIE McCARTHY SHOW *see* **THE CHARLIE McCARTHY SHOW**

438. THE EDGAR BERGEN HOUR. Variety, 60 min., CBS, 1955–1956.

A revised version of *The Charlie McCarthy Show* (see entry) wherein the series became an hour and much of the comedy (with Edgar Bergen's dummies Charlie McCarthy, Mortimer Snerd and Effie Klinker) took a backseat to music, songs and performances by guest stars. Also known as *The New Edgar Bergen Hour*.

Host: Edgar Bergen and Charlie McCarthy. ***Regulars:*** Gary Crosby, Carol Richards. ***Orchestra:*** Ray Noble.

439. EDITH ADAMS' FUTURE. Serial, 15 min., Mutual, 1941.

A daily drama about Edith Adams, a woman married for 35 years, as she struggles to contend with the various problems in her life, always dreaming of a future much brighter than handling major household chores.

Cast: Della Louise Orton (*Edith Adams*); Joseph Harding (*Husband*); Mary Louise Lantz (*Daughter*); Dolores Dahl (*Friend*). ***Announcer:*** John Adams.

THE EDITOR'S DAUGHTER *see* **MARY FOSTER, THE EDITOR'S DAUGHTER**

440. The Edward Everett Horton Show. Variety, 30 min., NBC, 1945.

A weekly program of comedy sketches featuring actor Edward Everett Horton as the host (he was assisted by a guest star each week). Les Tremayne did the announcing and Raymond Paige and his orchestra provided the music.

441. The Eileen Barton Show. Variety, 15 min., CBS, 1954.

A weekly program of popular songs with singer Eileen Barton. Joe King did the announcing and music was by the Alvy West Combo.

442. The Eileen Farrell Show. Variety, 15 and 30 min. versions, CBS, 1942–1946.

This program first ran as a 30-minute weekly outing (1942–43), then as a 15-minute, twice-weekly program (1944–46) and finally as a weekly half-hour (1946). It featured songs by soprano Eileen Farrell and the music of the CBS Symphony Orchestra under the direction of Charles Litcher. Stewart Young was the announcer.

443. The Electric Hour. Variety, 30 min., CBS, 1944–1946.

A program of music and songs sponsored by the Electric Companies of America. Nelson Eddy, the original host, was replaced by Anne Jamison and Bob Shanley in 1945. Vocal backing was provided by the Robert Armbruster Chorus; Frank Graham did the announcing; and Robert Armbruster and his orchestra provided the music.

Electric Theater *see* **Appendix**

444. Ella Fitzgerald. Variety, 15 min., NBC, 1940–1943.

Music and songs with vocalist Ella Fitzgerald and the music of the short-lived Ella Fitzgerald Orchestra.

445. Ellen Randolph. Serial, 15 min., NBC, 1939–1941.

The private life and personal problems of Ellen Randolph, the young wife of a missionary (George) as she struggles to save her marriage, which is threatened by her husband's belief that he is a failure. Also known as *The Story of Ellen Randolph*.

Cast: Elsie Hitz, Gertrude Warner (*Ellen Randolph*); John McGovern, Ted Jewett (*George Randolph*); Jackie Jordan (*Robert Randolph*); Helene Dumas (*Claire Clayton*); Florida Friebus (*Amy Brown*); Bernard Lenrow (*Dr. Lewis*); Macdonald Carey (*Ted Clayton*); Robert Regent (*Andy Barrett*); Jay Meredith (*Rena Fletcher*); Parker Fennelly (*Skipper*); Kathryn Bishop (*Agnes Foy*); Edward Trevor (*Carl Richmond*); George Wallach (*Peter Chang*); Maurice Franklin (*Dr. Keith*); Eloise Ellis (*Nadine*); Walter Burke (*Vince Kennedy*); Inge Adams (*La Ling*). ***Also:*** Ethel Owen (*Ellen's friend*); Mark Smith (*Doctor*). ***Announcer:*** Ford Bond.

446. Ellery Queen. Crime Drama, 60 min., CBS, 1939–1940; 30 min., NBC, 1942–1944; CBS, 1945–1947; NBC, 1947; ABC, 1947–1948.

Ellery Queen is a sophisticated gentleman detective and writer living in New York City. He rarely accepts a fee for his services (he considers it research) and finds additional material for his books by assisting his father, Inspector Richard Queen of the N.Y.P.D. Ellery's romantic interest, Nikki Porter, is also his secretary and the one who worries for him (he won't) when he is shot or beaten or when attempts are made on his life. Stories follow Ellery and Nikki as they investigate crimes. All the clues are given to the listener to enable him to solve the crime with—or before—Ellery. A guest "Armchair Detective" is present for each broadcast. This person (a celebrity) appears right before Ellery reveals the culprit to give his or her opinion. When this has been done, the program resumes and Ellery reveals the guilty party. Also known as *The Adventures of Ellery Queen*.

Cast: Hugh Marlowe, Carleton Young, Sydney Smith, ?*, Larry Dobkin (*Ellery Queen*); Santos Ortega, Bill Smith (*Richard Queen*); Marion Shockley, Barbara Terrell, Virginia Gregg, Charlotte Keane, Gertrude Warner

**In 1947 and 1948, the name of the actor portraying Ellery Queen was withheld in an attempt to make the fictitious character seem real.*

(*Nikki Porter*); Howard Smith, Ted de Corsia, Ed Latimer (*Sgt. Velie*); Arthur Allen (*Medical examiner*). ***Announcers:*** Ernest Chappell, Don Hancock, Roger Krupp, Paul Masterson. ***Organist:*** Chet Kingsbury, Rex Koury. ***Orchestra:*** Bernard Herrmann.

OPENING (from "One Diamond," 5/6/48)

ANNOUNCER: *Ellery Queen*. In the interest of a safer America, a happier American community, a more United States, the American Broadcasting Company and its affiliated stations bring you *Ellery Queen*, celebrated fighter of crime. As usual, Ellery invites you to match wits with him as he relates the mystery, and before revealing the solution, he gives you a chance to solve it. Tonight, Ellery's guest "Armchair Detective," who will represent you home armchair detectives, is the popular vocalist Miss Peggy Lee. And now here's Ellery Queen, your host for the next half-hour.

ELLERY: Thank you, Paul Masterson. Good evening, ladies and gentlemen. Tonight we meet Mr. Mark Gallows, who played a very dangerous game. I call it "One Diamond."

CLOSING

ELLERY: And there, ladies and gentlemen, you have the solution to our mystery. Thank you, Peggy Lee, for serving as our guest "Armchair Detective" this evening. As mementoes of the occasion, I have for you a copy of my latest mystery anthology, *The Queen's Awards, 1947*, and a subscription to *Ellery Queen Magazine*. This is Ellery Queen saying good night till next week and enlisting all Americans every night and every day in the fight against bad citizenship, bigotry and discrimination, the crimes which are weakening America.

ANNOUNCER: All names used on this program are fictitious and do not refer to real people either living or dead. The entire production was under the supervision of Ellery Queen. This is ABC, the American Broadcasting Company.

447. ELSA MAXWELL'S PARTY LINE. Gossip, 15 min., NBC Red, 1932–1939; NBC Blue, 1942; Mutual, 1943–1946.

A weekly program of gossip in which Elsa Maxwell, "the world's greatest party giver," related stories about the people she has known. Graham McNee assisted and did the announcing.

448. EMILY POST. Advice, 15 min., CBS, 1930–1931; NBC Blue, 1932–1933; 30 min., NBC Red, 1938.

Newspaper columnist Emily Post simply answered questions submitted by listeners.

449. EMOTION. Anthology, 30 min., NBC, 1949.

Stories designed to evoke emotion on the part of the listener. Dramatizations are written to place the subjects in emotional situations that require clear thinking to overcome. The situations, however, tend to worsen as the story unfolds and are meant to bring about tears, laughs or something as simple as a smile.

Host: Joseph Schildkraut. ***Music:*** Dr. Albert Harris. ***Producer:*** Andrew C. Love.

OPENING

HOST: Good evening, ladies and gentlemen, this is Joseph Schildkraut speaking. For the next half-hour, an unusual story will be presented to you. You may find it disturbing; yes, you may even find it shocking. However, we do promise you one thing, we promise you an emotion.

ANNOUNCER: This is *Emotion* starring Joseph Schildkraut.

CLOSING

HOST: Ladies and gentlemen, this evening you have heard our first experiment in *Emotion*. In the weeks to come, we invite you to explore with us the shadows of literature. We promise you an exciting journey along strange and seldom traveled paths of *Emotion*. Good night.

ANNOUNCER: This is NBC, the National Broadcasting Company.

EMPIRE BUILDERS *see* **APPENDIX**

450. ENCORE. Variety, 30 min., NBC, 12/8/52 to 3/16/53.

Baritone Robert Merrill as the host of a program of music and songs. Marguerite Piazza and the Ray Charles Chorus were the regulars; Kenneth Banghart did the announcing; and Meredith Willson and his orchestra provided the music.

451. ENDORSED BY DORSEY. Variety, 30 min., Mutual, 3/27/46 to 10/18/46.

A program of music and songs that replaced *The Tommy Dorsey Show* when the orchestra leader went on the road.

Host: Emerson Buckley. ***Regulars:*** Vera Holly, Buddy Merino, Bert Howell, the Chitterson Trio, the Clark Sisters, the Holidays. ***Orchestra:*** Sy Oliver.

452. Eno Crime Clues. Crime Drama, 15 min., CBS, 1931–1932; 30 min., NBC Blue, 1933–1936.

Spencer Dean is a world-famous private detective who is known as "The Manhunter." He and his assistant Dan Cassidy investigate crimes that go beyond the norm—crimes that require intellect, not brawn to solve. The program, sponsored by Eno Effervescent Salts, is more talk than action and presents all the clues the listener needs to solve the case along with Spencer. The program began as a 15-minute daily entry called *The Eno Crime Club*; in 1933 it became the half-hour *Eno Crime Clues. Other regular characters:* Jane Elliott, Spencer's romantic interest.

Cast: Edward Reese, Clyde North (*Spencer Dean*); Jack MacBryde (*Dan Cassidy*); Helen Choate (*Jane Elliott*).

OPENING

Announcer: *Eno Crime Clues.* In just a moment, ladies and gentlemen, the makers of Eno Effervescent Salts will present another thrilling "Manhunter" mystery, "The Blue Beard Room." [Commercial airs.] And now another thrill-a-minute "Manhunter" mystery by Stewart Sterling, "The Blue Beard Room," another action-packed radio riddle giving you a chance to play detective yourself. Match wits with the Manhunter; see how great a sleuth you really are. Listen carefully; you can solve the puzzle from the clues given in tonight's episode. We pick up the trail tonight in the living room of a gloomy old mansion...

453. Escape. Anthology, 30 min., CBS, 7/47 to 9/54.

High adventure dramatizations of people trapped in life and death situations. Their efforts to escape become the focal point of stories.

Narrators: William Conrad, Paul Frees. ***Recurring Performers:*** William Conrad, John Dehner, Paul Frees, Charles McGraw, Ben Wright. ***Announcers:*** William Conrad, Paul Frees, Elliott Lewis, Jack McCoy, George Walsh. ***Music:*** Ivan Ditmars, Cy Feuer, Leith Stevens. ***Producers:*** Norman MacDonnell, William Robson.

OPENING (typical; varies with each episode)

Announcer: You are isolated on a remote plantation in the crawling Amazon jungle and an immense army of ravenous ants is closing in on you, swarming in to eat you alive—a deadly black army from which there is no escape!

Narrator: We offer you *Escape*, designed to free you from the four walls of today for a half-hour of high adventure. Tonight we escape to the Amazon jungle and to a creepy, crawling terror as Carl Stevenson told it in his famous story, "Leiningen vs. the Ants."

454. Escape with Me. Anthology, 30 min., ABC, 1952.

A series of romantic adventure stories featuring a different cast each week. Kathi Norris served as the host and narrator; Don Pardo did the announcing.

455. Ethel and Albert. Comedy, 15 min., ABC, 1944–1950.

A humorous dialogue between Ethel and Albert Arbuckle, a happily married couple with a young daughter (Susy) who live in the small town of Sandy Harbor. Also titled *The Private Lives of Ethel and Albert.* Served as the basis for the television show of the same title.

Cast: Peg Lynch (*Ethel Arbuckle*); Richard Widmark, Alan Bunce (*Albert Arbuckle*); Madeleine Pierce (*Baby Susy*). ***Announcers:*** George Ansbro, Fred Cole, Cy Harrice, Don Lowe, Glenn Riggs, Herb Sheldon. ***Organists:*** Dolph Gobel, Rosa Rio, Lew White. ***Orchestra:*** Ralph Norman.

OPENING

Announcer: *The Private Lives of Ethel and Albert* starring Peg Lynch and Alan Bunce. Although our lives differ in many respects, everyday life offers many little sidelights that are familiar to everyone. You'll recognize the familiar moments in your daily routine when you hear *The Private Lives of Ethel and Albert.*

456. The Ethel Merman Show. Comedy, 30 min., NBC, 1949.

Music and songs coupled with a skit about Ethel Merman, a singer, and her friend Eddie McCoy as they struggle to produce a Broadway show backed by Homer Tubbs, a floor mop tycoon.

Cast: Ethel Merman (*Ethel Merman*); Leon Janney (*Eddie McCoy*); Allen Drake (*Homer Tubbs*). ***Producer:*** Kenneth MacGregor.

457. The Eve Young Show. Variety, 15 min., NBC, 1951.

Vocalist Eve Young as the host of a program of music and songs. Don Pardo did the announcing and the Norman Cloutier and Milton Katims orchestras provided the music.

458. The Evelyn Pasen Show. Variety, 30 min., CBS, 1945.

Twenty-year-old Met soprano Evelyn Pasen as the host of a weekly program of music and songs. Sidney Berry was the announcer and Bernard Herrmann conducted the CBS Columbia Concert Orchestra.

Evelyn Winters *see* **The Strange Romance of Evelyn Winters**

459. Ever Since Eve. Anthology, 15 min., ABC, 1954.

Serial-like stories that focus on women as they search for love and the ideal mate. Keith Morgan was the host and narrator.

460. The Eveready Hour. Variety, 60 min., NBC, 1926–1930.

The program sponsored by the National Carbon Company (makers of Eveready batteries), was a mix of music, comedy, songs, dramatic sketches, light opera, lectures and true-life stories. It first appeared in 1923 on WEAF in New York, making it radio's first variety series.

Regular Performers: Charles Mack and George Moran ("The Two Black Crows"), the Eveready Mixed Quartet, Max Jacob's String Quartet. ***Music:*** Nathaniel Shilkret.

461. Everybody Wins. Game, 30 min., CBS, 1948.

Contestants, chosen from the studio audience, compete in a series of question-and-answer rounds. Players who answer the most questions correctly receive a cash prize; losers are given a consolation prize (so everybody wins).

Host: Phil Baker. ***Announcer:*** Ken Roberts.

462. Everybody's Music. Variety, 30 min., CBS, 1938.

A weekly program that featured the broadcast premieres of original works by American composers. Henry M. Neely served as the host and commentator; Howard Barlow conducted the CBS Symphony Orchestra.

463. Everyman's Theater. Anthology, 30 min., NBC, 10/4/40 to 3/28/41.

A weekly series of original plays and adaptations by Arch Oboler. Top name guests appeared alongside a regular cast of supporting actors.

Host: Arch Oboler. ***Cast:*** Betty Caine, Raymond Edward Johnson, Bill Lipton, Gilbert Mack, Ann Shepherd, Luis Van Rooten. ***Music:*** Gordon Jenkins. ***Producer:*** Arch Oboler.

OPENING

Announcer: *Everyman's Theater*, written and created by Arch Oboler. Oxydol presents Miss Norma Shearer in a thrilling love story, "The Women Stayed at Home." And here is our writer-creator, Arch Oboler, who will introduce tonight's play.

Arch: The scene: a windswept coast. It is night; for once the sea is calm...

CLOSING

Arch: This is Arch Oboler. Tonight it has been a great privilege to bring you Norma Shearer in my play, "The Women Stayed at Home." All of us here and I know you out there are grateful to Miss Shearer for her stirring performance. With Miss Shearer were Hans Conried and Howard Duff. Good night.

464. Everything for the Boys. Variety, 30 min., NBC, 1944.

A wartime series of music, songs and short dramatizations geared to servicemen. Dick Haymes served as the host; Helen Forrest provided the vocals; and music was by Gordon Jenkins and his orchestra. Guests appeared in the dramatizations.

465. The Ex-Lax Big Show. Variety, 30 min., CBS, 1933–1934.

A program of music and songs sponsored by Ex-Lax and featuring vocalist Gertrude Niesen and the music of the Isham Jones Orchestra.

466. Exploring the Unknown. Anthology, 30 min., Mutual, 1945–1947; ABC, 1947–1948.

Stories of "science at work, searching for knowledge that will shape your future." Guests appeared in varying dramatizations sponsored by the Revere Copper and Brass Company. Sherman H. Dryer was the producer.

467. Exploring Tomorrow. Anthology, 30 min., Mutual, 1957–1958.

A twice-weekly program of stories that depict how science could affect the future of mankind. Adapted from stories appearing in *Astounding Science Fiction* magazine.

Host: John Campbell, Jr. ***Producer:*** Sanford Marshall.

OPENING

ANNOUNCER: The program you are about to hear is fiction, science fiction. We make no guarantees, however, how long it will remain fiction.

VOICE: *Exploring Tomorrow.*

ANNOUNCER: And now, here is your guide to these adventures of the mind, the editor of *Astounding Science Fiction* magazine, John Campbell, Jr.

HOST: We all believe pretty solidly that sooner or later almost any problem you can name is going to be solved. So, apparently, all you have to do is stand by and wait and it will soon be solved for you. I don't think that works right. There is another thing to consider—

ANNOUNCER: *Exploring Tomorrow.* Presented by the Mutual Broadcasting System in cooperation with L&M, today's most exciting cigarette, and the Kraft Foods Company, makers of delicious Kraft jellies and preserves; and Cape Coral, a beautiful waterfront wonderland on the western coast of Florida. In a moment, John Campbell returns with the story of "Time Heals."

CLOSING

ANNOUNCER: Join us each Wednesday and Friday night for fascinating adventures in *Exploring Tomorrow.* Produced and directed by Sanford Marshall here in New York. This is Mutual, the world's largest network.

468. The Fabulous Dr. Tweedy. Comedy, 30 min., NBC, 6/2/46 to 9/22/46.

Dr. Thaddeus Q. Tweedy is a befuddled Dean of Men at Potts College. He is a philosopher, and students find comfort in talking over their problems with him. Stories focus on the home and school life of Dr. Tweedy and the situations that develop when he gives advice but is not always sure it is the right advice, as chaos usually results—"Oh, no, I've done it again!" *Other regular characters:* Sidney Tweedy, Thaddeus's adopted son; Mary Potts, Sidney's fiancée (daughter of Alexander Potts, chairman of the board of Potts College); Timothy, a student; Col. Beauregard Jackson, Thaddeus's neighbor; Kitty Bell Jackson, Beauregard's sister. Thaddeus has a dog named Paulie; the college football team is the Potts Gophers; and Philbert the gopher is the team mascot.

Cast: Frank Morgan (*Thaddeus Q. Tweedy*); Harlan Stone, Jr. (*Sidney Potts*); Janet Waldo (*Mary Potts*); Harry Von Zell (*Timothy*); Gale Gordon (*Alexander Potts*); Will Wright (*Beauregard Jackson*); Sara Berner (*Kitty Bell Jackson*). ***Announcer:*** Bud Heistand. ***Music:*** Elliot Daniel.

OPENING

ANNOUNCER: *The Fabulous Dr. Tweedy,* written by Robert Riley Crutcher, and starring Frank Morgan.

CLOSING

ANNOUNCER: Here again is Frank Morgan and his thought for the week.

FRANK: My thought for today is fair play. Do unto others as they may do unto you, but don't let them catch you at it. Which brings me to my thought for the week: Never hit a fellow when he's down; he may get up and beat the stuffings out of you. Good night.

ANNOUNCER: This is NBC, the National Broadcasting Company.

469. The Falcon. Crime Drama, 30 min., NBC Blue, 1943–1944; ABC, 1944–1945; Mutual, 1945–1950; NBC, 1950–1952; Mutual, 1953–1954.

Michael Waring is a freelance private investigator based in New York City. He is known and feared by criminals as "The Falcon" and often takes the cases of the hopeless—people with the odds stacked against them who have no place else to turn. When everybody has an alibi except his client, Michael becomes a bit anxious; when he hears the police say, "Just because he's your client, it doesn't mean he can't be guilty," Michael steps into the arena, hoping to avoid violent confrontation by using his wits to trick a suspect into revealing his guilt. Stories relate his adventures as he and Nancy, his girlfriend and secretary, investigate crimes. Also known as *The Adventures of the Falcon*. *The Falcon* achieved great success with sponsor identification. To this day, Gem Blades is still associated with the show. However, Gem was not the sole sponsor. The second set of openings and closings listed represents the long-forgotten Kraft Foods sponsorship of the series.

Cast: Berry Kroeger, James Meighan, Les Damon, Les Tremayne, George Petrie (*Michael Waring*); Joan Banks, Elspeth Eric, Joan Alexander (*Nancy*); Mandel Kramer (*Sergeant Johnny Gleason*); Ken Lynch (*Sgt. Corbett*). ***Announcers:*** Russ Dunbar, Ed Herlihy. ***Organist:*** Bob Hamilton. ***Orchestra:*** Emerson Buckley, Harry Sosnik. ***Producer:*** Bernard L. Schubert.

OPENING (Gem Blades)

ANNOUNCER (over sounds of a ticking clock): Avoid five o'clock shadow.

VOICE: Use Gem Blades.

ANNOUNCER: Gem Razors and Gem Blades present the adventures of *The Falcon*.

SOUND: Phone rings.

MICHAEL (picking up receiver): Hello. Yes, this is the Falcon. Oh, Nancy, I'm glad you called. What's on the program for tonight? (*Laughs*) Well, it sounds like an awfully dead evening, baby, but you never can tell, tomorrow there may be mourning.

ANNOUNCER: Once again Gem Blades, the razor blades that will help you avoid five o'clock shadow, bring you the adventures of *The Falcon*. The Falcon, as you know, is Michael Waring, freelance detective, who's always ready with a hand for oppressed men and an eye for repressed women. So join him tonight when the Falcon learns "Murder Is a Family Affair."

CLOSING

ANNOUNCER: "Murder Is a Grave Situation." That is the title of next week's adventure of *The Falcon* when Mike Waring learns even those with double trouble can only die once. So be sure to listen next week at this time to another gay, exciting adventure of *The Falcon*. And, in the meantime, avoid five o'clock shadow with Gem Razors and Gem Blades. The adventures of *The Falcon* are based on the famous character created by Drexell Drake. James Meighan was starred as the Falcon. This is the Mutual Broadcasting System.

OPENING (Kraft Foods)

ANNOUNCER: This is Ed Herlihy, friends, inviting you on behalf of the Kraft Foods Company to listen to the adventures of *The Falcon* starring Les Damon. You met the Falcon first in his best-selling novels, then you saw him in his thrilling motion picture series. Now, join him on the air when the Falcon investigates "The Case of the Bellicose Boxer."

CLOSING

ANNOUNCER: "The Case of the Neighbor's Nightmare." That's the title of next week's adventure of *The Falcon* when Mike Waring learns that when someone tricks someone into losing his shirt, someone is likely to lose his life. So be sure to listen at this same time next week for another exciting adventure of *The Falcon*, brought to you by the Kraft Foods Company. The adventures of *The Falcon* are based on the famous character created by Drexell Drake and are produced by Bernard L. Schubert. Hear *Mr. and Mrs. Blandings* later; then it's Danny Kaye on *The Big Show* on NBC.

470. FALSTAFF'S FABLES. Satire, 5 min., ABC, 1949.

A five-minute program that presented parodies of classic children's stories. Alan Reed and his son, Alan Reed, Jr., did all the voices. Dick Tufeld was the announcer and organist John Duffy provided the music.

471. FAME AND FORTUNE. Variety, 30 min., NBC Blue, 1940–1941.

A weekly series wherein the compositions of amateur songwriters were performed by Frank Sinatra and Connie Haines. Studio audience applause determined the best amateur song and the writer received $100.

472. THE FAMILY HOUR. Variety, 45 min., CBS, 1941.

A program of light classical music with Deems Taylor as the host and commentator and the music of the Al Goodman Orchestra. Ross

Graham, Jack Smart, Gladys Swarthout and the Al Goodman Chorus were the regulars.

473. Family Skeleton. Serial, 15 min., CBS, 6/8/53 to 3/5/54.

The daily adventures of a young woman (Sarah Ann Spencer) and her efforts to find happiness. Mercedes McCambridge played Sarah; others in the cast were John Dehner, Forrest Lewis, Marvin Miller, Jeanette Nolan, Marilyn Steiner, Russell Thorson and Herb Vigran.

474. Family Theater. Anthology, 30 min., Mutual, 1947–1963.

Family-oriented radio dramas "for the next decade." Stories, while not overly religious, stressed family life and values, love and prayer. The series was the brainchild of Father Patrick Peyton, who convinced Mutual to provide a weekly half-hour of air time for nonsectarian entertainment. Major stars appeared in the dramas and sometimes served as the host for that episode (replacing Father Peyton for that evening's performance).

Host: Father Patrick Peyton. ***Announcers:*** Gene Baker, Tony LaFrano. ***Music:*** Harry Zimmerman.

OPENING (typical)

Announcer: *Family Theater* presents Dennis Morgan and Gene Lockhart. From Hollywood, the Mutual Network in cooperation with Family Theater presents transcribed "20,000 Leagues Under the Sea" starring Gene Lockhart. To introduce the drama, here is your host, Dennis Morgan [who would then begin the story].

CLOSING

Announcer: From Hollywood, *Family Theater* has presented "20,000 Leagues Under the Sea" starring Gene Lockhart. Dennis Morgan was your host. This series of *Family Theater* broadcasts is made possible by the thousands of you who feel a need for this type of programming, by the Mutual Network, which has responded to this need, and by the hundreds of stars of stage, screen and radio who give so unselfishly of their time and talent to appear on our *Family Theater* stage. To them, our humble thanks. *Family Theater* is broadcast throughout the world and originates in the Hollywood studios of the world's largest network. This is the Mutual Broadcasting System.

475. Famous Jury Trials. Anthology, 30 min., Mutual, 1936–1939; NBC Blue, 1940–1944; ABC, 1944–1949.

Dramatizations based on actual courtroom cases. Became the basis for the television series of the same title.

Cast: Maurice Franklin (*Judge*). ***Narrator:*** Roger DeKoven, DeWitt McBride. ***Announcers:*** Peter Grant, Hugh James, Roger Krupp.

OPENING

Judge: Gentlemen of the jury. You are the judge of evidence to be made before you. Be just and fear not, for the true administration of justice is the foundation of good government.

Announcer: *Famous Jury Trials*, dramatizations of cases taken from actual court history. The names of persons and places have been altered to protect those concerned.

476. Fannie Hurst Presents. Anthology, 30 min., ABC, 1944.

A weekly series of dramatizations based on stories written by Fannie Hurst (who also served as the host and narrator).

477. The Fanny Brice Show. Comedy, 30 min., CBS, 1944.

The story of an unpredictable teenage girl (Irma) and the problems she causes for all concerned when she tries to help people she believes are in trouble. Fanny Brice played the role of Irma; Hanley Stafford was her father (who was on the verge of a nervous breakdown); and Danny Thomas played the part of Jerry Dingle, the postman plagued by Irma's antics. Music was by Carmen Dragon and his orchestra.

478. Fashion Discoveries. Women, 30 min., NBC, 1941.

A weekly series of fashion tips and advice for women. Wynn Price was the host; he was assisted by Ruth Hopkins and Peggy Read.

479. The Fat Man. Crime Drama, 30 min., ABC, 1946–1951.

New York City is the setting for a hard-hitting detective series about Brad Runyon, an overweight private investigator known as "The Fat Man," as he wages a one-man battle against criminals. Based on the character created by

Dashiell Hammett. *Other regular characters:* Lila North, his secretary; and Police Sgt. O'Hara.

Cast: J. Scott Smart (*Brad Runyon*); Mary Patton (*Lila North*); Ed Begley (*Sgt. O'Hara*). ***Announcer:*** Charles Irving. ***Music:*** Bernard Green, Mark Winston.

OPENING

WOMAN: There he goes, into that drugstore. He's stepping on the scales.
SOUND: Coin dropping into the machine.
WOMAN: Weight 237 pounds.
SOUND: Card dropping.
WOMAN: Fortune ... danger! Who is it?
MAN: The Fat Man.
ANNOUNCER: The Norwich Pharmaceutical Company brings you the adventures of Dashiell Hammett's fascinating and exciting character, *The Fat Man*, a fast-moving criminologist who tips the scales at 237 pounds. Tonight's adventure starring J. Scott Smart in "A Window for Murder."

FATHER BROWN *see* **THE ADVENTURES OF FATHER BROWN**

480. FATHER KNOWS BEST. Comedy, 30 min., NBC, 1949–1954.

The white house at 607 Maple Street in the town of Springfield is the residence of the Anderson family: Jim, an insurance salesman; his wife, Margaret; and their children, Betty, Bud and Kathy. Betty, the eldest (called "Princess" by Jim), attends Springfield College. Bud, the middle child, is a mischievous teen who attends Springfield High School; Kathy, the youngest, called "Kitten" and "Angel" by Jim (and "Shrimp" by Bud), is a tomboy who is having a difficult time understanding the adult world. Jim and Margaret are the typical, all–American, good-natured parents and Jim's philosophy concerning children is simply, "Have 'em and leave 'em alone." Stories relate daily incidents in their lives. Served as the basis for the television series of the same title. *Other regular characters:* Elizabeth and Hector Smith, their neighbors; Billy Smith, their son.

Cast: Robert Young (*Jim Anderson*); June Whitley, Jean VanderPyl (*Margaret Anderson*); Rhoda Williams (*Betty Anderson*); Ted Donaldson (*Bud Anderson*); Norma Jean Nilsson, Helen Strong (*Kathy Anderson*); Herb Vigran (*Hector Smith*); Eleanor Audley (*Elizabeth Smith*); Sam Edwards (*Billy Smith*). ***Announcers:*** Bill Forman, Marvin Miller. ***Music:*** Roy Bargy.

OPENING

BETTY: Mother, are Post Forty Percent Bran Flakes really the best-tasting cereal of them all?
MARGARET: Well, your father says so, and *Father Knows Best.*
SONG: For goodness sake, eat Post Bran Flakes, so good and so good for you.
ANNOUNCER: Yes, it's *Father Knows Best*, transcribed in Hollywood and starring Robert Young as Father. A half-hour visit with your neighbors, the Andersons, and brought to you by America's largest-selling bran flakes, Post Forty Percent Bran Flakes, and Instant Postem, the good-tasting drink that's entirely caffeine free.

CLOSING

ANNOUNCER: Join us next week when we'll be back with *Father Knows Best* starring Robert Young as Jim Anderson. Until then, good night and good luck from the makers of Post Forty Percent Bran Flakes, America's largest-selling bran flakes, and Instant Postem, the drink that's entirely caffeine free. *Father Knows Best* has been transcribed in Hollywood. This is Bill Forman speaking. They're returning soon. Hear *Fibber McGee and Molly* on NBC.

481. FAULTLESS STARCH TIME. Variety, 15 min., ABC, 1949–1953.

A weekly program of music and songs sponsored by Faultless Starch. Ernie Lee originally hosted. He was replaced by Bob Atcher and Mary Jane Johnson. Franklyn Ferguson was the announcer and music was by the Caesar Giovannini Combo.

482. FAVORITE STORY. Anthology, 30 min., Syndicated, 1946–1949.

Dramatizations based on stories chosen by a weekly guest star. Also known as *My Favorite Story.*

Host: Robert Colman. ***Music:*** Robert Mitchell, Claude Sweetin.

OPENING

ANNOUNCER: Here's your invitation to radio's most dramatic half-hour—*Favorite Story.*

483. The FBI in Peace and War. Crime Drama, 30 min., CBS, 11/25/44 to 9/27/58.

Dramatizations based on the book *The FBI in Peace and War* by Frederick L. Collins. Stories are seen through the eyes of criminals (depicting their activities) with the FBI (represented by field agent Adam Sheppard) investigating and closing in for the arrest.

Cast: Martin Blaine (*Adam Sheppard*). ***Various Roles:*** Edith Arnold, Jackson Beck, Ralph Bell, Robert Dryden, Walter Greaza, John M. James, Frank Readick, Rosemary Rice. ***Announcers:*** Len Sterling, Warren Sweeney. ***Music:*** Vladimir Selinsky.

OPENING (from 6/10/53)

Announcer (over theme, the "March" from Prokofiev's "Love for Three Oranges"): *The FBI in Peace and War. The FBI in Peace and War*, brought to you by Brill Creme, the original creme hair grooming discovery that instantly improves your appearance. Brill Creme, the creme that's really not greasy, not messy, and—

Song: L-A-V-A, L-A-V-A.

Announcer: Lava, the soap that gets grimy hands cleaner faster than ordinary soaps ever can; and Nescafe Instant Coffee, the coffee with the richer, heart-of-the-bean flavor. Another great story based on Frederick L. Collins' copyrighted book, *The FBI in Peace and War*. Drama, thrills, action. Tonight's story, "The Traveling Man."

CLOSING

Announcer: The radio dramatizations of *The FBI in Peace and War* are written by Louis Pelletier and Jacques Finke. These programs are produced and directed by Betty Manderville. All names and characters used on the program are fictitious. Any similarity to persons living or dead is purely coincidental. This program is based on Frederick L. Collins' copyrighted book, *The FBI in Peace and War*, and is not an official program of the FBI. This is the CBS Radio Network.

484. Fibber McGee and Molly. Comedy, 30 min., NBC, 4/16/35 to 6/30/53; 15 min., NBC, 10/5/53 to 3/23/56.

Fibber McGee, the world's greatest liar, and his patient and adoring wife Molly reside at 79 Wistful Vista in the town of Wistful Vista (founded in 1892 and populated by 1002 people; elevation: 700 feet). Comedy stems from the situations that develop when people stop by to visit the McGees (usually when Fibber is trying to accomplish something) or by Fibber's constant habit of getting himself into trouble by telling exaggerated truths. This is the format that is known by most people. When the series premiered on April 16, 1935, it was virtually a variety program featuring the songs of Kathleen Wells, the music of Rico Martellis and his orchestra and the harmonica playing of Ronny and Van. The characters of Fibber McGee and Molly were a minor aspect of the program and featured their adventures as they drove across the country (under the sponsorship of Johnson's Auto Wax). On August 26, 1935, the format was altered when Johnson Wax decided to change the focus of its advertising from auto polish to floor wax. They chose to give the McGees a home of their own. This happened when Fibber won a home at 79 Wistful Vista with a two-dollar raffle ticket he bought from the Hagelmeyer Realty Development Company. (Four years later, when Fibber decided to trim an overgrown lilac bush in front of his house, he discovered he was living at 81 Wistful Vista, but he and Molly continued to use the 79 address as their legal residence.) Harlow Wilcox, the sponsor's spokesman, had a major role on the show, stopping by the McGees to convey the sponsor's message. Fibber called him "Waxy" and "Junior" while Molly addressed him as Mr. Wilcox. The program was also famous for the hall closet full of junk (when Fibber opened the closet, everything fell out and ended with the tinkling of a small bell. Fibber always responded with, "Gotta straighten out that closet one of these days").

Fibber's real name was Fibber. He was to have been named after his fourth cousin, Walpo J. Femmer, but the minister who performed the baptism had a head cold and pronounced the name as Fibber. Fibber was a member of the Elk's Club. The Wistful Vista *Gazette* was the town's only newspaper and WVIS was the radio station. Elm Street was lined with oak trees while Oak Street had elm trees. Everything in Wistful Vista seemed to be located at the intersection of 14th and Oak. Wherever Fibber was going—to the bank, car dealership or drug store—it was at this address. The recreation area was Dugan's Lake (where each year Fibber attempted to catch "Old Mulie," an evasive bass). Each week, the McGees hosted the Wistful Vista Literary, Pinochle and Drama Club in their living room. Also known as *The Johnson Wax Program* and *The Johnson Wax Program Starring Fibber McGee and Molly*. See also *Beulah, The Great Gildersleeve* and *The Marlin Hurt and Beulah Show* for information on the spinoff series. *Other regular characters:* Throckmorton P. Gildersleeve, the McGees' friend, owner of the Gildersleeve Girdle Company; Doc John Gamble (aka George Gamble); Mayor Homer LaTrivia; Wallace Wimple, the henpecked bird fancier; Rupert Blasingame, the Old Timer; Teeny, the annoying little girl next door (she has a pet dog named Margaret and said her father named her Martini because she was never as dry as he would have liked); Sis, another young girl who annoyed Fibber; Beulah, the McGees' maid (replaced by Lena); F. Ogden "Foggy" Williams, the weatherman; Molly's Uncle Dennis; Alice Deering, the McGees' boarder (when the housing shortage began during World War II, the McGees rented their spare bedroom to Alice, a man-crazy defense plant worker who constantly tied up their phone); Molly's friends Mrs. Abigail Uppington, Mrs. Wearybottom, Millicent Carstairs and Old Lady Weedledeck. Wallace referred to his wife as "Sweetie Face" and always carried his "bird book" with him; Fibber called Abigail "Uppy"; the Old Timer called Fibber "Johnny" and two characters were always mentioned but never heard: Myrt, the telephone operator, and Fred Nitny, Fibber's friend, who lived in Starved Rock, Illinois.

Cast: Jim Jordan (*Fibber McGee*); Marian Jordan (*Molly McGee/Teeny/Sis/Mrs. Wearybottom/Old Lady Weedledeck*); Hal Peary (*Throckmorton P. Gildersleeve*); Arthur Q. Bryan (*Doc Gamble*); Bill Thompson (*Wallace Wimple*); Cliff Arquette, Bill Thompson (*The Old Timer*); Marlin Hurt (*Beulah*); Jean Carroll (*Lena*); Gale Gordon (*Homer LaTrivia/F. Ogden Williams*); Bill Thompson, Ransom Sherman (*Uncle Dennis*); Shirley Mitchell (*Alice Deering*); Isabel Randolph (*Abigail Uppington*); Bea Benaderet (*Millicent Carstairs*); Jess Kirkpatrick (*Various roles*). ***Vocalists:*** Kathleen Wells, the Kingsman Quartet. ***Announcer:*** Harlow Wilcox. ***Orchestra:*** Rico Martellis, Billy Mills, Ted Weems.

OPENING (Original)

ANNOUNCER: The makers of Johnson Auto Wax present a new show featuring Rico Martellis, Kathleen Wells, those two harmoniacs, Ronny and Van, and starring that humbug of the highways, Fibber McGee, with his constant companion and severest critic, Molly.

CLOSING (Original)

ANNOUNCER: Don't forget next week at this same time, you have a bright and shining date with Johnson's Auto Wax and Fibber McGee and Molly. This is Harlow Wilcox speaking. Good night. This is the National Broadcasting Company.

OPENING (Revised)

ANNOUNCER: *The Johnson Wax Program* with Fibber McGee and Molly. The makers of Johnson Wax and Johnson self-polishing Glo-Cote present *Fibber McGee and Molly*, written by Don Quinn, music by the Kingsmen and Billy Mills Orchestra.

CLOSING (Revised)

ANNOUNCER: This is Harlow Wilcox speaking for the makers of Johnson Wax products for home and industry inviting you to be with us again next Tuesday night. Good night. This program has reached you from Hollywood. This is the National Broadcasting Company.

485. 51 EAST 51ST. Variety, 30 min., CBS, 1941.

Entertainment acts set against the background of the mythical Manhattan Cafe, located at 51 East 51st Street in New York City.

Host: Kay Thompson. ***Regulars:*** Erik Rhodes, Everett Sloane, Lionel Stander. ***Orchestra:*** Archie Bleyer.

486. FINDERS KEEPERS. Game, 30 min., NBC, 1944–1945.

Members of the studio audience compete. A dramatic cast enacts a scene that contains an error. The first player to spot and correct the mistake wins the round and a cash prize.

Hosts: Bob Sherry, Happy Felton. ***Dramatic Cast:*** Lee Brady, Julie Conway, Arthur Elms, Florence Halop. ***Orchestra:*** Jerry Jerome, Irving Miller.

487. THE FIRE CHIEF. Comedy, 30 min., NBC, 1932–1935.

A pioneering comedy series that featured a live studio audience and the star in full costume and makeup (based on Texaco's Fire Chief brand of gasoline). The comedy was basically Ed Wynn's vaudeville-like antics as he kidded with his announcer.

Host: Ed Wynn. ***Announcer:*** Graham McNamee. ***Orchestra:*** Eddy Duchin, Mark Warnow, Donald Voorhees.

OPENING

ANNOUNCER (over sirens): For speed, power and action, Texaco Fire Chief, the gasoline that's bought by more tourists than any other brand. And, for a sweeter running engine, Texaco, the motor oil that lasts longer and saves you money. Texaco service stations and dealers in all our 48 states present for your entertainment Eddy Duchin and his music, Graham McNamee and Ed Wynn, *The Fire Chief.*

488. THE FIRST HUNDRED YEARS. Comedy, 30 min., ABC, 1949.

The trials and tribulations of a young married couple played by Sam Edwards and Barbara Eiler. Also in the cast were Bea Benaderet, Joseph Kearns, Myra Marsh and Earle Ross. Owen James was the announcer.

489. FIRST NIGHTER. Anthology, 30 min., NBC Blue, 1930–1933; NBC Red, 1933–1936; CBS, 1937–1942; Mutual, 1944; CBS, 1945–1949.

A series of three-act plays performed by a cast of regulars. The Host, Mr. First Nighter, sat fourth row center at the Little Theater off Times Square where the play was supposedly performed.

Hosts (Mr. First Nighter): Charles P. Hughes, Bret Morrison, Marvin Miller, Don Briggs, Ed Prentiss.

Regular Performers: Don Ameche, Rye Billsbury, Betty Lou Gerson, Bob Jellison, Barbara Luddy, June Meredith, Olan Soule, Les Tremayne. ***Announcers:*** Rye Billsbury, Larry Keating, Vincent Pelletier. ***Orchestra:*** Caesar Petrillo, Eric Sagerquist, Frank Worth.

OPENING (from 3/11/48)

ANNOUNCER: Campana's *First Nighter* program from the Little Theater Off Times Square. Starring Olan Soule and Barbara Luddy with an all-star cast sent to you by Campana, the quality name in cosmetics. Broadway, theater time, and this evening there is a special date on the theater calendar because a new play is scheduled for its opening night performance at the Little Theater Off Times Square. What's more, you have front row seats with the genial First Nighter himself as your host. And here he is.

FIRST NIGHTER: Good evening, everybody. They say it's going to be a prompt curtain tonight, so let's be off, shall we? Here's my cab, won't you step in. All right, driver, let's go.

SOUND: Traffic noises.

ANNOUNCER: Up Broadway, across 42nd Street and into the famous Times Square district. Theater and supper clubs cluster in this area like pins in a pin cushion.

FIRST NIGHTER: Well, here we are.

VOICE: Have your tickets ready. Have your tickets ready, please.

VOICE: Good evening, Mr. First Nighter. The usher will show you to your seat.

FIRST NIGHTER: Thank you, we'll go right in. Here we are inside the theater, ladies and gentlemen, and I wish I had the time to name all the notables in the audience tonight, but about the play. It's a farce called "There's Something in the Air," written by Anthony Wayne. And, according to reports from those in the know, it promises a half-hour of hilarious entertainment. Olan Soule and Barbara Luddy headline the all-star cast. I see Frank Worth and his First Night Orchestra in the pit, and it's just about time for first curtain.

VOICE: Curtain time, curtain time.

FIRST NIGHTER: There's the signal for first curtain. The house lights are out and here's the play.

CLOSING

ANNOUNCER: The curtain falls on the final act of another original play from the Little Theater Off Times Square. Next week, ladies and gentlemen, we want to issue a special invitation to you and your family to join us again when another brand new play entitled "The Green Leprechaun" will be presented in the Little Theater Off Times Square. It's a love story, the kind that tugs at your heart strings as it puts a smile on your lips. Your whole family will enjoy it. Be sure to join us next week, same time, same station. And ladies, you'll never know how pretty you can be until you try Magic Touch. Now we move out of the theater and into the street.

VOICE: Your cab, Mr. First Nighter.

FIRST NIGHTER (entering cab): Good night.
ANNOUNCER: This is CBS, the Columbia Broadcasting System.

490. THE FIRST PIANO QUARTET. Variety, 30 min., NBC, 1945–1951.

A weekly series that featured arrangements of popular songs, light classical music and jazz arranged especially for four pianos. Gene Hamilton was the announcer and the pianists were Edward Edson, Adam Garner, Hans Horwitz, Frank Mittler, Vee Padwa and George Robert. Edwin Fadiman produced.

491. FISH POND. Game, 30 min., ABC, 8/13/44 to 10/1/44.

Players chosen from the studio audience are designated as fish. Each fish performs a routine (for example, a monologue, a song) that is judged by the "fish pond" judges (the studio audience). If the judges approve the performance, the fish is reeled in and the player receives a prize; if the judges disapprove, the fish is thrown back (loses).

Host: Win Elliot. ***Regulars:*** John Keller, Leon Weber, Jack McCarthy, Dorian St. George. ***Announcer:*** Jack McCarthy.

492. THE FITCH BANDWAGON. Variety, 30 min., NBC, 1937–1948.

The program, sponsored by Fitch Shampoo, originally featured performances by the name bands of the day (hence the title). The first regular host was added in 1944 (Dick Powell); a year later, the series became comedy-oriented (music mixed with various skits) when Cass Daley became the host. Phil Harris and Alice Faye continued the comedy aspect when they became hosts the following year.

Hosts: Dick Powell, Cass Daley, Phil Harris and Alice Faye. ***Regulars:*** Andy Devine, Henry Russell, Dink Trout. ***Announcer:*** Larry Keating. ***Orchestra:*** Phil Harris, Walter Scharf. ***Producer:*** Ward Byron.

OPENING

SONG: Laugh awhile, let a song be your smile, use Fitch Shampoo. Don't despair, use your head, save your hair, use Fitch Shampoo.
ANNOUNCER: *The Fitch Bandwagon*, brought to you by the F.W. Fitch Company, makers of those fine Fitch products, with yours truly, Larry Keating, Henry Russell, Dink Trout and our special guest for today, Glen Gray and the Casa Loma Orchestra. And starring Cass Daley.

493. FIVE MINUTE MYSTERIES. Anthology, 5 min., Syndicated, 1946.

A series of brief mystery presentations that were used by stations to fill time between programs. Rosa Rio provided the organ music and the regular cast (who performed different roles) consisted of Jackson Beck, Staats Cotsworth, Michael Fitzmaurice, Timmy Hyler, Abby Lewis, Frank Lovejoy and Ian MacAllister.

494. FIVE STAR JONES. Serial, 15 min., CBS, 1935–1936; NBC, 1936–1937.

The dramatic story of Tom Jones, a top-notch newspaper reporter who is known as "Five Star Jones." Tom works for the *Register* and is married to Sally; stories portray his life at work and at home.

Cast: John Kane (*Tom Jones*); Elizabeth Day (*Sally Jones*); Bill Johnstone (*Editor*). ***Producers:*** Anne Hummert, Frank Hummert.

THE FIX-IT-SHOP *see* **MEL BLANC'S FIX-IT-SHOP**

FLASH GORDON *see* **THE AMAZING ADVENTURES OF FLASH GORDON** and **THE AMAZING INTERPLANETARY ADVENTURES OF FLASH GORDON**

495. THE FLEISCHMANN YEAST HOUR. Variety, 60 min., NBC, 1929–1939.

The program, sponsored by Fleischmann Yeast, featured performances by top name guests, dramatic sketches, songs and music. See also *The Rudy Vallee Show*.

Host: Rudy Vallee. ***Regulars:*** Olsen and Johnson (John "Ole" Olsen) and Harold "Chic" Johnson). ***Sponsor's Spokesman:*** Dr. R.E. Lee. ***Announcer:*** Graham McNamee. ***Orchestra:*** The Connecticut Yankees. ***Producer:*** Rudy Vallee.

496. THE FLYING PATROL. Adventure, 15 min., NBC, 1941–1942.

Dramatizations based on the exploits of the Coast Guard Air Corps. Hugh Rowlands played the Coast Guard Chief and Sharon Grainger was his girlfriend. Other Coast Guards were played by Sidney Ellstrom, Bob Guilbert and Cliff Soubier. Also in the cast (playing various roles) were Kay Campbell, Mary Frances Desmond, Willard Farnum, Pat Murphy and Norma Jean Ross.

FLYWHEEL, SHYSTER AND FLYWHEEL *see* **APPENDIX**

FOLLOW THE MOON *see* **APPENDIX**

497. THE FORD SHOW. Variety, 30 min., NBC, 1945.

A weekly program of music and songs sponsored by the Ford Motor Company. Lawrence Brooks was the host; the Robert Russell Bennett Chorus and Orchestra provided the vocals and music.

498. THE FORD SUMMER HOUR. Variety, 60 min., CBS, 6/39 to 9/39.

A summer series of music and songs sponsored by the Ford Motor Company. James Melton served as the host; Audrey Marsh, Francis White and the Dixie Eight were the regulars; Donald Voorhees and his orchestra provided the music.

499. THE FORD SUMMER HOUR. Variety, 60 min., CBS, 7/41 to 9/41.

A Ford Motor Company–sponsored program of music and songs with host Meredith Willson. Gordon Gifford, Bud Mitchell, Jane Pickens, Linton Wells and Paul Wing were the regulars; additional vocals and music were provided by the Ford Orchestra and Chorus.

500. THE FORD SUNDAY EVENING HOUR. Variety, 60 min., CBS, 1934–1941; ABC, 1945–1946.

A Sunday evening program of light classical music sponsored by the Ford Motor Company. John Charles Thomas and Lawrence Tibbett were the hosts; Sir Thomas Beecham and W.J. Cameron were the regulars; music was provided first by the Detroit Symphony Orchestra, then by Eugene Ormandy and his orchestra.

501. FORD THEATER. Anthology, 60 min., NBC, 1947–1948; CBS, 1948–1949.

A weekly series of dramatic and comedy productions featuring top name guests from radio and Hollywood. Sponsored by the Ford Motor Company. Nelson Case was the announcer; Cy Feuer provided the music; Fletcher Markle was the producer.

502. FOREIGN ASSIGNMENT. Adventure, 30 min., Mutual, 1943–1944.

A World War II series about the assignments of Barry Brian, a foreign correspondent stationed in France, and his assistant, Carol Manning.

Cast: Bartlett Robinson, Maurice Wells, Jay Jostyn (*Barry Brian*); Vicki Vola (*Carol Manning*). ***Announcer:*** Joseph Julian. ***Music:*** Henry Sylvern.

503. FOREVER ERNEST. Comedy, 30 min., CBS, 4/29/46 to 7/22/46.

Ernest Fudge is a clerk at Spencer's Pharmacy in a small upstate New York town. He is timid and shy and afraid of everything and everyone (although he contends "I'm not afraid of everyone... I don't *know* everyone"). Ernest will go out of his way to help others and his girlfriend, Candy Lane, believes people take advantage of him. Although she loves him, she wishes he would change his wimpish ways. Ernest's efforts to please Candy and become the man of her dreams is the focal point of stories. *Other regular characters:* Duke, Ernest's friend, the fast-talker who helps get Ernest into trouble.

Cast: Jackie Coogan (*Ernest Fudge*); Lurene Tuttle (*Candy Lane*); Arthur Q. Bryan (*Duke*). ***Announcer:*** Dick Joy. ***Music:*** Billy May.

OPENING

ANNOUNCER: Here it is, *Forever Ernest*, a new radio series starring Jackie Coogan, Lurene Tuttle and Arthur Q. Bryan. The place? Oh, that's as familiar as Niagara Falls, as American as apple pie *à la* mode. Sure, you know Spencer's Drug Store all right, but it's possible you don't know Ernest Fudge. Ernest, played by Jackie Coogan, is assistant clerk, pharmacist and soda jerk; in fact, assistant everything in the place. At the moment, he's the one who needs assistance. Candy Lane, the girl of his dreams is seated at the soda fountain...

504. FOREVER TOPS. Variety, 25 min., ABC, 1946.

A weekly program featuring the top tunes of

the day. Paul Whiteman and his orchestra provided the music and vocals were by the Eugene Baird Chorus.

505. Fort Laramie. Western, 30 min., CBS, 1/56 to 10/56.

Dramatic events in the lives of the cavalrymen stationed at Fort Laramie, Wyoming, during the late 1800s, as seen through the eyes of Lee Quince, the captain.

Cast: Raymond Burr (*Capt. Lee Quince*); Vic Perrin (*Sgt. Ken Goerss*); Jack Moyles (*Major Daggett*); Harry Bartell (*Lt. Seiberts*). ***Announcer:*** Dan Cubberly. ***Music:*** Amerigo Moreno. ***Producer:*** Norman MacDonnell.

OPENING

Announcer: *Fort Laramie*, starring Raymond Burr as Capt. Lee Quince, specially transcribed tales of the dark and tragic ground of the wild frontier. The saga of fighting men who rode the rim of empire and the dramatic story of Lee Quince, captain of cavalry.

Frank Buck's Adventures *see* **The Jungle Adventures of Frank Buck**

506. The Frank Fay Show. Variety, 30 min., NBC Blue, 1941–1942.

A weekly series of music and songs coupled with various comedy sketches hosted by vaudeville comic Frank Fay. The program, sponsored by Tums, featured Bob Hannon, the vocal group Beverly and Her Boyfriends, and the music of Harry Salter and his orchestra.

507. The Frank Fontaine Show. Variety, 30 min., CBS, 1952.

A weekly program of music, songs and comedy with singer-comedian Frank Fontaine. Mary Jane Croft (and guests) appeared with Frank in skits; Helen O'Connell provided vocals; Harry Von Zell did the announcing, and Lud Gluskin and his orchestra provided the music.

Frank Merriwell *see* **The Adventures of Frank Merriwell**

508. The Frank Morgan Show. Variety, 30 min., NBC, 1944–1945.

The program, sponsored by Maxwell House Coffee, featured comedian Frank Morgan in various comedy skits; vocals by Carlos Ramirez; the announcing of Harlow Wilcox; and the music of Albert Stack and his orchestra. Robert Young was the master of ceremonies and Cass Daley and Eric Blore were the regulars.

Frank Race *see* **The Adventures of Frank Race**

509. The Frank Sinatra Show. Variety, 30 min., CBS, 1944–1945.

A weekly songfest with singer-actor Frank Sinatra. Vocalist Eileen Barton appeared regularly and music was provided by Axel Stordahl and his orchestra. Marvin Miller was the announcer. For information on Frank's other variety series, see *Light Up Time*, *Songs by Sinatra*, *To Be Perfectly Frank* and *Your Hit Parade*.

Frank Watanabe and the Honorable Archie *see* **Appendix**

510. The Frankie Laine Show. Variety, 30 min., CBS, 1951.

A weekly program of music and songs with singer Frankie Laine. Stuart Metz did the announcing and Freddy Martin and his orchestra provided the music.

511. The Fred Allen Show. Variety, 60 and 30 min. versions, CBS, 1932–1933; NBC, 1933–1940; CBS, 1940–1944; NBC, 1945–1949.

A weekly series of monologues, songs, jokes and outlandish skits. The regular performers were referred to as "The Mighty Allen Art Players" and three of Fred's most famous segments were "Portland's Comedy Spot" (conduced by Fred's wife, Portland Hoffa), "Town Hall News of the Week" and "Allen's Alley." In the latter, Fred strolled down an alley to ask the question of the week to four residents: Titus Moody, a transplanted New Englander; Senator Beauregard Claghorn, a politician from the South; Mrs. Pansy Nussbaum, a Jewish Bronxite who was married to the never-heard Pierre; and Ajax Cassidy, the Irishman who lived at the end of the alley—on Third Avenue in Manhattan. Also titled: *The Linit Show* (1932–1933), *The Salad Bowl Revue* (1933, when

***The Fred Allen Show* featured (left to right) Fred Allen, Kenny Delmar, Minerva Pious, Peter Donald and Parker Fennelly.**

sponsored by Hellmann's Mayonnaise), *The Sal Hepatica Revue* (1934, when sponsored by Ipana and Sal Hepatica). The year 1934 also saw the show as *Hour of Smiles* and *Town Hall Tonight*. In 1939, it became *The Fred Allen Show*; in 1940, when Texaco became the sponsor, it was called *Texaco Star Theater*.

Cast: Fred Allen (*Host*); Parker Fennelly (*Titus Moody*); Kenny Delmar (*Senator Beauregard Claghorn*); Minerva Pious (*Mrs. Pansy Nussbaum*); Peter Donald (*Ajax Cassidy*); Alan Reed (*Falstaff Openshaw*); Jack Smart (*Senator Bloat*). ***Regulars:*** Portland Hoffa Allen, Kenny Baker, Shirley Booth, John Brown, Charlie Cantor, Eileen Douglas, Larry Elliott, Wynn Murray, Alan Reed, Jack Smith, Ned Sparks, Walter Tetley. ***Vocalists:*** The Al Goodman Chorus, the John Brown Chorus, Ann, Lily and Mary DeMarco (The DeMarco Sisters), Hi, Lo, Jack and a Dame, the Hugh Martin Singers), the Merry Macs, the Town Hall Quartet. ***Announcers:*** Kenny Delmar, Arthur Godfrey, Harry Von Zell, Jimmy Wallington. ***Orchestra:*** Al Goodman, Lennie Hayton, Lou Katzman, Peter Van Steeden.

OPENING ("Town Hall Tonight")

ANNOUNCER: An hour of smiles, it's *Town Hall Tonight*, 60 minutes of fun and music brought to you by Ipana toothpaste; Ipana, for the smile of beauty. Fun with our star comedian, Fred Allen, music with Peter Van Steeden, new features, new laughs, it's *Town Hall Tonight.*

CLOSING

ANNOUNCER: We hope, ladies and gentlemen, that tonight's program has brought you all another hour of smiles and that you'll remember to be with us again next Wednesday. In the meantime, we hope you'll remember the product that makes this Fred Allen show possible, Ipana toothpaste for the smile of beauty.

FRED: Good night, ladies and gentlemen, and don't forget next Wednesday night for another hour of smiles in the old town hall.

This is Fred Allen saying good night.

ANNOUNCER: This is the Red Network of the National Broadcasting Company.

OPENING ("Texaco Star Theater")

ANNOUNCER: It's Texaco Time with Fred Allen, Portland Hoffa and Al Goodman and his orchestra. This is Arthur Godfrey saying you're welcome for Texaco dealers from coast to coast. Welcome to the *Texaco Star Theater* and the Texaco dealers whole-hearted help in keeping that car of yours going for the transportation you've got to have. And now, ladies and gentlemen, there's only one comedian in radio you can tune in to during a blackout who isn't bright enough to violate the law, and here he is, Fred Allen in person.

FRED: Thank you and good evening, ladies and gentlemen...

CLOSING

FRED: Next Sunday night, ladies and gentlemen, our guest will be Orson Welles. And now, Arthur, have you anything to add?

ARTHUR GODFREY: Just a scrap, Fred. The scrap pile in every city mounts higher and higher, but more is needed. You see, practically everything we need to win this war is made from scrap metal. Tanks, planes, aircraft carriers, everything. So, throw your scrap into the fight.

FRED: And thank you Arthur. This is Fred Allen speaking for Texaco dealers from coast to coast reminding you to drive under 35 miles per hour to save rubber and to drive into your Texaco dealer regularly to have your tires checked. Remember, you're welcome. Good night.

ANNOUNCER: This is the Columbia Broadcasting System.

OPENING ("The Fred Allen Show")

CHORUS: Mr. Allen, Mr. Allen.

ANNOUNCER: The makers of Blue Bonnet Margarine and Tender Leaf Tea present *The Fred Allen Show* with Fred's guest, Orson Welles. With Portland Hoffa, Minerva Pious as Mrs. Nussbaum, Alan Reed as Falstaff Openshaw, Parker Fennelly as Titus Moody. With the DeMarco Sisters and Al Goodman and his orchestra. And, until I show up as Senator Claghorn, my name is Kenny Delmar. And here he is, Fred Allen.

512. THE FRED ASTAIRE SHOW. Variety, 60 min., NBC, 9/8/36 to 8/31/37.

Dancer Fred Astaire as the host of a weekly program of music and songs. Jimmy Blair, Francia White and Trudy Wood provided the vocals; Charlie Butterworth supplied the light comic relief. Music was by Johnny Green and his orchestra. Jack Benny and Mary Livingston hosted the premiere episode due to Fred's engagement in Europe at the time. Astaire actually danced on a specially constructed four-foot square floor lined with microphones. The effect could have been faked with drum sticks, but Fred insisted that he dance because listeners tuned in to hear him dance. Also known as *The Packard Show*.

513. THE FRED BRADY SHOW. Variety, 30 min., NBC, 1943.

Music, songs and comedy with Fred Brady as the host. Joe DiRita, Charlie Kimper, Lou Lubin, Shirley Mitchell and Martha Tilton were the regulars; and Gordon Jenkins and his orchestra provided the music.

514. THE FRED KEATING SHOW. Variety, 30 min., Syndicated, 1940.

A weekly program of music, songs and light comedy with host Fred Keating and regulars George Jay, Peter Lind Hayes, Murray Marcellino, Sally Rand, Bobby Sherwood and Martha Tilton. Gary Breckner did the announcing and music was provided by Leon Leonardi and his orchestra.

515. THE FRED WARING SHOW. Variety, 15 and 30 min. versions, NBC, 1939–1950.

A program of music, songs and light comedy hosted by Fred Waring, leader of the Pennsylvanians Orchestra. The series is also known as *Chesterfield Time* (when sponsored by Chesterfield cigarettes) and *Victory Tunes* (during World War II when songs selected by servicemen were presented).

Host: Fred Waring. ***Regulars:*** Gordon Berger, Stuart Churchill, Ruth Cottingham, Donna Dae, Patsy Garrett, Livingston Gearheart, Gordon Goodman, Murray Kane, Hal Kanner, Lumpy Brannum, Poley McClintock, Virginia Morley, Les Paul, Lydia Perrone, Mac Perrone, Robert Shaw, Kay Thompson, Tom Waring, Joanne Wheatley, Jane Willson. ***Vocal Groups:*** Babs and Her Brothers, the Fred Waring Glee Club, Honey and the Bees, the McFarland Twins, Stella and the Fellas, the Three Girl Friends, the Twin Trio. ***Announcer:*** Bob

Fred Waring is surrounded by (left to right) Patsy Garrett, Jane Wilson, Honey Perron and Donna Dae on *The Fred Waring Show*.

Considine, Paul Douglas, Davis Ross. ***Orchestra:*** The Pennsylvanians.

516. THE FREDDY MARTIN SHOW. Variety, 30 min., CBS, 1954.

Dance band leader and saxophonist Freddy Martin as the host of a weekly series of music and songs with Johnny Corcoran, Bill Curtis and the Martin Men. Freddy Martin's orchestra provided the music.

517. THE FREE COMPANY. Anthology, 30 min., CBS, 1941–1942.

Dramatizations based on American ideals that featured top name actors (for example, John Garfield, Nancy Kelly, Agnes Moorehead,

Franchot Tone) and writers (for example, Maxwell Anderson, Stephen Vincent Benet, Ernest Hemingway, William Saroyan). Novelist James Boyd developed the program to combat World War II propaganda and show that our basic liberties were superior to the rest of the world. Actors and writers were not paid (they donated their time and talent); there were no commercials and the programs were uncontrolled (leaving some productions up for controversy as they were called un–American). Burgess Meredith was the host.

518. Free for All. Variety, 30 min., Mutual, 1943.

A weekly program of music, songs and comedy skits with Bill Grey, Betty Randall and Bob Stanley. Steve Shultz and His Katzenjammers provided the music.

519. The Fresh Up Show. Variety, 30 min., Mutual, 1945.

The program, sponsored by 7-Up soft drinks, featured music, songs and comedy sketches. Barry Grant served as the host. The regulars were Jim Backus, Lee Brady, Artie Elmer, Hildegarde Holliday, Walter Kinsella (as the Irish Policeman) and Annette Warren. Jerry Lawrence was the announcer and the music and choral backing was provided by the David Terry Orchestra and Chorus. Revised shortly after the premiere as the following title.

520. The Fresh Up Show. Comedy, 30 min., Mutual, 1945–1946.

Bert Wheeler is a clerk for Doc Fickett, the owner of Fickett's Drug Store in the town of Sunnydale. Bert is a timid soul who manages to become involved in everyone's problems while trying to solve his own—avoiding Doc's efforts to marry him off to his daughter, Viola, a girl who sees Bert as the man of her dreams. *Other regular characters:* Melville Fickett, Doc's British nephew; and Mr. Fuddle, Bert's henpecked friend.

Cast: Bert Wheeler (*Bert Wheeler*); Walter Kinsella (*Doc Fickett*); Annette Warren (*Viola Fickett*); Lee Brady (*Melville Fickett*); Artie Elmer (*Mr. Fuddle*). ***Vocalist:*** Ruth Davey. ***Announcer:*** Jerry Lawrence. ***Music:*** Dave Terry and the Fresh Up Orchestra and Chorus.

OPENING

ANNOUNCER: Fresh up with 7-Up, you like it, it likes you. The makers and distributors of 7-Up, America's fresh up drink, bring you *The Fresh Up Show* starring Bert Wheeler. Doc Fickett's Drug Store in Sunnydale is just like thousands of other drug stores throughout the United States. And the only reason you can't get service is because of the clerk who works there, Bert Wheeler…

521. Friendship Ranch. Variety, 30 min., NBC, 1944.

The bunkhouse on the Friendship Ranch was the setting for a children's series of country and western skits, songs and music. The regulars were Billy Daniels, Nancy Gonzales, Marilyn Gusten, Margie Hammer, Don Parker, Ronald Smith, Jack Vincent and the Warner Singers. Tex Antoine did the announcing

522. Front Page Farrell. Serial, 15 min., Mutual, 1941–1942; NBC, 1942–1954.

David Farrell is a top-notch reporter for the *Daily Eagle*, a crusading New York newspaper. He is married to Sally and has an impressive reporting record that has earned him the nickname "Front Page" Farrell. Stories follow David as he (assisted often by Sally) investigates crimes for stories.

Cast: Richard Widmark, Staats Cotsworth, Carleton Young (*David Farrell*); Florence Williams, Virginia Dwyer, Betty Garde (*Sally Farrell*); Ethel Intropide, Evelyn Varden (*Mrs. Howard; Sally's mother*); Robert Donley (*Police Lt. Carpenter*). ***Announcers:*** Bill Bond, James Fleming. ***Organists:*** Ann Leax, Rosa Rio. ***Producers:*** Anne Hummert, Frank Hummert.

OPENING

ANNOUNCER: We now present the exciting, unforgettable radio drama *Front Page Farrell*, the story of a crack newspaperman and his wife. The story of David and Sally Farrell. Today David is covering the story which he calls "The Blinding Light Murder Case."

523. Frontier Gentleman. Western, 30 min., CBS, 2/2/58 to 11/16/58.

When the editor of the *London Times* decides to do a series of reports about life on the American frontier of the 1880s, he assigns the task to reporter Jeremy Bryan (J.B.) Kendall, a former captain in the British Army in India. Stories follow Kendall as he writes his colorful and unusual accounts of the West—often becoming involved in the violence of the territory. (Kendall wears a shoulder holster and carries a knife in his boot. He receives $25 a month expenses and spent 98 days on a boat traveling from England to America; the ticket cost $300.)

Cast: John Dehner (Jeremy Bryan [J.B.] Kendall). ***Announcer:*** Johnny Jacobs. ***Music Conductor:*** Wilbur Hatch. ***Music Composer:*** Jerry Goldsmith. ***Producer:*** Tony Ellis.

OPENING

ANNOUNCER: *Frontier Gentleman.* Here with an Englishman's account of life and death in the West. As a reporter for the *London Times*, he writes his colorful and unusual stories; but as a man with a gun he lives and becomes part of the violent years in the new territories. Now, starring John Dehner, this is the story of Jeremy B. Kendall, *Frontier Gentleman.*

CLOSING

ANNOUNCER: Join us next week for another report from the *Frontier Gentleman.* This is the CBS Radio Network.

524. Frontier Town. Western, 30 min., Syndicated, 1952–1953.

Dos Rias is a ruthless frontier town of a century ago. Chad Remington is a lawyer who, together with his hard-drinking Irish companion Cherokee O'Bannon, risks his life to help clients.

Cast: Jeff Chandler, Reed Hadley (*Chad Remington*); Wayne Crosby (*Cherokee O'Bannon*). ***Announcer:*** Bill Forman. ***Music:*** Ivan Ditmars.

Fu Manchu *see* **The Shadow of Fu Manchu**

525. Fun for All. Variety, 30 min., CBS, 1952–1953.

A weekly program of music, comedy and game contests that involved members of the studio audience who received prizes for participating. Bill Cullen and Arlene Francis were the hosts; Bert Berman and Abe Goldman provided the organ music. Bill Cullen doubled as the announcer.

526. Fun in Print. Game, 30 min., CBS, 1940.

Players, chosen from the studio audience, comprised the amateur team that was pitted against a team of professional writers. Several question-and-answer rounds were played with the team scoring the most correct answers being declared the winners. Sigmund Spaeth was the host.

527. The Galen Drake Show. Variety, 60 min., CBS, 1954.

The program, aimed primarily at housewives, features informal chatter on everyday matters with host Galen Drake. The series also featured vocals by Stuart Foster, Betty Johnson and the Three Beaus and a Peep and the music of Bernard Leighton and his orchestra. Olin Trice did the announcing.

528. Game Parade. Game, 30 min., NBC Blue, 1943.

Five children are involved in a series of question-and-answer rounds wherein correct responses award the player a small cash prize. Arthur Elmer was the host and questioner; Renee Terry assisted him.

529. Gangbusters. Crime Drama, 30 min., NBC Blue, 1935; CBS, 1936–1940; NBC Blue, 1942–1944; ABC, 1944–1948; CBS, 1949–1954; Mutual, 1955–1957.

Dramatizations based on cases closed by the FBI. Following the rather loud opening theme (which gave rise to the expression "coming on like gangbusters"), a guest law enforcement official involved in the actual case appeared with the narrator to tell the story (which was heard using the flashback technique). At the end of each broadcast, a detailed description of a wanted criminal was broadcast. Hundreds of wanted men were apprehended as a result of these bulletins.

Host-Announcers: Charles Stark, Frank Gallop, Don Gardiner, Roger Foster, Les Griffith, H. Gilbert Martin. ***Narrators:*** Phillips H. Lord, John C. Hilley, Dean Carlton, Col. Norman Schwarzkopf, Lewis J. Valentine. ***Producer:*** Phillips H. Lord.

OPENING

ANNOUNCER: Now, *Gangbusters*, presented in cooperation with police and federal law enforcement departments throughout the United States. The only national program that brings you authentic police case histories.

SOUND: Marching feet, machine gun fire, police whistles.
ANNOUNCER: Sloan's Liniment presents *Gangbusters*. At war, marching against the underworld, from coast to coast, *Gangbusters*. Police, the G-Men, our government agents marching toward the underworld. Tonight *Gangbusters* presents "The Case of the Quincy Killers." What is known is that a railroad ticket in the hands of alert detectives could be a one-way ticket to the gallows. *Gangbusters* has asked the honorable Peter F. Hartman, former police chief, Quincy, Illinois, to narrate, by proxy, tonight's case. [He would then be introduced and the story would begin.]

CLOSING

ANNOUNCER (after case is summed up): And *Gangbusters'* congratulations to all the police officers whose brilliant investigation brought this crime to justice. [Over sirens and gun shots:] Tonight's case was dramatized by Stanley Niss and directed by Ted Corday with Bill Smith and Bill Zuckert in the leading roles. Don Gardiner speaking. *Gangbusters* is a Phillips H. Lord production.

THE GARRY MOORE–JIMMY DURANTE SHOW *see* **THE JIMMY DURANTE–GARRY MOORE SHOW**

530. THE GARRY MOORE SHOW. Variety, 60 min., CBS, 1949–1950.

An afternoon program of music, songs and comedy with host Garry Moore. Eileen Woods and Ken Carson provided the songs. Durward Kirby and Howard Petrie did the announcing; Irving Miller and his orchestra provided the music.

531. THE GARY CROSBY SHOW. Variety, 30 min., CBS, 1954–1955.

A program of music and songs with Gary Crosby (Bing Crosby's eldest son) and the music of Buddy Bergen and his orchestra. A guest assisted Gary on each broadcast.

532. GASLIGHT GAIETIES. Variety, 30 min., NBC, 1944.

A weekly program of music from the 1890s with singer Michael O'Shea as the host. Beatrice Kay and Sally Sweetland provided additional vocals; Charles "Bud" Dant and his orchestra supplied the music.

533. GASOLINE ALLEY. Drama, 15 min., NBC, 2/17/41 to 5/9/41.

A daily serial, based on the comic strip by Frank King, about Skeezix Wallet, a mechanic and part owner of the Wallet and Wumple Garage. *Other regular characters:* Nina Clock, Skeezix's girlfriend; Auntie Blossom; Ling Wee, the Chinese waiter.

Cast: Jimmy McCallion, Bill Idelson, Bill Lipton (*Skeezix Wallet*); Janice Gilbert, Jean Gillespie (*Nina Clock*); Cliff Soubier (*Wumple*); Irna Phillips (*Auntie Blossom*); Junius Matthews (*Ling Wee*).

OPENING

ANNOUNCER: Time to meet your friends at *Gasoline Alley*.
SOUND: Car being tuned up; phone ringing.
SKEEZIX: Hold it, Boomer, hold it till I get this phone. [Picks up phone] Wallet and Wumple Garage, Skeezix Wallet speaking. Oh, what's that? Yes, sir, we can fix it, we can fix anything on four wheels. Sure, we'll be waiting for you right here in Gasoline Alley.
ANNOUNCER: Yes, it's *Gasoline Alley*, the comic strip that's a favorite in a hundred great newspapers from coast to coast. In this episode, "The Adventure of the Hypnotized Hero," the boys get mixed up in quite a mish-mash of mesmerism, but right now a word from the friendly auto dealer in your town. [Commercial airs] And now, *Gasoline Alley*.

534. GATEWAY TO HOLLYWOOD. Drama, 30 min., CBS, 1938–1939.

Two undiscovered actors perform a playlet with an established celebrity. Thirteen such couples competed over a 13-week period and the couple whose performance was judged the best received a contract with RKO Radio Pictures.

Host: Jesse L. Lasky. ***Announcer:*** Ken Niles. ***Music:*** Wilbur Hatch.

535. THE GAY MRS. FEATHERSTONE. Comedy, 30 min., NBC, 4/18/45 to 10/10/45.

Mrs. Dora Featherstone is a well-meaning mother-in-law who lives with her daughter and son-in-law. She feels the need to remedy domestic problems, but finds her intentions backfiring and situations worsening. Her attempts to undo the damage comprised the heart of the series.

Cast: Billie Burke (*Mrs. Dora Featherstone*); Florence Lake (*Her daughter*); John Brown (*Her son-in-law*). ***Announcer:*** Marvin Miller. ***Orchestra:*** Eddy Howard.

536. Gay Nineties Revue. Variety, 60 min., CBS, 1939–1944.

Music, songs and comedy skits set against the background of the Granada, an 1890s-style nightclub in New York City.

Cast: Jack Norworth, Joe Howard (*Host/Club Proprietor*); Frank Lovejoy (*Broadway Harry*); Jack Arthur (*Danny Donovan*). ***Regulars:*** Don Costello, Billy Greene, Beatrice Kay, Ed Latimer, Lillian Leonard, Genevieve Rowe, the Club Men, the Elm City Four, the Floradora Girls. ***Announcer:*** John Reed King. ***Orchestra:*** Ray Bloch.

537. G.E. Circle. Variety, 15 min., NBC, 1931–1932.

A daytime program of household advice coupled with cooking tips, news, etiquette, music and songs. Also known as *The G.E. Home Circle*.

Host: Grace Ellis. ***Regulars:*** Bruce Barton, Heywood Broun, John Erskine, Emily Post, Jane Prestiss. ***Vocalist:*** Theodore Webb. ***Announcer:*** Ted Jewett. ***Organist:*** Eddie Dunbarn.

538. Gene and Glenn with Jake and Lena. Variety, 15 min., NBC, 1930–1932; 1939–1941.

Music, songs and comedy with Gene Carroll and Glenn Rowell, a comedy duo who also played music. The comedy segment was set at a boarding house (run by Lena) where Gene and Glenn lived. In addition to playing himself, Gene Carroll also did the voices of Lena and Jake (the handyman at the boarding house).

539. Gene Autry's Melody Ranch. Variety, 15 and 30 min. versions, CBS, 1940–1956.

Music, songs and playlets set against the background of the Melody Ranch (which was briefly called the Double M Ranch when sponsored by Doublemint Gum) in California. The playlet was a short western adventure that related the exploits of Gene Autry (a cowboy law enforcer) and his bumbling sidekick, Pat Buttram.

Host: Gene Autry. ***Regulars:*** Jim Boles, Pat Buttram, Scotty Harrel, Frank Mahoney, Nancy Mason, Tyler McVey, Alvino Rey. ***Vocal Groups:*** The Blue Jeans, the Cass Country Boys, the Johnny Bond Trio, the King Sisters, the Pinafors. ***Announcers:*** Lou Crosby, Charles Lyon. ***Orchestra:*** Carl Cotner, Paul Sills.

OPENING

ANNOUNCER: Howdy, folks, and welcome to *Melody Ranch* with Gene Autry.

GENE (singing): I'm back in the saddle again, out where a friend is a friend [applause begins].

ANNOUNCER: Yes, transcribed, your friendly local merchants who sell and display healthful, refreshing and delicious Doublemint chewing gum invite you to meet all the folks here at Melody Ranch.

540. The General Electric Theater. Anthology, 30 min., CBS, 7/9/53 to 10/1/53.

Dramatic presentations sponsored by General Electric and also known as *G.E. Stereo Theater* (it was the first network radio series to be broadcast on FM in stereo). A cast of regulars performed the various stories.

Cast: Joseph Cotten, Helen Hayes, Dina Merrill, Agnes Moorehead, Cyril Ritchard, Peter Ustinov. ***Announcer:*** Ken Carpenter. ***Music:*** Wilbur Hatch.

General Motors Concerts *see* **Appendix**

541. Gentleman Adventurer. Adventure, 30 min., Mutual, 4/17/48 to 8/28/48.

Drake and Company is an ages-old Philadelphia-based company specializing in marine and ocean insurance. Alan Drake, the nephew of the owner (Uncle Dan Drake), is a troubleshooter who travels around the world to investigate claims filed against the company. He is assisted by Steve Lawlor, an impatient investigator who attracts women as easily as he does trouble. They travel to the four corners of the globe investigating claims and often become involved in the personal problems of their clients. Also known as *Special Agent*.

Cast: James Meighan (*Alan Drake*); John

Larkin, Lyle Sudrow (*Steve Lawlor*). ***Announcer:*** Don Fredericks. ***Music:*** Morris Mamorsky, Chet Kingsbury. ***Producer:*** Herb Rice.

OPENING

ANNOUNCER: Mutual presents *Gentleman Adventurer* starring James Meighan as Alan Drake. The man called Alan Drake is the last of his name. He earns his living in a remarkable way. He's a troubleshooter, an investigator for the ancient company, Drake and Company, insurers of shipping who protect all comers against piracy on the high seas or robbery on the open road anywhere in the world. Tonight's adventure, "The Bandit and the Blonde."

CLOSING

ANNOUNCER: You have heard a complete episode of *Gentleman Adventurer*, the life of Alan Drake, starring James Meighan in the title role. Featured was John Larkin as Steve Lawlor. The entire program is under the direction of Herbert Rice. Don Frederick speaking. This is the Mutual Broadcasting System.

542. THE GEORGE BURNS AND GRACIE ALLEN SHOW. Comedy, 30 min., NBC, 9/20/45 to 5/17/50.

The house at 316 North Campden Drive in Beverly Hills, California, provided the basic setting for a weekly visit with George Burns, a "straight man" who was married to comedienne Gracie Allen, a dimwitted woman who could complicate any situation (George's efforts to undo the problems Gracie caused was the series' actual focal point). This version of George and Gracie's long radio career was the basis for their 1950–58 television series of the same title. The program was sponsored by Maxwell House Coffee and was originally titled *Maxwell House Coffee Time* (1945–49), then *The Amident Toothpaste Show* (1949–50). For information on the other Burns and Allen radio shows, see the following titles: *The Adventures of Gracie* (1934–35); *Campbell's Tomato Juice Program* (1935–37); *The Chesterfield Program* (1937–38); *The Hinds Honey and Almond Cream Program* (1939–40); *The Hormel Program* (1940–41); *The Robert Burns Panatela Program* (1932–33); *The Swan Soap Show* (1941–45); and *The White Owl Program* (1933–34). *Other regular characters:* Blanche and Harry Morton, George's neighbors; Clara, Muriel and Tootsie, Gracie's friends; the Happy Postman (who was not so happy after a confrontation with Gracie; his never-heard wife was Bertha). George's phone number was given as Gladstone 1131 and much comedy stemmed from George's conversations with Gracie about her less-than-intelligent family.

Cast: George Burns (*George Burns*); Gracie Allen (*Gracie Allen*); Bea Benaderet (*Blanche Morton*); Gale Gordon, Hal March (*Harry Morton*); Mel Blanc (*The Happy Postman*); Elvia Allman (*Tootsie Stagwell*); Margaret Brayton (*Clara Bagley*); Sara Berner (*Muriel*). ***Regulars:*** Jim Backus, Dawn Bender, Tommy Bernard, Hans Conried, Lois Corbett, Richard Crenna, Barbara Eiler, Verna Felton, Bill Goodwin, Sandra Gould, Bob Jellison, Joseph Kearns, Sheldon Leonard, Cathy Lewis, Elliott Lewis, Wally Maher, Lou Merrill, Marvin Miller, Frank Nelson, Isabel Randolph, Mary Lee Robb, Dick Ryan, Doris Singleton, Eric Snowden, Irene Tedrow, Lurene Tuttle, Veola Vonn, Ernie Whitman, Paula Winslow, Ann Whitfield. ***Announcers:*** Bill Goodwin, Toby Reed. ***Vocalists:*** The Les Paul Trio. ***Music:*** The Maxwell House Orchestra (conducted by Harry Lubin, Meredith Willson).

OPENING

GRACIE: Another cup of Maxwell House Coffee, George?

GEORGE: Sure, pour me another cup, Gracie.

GRACIE: You know, Maxwell House is always good to the last drop.

GEORGE: And that drop's good, too.

ANNOUNCER: Yes, it's *Maxwell House Coffee Time* starring George Burns and Gracie Allen. With our special guest for tonight, Richard Widmark, yours truly, Toby Reed, Bea Benaderet, Harry Lubin and the Maxwell House Orchestra and Bill Goodwin. For America's Thursday night comedy enjoyment, it's George and Gracie. And for America's everyday coffee drinking enjoyment, it's Maxwell House, always good to the last drop.

CLOSING

ANNOUNCER: Join us against next Thursday when we'll all be back. George Burns, Gracie Allen, Bill Goodwin, Harry Lubin and the Maxwell House Orchestra, and yours truly, Toby Reed. And now, here are our stars:

GEORGE: Good night, everyone.

GRACIE: Until next Thursday, good night.

ANNOUNCER: Until next Thursday when Jane Wyman will be our guest, good night and

George Burns and Gracie Allen starred in *The George Burns and Gracie Allen Show* from 1945 to 1950.

good luck from the makers of Maxwell House, America's favorite brand of coffee, always good to the last drop. This is NBC, the National Broadcasting Company.

543. George Jessel Salutes. Variety, 30 min., ABC, 1953–1954.

A weekly program paying tribute to servicemen's clubs with host George Jessel, a former vaudeville comic and brilliant after-dinner speaker known as the Toastmaster General of the United States. Tony Bovaar, Shirley Haimer and John Steele handled the songs; Paul Whiteman and his orchestra provided the music. See also *Thirty Minutes in Hollywood*.

544. The George O'Hanlon Show. Comedy, 30 min., Mutual, 1948.

The story of a not-too-bright husband (George O'Hanlon), his patient and understanding wife (Lurene Tuttle), his chiseling best friend (Cliff Young) and his overbearing boss (Alan Reed). Harry Zimmerman and his orchestra provided the music.

545. Get Rich Quick. Game, 30 min., ABC, 1948.

A dramatic skit is performed on stage. A telephone call is then placed by the host to a listener (chosen by postcard selection). If the listener identified the person, place or thing represented by the skit, he or she won $25.

Host: Johnny Olsen. ***Announcer:*** Jimmy Blaine. ***Music:*** Ivan Ditmars.

546. Gibbs and Finney, General Delivery. Comedy, 30 min., NBC Blue, 1942.

Gideon Gibbs and Asa Finney are friends who open a livery stable in a small New England town during the gas and rubber shortage of World War II. Stories follow their mishaps as they struggle to make their new venture work.

Cast: Parker Fennelly (*Gideon Gibbs*); Arthur Allen (*Asa Finney*); Ethel Owen (*The Widow*); Roy Fant (*The Printer*). ***Vocalists:*** Paul Parks, Walter Scanlon.

547. The Gibson Family. Comedy, 60 min., NBC, 1934–1935.

Original music compositions were coupled with a serialized look at daily events in the lives of the Gibsons, a not-so-typical American family: parents Dot and Bob; their daughter, Sally; Bob's wealthy parents (Mother and Father); and Awful, the butler.

Cast: Loretta Clemens (*Dot Gibson*); Jack Clemens, Al Dary (*Bob Gibson*); Adele Ronson (*Sally Gibson*); Bill Adams (*Father*); Anne Elstner (*Mother*); Ernest Whitman (*Awful*). ***Vocalists:*** Lois Bennett, Conrad Thibault. ***Announcer:*** Jimmy Wallington. ***Orchestra:*** Donald Voorhees.

548. The Ginny Simms Show. Variety, 30 min., CBS, 1945–1947.

A weekly program of music and songs with vocalist Ginny Simms as the host. Don Wilson did the announcing and Frank DeVol and his orchestra provided the music. The program, sponsored by Borden Milk, featured guest vocalists assisting Ginny.

549. Ginny Simms Song Book. Variety, 15 min., ABC, 1950–1951.

A shortened version of the above title that featured songs by vocalist Ginny Simms. Frank Graham did the announcing and the Buddy Cole Trio supplied the music.

550. Girl Alone. Serial, 15 min., NBC, 1936–1941.

Dramatic events in the life of Patricia Rogers, a society woman seeking to find someone who will love her for herself, not her wealth.

Cast: Betty Winkler (*Patricia Rogers*); Joan Winters (*Alice Warner*); Don Briggs, Pat Murphy, Arthur Jacobson (*Scoop Curtis*); June Travis (*Stormy Curtis*); Henry Hunter (*Scott*); Laurette Fillbrandt (*Virginia*); Les Damon, Karl Weber, Syd Simons (*John Knight*); Betty Lou Gerson (*Helen Adams*); Jane Logan (*Stella Moore*); Willard Waterman, Ted Maxwell (*Leo Warner*); Kathryn Card (*Kate*); Herbert Nelson (*Dick Conover*); Hope Summers (*Clara*); Bob Jellison (*Lewis*); Fran Carlon (*Ruth Gardner*); Betty Caine (*Tess Monroe*). ***Announcer:*** Charles Lyon.

551. Girl from Paris. Variety, 15 min., NBC, 1951.

A weekly program of music and songs with vocalist Jane Morgan and the music of Andrew Ackers and his orchestra. The title was derived from Jane's trip to Paris at the time.

552. Give and Take. Game, 30 min., CBS, 1945–1953.

A contestant, chosen from the studio audience, selected a gift from an on-stage prize table. A series of question-and-answer rounds followed that awarded the player the prize if he successfully answered all the questions.

Host: John Reed King. ***Announcer:*** Jim Brown.

553. Glamour Manor. Variety, 30 min., ABC, 1944–1947.

A daytime program of music, songs and comedy set at the Glamour Manor Hotel (where anything could happen and usually did).

Host: Kenny Baker (as the hotel manager). ***Regulars:*** Cliff Arquette, Jack Bailey, Bea Benaderet, Barbara Eiler, John McIntire, Tyler McVey, "Smilin' Jack" Smith, Hal Stevens, Lurene Tuttle, Don Wilson. ***Announcers:*** Rod O'Connor, Terry O'Sullivan. ***Orchestra:*** Charles Hale, Harry Lubin.

Cast members perform on the daytime variety program *Glamour Manor*.

554. The Glenn Miller Show. Variety, 30 min., CBS, 1939–1942.

A program of big band music and songs with orchestra leader Glenn Miller as the host. Tex Beneke, Ray Eberle, Marian Hutton and Paula Kelly and the Modernaires were the regulars. The Glenn Miller Orchestra provided the music.

555. The Gloom Chasers. Variety, 30 min., Mutual, 1939.

A weekly program of songs and comedy skits designed to make the audience happy. Allen Courtney was the host; Red Dave and Eleanor Sherry, the regulars; and music was furnished by the Lea Freaudberg Orchestra. An earlier, 15-minute version appeared on NBC in 1931 featuring the antics of Col. Lemuel Q. Stoopnagle (Frederick Chase Taylor) and his friend Budd (Budd Hulick).

556. Gloria Carroll Entertains. Variety, 15 min., Syndicated, 1947.

Music and songs with host/vocalist Gloria Carroll and the Three Embers.

557. Go for the House. Game, 30 min., ABC, 1948–1949.

Seven couples compete in a series of seven question-and-answer rounds. At the end of each round, the lowest scoring couple is disqualified; the remaining couples each receive household furnishings and the option to either quit with what they have already won or continue and risk the loss of everything on the next round. If players correctly answered the questions in all seven categories, they won a small cottage. Players who continued but failed to reach the last level of competition lost their household furnishings but received a consolation prize.

Host: John Reed King. ***Announcer:*** Doug Browning. ***Organist:*** George Benninger.

558. The Gold and Silver Minstrels. Variety, 30 min., Mutual, 1946.

Cast of *The Goldbergs* included (left to right) James Waters, Roslyn Siber, Gertrude Berg and Alfred Ryder.

A weekly program of music and songs featuring a cast of regular performers and performances by guest artists.

Host: Roland Winters. ***Regulars:*** Jimmy Carroll, Betty Mulliner, "Happy" Jim Parsons, the Gold and Silver Quartet and Trio. ***Announcer:*** Ted Brown. ***Orchestra:*** Ray Bloch.

559. The Goldbergs. Comedy-Drama, 15 and 30 min. versions, NBC Blue, 1929–1931; NBC Red, 1931–1934; Mutual, 1936; CBS, 1938–1950.

The apartment house at 1038 East Tremont Avenue in the Bronx, New York, is home to several Jewish families, including Molly Goldberg, her husband Jake and their children Rosalie and Sammy. Molly is the typical, caring mother and all-around problem solver; stories, which are somewhat serial-like in presentation, relate true-to-life events in the lives of the Goldbergs. The program was originally titled *The Rise of the Goldbergs* and ran for 30 minutes in 1949 and 1950. Although *The Goldbergs* became a television series (1949–56), a little-known test film was produced for NBC in 1948; called "Whistle, Daughter, Whistle," it served as the pilot for the video version. Here, Molly (Gertrude Berg) and her neighbor Mrs. Bloom (Minerva Pious) attempt to arrange a marriage between Molly's daughter Rosalie (Lenore Conegran) and Mrs. Bloom's son Mickey (John Harvey).

Cast: Gertrude Berg (*Molly Goldberg*); James R. Waters (*Jake Goldberg*); Roslyn Siber (*Rosalie Goldberg*); Alfred Ryder, Everett Sloane (*Sammy Goldberg*); Menasha Skulnik, Eli Mintz (*Uncle David*); Minerva Pious (*Mrs. Bloom*); Howard Merrill (*Mickey Bloom*); Arnold Stang, Eddie Firestone, Jr. (*Seymour Fingerhood*); Bruno Wick (*Mr. Fowler*); Tito Vuolo (*Uncle Carlo*); Joan Tetzel (*Jane Brown*); Sidney Slon (*Solly*).

OPENING

Molly: Yoo hoo, is anybody...

Announcer: There's Molly, folks—that means your friends the Goldbergs are here.

560. Good Listening. Game, 30 min., CBS, 1943.

The format called for contestants to answer questions based on a medley of vocal clues that were constantly interrupted by plants in the studio audience. A player won money ($3, $6, or $9) based on how many questions he could answer that were related to the interrupted songs.

Host: Lionel Kaye. ***Vocalists:*** The Three Chances. ***Orchestra:*** Van Alexander.

561. Good News. Variety, 60 min., NBC, 1937–1939; 30 min., NBC, 1939–1940.

The original format dramatized films produced by Metro-Goldwyn-Mayer. Guests served as the host (as well as the players) and music was supplied by Meredith Willson and his orchestra. Shortly after, the format changed to present comedy acts with regulars Fanny Brice and Frank Morgan. When the show switched to a half-hour format, Mary Martin became a part of the cast. Meredith Willson continued to supply the music and a name guest continued to host and perform.

562. The Goodrich Silvertown Orchestra. Variety, 30 min., NBC, 1929–1936.

A program of music and songs sponsored by the B.F. Goodrich Tire Company, makers of the now-extinct Silvertown Tires. Joseph M. White, a singer known as "The Silver Masked Tenor," hosted the program. The Boswell Sisters were regular performers and Phil Carlin did the announcing. Music was provided by the Milton Rittenberg, Jack Shilkret and B.A. Rolfe orchestras.

563. The Goodwill Hour. Advice, 30 min., Mutual, then NBC Blue, 1937–1944.

"You have a friend and adviser in John J. Anthony," said the announcer, and people with personal problems stepped up to the microphone to bare their souls and receive free help from John J. Anthony, a man who professed to having three university degrees. In reality, he was a high school dropout named Lester Kroll. Participants were always cautioned not to give names and not to touch the microphone. Roland Winters did the announcing.

564. The Goon Show. Comedy, 30 min., NBC, 1954–1958.

A British series about a group of goons, "people of inarticulate language with one-cell brains who think in the fourth dimension," who are anti-everything and whose sole purpose is first to destroy the British Empire, then the rest of the world. Every known effect that broadcasting had to offer was used to present the stories—all of which revolved around one Netty Seagoon, a man of many occupations, yet completely naive and stupid. His adventures in a world of dimwitted buffoons was the basis of the series. *Other regular characters:* Eccles, the idiot; Major Denis Bloodnok, Indian Army, retired; Bluebottle, the character who always reads the stage directions in his script; Hercules Grytpype-Thynne, the chief villain; Morarity, the evil being bent on conquering the world; Henry Cron, a seemingly feeble old man.

Cast: Harry Seacombe (*Netty Seagoon*); Peter Sellers (*Bluebottle/Henry Cron/Major Denis Bloodnok/Hercules Grytpype-Thynne*); Spike Milligan (*Eccles the Idiot/Morarity*). ***Regulars:*** The Ray Ellington Quartet. ***Vocalist:*** Max Geldry. ***Announcer:*** Wallace Greenslade. ***Orchestra:*** Wally Stark.

565. The Gordon MacRae Show. Variety, 15 min., CBS, 1945–1946; NBC, 1946–1947.

A program of music and songs with singer-actor Gordon MacRae as the host. Vocalists Marian Bell and Sheila Stevens were the regulars; the Archie Bleyer and Johnny Guarneri orchestras provided the music. Dan Seymour did the announcing.

566. The Gracie Fields Show. Variety, 5 min., NBC Blue, 1942; 15 min., NBC Blue, 1942–1943; 30 min., ABC, 1944–1945; Mutual, 1951–1952.

A program of music and songs with British singer-comedienne Gracie Fields. She was assisted by Bob Burns, Don Hancock, and the Spartan Quartet. Bill Goodwin did the announcing and musical backing was provided by the Lew Briney, Carl Hoffman and Harry Sosnik orchestras. Before expanding to 15, then 30 minutes, a week, a five-minute version was broadcast nightly and featured one song and one story by Fields.

567. Gramps. Comedy, 30 min., NBC, 7/2/47 to 8/20/47.

The story of a small-town newspaper editor (played by Craig McDonnell), his wife (Anne Seymour) and their two children (Joan Lazer, Edwin Bruce). Gramps (Edgar Stehli), a well-meaning old codger who has a knack for innocently starting trouble, comes for a visit and decides to stay.

568. Granby's Green Acres. Comedy, 30 min., NBC, 7/3/50 to 8/21/50.

John Granby is an exasperated bank clerk who decides to get away from it all and begin a new life as a farmer with his wife (Iris) and daughter (Lisa). His dreams are shattered when he discovers that his Green Acres farm is a broken-down nightmare. Stories follow John as he attempts to operate a farm despite the objections of a family who want to move back to the city. A television version based on this concept became *Green Acres* with Eddie Albert and Eva Gabor.

Cast: Gale Gordon (*John Granby*); Bea Benaderet (*Iris Granby*); Louise Erickson (*Lisa Granby*); Parley Baer (*Eb, their handyman*). ***Music:*** Opie Cates.

569. Grand Central Station. Anthology, 30 min., NBC Blue, 1937–1938; CBS, 1938–1940; NBC Blue, 1940–1941; CBS, 1941; NBC Red, 1941–1942; CBS, 1944–1952; ABC, 1954.

A long-running series of human interest stories that usually begin in Grand Central Station, a major rail terminal in New York City. Incidents in the life of a passenger either departing or arriving at the station would become the subject of the evening's story (with the action most always shifting to areas outside the station). It is interesting to note that during the opening theme, sounds of steam engines are heard inside the station. This would have been an extreme health hazard due to the smoke exhaust from the engine's boiler; only electric engines were permitted.

Narrators: Jack Arthur, John Reed King, Alexander Scourby. ***Announcers:*** George Baxter, Ken Roberts, Tom Shirley. ***Music:*** Lew White. ***Producers:*** Himan Brown, Martin Horrell.

OPENING

Announcer: Pillsbury Sno-Sheen Cake Flour brings you *Grand Central Station*. As a bullet seeks its target, shining rails in every part of our great country are aimed at Grand Central Station, heart of the nation's greatest city. Drawn by the magnetic force of the fantastic metropolis, day and night great trains rush toward the Hudson River, sweep down its eastern bank for 140 miles, flash briefly by the long red row of tenement houses south of 125th Street, dive with a roar into a two-and-one-half mile tunnel which burrows between the glitter and swank of Park Avenue. And then, Grand Central Station, crossroads of a million private lives, gigantic stage on which are played a thousand dramas daily.

570. Grand Hotel. Anthology, 30 min., Local Chicago, 1930–1933; NBC Blue, 1933–1936; NBC Red, 1936–1937; NBC Blue, 1937–1938; CBS, 1940; NBC, 1944–1945.

Dramatizations based on incidents in the lives of the guests who book rooms at the Grand Hotel. Based on the novel by Vicki Baum. The only regular was the telephone operator (who opened each show and made connections between rooms).

Cast: Betty Winkler, Luise Barclay (*Telephone Operator*). ***Cast*** (various roles): Don Ameche, Jim Ameche, Jean David, Henry Drew, Charles Eggleston, Betty Lou Gerson, Anne Seymour, Les Tremayne. ***Announcer:*** Vincent Pelletier. ***Organist:*** Dave Bacal. ***Producer:*** Joe Ainley.

571. Grand Marquee. Anthology, 30 min., NBC, 1946–1947.

A weekly series of comedy and drama presentations featuring a regular male and female lead with guests in supporting roles.

Cast: Jim Ameche, Olan Soule (*Male lead*); Beryl Vaughn (*Female lead*). ***Announcer:*** George Stone. ***Music:*** Joseph Gallichio.

OPENING

Announcer: The National Broadcasting Company's *Grand Marquee*. Grand Marquee, lighted by stars, twinkling, glowing, blazing with various lights and colors against the sky. The National Broadcasting Company's fabulous billboard announces another exciting evening in the world of make-believe. Tonight, the *Grand Marquee* offers Irwin Weinhausen's laugh-packed comedy "Hold It Please," starring Jim Ameche. And now to greet you and set the scene for tonight's merriment, here is your *Grand Marquee* star himself, Jim Ameche.

Jim: Thank you, George Stone, and good evening, ladies and gentlemen. Tonight's play concerns a photographer who has a very unusual idea...

572. The Grand Ole Opry. Variety, 30 min., NBC, 1939–1957.

A program of country and western music that, while only broadcast on NBC for 18 years, began on WSM radio in Nashville in 1925 and is still running in 1997, making it the longest running program in radio history. The original program was titled *The WSM Barn Dance* and became *The Grand Ole Opry* in 1926. In October 1939, when the program was broadcast for five hours on Saturday nights, NBC picked up 30 minutes of the show under the sponsorship of Prince Albert Pipe Tobacco. George D. Hay, known as "The Solemn Old Judge," was the host; Whitey Ford, "The Duke of Paducah," was the emcee for the NBC version; and Louie Buck and Dave Stone were the announcers.

573. Grand Slam. Game, 30 min., CBS, 1943–1953.

A question, submitted by a listener, was divided into five parts. If a contestant could answer each part correctly, he had a "grand slam" and won a $100 savings bond. If, at any time during the questioning, the contestant responded incorrectly, he was disqualified and the listener who submitted the question won $5. The game segment was coupled with music and songs.

Host: Irene Beasley. ***Assistant-Announcer:*** Dwight Weist. ***Pianist:*** Bob Downey. ***Organist:*** Abe Goldman. ***Producer:*** Irene Beasley.

Grandpa Burton *see* **Appendix**

574. The Grape Nuts Program. Comedy, 30 min., NBC, 4/12/37 to 8/11/38.

George Burns and Gracie Allen's first series for NBC (after starring in the CBS series *The Adventures of Gracie*, *Campbell's Tomato Juice Program*, *The Robert Burns Panatela Program* and *The White Owl Program*; see titles for information). Stories relate comical events of a scatterbrained, man-chasing woman (Gracie Allen) and her level-headed friend, the recipient of her antics, George Burns. (George and Gracie were not husband and wife in the series, just friends.) The program, sponsored by the General Foods Corporation, makers of Post Grape Nuts Cereal, also featured parodies on plays and movies and "The Grape Nuts Nutsey Rhyme" (wherein Gracie told silly rhymes).

Hosts: George Burns, Gracie Allen. ***Regulars:*** John Conte, Dick Foran, Tony Martin. ***Announcers:*** Ronald Drake, Ken Niles. ***Orchestra:*** Jan Garber, Ray Noble.

575. Grapevine Rancho. Variety, 30 min., CBS, 1943–1944.

A weekly program of country and western music and songs with host Ransom Sherman, vocalist Carlos Ramirez and the music of Lud Gluskin and his orchestra.

576. The Gray Gordon Show. Variety, 30 min., NBC, 1936–1939.

Music and songs with host/orchestra leader Gray Gordon. Cliff Bradden and Shirley Lane and the Lane Sisters were the vocalists; music was provided by the Gray Gordon Orchestra.

577. The Great Adventure. Anthology, 30 min., ABC, 1951.

Dramatizations of America's development through the progress of science and industry. Westbrook Van Voohis was the narrator.

578. The Great Day. Game, 30 min., Mutual, 1952.

Selected servicemen appeared before the microphones to relate a story why $100 should be awarded to him. The most impressive story, as determined by studio audience applause, earned the serviceman the $100. John Reed King was the host.

579. The Great Gildersleeve. Comedy, 30 min., NBC, 1941–1958.

A spinoff from *Fibber McGee and Molly* wherein Throckmorton P. "Gildy" Gildersleeve was portrayed as a friend of the McGees and the owner of the Gildersleeve Girdle Factory in the town of Wistful Vista. When his brother-in-law Ed Forrester, the owner of a used car lot in Summerfield, dies, Gildersleeve leaves town to take over Ed's affairs and find a home for his two children, Evelyn (later to become Marjorie) and Leroy Forrester. When Throckmorton applies to become the administrator of the Forrester estate, Judge Hooker feels that Gildersleeve's best interests are not for the chil-

Great Gildersleeve **stars (left to right) Marylee Robb (Marjorie), Willard Waterman (Gildy) and Walter Tetley (Leroy).**

dren and stipulates that he must post a $50,000 bond and account to him for every penny that he spends. With no other choice but to stay in Summerfield (to make the estate pay or go to jail for contempt), Gildy moves into the Forrester home and eventually settles down (he sells his girdle factory and becomes the water commissioner of Summerfield). Stories follow Gildersleeve's various misadventures as a ladies' man, foster uncle to two mischievous children, and public official as he struggles to make a new life for himself. *Other regular characters:* Birdie Lee Coggins, Gildy's maid; Richard Peavy, the druggist; Floyd, the barber; Leila Ranson, the Southern belle on whom Gildy has a crush; Rumson Bullard, Gildy's obnoxious neighbor (with whom he is always feuding); Kathryn Milford and Adeline Fairchild, two women seeking Gildy's heart; Bronco Thompson, Marjorie's boyfriend (they married in 1950); Craig Bullard, Rumson's son; Eve Goodwin, the school principal Gildy dated. Judge Hooker's first name was given as both Amos Alonzo and Horace; Gildy is a member of the Jolly Boys Club; Birdie is a member of a club called the Order of the Daughters of Cleopatra. Leroy calls his uncle "Unk" and Marjorie calls him "Unkie." Gildy first lived on Parside Avenue, then at 2100 Burnside Avenue; Eve lived on Laurel Avenue. Marjorie attended Summerfield High School; Leroy, Summerfield Grammar School; Gildy's phone number: Summerfield 2371. Served as the basis for the television series of the same title.

Cast: Hal Peary, Willard Waterman (*Throckmorton P. Gildersleeve*); Lurene Tuttle (*Evelyn Forrester*); Louise Erickson, Marylee Robb (*Marjorie Forrester*); Walter Tetley (*Leroy Forrester*); Lillian Randolph (*Birdie Lee Coggins*); Earle Ross (*Judge Hooker*); Richard Legrand, Forrest Lewis (*Peavey*); Arthur Q. Bryan (*Floyd*); Shirley Mitchell (*Leila Ransom*); Gale Gordon (*Rumson Bullard*); Tommy Bernard (*Craig Bullard*); Richard Crenna (*Bronco Thompson*); Cathy Lewis (*Kathryn Milford*); Una Merkel (*Adeline Fairchild*); Bea Benaderet (*Eve Goodwin*). ***Announcers:*** Ken Carpenter, John Easton, John Laing, Ken Roberts, John Wald, Harlow Wilcox. ***Orchestra:*** Robert Armbruster, Jack Meakin, Billy Mills, Claude Sweetin.

OPENING

ANNOUNCER: The Kraft Food Company presents *The Great Gildersleeve*. It's *The Great Gildersleeve* starring Hal Peary and brought to you by the Kraft Food Company, makers of Parkay Margarine and a complete line of famous quality food products. Now let's peep into the world of Summerfield and see what goes on there...

580. GREAT GUNNS. Comedy, 30 min., Mutual, 5/8/41 to 9/25/41.

The trials and tribulations of the Gunns, a former stage family who are attempting (without much success) to live a life apart from the world of show business. *Regular characters:* Chris and Veronica Gunn, the parents; Buster Gunn, their son; Pop Gunn, Chris's father; Gloomy, their butler; Moe, their agent; Lorson Snells, the producer.

Cast: Bret Morrison (*Chris Gunn*); Barbara Luddy (*Veronica Gunn*); Bob Jellison (*Buster Gunn*); Phil Lord (*Pop Gunn*); Marvin Miller (*Gloomy/Moe/Lorson Snells*). ***Announcer:*** Marvin Miller. ***Music:*** Harold Stokes. ***Producer:*** William Bacher.

581. THE GREAT MERLINI. Crime Drama, 30 min., NBC, 1950.

The Great Merlini (no other name given) is a master illusionist and escape artist who has made it his hobby to battle the criminal element. Stories follow his efforts to help the police solve baffling crimes. *Other regular characters:* Julie Boyd, his assistant; Police Inspector Gavigan.

Cast: Chester Morris (*The Great Merlini*); Barbara Cook (*Julie Boyd*); Robert Noe (*Inspector Gavigan*).

582. THE GREATEST STORY EVER TOLD. Anthology, 30 min., ABC, 1947–1956.

Religious dramas based on events in the life of Jesus Christ that were adapted from the book of the same name by Fulton Oursler. Warren Parker played Jesus, the only regular character on the program. Norman Rose did the announcing and music was by Jacques Belasco.

583. THE GREEN HORNET. Crime Drama, 30 min., Local Detroit, 1936–1938; Mutual, 1938–1939; NBC Blue, 1939–1940; Mutual, 1940–1941; NBC Blue, 1942–1944; ABC, 1945–1952.

After building the *Daily Sentinel* into one of America's greatest newspapers, editor Dan Reid turns over the management to his playboy bachelor son Britt, hoping the responsibility will mature him, and secretly hires ex-cop Mike Axford to watch over Britt's activities. Britt is instilled with his father's goal and, like his great-grand-uncle John Reid (The Lone Ranger), he begins a crusade to protect the rights and lives of decent citizens. He adapts the masked guise of the Green Hornet (the symbol of the insect that is most deadly when aroused) and establishes a base in an abandoned building next to his apartment. He then reveals his true identity to only one other person—Kato, his Oriental houseboy. Considered criminals and wanted by the police, the Green Hornet and Kato avenge crime as semi-fugitives, always disappearing before the authorities arrive. Britt used a gun that emitted gas and left criminals unconscious for the police to apprehend; his car was called the *Black Beauty*. Kato's nationality changed from Japanese to Filipino on December 7, 1941, when the United States declared war on Japan. *Other regular characters:* Lenore "Casey" Case, Britt's secretary; Ed Lowry, a reporter; Clicker Binney, the photographer; the Newsboy (who appeared at the end to shout "Read All About It"). The paper's competition was the *Clarion*.

Cast: Al Hodge, Bob Hall, Donovan Faust, Jack McCarthy (*Britt Reid/The Green Hornet*); Raymond Hayashi, Rollon Parker, Michael Tolan (*Kato*); Lee Allman (*Lenore Case*); Patricia Dunlap (*Clicker Binney*); Jim Irwin, Gil Shea (*Mike Axford*); Jack Petruzzi (*Ed Lowry*); Rollon Parker (*Newsboy*). ***Announcers:*** Bob Hite, Hal Neal, Mike Wallace, Charles Woods.

OPENING

ANNOUNCER (over theme, "Flight of the Bumble Bee"): *The Green Hornet*. He hunts the biggest of all game, public enemies that even the G-Men cannot reach. *The Green Hornet*. With his faithful valet, Kato, Britt Reid, daring young publisher, matches wits with the underworld, risking his life that criminals and racketeers, within the law, may feel its weight by the sting of *The Green Hornet*. Ride with Britt Reid as he races toward another thrilling adventure as *The Green Hornet* rides again.

CLOSING

ANNOUNCER: The story you have just heard is a copyrighted feature of the Green Hornet, Incorporated. The events depicted in the drama are fictitious. Any similarity to persons living or dead is purely coincidental.

584. THE GREEN LAMA. Crime Drama, 30 min., CBS, 6/5/49 to 8/20/49.

Jethro DuMont is a wealthy young American who acquires special powers after ten years of study in Tibet. Because of his great wisdom, his willingness to devote his life to fighting crime, and his powers of concentration, he becomes the Green Lama, a mysterious figure for justice (he chose the color green because it is one of the six sacred colors of Tibet and the symbol for justice). Stories follow Jethro as he and his Tibetan assistant Toku use the powers of the Lama to battle evil.

Cast: Paul Frees (*Jethro DuMont*); Ben Wright (*Toku*). ***Announcer:*** Larry Thor. ***Music:*** Richard Aurandt.

OPENING

ANNOUNCER: Time now for another exciting adventure from the files of Jethro DuMont. Jethro DuMont, a wealthy young American who, after ten years in Tibet, returned as the Green Lama to amaze the world with his amazing powers in his single-handed fight against injustice and crime.

585. GREEN VALLEY, U.S.A. Serial, 30 min., CBS, 1942–1944; Mutual, 1944.

Dramatic incidents in the lives of the people of Green Valley, a small, rural town.

Cast: Ed Begley, Frank Behrens, Alan Devitt, Elspeth Eric, Gilbert Mack, Ann Shepherd, Richard Widmark. ***Narrators:*** Henry M. Neeley, Santos Ortega. ***Music:*** Emery Deutsch. ***Producer:*** Himan Brown.

586. THE GROUCHO MARX SHOW. Variety, 30 min., CBS, 1943.

A weekly program of music, songs and comedy skits with comedian Groucho Marx as the host. Donald Dickson and Virginia O'Brien were the regulars. Songs and music were provided by the Robert Armbruster Orchestra and Chorus.

587. GUESS WHERE. Game, 30 min., Mutual, 1939.

A dramatization, depicting a specific place, was enacted. Players who were able to identify the subject of the skit received a cash prize. June Walker was the host. Charles Cantor, Wilbur "Budd" Hulick and Jack Johnson assisted her.

588. GUEST STAR. Anthology, 15 min., Syndicated, 1943–1962.

A public service program (to promote the sale of U.S. Savings Bonds) wherein a different star appeared in a short dramatic or musical sketch.

Announcers: Jeff Barker, John Conte. ***Music:*** The Savings Bond Orchestra conducted by David Rose, Harry Sosnik.

OPENING

ANNOUNCER: The United States Savings Bond Division presents *Guest Star*. How do you do, ladies and gentlemen, this is Jeff Barker greeting you on behalf of *Guest Star*, the transcribed feature program brought to you by this station and the United States Savings Bond as a public service. With it we bring you this message—a secure future for yourself and your family is yours if you save for it through the regular purchase of United States Savings Bonds. Today's guest is the well-known motion picture star, Mr. Humphrey Bogart. He is featured in a brief episode based on early Mexican history called "Incident in Freedom" by Morton Freedman. Here is Mr. Humphrey Bogart...

CLOSING

ANNOUNCER: You have been listening to *Guest Star*, a transcribed feature program brought to you by this station each week at this time as a public service. Today's guest was the noted screen actor Mr. Humphrey Bogart, who appeared by special arrangement with Santana Productions. Join us again next week when we'll have another fine star on our program.

589. THE GUIDING LIGHT. Serial, 15 min., NBC, 1937–1947; CBS, 1947–1956.

The dramatic story of Dr. John Ruthledge, a minister in the small town of Five Points. The series later focused on the lives of the Bauer family and served as the basis for the television series of the same title.

Cast: Arthur Peterson (*John Ruthledge*); Sarajane Wells, Mercedes McCambridge (*Mary Ruthledge*); Laurette Fillbrandt (*Trudy Bauer*); Lyle Sudrow (*Bill Bauer*); Jone Allison (*Meta Bauer*); Ed Prentiss (*Ned Holden*); Jane Webb (*Peggy*); Sharon Grainger (*Phyllis Gordon*); Annette Harper (*Sister Lillian*); Ruth Bailey, Charlotte Manson (*Rose*); Betty Arnold (*Iris Marsh*); Betty Lou Gerson (*Charlotte Brandon*); Hugh Studebaker (*Charles Matthews*); Mary Lansing (*Julie Collins*); Eloise Kummer (*Norma Greenman*); Ken Griffin (*Edward Greenman*); Alma Samuels (*Sister Ada*); Gail Henshaw (*Laura Martin*); Raymond Edward Johnson (*Gordon Ellis*); Frank Behrens (*Rev. Tom Bannion*); Margaret Fuller, Muriel Bremner (*Fredericka Lang*); Bret Morrison (*Clifford Foster*); Sam Edwards, Leonard Waterman (*Roger Collins*); Sam Wanamaker, Phil Dakin, Marvin Miller, Raymond Edward Johnson (*Ellis Smith*); Sidney Breese (*Dr. McNeill*). ***Announcers:*** Herbert Allen, Clayton "Bud" Collyer, Fort Pearson. ***Music:*** Chet Kingsbury. ***Producer:*** Joe Ainley.

OPENING

ANNOUNCER (over theme, "Aphrodite"): *The Guiding Light*, created by Irna Phillips and brought to you by Procter and Gamble, makers of Ivory Soap.

590. THE GULF SCREEN GUILD THEATER. Anthology, 30 min., CBS, 1939.

Radio adaptations of well-known motion pictures sponsored by Gulf Oil. The actors who appeared did not receive a fee for their services. Their pay was donated to the Motion Picture Relief Fund to help build a home for retired actors. Presentations include:

The Strawberry Blonde. James Cagney and Jack Carson as two turn-of-the-century men trying to outdo each other to win the hand of the town beauty (Olivia deHavilland).

If Only She Could Cook. Humphrey Bogart, Alice Faye and Herbert Marshall in the story of a man and woman who pose as a butler and cook to relieve their financial burdens.

Mr. Jinx Goes to Sea. Bing Crosby, Jean Parker and Andy Devine in a story about a young man who joins the Navy despite the fact that his family is jinxed when it comes to the sea.

His Girl Friday. Rosalind Russell and Cary Grant as a girl reporter and her wise-cracking editor.

The Amazing Dr. Clitterhouse. Humphrey Bogart and Edward G. Robinson in the story of a prominent doctor who joins the underworld to do research.

Host: Roger Pryor. ***Announcers:*** Claude Easton, Harry Von Zell. ***Music:*** Oscar Bradley and the Gulf Orchestra.

OPENING

ANNOUNCER: *The Gulf Screen Guild Theater*. Your host, the director of the stars' own theater, Roger Pryor.

PRYOR: Good evening, everyone. Your neighborhood good Gulf dealer and the Gulf Oil Company welcome you once again to *The*

***Gunsmoke* featured (left to right) Howard McNear, William Conrad, Georgia Ellis and Parley Baer.**

Gulf Screen Guild Theater. Tonight we present Humphrey Bogart and Alice Faye in "If Only She Could Cook."

591. The Gulf Show. Variety, 30 min., NBC Blue, then CBS, 1933–1935.

A weekly program of comedy monologues coupled with music and songs with host Will Rogers, the Revelers vocal group and the music of the Al Goodman and Frank Tour orchestras. Harry Von Zell did the announcing.

592. The Gumps. Comedy-Drama, 15 min., CBS, 1934–1937.

Events in the lives of the Gumps, a not-so-typical American family: Andy, his wife Min and their son Chester. Based on the comic strip by Sidney Smith.

Cast: Wilmer Walter (*Andy Gump*); Agnes Moorehead (*Min Gump*); Lester Jay, Jackie Kelk (*Chester Gump*). ***Announcer:*** Ralph Edwards. ***Producer:*** Himan Brown.

593. Gunsmoke. Western, 30 min., CBS, 4/26/52 to 6/18/61.

The dramatic story of Matthew "Matt" Dillon, a U.S. marshal maintaining law and order in Dodge City, Kansas, during the late 1800s. *Other regular characters:* Chester Proudfoot, his deputy; Kitty Russell, owner of the Long Branch Saloon; Doc Adams, the town physician. Matt's office is on Front Street; Matt and Chester have coffee at Del Monico's Cafe. Served as the basis for the television series of the same title.

Cast: William Conrad (*Matt Dillon*); Parley Baer (*Chester Proudfoot*); Georgia Ellis (*Kitty Russell*); Howard McNear (*Doc Adams*). ***Announcers:*** George Fenneman, George Walsh. ***Music:*** Rex Koury. ***Producer:*** Norman MacDonnell.

OPENING

Announcer (over horse riding and gunshots): Around Dodge City and the territory out west, there is just one way to handle the killers and the spoilers and that is with the U.S. marshal and the smell of *Gunsmoke*. [Over theme music:] *Gunsmoke*, starring William Conrad, the transcribed story of the violence that moved west with young America and the story of a man who moved with it.

MATT: I'm that man, Matt Dillon, United States marshal, the first man they look for and the last they want to meet. It's a chancy job and makes a man watchful and a little lonely.

CLOSING

MATT (after summing up the episode): Next week, trouble comes to Dodge when two men claim title to the same area. And that was the West. Good night.

ANNOUNCER: *Gunsmoke*, produced and directed by Norman MacDonnell, stars William Conrad as Matt Dillon, U.S. marshal... This is CBS, the Columbia Broadcasting System.

594. GUY LOMBARDO TIME. Variety, 30 min., CBS, 1938.

"The sweetest music this side of Heaven" with host/orchestra leader Guy Lombardo. Mindy Carson, Kenny Gardner, Bill Flannigan, Billy Leach, Ogden Nash and Don Rodney were the regulars. Also appearing were Guy's sister (Rosemarie) and brothers (Lebert, Carmen and Victor Lombardo). Andre Baruch was the announcer and the Guy Lombardo Orchestra provided the music. See also *Lombardo Land, U.S.A.* and *Musical Autographs*.

595. HAL KEMP IS ON THE AIR FOR GRIFFIN. Variety, 30 min., CBS, 1938–1939.

A weekly program of music and songs that is also known as *Time to Shine*. Orchestra leader Hal Kemp hosted and supplied the music. The program was sponsored by Griffin Shoe Polish.

OPENING

ANNOUNCER: *Hal Kemp Is on the Air for Griffin*.

SONG: It's time to shine, shine your shoes and you'll wear a smile; shine your shoes and you'll be in style. Griffin polish shines the best ... everybody get set, it's time to shine.

ANNOUNCER: And here's Hal Kemp.

596. THE HAL MCINTYRE SHOW. Variety, 30 min., ABC, 1945.

A program of music and songs with orchestra leader Hal McIntyre as host. Ruth Gaynor, Al Noble and Johnny Turnbull were the regulars and music was supplied by the Hal McIntyre Orchestra.

THE HAL PEARY SHOW *see* **THE HAROLD PEARY SHOW—HONEST HAROLD**

597. THE HALL OF FANTASY. Anthology, 30 min., Mutual, 1945.

Tales of the supernatural in which the Prince of Darkness often triumphed. Organist Harold Turner provided the music and Richard Thorne was the producer.

OPENING

ANNOUNCER: And now, *The Hall of Fantasy*. Welcome to *The Hall of Fantasy*, welcome to this series of radio dramas dedicated to the supernatural, the unusual and the unknown. Come with me, my friends, we shall descend to the world of the unknown and forbidden, down to the depths where the veil of time is lifted and the supernatural reigns and peaks. Come with me and listen to the tale of "The Wild Huntsman," an original tale of fantasy by Richard Thorne.

THE HALLMARK CHARLOTTE GREENWOOD SHOW *see* **THE CHARLOTTE GREENWOOD SHOW**

598. THE HALLMARK HALL OF FAME. Anthology, 30 min., CBS, 1953–1955.

A slightly revised version of "The Hallmark Playhouse" (next entry) that phased out dramas based on contemporary literature to focus on biographical dramas from American and world history. Lionel Barrymore served as the host; Frank Gast was the announcer and music was provided by Lyn Murray. Sponsored by Hallmark Greeting Cards.

599. THE HALLMARK PLAYHOUSE. Anthology, 30 min., CBS, 1948–1953.

A weekly series of dramatizations sponsored by Hallmark Greeting Cards. Jean Holloway wrote all the adaptations (from contemporary literature) and top name radio and Hollywood personalities appeared in the stories. Served as the basis for *The Hallmark Hall of Fame* television series. See also the prior title.

Host-Narrator: James Hilton. ***Announcer:*** Frank Gast. ***Music:*** Lyn Murray. ***Producer:*** Dee Engelbach.

OPENING (from 12/24/48)

ANNOUNCER: Remember, a Hallmark card when you care enough to send the very best. Tonight, from Hollywood, the makers of Hallmark Greeting Cards bring you Mr. James Hilton and "The Story of Silent Night" on *The Hallmark Playhouse*. Each week, Hallmark brings you outstanding stories chosen by one of the world's best-known authors, Mr. James Hilton. Before we begin, here is a Christmas message from the folks at Hallmark and the friendly stores where Hallmark cards are sold. A special Hallmark Christmas card from all of us to all of you that comes with sincerity and brings our friendly greetings too. So, to the wishes you've received, please add our wishes for Christmas cheer and, by the way, it's sure been grand to have you with us through the year. And now it's Hallmark's pleasure to present the distinguished novelist, Mr. James Hilton.

HILTON: Good evening, ladies and gentlemen. This is James Hilton. Tonight on our *Hallmark Playhouse* we'll tell you the story of how that wonderful Christmas song, "Silent Night," came to be written 130 years ago tonight.

CLOSING

HILTON: You have heard the story of a miracle, a miracle that was born one "Silent Night."

ANNOUNCER: Before James Hilton returns to tell you about our story for next week, I would like to tell you about Hallmark New Year's cards. They're bright and gay as a New Year's party. They're a thoughtful expression of friendship... Remember, these are Hallmark cards—when you care enough to send the very best. Here again is James Hilton.

HILTON: The story of "Silent Night" and the music you have just heard has all the beauty and joy and happiness of Christmas. There is nothing anyone can add to it. And now, for all of us here in the playhouse, for everyone who is proudly a member of the Hallmark family, we wish you, our friends, a very, very merry Christmas. Until next Thursday then, this is James Hilton saying good night.

ANNOUNCER: Look for Hallmark cards that are sold only in stores that have been carefully selected to give you expert and friendly service. Remember, Hallmark cards when you care enough to send the very best. This is Frank Gast saying good night to you all until next week at this same time when James Hilton returns to present Herbert Marshall in "Lost Horizon." This program came to you from the Hallmark Playhouse. This is CBS, the Columbia Broadcasting System.

600. THE HALLS OF IVY. Comedy, 30 min., NBC, 1/6/50 to 6/25/52.

Incidents that befall the mythical Ivy College in Ivy, U.S.A., its students and faculty as seen through the eyes of Dr. William Todhunter Hall, the president, and his wife, Victoria Cromwell-Hall, a former showgirl who now teaches English. William and Victoria live on campus at Number 1 Faculty Row. William first saw Victoria perform in the play "Give Them Tears." He attended 26 performances before he could work up the courage to ask her for a date. Victoria calls William by the pet name "Toddy Bear" and the college radio station is XIVY. *Other regular characters:* Penny, their maid; Prof. Jeremiah Warren; Prof. Heathcliff; Clarence Wellman, the Chairman of the Board of Ivy; Mr. Meriwether, a wealthy contributor to the college and a member of the Board of Directors.

Cast: Ronald Colman (*Dr. William Hall*); Benita Hume (*Victoria Hall*); Gloria Gordon (*Penny*); Arthur Q. Bryan (*Prof. Jeremiah Warren*); Alan Reed (*Prof. Heathcliff*); Herb Butterfield (*Clarence Wellman*); Willard Waterman (*Mr. Meriwether*). ***Announcer:*** Ken Carpenter. ***Music:*** Henry Russell.

OPENING (from 1/6/50)

ANNOUNCER: Good evening, this is Ken Carpenter saying welcome to the world premiere of the Mr. and Mrs. Ronald Colman show, *The Halls of Ivy*, sponsored by the Joseph Schlitz Brewing Company, makers of Schlitz, the beer that made Milwaukee famous. And now, *The Halls of Ivy*.

SONG: Oh, we love the Halls of Ivy that surround us here today, and we shall not forget though we be far, far away...

ANNOUNCER: Welcome to Ivy, the town of Ivy and Ivy College. Ivy College is co-educational and nonsectarian and its age is indicated by the fact that until recently, the curriculum required two years of Greek. Ivy is all–American; its student body is a pretty fair cross-section of the country's youthful seekers of knowledge. Dr. William Todhunter Hall, Ph.D., LLD and M.A. is president of Ivy… [The story would then begin.]

CLOSING

ANNOUNCER: We'll be seeing you next week at this time at *The Halls of Ivy* starring Mr. and Mrs. Ronald Colman. *The Halls of Ivy* was created by Don Quinn and presented by the Joseph Schlitz Brewing Company of Milwaukee, Wisconsin. Ken Carpenter is speaking.

SONG: Oh, we love the Halls of Ivy that surround us here today, and we shall not forget though we be far, far away…

ANNOUNCER: This is NBC, the National Broadcasting Company.

601. HANNIBAL COBB. Crime Drama, 30 min., ABC, 1/9/50 to 5/11/51.

A daily series about the adventures of Hannibal Cobb, a private detective who takes a personal interest in his clients. Stories are often told from the point of view of Cobb's clients, rather than from Hannibal's perspective. Cobb's address was 17 South Jackson.

Cast: Santos Ortega (*Hannibal Cobb*). ***Announcer:*** Les Griffith. ***Organist:*** Rosa Rio.

OPENING

ANNOUNCER: *Hannibal Cobb* starring Santos Ortega. Each weekday at this time, the American Broadcasting Company brings you *Hannibal Cobb* as you'll find him in the "Photocrime" pages of *Look* magazine. And now, a dramatic story of human conflict told from the point of view of someone closely involved in tonight's case.

CLOSING

ANNOUNCER: Be sure to be with us each weekday at this time when *Hannibal Cobb* will bring you another exciting story of human conflict. Santos Ortega starred as Hannibal Cobb. This is ABC, the American Broadcasting Company.

602. HAP HAZARD. Comedy, 30 min., NBC, 7/1/41 to 9/23/41.

Comedy sketches set at Crestfallen Manor, a rustic hotel with numerous problems. Hap Hazard was the proprietor. He was assisted by Mr. Pittaway and Cyclone, the handyman. Crestfallen Manor was part of the Stop and Flop Motel Chain.

Cast: Ransom Sherman (*Hap Hazard*); Cliff Soubier (*Mr. Pittaway*); Ray Grant (*Cyclone*); Elmira Roessler (*Waitress*); Mary Patton (*Waitress*). ***Vocalist:*** Edna O'Dell. ***Announcers:*** Ben Gage, Durward Kirby, Harlow Wilcox. ***Orchestra:*** Gordon Jenkins, Billy Mills.

603. THE HAPPINESS BOYS. Variety, 15 min., NBC Blue, 1926–1938.

A program of comic songs and sentimental ballads with Billy Jones and Ernie Hare, radio's first big stars (they began on local New York radio in 1921). Ben Selvin and his orchestra supplied the music. Jones and Hare were first called the Happiness Boys (when sponsored by Happiness Candies), then the Interwoven Pair (for Interwoven Sox), the Flit Soldiers (for Standard Oil) and the Tasty Breadwinners (for Tasty Yeast Bakers).

604. THE HAPPY GANG. Variety, 30 min., Syndicated, 1946.

A Canadian series of music, songs and comedy that was produced in 1937, but heard for the first time in the United States in 1946. Comedian Bert Pearl was the host. He was assisted by Eddie Allen, Hugh Bartlett, Cliff McKay, Jimmy McNamara, Blain Mothe, Joe Nios, Bob Semly and Kathleen Stakes.

605. HAPPY ISLAND. Variety, 30 min., ABC, 1944–1945.

Life in the mythical kingdom of Happy Island as seen through the eyes of King Bubbles, its kind-hearted ruler. Songs and musical selections follow each comedy skit: the opening monologue by King Bubbles; the King's visit to Worry Park (where people with problems find comical comfort from the king); a trip through the Happy Island Department Store; a story by King Bubbles to his niece, Beulah; the Happy Island Good Deed of the Day (where the king performs his weekly good deed) and the concluding segment, a Happy Thought from Happy Island. The program was sponsored by Borden Milk and featured the company mascot Elsie the Cow in commercials.

Cast: Ed Wynn (*King Bubbles*); Lorna Lynn (*Beulah*); Hope Emerson (*Elsie the Cow*). ***Regulars:*** Jackson Beck, Natalie Core, Winifred

Hoeney, Craig McDonnell, Ron Rawson, Rolfe Sedan, Amy Sedell. ***Vocalists:*** Evelyn Knight, Jerry Wayne. ***Announcers:*** Jackson Beck, Paul Masterson. ***Orchestra:*** Mark Warnow.

OPENING

ANNOUNCER: Borden Milk welcomes everybody to *Happy Island*. And here is Ed Wynn as its hilarious majesty, King Bubbles.

606. HAPPY JACK TURNER. Variety, 15 min., NBC, 1932–1941.

A long-running program of music and songs with Jack Turner, a pianist who provided his own musical backing.

607. HAPPY JIM PARSONS. Variety, 15 min., NBC, 1940.

A weekly program of music and songs hosted by singer Jim Parsons. Irving Kaufman was the announcer.

608. THE HARDY FAMILY. Comedy, 30 min., Mutual, 1/3/52 to 1/1/53.

The house at 342 Maple Street in the town of Carvel is the residence of the Hardy family: James, a prestigious judge, his wife Emily and their son Andy. Andy is the typical American young man interested in cars and girls, but not necessarily in that order. He has a hot rod, a girl (Polly Benedict) and a best friend (Beasey), and stories relate Andy's misadventures with all three. Beasey is usually drawn into Andy's troubles, and having Beasey for a friend doesn't insure one of getting out of trouble. More complicated, yes; resolved, no. Polly is sweet and romantic and loves Andy, but worries about her reputation (she is shy about showing affection in public and constantly tells Andy, "No smooching on the front porch"). As for Andy's car, well, a larger allowance would help as it is always in need of repairs and parts. Based on the motion picture series.

Cast: Mickey Rooney (*Andy Hardy*); Lewis Stone (*James Hardy*); Fay Holden (*Emily Hardy*); Richard Crenna (*Beasey*); Eleanor Tannen (*Polly Benedict*). ***Announcers:*** Herb Allen, Jack McCoy. ***Music:*** Jerry Fielding.

OPENING

ANNOUNCER: From Hollywood, here's Mickey Rooney, Lewis Stone and Fay Holden in *The Hardy Family*. We're proud to present *The Hardy Family* based on the famous Metro-Goldwyn-Mayer motion picture series, which brought to life to millions and reflected the common joys and tribulations of the average American family. And now, here they are, the same great stars in the parts they created on the screen, Lewis Stone, Mickey Rooney and Fay Holden, *The Hardy Family*.

609. THE HAROLD PEARY SHOW—HONEST HAROLD. Comedy, 30 min., CBS, 9/10/50 to 6/13/51.

"The Homemaker" is a radio program broadcast over station KHJP in the small town of Melrose Springs. The program starts at ten in the morning and stars "Honest" Harold Hemp, a local personality who sings, tells jokes and offers advice to housewives—"to give them a break from their housework." Harold lives with his mother and his ten-year-old nephew Marvin, who has come to stay with him (he attends fifth grade at Melrose Springs Grammar School). Stories relate Harold's misadventures with the various characters he encounters and his efforts to become a father to Marvin. *Other regular characters:* Gloria, the station switchboard manager; Doc Yak Yak, Hal's friend; Pete the Policeman; Miss Turner, the schoolteacher.

Cast: Harold Peary (*"Honest" Harold Hemp*); Jane Morgan, Kathryn Card (*Mrs. Hemp*); Sammy Ogg (*Marvin*); Gloria Holliday (*Gloria*); Joseph Kearns (*Doc Yak Yak*); Parley Baer (*Pete*); June Witley (*Miss Turner*). ***Announcer:*** Bob LeMond. ***Music:*** Jack Meakin.

OPENING

ANNOUNCER: *The Harold Peary Show*. And now, Harold Peary as Honest Harold, the Homemaker.

CLOSING

ANNOUNCER: You have just heard *The Harold Peary Show—Honest Harold*. Stay tuned now for *The Bing Crosby Show* which follows immediately on most of these CBS stations. This is Bob LeMond speaking.

610. HAROLD TEEN. Comedy, 30 min., Mutual, 1941–1942.

Harold Teen is a young adolescent with a knack for finding trouble. Stories, based on the comic strip by Carl Ed, relate Harold's various mishaps as he struggles to cope with life. *Other regular characters:* Shadow Smart, his best friend; Lillums Lovewell, his girlfriend; Cynthia, the girl who has a crush on Harold; Beezie

Jenks and Josie, Harold's friends; Harold and Beezie's fathers.

Cast: Charles Flynn, Willard Farnum, Eddie Firestone, Jr. (*Harold Teen*); Bob Jellison (*Shadow Smart*); Loretta Poynton, Eunice Yankee (*Lillums Lovewell*); Rosemary Garbell (*Josie*); Marvin Miller (*Beezie Jenks*); Willard Waterman (*Harold's father*); Jack Spencer (*Beezie's father*). ***Announcer:*** Marvin Miller.

611. Harry James and His Orchestra. Variety, 15 and 30 min. versions, CBS, 1942–1945.

A weekly program of music and songs with trumpeter Harry James as the host. Buddy DeVito and Kitty Kallen were the vocalists and the Harry James Orchestra provided the big band music.

612. The Harry Savoy Show. Variety, 30 min., Mutual, 1946.

A weekly program of music and songs with host Harry Savoy and vocalists Vera Holly and the Murphy Sisters Trio. John Gart and his orchestra provided the music.

613. Harv and Esther. Variety, 30 min., CBS, 1935–1936.

Comedy skits about a husband and wife (Harv and Esther) coupled with music and songs. The program was sponsored by International Harvester and the character names of Harv and Esther were derived from the word Harvester.

Cast: Alan Reed (*Harv*); Audrey Marsh (*Esther*). ***Vocalists:*** Jack Arthur, the Rhythm Girls. ***Orchestra:*** Vic Arden.

614. Harvest of Stars. Variety, 30 min., NBC, 1945–1950.

A weekly program of music and songs sponsored by International Harvester. Raymond Massey was the first to host; he was replaced by soloist James Melton. Don Hancock did the announcing and music was provided first by the Howard Barlow, then the Frank Black Orchestra.

615. Harvey and Dell. Serial, 15 min., NBC Blue, 1940–1942; CBS, 1942.

Dramatic incidents in the lives of a three-member family: Harvey, the father (played by Dwight Meade); Dell, his wife (Doris Meade); and Dorothy (Dorothy Meade), their daughter.

616. Hashknife Hartley. Western, 30 min., Mutual, 1950–1951.

The West of a century ago was the setting for a weekly series about the adventures of two roaming cowboys: the happy-go-lucky Hashknife Hartley and his sidekick, Sleepy Stevens.

Cast: Frank Martin (*Hashknife Hartley*); Barton Yarborough (*Sleepy Stevens*). ***Host-Narrator:*** W.C. Tuttle. ***Announcer:*** Don McCall. ***Music:*** Harry Zimmerman.

OPENING

Announcer: This is W.C. Tuttle's famous adventure story of Hashknife Hartley and Sleepy Stevens starring Frank Martin as Hashknife Hartley and Barton Yarborough as Sleepy Stevens. Here now is the creator of these rough and tumble cowboys, W.C. Tuttle himself, ready to begin today's story called "Range War."

Tuttle: Howdy, folks. Hashknife Hartley and Sleepy Stevens are riding along...

617. The Haunting Hour. Anthology, 30 min., Syndicated, 1946.

Suspense dramatizations that feature a different cast and story each week.

OPENING

Announcer: No! No! Stay where you are. Do not break the stillness of this moment! For this is a time of mystery, a time when the imagination is free and moves swiftly. This is *The Haunting Hour*!

618. Have Gun—Will Travel. Western, 30 min., CBS, 11/23/58 to 11/27/60.

Paladin (no other name given) is a former Army officer turned professional gunman for hire. He is based in the Hotel Carlton in San Francisco (1875) and has a calling card that reads "Have Gun—Will Travel. Wire Paladin. San Francisco." Stories, based on the television series of the same name, relate Paladin's exploits as he uses his experience to help people unable to protect themselves. Paladin is a loner with few friends and a wide reputation. He has an eye for the ladies and a taste for fine wine and food. *Other regular characters:* Hey Boy, his servant; Miss Wong, a hotel maid who is Hey Boy's girlfriend.

Cast: John Dehner (*Paladin*); Ben Wright (*Hey Boy*); Virginia Gregg (*Miss Wong*). ***Announcer:*** Hugh Douglas. ***Producer:*** Norman MacDonnell.

OPENING

ANNOUNCER: *Have Gun—Will Travel*, starring Mr. John Dehner as Paladin. San Francisco, 1875, the Carlton Hotel, headquarters of the man called Paladin.

CLOSING

ANNOUNCER: *Have Gun—Will Travel*, created by Herb Meadow and Sam Rolfe, is produced by Norman MacDonnell and stars John Dehner as Paladin. Hugh Douglas speaking. Join us again next week for more *Have Gun—Will Travel.*

619. Hawaii Calls. Variety, 30 min., Mutual, 1945–1963.

A weekly program of music and songs from Hawaii. Webley Edwards served as the host and commentator and Jim Wahl was the announcer. Al Kealoha, Danny Sinclair and Perry and His Singing Surfsiders were the regulars. The program began as a local series in Hawaii in 1935.

620. Hawk Durango. Western, 30 min., CBS, 1946–1948.

The original concept (1946–47) dealt with the adventures of Hawk Durango, a saloon owner in the Old West, and his sidekick, Brazos John. After one year, the format changed to focus on the exploits of Hawk Larabee, a cattleman who owned the Black Mesa Ranch, and his sidekick, Sombre Jones.

Cast (Hawk Durango): Elliott Lewis (*Hawk Durango*); Barton Yarborough (*Brazos John*). ***Cast (Hawk Larabee):*** Barton Yarborough (*Hawk Larabee*); Barney Phillips (*Sombre Jones*). ***Announcer:*** James Matthews. ***Music:*** Wilbur Hatch.

Hawk Larabee *see* **Hawk Durango**

621. Hawthorne TBA. Variety, 30 min., NBC, 1953.

A weekly program of music and songs featuring performances by guests. Jim Hawthorne served as the host; John Storm did the announcing; and Robert Armbruster and his orchestra supplied the music.

622. Hear It Now. Documentary, 60 min., CBS, 1950–1951.

A weekly program that replayed famous events previously heard on the air. Interviews and reports from around the world were also a part of the program. Edward R. Murrow was the host and narrator; music was supplied by Alfredo Antonini and his orchestra. Edward R. Murrow and Fred W. Friendly were the producers.

623. Heart Throbs of the Hills. Variety, 15 min., 4/39 to 6/39.

An updated, transcribed version of *Hillbilly Heart Throbs* (see entry) that, like the original series, presented dramatizations based on old folk songs.

Cast: Bella Allen, Margaret Johnson, Travis Johnson, Robert Porterfield, Ethel Park Richardson, Johnnie Rogers, Robert Strauss. ***Announcer:*** Kelvin Keech. ***Music:*** The Hilltop Harmonizers. ***Producer:*** Ethel Park Richardson.

624. Heartbreak Theater. Anthology, 30 min., Syndicated, 1956–1977.

Stories of the Salvation Army and its role in our society. Marvin Miller, Macdonald Carey and C.P. MacGregor were the hosts and narrators. The program, sponsored by the Salvation Army, was produced by C.P. MacGregor.

625. Hearthstone of the Death Squad. Crime Drama, 30 min., CBS, 8/30/51 to 9/17/52.

"You're more clever than I gave you credit for!" is a familiar expression from criminals when they are apprehended by Inspector Hearthstone, a brilliant Scotland Yard detective, who uses trickery to outwit and capture villains. Hearthstone is with the Death Squad Division of the Metropolitan Police Department in London and stories follow his intense investigations into murders. He is assisted by Detective Sam Cook. Originally broadcast as a segment of *Mystery Theater*.

Cast: Alfred Shirley (*Inspector Hearthstone*); James Meighan (*Sam Cook*). ***Announcer:*** Harry Cramer.

OPENING (from 1/10/52)

ANNOUNCER: And now, *Hearthstone of the Death Squad* in "The Terrifying Letter Murder Case." Tonight we again present the famous Hearthstone of the Death Squad, implacable manhunter of the Metropolitan Police in one of his greatest investigations entitled "The Terrifying Letter Murder Case." And now, Inspector Hearthstone in "The Terrifying Letter Murder Case."

CLOSING

ANNOUNCER: And thus, Hearthstone of the

Death Squad writes *solved* in the files of "The Terrifying Letter Murder Case." The part of Inspector Hearthstone was played by Alfred Shirley. Written by Frank Hummert, directed by Henry Howard, and is a presentation of CBS Radio.

626. Heart's Desire. Human Interest, 30 min., Mutual, 1946–1948.

A letter submitted by a listener is read to the studio audience. The contents reveal a sad story in which the writer explains why he or she needs a specific item. The studio audience votes on each letter (via applause) and the most deserving individuals receive the item they requested. Ben Alexander served as the host.

627. The Hedda Hopper Show. Variety, 30 min., NBC, 1950–1951.

Celebrity interviews, editorial comments, comedy skits and gossip with Hedda Hopper, a former actress turned Hollywood gossip columnist. Hedda Hopper hosted and Frank Worth and his orchestra provided the music.

628. Hedda Hopper's Hollywood. Interview, 15 min., NBC, 1939–1944;CBS, 1944.

A daily program of celebrity interviews with Hollywood gossip columnist Hedda Hopper as the host. Music was provided by Richard Aurandt and his orchestra.

629. The Helen Hayes Theater. Anthology, 30 min., NBC Blue, 1935–1937; CBS, 1945–1946.

A weekly series of dramatizations starring Helen Hayes as the host and female lead (guests appeared as the male lead).George Bryan did the announcing and music was supplied by Mark Warnow and his orchestra.

630. Helen Holden: Government Girl. Drama, 15 min., Mutual, 1941.

The romance, intrigues and adventures of Helen Holden, a U.S. government agent in Washington, D.C., at the outbreak of World War II. *Other regular characters:* Mary Holden, her aunt, a newspaper correspondent; David, Helen's romantic interest.

Cast: Nancy Ordway (*Helen Holden*); Nell Fleming (*Mary Holden*); Robert Pollard (*David*). ***Announcer:*** Frank Blair.

631. Hello. Variety, 15 min., NBC, 1943.

A weekly program of music and songs with vocalist Louise King as host and the music of Joseph Gallichio and his orchestra.

632. Hello, Peggy. Serial, 15 min., NBC, 1937–1938.

A daily drama about the struggles of young marrieds Peggy and Ted Hopkins. Eunice Howard played Peggy and Alan Bunce was Ted.

633. A Helping Hand. Anthology, 15 min., CBS, 10/13/41 to 1/30/42.

Short dramatizations that depict the plight of people faced with real-life problems. Following the drama, the host appears to present possible solutions to the circumstances presented in the story.

Host: John J. Anthony. ***Announcer:*** Don Hancock. ***Organist:*** Elsie Thompson.

OPENING

Announcer: The makers of Ironized Yeast present *A Helping Hand. A Helping Hand* is a new program dedicated to public service and conducted by John J. Anthony, nationally famous counselor on human problems, author of the well-known book *Marriage and Family Problems and How to Solve Them*, and founder of the Marital Relations Institute. And now, here is Mr. Anthony [who would then tell the audience of the problem to be dramatized].

634. Helpmate. Serial, 15 min., NBC, 9/22/41 to 6/30/44.

Incidents in the daily lives of three married couples who are also neighbors: Linda and Steve Harper, Grace and Clyde Marshall and Holly and George Emerson.

Cast: Arlene Francis, Fern Parsons (*Linda Harper*); Myron McCormick, John Larkin (*Steve Harper*); Judith Evelyn (*Grace Marshall*); Karl Weber (*Clyde Marshall*); Beryl Vaughn (*Holly Emerson*); Sidney Ellstrom (*George Emerson*). ***Producers:*** Anne Hummert, Frank Hummert.

635. The Henry Morgan Show. Comedy, 15 min., N.Y. (WOR), 1940–1943; 30 min., ABC, 1946–1947; NBC, 1949–1950.

A weekly series of monologues, songs, music and comedy skits. The program began locally in New York with occasional appearances on the full Mutual network. At this time, Morgan's show aired six times a week and consisted primarily of recorded music (which Henry chose from his record collection) and acerbic comedy with Morgan bad-mouthing everyone and everything (including his sponsors). When the series became a half-hour, "the bad boy of radio" continued his off-the-wall remarks (aimed mostly at his sponsors) and coupled them with various comedy skits and performances by guest stars. Morgan's local show was originally called *Meet Mr. Morgan* and then *Here's Morgan*. Eversharp razor blades, Life Savers candy, Shell gasoline, Adler Elevator Shoes, Lifebuoy Soap, Ironized Yeast and Pall Mall cigarettes were among the sponsors needled by Morgan.

Host: Henry Morgan. ***Regulars:*** Art Carney, Kenny Delmar, Florence Halop, Charles Irving, Lisa Kirk, Madaline Lee, Alice Pearce, Minerva Pious, Arnold Stang. ***Vocalists:*** The Billy Williams Choir. ***Announcers:*** Art Ballinger, Ben Grauer, Ed Herlihy, Charles Irving, Durward Kirby, David Ross, Dan Seymour. ***Orchestra:*** Bernie Green, Milton Katims.

OPENING

HENRY (over music of "For He's a Jolly Good Fellow"): Good evening *any*body.

ANNOUNCER: Here's Morgan.

636. HER HONOR, NANCY JAMES. Serial. 15 min., CBS, 1938–1939.

Dramatic incidents in the life of Nancy James, a judge in the Court of Common Relations in Metropolis City. *Other regular characters:* Richard Wharton, the mayor; Anthony Hale, the D.A.; Evelyn Wharton, Richard's wife.

Cast: Barbara Weeks (*Nancy James*); Joseph Curtin (*Richard Wharton*); Ned Wever (*Anthony Hale*); Kay Strozzi (*Evelyn Wharton*). ***Announcer:*** Frank Gallop.

HERB SHRINER TIME *see* **ALKA-SELTZER TIME**

637. HERCULE POIROT. Crime Drama, 30 min., Mutual, 1945–1947.

The house at 14 Farraway Street in London, England, is residence to Hercule Poirot, a brilliant Belgian detective who uses his wits to outsmart criminals. Stories, based on the character created by Agatha Christie, relate Poirot's efforts to solve various crimes, mostly murders. When the program's title switched to *The New Adventures of Hercule Poirot* in 1947, Hercule took up residence at the New White Haven Mansion. Harold Huber played Poirot and each episode was introduced by Agatha Christie (via shortwave from London).

OPENING

ANNOUNCER: Agatha Christie's Poirot. From the thrill-packed pages of Agatha Christie's unforgettable stories of corpses, clues and crimes, Mutual brings you, complete with bowler hat and raised mustache, your favorite detective, Hercule Poirot, starring Harold Huber in "The Case of the Careless Victim."

638. HERE COMES ELMER. Comedy, 30 min., CBS, 12/9/44 to 6/30/45.

The warm weather replacement for *Al Pearce and His Gang* that dealt with the mishaps of Elmer Blurt, a super salesman (in his own mind) who could never seem to sell anything. Elmer lived at the Puny Plaza Hotel where his friend Arlene worked the switchboard.

Cast: Al Pearce (*Elmer Blurt*); Arlene Harris (*Arlene*). ***Vocalists:*** The Smart Set. ***Announcer:*** Wendell Niles. ***Orchestra:*** Mickey Sillette.

639. HERE COMES MCBRIDE. Crime Drama, 30 min., NBC, summer of 1949.

Rex McBride is a tough private insurance investigator based in Los Angeles. He is the cops' number one suspect in cases ("He just looks to be guilty") and girls think of him "as a poor schnook who can't afford fancy restaurants" ("But I can, that's why I have an expense account"). Stories follow Rex's light-hearted adventures when his seemingly simple cases involve him with murder and mayhem.

Cast: Frank Lovejoy (*Rex McBride*). ***Announcer:*** Art Ballinger. ***Organist:*** Hank Sylvern. ***Producer:*** Warren Lewis.

OPENING

ANNOUNCER (over opening theme of "Here Comes the Bride"): *Here Comes McBride*! Out of the pages of Cleave F. Adams' popular novels, NBC presents an exciting new detective series, *Here Comes McBride* starring Frank Lovejoy.

CLOSING

ANNOUNCER: You have been listening to the first in a new mystery series, *Here Comes McBride*, starring Frank Lovejoy and based on the popular fiction character created by Cleave F. Adams. The program was directed by Warren Lewis. This is NBC, the National Broadcasting Company.

640. HERE'S HOWE. Human Interest, 15 min., Mutual, 1945.

A short-lived program wherein host Pete Howe discussed strange facts.

641. HERE'S TO ROMANCE. Variety, 30 min., CBS, 1943–1945.

A weekly program of music, songs and dramatic skits. Buddy Clark and Dick Haymes were the hosts; vocals were by Martha Tilton and the David Broekman Chorus. Jim Ameche did the announcing and music was by the David Broekman (and later) Ray Bloch orchestras.

642. HERE'S TO ROMANCE. Variety, 15 min., CBS, 1947.

A weekly program of music and songs with Phil Hanna as the host. Vocals were by Betty Brewer and Her Boyfriends. Durward Kirby did the announcing and Phil Davis and his orchestra provided the music.

643. THE HERMIT'S CAVE. Anthology, 30 min., Syndicated, 1940–1943.

Grisly tales of murder and the supernatural as told by an old character called the Hermit (who stood at the mouth of his cave and warned people with weak hearts not to listen).

Cast: Mel Johnson (*The Hermit*). ***Producers:*** William Conrad, Bill Forman.

OPENING

ANNOUNCER: And now the Hermit.

SOUND: Howling dogs and crackling wind.

HERMIT: Heh, heh, heh, heh, heh, heh, heh. Ghost stories, weird stories, murder, too. Heh, heh, heh, heh, heh, heh. The Hermit knows of them all. Turn out your lights, turn them out. Ahhhh, have you heard the story, "The Blackness of Terror"? Hmmmmmmm? Then listen while the Hermit tells you the story. Heh, heh, heh, heh, heh.

CLOSING

HERMIT: Turn on your lights, turn them on. Heh, heh, heh, heh, heh. I'll be back, pleasant dreams. Heh, heh, heh, heh, heh.

ANNOUNCER: All characters, places and occurrences mentioned in *The Hermit's Cave* are fictitious and similarities to persons, places or occurrences are purely coincidental.

644. HIDDEN STARS. Variety, 30 min., NBC, 1940.

A program of music and songs that featured a performance by an up-and-coming star. Orrin Tucker was the host; Bonnie Baker and Jack Bartell the regulars; the Bobby Guardi Quartet supplied the music.

645. HIGH ADVENTURE. Anthology, 30 min., Mutual, 1947–1954.

Originally a series of dramatizations detailing the experiences of ordinary people suddenly projected into unusual circumstances. The revised format focused on the experiences of the High Adventure Society, a fictitious club whose members appeared to relate the various life and death situations they encountered and overcame.

Host-Narrators: Henry Norell, George Sanders. ***Announcer:*** Phil Tonkin. ***Music:*** Jim Boles, Sylvan Levin.

646. HIGHWAY PATROL. Crime Drama, 15 min., Mutual, 1943.

The work of the men of the U.S. Highway Patrol as depicted through the activities of Cpl. Steve Taylor and Mike Gallager, state troopers who risked their lives to keep our highways safe.

Cast: Michael Fitzmaurice (*Steve Taylor*); John McGovern (*Mike Gallager*).

647. HIGHWAYS IN MELODY. Variety, 30 min., NBC, 1944–1948.

A weekly program that mixed popular standards with light classical music. Roland Winters served as the host and commentator. Dorothy Kirsten and the Ken Christy Chorus provided the vocals; Ford Bond did the announcing and Paul LaValle and his orchestra provided the music.

648. Hilda Hope, M.D. Serial, 15 min., NBC, 1939–1940.

The dramatic story of Hilda Hope, a dedicated female physician. Selena Royle played Hilda Hope and others in the cast were Vera Allen, Richard Gordon, House Jameson and Ann Shepherd. Charles Paul provided the organ music.

649. Hildegarde. Variety, 30 min., NBC, 1943.

A program of music and songs with Hildegarde Loretta Sell, a singer-pianist known as "The Incomparable Hildegarde." Radcliffe Hall did the announcing and Bob Grant and his orchestra provided the music.

650. Hildegarde's Radio Room. Variety, 30 min., CBS, 1946–1947.

Music and songs with "The Incomparable Hildegarde" (Hildegarde Loretta Sell) as the host. Weekly guests performed alongside Hildegarde (a singer-pianist); comical pianist Oscar Levant was the regular. Harry Sosnik and his orchestra provided the music and the program was sponsored by the Campbell Soup Company.

651. Hillbilly Heart Throbs. Anthology, 15 min., NBC, 5/23/33 to 10/27/38.

Dramas based on old folk songs and presented like a musical play. Also known as *Dreams of Long Ago*. See also *Heart Throbs of the Hills* for a revised version of this series.

Cast: Curtis Arnell, Ray Collins, Clayton "Bud" Collyer, Brian Donlevy, Anne Elstner, Billy Halop, Florence Halop, Agnes Moorehead, Ethel Park Richardson. ***Vocalists:*** Frank Luther, Carson Robinson, the Vass Family. ***Producer-Writer:*** Ethel Park Richardson.

652. Hilltop House. Serial, 15 min., CBS, 1937–1941.

Dramatic incidents in the life of Bess Johnson, matron of the Hilltop House Orphanage in the town of Glendale. Stories stressed her struggles to choose between sacrificing love to raise the children of other women. See also *The Story of Bess Johnson*, the spinoff series.

Cast: Bess Johnson (*Bess Johnson*); Grace Matthews, Jan Miner (*Julie Erickson*); Janice Gilbert (*Jean Adair*); Jim Donnelly (*Jerry Adair*); Vera Allen (*Grace Doblen*); Carleton Young, Spencer Bentley (*Dr. Clark*); John Moore (*Jeffrey Barton*); Irene Hubbard (*Thelma Gidley*); Estelle Levy (*Stella Rudnick*); Jeanne Elkins (*Pixie Osborne*); Dorothy Lowell (*Linda Clark*); Gee Gee James (*Tulip Elson*); Alfred Swenson, Jack Roseleigh (*Paul Hutchinson*); Lilli Darvas (*Hannah*); Alvin Sullum (*Kevin Burke*); James Van Dyk (*Ed Crowley*); Edwin Bruce (*David Findlay*); Evelyn Streich (*Gwen Barry*); Jerry Tucker (*Roy Barry*); Joseph Curtin (*Steve Cortland*); Jay Jostyn (*Frank Klabber*). ***Organist:*** Chet Kingsbury. ***Producer:*** Ed Wolfe.

OPENING

Announcer: *Hilltop House*, starring Bess Johnson, is dedicated to the women of America. *Hilltop House*, the dramatic story of a woman who must choose between love and the career of raising other women's children.

653. The Hinds Honey and Almond Cream Program. Comedy, 30 min., CBS, 10/4/39 to 6/26/40.

Skits that revolve around the antics of George Burns and Gracie Allen in a revamped version of their prior show, *The Chesterfield Program* (which see). New to the cast is Bubbles, Gracie's overweight friend. George and Gracie are singles (friends) and many sketches revolve around Gracie's efforts to find a man (never realizing that George is the right one for her). Music and songs are coupled with the comedy segments. Sponsored by Lehn and Fink Products, makers of Hinds Honey and Almond Cream (a skin lotion).

Cast: George Burns (*George Burns*); Gracie Allen (*Gracie Allen*); Mary Kelly (*Bubbles*). ***Regulars:*** Ted Allen, Mary Kelly, Elliott Lewis, Gene Loughlin, Hal Rourke, Pauline Swanson. ***Vocalist:*** Frank Parker. ***Announcer:*** Truman Bradley. ***Orchestra:*** Ray Noble.

654. His Honor the Barber. Comedy, 30 min., NBC, 10/16/45 to 4/9/46.

Vincent County is a small city of 3,543 people on the outskirts of Colorado. Bernard Fitz is the town's judge (who presides in District Court Number One) and operator of a barber shop on the side. McGrath is the town's sheriff and a thorn in Fitz's side. The judge is a sympathetic man who believes in a humanistic interpretation of the law. McGrath, "Vincent's own little Hitler," believes in a by-the-books punishment for lawbreakers. Their clash, along with Judge Fitz's efforts to deal with problems at home (he lives with his niece, Susan) and at work, are the focal point of stories. *Other regular characters:* Joel Pearson, the lawyer.

Cast: Barry Fitzgerald (*Judge Bernard Fitz*); William Green (*Sheriff McGrath*); Dawn Bender (*Susan Fitz*); Leo Cleary (*Joel Pearson*). ***Announcer:*** Frank Martin. ***Music:*** Opie Cates. ***Producer:*** Carlton E. Morse.

OPENING

VOICE: District Court Number One in the court house of Vincent County on the twenty-seventh day of November 1945, is convened. Judge Bernard Fitz presiding.

ANNOUNCER: Ballantine, America's largest-selling ale, presents Barry Fitzgerald starring in *His Honor, the Barber*, written and produced by Carlton E. Morse.

655. Hit the Jackpot. Game, 30 min., CBS, 6/29/48 to 12/27/49.

Members of the listening audience were involved. Clues to a mystery phrase were presented in either song or story. A postcard was selected and a call placed to that listener. If the listener could guess the mystery phrase, he or she won a lavish prize.

Host: Bill Cullen. ***Vocalists:*** The Ray Charles Singers. ***Announcers:*** George Bryan, Richard Stark. ***Orchestra:*** Al Goodman. ***Producers:*** Mark Goodson, Bill Todman.

656. The Hoagy Carmichael Show. Variety, 15 min., CBS, 1946–1948.

Orchestra leader and composer Hoagy Carmichael as the host of a weekly program of music and songs. Buddy Cole, Phil Stevens and Shirlee Turner were the regulars; Bob Lemond did the announcing; and the Hoagy Carmichael Orchestra provided the music.

657. Hobby Lobby. Human Interest, 30 min., CBS, 1937–1938; NBC Red, 1938; NBC Blue, 1938–1939; CBS, 1939–1946; Mutual, 1949.

The program showcased the usual and unusual hobbies of ordinary people. The title was derived from a segment wherein a guest celebrity appeared to "lobby his hobby."

Host: Dave Elman. ***Announcers:*** Alan Kent, Harry Von Zell. ***Orchestra:*** Ted Rapf, Harry Salter, Harry Sosnik.

658. Hogan's Daughter. Comedy, 30 min., NBC, 6/21/49 to 9/14/49.

Phyllis Hogan, the red-haired, blue-eyed daughter of Tom and Kate Hogan, feels that nothing nice ever happens to her or her family. She believes that "them that has, gets" and wishes that she too could catch a break. Phyllis constantly looks for work, but can't seem to find any (she attended the Dalgrim Business School, got a B-minus in typing and hopes to become a secretary). She has a boyfriend, TV repairman Marvin Gaffney, a confidante (LaVerne) and numerous problems. Phyllis is not the type to take things lying down and her efforts to overcome the causes of aggravation in her life is the focal point of stories. The Hogans live in an apartment in Manhattan on East 53rd Street; Tom's favorite hangout is O'Meara's Bar; Phyllis and LaVerne have lunch each day at the Gypsy Tea Shop; and Phyllis' lucky number is 26.

Cast: Shirley Booth (*Phyllis Hogan*); Howard Smith (*Tom Hogan*); Betty Garde (*Kate Hogan*); Everett Sloane (*Marvin Gaffney*); Betty Garde (*LaVerne*); Johnny Roventini (*Johnny the bellboy; commercial spokesman*). ***Announcer:*** Ken Roberts. ***Music:*** Bernard Green.

OPENING

ANNOUNCER: Philip Morris presents *Hogan's Daughter* starring Shirley Booth.

JOHNNY: Call for Philip Mor-rees, call for Philip Mor-rees.

ANNOUNCER: It's a wonderful feeling to wake up fresh with no cigarette hangover. Yes, you'll be glad tomorrow when you smoke Philip Morris today.

JOHNNY: Call for Philip Mor-rees.

ANNOUNCER: And now *Hogan's Daughter* starring Shirley Booth.

CLOSING

ANNOUNCER: Listen again next week for *Hogan's Daughter*. Until then—

JOHNNY: Call for Philip Mor-rees.

ANNOUNCER: Friends, remember this. If you're tired of cigarette hangover, call for the one cigarette that gives you a milder, fresher, cleaner smoke. Yes, from now on—

JOHNNY: Call for Philip Mor-rees.

ANNOUNCER: Good night, Johnny, see you next Tuesday, same time, same station when Philip Morris will again present Shirley Booth as *Hogan's Daughter*, written by John Wheaton and Sam Moore. Until then—

JOHNNY: Call for Philip Mor-rees.

ANNOUNCER: Smoke a pipe? You get real solace, comfort and pleasure from Revelation Pipe Tobacco ... only 15 cents. Try Revelation. All names and characters used on this program are fictitious. This is Ken Roberts saying good night from Philip Morris. This is NBC, the National Broadcasting Company.

659. HOLIDAY FOR MUSIC. Variety, 30 min., CBS, 1946.

A weekly program of music and songs with vocalist Kitty Kallen as the host. Curt Massey was regularly featured and David Rose and his orchestra provided the music.

660. HOLLAND HOUSEWARMING. Variety, 30 min., NBC, 1941.

Each week a guest of honor was given a housewarming party featuring music and songs—all sponsored by Holland Furnaces. The program is also known as *Housewarming*. The first broadcast was called "Holland Housewife" and featured actress Merle Oberon as the host.

Host: Don McNeill. ***Regulars:*** Bob Jellison, Hilda Graham, Ed Prentiss, Curt Roberts, Sharon Lee Smith. ***Announcer:*** Verne Smith. ***Orchestra:*** Benny Goodman.

661. HOLLYWOOD AIRPORT. Anthology, 30 min., ABC, 2/3/54 to 6/2/54.

Dramatizations set against the background of Hollywood Airport and based on stories appearing in *Photoplay* magazine. The stories are seen through the eyes of Cal York, a *Photoplay* columnist.

Cast: Joe Heigesen (*Cal York/Host/Narrator*). ***Announcer:*** Dorian St. George.

662. HOLLYWOOD CALLING. Game, 60 and 30 min. versions, NBC, 1949–1950.

The program was designed to test the listening audience's knowledge of film personalities and movies. A postcard was selected and a name film personality telephoned the listener to ask him questions regarding a film. If the player could identify the subject of the questions, he won a cash prize.

Host: George Murphy. ***Producer:*** Victor Knight.

663. HOLLYWOOD HOTEL. Anthology, 60 min., CBS, 1934–1938.

The program combined variety performances with dramatic productions set against the background of the swank Hollywood Hotel. Top name Hollywood stars were featured in the radio dramas.

Host: Louella Parsons. ***Emcees:*** Dick Powell, Fred MacMurray, Herbert Marshall, William Powell. ***Telephone Operator:*** Duane Thompson. ***Vocalist:*** Anne Jamison. ***Announcer:*** Ken Niles. ***Orchestra:*** Ted Fiorito, Raymond Paige. ***Producer:*** Bill Bacher.

664. HOLLYWOOD JACKPOT. Game, 30 min., CBS, 1946.

Selected members of the studio audience competed in various game contests for merchandise prizes. Kenny Delmar was the host and Bill Cullen did the announcing. Louis Cowan produced.

665. HOLLYWOOD LOVE STORY. Anthology, 30 min., NBC, 1951–1953.

Fictional romances based on stories appearing in *Photoplay* magazine. Alexander Scourby served as the host and narrator.

666. HOLLYWOOD MYSTERY TIME. Drama, 30 min., NBC Blue, 1944; ABC, 1944–1945.

The program was originally a weekly series of dramatizations featuring Carleton Young and Gloria Blondell as the male and female leads (guests appeared in supporting roles). In 1945, the format changed to focus on the cases of a movie producer (Jim Laughton) who worked as a private detective on the side. He was assisted by his secretary, Gloria Dean.

Cast: Carleton Young (*Jim Laughton*); Gloria Blondell (*Gloria Dean*). ***Announcer:*** Jim Doyle. ***Music:*** Ernest Gill.

667. HOLLYWOOD OPEN HOUSE. Variety, 30 min., Syndicated, 1946–1947.

A weekly program of music and songs first hosted by orchestra conductor Enric Madriquera. Jim Ameche became the host in 1947. Harry Cool, Jerry Cooper and Patricia Gilmore were the regulars. Jim Ameche did the announcing and music was provided by the Enric Madriquera and Ray Bloch orchestras.

668. Hollywood Players. Anthology, 30 min., CBS, 1946–1947.

A weekly series of adaptations of major motion pictures, novels and stage productions featuring a cast of regulars (Claudette Colbert, Bette Davis, Joan Fontaine, Paulette Goddard and Gregory Peck). Frank Bingham did the announcing and music was by Bernard Katz.

669. Hollywood Playhouse. Anthology, 30 min., NBC Blue, 1937–1939.

Dramatic presentations featuring top name performers. Jim Ameche, Charles Boyer, Herbert Marshall, Gale Page and Tyrone Power served as the hosts over its two-year run. Music was by Harry Sosnik and his orchestra.

670. Hollywood Premiere. Anthology, 30 min., CBS, 1941.

Dramatic productions that featured well-known stars. The performers worked without pay for air time to plug their upcoming movies. Hollywood gossip columnist Louella Parsons was the host.

671. Hollywood Preview. Anthology, 30 min., CBS, 1946.

Short dramatizations based on forthcoming motion pictures. Knox Manning served as the host and Hal Hudson was the producer.

672. Hollywood Showcase. Variety, 30 min., CBS, 1948.

A weekly program of music, songs and comedy with Mickey Rooney as the host. Dave Barry, Buddy Cole, Barbara Fuller and Julie Wilson were the regulars; Bob Lemond did the announcing; and music was by Lud Gluskin and his orchestra.

673. Hollywood Sound Stage. Anthology, 30 min., CBS, 1951–1952.

Dramatic productions in which established performers donated their earnings to help support the Motion Picture Relief Fund. Hugh Douglas did the announcing and Alexander Courage supplied the music.

674. Hollywood Star Showcase. Anthology, 30 min., CBS, 1950–1951; ABC, 1951–1952; NBC, 1951–1953.

A weekly series of original dramatic productions featuring top name film stars. Herb Rawlinson and Orville Anderson were the hosts; Norman Brokenshire was the announcer; and music was provided by the Jeff Alexander and Basil Adlam orchestras. The program is also known as *Hollywood Star Playhouse*.

675. Hollywood Star Theater. Anthology, 30 min., NBC, 1947–1952.

The format featured an established star performing with a promising young actor in a story that was especially written for that person. Don Wilson was the announcer and Jeff Alexander and his orchestra provided the music. The program is also known as *Hollywood Star Preview*, *Hollywood Theater* and *Tums Hollywood Theater* (when sponsored by Tums antacid).

676. Hollywood Star Time. Anthology, 15 min., ABC, 1944–1945; 30 min., CBS, 1946–1947.

The original quarter-hour format featured interviews with celebrities. When the series switched to a half-hour format, it presented radio adaptations of well-known motion pictures.

Host: Herbert Marshall. ***Announcer:*** Wendell Niles.

OPENING (from 2/15/47)

Announcer: You're twice as sure with two great names—Frigidaire and General Motors. Frigidaire presents *Hollywood Star Time* direct from Hollywood. Tonight, the radio production of Columbia Pictures' delightful comedy, *Talk of the Town*, starring Cary Grant, Marguerite Chapman and your Saturday evening host, Herbert Marshall.

CLOSING

Announcer: Until next Saturday at this same time then, here is our Saturday evening host, calling it a day with his familiar—

Host: As ever, Herbert Marshall, good night.

Announcer: This is Wendell Niles speaking for Frigidaire, made only by General Motors. Good night.

677. Hollywood Tour. Human Interest, 15 min., ABC, 1947.

Cal York, columnist for *Photoplay* magazine, as host of a program that mixed celebrity interviews with tours of Hollywood. A woman, chosen from the studio audience, was asked a question submitted by a listener. If she correctly answered it, she received the tour and returned on the next broadcast to relate her experiences. Dresser Dahlstead did the announcing.

678. Hollywood Whispers. Gossip, 15 min., Mutual, 1938–1942.

A program of gossip with host George Fisher. The program is also known as *The George Fisher Show*.

679. Home Folks. Variety, 15 min., CBS, 1952.

A weekly program of music and songs sponsored by the Quaker Oats Company. Owen Bradley was the host. The Aunt Jemima Quartet provided the music and vocals were by Ernest Tubb and the Beasley Sisters.

680. Home of the Brave. Serial, 15 min., CBS, 1/6/41 to 9/19/41.

The story, set in the small town of New Chance, Colorado, follows events in the lives of two people: Joe, a telephone lineman, and Casino, the girl he loves, but who does not love him.

Cast: Tom Tully, Ed Latimer (*Joe*); Jeanette Nolan, Sammie Hill (*Casino*); Richard Widmark, Vincent Donehue (*Neil Davisson*); Jone Allison (*Lois Davisson*); Alan Bunce (*Spencer Howard*); Ted de Corsia (*Patrick Mulvaney*); Ed Latimer (*Doc Gordon*). ***Organist:*** Charles Paul.

681. Home Sweet Home. Serial, 15 min., NBC, 1934–1936.

Dramatic incidents in the lives of Lucy and Fred Kent, a married couple with a young son (Dick) who are struggling to make ends meet so that one day they can have "a home sweet home of their own."

Cast: Harriet MacGibbon (*Lucy Kent*); Cecil Secrest (*Fred Kent*); Billy Halop (*Dick Kent*). ***Announcers:*** George Ansbro, John Monks.

682. Home Town, Unincorporated. Variety, 30 min., NBC, 1939.

An entertainment session of music, songs and comedy set against the background of a fictional locale populated by 498 people.

Host: Cliff Soubier (as Capt. Barney Barnett). ***Regulars:*** Van Dyne, Marlin Hurt, Hugh Studebaker, Dick Todd, Virginia Verrill. ***Orchestra:*** Robert Strong, Robert Trendler.

Honest Harold *see* **The Harold Peary Show—Honest Harold**

683. Honeymoon in New York. Interview, 25 min., NBC, 1947–1949.

An engaged couple is brought before the microphones and interviewed. They relate various aspects of their lives and receive merchandise prizes for participating.

Host: Durward Kirby. ***Vocalist:*** Joy Hodges. ***Announcer:*** Herb Sheldon. ***Orchestra:*** Jerry Jerome. ***Producer:*** George Voutsas.

The Honeymooners *see* **Appendix**

684. Hoofbeats. Western, 15 min., Syndicated, 1937–1938.

The program, sponsored by Post Grape Nuts Flakes cereal, told of the adventures of Buck Jones, an easygoing cowboy who rode a horse named Silver. Charles "Buck" Jones, a film star of the era, played Buck Jones and the program was announced by a character identified only as the Old Wrangler.

OPENING

Wrangler (over hoofbeats): Howdy, folks, you'll be mighty glad to hear, I reckon, that the makers of Grape Nuts Flakes, that's America's most famous cereal in flake form, are gonna bring you America's most famous cowboy, hard ridin', hard hittin', hard to beat, everybody's favorite, Buck Jones.

685. Hook 'n' Ladder Follies. Variety, 30 min., NBC, 1943–1944.

A program of country and western music, songs and comedy with Ralph Dumke as the host, Capt. Walt. He was assisted by the bumbling Stringbean Crachet (played by Wilbur "Budd" Hulick). Ed Durlocker, Carson Robinson and the Song Spinners were the regulars. Frank Novack and his orchestra supplied the music.

Hookey Hall *see* **Rocking Horse Rhythms**

686. The Hoosier Hot Shots. Variety, 30 min., Mutual, 1950–1951.

Music and comedy with Frank Kettering, Paul Trietsch, Ken Trietsch and Otto Ward, a novelty musical group known as the Hoosier Hot Shots (much like Spike Jones and His City Slickers band). Vocals were by Anita Gordon and Fort Pearson was the announcer.

687. The Hoover Sentinels Serenade. Variety, 30 min., NBC, 1934–1935.

A Sunday afternoon program of light concert music with Ernestine Schumann-Heink of the Metropolitan Opera as the host. Josef Koestner conducted the orchestra and Hoover Vacuum Cleaners sponsored the program.

688. Hop Harrigan. Adventure, 15 min., NBC Blue, 1942–1944; ABC, 1944–1945; Mutual, 1946–1948.

An adaptation of the All-American comic book hero Hop Harrigan, a daring air ace, and his never-ending battle against evil. *Other regular characters:* Gale Nolan, his girlfriend; Tank Tinker, his mechanic.

Cast: Chester Stratton, Albert Aley (*Hop Harrigan*); Mitzi Gould (*Gale Nolan*); Ken Lynch, Jackson Beck (*Tank Tinker*). ***Announcer:*** Glenn Riggs.

OPENING

Announcer: Presenting Hop Harrigan, America's Ace of the Airwaves.

Hop (over plane-in-flight sounds): CX-4 calling control tower, CX-4 calling control tower. Standing by. Okay, this is Hop Harrigan coming in.

Announcer: Yes, it's America's Ace of the Airwaves, coming in for another transcribed episode in the adventures of *Hop Harrigan*.

689. Hopalong Cassidy. Western, 30 min., Mutual, 1950; CBS, 1950–1952.

A radio version of the television series of the same name about Hopalong Cassidy, a rancher and owner of the Bar 20 Ranch (near the town of Blackton Bend). Hopalong, who rode a horse named Topper, was assisted by Jack "California" Carlson, and was more of a crime fighter than cattle rancher, battling the evil elements of the Old West of the 1890s.

Cast: William Boyd (*Hopalong Cassidy*); Andy Clyde, Joe DuVall (*Jack "California" Carlson*). ***Music:*** Albert Glasser. ***Producer:*** Walter White, Jr.

William Boyd starred in the radio version of *Hopalong Cassidy*.

OPENING

Announcer: With action and suspense out of the Old West comes the most famous hero of them all, *Hopalong Cassidy*, starring William Boyd. The ring of the silver spurs heralds the most amazing man ever to ride the prairies of the early West, Hopalong Cassidy. The same Hoppy you cheer in motion pictures and the same California you've laughed at a million times. Raw courage and quick shooting have built a legend around this famous hero. Hopalong is a name to be feared, respected and admired, for this great cowboy rides the trails of adventure and excitement. William Boyd as Hopalong Cassidy and Andy Clyde as California. And now, another exciting story of the early West, "Hoppy and the Iron Horse."

CLOSING

Announcer: And so an exciting adventure ends for Hoppy and California. They'll get back to the Bar 20 just around round-up time and settle down to a peaceful ranch life. But we've a hankering it won't last for very long. Somewhere there'll be trouble and that's when Hoppy will ride out into another dangerous escapade. *Hopalong Cassidy* starring William Boyd is transcribed and produced in the West by Walter White, Jr. All stories are based upon the characters by Clarence E. Mulford. This is a Commodore Production.

690. The Horace Heidt Show. Variety, 30 min., NBC Blue, 1944.

A weekly program of music and songs with orchestra leader Horace Heidt as the host. Fred Lowery, Bob Matthews and Henry Russell were the regulars and music was by the Horace Heidt Orchestra.

691. Horatio Hornblower. Adventure, 30 min., ABC, 1953–1954.

A British-produced series about Horatio Hornblower, a captain with the Royal Navy who commands the ship HMS Firedrake during the early 1800s. His adventures as he battles evil while on assignment in the Baltic Sea is the focal point of the series (which is based on the novel by C.S. Forester).

Cast: Michael Redgrave (*Horatio Hornblower*). ***Music:*** Sidney Torch.

OPENING

Voice: Call all hands, straight to quarters.

Voice: Roll out the guns. Sights on target. Fire!

Announcer: Presenting Michael Redgrave as C.S. Forester's indomitable man of the sea, Horatio Hornblower.

692. The Hormel Program. Comedy, 30 min., NBC, 7/1/40 to 3/24/41.

Comedy skits that revolve around the antics of comedian George Burns and his wife Gracie Allen. Sponsored by the George A. Hormel Packing Company, makers of Spam.

Hosts: George Burns, Gracie Allen. ***Announcer:*** John "Bud" Heistand. ***Regulars:*** Irving Lee, the Smoothies Three. ***Orchestra:*** Artie Shaw.

693. Hot Copy. Drama, 30 min., NBC, 1941–1944; ABC, 1944.

Events in the life of Patricia Murphy, a syndicated newspaper columnist and reporter. Eloise Kummer first played the role of Patricia; she was replaced by Fern Parsons. Music was by the Roy Shield Orchestra.

Hotel for Pets *see* **Appendix**

694. The Hotpoint Holiday Hour. Anthology, 60 min., CBS, 1950.

A weekly series of dramatic productions sponsored by Hotpoint Appliances. Mel Ferrer served as the host and narrator and Marvin Miller did the announcing.

695. The Hour of Charm. Variety, 30 min., CBS, 1934–1936; NBC, 1936–1946.

A weekly program of music and songs featuring Phil Spitalny and His All-Girl Orchestra. Arlene Francis was the host and Evelyn Kaye Klein (billed as "Evelyn and Her Magic Violin"), Hollace Shaw, Katharine Smith and Viola Schmier were the regulars. Ron Rawson and Richard Stark were the announcers.

The Hour of Smiles *see* **The Fred Allen Show**

696. The House Beside the Road. Drama, 30 min., CBS, 1932–1934.

A weekly mix of light comedy and drama about "the poignant, homey little tales of the simple kindness of Ma and Pa." Also known as *The Wayside Cottage*.

Cast: Vivia Ogden (*Ma*); William Adams (*Pa*); Mary Smith (*Evelyn Dale*); Ethel Park Richardson (*Aunt Julie*); Warren Colston (*David Minor*). ***Also:*** Fannie Mae Baldridge, Anne Elstner, Jackie Kelk, Ruth Russell, Laddie Seaman, Walter Tetley.

697. A House in the Country. Comedy-Drama, 15 min., NBC Blue, 1941–1943.

Joan and Bruce are a young city couple who decide to get away from it all and move to the peace and quiet of the country. Stories relate amusing incidents in their lives as they attempt to adjust to new surroundings.

Cast: Frances Chaney, Joan Banks, Patsy Campbell (*Joan*); John Raby, Lyle Sudrow (*Bruce*); Parker Fennelly (*Sam, their friend*); Sam Poletchek, Ed Latimer (*Handyman*); Raymond Knight (*Shopkeeper*); Abby Lewis (*Telephone operator*). ***Announcers:*** Clayton "Bud" Collyer, Hugh James. ***Music:*** John Gart.

698. House of Glass. Comedy, 25 min., NBC, 10/23/53 to 3/12/54.

Barney Glass and his wife Bessie, who doubles as the cook, run the House of Glass, a resort hotel in New York's Catskill Mountains. Stories relate the comical situations that develop as they struggle to operate their establishment. Created by Gertrude Berg.

Cast: Joseph Buloff (*Barney Glass*); Gertrude Berg (*Bessie Glass*); Ann Thomas (*Sophie, the waitress*). ***Music:*** Milton Katims.

699. The House of Mystery. Anthology, 15 and 30 min. versions, Mutual, 1945–1949.

Originally, in its quarter-hour format, a series of scary stories read by the host ("The Mystery Man") to an audience of children. In 1945, when the series switched to a half-hour format, it became a weekly dramatization of a horror story geared to children.

Cast: John Griggs (*Roger Elliott, the Mystery Man*).

OPENING

Announcer: This is *The House of Mystery.*

Host: Good evening. This is Roger Elliott, otherwise known as the Mystery Man, welcoming you to another story-telling session here at *The House of Mystery.*

700. The House on Q Street. Drama, 25 min., NBC Blue, 11/4/43 to 3/9/44.

A large boarding house on Q Street in Washington, D.C., was the setting for a weekly peek at society as seen through the eyes of its occupants: the housekeeper; an ex–Senator; his daughter; a Russian ex–Countess (still devoted to the Soviet cause); a British army officer; and a U.S.–educated Chinese Embassy representative.

Cast: Jessie Royce Landis (*Housekeeper*); Douglas C. Holm (*Senator*); Celeste Holm (*His daughter*); Adelaide Klein (*Russian countess*); Eric Dressler (*British army officer*); Ed Begley (*Chinese representative*). ***Also:*** Cameron Andrews, Donald Bain, Stanley Bell.

701. House Party. Variety, 30 min., CBS, 1945–1967.

A long-running casual program of chatter, music, songs, advice for housewives and audience participation for prizes. Art Linkletter served as the host; Larrie Harper and Jack Slattery were the announcers; and the Muzzy Marcellino Trio provided the music. The program is also known as *Art Linkletter's House Party* and served as the basis for the television series of the same title.

702. Houseboat Hannah. Serial, 15 min., Mutual, 1936–1938; NBC Blue, 1938–1941.

Events in the life of Hannah O'Leary and her husband Dan, cannery workers who lived on a houseboat in San Francisco.

Cast: Henrietta Tedro, Doris Rich (*Hannah O'Leary*); Norman Gottschalk (*Dan O'Leary*); Bonnie Kay (*Margery Davis*); Les Damon, John Larkin (*James Nichols*); Nancy Douglass (*Barbara Hughes*); Jim Andelin (*Clem*); Virginia Dwyer (*Ellen Smith*); Carl Kroenke (*Alec Ferguson*).

Announcers: Gene Baker, Olan Soule. ***Producers:*** Anne Hummert, Frank Hummert.

703. How To. Human Interest, 30 min., CBS, 10/7/51 to 12/2/51.

An edited version of the television series soundtrack. A person with a problem is brought on stage. The host and panelists then attempt to resolve the difficulty presented by the guest.

Host: Roger Price. ***Panelists:*** Stanley Adams, Anita Martel, Leonard Stern. ***Announcer:*** Bob Lemond.

704. The Howard Miller Show. Variety, 15 min., CBS, 1955.

A program of music and songs that featured performances by guests. Howard Miller was the host and Ed Joyce did the announcing.

705. Howdy Doody. Children, 60 min., NBC, 12/15/51 to 9/12/53.

An audio version of the television series soundtrack that relates the efforts of a circus troupe to perform in the town of Doodyville against the wishes of Phineas T. Bluster, a mean old man who is opposed to people having fun. *Regular characters:* Buffalo Bob Smith, the host; Howdy Doody, the red-haired, freckle-faced boy (a puppet); Clarabell Hornblow, the clown who "talked" by squeaking a horn; Princess Summer-Fall-Winter-Spring; Dilly Dally (a puppet); the Flubadub, the main circus attraction (a puppet).

Cast: Bob Smith (*Buffalo Bob Smith/Voice of Howdy Doody*); Bob Nicholson (*Clarabell Hornblow*); Judy Tyler (*Princess Summer-Fall-Winter-Spring*); Dayton Allen (*Voice of Phineas T. Bluster/Flubadub*); Bill LeCornec (*Dilly Dally*). ***Music:*** Edward Kean.

OPENING

Buffalo Bob: Say, kids, what time is it?

Kids: Howdy Doody time.

Song: It's Howdy Doody time, it's Howdy

Doody time, Bob Smith and Howdy too, say Howdy Doo to you. Let's give a rousing cheer, 'cause Howdy Doody's here; it's time to star the show, so kids, let's go.

706. Howie Wing. Adventure, 15 min., CBS, 10/3/38 to 6/30/39.

Howie Wing is a daring young air ace with the Cadet Aviation Corps who later became a co-pilot for Capt. Harvey, the owner of a South American airline. His exploits as he battles corruption, especially the evil Burton York, are the focal point of stories. *Other regular characters:* Donna Cavendish, Howie's girlfriend; and Typhoon Tootel, Howie's mechanic.

Cast: William Janney (*Howie Wing*); Mark Parker (*Donna Cavendish*); Neil O'Malley (*Capt. Harvey*); Robert Strauss (*Typhoon Tootel*); Raymond Bramley (*Burton York*).

707. How'm I Doin? Game, 30 min., NBC, 1/9/42 to 10/1/42.

Two contestants compete and each receive $30. Three questions are posed to them by the host. Each correct answer adds $10 to a player's score; an incorrect response deducts $10. Players are defeated when they run out of money; winners keep what they have earned.

Host: Bob Hawk. ***Announcer:*** Bert Parks. ***Orchestra:*** Vaughn Monroe.

708. How's the Family? Game, 30 min., Mutual, 1953.

A question-and-answer session wherein married couples compete against each other for merchandise prizes. Marshall Kent served as the host and Pierre Andre did the announcing.

709. Hy Gardner Calling. Gossip, 15 min., NBC, 1952.

A program of celebrity gossip with newspaper columnist Hy Gardner as the host and reporter. Also known as *The Hy Gardner Show*.

710. I Deal in Crime. Crime Drama, 30 min., ABC, 1/21/45 to 10/18/47.

"Money and I are strangers," says Ross Dolan, a private detective with an office on the fourth floor (Room 404) in the Melrose Building in Los Angeles. Ross has been an investigator for ten years and charges $25 a day plus expenses. Dolan, an ex–Navy man, is a bit rough around the edges, advertises his services in the *Chronicle* and takes whatever jobs can make him money. Stories follow Ross as he tackles cases that most often involve him with murder. Ross carries a .38 "and I've got a permit for it." The police also warn him to keep his nose clean. "I do," he responds, "that's why I carry a box of Kleenex."

Cast: William Gargan (*Ross Dolan*). ***Announcer:*** Dresser Dahlstead. ***Music:*** Skitch Henderson.

OPENING

Ross: *I Deal in Crime.*

Announcer: The American Broadcasting Company presents *I Deal in Crime* starring William Gargan.

Ross: My name is Ross Dolan and in case you're inclined to say what, pull up a chair and listen to this. I've been a private investigator for ten years, except for a short hitch in Uncle Sugar's Navy. I've been a seaman on an L.S.T., a gunner on a PT boat, even made a parachute jump. But just yesterday, they [the Navy] decided to get along without me, so I found myself on my way back to my old hangout… [He would then begin the story.]

CLOSING

Announcer: Don't forget to listen again next week, same time, when you will hear William Gargan say—

Ross: *I Deal in Crime.*

Announcer: *I Deal in Crime* starring William Gargan is a presentation of the American Broadcasting Company. *I Deal in Crime* came to you from Hollywood. This is ABC.

711. I Fly Anything. Adventure, 30 min., ABC, 11/29/50 to 7/19/51.

"Anything, any time, anywhere. *I Fly Anything*," is the motto of Dockery Crane, a freelance pilot (of a DC-4) who will take any legal flying assignment to make money. Dockery is assisted by Buzz, his one-man crew, and June, his secretary, who fills a jug with coffee for every flight ("She likes coffee over the ocean; she's funny that way"). Stories relate their exploits as they risk their lives to transport cargo and passengers to their destination.

Cast: Dick Haymes (*Dockery Crane*); George Fenneman (*Buzz*); Georgia Ellis (*June*). ***Announcers:*** Jay Arlen, Lou Cook. ***Music:*** Basil Adlam, Rex Maupin. ***Producers:*** Frank Cooper, Sy Fisher.

OPENING

SOUND: Airplane in flight.

ANNOUNCER: *I Fly Anything* starring Dick Haymes as air cargo pilot Dockery Crane.

CRANE: Crago 91743 to LaGuardia tower, requesting landing instructions, please. Over.

VOICE: LaGuardia to 91743. You're number two to land. Visibility seven miles. Winds northwest 290 degrees, 20 miles. Altimeter setting of 025. You will be clear to land on runway two-one. Is that you, Crane?

CRANE: That's me, Dockery Crane.

VOICE: What are you bringing into our fair city this time, Crane? Cabbages, kings or crumbuns?

CRANE: No, you're wrong all the way, Buster. I'm bringing in a dent in my rudder and a gram of drugs and a date with death. You know me, *I Fly Anything*!

ANNOUNCER: Transcribed, the American Broadcasting Company presents Dick Haymes as fast-moving, hard-hitting, romantic air cargo pilot Capt. Dockery Crane in *I Fly Anything*.

CRANE: My name is Dockery Crane and my business is the Wild Blue Yonder business; pickup and delivery business by air. You get yourself a hangar, a crew, a secretary and a big teletype machine and a certificate from the C.A.B. and a great big pile of hope and your motto is "Anything, any time, anywhere. *I Fly Anything*."

CLOSING

ANNOUNCER: You have been listening to the fifth in a series starring Dick Haymes as air cargo pilot Docker Crane in *I Fly Anything*. And there goes the teletype with next week's cargo load—

JUNE: Doc, an urgent on the teletype. A man by the name of Brad Barton wants to know if you will fly up to the timber country of Northern Minnesota to pick up a passenger.

CRANE: Tell him sure, "Anything, any time, anywhere, I Fly Anything."

ANNOUNCER: *I Fly Anything* starring Dick Haymes was produced by Frank Cooper and Sy Fisher in association with the American Broadcasting Company. This program has come to you from Hollywood and was transcribed from ABC, the American Broadcasting Company.

712. I LOVE A MYSTERY. Adventure, 15 and 30 min. versions, NBC Red, 1939–1940; NBC Blue, 1940–1942; CBS, 1943–1944; Mutual, 1949–1952.

During the bombing of Shanghai at the outset of World War II, three globe-trotting adventurers (Doc Long, Jack Packard and Reggie York) were captured and sent to prison. The three became friends and vowed to roam the world and battle evil. After escaping, they formed the A-1 Detective Agency and began their quest. Stories, presented in a serialized format, relate their exploits as they risk their lives to help others (their agency's slogan: "No job too tough, no mystery too baffling"). In 1940, after the death of Walter Paterson (who played Reggie), the role of the agency secretary, Jerri Booker, was expanded to accompany Jack and Doc on assignments. Doc had the ability to get out of tight spots by picking locks; Jack had an analytical mind; Reggie was exceptionally strong; and Jerri had a natural ability for sleuthing. In 1949, after the series had been off the air for five years, it returned to the air (Mutual) with Russell Thorson, Tony Randall and Jim Boles as the adventurers. See also *I Love Adventure*.

Cast: Barton Yarborough, Jim Boles (*Doc Long*); Michael Raffetto, Jay Novello, John McIntire, Russell Thorson (*Jack Packard*); Walter Paterson, Tony Randall (*Reggie Yorke*); Gloria Blondell (*Jerri Booker*). ***Producer:*** Carlton E. Morse.

OPENING

ANNOUNCER: The makers of Fleischmann Yeast present *I Love a Mystery. I Love a Mystery*, presenting the latest adventures of Jack, Doc and Reggie, specialists in crime and adventure, now following the Chinese pirate map of P. Wy Ling.

713. I LOVE ADVENTURE. Adventure, 30 min., ABC, 4/25/48 to 7/18/48.

A 13-episode continuation of the series *I Love a Mystery* (see prior title) that appeared one year before its 1949 renewal. The original adventures of the members of the A-1 Detective Agency ended in 1944 when Doc and Jack closed the company and went to work for Uncle Sam. After the war, Doc, Jack and Reggie (who was brought back) were recruited by a London-based organization dedicated to battling global crime. Stories follow their exploits as they risk their lives to battle the enemies of the free world.

Cast: Barton Yarborough (*Doc Long*);

Michael Raffetto (*Jack Packard*); Tom Collins (*Reggie Yorke*). ***Host-Announcer:*** Dresser Dahlstead. ***Organist:*** Rex Koury.

714. I Love Lucy. Comedy, 30 min., CBS, 1952.

The brownstone at 623 East 68th Street in Manhattan is owned by Fred and Ethel Mertz. Lucy Ricardo and her husband Ricky, a bandleader at the Tropicana Club, live above them (in Apartment 3-B). The four are best friends, although they have their differences at times and are at each other's throats. Fred and Ethel are former vaudeville entertainers; Fred is stingy and Ethel actually owns the building. Ricky is a level-headed Cuban who married Lucy in 1942. Lucy is somewhat scatterbrained and longs for a career in show business—something Ricky opposes. Stories relate the chaos that results when Lucy schemes to get her way—often dragging Fred and Ethel into her plots. A simulcast of the television series with narration added to explain the visual scenes.

Cast: Lucille Ball (*Lucy Ricardo*); Desi Arnaz (*Ricky Ricardo*); William Frawley (*Fred Mertz*); Vivian Vance (*Ethel Mertz*). ***Announcers:*** Johnny Jacobs, John Stevenson. ***Narrator:*** Desi Arnaz. ***Music:*** Wilbur Hatch. ***Commercial Spokesman:*** Johnny Roventini (Johnny the Bellboy).

OPENING

ANNOUNCER: Philip Morris, America's most enjoyable cigarette, presents Lucille Ball and Desi Arnaz in *I Love Lucy*.

JOHNNY: Call for Philip Mor-rees. Call for Philip Mor-rees.

ANNOUNCER: Ladies and gentlemen, you can stop worrying about cigarette irritation and start smoking for pleasure... Philip Morris is free from sources of irritation used in the manufacture of all other leading cigarettes... You'll be glad tomorrow you smoked Philip Morris today.

JOHNNY: Call for Philip Mor-rees.

ANNOUNCER: And now by transcription, let's join Lucille Ball and Desi Arnaz as Lucy and Ricky Ricardo in *I Love Lucy*.

RICKY: Hello, I'm Ricky Ricardo and I'm the guy who loves Lucy. The whole thing started ten years ago. I had just come to this country from Cuba and I didn't know much about your customs. The first girl I had a date with was Lucy. It was a romantic night and after all, I had a reputation to live up to as a Latin lover. I kissed her good night. It was right then that she told me that under the Constitution of the United States of America, if a man kisses a girl he had to marry her. One lousy trick, but I didn't care because after all, if I didn't marry her, I would have married someone else. And Lucy, just like any other American girl, was pretty, charming, witty and partly insane. She's always doing these crazy things. Take the other night for instance...

715. I Want a Divorce. Drama, 30 min., Mutual, 10/18/40 to 4/18/41.

Bittersweet dramatizations that depict the incidents that lead a couple to divorce court. Stories are rather poignant and detail the heartbreak of divorce and the outcome such situations have on all concerned, especially if children are involved.

Cast: Joan Blondell (*Leading lady*); Conrad Binyon (*Various roles*). ***Host:*** Cal York. ***Announcer:*** Herb Allen. ***Music:*** David Rose.

OPENING (from "Child Custody," 3/7/41)

ANNOUNCER: Starring Joan Blondell in *I Want a Divorce*.

VOICE: Judge, I want a divorce.

JUDGE: Divorce granted.

VOICES: I want a divorce. I want a divorce. I want a divorce.

ANNOUNCER: Faster, faster, even faster does the divorce mill grind away yesteryear's happiness. Why? Why? Why?, ask millions. Listen to *I Want a Divorce*, the copyrighted program approved by many leaders of church and state, the program that dramatizes the real-life happenings in other people's marriages. Broadcast coast to coast from Hollywood each week at this hour. And now here is Cal York, Hollywood correspondent for *Photoplay Movie Mirror* magazine, to tell you about tonight's *I Want a Divorce* play.

CAL: Does motherhood give a woman the sole right to demand the custody of her children merely because she is their mother? In our story, Carol Parker, portrayed by our lovely star, Joan Blondell, presents this issue.

CLOSING

ANNOUNCER: And so ends another *I Want a Divorce* play emphasizing the fact that in the difficult and unforgettable problems of divorce, parents, whether they accept it or not, do have an obligation to their children and every mother must earn her right to them. In just a moment, Cal York will bring Miss Blondell back to the microphone. [Commercial airs.] And now here's Cal York with Joan Blondell.

CAL: Well, it was an interesting drama tonight, Joan, very well played. What about next week's show?

JOAN: It's a story about a woman's influence on her husband... I hope you will be listening. Good night.

CAL: We'll all be present. Good night everyone.

JOAN: Good night.

ANNOUNCER: All names mentioned in tonight's play are fictitious. Any similarity to actual persons is purely coincidental. Joan Blondell is soon to appear with Dick Powell in the Universal picture *Model Wife*. This is the Mutual Broadcasting System.

716. I WAS A COMMUNIST FOR THE FBI. Drama, 30 min., Syndicated, 1952–1953.

A fact-based series that recounts the experiences of Matt Cvetic, a double agent who, for nine years, infiltrated the Communist Party in the United States to report regularly to the FBI on cell operations. Dana Andrews played the role of Matt Cvetic.

OPENING

MATT: *I Was a Communist for the FBI.*

ANNOUNCER: Starring Dana Andrews in an exciting tale of danger and espionage, *I Was a Communist for the FBI*. You are about to hear a strange story; names, dates and places are, for obvious reasons, fictional, but many of these incidents are based on actual experiences of Matt Cvetic who, for nine fantastic years, lived as a Communist for the FBI. Here is our star, Dana Andrews as Matt Cvetic.

MATT: You can read it in the official report, the whole story of my life as a Communist for the FBI. I was in the party. I saw it work. For nine years I recorded the Communist conspiracy against the United States from within. This is part of the story. [The episode would then begin.]

717. ICE BOX FOLLIES. Variety, 30 min., ABC, 1/24/45 to 7/22/45.

A program of music, songs and light comedy sponsored by Hire's Root Beer Soda. Wendell Niles served as the host. Mel Blanc provided comic relief; vocals were by Don Prindle and Gale Robbins; Harlow Wilcox did the announcing; and Billy Mills and his orchestra provided the music.

718. ILKA CHASE'S PENTHOUSE PARTY. Variety, 30 min., CBS, 6/6/41 to 12/31/41.

A weekly program of music and songs with actress Ilka Chase as the host. Judith Anderson, Yvette Harris and Elizabeth Huston were the regulars and Paul Barton and his orchestra provided the music.

719. I'LL FIND MY WAY. Serial, 15 min., Mutual, 1941.

The story of a small-town girl with ambitions of becoming an actress. Her dreams, however, are hindered by her father's newspaper which sidetracks her as she struggles to save it.

Cast: Phyllis Jeanne (*Girl*); Jack Preston (*Father*); Arch Schmidt (*Printer*); Leonard Sherer (*Doctor*); Billy Kenton (*City intruder*).

720. IMPERIAL TIME. Variety, 15 min., Mutual, 1941.

A program of music and songs sponsored by Imperial margarine. Singer Mary Small served as the host with additional vocals by the Boy Friends. Dan Seymour did the announcing and Phil Wall and his orchestra supplied the music.

721. INDICTMENT. Crime Drama, 30 min., CBS, 1956–1959.

Various stories that detail the work of an assistant district attorney as he goes about gathering the evidence needed to bring a case "to a swift indictment." The program is based on the experiences of Eleazar Lipsky, a former assistant district attorney in New York City. Edward McCormick played the assistant D.A. and Tom Russo was the police detective who worked with him.

OPENING

ANNOUNCER: *Indictment*, a formal written charge of crime, is the basis for trial of the accused. *Indictment*! The story you are about to hear is from New York City and is based on stories of the criminal law with authentic procedures as detailed by Eleazar Lipsky, former assistant District Attorney of

New York. It is the assistant district attorney who directs criminal investigations, assembles facts and witnesses and brings the case to a just indictment.

722. INFORMATION PLEASE. Game, 30 min., NBC Blue, 1938–1940; NBC Red, 1940–1946; CBS, 1946–1947; Mutual, 1947–1951.

The program tested a panel's knowledge of various subjects. Questions were submitted by listeners who received cash or merchandise prizes if they stumped the panel.

Host: Clifton Fadiman. ***Panel:*** Franklin P. Adams, Milton Cross, John Gunther, John Kiernan, Oscar Levant. ***Announcers:*** Don Baker, Milton Cross, Ben Grauer, Ed Herlihy, Jay Jackson. ***Music:*** Joe Kahn.

OPENING

ANNOUNCER: It's half-past eight, New York time, time to wake up, America, and stump the experts. Each week at this time, Lucky Strike sets up a board of four know-it-alls for you to throw questions at. For every question we use, Lucky Strike pays out $10 plus a copy of the new "Information Please Quiz Book." If your question stumps us, you get $25 more plus a 24-volume set of the current Encyclopedia Britannica. Send your questions to Information Please, 480 Lexington Avenue, New York City. If our editorial staff edits your question a bit, don't fret over it. In case of duplication, *Information Please* uses the questions that were received first. And now light up a Lucky Strike as I present our master of ceremonies, the literary critic of the *New Yorker* magazine, Clifton Fadiman.

CLIFTON: Good evening, ladies and gentlemen. Let me remind you again, *Information Please* is completely unrehearsed and ad-libbed from beginning to end...

723. INNER SANCTUM MYSTERIES. Anthology, 30 min., NBC Blue, 1941–1943; CBS, 1943–1950; ABC, 1950–1951; CBS, 1952.

A weekly series of mystery and suspense productions bordering on the supernatural. The program was originally titled *The Squeaking Door* (for its trademark squeaking door effect in the opening theme) and is also known as *Inner Sanctum*. Stories include:

Elixir Number 4. Richard Widmark in a tale about a man who discovers a potion that produces eternal life.

The Vengeful Corpse. Barbara Weeks and Karl Swenson in a story about a woman, burned as a witch in seventeenth-century Salem, who returns to seek revenge.

The Wailing Wall. Boris Karloff as a man who murders his wife, buries her in the basement, then is haunted by the moanings of her spirit.

Death Across the Board. After killing a man in self-defense, a doctor (Raymond Massey) finds he is a chess piece in a cleverly conceived plot using real people instead of chessmen.

Hosts: Raymond Edward Johnson, Paul McGrath, House Jameson, Mary Bennett. ***Announcers:*** Allen C. Anthony, Ed Herlihy, Dwight Weist. ***Music:*** John Hicks. ***Producer:*** Himan Brown.

OPENING

ANNOUNCER: Lipton Tea and Lipton Soups present *Inner Sanctum Mysteries*.

SOUND: A creaking door opening.

HOST: Good evening, friends of the Inner Sanctum. This is your host to welcome you in through the squeaking door for another half-hour of horror.

CLOSING

HOST: Now it's time to close the door of the Inner Sanctum until next week when Lipton Tea and Lipton Soups bring you another Inner Sanctum mystery. Until then, good night ... pleasant dreams.

SOUND: Squeaking door closes.

724. THE INSIDE STORY. Anthology, 30 min., NBC Blue, 1939.

Dramatizations based on current news events and incidents in the lives of interesting people. Fred Sullivan served as the host; the Gilbert Welty Orchestra provided the music.

INSPECTOR HEARTHSTONE OF THE DEATH SQUAD *see* **HEARTHSTONE OF THE DEATH SQUAD**

725. INSPECTOR MARK SABRE. Crime Drama, 30 min., ABC, 1952–1954.

"He's just a city detective working for peanuts," say the wealthy when Mark Sabre, an inspector with the Homicide Bureau of the

Los Angeles Police Department, is assigned to investigate a high profile case. To the scoundrels who break the law, Sabre is "just a dumb flatfoot." But no matter what their social status, Sabre treats each with the same objective—"to get the truth." Sabre is tough "and packs a wallop with that left" (although he prefers to quietly question a suspect rather than beat the answer out of him). Mark is assisted by Tim Maloney, an easily aggravated sergeant who lets the suspects get the best of him ("We better get out of here before I become as loony as the rest of them"). Stories follow their case investigations as Mark uses deductive reasoning to solve crimes. Broadcast as *Mystery Theater*, but also known as *Inspector Mark Sabre* and *Mark Sabre*. After solving "The Case of the Portrait in Red," this conversation occurred:

MARK: And that closes the file on "The Case of the Portrait in Red."

TIM: I'm certainly glad to see the end of it, Mark. Never in all my years on the force have I seen so many screwballs in one evening.

MARK: Now watch what you say, Tim, I may go into show business myself.

TIM: As a technical adviser?

MARK: Certainly not. They want me to play the lead on a radio show called *Mystery Theater*.

TIM: Have you no pride, man? And what's to become of me if there's another case like this? Who'll be here to protect me?

MARK: Oh, you're right Tim, it wouldn't be fair to you. I guess I'll have to turn it down.

TIM: You're a darlin' man, Inspector, a darlin' man.

Cast: Bill Johnstone, Robert Carroll (*Mark Sabre*); James Westerfield (*Tim Maloney*). ***Announcer:*** Roger Forster. ***Music:*** Clark Whipple.

OPENING

ANNOUNCER: Phillips Milk of Magnesia and Bayer Aspirin bring you *Mystery Theater*, transcribed, and Inspector Mark Sabre of the Homicide Squad ... and tonight's story "The Case of the Portrait in Red."

CLOSING

ANNOUNCER: Tonight's story, "The Case of the Portrait in Red," was written by Robert Talman. The names of all characters in tonight's dramatization are fictitious and any resemblance to living persons is purely coincidental. Listen again next week to *Mystery Theater* and "The Case of the Voice of Death." Roger Forster speaking. This program has come to you from New York. America is sold on ABC, the American Broadcasting Company.

726. INSPECTOR THORNE. Crime Drama, 30 min., NBC, 7/20/51 to 9/27/51.

A British-produced series with Karl Weber as Inspector Thorne, a brilliant investigator with the Homicide Bureau of New Scotland Yard. He was assisted by Sgt. Muggin (played by Danny Ocko).

OPENING

ANNOUNCER: And now, the National Broadcasting Company presents *Inspector Thorne* in "The Dark Cigarette Murder Case." Tonight, the National Broadcasting Company presents the exploits of the spectacular young Inspector Thorne of the Homicide Bureau, whose investigations rank with many of the most celebrated ones in the annals of crime fiction. An investigator smart enough to claim he is dumb and modest enough to believe it. Tonight, Inspector Thorne turns to "The Dark Cigarette Murder Case."

727. THE INTIMATE REVUE. Variety, 30 min., NBC, 1934–1935.

A weekly program of music and songs with Bob Hope as the host (who provided his own brand of light comedy). Jane Froman and James Melton provided the songs and Al Goodman and his orchestra supplied the music.

728. INTO THE LIGHT. Serial, 15 min., NBC Blue, 1941–1942.

A daily drama about a beautiful young woman (Tanya) and the healing influence she has on two bickering brothers.

Cast: Margo (*Tanya*); Peter Donald (*First brother*); Martin Wolfson (*Second brother*); Mitzi Gould (*Emily*); Chassie Allen (*Ma Owen*); Morris Carnovsky (*Mr. Kriss*). ***Also:*** Peter Capell, Margaret Foster.

729. IODENT DRESS REHEARSAL. Variety, 30 min., NBC Blue, 1936–1937.

Music, songs and comedy with comedian Pinky Lee and actress Mabel Albertson as "The Countess of Kleptomania." Tenor Morton Bowe provided the songs and music was by Joe Rines and his orchestra.

The Irene Dunn–Fred MacMurray Show *see* **Bright Star**

730. Irene Rich Dramas. Anthology, 15 min., NBC Blue, then CBS, 1933–1944.

Weekly dramatizations featuring top name radio performers. Irene Rich, a former silent film star, served as the host and female lead (guests appeared as her leading man). Frank Goss, Ed Herlihy and Marvin Miller did the announcing.

731. Island Venture. Adventure, 30 min., CBS, 11/22/45 to 6/20/46.

Gil Berry is an ex–Navy pilot turned owner of an air freight line in the South Pacific. His adventures, as he attempts to maintain the line, are dramatized. *Other regular characters:* Trigger Brett, his partner; Mendoza, the owner of a cargo line; Chula, the island big shot; Mendoza's daughter.

Cast: Jerry Walter (*Gil Berry*); Hugh Rowlands (*Trigger Brett*); Clare Boreum (*Mendoza*); Willard Waterman (*Chula*); Jane Webb (*Mendoza's daughter*). ***Also:*** Norman Gottschalk, Jonathan Hole, Ken Nordine.

732. It Can Be Done. Anthology, 30 min., NBC Blue, then CBS, 1937–1939.

Edgar Guest, a popular poet of the era, was host to a series of dramatizations based on the experiences of a weekly guest star.

733. It Happened in Hollywood. Variety, 15 min., CBS, 1939.

A weekly program of music and songs with John Conte as the host; vocals by Martha Mears; comedy from Helen Troy as the telephone operator; and music with Eddie Dunstedter and his orchestra.

734. It Happened in 1955. Anthology, 15 min., Mutual, 1945.

Short dramas depicting how life could be ten years into the future. Del Sharbutt was the host.

735. It Happens Every Day. Interview, 5 min., CBS, 1952.

A short program of interviews with people with unusual stories to tell. Arlene Francis was the host and Bill Cullen did the announcing.

736. It Pays to Be Ignorant. Comical Game, 30 min., Mutual, 1942–1944; CBS, 1944–1949.

A contestant is first interviewed, then picks a question from "The Dunce Cap." The question is read (for example, "From what state do we get Hawaiian canned pineapple?") and three "ignorant" panelists provide comic answers while evading the correct response. A cash prize of $23.90 is awarded to the contestant for facing the panel. The program began locally in New York in 1940 over WOR.

Host: Tom Howard. ***Panel:*** Lulu McConnell, Harry McNaughton, George Shelton. ***Vocal Groups:*** The Esquires, the Townsmen Quartet. ***Closing Theme Vocal:*** Al Madru. ***Announcer:*** Ken Roberts, Richard Stark. ***Musical Director:*** Tom Howard, Jr. ***Orchestra:*** Doc Novak. ***Producer:*** Tom Howard.

OPENING

Host: What is a reigning beauty?

Panelist: A girl who is all wet.

Host: Correct, pay that man eight dollars. If four frankfurters cost ten cents, what is five hundred frankfurters?

Panelist: A lot of baloney.

Host: Correct, pay that man nine dollars because—

Announcer: *It Pays to Be Ignorant.* Yes, *It Pays to Be Ignorant*, a zany half-hour with those masters of insanity, Harry McNaughton, George Shelton and Lulu McConnell, and featuring Doc Novak's orchestra. And now here's the man who proves *It Pays to Be Ignorant*, Tom Howard.

CLOSING

Song: It pays to be ignorant, to be dumb, to be dense, to be ignorant. It pays to be ignorant, just like me...

Announcer: This is Ken Roberts reminding you to be with us again next week, same time, same station for more zany fun on *It Pays to Be Ignorant.*

737. It Takes a Woman. Anthology, 5 min., Syndicated, 1945.

Capsule dramas (designed as a filler program) that depict women in a sentimental but heroic light. Frankie Burke, who appeared in stories, also played Frances Scott, the host and narrator.

738. It's a Crime, Mr. Collins. Crime Drama, 30 min., Mutual, 1956–1957.

"He's wonderful at murder"—solving them, that is, says Gail Collins, the wife of private detective Greg Collins. No matter what the police think, if Greg feels a client is innocent, he will do what it takes to prove it. Stories, which relate Greg's case investigations, are narrated by Gail as she tells her Uncle Jack about Greg's latest caper.

Cast: Tom Collins, Mandel Kramer (*Greg Collins*); Gail Collins (*Gail Collins*); Richard Denning (*Uncle Jack*).

OPENING

VOICE: *It's a Crime, Mr. Collins.*

GAIL: It surely is. After all, how would you feel if you found that your husband had a fan and then found out that the fan belonged to a fan dancer? Yes, it's Gail Collins here and in a moment I'll be back to set the stage for our puzzling crime. [After a commercial, Gail sets up the plot for the evening's story.]

CLOSING

GREG: Well, folks, Gail and I hope you enjoyed our adventure, "The Pink Lady." Be sure to visit us next week for another puzzling murder where there's crime and romance. There you will find Mr.—

GAIL: And Mrs. Collins.

739. IT'S A LIVING. Human Interest, 30 min., Mutual, 1948–1949.

Interviews with people with strange or unusual jobs. Ben Alexander was the host.

740. IT'S ALWAYS ALBERT. Comedy, 30 min., CBS, 1948.

Events in the life of Albert, a happy-go-lucky young composer unable to find work.

Cast: Arnold Stang (*Albert*); Jan Murray (*His brother*); Pert Kelton (*Albert's girlfriend*). ***Announcer:*** George Bryan. ***Music:*** Jack Miller.

741. IT'S HIGGINS, SIR. Comedy, 30 min., NBC, 7/3/51 to 9/25/51.

Philip Roberts, his wife Elizabeth and their children (Nancy, Debbie and Tommy) are an average American family whose lives suddenly change when a titled British relative (Sir Reginald Robertson) dies and they inherit a Queen Anne silver service (worth $10,000) and Higgins, a prim and proper English butler. Stories focus on the misadventures that occur as Higgins attempts to adjust to a new homeland and his new employers attempt to adjust to him. Philip is a lawyer with the firm of Bascomb, Finefeather, Blantz, Banweiler, Pinza and Roberts. Higgins calls the girls "Miss Nancy," and "Miss Deborah" and Tommy "Master Thomas." Nancy is in high school; Debbie is a tomboy who loves sports, snakes, toads and centipedes; and Tommy is the closest one to Higgins (able to relate and help him out of scrapes).

Cast: Harry McNaughton (*Higgins*); Vinton Hayworth, Arthur Cole (*Philip Roberts*); Peggy Allenby, Vera Allen (*Elizabeth Roberts*); Denise Alexander (*Debbie Roberts*); Charles Nevil (*Tommy Roberts*); Pat Hosley (*Nancy Roberts*).

OPENING

HIGGINS: There's no Mister. It's just *Higgins*, sir.

ANNOUNCER: The National Broadcasting Company presents a new comedy series, *It's Higgins, Sir*, created and transcribed by Paul Harrison and starring Harry McNaughton as Higgins. A butler in the home of an average American family appears unusual to say the least. But when the butler is left to the family in a will, along with a Queen Anne silver service worth at least $10,000, that's news… [The story would then begin.]

742. IT'S THE BARRYS. Comedy, 15 min., NBC, 1953.

Events in the life of the Barry family: Jack, the bumbling husband; Marcia, his level-headed wife; and Jeff, their son.

Cast: Jack Barry (*Jack Barry*); Marcia Van Dyke (*Marcia Barry*); Jeff Barry (*Jeff Barry*).

743. IT'S UP TO YOU. Game, 30 min., NBC Blue, 1939.

Two players are assigned a task (for example, reciting "Mary Had a Little Lamb" or talking oneself out of a parking ticket) that each has to perform to the best of his or her ability. The winner is chosen by studio audience applause and receives merchandise prizes. Dale Baxter was the host.

744. JACK AND CLIFF. Variety, 30 min., NBC, 6/9/48 to 9/15/48.

Music, songs and comedy sketches that revolve around Jack Pearl's Baron Munchausen character (a teller of tall tales).

Hosts: Jack Pearl, Cliff Hall. ***Regulars:*** Johnny Gibson, Bernie Gould, Dick Karlan, Craig McDonnell, Joe O'Brien, Byrna Robinson, Hazel Shermet, Ann Thomas, Eve Young, the Jack Allison Quartet. ***Announcer:*** Bob Sherry. ***Orchestra:*** Milton Katims.

745. JACK ARMSTRONG, THE ALL-AMERICAN BOY. Adventure, 15 and 30 min., versions, CBS, 1933–1936; NBC, 1936–1941; Mutual, 1941–1942; NBC Blue, 1942–1944; ABC, 1944–1949.

The original format followed the adventures of Jack Armstrong, a super athlete and honor student at Hudson High School. It later dealt with Jack's adventures in exotic locales with his cousins, Billy and Betty Fairfield, and their uncle, Jim Fairfield, a pilot who owned a plane called the *Silver Albatross*. In 1946, Uncle Jim and Betty were dropped and replaced by Vic Hardy, a crime investigator who joined Jack and Billy in their battle against evil. During World War II, the Write-a-Fighter Corps was instituted and promoted on the program. Over 1,000,000 people joined and members promised to write at least one letter a month to servicemen, sell war bonds, plant victory gardens and collect scraps of tin, paper and rubber. See also *Armstrong of the SBI*.

Cast: St. John Terrell, Jim Ameche, Don Ameche,* Stanley Harris, Charles Flynn, Michael Rye (*Jack Armstrong*); Murray McLean, John Gannon, Roland Butterfield, Milton Guion, Dick York (*Billy Fairfield*); Scheindel Kalish, Sarajane Wells, Loretta Poynton, Patricia Dunlap (*Betty Fairfield*); James Goss (*Uncle Jim Fairfield*); Ken Griffin (*Vic Hardy*); Arthur Van Slyke, Olan Soule (*Coach Hardy, athletic director at Hudson High*). ***Vocals:*** The Norsemen. ***Announcers:*** Truman Bradley, Paul Douglas, Bob McKee, Franklyn McCormack, David Owen, Ed Prentiss, Tom Shirley.

OPENING

ANNOUNCER: *Jack Armstrong, the All-American Boy* is on the air in person to get you to eat Wheaties. Fellows, girls, hang on for thrills, excitement, adventure. Today, Wheaties brings you a story of champions in action.

VOICES (echoing): Jack Armstrong, Jack Armstrong, Jack Armstrong, Jack Armstrong, the All-American Boy.

SONG: Wave the flag for Hudson High boys, show them how we stand. Ever shall our team be champions known throughout the land.

ANNOUNCER: Wheaties, breakfast of champions, brings you the thrilling adventures of *Jack Armstrong, the All-American Boy*.

CLOSING

ANNOUNCER: Be sure to listen in at this same time tomorrow evening to find out what happens next. Fellows, girls, ask your mother for Wheaties. Tell her Wheaties are the whole wheat cereal that actually supplies the same amount of heat-producing units you need for body warmth these cold winter mornings as hot cereals do. Fix that famous breakfast of champions with plenty of milk, cream or sugar, and some bananas. You'll say, just like Jack Armstrong says, "Wheaties and bananas are a great combination." This is David Owen saying good-bye for Jack Armstrong and the maker of Wheaties.

SONG: Try Wheaties, they're whole wheat with all of the bran. Won't you try Wheaties ... they're crispy, they're crunchy the whole year through. Jack has them, never tires of them and neither will you. Just buy Wheaties, the best breakfast food in the land.

746. THE JACK BENNY PROGRAM. Comedy, 30 min., CBS, 1932–1933; NBC, 1933–1948; CBS, 1949–1955.

A situation comedy that portrayed the home and working life of comedian Jack Benny. At work, the stage of his radio program, Jack had misadventure with his cast and crew. At home (366 North Camden Drive in Hollywood), the audience was given just a glimpse into the private life of the perennially 39-year-old entertainer. Jack was rather tight with his money and had a booby-trapped vault in his basement; parting with money was a most difficult task for him to perform. Jack also had a run-down car (a Maxwell), a parrot (Polly) and a Polar Bear named Carmichael (who lived in the outer basement "and once ate a gasman"). Jack's endless attempts to play the violin and his feuds with Fred Allen and Phil Harris were also part of the program. *Other regular characters:* Rochester Van Jones, Jack's valet; Mary Livingston, Jack's girlfriend (she had a sister

**Note: Don Ameche took over for his brother Jim in 1933. When Don became a film actor, Jim returned to the role and played it until 1938.*

Jack Benny was the central figure of the long-running *Jack Benny Program*.

named Babe, and Jack constantly joked about her); Don Wilson, Jack's announcer; Dennis Day, Jack's vocalist; Phil Harris, Jack's orchestra leader (who loved to drink, gamble and play pool); Prof. Andre LeBlanc, Jack's exasperated violin teacher; Mabel and Gertrude, the telephone operators; Schlepperman and Mr. Kitzel, the Jewish foils; T. Wimley, the sound man; the Train Announcer ("Anaheim, Azusa and Cuc-a-monga"); Martha and Emily, the old ladies with a crush on Jack; Dennis Day's mother. The series, also known as *The Jell-O Program* and *The Lucky Strike Program*, moved to television in 1950.

Cast: Jack Benny (*Jack Benny*); Eddie Anderson (*Rochester Van Jones*); Mary Livingston (*Mary Livingston*); Dennis Day (*Dennis Day*); Don Wilson (*Don Wilson*); Phil Harris (*Phil Harris*); Sara Berner (*Mabel*); Bea Benaderet (*Gertrude*); Mel Blanc (*Prof. LeBlanc/Jack's car/Jack's parrot/Carmichael/Train Announcer/T. Wimley*); Sam Hearn (*Schlepperman*); Artie Auerbach (*Mr. Kitzel*); Jane Morgan (*Martha*); Gloria Gordon (*Emily*); Verna Felton (*Dennis's mother*). ***Also*** (Various roles): Andy Devine, Sheldon Leonard, Frank Nelson, Blanche Stewart. ***Vocalists:*** Kenny Baker, Michael Bartlett, Dennis Day, James Melton, Frank Parker, Larry Stevens, the Sportsmen Quartet. ***Announcers:*** Kenny Delmar, Paul Douglas, George Hicks, Don Wilson. ***Orchestra:*** Frank Black, Bob Crosby, Johnny Green, Phil Harris, George Olsen, Ted Weems. ***Producers:*** Irving Fein, Hilliard Marks.

Note: Jack Benny's early programs were in no way like the one listed above or what most people remember. In the early 1930s, Jack was simply the host of a program of music and songs (he introduced the segments and joked between each performance). Ethel Shutta was the vocalist on these early programs and George Olsen and his orchestra provided the music.

OPENING (from Jack's first show, 5/2/32)

ANNOUNCER: Tonight, Canada Dry, the champagne of ginger ale, presents a series of programs to advertise the new made-to-order Canada Dry, which you can now buy by the glass at drug stores and soda fountains. This series will feature George Olsen and his music, Miss Ethel Shutta, the star of many Broadway successes and that suave comedian, dry humorist and famous master of ceremonies, Jack Benny.

JACK: Ladies and gentlemen, this is Jack Benny talking and this is my first appearance on the air professionally; by that I mean I'm finally getting paid... I'm supposed to be a sort of master of ceremonies and tell you all the things that will happen ... and also talk about Canada Dry, made to order by the glass... So, ladies and gentlemen, a master of ceremonies is really a fellow who's unemployed and gets paid for it...

CLOSING

JACK: That, ladies and gentlemen, was the last number on our first show on the second of May. I hope you will be with us again next Wednesday. Well, good night then.

ANNOUNCER: Ladies and gentlemen, we are concluding the first program in a new series sponsored by Canada Dry... Canada Dry has presented Jack Benny, Ethel Shutta and George Olsen and his music. The same group of artists will be with you at this time Wednesday evening. This is the National Broadcasting Company.

OPENING (from Jack's last show, 5/22/55)

ANNOUNCER: *The Jack Benny Program*, transcribed and presented by Lucky Strike, the cigarette that tastes better.

SONG: Light up a Lucky, it's light-up time. Be happy, go Lucky, it's light-up time. For the taste that you like, light up a Lucky Strike; relax, it's light-up time.

ANNOUNCER: *The Lucky Strike Program* starring Jack Benny, with Mary Livingston, Rochester, Dennis Day, Bob Crosby and yours truly, Don Wilson. And now, ladies and gentlemen, we come to the last Jack Benny show of the month; it's also the last program of the current series; as a matter of fact, it's the last show of the season. So now I bring you the man I thought wouldn't last, Jack Benny.

JACK: Thank you, thank you, this is Jack Benny talking...

747. JACK BUNDY'S CARNIVAL. Variety, 30 min., Mutual, 1944–1945.

A weekly program of music, songs and comedy with host Jack Bundy. Guests appeared with the regulars (Monica Lewis and Bob Shepherd) and Bob Stanley and his orchestra provided the music.

748. THE JACK CARSON SHOW. Comedy, 30 min., CBS, 1943–1946.

Music and songs coupled with comedy skits that are set at 22 North Hollywood Lane, the home of comedian Jack Carson in Hollywood, California. Like *The Jack Benny Program*, sketches relate Carson's hectic home life as he contends with relatives, friends and neighbors.

Cast: Jack Carson (*Jack Carson*); Arthur Treacher (*Tristan, the Butler*); Eddie Marr (*Jack's press agent*); Dave Willock (*Tugwell, Jack's nephew*); Norma Jean Nilsson (*Little girl next door*); Elizabeth Patterson (*Aunt Sally*); Mel Blanc (*Hubert Peabody*); Jane Morgan (*Mrs. Foster*). ***Regulars:*** Doris Drew, Anita Ellis, Johnny Richards, Tony Romano, Maxie Rosenbloom, Hanley Stafford, the King Sisters. ***Announcers:*** Hy Averback, Howard Petrie, Del Sharbutt, Bob Stewart. ***Orchestra:*** Ray Chamberlain, Charles "Bud" Dante, Walter Gross, Freddy Martin, Johnny Richards. ***Producers:*** Sam Fuller, Victor Knight.

749. The Jack Coffey Show. Variety, 30 min., NBC Blue, 1941.

Music and songs with orchestra leader Jack Coffey as the host. Vocals were by Beverly Blayne, Dick Kapi and Three Smart Girls. Jack Coffey and his orchestra provided the music.

750. The Jack Haley Show. Variety, 30 min., NBC, 1937–1938; CBS, 1938–1939.

Music, songs and skits with comedian Jack Haley as the host. Artie Auerbach, Lucille Ball and Virginia Verrill were the regulars and Ted Fiorito and his orchestra supplied the music. The program, sponsored by Log Cabin pancake syrup, is also known as *The Log Cabin Jamboree*.

751. The Jack Kirkwood Show. Variety, 15 min., NBC, 1943–1944; CBS, 1944–1946.

A nightly program of music, songs and comedy set against the background of the Madhouse Little Theater. See also *Mirth and Madness*.

Host: Jack Kirkwood. ***Regulars:*** Lee Albert, Gene Lavalle, Lillian Leigh, Jean McKean, Don Reid. ***Announcers:*** Steve Dunne, Jimmy Wallington. ***Organists:*** Gaylord Carter, Lud Gluskin. ***Orchestra:*** Irving Miller.

752. Jack Oakie's College. Variety, 60 min., CBS, 12/29/36 to 3/22/38.

A weekly program of music, songs and vaudeville-like skits presided over by Prof. Jack Oakie, the head of a mythical college that majored in fun. Guests appeared as the student body (who also supplied the laughs and songs). A young Judy Garland was the featured vocalist and Benny Goodman and his orchestra provided the music.

753. The Jack Paar Show. Variety, 30 min., NBC, summers of 1947, 1948, 1949.

A program of music, songs, chatter and comedy that replaced *The Jack Benny Program* for three summers.

Host: Jack Paar. ***Regulars:*** Hans Conried, Trudy Erwin, Florence Halop, Carol Richards, Martha Stewart, the Page Cavanaugh Trio, Jud Conlon's Rhythmaires. ***Announcers:*** Hy Averback, Frank Nelson. ***Orchestra:*** Jerry Fielding.

754. The Jack Pearl Show. Comedy, 30 min., NBC, 1932–1937.

Music and songs coupled with skits built around Baron Munchausen, a teller of tall tales who spoke with a German accent, and his straight-man Sharlie, who listened but seriously doubted the Baron's stories. Before ending, the format switched to focus on a German tavern keeper named Peter Pfeiffer, who also had a knack for stretching the truth. See also *Jack and Cliff*. Also known as *The Raleigh and Kool Program* (when sponsored by Raleigh and Kool cigarettes).

Cast: Jack Pearl (*Host/Baron Munchausen/Peter Pfeiffer*); Cliff Hall (*Sharlie*); Mae Questel (*Dizzy secretary*). ***Regulars:*** Charlie Hall, Jean Merrill, Brad Reynolds. ***Announcer:*** Frank Gallop. ***Orchestra:*** Morton Gould.

755. The Jack Pepper Show. Variety, 30 min., CBS, 1944.

A weekly program of music, songs and comedy with comedian Jack Pepper as host. Jackson Beck, Art Carney, Sandra Gould, Dan Ocko, Mickey O'Day, Jeri Sullivan and the Murphy Sisters were the regulars. Tip Corning did the announcing and Mitchell Ayres and his orchestra provided the music.

756. The Jack Smith, Dinah Shore, Margaret Whiting Show. Variety, 15 min., CBS, 1950.

A daily program of music and songs featuring vocalists Jack Smith, Dinah Shore and Margaret Whiting.

Host (Monday and Friday evenings): Margaret Whiting. ***Announcer:*** Bob Stevenson. ***Orchestra:*** Frank DeVol. ***Hosts*** (Tuesday, Wednesday and Thursday evenings): Dinah Shore, Jack Smith. ***Announcer:*** Bob Stevenson. ***Orchestra:*** Frank DeVol.

757. The Jack Smith Show. Variety, 15 min., CBS, 1943–1950.

A daily program of music and songs with Jack Smith, a popular tenor who was called "The singer with a Smile in His Voice." Dinah Shore and Margaret Whiting assisted with the vocals and the Earl Sheldon and Frank DeVol orchestras provided the music. Dan Hancock did the announcing. See also the prior title.

758. The Jack Webb Show. Satire, 30 min., ABC, 1946.

Clever spoofs of radio programs with Jack Webb (of *Dragnet* fame) as a comedian and the star of a program so undramatic that it is hard to associate such a series with his career. But it happened. Music and songs were coupled with skits; and each week "It's Contest Time" offered "a peachy keen prize" for the writer of the best letter explaining, "How to get *The Jack Webb Show* off the air." Skits included:

1. "Facts on File." Fred Fact (Jack Webb) related "facts that are facts and that's a fact."

2. "Is it Dick Tracy? Is it Sherlock Holmes? Is it Mr. North? Is it Mrs. North? Is it the Thin Man?, the Fat Man?, the Saint?, the Whistler?, the Green Hornet?, the spider, the cat, the dog, the mouse? No, it's the Razor—he's sharp. Another first for radio, the true adventures of the Razor. Tonight's story, another close shave for the Razor entitled 'The Case of the Confused Keyhole.'"

3. A program for sad people entitled "The Misery Hour" with Terry Tear (Jack Webb) as the host.

Host: Jack Webb. ***Regulars:*** John Galbraith, Clancy Hayes, Phil Vivaro, the Ragadiers. ***Vocalist:*** Nora McNamara. ***Announcer:*** John Galbraith. ***Orchestra:*** Phil Vivaro.

OPENING (from 4/17/46)

ANNOUNCER: This week, the major league baseball season opens. In keeping with this, the American Broadcasting Company brings you the first foul ball of the season, *The Jack Webb Show* in its fifth consecutive strikeout. Nothing new has been added... Oh, yes, a wonderful gal with a wonderful voice has made a terrible mistake tonight. Midge Williams has agreed to set her career back ten years with a guest appearance on *The Jack Webb Show*. I'm gonna find a nice quiet room until this whole thing blows over. Why don't you do the same thing?

CLOSING

JACK: This is Jack Webb. Give us another chance next Wednesday at nine-thirty, won't you? Good night, gang.

ANNOUNCER: This is ABC, the American Broadcasting Company.

759. THE JACKIE GLEASON–LES TREMAYNE SHOW. Variety, 30 min., NBC, 1944.

A weekly program of music, songs and comedy that featured comedian Jackie Gleason and dramatic actor Les Tremayne as the co-hosts. Patsy Garrett and Andy Russell were the regulars (assisted by guests in songs and comedy skits) and Hank Levin and Henry Sylvern provided the music.

760. JACK'S PLACE. Variety, 85 min., CBS, 10/12/53 to 1/1/54.

A lavish program of variety performances by guests that came too late to radio. (Television had killed off NBC's *The Big Show*, and this CBS attempt also failed to capture an audience. The program was cut five minutes to make room for a newscast.) Jack Gregson hosted and Mary Mayo provided the vocals. John Hicks did the announcing.

761. THE JAILBUSTERS. Variety, 15 min., CBS, 1945.

A daily program of music and songs with a group called the Jailbusters (Everett Barkstable, Orville Brooks, Theodore Brooks, J.C. Ginyard and George McFadden).

762. THE JAMES AND PAMELA MASON SHOW. Anthology, 30 min., NBC, 7/14/19 to 9/1/49.

A weekly series of light dramatizations featuring husband-and-wife actors James and Pamela Mason as the leads. Lurene Tuttle appeared in various supporting roles and Frank Barton did the announcing. Music was by David Raksin and his orchestra.

763. THE JAMES MELTON SHOW. Variety, 30 min., CBS, then NBC, 1944–1946.

Music and songs with host James Melton, a popular tenor of the era. Joan Roberts provided additional vocals and Jimmy Wallington did the announcing. Al Goodman and his orchestra provided the music.

764. THE JAN AUGUST SHOW. Variety, 15 min., CBS, 1947.

Pianist Jan August as the host of a program of music and songs sponsored by Revere cameras. Tony Esper, Monica Lewis and Chick Robertson were the regulars. Ken Roberts did the announcing and Jan August supplied the music.

765. JANE ACE, DISC JOCKEY. Variety, 30 min., NBC, 1951–1952.

Jane Ace (of the program *Easy Aces*) as a disc jockey spinning records and relating light nonsense. Jane Ace played herself and Don Pardo did the announcing.

766. Jane Arden. Serial, 15 min., NBC Blue, 1938–1939.

Dramatic events in the life of Jane Arden, a reporter for the *Bulletin*, a crusading metropolitan newspaper.

Cast: Ruth Yorke (*Jane Arden*); Florence Freeman (*Betty Harrison*); Helene Dumas (*Louise West*); Richard Gordon (*Jane's father*); Betty Garde (*Jane's mother*); Bill Baar (*Jack Fraser*); Maurice Franklin (*E.J. Walker*); Frank Provo (*Bob Brandon*). ***Music:*** Howard Smith.

767. The Jane Froman–Don Ross Show. Variety, 30 min., NBC, 1937.

The 1937 replacement for *The Jack Benny Program*. Don Ross was the host; vocals were by Jane Froman and the Tune Twisters; comedy came from Freddie Lightner; the Al D'Artega Orchestra supplied the music. Also known as *The Jell-O Summer Show*.

768. The Jane Froman–Jan Peerce Show. Variety, 30 min., CBS, 1939.

Music and songs with vocalist Jane Froman and tenor Jan Peerce as the hosts. Erno Rapee and his orchestra supplied the music.

769. The Jane Froman Show. Variety, 30 min., CBS, 1938.

A weekly program of music, songs and light comedy with vocalist Jane Froman as the host. Hugh Herbert and Ted Husing were the regulars and Dick Himber and his orchestra supplied the music.

770. The Jane Pickens Show. Variety, 30 min., NBC, 1948.

A weekly program of music and songs with soprano Jane Pickens. Jack Liltz and the Norman Cloutier Chorus supported her in songs. Robert Warren did the announcing and Norman Cloutier and his orchestra provided the music. The program is also known by its 1956–57 title, *Pickens' Party*.

771. The Janette Davis Show. Variety, 15 min., ABC, 1946–1948; CBS, 1948.

A nightly program of music and songs with vocalist Janette Davis as the host. Lee Vines did the announcing and the Archie Bleyer and Howard Smith orchestras provided the music.

Jane Froman headlined *The Jane Froman Show* in 1938.

772. Jason and the Golden Fleece. Adventure, 30 min., NBC, 10/21/52 to 7/19/53.

The Golden Fleece is a 60-foot sailing vessel for hire that is captained by a man named Jason. Jason is also the owner of a bar on the 800 block in the French Quarter of New Orleans. Stories relate his adventures as he and his bartender and first mate, Louie DuMont, become involved in the personal problems of their passengers.

Cast: Macdonald Carey (*Jason*); William Conrad (*Louie DuMont*). ***Music:*** Frank Worth.

OPENING

Sound: Voice yelling "Raspberries, raspberries."

Jason: New Orleans is dirty and damp, but I like it here. I like the chant of the coal peddler as he walks past my bar on Bourbon Street. I like the call of the blackberry woman who is still singing the same song she sang when pirates hid their loot in Jean Lafitte's blacksmith shop in the French Quarter. And I like the Mississippi, where a man and his boat can find a dream. Yea, I like

New Orleans. They call me Jason; I call my boat *The Golden Fleece.*

ANNOUNCER: NBC presents *Jason and the Golden Fleece* starring Macdonald Carey.

773. JAY STEWART'S FUN FAIR. Variety, 30 min., ABC, 5/21/49–9/24/49.

The format called for participants to exhibit their pets, submit to capsule interviews and compete in various quizzes for prizes. Jay Stewart was the host and Lou Cook did the announcing.

774. THE JEAN GABLON SHOW. Variety, 15 min., CBS, 1946.

Music and songs with host Jean Gablon and the backing of Paul Baron and his orchestra.

THE JEDDO HIGHLANDERS *see* **APPENDIX**

775. JEFF REGAN, INVESTIGATOR. Crime Drama, 30 min., CBS, 1948–1950.

The International Detective Bureau is a Los Angeles–based firm run by Anthony J. Lyon, a somewhat unethical chap who sees the business only as a means by which to make money. His clients, however, prefer tough but discreet investigators. When such a man is needed, Lyon assigns the case to Jeffrey "Jeff" Regan, the man who will get the job done their way—with no fanfare. Stories follow Jeff's case investigations as he strives to please Lyon (a greedy boss) and desperate clients. Jeff earns $10 a day plus expenses and refers to Anthony's office as "the Lyon's Den." Jeff is sometimes called "the Lyon's Eye" by clients. Although Anthony claims, "International is in business to make people happy," Jeff disagrees and never actually explains why he keeps his job—"It feels good when I get the job done. But he doesn't care whether it's homicide, arson, a lost daughter or people just getting kicked around. He's in it for the money. And me, I don't know, I don't know." *Other regular characters:* Melody, Lyon's receptionist. Jack Webb, first to play the part, left in 1949 to play Sgt. Joe Friday on *Dragnet.*

Cast: Jack Webb, Frank Graham (*Jeff Regan*); Wilms Herbert, Frank Nelson (*Anthony J. Lyon*); Laurette Fillbrandt (*Melody*). ***Announcer:*** Marvin Miller. ***Music:*** Del Castillo. ***Producer:*** Gordon D. Hughes.

OPENING

JEFF: My name is Jeff Regan. I work for Anthony J. Lyon, head of the International Detective Bureau. He doesn't care where the money comes from, just so long as it comes his way. He cashes in on trouble, and for him it pays off; for me, it's work.

ANNOUNCER: Here's the kind of adventure you've been waiting to hear. Hard-boiled action and mystery with radio's most exciting private detective—Jeff Regan. So stand by for trouble and suspense in tonight's story of "The Prodigal Daughter." And now, here's Jack Webb as Jeff Regan.

CLOSING

ANNOUNCER: Remember, it's CBS, same time next week for hard-boiled action and mystery with radio's most exciting private detective, Jeff Regan, as he tells the story of "The Lonesome Lady." This is CBS, the Columbia Broadcasting System.

THE JELL-O PROGRAM *see* **THE JACK BENNY PROGRAM**

THE JELL-O SUMMER SHOW *see* **THE JANE FROMAN–DON ROSS SHOW**

776. THE JERRY COOPER SHOW. Variety, 15 min., NBC, 12/4/34 to 4/2/35.

A weekly program of music and songs with vocalist Jerry Cooper as the host. The DeVore Sisters, the Eight Men and the Smoothies (vocal groups) were the regulars. Jimmy Leonard did the announcing and William Stoees and his orchestra provided the music.

777. THE JERRY LESTER SHOW. Variety, 30 min., CBS, 7/25/43 to 1/6/44.

Music, songs and comedy hosted by comedian Jerry Lester (who was assisted by guests in sketches). Vocals were by Diane Courtney and Ray Sinatra and Fred Uttal did the announcing.

778. THE JERRY WAYNE SHOW. Variety, 30 min., Mutual, 1942–1945.

A weekly program of music and songs with host/vocalist Jerry Wayne. Carole Candes, Hope Emerson, Lorna Lynn and Craig McDonnell were the regulars. The Jeff Alexander Chorus provided vocal backing and Dan Seymour did the announcing. Music was by the Alvy West Band and the Jeff Alexander Orchestra. See also *Melody Lane with Jerry Wayne*.

779. The Jim Backus Show. Variety, 30 min., Mutual, 1947–1948.

A weekly program of comedy skits with host Jim Backus and regulars Jerry Hausner, Frances Robertson and Dink Trout. Frank Graham did the announcing.

780. The Jim Backus Show. Variety, 60 min., ABC, 1957–1958.

Music, songs and comedy skits with Jim Backus as the host. Betty Ann Grove and Jack Haskell were the vocalists and Elliot Lawrence and his orchestra supplied the music.

781. The Jim Backus Vaudeville Show. Variety, 30 min., CBS, 1942.

A weekly series recreating the music, songs and slapstick-like comedy of vaudeville. Jim Backus was the host; Mary Small and the Eight Balls of Fire were the regulars; and Jeff Alexander and his orchestra provided the music.

Jimmy Allen *see* **The Air Adventures of Jimmy Allen**

782. Jimmy Carroll Sings. Variety, 15 min., CBS, 1945.

A program of music and songs with vocalist Jimmy Carroll as the host. The Ken Christy Chorus assisted Jimmy and Ted Dale and his orchestra provided the music.

783. The Jimmy Dorsey Show. Variety, 30 min., CBS, 1950.

A weekly program of big band music with orchestra leader Jimmy Dorsey as the host. Claire Hogan and Kenny Martin provided the vocals; Bob Shipley did the announcing; the Jimmy Dorsey orchestra provided the music.

784. The Jimmy Durante–Garry Moore Show. Variety, 30 min., NBC, 1943–1945; CBS, 1945–1947.

A weekly series of skits, songs and performances by guest stars featuring the talents of comedians Jimmy Durante and Garry Moore (who alternated billing; one week it was as listed above; next it was *The Garry Moore-Jimmy Durante Show*). Also known as *Comedy Caravan*.

Hosts: Jimmy Durante, Garry Moore. ***Regulars:*** Elvia Allman (*Cuddles Bongschnook*), Georgia Gibbs, Florence Halop (*Hot Breath Houlihan*), Susan Ellis, Jeri Sullivan, Alan Young. ***Announcer:*** Howard Petrie. ***Orchestra:*** Xavier Cugat, Roy Bargy.

OPENING

Sound: Phone rings.

Garry (picking up receiver): Hello, Rexall Drug Show, Garry Moore speaking.

Jimmy: Hello, Junior, this is Jimmy.

Garry: Jimmy Durante, where are you?

Jimmy: Can't get down to the show. I was at the beach and three girls buried me in the sand.

Garry: Well, so what?

Jimmy: Well, come and get me. I forgot where they buried me.

Announcer: Your Rexall Drug Store presents Jimmy Durante and Garry Moore—*The Jimmy Durante–Garry Moore Show* with Jeri Sullivan, Roy Bargy and his orchestra and yours truly, Howard Petrie. Brought to you by your friendly Rexall Drug Store. Rexall, an old familiar name that has always stood for quality and value.

CLOSING

Garry: Good night, Mr. Durante.

Jimmy: Good night, Mr. Moore.

Garry: Good night, everybody.

Jimmy: Good night, folks.

Announcer: We'll be looking for you next Friday night, same time, same station when we'll be back with another *Jimmy Durante–Garry Moore Show* for Rexall Drug Stores. In the meantime, visit the friendly Rexall druggist who brings you these fine programs. And remember, you can depend on any drug product that bears the Rexall name. Tune in again next Friday night for Roy Bargy and his orchestra, Jeri Sullivan, yours truly, Howard Petrie—

Jimmy: And Jimmy Durante.

Garry: And Garry Moore.

Jimmy: In person.

Announcer: This is CBS, the Columbia Broadcasting System.

785. The Jimmy Durante Show. Variety, 30 min., NBC, 1947–1950.

A weekly series of songs and skits that

picked up where the previous title left off (but without Garry Moore). Also titled *The New Jimmy Durante Show* and also known as *The Rexall Show*.

Host: Jimmy Durante. ***Regulars:*** Barbara Jo Allen (*Vera Vague*), Candy Candido, Florence Halop (*Hot Breath Houlihan*), Arthur Treacher. ***Announcer:*** Howard Petrie. ***Orchestra:*** Roy Bargy.

OPENING

ANNOUNCER: Good health to all from Rexall. From Hollywood, *The Jimmy Durante Show*.

JIMMY (singing): Ink a dink a dink, a dink a do, a dink a dee, oh what a beautiful day...

ANNOUNCER: Yes, it's *The Jimmy Durante Show* with Arthur Treacher, Candy Candido, Roy Bargy and his orchestra, yours truly, Howard Petrie, and our special guest for tonight, Bing Crosby. And now, here's Jimmy.

CLOSING

JIMMY: Good night ladies and gentlemen, thanks for listening in. And good night Mrs. Calabash, wherever you are.

ANNOUNCER: *The Jimmy Durante Show* has been brought to you by your friendly neighborhood Rexall Drug Store—good health to all from Rexall. This is Howard Petrie wishing you a pleasant good night until next week at this same time when NBC will again bring you *The Jimmy Durante Show*. This is NBC, the National Broadcasting Company.

786. THE JIMMY EDMONDSON SHOW. Variety, 30 min., NBC, 1946.

Music, songs and comedy with Jimmy Edmondson, a comic known as "Prof. Backwards" (he spells and pronounces words from end to start). Nanette Fabray, Juano Hernandez, Patricia Hosley, Art Kahl, Florence MacMichael and the Esquire Quartet were the regulars. Bob Sherry did the announcing and Jerry Jerome and his orchestra supplied the music.

787. JIMMY GLEASON'S DINER. Comedy, 30 min., ABC, 1945–1946.

Jimmy Gleason's Diner is a small eatery located near a film studio in Hollywood, California. It is owned by a former movie actor Jimmy Gleason and his wife, Lucille. Stories relate the exchange of conversation between them and their customers.

Cast: Jimmy Gleason (*Jimmy Gleason*); Lucille Gleason (*Lucille Gleason*). ***Also:*** Willie Best, Ken Christy, Joseph Kearns. ***Music:*** The ABC Staff Orchestra.

788. THE JO STAFFORD SHOW. Variety, 15 and 25 min. versions, ABC, 1948–1949; CBS, 1953.

A weekly program of music and songs with vocalist Jo Stafford as the host. Clark Dennis and the Starlighters were the regulars. Marvin Miller and Johnny Jacobs did the announcing. The Page Cavanaugh Trio and the Paul Weston Orchestra provided the music.

THE JOAN BENOIT SHOW *see* **APPENDIX**

789. THE JOAN BROOKS SHOW. Variety, 15 min., CBS, 1945.

A program of music and songs with vocalist Joan Brooks and the music of Archie Bleyer and his orchestra.

790. THE JOAN DAVIS SHOW. Comedy, 30 min., CBS, 1945–1947.

Joanie's Tea Room is a quaint little shop in the town of Swanville, U.S.A. It is run by Joan Davis, a slightly scatterbrained, likable, well-meaning young woman who is having a difficult time keeping her business out of the red. She is assisted by Andy and Harry and stories follow Joan's efforts to keep her shop out of the hands of her creditors (the bank) and her involvement with the various characters who inhabit the shop. *Other regular characters:* Barbara Weatherbee, the rich and spoiled daughter of the bank president (Josh Weatherbee, whom she calls "Pater"); Rosella Hipperton III, Joan's overweight friend (whom Joan calls "Hippy"); Seranis, Joan's lazy, unemployed brother-in-law (her sister Tallulah's husband). Joan is in love with Andy, but Andy (who sings a romantic song between acts) is not as romantic as Joan would like. Harry has just the opposite problem: Mrs. Hipperton has eyes for him—but he has no interest in her. See also the following title.

Cast: Joan Davis (*Joan Davis*); Andy Russell (*Andy/Seranis*); Harry Von Zell (*Harry/Josh Weatherbee*); Shirley Mitchell (*Barbara Weatherbee*); Verna Felton (*Rosella Hipperton III*). ***Announcer:*** Harry Von Zell. ***Music:*** Paul Weston.

OPENING

ANNOUNCER: *The Joan Davis Show.*

SONG: Poor Joan, ain't got nobody; she's nobody's sweetheart now.

ANNOUNCER: Featuring the romantic singing of Andy Russell, with a great comedy cast including Verna Felton, Shirley Mitchell and the music of Paul Weston and his orchestra. And here's the star of our show, America's Queen of Comedy, Joan Davis.

JOAN: Thank you, thank you very much. [She would then begin the show.]

791. JOAN DAVIS TIME. Comedy, 30 min., CBS, 1947–1949.

A revised version of the prior title. Events in the day-to-day life of Joan Davis, a misadventure-prone young woman who is also the owner of Joanie's Tea Room in the town of Swanville, U.S.A. Joan's efforts to improve her life and find a steady boyfriend were the focal point of the series. Joan feels her life is in a rut and has had several boyfriends, but is still searching for Mr. Right. Henry Crabtree was her first boyfriend (junior high school). They would meet after football practice and he would carry her football shoes home for her. After high school, she met Punchy Callahan, a prizefighter who had "a soft spot in his head" for her. She then met a cowboy named "Two Gun" Tex Hayes while at a party, sitting in a corner watching other people having a good time. She now likes Freddy Neidermeyer, but he has no real romantic interest in her. The various characters who frequent the shop and the zany people Joan meets wherever she goes also test Joan's endurance as she struggles to keep her sanity. *Other regular characters:* Mabel, her girlfriend; Lionel, the tea shop manager. Also known as *Joanie's Tea Room*. See also *Leave It to Joan*, Joan's 1949–1950 series.

Cast: Joan Davis (*Joan Davis*); Sharon Douglas (*Mabel*); Lionel Stander (*Lionel*). ***Regulars*** (various roles):Hans Conried, Verna Felton, Andy Russell. ***Also:*** The Choraleers. ***Announcers:*** Ben Gage, Bob Lemond, Harry Von Zell. ***Orchestra:*** Lud Gluskin, John Rarig, Paul Weston. ***Producer:*** Dick Mack.

OPENING

ANNOUNCER: Well, there's no question about it. From coast to coast, it's *Joan Davis Time.*

CHORUS: It's *Joan Davis Time.*

ANNOUNCER: During the time you spend with Joan Davis tonight, you'll hear the voice of her special guest, that talented young man who's been spreading laughter from coast to coast, Peter Lind Hayes, plus a supporting cast featuring Lionel Stander, Hans Conried, the music of John Rarig's orchestra, the Choraleers singing quintet and yours sincerely, Ben Gage. And now, it's time to meet the star of our show, America's Queen of Comedy, Joan Davis.

CLOSING

ANNOUNCER: Don't forget there's more good fun and music coming up next week, coast to coast, when a very special guest will drop in to see Joanie, none other than the hilarious fugitive from *Duffy's Tavern*, Clifton Finnegan. So, remember, if anybody asks you what time it is at this time, tell them it's *Joan Davis Time*. This is CBS, the Columbia Broadcasting System.

JOANIE'S TEA ROOM *see* **JOAN DAVIS TIME**

792. JOE AND ETHEL TURP. Comedy, 15 min., CBS, 1/4/43 to 9/24/43.

Humorous events in the lives of Joe and Ethel Turp, a married couple beset with problems. Based on the characters created by Damon Runyon.

Cast: Jackson Beck (*Joe Turp*); Patsy Campbell (*Ethel Turp*); Jack Smart (*Uncle Ben*); Art Carney (*Billy Oldham*). ***Organist:*** Fred Fiebel. ***Producer:*** Larry Berns.

793. JOE AND MABEL. Comedy, 30 min., NBC, 2/13/41 to 9/27/42.

Joe Sparton and Mabel Stooler are lovers who have vastly different opinions about marriage. Joe is a Brooklyn cab driver. He is hardworking, level-headed and not ready for marriage. Mabel is beautiful, stubborn, a bit scatterbrained and ready to tie the knot. She works as a manicurist in Manhattan and is dead set on convincing Joe that she would make the perfect wife for him. Stories follow their romantic ups and downs as Mabel schemes to change Joe's mind about marriage. *Other regular characters:* Adele, Mabel's mother; Sherman, Mabel's mischievous 12-year-old brother (he is a schemer and, Joe feels, "an annoying object to me and Mabel's relationship"); Mike, Joe's cabbie friend (their favorite hangout is the Coffee Pot); Dolly, Mike's girlfriend, "the dish from Flatbush."

Cast: Ted de Corsia (*Joe Spartan*); Ann Thomas (*Mabel Stooler*); Betty Garde (*Adele Stooler*); Jack Grimes (*Sherman Stooler*); Walter Kinsella (*Mike*); Jean Ellyn (*Dolly Dunkle*). ***Announcer:*** George Putnam.

OPENING

ANNOUNCER: It's time to meet *Joe and Mabel* again, those very human beings. Irving Gaynor Neiman brings you another story of the far-from-placid lives of Joe, loquacious cabbie, and his spirited girlfriend Mabel. And throw in for good measure another glimpse of Sherman, Mabel's kid brother, and of course, Joe's cabbie friend, Mike. Well, today we have a look at what happened on Valentine's Day. Wait a minute, here's Joe to tell you about it...

794. The Joe DiMaggio Show. Children, 30 min., CBS, 1949–1950.

A Saturday morning series that featured short dramatizations based on the lives of sports figures and quiz segments wherein children were asked sports-related questions in return for prizes.

Host: Joe DiMaggio. ***Co-Host:*** Jack Barry. ***Dramatic Cast:*** Jackson Beck, Charles Irving, Leon Janney, Adelaide Klein, Charlotte Manson. ***Announcer:*** Ted Brown. ***Music:*** Arlo Hults.

795. The Joe E. Brown Show. Variety, 30 min., CBS, 1938–1939.

A weekly program of music, songs and comedy skits with comedian Joe E. Brown as the host. Bill Demming, Frank Gill and Margaret McCrae were the regulars and Harry Sosnik and his orchestra provided the music.

796. Joe Palooka. Comedy, 15 min., Syndicated, 1945.

A radio adaptation of the comic strip by Ham Fisher about a heavyweight boxer named Joe Palooka, a clean-living, moral champ ignorant of gambling, fixed fights, blonde sirens and night clubs. *Other regular characters:* Ann Howe, his girlfriend; Knobby Walsh, his manager; Clyde, his trainer.

Cast: Norman Gottschalk, Alan Reed, Karl Swenson (*Joe Palooka*); Elmira Roessler, Elsie Hitz, Mary Jane Higby (*Anne Howe*); Frank Readick, Hal Lansing (*Knobby Walsh*); Murray Forbes (*Clyde*).

797. The Joe Penner Show. Comedy, 30 min., CBS, 1933–1935.

A weekly series of comedy skits, songs and performances by guests. The program, sponsored by Fleischmann's Yeast, is also known as *The Baker's Broadcast*. See also *The Park Avenue Penners*.

Host: Joe Penner. ***Regulars:*** Roy Atwell, Jim Bannon, Russ Brown, Harriet Hilliard, Harry Holcombe, Tommy Lane, Dick Merrill, Dick Ryan, Kenny Stevens. ***Music:*** Ozzie Nelson, Jacques Renard.

798. Joe Powers of Oakville. Variety, 30 min., CBS, 1946.

A weekly program of music, songs, comedy sketches and capsule dramatizations with host Joe Powers. David Anderson, Richard Leonard, Julian Noa, Elizabeth Reller and Helen Shields were the regulars. George Sherman and his orchestra provided the music.

799. The John Charles Thomas Show. Variety, 30 min., NBC, 1943–1946.

Music and songs with John Charles Thomas, a Metropolitan Opera baritone. John Nesbitt hosted a short segment called "The Passing Parade" (where events of the past were recalled); the Ken Darby Singers were regulars; Victor Young and his orchestra provided the music.

800. The John Conte Show. Variety, 5 min., ABC, 1952.

A filler program of songs with John Conte as the host and the music of the John Magnate Trio.

801. The John Kirby Show. Variety, 30 min., CBS, 1940.

Music and songs with orchestra leader John Kirby as the host. Maxine Sullivan and the Golden Gate Quartet provided the vocals and John Kirby and his orchestra supplied the music.

802. John Steele, Adventurer. Anthology, 30 min., Mutual, 1949–1956.

Various tales of danger and excitement as told by John Steele, a fictional adventurer. Don Douglas played John Steele and Sylvan Levin provided the music.

OPENING

ANNOUNCER: Take one man with an iron sense

of justice, put him in a lonely canyon with a desperate killer—that's our story for tonight, "Trail's End," taken from the files of *John Steele, Adventurer*.

STEELE: Hello, friends, this is John Steele. If you like stories of suspense and action, you've come to the right place because our specialty is curling hair and wearing out the edges of seats. This week's tale takes us out to the empty prairies of the far west where a good friend of mine lived a very absorbing story. I first met George Brennan when I was managing the White Swan Cafe out in Silverton. But here he is to tell you about it himself, George.

GEORGE: I guess being sheriff is about the most thankless job a man could ask for...

803. JOHNNY DESMOND GOES TO COLLEGE. Variety, 30 min., ABC, 1950.

A weekly program of music and songs set against a college motif. Vocalist Johnny Desmond served as the host; Doris Drew, the Four Vagabonds and the George Barnes Octet were the regulars. Rex Maupin and his orchestra provided the music.

804. A JOHNNY FLETCHER MYSTERY. Crime Drama, 30 min., NBC, 1945–1946; ABC, 5/30/48 to 9/5/48.

Johnny Fletcher and his partner Sam Kragg are two down-on-their-luck, unemployed gents who scheme to make money—from selling books to displaying Sam's abilities as a strongman. However, no matter what they are doing, a damsel in distress manages to find them—and cry her woes to them. Johnny has a soft heart for such things and will gladly use his training as a detective to take such cases—for whatever money they can afford (in the episode, "The Navy Colt," for example, Johnny's fee was $10). Sam is always a bit hesitant and feels "beautiful dames is trouble." But he assists, and together their exploits are detailed as they become private detectives to help others. Johnny and Sam reside at the Eagle Hotel.

Cast: Albert Dekker, Bill Goodwin (*Johnny Fletcher*); Mike Mazurki, Sheldon Leonard (*Sam Kragg*). ***Announcers:*** Owen James, John Storm. ***Music:*** Buzz Adlam.

OPENING

SAM: Johnny, I don't like this. Something tells me we shudda minded our own business.

JOHNNY: Look, Sam, helping a damsel in distress is your business, my business, everybody's business.

SAM: What's a damsel?

JOHNNY: Well, a dame.

SAM: Well, okay then. It's your business. I want no part of it.

ANNOUNCER: Yes, it's time for another *Johnny Fletcher Mystery*, brought to you by the National Broadcasting Company and starring Albert Dekker as Johnny Fletcher and Mike Mazurki as Sam Kragg in Frank Gruber's best selling murder mystery, "The Navy Colt."

CLOSING

ANNOUNCER: Be sure to be with us next week when we bring you another best selling *Johnny Fletcher Mystery* by Frank Gruber entitled "The Mighty Blockhead." This program was produced in Hollywood's Radio City. This is NBC, the National Broadcasting Company.

805. THE JOHNNY GREEN SHOW. Variety, 30 min., CBS, 1939.

A program of music, songs and short dramatizations with orchestra leader Johnny Green as the host. Genevieve Rose provided the vocals and Johnny Green and his orchestra supplied the music.

806. THE JOHNNY LONG SHOW. Variety, 30 min., NBC, 1939.

Orchestra leader Johnny Long as the host of a weekly program of music and songs. Helen Young was the featured vocalist (she was assisted by guests) and the Johnny Long Orchestra provided the music.

807. JOHNNY LUJACK OF NOTRE DAME. Drama, 30 min., ABC, 1949.

Fictionalized yarns centered around Johnny Lujack, a former Notre Dame quarterback, who helps people in trouble. Johnny Lujack played himself and Ed Prentiss played his sidekick. Boris Aplon supplied the music.

808. THE JOHNNY MACK BROWN SHOW. Variety, 30 min., CBS, 1939.

A program of country and western music with movie cowboy Johnny Mack Brown as the host. Isleta Gayle was the featured vocalist (assisted by guests) and the Texas Rangers supplied the music. The program is also known as *Under Western Skies*.

809. Johnny Madero, Pier 23. Crime Drama, 30 min., Mutual, 4/24/47 to 9/4/47.

San Francisco's waterfront provided the background for an action series about Johnny Madero, a freelance detective who was based on Pier 23—where he rented boats, but would do whatever else he could to make money.

Cast: Jack Webb (*Johnny Madero*). ***Music:*** Harry Zimmerman.

OPENING

ANNOUNCER: And now Jack Webb in *Johnny Madero, Pier 23*. [Johnny would then tell the listener about the evening's story.]

810. The Johnny Mercer Show. Variety, 60 min., CBS, 1953.

A weekly program of music and songs with vocalist Johnny Mercer as the host. The Notables and the Roger Wayne Chorale were the regulars. Johnny Jacobs did the announcing and music was provided by the Paul Smith Trio.

811. Johnny Mercer's Music Shop. Variety, 15 min., NBC, 1944–1945.

A program of music and songs with singer Johnny Mercer as the host. Ella Mae Morse, Jo Stafford and the Pied Piers were the regulars. Wendell Niles did the announcing and music was by Paul Weston and his orchestra.

812. The Johnny Morgan Show. Variety, 30 min., NBC, 1946.

A weekly program of music, songs and light comedy with host Johnny Morgan. Jack Arthur, Norman Brokenshire, Bill Keene, Walter Kinsella, Gloria Mann and the Smoothies were the regulars. Jack Costello did the announcing.

813. Johnny Nighthawk. Audition (Adventure), 30 min., produced in 1954.

John Stevens is a licensed transport pilot. He is nicknamed "Johnny Nighthawk" and owns an air service (Stevens Air Transport) that is in dire financial straits. Johnny thrives on trouble, and when people look for a man who won't reject their propositions or turn down dangerous assignments, they seek out Johnny Nighthawk. Johnny has special rates for special people; his partner, Benny Corrigan, believes "special rates mean special trouble." Johnny's one-plane airline is based in Los Angeles and he believes that his luck is going to change—"I can feel it in my bones." The proposed series was to relate Johnny's adventures as he becomes involved with unscrupulous characters and their shady dealings. In the audition episode, Johnny becomes involved in a crooked scheme to transport a valuable Ming Llama statue.

Cast: Howard Duff (*Johnny Nighthawk*); Dave Willock (*Benny Corrigan*).

814. Johnny Olsen's Luncheon Club. Variety, 25 min., ABC, 1950.

An afternoon program of music, songs and chatter with Johnny Olsen and his wife Penny as the hosts. Bob Maurer did the announcing and organist Al Greiner supplied the music.

815. Johnny Presents. Variety, 30 min., NBC, 1939–1946.

A program of varied entertainment sponsored by Philip Morris cigarettes (its living trademark was a bellboy named Johnny who would open each program in a shrill voice with "Call for Philip Mor-rees, call for Philip Mor-rees," followed by the announcer saying, "*Johnny Presents*"). Music and songs were the main feature of the program and two dramatic skits were also presented over the course of the series' run: "Nancy Bacon, Reporting" (about a female reporter) and "William and Mary" (about the struggles of young marrieds).

Cast: Johnny Roventini (*Johnny*); Una Merkel (*Nancy Bacon*); Roland Young (*William*); Cornelia Otis Skinner (*Mary*). ***Host:*** Barry Wood. ***Vocalists:*** Ginny Simms, the Marsh Sisters, the Ray Bloch Chorus. ***Announcer:*** Ken Roberts. ***Orchestra:*** Ray Bloch.

816. John's Other Wife. Serial, 15 min., NBC, 1936–1942.

Dramatic incidents in the life of John Perry, owner of Perry's Department Store, who is married (to Elizabeth) but also romantically involved with his "other wife," his secretary, Martha Curtis.

Cast: Hanley Stafford, Matt Crowley, Luis Van Rooten, Richard Kollmar, William Post, Jr., Joseph Curtin (*John Perry*); Adele Ronson, Erin O'Brien-Moore (*Elizabeth Perry*); Phyllis Welch, Rita Johnson (*Martha Curtis*); Joan Banks (*Roberta Lansing*); Franc Hale (*Annette*); John Kane (*Lanny*); Elaine Kent, Patricia Holbrook (*Carolyn Prince*); Mary Cecil, Nell Harrison, Virginia Ogden (*Grandmother*); Alan Bunce (*Dr. Tony Chalmers*); Ethel Blume (*Evelyn*); Irene Hubbard, Lyda Kane (*Molly*); Alexander Kirkland (*Curt Lansing*); Alice Reinheart (*Judy*). ***Theme Composer:*** ("The Sweetest Story Ever Told"): Stanley Davis. ***Producers:*** Anne Hummert, Frank Hummert.

OPENING

ANNOUNCER: And now for the dramatic story of *John's Other Wife* [a recap of the prior episode would then follow].

817. THE JOHNSON FAMILY. Comedy-Drama, 15 min., Mutual, 1941–1950.

An unusual, long-running daily program about a Negro family, their friends, relatives and neighbors in a small Southern community. All the parts were played by Jimmy Scribner, a Caucasian who also wrote, produced and provided the banjo music for the show.

THE JOHNSON WAX PROGRAM *see* **FIBBER MCGEE AND MOLLY**

818. JONATHAN TRIMBLE, ESQUIRE. Drama, 30 min., Mutual, 1946.

A small city of 60,000 people in the year 1905 was the setting for a light dramatic series about Jonathan Trimble, "a crochety old conservative" newspaper editor who loved the simple life and who was opposed to the progress that was rapidly changing his comfortable world. *Other regular characters:* Alice Trimble, his wife; Mildred, their maid.

Cast: Donald Crisp, Gale Gordon (*Jonathan Trimble*); Irene Tedrow (*Alice Trimble*); Jean Gillespie (*Mildred*). ***Also:*** Ruth Barnett, Art Gilmore, Jack Mather, Victor Rodman, Earle Ross, Leora Thatcher, Roderick Thomas. ***Announcer:*** Tony LeFrano. ***Music:*** Jack Meakin.

819. JONES AND I. Comedy, 30 min., ABC, 9/30/45 to 3/24/46.

Humorous events in the lives of Sally Jones, a pretty 18-year-old girl who sees life as being a wife and mother, and Jack Scott, her "unofficial" fiancé, the man she longs to marry, but who is not prepared to take that walk down the aisle. Sally's efforts to convince Jack oth-

Alice Reinheart appeared daily in the serial *John's Other Wife.*

erwise was the focal point of the series—a situation complicated by Ned Scott, Jack's misguided uncle and mentor.

Cast: Sammie Hill (*Sally Jones*); Scott Farnsworth (*Jack Scott*); Mason Adams (*Ned Scott*). ***Also:*** Lorna Lynn, John Monks, Ethel Owen, Betty Philson, Amzie Strickland, Ann Thomas, Jerry Tucker. ***Organist:*** Charles Paul.

JOYCE JORDAN, GIRL INTERNE *see* **JOYCE JORDAN, M.D.**

820. JOYCE JORDAN, M.D. Serial, 15 min., CBS, 1937–1944; NBC, 1944–1948; ABC, 1951–1952; NBC, 1954–1955.

The program, which began as *Joyce Jordan, Girl Interne*, related dramatic incidents in the life of Joyce Jordan, a young doctor with a practice in the small town of Preston. In 1942, when Joyce passed her medical exams, she found employment at a large city hospital and the series title became *Joyce Jordan, M.D.*

Cast: Rita Johnson, Ann Shepherd, Betty Winkler, Elspeth Eric, Gertrude Warner, Fran Carlon (*Joyce Jordan*); Ethel Owen (*Cassie*); Myron McCormick (*Paul Sherwood*); Erik Rolf (*Dr. Hans Simons*); Lesley Woods (*Margot Sherwood*); Richard Widmark (*Dr. Alan Webster*); Irene Hubbard (*Dr. Tracy*); Ethel

Cast members on the set of *Joyce Jordan, M.D.*

Owen, Eda Heinemann (*Dr. Molly Hedegrow*); Alan Devitt (*Roger Walton*); Patricia Ryan (*Myra Lee*); Raymond Edward Johnson (*Dr. Cliff Reed/Dr. Alexander Grey*); Boyd Crawford (*Greg Ogden*); Ethel Blume (*Gloria Blaine*); Frank Lovejoy (*Victor Manion*); Vera Allen (*Ada Manion*); Charles Webster (*Mike Malone*); James Monks (*Edgar Jarvis*). ***Announcers:*** Ron Rawson, Ken Roberts. ***Producer:*** Himan Brown.

OPENING

ANNOUNCER: Dreft, America's favorite brand for dishes presents *Joyce Jordan, M.D.* If doing dishes gets you down, you'll love that new Dreft. It does dishes far quicker, easier, far better than any soap in the world… This new Dreft is wonderfully mild, too. If dishwashing is a headache, you'll love that new Dreft. And now *Joyce Jordan, M.D.*

CLOSING

ANNOUNCER: This is Ron Rawson inviting you to listen again to *Joyce Jordan, M.D.*, brought to you by Procter and Gamble, makers of Dreft, America's favorite brand for dishes. It's new, it's improved, it's better than ever, Dreft. Listen Monday at this same time for *Joyce Jordan, M.D.* And be sure to stay tuned now for *This Is Nora Drake*, which follows immediately over most of these NBC stations. This is NBC, the National Broadcasting Company.

821. THE JUDGE. Crime Drama, 30 min., CBS, 1952.

The story of a retired judge who draws on his long experience behind the bench to help the police capture criminals. John Dehner played the judge and Lawrence Dobkin was the police lieutenant he assisted. Dan Cubberly did the announcing and Leith Stevens supplied the music.

822. JUDY AND JANE. Serial, 15 min., NBC Blue, 1932–1943.

The conflicts, tensions, romances and struggles of everyday life as heard through the experiences of Judy and Jane, two young women who are also best friends.

Cast: Joan Kay, Margaret Calvert (*Judy*); Margaret Evans, Donna Reade, Ireene Wicker, Betty Ruth Smith (*Jane Lee*); Marvin Miller (*Dr. Bishop*); Harry Holcombe (*Chick Reading*); Jack Lloyd (*Reginald*); Walter Wicker (*Jim Sargent*). ***Announcer:*** Jack Brinkley. ***Producers:*** Anne Hummert, Frank Hummert.

OPENING

ANNOUNCER: *Judy and Jane*, sponsored by Folger's, the coffee that's been handed down from mother to daughter for almost a hundred years. And now, the dramatic story of *Judy and Jane*.

CLOSING

ANNOUNCER: This transcribed adventure of *Judy and Jane* is brought to you by the Folger Coffee Company. We'll be back with you tomorrow at this same time. Until then, this is Jack Brinkley bidding you good-bye for Folger's Coffee—there's a mountain of flavor in every spoonful.

823. THE JUDY CANOVA SHOW. Comedy, 30 min., CBS, 1943–1944.

Judy Canova is a country girl who lives in the rural town of Cactus Junction. In an effort to find a man and improve her social status, she moves to California to live with her Aunt Aggie, a sophisticated woman who Judy hopes can change her backwoods style. Stories relate Judy's antics with friends and family and her efforts to impress Benchley Botsford, the man who has captured her heart (she constantly schemes to be alone with him but something always interferes with her plans). Judy also sings several songs: one after the opening theme, another during the show and one before the closing. *Other regular characters:* Geranium, Aggie's maid; Pedro, the Mexican handyman (his weekly line: "Pardon me for talking in your face, Senorita"); Mr. and Mrs. Simpson, Aggie's neighbors; their son, Monroe, who has a cat named Ben Her ("I called him Ben until "he" had kittens") and a baby brother called Baby Bubakins, a nightmare of an infant Judy sometimes babysits. See also the following two titles.

Cast: Judy Canova (*Judy Canova*); Ruth Perrott, Verna Felton (*Aunt Aggie*); George Dietz (*Benchley Botsford*); Ruby Dandridge (*Geranium*); Mel Blanc (*Pedro*); Gale Gordon, Joseph Kearns (*Mr. Simpson*); Tommy Bernard (*Monroe Simpson*); Jerry Hausner (*Baby Bubakins*). ***Regulars*** (Various Roles): Elvia Allman, Hans Conried. ***Vocalists:*** The Sportsmen Quartet. ***Announcers:*** Ken Niles, Howard Petrie, Verne Smith. ***Orchestra:*** Opie Cates, Charles "Bud" Dante, Gordon Jenkins.

OPENING

ANNOUNCER: *The Judy Canova Show* with Mel Blanc, Ruby Dandridge, Joe Kearns, Ruth Perrott, George Dietz, Jerry Hausner, Tommy Bernard, the Sportsmen Quartet, Opie Cates and his orchestra and starring Judy Canova. [Judy would then appear and sing a song before beginning the comedy.]

824. THE JUDY CANOVA SHOW. Comedy, 30 min., NBC, 1945–1950.

A revised version of the prior title that establishes Judy Canova as a film actress with her own weekly radio series. She lives in California with her maid (Geranium) and she has a publicity agent (Gordon Mansfield) and a best friend and advisor (Patsy Pierce, a former silent screen star). Stories relate events in Judy's life at home and at the radio station. Judy sings a song between each act. *Other regular characters:* Pedro, the Mexican handyman.

Cast: Judy Canova (*Judy Canova*); Gale Gordon (*Gordon Mansfield*); Verna Felton (*Patsy Pierce*); Ruby Dandridge (*Geranium*); Mel Blanc (*Pedro*). ***Regulars*** (Various Roles): Joseph Kearns, George Neise. ***Vocalists:*** The Sportsmen. ***Announcer:*** Howard Petrie. ***Orchestra:*** Charles "Bud" Dant.

OPENING

ANNOUNCER: From Hollywood, *The Judy Canova Show*, brought to you each week by the Colgate Palmolive Company, makers of Halo Shampoo to glorify your hair, and the new 1948 Super Suds with extra suds for extra whiteness. *The Judy Canova Show* with Mel Blanc, Ruby Dandridge, Joe Kearns, Gale Gordon, George Neise, Verna Felton, the Sportsmen, Charles Dant and his orchestra and starring Judy Canova.

CLOSING

ANNOUNCER: *The Judy Canova Show* is written by Fred Fox, Henry Hoople with John Ward and is produced and directed by Joe Rines. This is Howard Petrie asking you to use Halo Shampoo to glorify your hair, and the new 1948 Super Suds with extra suds for extra whiteness. And now, here's Judy.

JUDY: Thank you Howard. And folks, it was awfully nice being with you tonight; and I hope we'll all be together again next Saturday night. In the meantime, please don't forget the two products that bring us to you each week, Halo Shampoo and Super Suds. This is Judy Canova from Hollywood singing, "Go to sleep-y, little baby; go to sleep-y, little baby. When you wake, you'll patty-patty-cake; and ride a shiny little po-o-ny..."

ANNOUNCER: Stay tuned to Kay Kyster with his *Kollege of Musical Knowledge* which follows immediately. This is NBC, the National Broadcasting Company.

825. THE JUDY CANOVA SHOW. Comedy, 30 min., NBC, 1950–1951.

A revamped version of the prior title that continues to find Judy Canova playing herself, the noted film comedian and radio actress. Judy lives in California, has many fans and two steady boyfriends—Hubert Updyke, a multi-millionaire, and Joe Crunchmiller, a poor taxi cab driver. Judy is in love with both of them, but can't choose between them. Both are constantly trying to impress her, and Judy's efforts to discover which one is the right man for her is the subplot of stories, which focus on Judy's mishaps at home, where she encounters a wide variety of strange characters. *Other regular characters:* Geranium, Judy's maid; Pedro, the Mexican handyman; Patsy Pierce, Judy's friend, a former silent screen star.

Cast: Judy Canova (*Judy Canova*); Ruby Dandridge (*Geranium*); Jim Backus (*Hubert Updyke*); Sheldon Leonard (*Joe Crunchmiller*); Mel Blanc (*Pedro*); Verna Felton (*Patsy Pierce*); Hans Conried (*Various Roles*). ***Vocalists:*** The Southerners. ***Announcer:*** Howard Petrie. ***Orchestra:*** Charles "Bud" Dant. ***Producer:*** Joe Rines.

OPENING

ANNOUNCER: From Hollywood, *The Judy Canova Show*, with Mel Blanc, Ruby Dandridge, Verna Felton, Sheldon Leonard, Jim Backus, the Southerners, Charles Dant and his orchestra and starring Judy Canova [who would begin the show with a song].

CLOSING

JUDY: Folks, it was awfully nice being with you tonight. This is Judy Canova from Hollywood saying good night, everyone.

826. JUDY, JILL AND JOHNNY. Variety, 30 min., Mutual, 1946–1947.

A Saturday afternoon program of music and songs with Susan Douglas (as Judy), Susan Thorne (as Jill) and Johnny Desmond (as Johnny). Bert Parks did the announcing and music was provided by the Casa Loma and Claude Thornhill orchestras.

827. JUKE BOX JURY. Variety, 30 min., CBS, 1954–1956.

A new or soon-to-be-released song is performed by a guest celebrity or by the composer himself. A panel of guests (celebrities and people associated with the music world) then rate the value of the song—whether it will be a hit or a miss. Served as the basis for the *Peter Potter's Juke Box Jury* television series.

Host: Peter Potter. ***Announcer:*** Johnny Jacobs.

828. THE JULIUS LA ROSA SHOW. Variety, 10 min., CBS, 1953.

A short program of music and songs with singer Julius La Rosa as the host. The Wanderers provided vocal backing and music was provided by the Russ Case Orchestra.

829. JUMBO. Musical Comedy, 30 min., NBC, 10/29/35 to 4/21/36.

The Considine Wonder Show is a small traveling circus in financial difficulty. The circus is owned by Johnny Considine and his daughter Mickey. The Mulligan Circus is their competition (and stealing all their business). The circus owners are also rivals but their children (Mickey and Matt Mulligan) are lovers, a situation that causes additional problems when they are forbidden to see each other, but plan secret rendezvous. Stories follow events in the lives of the circus personnel as Considine struggles to live up to a show business tradition, "The Show Must Go On." Helping Considine is Claudius "Brainy" Bowers, a fast-talking con artist who is the show's press agent (he has promised Mickey that "somehow I'll save the show") and Jellico, Considine's agent. The main attraction of the Considine Wonder Show is Jumbo, "The Wonder Elephant." When a scene is established (for example, Mickey and Matt meeting), the characters break into a song (as in a Broadway musical). Sponsored by Texaco Fire Chief Gasoline and based on the play by Billy Rose. Also known as *The Jumbo Fire Chief.*

Cast: Jimmy Durante (*Claudius Bowers*); Gloria Grafton (*Mickey Considine*); Donald Novis (*Matt Mulligan*); Arthur Sinclair (*John A. Considine*); A.P. Kaye (*Jellico*). ***Announcer:*** Louis Witten. ***Orchestra:*** Adolph Deutsch. ***Producer:*** Billy Rose. ***Vocalists:*** Charles Henderson and the Singing Razorbacks.

OPENING

SOUND: A siren.

ANNOUNCER: Texaco is on the air. Texaco service stations and dealers from coast to coast present the new *Jumbo Fire Chief* program. We are broadcasting from the Sawdust Ring of the New York Hippodrome, scene of the most spectacular show of all time, an actual audience of 4500 people is present and we have asked them not to laugh or applaud so that you may better enjoy the program. The story is written by Ben Hecht and Charles MacArthur, with original songs by Richard Rodgers and Lorenz Hart. All under the personal supervision of Billy Rose.

CLOSING

ANNOUNCER: Louis A. Witten speaking for the Texaco Company, inviting you to tune in again next Tuesday for the *Jumbo Fire Chief* program for the further adventures of the Considine Wonder Show. And remember, whenever you hear the siren and bells, think of Texaco. This is the National Broadcasting Company.

830. THE JUNE HYND GUEST BOOK. Talk, 15 min., NBC Blue, then NBC Red, 1937–1940.

An afternoon program of chatter and celebrity interviews with hosts June Hynd and Alma Kitchell. Also known as *Let's Talk It Over*.

831. JUNE'S MY GIRL. Audition (Comedy), 30 min., NBC, 10/4/48.

Hoping to make her mark in the business world, June Morgan leaves her home in Little Falls, New York, and heads for Manhattan. She finds a room at the Dolly Madison Hotel and a job at the Nichols Employment Agency, a company run by a tightwad (Mr. Nichols) and in financial difficulty. June is very pretty, constantly being wooed by men, and has a generous heart. The proposed series was to focus on the situations that develop as June tries to help others. The audition episode finds June seeking a companion for a rich client's spoiled son (Cabot Van Cleave) on a world cruise. *Other regular characters:* Jimmy Crain, an executive with the Second National Bank (he has been assigned to monitor the agency and get it back on its feet); Ollie, the agency's Swedish janitor; Ned, Jimmy's friend.

Cast: Diana Lynn (*June Morgan*); Harry Bartell (*Jimmy Crain*); Alan Reed (*Mr. Nichols*); Parley Baer (*Ollie*); Tony Barrett (*Ned*). ***Announcer:*** Jay Stewart. ***Music:*** Felix Mills. ***Producer:*** Thomas A. MacAvity.

OPENING

ANNOUNCER: We present a brand new comedy show entitled *June's My Girl*, and as her boyfriend Jimmy just said, "What a girl!" Our June is played by the lovely young screen star, whom you'll remember from her roles in *When Our Hearts Were Young and Gay*, *Miracle at Morgan's Creek* and her newest picture, *Ruthless*, Diana Lynn. And now let's settle back, relax and listen to *June's My Girl*.

CLOSING

ANNOUNCER: We hope you liked the show and you'll find an important spot for it in your future radio plans. This is Jay Stewart saying thanks for listening. This is NBC, the National Broadcasting Company.

832. THE JUNGLE ADVENTURES OF FRANK BUCK. Adventure, 15 min., NBC, 1932–1934; Mutual, 1934.

"In the jungle, there is always danger. That is the keynote of the jungle, where death lurks in every shadow, behind every tangle of matted vines, beneath every leaf of rotted foliage. You don't go looking for danger. It looks for you," says Frank Buck about his job—capturing wild animals for zoos and circuses and always vowing to bring 'em back alive. But capturing the wild beasts is not the only thing he does. There are the unscrupulous who prey on the helpless and there are the menacing superstitions of the jungle (for example, women who can turn themselves into tigers). Stories relate Buck's adventures in dealing with the various hazards of his work. *Other regular characters:* Ollie, Frank's assistant. A cast is not identified.

OPENING

BUCK: I had 24 hours to trap a man-eating tiger

or a lovely lady would meet death by torture. That's the story of "The Ghost Tiger of Fungahi."

ANNOUNCER: From the tangled wilds of Borneo, to the mystic mountains of Tibet, to the fierce jungles of Malaya, RKO Radio Pictures presents *Bring 'Em Back Alive*—filmed in the depths of the Malayan jungle, the only wild animal picture that can never be duplicated, Frank Buck's original *Bring 'Em Back Alive* is authentic, thrilling, packed with action and suspense. The dramatic story of the jungle, the land of the short shadows. Survival of the fittest is the law of life. See Frank Buck in *Bring 'Em Back Alive*. And now, for the first time on the air, RKO presents *The Jungle Adventures of Frank Buck*.

CLOSING

ANNOUNCER: Killers of the jungle! A mad elephant on the rampage! A battle royal between a 30-foot python and a tiger! See *Bring 'Em Back Alive*! RKO Radio Pictures has presented a jungle adventure of Frank Buck. In this series of original radio dramas, all characters are impersonated. See and hear Frank Buck in person in his great wild animal picture, the original *Bring 'Em Back Alive*. Filmed in the depths of the Malayan jungle, the only wild animal picture which can never be duplicated. *Bring 'Em Back Alive* is authentic, thrilling, packed with action, danger, suspense. It's the picture for every member of the family; an exciting experience in motion picture entertainment. See the most ferocious jungle killers in their native haunts. See *Bring 'Em Back Alive*. It's another great RKO Radio Picture.

Note: The radio series is also known as *Bring 'Em Back Alive* and *Frank Buck's Adventures*.

833. JUNGLE JIM. Adventure, 15 min., Syndicated, 1935–1954.

A radio adaptation of the comic strip by Alex Raymond. Jim Bradley, a jungle guide, and his sidekick Kolu battle the forces of evil (usually from their enemy, the diabolical Shanghai Lil).

Cast: Matt Crowley (*Jungle Jim Bradley*); Juano Hernandez (*Kolu*); Franc Hale (*Shanghai Lil*). Gerald Mohr replaced Matt Crowley as Jungle Jim for a brief period in 1938. ***Announcers:*** Roger Krupp, Glenn Riggs. ***Producer:*** Jay Clark.

OPENING

ANNOUNCER: Presenting the adventures of *Jungle Jim*. The thrilling adventures of *Jungle Jim* are presented each Sunday in the *Comic Weekly*, the world's greatest pictorial supplement of humor and adventure. In *Comic Weekly*, each page is printed in full color and is distributed everywhere as an integral part of your Hearst Sunday newspaper. And now to today's exciting episode in the adventures of *Jungle Jim*.

834. JUNIOR JUNCTION. Children, 30 min., ABC, 1946–1952.

A daytime program of music, songs and games for children with Jack Lester as the host. Peggy Murdock and Bill Snary were the regulars and music was provided by Bruce Case and his orchestra.

835. JUNIOR MISS. Comedy, 30 min., CBS, 1942; CBS, 1948–1954.

Judy Graves is the "Junior Miss" of the title, a pretty but unpredictable 15-year-old bundle of dynamite who lives with her parents (Harry and Grace) and her 16-year-old boy-crazy sister Lois in an apartment at 36 East 82nd Street in Manhattan. Stories follow Judy's various misadventures at home and at school. *Other regular characters:* Hilda, their maid; Fuffy Adams, Judy's girlfriend (whom she calls "Fuff").

Cast: Shirley Temple, Barbara Whiting (*Judy Graves*); Elliott Lewis, Gale Gordon (*Harry Graves*); Margaret Lansing, Sarah Selby (*Grace Graves*); K.T. Stevens, Barbara Eiler, Peggy Knudson (*Lois Graves*); Myra Marsh (*Hilda*); Priscilla Lyon, Beverly Wills (*Fuffy Adams*). ***Announcers:*** Johnny Jacobs, Jimmy Wallington. ***Music:*** Bill Saborinsky, Walter Schumann.

OPENING

JUDY: Philosophers have said that there's a place for everything and everyone in this world. I wish we 15 year olds could get located.

ANNOUNCER: It's time for *Junior Miss*, another in the transcribed series of programs based on the delightful characters created by Sally Benson with Gale Gordon as Harry Graves and starring Barbara Whiting.

CLOSING

ANNOUNCER: *Junior Miss*, based on the famous

stories by Sally Benson, is written for radio by Henry Garson; Mr. Garson directed. In the cast are Barbara Whiting—

BARBARA: I'm Judy Graves.

ANNOUNCER: Gale Gordon—

GALE: Harry Graves.

ANNOUNCER: Sarah Selby—

SARAH: Mrs. Graves.

ANNOUNCER: Peggy Knudsen—

PEGGY: Lois Graves.

ANNOUNCER: Myra Marsh—

MYRA: The Graves' maid, Hilda.

ANNOUNCER: And Beverly Wills—

BEVERLY: Fuffy Adams.

ANNOUNCER: This is Johnny Jacobs inviting you to listen to *Junior Miss* transcribed again next week at this same time.

Note: Shirley Temple portrayed Judy in 1942 but the show folded after a short run due to its high production costs ($12,000 an episode).

JUNIOR NURSE CORPS *see* **APPENDIX**

836. JUST EASY. Variety, 60 min., ABC, 1954.

Music and songs with host Jack Gregson, vocalist Peggy Ann Ellis and the music of Bobby Hackett and his orchestra.

837. JUST ENTERTAINMENT. Variety, 15 min., CBS, 1956.

A program of country and western music with Pat Buttram as the host. Jack Holloran and Betty Martin were the regulars and music was by the Pat Buttram Band.

838. JUST ENTERTAINMENT. Variety, 25 min., CBS, 1946.

Actor Burgess Meredith as the host to a program of music and songs with vocalists Lenny Colyer, Gogi Grant, Mahalia Jackson and the Four Lads as regulars. Joe Foss did the announcing and music was by Caesar Petrillo and his orchestra.

839. JUST FOR YOU. Variety, 60 min., NBC, 1954.

A program of music and songs featuring performances by guests. Eddy Howard was the host; Dick Noble did the announcing; and music was by the Twelve Piece WMAQ Staff Orchestra (the NBC affiliate in Chicago, from where the program was broadcast).

840. JUST NEIGHBORS. Comedy, 30 min., NBC Blue, 1938.

The philosophy of Bess, Carrie and Sue, three talkative neighbors with adjoining back porches who gather each day to discuss life. Kathryn Card played Bess; Betty Caine was Carrie; and Helen Behmiller portrayed Sue. The program was originally titled *The Three Flats*.

841. JUST PLAIN BILL. Serial, 15 min., CBS, 1933–1936; NBC, 1936–1955.

Events in the life of Bill Davidson, a kindly and philosophical barber in the small town of Hartville, his married daughter, Nancy Donovan, and Nancy's husband, Kerry Donovan.

Cast: Arthur Hughes (*Bill Davidson*); Ruth Russell (*Nancy Donovan*); James Meighan (*Kerry Donovan*); Ara Gerald (*Kathleen Chatton*); Macdonald Carey (*Jonathan Hillery*); Audrey Egan (*Shirley King*); Charlotte Lawrence (*Reba Britton*); Elizabeth Day (*Margaret Burns*); Charles Eggleston (*Humphrey Fuller*); Ann Shepherd (*Pearl Sutton*); William Woodson (*John Britton*). ***Announcers:*** Andre Baruch, Fielden Farrington, Ed Herlihy, Roger Krupp. ***Producers:*** Anne Hummert, Frank Hummert.

OPENING

ANNOUNCER: Now to the many friends who wait for him, we present *Just Plain Bill*, barber of Hartville. The story of a man who might be living right next door to you; the real-life story of people just like people we all know.

CLOSING

ANNOUNCER: Listen for *Just Plain Bill* on this station at this same time on Monday. This is Roger Krupp saying good-bye for *Just Plain Bill* and the Whitehall Pharmaceutical Company, makers of Anacin and many other dependable, high-quality drug products.

842. JUVENILE JURY. Children, 30 min., Mutual, 1946, 1951; NBC, 1952–1953.

A panel of five children attempt to answer questions, submitted by guests or listeners, concerning problems faced by the younger generation. Served as the basis for the television series of the same title.

Host: Jack Barry. ***Announcer:*** John Scott. ***Producer:*** Dan Enright.

843. The Kaiser Traveler. Variety, 15 min., ABC, 1949.

A program of music and songs sponsored by Kaiser Aluminum and starring folk singer Burl Ives. Cy Harrice was the announcer.

844. Kaltenmeyer's Kindergarten. Comedy, 30 min., NBC, 1933–1940.

A program of comedy skits for children that was set at the Nonsense School of the Air. Prof. August Kaltenmeyer, D.U.N. (Doctor of Utter Nonsense), was the dean and he was assisted by Izzy Finkelstein. Other characters who inhabited the schoolhouse were Mickey Donovan and Gertie Glump; Chauncey the bum; Cornelius Callahan, the local tough guy; Yonny Yohnson, the Swede; and Percy Van Schuyler. In 1940, the series became *Kindergarten Kapers* and the dean became Prof. Ulysses S. Applegate (U.S.A.) due to American resentment of Germans.

Cast: Bruce Kamman (*August Kaltenmeyer/ Ulysses S. Applegate*); Johnny Wolf (*Izzy Finkelstein*); Jim Jordan (*Mickey Donovan*); Marian Jordan (*Gertie Glump*); Sidney Ellstrom (*Chauncey*); Cecil Roy (*Daisy Dean*); Billy White (*Cornelius Callahan*); Thor Ericson (*Yonny Yohnson*); Merrill Fugit (*Percy Van Schuyler*). ***Vocalists:*** The Escorts and Betty. ***Orchestra:*** Harry Kogen.

845. Kate Hopkins, Angel of Mercy. Serial, 15 min., Syndicated, 1939–1940; CBS, 1940–1942.

Dramatic events in the life of Kate Hopkins, a widowed nurse in the town of Forest Hills (located in the Sleeping Elephant Mountains). *Other regular characters:* Tom Hopkins, her son; Robert and Jessie Atwood, Kate's friends.

Cast: Helen Lewis, Margaret MacDonald (*Kate Hopkins*); Ned Wever, Clayton "Bud" Collyer (*Tom Hopkins*); Raymond Edward Johnson (*Robert Atwood*); Constance Collier (*Jessie Atwood*).

846. Kate Smith.

Singer Kate Smith was the host of a number of programs featuring music and songs. Kate, "The Songbird of the South," was known for introducing the Irving Berlin song "God Bless America"; "When the Moon Comes Over the Mountain" was her theme song. Andre Baruch and Ted Collins were her announcers and Jack Miller and his orchestra provided the music. *The Series:*

Kate Smith Sings, 15 min., CBS, 1931.

Kate Smith and Her Swanee Music, 15 min., CBS, 1931–1934.

Kate Smith's Matinee Hour, 60 min., CBS, 1934.

Kate Smith's New Star Revue, 30 min., CBS, 1934–1935.

The Kate Smith Hour, 60 min., CBS, 1935. Revised, CBS, 1937–1945.

Kate Smith's Coffee Time, 15 min., CBS, 1935–1936.

Kate Smith's A&P Bandwagon, 60 min., CBS, 1936–1937.

Kate Smith Speaks, 15 min., CBS, 1938–1947; Mutual, 1947–1951.

Kate Smith Sings, 30 min., CBS, 1945–1947; Mutual, 1948–1951.

Kate Smith Calling, 2 hrs., ABC, 1949–1950 (featured Kate telephoning listeners).

The Kate Smith Show, 25 min., NBC, 1951–1952; 30 min., Mutual, 1958–1959.

847. The Kathy Godfrey Show. Variety, 25 min., CBS, 1955.

Kathy Godfrey as the host of a weekly program of music and songs. Bob Hite did the announcing and music was provided by Norman Leyden and his orchestra.

Katie's Daughter *see* **Appendix**

848. Kay Fairchild, Stepmother. Serial, 15 min., CBS, 1938–1942.

The program, also known as *Stepmother*, is set in the town of Walnut Grove and tells the dramatic story of Kay Fairchild and her efforts to raise Peggy and Bud, her husband John's children from a previous marriage.

Cast: Sunda Love, Janet Logan, Charlotte Manson (*Kay Fairchild*); Francis X. Bushman, Bill Green, Charles Penman, Willard Waterman (*John Fairchild*); Peggy Wall, Barbara Fuller (*Peggy Fairchild*); Cornelius Peeples (*Bud Fairchild*); Ethel Owen, Donelda Curry, Betty Arnold (*Genevieve Porter*); Bess McCammon (*Mrs. Fairchild*); Edith Davis, Guila Adams (*Mattie*); John Larkin, Robert Guilbert (*Bert Weston*); Cornelia Osgood (*Adella Winston*); Harry Elders (*David Houseman*). ***Announcers:*** Carlton KaDell, Roger Krupp.

Kate Smith and guest Babe Ruth in "Kate Smith's Coffee Time," on CBS in 1936.

OPENING

ANNOUNCER: Can a stepmother successfully raise another woman's children? Colgate All-Purpose Tooth Powder presents the real-life story of Kay Fairchild, our stepmother who tries. Now, Colgate Tooth Powder presents *Kay Fairchild, Stepmother*. David Houseman wants to win Kay Fairchild away from her husband and he justifies this unorthodox ambition with the claim he loves her and John doesn't.

CLOSING

ANNOUNCER: Well, Peg is lined up in favor of Kay divorcing her husband and marrying David Houseman. Tomorrow, she goes to work to put her idea into practice. Tune in again tomorrow and every day, Monday through Friday, for *Kay Fairchild, Stepmother*, brought to you by Colgate All-Purpose Tooth Powder. This is Carlton KaDell. This is the Columbia Broadcasting System.

849. Kay Kyser's Kollege of Musical Knowledge. Variety, 30 min., NBC, 1938–1939; Mutual, 1939–1940; NBC, 1940–1948; ABC, 1948–1949.

Musical numbers coupled with quiz segments that found the host (called "The Old Professor" or just "Fess") dressed up in an academic cap and gown. Selected players from the studio audience competed and questions were divided into midterms and final exams. A mystery selection was played by the orchestra and players, who were given generous clues by the Old Professor, had to identify the song's title. A prize was awarded to the player if he was correct. If a player could not guess the song title, the studio audience (called students) shouted out the correct song title. Served as the basis for the television series of the same title.

Host: Kay Kyser. ***Regulars:*** Harry Babbitt, Mervyn Bogue (as Ish Kabibble, a novelty singer), Phil Harris, Don Leslee, Sully Mason, Shirley Mitchell, Ginny Simms, Diane Templeton, the Campus Kids, the King Sisters (Alyce, Donna, Louise and Yvonne), the Town Criers. ***Announcers:*** Bill Forman, John Heistand, Ken Niles, Verne Smith. ***Orchestra:*** Kay Kyser. ***Producer:*** Frank O'Connor.

850. Keep 'Em Rolling. Variety, 30 min., Mutual, 11/9/41–5/17/42.

Dramatizations, music, songs and chatter sponsored by the U.S. government. George S. Kaufman was the host and Morton Gould and his orchestra supplied the music. Top names in radio, Hollywood and Broadway performed on the program.

OPENING

Voice: Remember Pearl Harbor!

Announcer: *Keep 'Em Rolling*. The War Production Board in cooperation with WOR/Mutual presents the twenty-fourth in this weekly series of programs of entertainment and information about America's united war effort. Tonight's guests include the dynamic star of stage and screen, John Garfield; radio's popular songstress Wynn Murray; the young composer-conductor Morton Gould and the orchestra. Your master of ceremonies is one of the most distinguished figures of the contemporary theater, the well-known author and playwright, George S. Kaufman.

851. Keeping Up with Rosemary. Drama, 30 min., NBC, 7/4/42 to 9/12/42.

Events in the life of a female magazine reporter named Rosemary. Fay Wray played the part of Rosemary; Henry M. Neeley was her father; Ruth McDevitt portrayed her mother; Billy Norman and Raymond Ives were her brothers; Ben Lockwood was Rosemary's romantic interest; Sydney Smith played the managing editor of the magazine; and Joseph Julian was the editor's assistant. Joseph Stopak provided the music.

852. Keeping Up with Wigglesworth. Comedy, 15 min., Syndicated, 1945.

Humorous incidents in the life of a misadventure-prone young man named Snuffy Wigglesworth.

Cast: Jack Ayres (*Snuffy Wigglesworth*). ***Also:*** Bill Adams, Floyd Buckley, Marilyn Erskine, Eunice Howard, Charles Miller, Anthony Rivers. ***Announcer:*** Matt Crowley. ***Music:*** Lloyd Shaffer.

853. Keepsakes. Variety, 30 min., NBC Blue/ABC, 1943–1944; ABC, 1944.

A weekly program of nostalgic songs and musical numbers. Dorothy Kirsten was the host; Mack Harrell did the announcing; and the Harry Sosnik orchestra and chorus provided the music and vocal backing for Miss Kirsten.

854. Kelly's Courthouse. Game, 30 min., NBC Blue, 4/20/44 to 6/8/44.

Selected members of the studio audience were involved. A six-minute mystery vignette was performed, but stopped before disclosing the culprit. Three musical clues were provided to help contestants solve the mystery. The first player to correctly uncover the guilty party received a $25 war bond. If a player gave an incorrect response, a gunshot was heard and that player was disqualified.

Host: Fred Uttal. ***Cast:*** John Aulicino, Sanford Bichart, Phyllis Clarke, Don Douglas, Roger Krupp, Bryna Raeburn. ***Announcer:*** Dan Seymour. ***Organist:*** Henry Sylvern. ***Orchestra:*** Joseph Stopak.

855. The Ken Banghart Show. Variety, 15 min., NBC, 1947.

Music and songs with host Ken Banghart.

Arthur Gray provided additional vocals and Jack Costello did the announcing.

856. The Ken Carson Show. Variety, 30 min., Mutual, 1945.

Vocalist Ken Carson as the host of a weekly program of music and songs. The Little Sisters were the regulars and Harry Zimmerman and his orchestra provided the musical backing.

857. The Ken Murray Show. Variety, 30 min., NBC, 1932–1933; CBS, 1936–1937.

Music, songs and comedy skits with comedian Ken Murray (who would become famous for his home movies of Hollywood celebrities). Eve Arden, Tony Labriola, Phil Regan, Shirley Ross and Marilyn Stuart were the regulars. Music was by the Lud Gluskin and Russ Morgan orchestras.

Kindergarten Kapers *see* **Kaltenmeyer's Kindergarten**

858. The King Cole Trio. Variety, 15 min., NBC, 1946–1948.

A program of music and songs featuring singer-pianist Nat King Cole. Ted Pearson was the host and music was by the Nat King Cole Trio. The program is also known as *King Cole Trio Time.*

King for a Night *see* **The King's Men**

859. The King's Men. Variety, 30 min., NBC, 1949.

A program of music and songs featuring top name guests performing with the King's Men Quartet (Ken Darby, Jan Dodson, Bud Linn, Rod Robinson). Ken Niles and Harlow Wilcox did the announcing; Elliot Daniel and his orchestra provided the music. The program is also known as *King for a Night.*

860. King's Row. Serial, 15 min., NBC, 2/26/51 to 2/29/52.

The dramatic story of Parris Mitchell, a doctor in the town of King's Row. Based on the novel by Henry Bellamann.

Cast: Francis DeSales (*Dr. Parris Mitchell*); Charlotte Manson (*Randy Monaghan*); Charlotte Holland (*Elsie Mitchell*); Jim Boles (*Fulmer Green*). ***Announcer:*** John McDougall. ***Music:*** Burt Buhrmann.

861. Kiss and Make Up. Game, 30 min., CBS, 1946.

Married couples, situated in a staged courtroom, were brought before the bench and asked to air their grievances. A panel of studio audience members decided which mate was at fault. The penalty: kiss and make up.

Host-Judge: Milton Berle. ***Vocalists:*** The Murphy Sisters. ***Orchestra:*** Harry Salter.

862. Kitty Foyle. Serial, 15 min., CBS, 1942–1944.

Dramatic incidents in the life of Kitty Foyle, a poor girl in love with a wealthy man (Wynn Strafford). The program is a first-person account with flashbacks being used to recall Kitty's experiences. Based on the novel by Christopher Morley.

Cast: Julie Stevens (*Kitty Foyle*); Victor Thorley (*Wynn Strafford*); Mark Smith (*Pop Foyle*); Amanda Randolph (*Maid*). ***Announcer:*** Mel Allen.

863. Kitty Keene. Serial, 15 min., CBS, 1937; Mutual, 1938–1941.

A daily drama about Kitty Keene, a female private detective who runs an agency called Kitty Keene, Incorporated. Stories are a portrait of her life at work and with her family (her husband Bob Jones and daughter Jill). Kitty uses her maiden name for business.

Cast: Beverly Younger, Gail Henshaw, Fran Carlon (*Kitty Keene*); Bob Bailey, Dick Wells (*Bob Jones*); Dorothy Gregory, Janet Logan (*Jill Jones*); Carlton KaDell, Bill Bouchey, Ken Griffin (*Charles Williams*); Chuck Grant (*Buzzer Williams*); Ian Keith (*Humphrey Manners*); Louise Fitch (*Anna*); Loretta Poynton (*Pearl Davis*). ***Producers:*** George Fogel, Anne Hummert, Frank Hummert, Alan Wallace.

864. Knickerbocker Playhouse. Anthology, 30 min., CBS, 1939; NBC, 1940–1942.

Light dramas and comedies (all written especially for radio) with Elliott Lewis as the host, Mr. Knickerbocker, a distinguished gentleman who ushered listeners through a rear entrance of a theater so they could "watch" the evening's story from backstage. Marvin Miller and Betty Winkler were regular performers and Gene Baker did the announcing. Music was by the Carl Hohengarten Orchestra.

KOLLEGE OF MUSICAL KNOWLEDGE *see* **KAY KYSER'S KOLLEGE OF MUSICAL KNOWLEDGE**

865. THE KORN KOBBLERS. Variety, 15 min., NBC Blue, 1942–1944; Mutual, 1944–1947.

A program of country and western music and songs with the Korn Kobblers, a novelty orchestra consisting of Marty Gould, Stan Frittle, Charles Koening, Nels Loakso, Howard McElroy and Harry Turner. Alan Courtney did the announcing.

866. THE KRAFT MUSIC HALL. Variety, 60 min., NBC, 1933–1942; 30 min., NBC, 1942–1949.

A long-running program of music, songs and comedy sponsored by the Kraft Foods Company. The program was originally a showcase for Paul Whiteman and his orchestra, but evolved into a standard variety show featuring performances by top name guests in 1934.

Hosts: Deems Taylor (1933), Al Jolson (1933–1934), Bing Crosby (1935–1946), Eddie Foy, then weekly guests (1946–1947), Al Jolson (1947–1949). ***Summer Edition Hosts:*** Don Ameche, Bob Crosby, Nelson Eddy, Dorothy Kirsten, Frank Morgan. ***Regulars:*** Victor Borge, Connee Boswell, Bob Burns, Peggy Lee, Jerry Lester, Mary Martin, Marilyn Maxwell, the Charioteers, the Music Maids and Hal. ***Announcers:*** Ken Carpenter, Roger Krupp, Don Wilson. ***Orchestra:*** Robert Armbruster, Lou Bring, Jimmy Dorsey, John Scott Trotter, Paul Whiteman.

867. KUKLA, FRAN AND OLLIE. Children, 10 min., NBC, 1952–1953.

A daily program for the small fry based on the television series of the same title. Stories were simply the exchange of conversation between a live host (Fran) and several puppets who inhabited the Kuklapolitan Theater: Kukla, a bald, round-nosed boy; Ollie, the snaggletoothed dragon; Beulah Witch; and Madame Ooglepuss. Fran Allison was the host and Burr Tillstrom, the creator and producer, supplied the puppet voices and music.

868. THE LA PALINA SMOKER. Variety, 15 min., CBS, 1927–1930.

Music and songs with singer-pianist Harry Link. The program was sponsored by Paley's Congress Cigars, a company owned by William S. Paley (the man who bought CBS in 1928).

869. LADIES BE SEATED. 30 min., NBC Blue/ABC, 6/26/44 to 7/20/50.

The basic format involved female members of the studio audience participating in a series of stunts for prizes. Interviews, guests and sing-alongs were also part of the program. *Ladies Be Seated* became a five-week experimental television series on DuMont (2/25/45 to 3/24/45) with Johnny Olsen and his wife Penny hosting the festivities. ABC next picked up the project for a short-lived television series (4/22/49 to 6/17/49) with Tom Moore as the host.

Host: Ed East, Polly East, Jimmy Blaine, Johnny Olsen, Penny Olsen, Tom Moore. ***Announcers:*** George Ansbro, Helen Rhodes. ***Music:*** The Buddy Weed Trio. ***Producer:*** Harvey Marlowe.

870. LADIES FAIR. Variety, 30 min., Mutual, 1/23/50 to 1/1/54.

A daytime program of songs, music, games and quizzes aimed at the female listener. Tom Moore was the host; Holland Engle and Don Gordon did the announcing; and organists Herbert Foote and Porter Heaps provided the music.

THE LADY ESTHER SCREEN GUILD PLAYHOUSE *see* **SCREEN GUILD THEATER**

871. LAND OF THE LOST. Adventure, 30 min., ABC, 1944–1945; Mutual, 1945–1946; ABC, 1947–1948.

The lake near the home of Isabel and Billy Hewson is very special. It can lead to an undersea world called the Land of the Lost, a place where all lost articles on earth find a home. One day, while at the lake, Isabel and Billy befriend Red Lantern, a talking fish from King Findol's Court (ruler of the Land of the Lost), who takes them through a secret tunnel under the lake to the Land of the Lost. Billy and Isabel are able to breathe underwater by the Magic Seaweed and stories relate their adventures as they become involved with the various sea creatures, some of whom face danger from the evils of the deep. Each week, the program offered prizes for seven boys and seven girls whose letter, telling why they want a lost belonging returned, were selected by a panel. While the actual item could not be returned, the nearest possible duplicate was sent. The program segment was called *Lucky Seven Time*; listeners were called Pollywogs; and the show's slogan was "Never Say Lost."

Cast: Isabel Manning Hewson (*Isabel, adult; narrator*); Betty Jane Tyler (*Isabel, child*); Raymond Ives (*Billy Hewson*); Junius Matthews, William Keene, Art Carney (*Red Lantern*). ***Announcer:*** Michael Fitzmaurice. ***Music:*** Gene Porozzo. ***Vocal Arrangements:*** Peggy Marshall. ***Producer:*** Isabel Manning Hewson.

OPENING

ANNOUNCER: Lost anything lately, you listeners? Then stay tuned to this station. You may hear surprising news about it in our fantasy, *Land of the Lost*, with prizes for lucky winners at the end. The Mutual Broadcasting System presents the *Land of the Lost* and its discoverer, the well-known storyteller, Isabel Manning Hewson.

ISABEL: Time to catch an ocean current everyone, time to travel down, down to the bottom of the sea, to that enchanted kingdom, the Land of the Lost. No wonder all lost things up on Earth come to life there. For it is the loveliest place you ever dreamed of. With its white sand and pearly palaces, all a-shimmer with pale green light. My brother Billy and I never tired of visiting the Land of the Lost. Every week our faithful friend, the wise-talking fish Red Lantern, would take us down through the tunnel under the lake that led to the ocean. Soon we'd be speeding along on an express current and before you could say "Popping Perriwinkles," we'd reach our destination.

RED LANTERN: All off, Pollywogs, it's the Land of the Lost.

ISABEL: And there's the magic seaweed curtain waiting to open for us… [The story would then begin.]

CLOSING

ISABEL: Remember our motto, "Never Say Lost."

ANNOUNCER: Remember, too, at this time next week, you may be hearing your name as a winner on "Lucky Seven Time." Get your letters off as soon as possible telling us about anything you've lost. It makes no difference whether it's a collar button or a diamond ring. You'll receive the nearest possible duplicate if, in the opinion of our judges, you've sent in one of the most interesting letters telling why you want a lost possession returned… Join us next week when Isabel and Billy get mixed up with a high-jumping Tiddlywink and Slippery Jack of Spades in the queerest places yet, the Big Game Preserve. Be with us next week, same time, same station when Isabel Manning Hewson takes you again to the Land of the Lost. The *Land of the Lost* is an original story by Isabel Manning Hewson. This is the Mutual Broadcasting System.

872. THE LANNY ROSS SHOW. Variety, 30 and 15 min. versions, CBS, then Mutual, 1939–1952.

A program of music and songs with tenor Lanny Ross as the host. Louise Carlyle and Evelyn Knight provided additional vocals. Jimmy Blaine, Nelson Case, Jean Paul King and John Scott were the announcers. Music was by the Buddy Weed Trio, the Al Fannell Trio, the Herman Chittison Trio and the Will Lorin Orchestra.

873. THE LARRY CARR SHOW. Variety, 15 min., CBS, 1946.

Music and songs with vocalist Larry Carr as the host. John Tillman did the announcing and Howard Smith and his orchestra provided the music.

874. THE LARRY CLINTON SHOW. Variety, 30 min., NBC, 1938.

Music and songs with orchestra leader Larry Clinton as the host. Bea Wain was the regular vocalist (she was accompanied by guests) and the Larry Clinton Orchestra provided the music.

875. LASSIE. Adventure, 15 min., ABC, then NBC, 1947–1950.

Narrated stories about a wandering collie (given various names by the people she comes in contact with) as she befriends both humans and animals in her travels. Lassie's reactions (barks, whines, growls and panting) are heard as the story unfolds. Based on the *Lassie* motion picture series and sponsored by Red Heart Dog Food.

Storytellers: Gayne Whitman, Rudd Weatherwax. ***Dog Imitations:*** Earl Keen. ***Announcer:*** Charles Lyon. ***Organist:*** John Duffy. ***Producer:*** Frank Perrin.

OPENING

SOUND: Lassie barking.

ANNOUNCER: From Hollywood, John Morrill and Company, makers of Three Flavor Red Heart, America's favorite dog food, presents Metro-Goldwyn-Mayer's lovable motion picture star, *Lassie*. Ladies and gentlemen, today Lassie plays the part of a beautiful collie named Beauty in our story entitled "The Long Trip Home."

CLOSING

ANNOUNCER: Next week, Lassie plays the part of a dog named "Hoiman" in that amusing comedy titled "Hoiman's Pups." Now don't miss it. *Lassie* is presented each week at this time by John Morrill and Company, makers of Three Flavor Red Heart, America's favorite dog food. Lassie appeared by arrangement with Metro-Goldwyn-Mayer, who invite you to see their Technicolor musical *Annie Get Your Gun*, starring Betty Hutton and Howard Keel. The *Lassie* show is produced and transcribed in Hollywood by Frank Perrin and directed by Harry Stewart. This is Charles Lyon. Ralph Edwards brings you *Truth or Consequences* tonight on NBC.

876. LATITUDE ZERO. Science Fiction, 30 min., NBC, 6/7/41 to 9/27/41.

While fishing off the coast of Alaska, the men of a boat called *The Hope* discover a submarine embedded on the beach of a remote island. The vessel has a smooth shell (no rivets or plates), the insignia of a horseshoe and appears to be over 250 feet long. After determining that the sub is not American, Japanese or Russian, they hear an SOS tapping coming from inside the sub. Brock Spencer, captain of *The Hope*, returns the code, asking for a way into the sub. A message is returned that instructs Brock to a secret hatchway under a six-inch gun. Brock and his shipmates Tibbs Canard and Bert Collins enter the sub to discover Capt. Craig MacKenzie and his bodyguard Simba, a six-foot, five-inch black man with incredible strength. They also learn that MacKenzie is an alien from a world beneath the sea called Latitude Zero and that the submarine, called *The Omega* (the horseshoe is its Greek symbol), was built in 1805. MacKenzie and Simba are capable of piloting the sub alone. They were transporting prisoners when an escape attempt was made that cost the prisoners their lives and wounded both Simba and MacKenzie. The sub beached itself; the fresh air let in by Brock and his men revived them. Brock, Tibbs and Bert soon find their lives changed when MacKenzie asks for their help in returning to Latitude Zero. Serialized stories relate their adventures as they battle the enemies of the undersea world (in particular, the evil Lucretia).

Cast: Lou Merrill (*Capt. Craig MacKenzie*); Bruce Payne (*Capt. Brock Spencer*); Jack Zoller (*Tibbs Canard*); Ed Max (*Bert Wheeler*); Charlie Lung (*Simba*); Anne Stone (*Lucretia*).

OPENING

VOICE: Longitude 180 degrees, 12 minutes.

VOICE: Latitude Zero.

VOICE: All hands at stations. Stand by for dive.

ANNOUNCER: The National Broadcasting Company presents—

VOICE: *Lat-i-tude Zerrrooooo*.

ANNOUNCER: *Latitude Zero*. Adventure fans, tonight begins the first episode of the most exciting and fabulous adventure story you've ever heard, *Latitude Zero*, especially written for radio by Ted Sherdeman. A story of five men against the world; heroic men with ideals and courage and strength to fight for them in Latitude Zero.

CLOSING

ANNOUNCER: Next week, same day, same station, don't miss the thrilling revelations of the mysterious Capt. MacKenzie, builder of *The Omega*, the strange submarine from the unknown port. You'll find thrills, action and adventure on the next installment of—

VOICE: *Lat-i-tude Zerrrooooo*.

ANNOUNCER: *Latitude Zero*, especially written for radio by Ted Sherdeman, originates in Hollywood's Radio City. This is the National Broadcasting Company.

877. THE LAUGH AND SWING CLUB. Variety, 30 min., Mutual, 1946.

A weekly program of music and songs coupled with comedy sketches. Comedian Morey Amsterdam was the host and Del Casino,

Henry Morgan and Mabel Todd were the regulars. Music was by Van Alexander and his orchestra.

878. Lavender and New Lace. Variety, 15 min., NBC, 1934.

A program of music and songs with Sylvia Marlowe, a harpsichordist, as the host. Joan Brooks and Felix Knight were the vocalists; Glenn Riggs did the announcing; and William Wilgus was the producer.

879. Lavender and Old Lace. Variety, 15 min., CBS, 1934–1936; NBC Blue, 1936.

Music and songs featuring singers Lucy Monroe, Frank Munn and Fritzi Scheff. Abe Lyman and his orchestra provided the music and Anne and Frank Hummert produced.

880. The Lawrence Welk Show. Variety, 30 min., ABC, 6/1/49 to 11/16/57.

A weekly program of dance music that led to TV's popular and long-running *Lawrence Welk Show*. In 1949, when the program was sponsored by Miller High Life Beer, the program was called *The Lawrence Welk High Life Revue*. Ted Brown was the host; Dick Hall, Helen Ramsey and Roy Waldrum were the regulars; Bob Orrin did the announcing; music was by the Lawrence Welk Orchestra.

881. Lawyer Q. Game, 30 min., NBC Blue, 1941.

An actual criminal case was reenacted by a cast of regular performers. Practicing lawyers appeared following the dramatization and presented a capsule summary to a jury of 12 studio audience members. After a brief deliberation (a commercial break), each juror gave his opinion as to whether the defendant was guilty or innocent. The actual court decision is revealed and a cash prize is awarded to each juror who matched the original verdict.

Host: Karl Swenson. ***Cast:*** Eleanor Audley, Joseph Julian, Ronald Liss, Neil O'Malley. ***Announcer:*** Dennis James.

882. Lawyer Tucker. Comedy, 30 min., CBS, 1947.

Dan Tucker is an attorney with a big heart who has his own ideas as to how the law should be administered. Stories focus on the bickering that results when he and his liberal-minded junior partner clash over a case.

Cast: Parker Fennelly (*Dan Tucker*); Maurice Wells (*Junior partner*); Mae Shutts (*Dan's sister*). ***Also:*** Arthur Anderson, Cameron Andrews, Ted Osborne.

Lazy Dan *see* **Appendix**

883. Leave It to Joan. Comedy, 30 min., CBS, 1949–1950.

Joan Davis is a salesgirl at Wollock's Department Store. She lives at home with her father, Police Sgt. "Pops" Davis, and stories (mostly at the department store) relate her experiences with the staff: Simon Hackaday, the manager; Penny Prentiss, secretary to the boss; and Tom Hinkle, the store detective. Each episode involves a special guest star and Joan sings when the occasion permits. Pops calls Joan "Tootsie."

Cast: Joan Davis (*Joan Davis*); Shirley Mitchell (*Penny Prentiss*); Andy Russell (*Tom Hinkle*); Harry Von Zell (*Simon Hackaday*); Joseph Kearns (*Pops Davis*). ***Announcer:*** Ken Niles. ***Music:*** Lyn Murray.

OPENING

Announcer: Well, as I live and breathe, it's got a hole in the head, it's a Roytan Cigar.

Joan: I breathe too when they say I've got a hole in my head. I'm Joan Davis.

Chorus: *Leave It to Joan.*

Announcer: Roytan, the cigar that breathes, presents *Leave It to Joan* with the music of Lyn Murray and our very special guest, Al Jolson. And starring America's Queen of Comedy, Joan Davis. Man to man, smoke Roytan, the cigar that breathes. Yes, breathes. The famous breathing channel in each Roytan cigar makes it easy drawing. So breathe in that mellow richness, breathe in that fragrant aroma... man to man, you're missing something until you smoke Roytan, the cigar that breathes. Light up a Roytan and—

Chorus: *Leave It to Joan, Leave It to Joan.*

CLOSING

Announcer: *Leave It to Joan* stars Joan Davis. Man to man, smoke Roytan, the cigar that breathes. And as I live and breathe, this is Ken Niles smoking a Roytan. Joan Davis will be heard at this same time next week. Good night. This is CBS, the Columbia Broadcasting System.

884. Leave It to Mike. Comedy, 30 min., Mutual, 1945–1946.

Events in the life of Mike McNally, a misadventure-prone young man with a marriage-minded girlfriend (Dinny) and a slave-driving boss (Mr. Berkeley).

Cast: Walter Kinsella (*Mike McNally*); Joan Alexander (*Dinny*); Jerry Macy (*Mr. Berkeley*); Hope Emerson (*Berkeley's wife*).

885. Leave It to the Girls. Discussion, 30 min., Mutual, 1945–1949.

A panel of four well-known women answer questions submitted by listeners (who each receive $10). Following the discussion, a male guest (usually a celebrity) appears "to defend the men of America." The program, which served as the basis for the television series of the same title, began as a serious discussion concerning problems, but soon evolved into a light comedy with humorous questions and equally humorous responses.

Moderators: Dorothy Kilgallen, Elissa Landi, Maggi McNellis, Paula Stone. ***Regular Panelists:*** Constance Bennett, Robin Chandler, Hedda Hopper, Eloise McElhone. ***Question Man:*** Ted Malone. ***Announcers:*** Andre Baruch, Tiny Ruffner. ***Producer:*** Martha Roundtree.

OPENING (from 11/16/46)

ANNOUNCER: Mutual presents *Leave It to the Girls*. Well, good evening, ladies and gentlemen, this is Tiny Ruffner inviting you for the fastest half-hour in radio; 30 minutes of rapid-fire entertainment from four of the most glamorous and successful girls in all of America: Eloise McElhone, Florence Pritchard, Patricia Bright and Maggi McNellis.

886. Lefty. Comedy, 30 min., CBS, 1946.

A baseball-accented sitcom about the antics of a southpaw pitcher named Lefty. Jack Albertson portrayed Lefty; Joan Alexander was the society reporter; Maxine Stuart played Lefty's secretary.

Leonidas Witherall *see* **The Adventures of Leonidas Witherall**

887. The Les Paul and Mary Ford Show. Variety, 15 min., Mutual, 1950–1951; 10 min., Mutual, 1955.

A program of music and songs with guitarist Les Paul and his wife, vocalist Mary Ford. Vocalists Bob Pollard and Eileen Pollard were the regulars on the 1955 version.

888. Let George Do It. Crime Drama, 30 min., Mutual, 1946–1950; Syndicated, 1950–1954.

George Valentine is a former cop turned private investigator who operates out of a fifth floor office in a Manhattan building. George has an adventurous spirit, an abundance of energy, but not too much money. To acquire cases, George places an ad in the newspaper that reads, "Personal notice. Danger is my stock and trade. If the job is too tough for you to do, you've got a job for me. George Valentine. Box 13." Stories follow his efforts to solve the cases that result from the ad. *Other regular characters:* Sonny Brooks, his assistant; Clair Brooks, Sonny's sister and George's secretary (whom he calls "Brooksie"); Caleb, the building elevator operator.

Cast: Bob Bailey (*George Valentine*); Frances Robinson, Virginia Gregg, Shirley Mitchell (*Clair Brooks*); Eddie Firestone, Jr. (*Sonny Brooks*); Joseph Kearns (*Caleb*). ***Announcer:*** John Easton. ***Music:*** Charles "Bud" Dant, Eddie Dunstedter.

OPENING

GEORGE: Personal notice. Danger is my stock and trade. If the job is too tough for you to handle, you've got a job for me, George Valentine. Write for full details.

ANNOUNCER: Standard Oil of California invites you to *Let George Do It*. Tonight, "Crime of Passion," another adventure of George Valentine.

889. Let Yourself Go. Variety, 30 min., CBS, 1944–1945.

A weekly program of music, songs and comedy sponsored by Eversharp pens and pencils.

Host: Milton Berle. ***Regulars:*** Joe Besser, Connie Russell. ***Announcer:*** Ken Roberts. ***Orchestra:*** Ray Bloch, Jacques Renard.

OPENING

ANNOUNCER: Eversharp invites you to *Let Yourself Go* and you'll always go right with Eversharp.

SONG: Buy Eversharp, buy Eversharp for writing pleasure. Buy Eversharp, buy Eversharp, they'll be forever.

ANNOUNCER: Yes, *Let Yourself Go*, starring Milton Berle, with Ray Bloch and his orchestra, Connie Russell and Joe Besser. Presented by Eversharp, world's leading manufacturer of fountain pens, repeater pencils, lead and desk sets. Tonight, Eversharp presents the secret ambition of the star of stage and screen, Al Jolson. And now, here's the entertainment you've been waiting for, the fellow who let himself go and wound up being Ziegfeld's biggest folly, Milton Berle.

890. LET'S BE CHARMING. Variety, 15 min., Mutual, 1943–1944.

A daily program of music and household advice for women with Pat Barnes and Julia Sanderson as the hosts. Music was by the John Gart and Nathan Shilkret orchestras.

891. LET'S BE CRAZY. Variety, 30 min., CBS, 1940.

A weekly program of music and songs with Dale Evans (wife of Roy Rogers) and Tom Moore as the hosts. Caesar Petrillo and his orchestra provided the music.

892. LET'S DANCE. Variety, 3 hrs., NBC, 1934–1935.

A lengthy Saturday night program of music that was divided into three one-hour segments: mellow songs with the NBC House Orchestra (led by Kel Murray); jazz with Benny Goodman; and Latin music with Xavier Cugat.

893. LET'S DANCE, AMERICA. Variety, 30 min., CBS, 1948.

A weekly program of dance music with Fred Robbins as the host. Music was provided by the Tex Beneke and Skitch Henderson orchestras.

894. LET'S LAUGH AND GET ACQUAINTED. Interview, 30 min., NBC, 1946.

A couple, chosen from the studio audience, appeared on stage and discussed various topics of interest with the host. Merchandise prizes were given to each couple for participating. Jack Gregson was the host and Hal Gibney and Don Stanley did the announcing.

895. LET'S LISTEN TO HARRIS. Variety, 30 min., NBC Blue, 1933–1934.

Orchestra leader Phil Harris as the host of a program of Big Band music and songs. Vocalist Leah Ray provided the songs and the Phil Harris Orchestra supplied the music. Also known as *The Phil Harris Orchestra*.

896. LET'S PLAY REPORTER. Game, 30 min., NBC, 1943.

A contestant, chosen from the studio audience, takes on the role of a newspaper reporter. A story submitted by a listener is told to the reporter by the host. Following the story, the reporter is asked to relate certain aspects of the story. Each correct response earns the reporter one dollar.

Host: Frances Scott. ***Assistants:*** Bob Denton, James L. Kilgallen. ***Orchestra:*** Jack Martin.

897. LET'S PRETEND. Children, 30 min., CBS, 1930–1954.

Original dramatizations coupled with adaptations of fairy tales and classic stories. Originally titled *The Adventures of Helen and Mary* (1930–1934), then *In the Land of Let's Pretend* (1934–1937) and finally *Let's Pretend* (1937–1954). Cream of Wheat was the long-time sponsor of the show.

Cast: Bill Adams, Bill Lipton (*Uncle Bill, the Host*); Marilyn Erskine (*Fairy Godmother*); Miriam Wolfe (*Witch*); Brad Barker, Harry Swan (*Animal Imitations*). ***Child Performers*** (varied greatly from year to year; listed is the cast from 1939): Albert Aley, Arthur Anderson, Vivian Block, Kenneth Darby, Jack Grimes, Jackie Jordan, Estelle Levy, Jimmy Lydon, Patricia Reardon, Patricia Ryan, Jane Tyler. ***Music:*** Maurice Brown. ***Producer:*** Nila Mack.

OPENING

SONG: Hello, hello, come on, let's go, it's time for *Let's Pretend*. The gang's all here and standing here is Uncle Bill your friend. The story is exciting, it's fun right to the end, so now you know, do as you're told, get set for *Let's Pretend*.

ANNOUNCER: Yes, it's radio's outstanding children's theater, *Let's Pretend*, created by Nila Mack.

BILL: Well, hello, Pretenders.

KIDS: Hello, Uncle Bill.

BILL: Are you all ready for a story?

KIDS: Let's go!

BILL: Let's go is right. Today, "The Story of the Twelve Dancing Princesses."

Nila Mack (center) with a 1940 group of Pretenders on *Let's Pretend*.

898. LET'S TALK HOLLYWOOD. Game, 30 min., NBC, 7/4/48 to 9/26/48.

Celebrity guests attempted to answer questions submitted by listeners. Home audience members whose questions stumped the guests received an RCA television set as a prize.

Host: George Murphy. ***Panelists:*** Eddie Bracken, Edith Gwynne, Erskine Johnson. ***Announcer:*** Hy Averback.

LET'S TALK IT OVER *see* **THE JUNE HYND GUEST BOOK**

899. THE LIBERACE SHOW. Variety, 30 min., Syndicated, 1954–1955.

A weekly program of music with pianist Liberace that was based on his then-current syndicated television series. His brother George Liberace supplied the musical background.

900. The Life and Love of Dr. Susan. Serial, 15 min., CBS, 1939–1940.

Events in the life of Susan Chandler, a doctor in the small town of Valleydale. Susan was the mother of twins (Dickie and Marilyn) and shared a practice with her father-in-law, Dr. Howard Chandler (Susan's husband, Dr. John Chandler, was reported missing in South America). Stories centered on Susan as she struggled to raise her children, attend patients and help Howard (a stubborn man with old-fashioned ideas) save his failing practice.

Cast: Eleanor Phelps (*Dr. Susan Chandler*); Tommy Hughes (*Dickie Chandler*); Gloria Mann (*Marilyn Chandler*); Fred Barron (*Dr. Howard Chandler*); Mary Cecil (*Miranda Chandler*); Mary Mason (*Nancy Chandler*); Alexander Kirkland (*Dr. Halliday*); Elspeth Eric (*Abby Bradford*). ***Announcer:*** Frank Luther. ***Organist:*** Richard Leibert.

901. Life Begins. Serial, 15 min., CBS, 1940–1941.

A daily drama about the life and loves of a young woman named Martha Webster and her experiences with the wealthy Craig family. Also known as *Martha Webster*.

Cast: Bess Johnson (*Martha Webster*); Carleton Young (*Winfield Craig*); Toni Gilman (*Virginia Craig*); Jimmy Donnelly (*Richard Craig*); Betty Philson (*Lucy Craig*); Ray Collins (*Alvin Craig*); Donald Cook (*Dick Young*); Margaret MacDonald (*Holly*); Agnes Moorehead (*Mrs. Riley*); Eddie Ryan (*Don Cavanaugh*); Jeanette Nolan, Gretchen Davidson (*Kay Smith*); Tom Tully (*Jim Carroll*). ***Also:*** Floyd Buckley, Eleanor Phelps, Everett Sloane. ***Announcer:*** Ken Roberts.

902. Life Begins at 80. Discussion, 30 min., Mutual, then ABC, 1948–1953.

Senior citizens discuss issues either submitted by home listeners or presented by guests. Became the basis for the 1950–1956 television series of the same name with Jack Barry as the host. Jack Barry also hosted the radio version and Dan McCullough did the announcing. Dan Enright was the producer.

903. Life Can Be Beautiful. Serial, 15 min., CBS, then NBC, 1938–1954.

Carol "Chichi" Conrad is a small-town girl who was adopted and raised by the kindly "Papa" David Solomon, the owner of the Slightly Read Bookshop. Stories focus on "Papa David" (as he helps people in need) and on Carol's romantic relationships, most notably with Stephen Hamilton, a crippled man who worked for Papa David and whom she later married, and with Toby Nelson, the man who pursued Carol after Stephen's death.

Cast: Alice Reinheart, Teri Keane (*Carol Conrad*); Ralph Locke (*Papa David Solomon*); Carl Eastman (*Toby Nelson*); John Holbrook, Earl Latimer (*Stephen Hamilton*); Roger DeKoven (*Dr. Myron Henderson*); Agnes Moorehead, Ethel Owen (*Nellie Conrad*); Humphrey Davis (*Al Douglas*); Clayton "Bud" Collyer (*Logan Smith*); Ruth Yorke (*Maybelle Owens*); Peggy Allenby (*Nurse Kimball*); Ruth Weston (*Muriel Kellogg*); Mitzi Gould (*Tita Yates*). ***Announcers:*** Bob Dixon, Ed Herlihy, Don Hancock, Ralph Edwards, Ron Rawson. ***Organist:*** Herschel Leucke. ***Producer:*** Don Becker.

OPENING

Announcer: John Ruskin wrote: "Whenever money is the principal object of life, it is both got ill and spent ill and does harm in both getting and spending. When getting and spending happiness is our aim, life can be beautiful." *Life Can Be Beautiful* is an inspiring message of faith drawn from life, written by Carl Bixby and Don Becker and brought to you by Spic and Span. No soap, no other cleanser, nothing in America cleans painted walls, woodwork and linoleum like Spic and Span.

904. A Life in Your Hands. Drama, 30 min., NBC, 1949–1952.

Jonathan Kegg is a wealthy, retired lawyer who has become a Friend of the Court. Stories follow his experiences when he steps in to impartially cross-examine witnesses during criminal procedures when justice is threatened.

Cast: Ned LeFevre, Lee Bowman, Carlton KaDell (*Jonathan Kegg*). ***Narrators:*** Carlton KaDell, Myron Wallace. ***Announcer:*** Ken Nordine.

905. The Life of Irene Castle. Drama, 15 min., Syndicated, 1931–1934.

Serialized stories based on the life of Irene Castle, "the best-dressed woman in America." Irene Rich played herself and the program was sponsored by Formfit Bras.

906. The Life of Mary Sothern. Serial, 15 min., Mutual, 1935–1937; CBS, 1937–1938.

Dramatic incidents in the life of Mary Sothern and her friends, Danny and Phyllis Stratford.

Cast: Linda Carlon, Minabelle Abbott, Betty Caine (*Mary Sothern*); Jack Zoller, Joseph Julian, Leon Janney (*Danny Stratford*); Florence Golden (*Phyllis Stratford*); Bess McCammon (*Alice Sanders*); Rikel Kent (*Jerome Sanders*); Jay Jostyn (*Max Tilley*). ***Announcer:*** Ken Roberts.

The Life of Mortimer Meek *see* **Meet Mr. Meek**

907. The Life of Riley. Comedy, 30 min., CBS, 1941; ABC, 1944–1945; NBC, 1945–1951.

Chester A. Riley is a riveter for the Stevenson Aircraft Company in Los Angeles. He earns $59.20 a week (1949) and began working for Carl Stevenson when he opened the plant in 1941. Chester is married to the former Margaret "Peg" Barker of Brooklyn, New York (his home town), and is the father of two children: Barbara (nicknamed Babs) and Chester A. Riley, Jr. (called Junior). He lives at 1313 Blue View Terrace and his next door neighbor, Jim Gillis, is also his best friend. (Jim is from Brooklyn, works alongside Chester and is married to Olive, whom he calls "Honeybee.") Stories relate incidents in the life of Riley, a constant bumbler who is seeking a better life for himself and his family. *Other regular characters:* Digby "Digger" O'Dell, the "Friendly Undertaker" (who always appeared when Riley was down in the dumps to help "cheer" him up; he opened with "Hello, it is I, Digby O'Dell, the Friendly Undertaker" and closed with, "I better be shoveling off"); Waldo Binney, Riley's friend, who lived at Ocean Park. Chester and Jim were members of a lodge called the Brooklyn Patriots of Los Angeles; Jim has a son named Egbert; Digger's wife was named Hilda and he had a son named Clay. Babs attended State University (1950) and Riley's catchphrase was "What a revoltin' development *this* is." While the radio version did spawn a television version with Jackie Gleason as Riley (1949–1950) and later William Bendix in the title role (1953–1958), NBC attempted two live television test programs based on the radio series in 1948. Herb Vigran played Chester on 4/13/48 and Buddy Gray was Riley on 4/20/48. Alice Drake was Peg; Arlene Becker played Babs; Lou Krugman was Jim; and Jo Gilbert played Honeybee.

Cast: Lionel Stander, William Bendix (*Chester A. Riley*); Grace Coppin, Paula Winslow, Georgia Backus (*Peg Riley*); Peggy Conklin, Sharon Douglas, Barbara Eiler (*Babs Riley*); Jack Grimes, Scotty Beckett, Conrad Binyon, Bobby Ellis, Tommy Cook (*Junior Riley*); John Brown (*Jim Gillis/Digby "Digger" O'Dell*); Shirley Mitchell (*Honeybee Gillis*); Dink Trout (*Waldo Binney*); Alan Reed, Ken Christy (*Carl Stevenson*). ***Announcers:*** Ken Carpenter, Ken Niles, Jimmy Wallington. ***Music:*** Lou Kosloff. ***Producer:*** Irving Brecher.

OPENING

Announcer: Prell brings you *The Life of Riley.* Prell, the shampoo that removes unsightly dandruff, leaves hair radiantly lovely; as Tallulah says—

Song: I'm Tallulah, the tube of Prell, and I'll make your hair look swell; it'll shine, it'll glow ... for radiant hair, get a-hold of me, Tallulah, the tube of Prell Shampoo.

Announcer: And now *The Life of Riley* with William Bendix as Riley.

CLOSING

Announcer: Procter and Gamble invites you to be with us again next week to hear *The Life of Riley* with William Bendix. Mrs. Riley is Paula Winslow; Digger O'Dell is John Brown. *The Life of Riley* is produced by Irving Brecher by arrangement with Universal-International Pictures. Jimmy Wallington speaking.

908. Life with Charlotte. Variety, 30 min., NBC, 1944.

Music, songs and comedy sketches set against the background of the Greenwood Boarding House in Washington, D.C. Charlotte Greenwood played herself, as the owner of the boarding house (the series host). Arthur Q. Bryan and Shirley Mitchell were the regulars; the Three Hits and a Miss were the vocalists; and Matty Malneck and his orchestra provided the music. See also *The Charlotte Greenwood Show* for the revised version of this series.

909. Life with Luigi. Comedy, 30 min., CBS, 9/21/48 to 3/3/53.

With a devious plan to get his overweight

daughter Rosa married, a man named Pasquale, the owner of Pasquale's Spaghetti Palace, arranges for his friend Luigi Basco to join him in Chicago's Little Italy. When Luigi arrives in Chicago from Italy, he opens an antique shop (Luigi Basco Antiques at 21 North Halstead Street), and stories follow Luigi's efforts to run his business and avoid Pasquale's endless attempts to marry him off to Rosa. Each episode opens and closes with Luigi writing a letter to his Mama Basco in Italy telling her of his experiences. Luigi's dream is to become an American citizen and his most treasured item is a bust of George Washington. Pasquale calls Luigi "Cabbage Puss" and "Banana Nose." *Other regular characters:* Miss Spaulding, Luigi's night school teacher; Luigi's classmates and friends, Horowitz, Schultz and Peterson. Served as the basis for the television series of the same title.

Cast: J. Carrol Naish (*Luigi Basco*); Alan Reed (*Pasquale*); Jody Gilbert (*Rosa*); Mary Shipp (*Miss Spaulding*); Joe Forte (*Horowitz*); Hans Conried (*Schultz*); Ken Peters (*Peterson*). ***Announcers:*** Bob Lemond, Charles Lyon. ***Music:*** Lud Gluskin. ***Producers:*** Cy Howard, Pat Burton.

OPENING

ANNOUNCER: The makers of Wrigley's Spearmint chewing gum invite you to enjoy life, *Life with Luigi*, a comedy starring that celebrated actor, Mr. J. Carrol Naish, with Alan Reed as Pasquale. Friends, the makers of Wrigley's Spearmint Chewing Gum are glad to bring you *Life with Luigi* because they feel it is a friendly, good-natured show that offers you relaxation and enjoyment. And you know Wrigley's Spearmint Chewing Gum offers you relaxation and enjoyment too ... so chew Wrigley's Spearmint Gum often, every day. Millions enjoy it and you will too. Now, Wrigley's Spearmint Chewing Gum brings you Luigi as he writes another letter describing his adventures in America to his Mama Basco in Italy. [The episode would then begin as Luigi reads his letter.]

CLOSING

ANNOUNCER: The makers of Wrigley's Spearmint Chewing Gum invite you to listen next week at this same time when Luigi Basco writes another letter to Mama Basco in Italy. *Life with Luigi* is a Cy Howard production. This is the CBS radio network.

910. THE LIFEBUOY PROGRAM. Variety, 30 min., NBC, 1936–1939.

A weekly program of music, songs and comedy with vaudeville performer Al Jolson (who sang sentimental songs of the South in blackface). The program, sponsored by Lifebuoy Soap, is also known as *The Al Jolson Show*.

Host: Al Jolson. ***Regulars:*** Douglas Corrigan, Harry Einstein, Martha Raye. ***Announcer:*** Tiny Ruffner. ***Music:*** Lud Gluskin.

OPENING

ANNOUNCER: From New York City we bring you *The Lifebuoy Program* starring Al Jolson and our special guest star, Gail Patrick, and Connee Boswell with Lud Gluskin and his orchestra. And now, Al Jolson.

911. LIGHT OF THE WORLD. Anthology, 15 min., NBC, then CBS, 1940–1950.

Dramatizations based on stories from the Bible that were modernized and presented in serial form. Bret Morrison narrated each story (as "The Speaker"). Ted Campbell, Jim Fleming and Stuart Metz were the announcers; Clark Whipple provided the organ music; and Anne Hummert and Frank Hummert were the producers.

912. LIGHT UP TIME. Variety, 15 min., NBC, 1949–1950.

A daily program of music and songs with Frank Sinatra as the host. Vocalists Dorothy Kirsten and Margaret Whiting were the regulars; Don Wilson did the announcing; and the Jeff Alexander orchestra and chorus provided the music and choral backing.

913. LIGHTS OUT. Anthology, 30 min., NBC, 4/17/35 to 8/1639; CBS, 10/6/42 to 9/28/ 43; NBC, 7/14/45 to 9/1/45; 7/6/46 to 8/24/46; ABC, 7/16/47 to 9/3/47.

A weekly series of suspense tales dealing with the occult and the supernatural. The program, created by Wyllis Cooper, premiered over station WENR in 1934. It became a network show (NBC Red) on April 17, 1935, and in 1936 Arch Oboler became the new producer. The 15-minute version ran from 1/1 to 4/18/34; the half-hour edition comprised the remainder of the run. The series is famous for using the most gruesome sound effects ever heard on radio up to this time (for example, dripping maple syrup for blood; frying bacon for the effect of an electric chair execution).

Host: Wyllis Cooper (1934–1936); Arch Oboler (1936–1939; 1942–1946); Boris Karloff (1947). ***Announcers:*** Bob Lemond, George Stone. ***Music:*** Leith Stevens. ***Producers:*** Wyllis Cooper, Arch Oboler.

EARLY OPENING

ANNOUNCER: This is the witching hour. It is the hour when dogs howl and evil is let loose on a sleeping world. Want to hear about it? Then turn out your lights!

LATER OPENING

ANNOUNCER: *Lights Out* everybody.

SOUND: Gong.

ANNOUNCER: It ... is ... later ... than ... you ... think.

HOST: This is Arch Oboler bringing you another in our series of stories of the unusual. And once again we caution you. These *Lights Out* stories are definitely not for the timid soul. So we tell you calmly and very sincerely, if you frighten easily, turn off your radio now.

914. L'IL ABNER. Comedy, 15 min., NBC, 11/20/39 to 12/6/40.

Humorous incidents in the lives of the residents of Dog Patch, U.S.A., the rural community created by cartoonist Al Capp. Particular focus is on the relationship between the naive L'il Abner Yokum and Daisy Mae Scruggs, the most beautiful girl in the community.

Cast: John Hodiak (*L'il Abner Yokum*); Laurette Fillbrandt (*Daisy Mae Scruggs*); Hazel Dopheide (*Mammy Pansy Yokum*); Clarence Hartzell (*Pappy Lucifer Ornamental Yokum*). ***Announcer:*** Durward Kirby. ***Producer:*** Wynn Wright.

915. LILAC TIME. Instruction, 30 min., CBS, 1934–1935.

A weekly program of dance music and instruction with dancer Arthur Murray describing dance steps as the music played. Carol Oxford provided vocal backing.

916. LINCOLN HIGHWAY. Anthology, 30 min., NBC, 1940–1942.

Dramatizations of supposedly true stories that occurred along the highway of Route 30. Top name stars from Hollywood, Broadway and radio appeared in the stories.

Host-Narrator: John McIntire. ***Music:*** Jack Arthur (also the theme vocalist).

OPENING

SONG: Hi there, neighbor, going my way, east or west on the Lincoln Highway? Hi there, Yankee, give out with a great big thankee, this is God's country.

ANNOUNCER: Yes, it's *Lincoln's Highway*, with your host, Mr. John McIntire.

917. LINDA'S FIRST LOVE. Serial, 15 min., Syndicated, 1939–1950.

The story of a young woman (Linda) and her search for happiness. While the program chronicled several romantic situations involving Linda, the title refers to a long-running storyline wherein Linda, a poor girl who works in a department store, tries to carry on a romance with a young and wealthy playboy (Kenneth Woodruff) despite objections from both families. Complicating the situation is Danny Grogan, a young man from Linda's social class, who has fallen in love with her. Although the program ran for 11 years, detailed cast information remains evasive.

Cast: Arline Blackburn (*Linda*); Karl Swenson (*Danny Grogan*). ***Announcers:*** Andre Baruch, Roger Forster.

OPENING

ANNOUNCER: The Kroger Grocery and Baking Company brings you, transcribed, *Linda's First Love*, the true-to-life story of a young girl; a girl in love with the world about us and in love with the wealthy young Kenneth Woodruff. She is a shop girl; he is a young society man. The romance is frowned upon by Linda's friends and family and Linda faces the world with her dreams of happiness alone.

918. THE LINE-UP. Crime Drama, 30 min., CBS, 7/6/50 to 2/20/53.

A gritty police drama that follows the investigations of Lt. Ben Guthrie and sergeants Matt Grebb and Peter Carter, plainclothes detectives with the San Francisco Police Department. The program begins with the suspects in a case being placed in a line-up where a witness "sees" and hears their cross-examination by the police. The investigation is then begun and the program details the step-by-step methods used to bring the case to a just end. Served as the basis for the television series of the same title.

Cast: Bill Johnstone (*Ben Guthrie*); Joseph

Kearns, Wally Maher (*Matt Grebb*); John McIntire, Jack Moyles (*Peter Carter*). ***Announcer:*** Dan Cubberly. ***Music:*** Eddie Dunstedter. ***Producers:*** Jaime Del Valle, Elliott Lewis.

OPENING

ANNOUNCER: Ladies and gentlemen, we take you now by transcription behind the scenes at a police headquarters in a great American city where, under the cold glaring lights, will pass before us the innocent, the vagrant, the thief, the murderer. This is *The Line-up*.

THE LINIT SHOW *see* **THE FRED ALLEN SHOW**

919. LISTEN TO A LOVE SONG. Variety, 30 min., CBS, 1946.

Romantic music and songs with vocalist Tony Martin as the host. The Al Stack Orchestra and Chorus provided the music and vocal backing. Jimmy Wallington did the announcing.

920. LISTENING POST. Anthology, 30 min., ABC, 1944–1948.

Dramatizations based on stories appearing in the *Saturday Evening Post*. Bret Morrison was the host and narrator and Clayton "Bud" Collyer did the announcing.

921. LITTLE ITALY. Drama, 15 min., CBS, 1933–1934.

A daily serial that mixes drama with light comedy to relate incidents in the lives of an Italian-American family.

Cast: Himan Brown (*Papa*), Ruth Yorke (*Mama*); Rose Keane (*Beatrice*), Ned Wever (*Nicholas*), Alfred Corn [Alfred Ryder] (*Tony*). ***Producer:*** Himan Brown.

LITTLE JACKIE LITTLE *see* **APPENDIX**

922. LITTLE OL' HOLLYWOOD. Variety, 30 min., NBC Blue, 1940–1942.

A weekly program of music, talk and songs from Hollywood with Ben Alexander as the host. Gogo DeLys provided the songs and Gordon Jenkins and his orchestra supplied the music.

923. LITTLE ORPHAN ANNIE. Adventure, 15 min., NBC Blue, 1931–1936; NBC Red, 1936–1940; Mutual, 1940–1942.

A radio adaptation of the comic strip by Harold Gray about an adorable orphan girl named Annie, her dog Sandy, and Oliver "Daddy" Warbucks, the billionaire who looks out for her. Many of Annie's adventures are set in and around the farm of Ma and Pa Silo, the kindly old couple who care for Annie when Daddy Warbucks is away on business. The Silo farm is located on the outskirts of the town of Simmons Corners and Annie's best friend, Joe Corntassle, assists her in her quest to help people—at home and abroad (when they travel with Daddy Warbucks). When situations get tough and Annie must make a decision that will affect both her and Joe, Joe will do whatever Annie feels is right—"Just go ahead and decide, I'm with you." "Leapin' lizards" and "Jumpin' grasshoppers" are Annie's favorite expressions; the Silo farm is located at RFD #1; Ryder's Drug Store is Annie and Joe's favorite hangout; the *Gazette* is the town's newspaper; and the Emporium is the general store. The program was sponsored by Ovaltine and a great deal of time (four to six minutes on a 15-minute show) was used to offer premiums and sell the product.

Cast: Shirley Bell, Janice Gilbert (*Little Orphan Annie*); Allan Baruck, Mel Torme (*Joe Corntassle*); Stanley Andrews, Henry Saxe, Boris Aplon (*Oliver "Daddy" Warbucks*); Henrietta Tedro (*Ma Silo*); Jerry O'Mera (*Pa Silo*); Brad Barker (*Sandy*). ***Announcer:*** Andre Baruch (as Uncle Andy).

OPENING (from 10/22/35)

SONG: Who's that little chatterbox, the one with pretty auburn locks, whom do you see, it's Little Orphan Annie. She and Sandy make a pair, they never seem to have a care, cute little she, it's Little Orphan Annie.

ANNOUNCER: Well, here it is, 5:45 again, the time when you hear *Little Orphan Annie* before drinking your Ovaltine every night. Attention everybody, please. Tonight's the night when you're going to hear about the big surprise that's coming for you. Yes, sir, the most beautiful and thrilling surprise Annie has ever had for her radio friends. Something absolutely new and different from anything ever heard over the radio before. So get your pencil and paper quick, so you won't miss a single word of the big news

I'll be telling you the very minute the adventure is over tonight. And now for Annie's big surprise party. Remember, Joe is keeping Annie away from the farm so...

CLOSING

ANNOUNCER: Attention now, everybody, please. Here's the big news of the big surprise that Orphan Annie has for you... We are going to give you a chance to get a birthday ring just like Annie's ... a ring with your own birthstone in it... Absolutely different than any ring offered on the radio before... This birthday ring Annie will send you is a genuine gold plated ring ... it's finished in genuine 24-karat gold plate. On top of that, it has a special rose-gold finish... Another thing, this Little Orphan Annie Birthday Ring is a big ring... It's five-eighths of an inch across the top ... and what's more, this Orphan Annie Birthday Ring is an automatic fitting ring, so no matter how big or small your finger is, it will fit you exactly right... And here's the biggest thrill of all. Wait until you see the birthstone that is set in this ring. It's a handmade, simulated birthstone, actually imported from Europe, just like the stone that Daddy Warbucks sent to Annie... And best of all, the ring you get will have your own particular birthstone in it ... for example, if your birthday comes in October, the same as Annie's, you'll get a beautiful simulated rose zircon in your ring... And listen to what else Annie puts on this ring for you. Right next to the stone, where everybody can see it, it shows the month you were born in, spelled out right in the middle... Boy oh boy, did you ever dream of having a big shiny gold-plated birthday ring like that for your very own? You can't buy Little Orphan Annie Birthday Rings like this anywhere because they've been made up especially for Annie's radio friends—you boys and girls who drink Ovaltine regularly. And you can get this ring for only ten cents and one Ovaltine aluminum seal. Just think of getting a bargain like that. So send in right away... Now here's all you have to do. Just print your name and address plainly on a piece of paper. Next put down your birthday month ... then just mail it in ... with ten cents in coin to Little Orphan Annie, Chicago, Illinois... That's all you do... Say, I'll bet boys and girls everywhere will be sending in for their rings this very night... So ask your mother to get you a can of Ovaltine ... because even if you have some now, you'll be needing another can soon anyway... So get busy right now and don't forget to be here right on time Monday at 5:45 to hear the exciting things that will be happening to Annie next. We'll see you Monday at 5:45, friends. Good-bye.

924. LIVE LIKE A MILLIONAIRE. Variety, 30 min., NBC, 1950–1951; ABC, 1952–1953.

The original format found children introducing their talented parents, who performed for the home and studio audience. In 1951, when the series was adapted to television, the format changed slightly to showcase the talents of hopeful actors and singers. In each format, studio audience applause determined the winner. While winners in both formats sought possible discovery, each was awarded (as a prize) one week's tax on a million dollars.

Host: Jack McCoy. ***Announcer:*** John Nelson. ***Music:*** Ivan Ditmars.

925. THE LIVES OF HARRY LIME. Adventure, 30 min., Syndicated, 1952–1953.

A radio adaptation of the feature film *The Third Man*, about Harry Lime, an international rogue and confidence man who moved from country to country—always remaining one step ahead of the law—and always fleecing people who needed to be taught a lesson. When asked, "What is your business, Mr. Lime?", Harry would respond, "I dabble. I dabble in assorted things." Also known as *The Third Man*.

Cast: Orson Welles (*Harry Lime*). ***Music:*** Anton Karas. ***Producer:*** Harry Alan Towers.

OPENING

ANNOUNCER: Presenting Orson Welles as "The Third Man." [Over zither music:] *The Lives of Harry Lime*, the fabulous stories of the immortal character originally created in the motion picture *The Third Man*, with zither music by Anton Karas.

SOUND: A gun shot.

ORSON: That was the gun shot that killed Harry Lime. He died in a sewer beneath Vienna, as those of you know who saw the movie *The Third Man*. Yes, that was the end of Harry Lime, not the beginning. Harry Lime had many lives, and I can recount all of them.

How do I know? It's very simple. Because my name is Harry Lime.

The Log Cabin Jamboree *see* **The Jack Haley Show**

926. Lombardo Land, U.S.A. Variety, 30 min., Mutual, 1949–1946.

A weekly program of music and songs with orchestra leader Guy Lombardo as the host. Carmen, Lebert, Rosemarie and Victor Lombardo were the regulars and David Ross did the announcing. The Guy Lombardo Orchestra provided the music. See also *Guy Lombardo Time* and *Musical Autographs*.

927. Lone Journey. Serial, 15 min., NBC, 1940–1943; CBS, 1946–1947; ABC, 1951–1952.

Dissatisfied with life in Chicago, businessman Wolfe Bennett and his wife Nita retreat to the Judith Mountain area of Montana where they purchase the Spear T. Ranch. Stories follow their efforts to begin a new life.

Cast: Les Damon, Reese Taylor, Staats Cotsworth, Henry Hunter (*Wolfe Bennett*); Betty Winkler, Claudia Morgan, Betty Ruth Smith, Eloise Kummer, Olive Deering, Charlotte Holland (*Nita Bennett*); Vinton Hayworth (*Port*); Lesley Woods (*Matron*); Polly Rowles (*Nita's aunt*); Nancy Osgood (*Wolfe's mother*); Dorothy Lovell (*Cecily Andrews*); James Meighan (*Cullen Andrews*); John Gibson (*Jim Matthews*); Geraldine Kay (*Kyle King*); Betty Caine, Ginelle Gibbs (*Lelia Matthews*); Grace Valentine, Bess McCammon (*Jesse King*); Charlotte Holland, Laurette Fillbrandt (*Sydney McKenzie*). ***Also:*** Joan Alexander, Dolores Gillis, Marilyn Monk, Minerva Pious. ***Narrator:*** Charles Woods. ***Announcers:*** Nelson Case, Durward Kirby, Henry Morgan, Richard Stark.

928. The Lone Ranger. Western, 30 min., Mutual, 1933–1942; NBC Blue, 1942–1944; ABC, 1944–1954.

A group of six Texas Rangers, trailing the notorious Butch Cavendish Hole-in-the-Wall Gang, stop as they approach the canyon passage to Bryant's Gap. Their scout, who is secretly working for Butch, returns and informs Capt. Dan Reid that the passage is clear. As the Rangers ride in, they are trapped and downed by the Cavendish Gang. Believing that all the Rangers are dead, the gang rides off. Later that afternoon, Tonto, an Indian riding through the canyon, finds a lone survivor, John Reid, the captain's brother. Tonto nurses Reid's wounds. When he regains consciousness, Reid recalls Tonto, an Indian he befriended years ago, the childhood companion who called him "Kemo Sabe" (translated as both Faithful Friend" and "Trusted Scout"). To convince Cavendish that all the Rangers were killed, Tonto digs six graves—the sixth marked with the name John Reid—to conceal the fact that one ranger had lived to avenge the others—as the Lone Ranger. At Tonto's suggestion, Reid fashions a mask from his brother's black vest and, posing as an outlaw, he tracks down and apprehends the Cavendish Gang.

Bearing the trademark of the silver bullet, the Lone Ranger and Tonto rode the Western plains of the 19th century striving to maintain law and order in a wild and lawless era. *Other regular characters:* Dan Reid, the Ranger's nephew; Thunder Martin, a rancher who was also the Ranger's friend. The Ranger's horse was named Silver; Tonto had three horses: White Feather, Paint and Scout; Dan's horse was named Victor. The only reward the Ranger wanted was to make the West good and great and free of outlaws. He never shot to kill. The only person ever killed by him was Butch Cavendish. He avenged his brother's death by putting Cavendish in jail on murder charges. However, while awaiting execution, Cavendish broke out of Federal prison and tracked Reid to the same spot where he killed Dan. After a fierce gun battle, Cavendish became the only victim of the Ranger's silver bullet. Served as the basis for the television series of the same title with John Hart and Clayton Moore as the Lone Ranger and Jay Silverheels as Tonto.

Cast: George Seaton, Jack Deeds, Earl Graser, Brace Beemer, John Todd, Jim Jewell (*John Reid/The Lone Ranger*); John Todd (*Tonto*); Ernie Stanley, James Lipton, Dick Beals (*Dan Reid*); Jay Michael (*Butch Cavendish*); Paul Hughes (*Thunder Martin*). ***Announcer-Narrators:*** Brace Beemer, Fred Foy, Harold Golder, Bob Hite, Charles Woods. ***Producers:*** James Jewell, Fran Striker, George W. Trendle.

OPENING

Ranger: Hi-yo, Silver!

Announcer (over "William Tell Overture"

theme): A fiery horse with the speed of light, a cloud of dust and a hearty hi-yo, Silver. The Lone Ranger! With his faithful Indian companion Tonto, the daring and resourceful masked rider of the plains led the fight for law and order in the early western United States. Nowhere in the pages of history can one find a greater champion of justice. Return with us now to those thrilling days of yesteryear. From out of the past come the thundering hoofbeats of the great horse Silver. The Lone Ranger rides again!

RANGER: Come on, Silver, let's go, big fellow! Hi-yo, Silver, away!

CLOSING (typical)

BANKER: That's the man I saw in the Sheriff's office.

SHERIFF: Well, if it wasn't for him, the crooks would have made off with all the money in your bank.

BANKER: By gosh, I reckon you're right, Sheriff. Just who is he?

SHERIFF: By golly, don't you know? He's the Lone Ranger!

RANGER (riding off): Hi-yo, Silver, awaaaaay!

ANNOUNCER: This is a feature of the Lone Ranger, Incorporated. Created and produced by George W. Trendle, directed by Charles B. Livingston and edited by Fran Stryker. The part of the Ranger is played by Brace Beemer. This is Fred Foy speaking.

Note: The Lone Ragner got the metal for his bullets from a silver mine that he inherited from the family (it was mined by an oldtimer named Jim). While it is a known fact that Tonto had seen the Lone Ranger unmasked, two other people had also seen Reid without his mask. In 1942, Reid granted the last request of Grandma Frisby, the elderly woman who raised Dan, to see him without his mask. In the twentieth anniversary episode of 1953, the story of the Ranger's revenge on Butch Cavendish was retold. As Butch lay dying at the foot of a cliff, the Ranger unmasked for him. Butch's final words were, "Wished I could have died without knowing."

929. THE LONE WOLF. Crime Drama, 30 min., Mutual, 6/29/48 to 1/1/49.

"Michael Lanyard is a sucker for a pretty girl," and if there is a beautiful girl in distress, Michael Lanyard will be there to help. If his buddies are having a drink, Michael does too—milk. ("It must be a taste I acquired as a child," he says of the situation when people stare at him.) Michael is tall and handsome and girls like to be with him; but to Michael, they are most often trouble. But trouble is Michael's business and it's a business he likes. Michael, a private detective who works alone (called "The Lone Wolf"), doesn't like murders—but they seem to happen in his presence and his efforts to solve the crimes are the focal point of the series. Michael is reluctant to use violence, but if the situation calls for it, he will (and he always apologizes to the audience for doing so). Michael's favorite hangout is the Silver Sea Shell Bar and Grill.

Cast: Gerald Mohr, Walter Coy (*Michael Lanyard*). ***Announcer:*** Bob Anderson. ***Music:*** Rex Koury.

OPENING

SOUND: Knocks on a door.

GIRL: Who is it?

VOICE: Michael Lanyard.

GIRL (opening the door): The Lone Wolf.

MICHAEL: May I come in?

ANNOUNCER: Michael Lanyard returns in the adventures of *The Lone Wolf* in our story for tonight, "The Golden Santa." Mutual presents the adventures of *The Lone Wolf*, based on the famous character from American fiction by Louis Joseph Vance and known the world over for more than a quarter of a century. With Walter Coy as the Lone Wolf.

CLOSING

ANNOUNCER: Now once again, here is our star, Walter Coy, who returns as Michael Lanyard with a word about next week.

MICHAEL: Next week, it's the story of "The Thoughtful Thief," in which a crook obligingly announces the time and place of his theft in advance, which causes all the valuables to be locked in a vault which is completely foolproof. The only trouble is, the thief isn't a fool. Listen, won't you?

ANNOUNCER: And now this is Bob Anderson reminding you to join us again next week, same time, same station for another adventure of *The Lone Wolf*. This program came to you from Hollywood. This is the Mutual Broadcasting System.

930. LONELY WOMEN. Serial, 15 min., NBC Blue, 6/29/42 to 12/10/43.

The Towers Hotel for Women was the setting for this World War II drama about the feelings of loneliness experienced by several women whose men were off to war. Particular focus was on Judith Clark, a secretary, and her friend, Marilyn Larimore, a model.

Cast: Barbara Luddy (*Judith Clark*); Betty Lou Gerson (*Marilyn Larimore*); Harriette Widmer (*Peggy*); Eileen Palmer (*Judy Evans*); Reese Taylor (*George Bartlett*); Florence Brower (*Helen*); Nanette Sargent (*Nora*); Les Tremayne (*Jack Crandall*); Patricia Dunlap (*Bertha Schultz*); Virginia Payne (*Bertha's mother*); Murray Forbes (*Bertha's father*); Herb Butterfield (*Chester Colby*); Muriel Bremner (*Edith Crandall*); Kay Campbell (*Laura Richardson*). ***Announcers:*** Fort Pearson, Marvin Miller. ***Organist:*** Bernice Yanocek. ***Producer:*** Carl Webster.

931. LONESOME GAL. Men, 15 min., Syndicated, 1947–1951.

An unusual program geared to the male audience. The title character, who was anonymous and wore a mask when playing the role, talked with as seductive a voice as had been heard on radio. She treated her entire audience as one and rambled on with chatter in an intimate vein, directed to her male listeners. Her soft, mellow tones suggested that she can be looked upon as a lover, friend or companion. The "Lonesome Gal" opened the program and immediately played up the sex motif; the program itself was interspersed with talk and music. Disc jockey Jean King played the title role and the program was originally titled *The Lonesome Girl.*

932. THE LONGINES SYMPHONETTE. Variety, 30 min., CBS, then Mutual, NBC, ABC, 1943–1958.

A program of concert music sponsored by the Longines-Wittnauer Watch Company, makers of "The World's Most Honored Watch." Frank Knight was the host and announcer and the orchestras of Macklin Marrow and Michel Piastro provided the music.

933. LOOK YOUR BEST. Women, 30 min., CBS, 1950.

A program of beauty tips and advice for women. Richard Willis was the host and Bill Shipley did the announcing.

934. LORA LAWTON. Serial, 15 min., NBC, 1943–1950.

Originally the story of a housekeeper (Lora Lawton) and her romance with Peter Carver, a wealthy businessman (owner of the Carver Shipbuilding Company) in Washington, D.C. Stories later followed events in their lives when they married and faced opposition from Peter's family.

Cast: Joan Tompkins, Jan Miner (*Lora Lawton*); James Meighan, Ned Wever (*Peter Carver*); Ethel Wilson (*May Case*); Fran Carlon (*Helene Hudson*); Carol Summers (*Octavia*); Marilyn Erskine, Charita Bauer (*Gail Carver*); James Van Dyke (*Clyde Houston*); Lawson Zerbe (*Rex Lawton*); Elaine Kent (*Iris Houston*); Walter Greaza (*Russ*). ***Also:*** Spencer Bentley, Staats Cotsworth, Michael Fitzmaurice, Sammie Hill, Helen Shields. ***Announcer:*** Ford Bond. ***Organist:*** Ted Steele. ***Producers:*** Anne Hummert, Frank Hummert.

935. LORENZO JONES. Serial, 15 min., NBC, 4/26/37 to 9/30/55.

Lorenzo Jones is a garage mechanic who spends most of his time inventing seemingly useless gadgets. The light-hearted comedy stories focus on Lorenzo, whose good-natured heart gets him into various predicaments. *Other regular characters:* Belle Jones, his wife; Abby Matson, their friend; Sandy Matson, Abby's husband; Jim Barker, Lorenzo's employer; Irma Barker, Jim's wife.

Cast: Karl Swenson (*Lorenzo Jones*); Betty Garde, Lucille Wall (*Belle Jones*); Jean McCoy (*Abby Matson*); Joseph Julian (*Sandy Matson*); John Brown (*Jim Barker*); Nancy Sheridan, Mary Wickes, Grace Keddy (*Irma Barker*). ***Announcer:*** Don Lowe. ***Organists:*** Ann Leaf, Rosa Rio. ***Producers:*** Anne Hummert, Frank Hummert.

OPENING

ANNOUNCER: Now smile awhile with Lorenzo Jones and his wife Belle. We all know couples like lovable and practical Lorenzo Jones and his dedicated wife Belle. Lorenzo's inventions have made him a character to the town, but not to Belle who loves him. Their struggle for security is anybody's story, but somehow with Lorenzo it has made more smiles than tears.

936. THE LOUELLA PARSONS SHOW. Gossip, 15 min., ABC, 1946–1951.

A daily program of Hollywood gossip with

(Left to right) Lucille Wall, Joseph Julian and Karl Swenson were featured in *Lorenzo Jones*.

columnist Louella Parsons. Marvin Miller and Verne Smith were the announcers.

OPENING

ANNOUNCER: Woodbury, for the skin you love to touch. Woodbury brings you direct from Hollywood, Hollywood's best-known, best-loved reporter, Louella Parsons, with exclusive news about your favorite stars, direct from the glamour center of the world. And now, here she is, Louella Parsons.

LOUELLA: Hello to all of you from Hollywood... Believe it or not, censorship has reared its ugly head on 17-year-old Shirley Temple on whose new picture *Kiss and Tell*, Chicago has given a pink ticket meaning it's suitable only for adults...

LOUISA *see* **APPENDIX**

937. THE LOUISE FLOREA SHOW. Variety, 15 min., NBC Blue, 1938.

Music and songs with vocalist Louise Florea as the host. Jessie Crawford provided the organ music and Leopold Spitalny supplied the orchestra backing.

938. LOUISE MASSEY AND THE WESTERNERS. Variety, 15 min., NBC Blue, 1936.

A program of country and western music and songs with singer Louise Massey as the host. Her brothers, Allen (banjo player) and Curt Massey (singer-violinist) assisted her. Milt Mable and Larry Wellington were the regulars and the Westerners provided the music.

939. LOVE NOTES. Women, 5 min., Syndicated, 1945.

A short program of romantic poetry readings with Jerry Wayne as the host. Ben Grauer did the announcing.

940. LOVE STORY THEATER. Anthology, 30 min., Mutual, 1946–1947.

A weekly program of dramas focusing on love and romance with Jim Ameche as the host. Sylvan Levin and his orchestra provided the music and top name guests performed in the stories.

941. Lovely Lady. Women, 30 min., NBC, 1940.

A weekly program of fashion news, beauty tips and advice for women. John Slanton was the host and fashion commentator; Lester Harding assisted him and did the announcing; and Milton Shrednik and his orchestra provided the music.

942. Lucky Stars. Variety, 30 min., NBC, 1946.

The program features performances by promising (but undiscovered) talent. Jack Kiltie was the host; Lynn Collier, Bob Houston, Marie Ragndahl and the Smoothies were the regulars; Leopold Spitalny and his orchestra provided the music.

The Lucky Strike Program *see* **The Jack Benny Program**

943. Luke Slaughter of Tombstone. Western, 30 min., CBS, 1958.

Following the Civil War, cavalryman Luke Slaughter returns to his home in Arizona and begins the Slaughter Cattle Ranch just outside the town of Tombstone. When the series begins (1880s), Luke has established himself as a powerful force in the state; a man who has a thriving business and a man to whom others can look for help in times of need. Luke is an amateur historian. He has a collection of wanted posters and keeps track of outlaws still on the loose. Although Luke is a cattle rancher, he spends more time upholding the law than ranching, and stories follow his exploits as he risks his life to fight evil. *Other regular characters:* Wichita Bagby, his sidekick; Clint Wallace, the sheriff.

Cast: Sam Buffington (*Luke Slaughter*); Junius Matthews (*Wichita Bagby*); Charles Seel (*Clint Wallace*); Vic Perrin (*Various roles*). ***Music:*** Wilbur Hatch. ***Producer:*** William N. Robson.

OPENING

Luke: Slaughter's my name, Luke Slaughter. Cattle's my business. It's a tough business, it's a big business. I've got a big stake in it. There's no man west of the Rio Grande big enough to take it from me.

Announcer: *Luke Slaughter of Tombstone.* Civil War cavalryman turned Arizona cattleman. Across the territory from Yuma to Fort Defiance; from Flagstaff to the Wachukas and below the border from Chiwawa to Sonora, his name was respected or feared—depending which side of the law you were on. Man of vision, man of legend—*Luke Slaughter of Tombstone.*

CLOSING

Announcer: Next week at this time we return with—

Luke: Slaughter's the name, Luke Slaughter. When we meet up again you can call me that. Luke Slaughter.

Announcer: This is the CBS radio network.

944. Lulu and Johnny. Variety, 15 min., NBC Blue, 1943.

A program of music and songs with singers Lulu Bates and Johnny Morgan. Joe Rines and his orchestra provided the music.

945. Lum and Abner. Comedy, 15 min., NBC Red, 1931–1933; Mutual, 1934–1935; NBC Blue, 1935–1938; CBS, 1938–1940; NBC Blue, 1941–1944; ABC, 1944–1947.

Comical events in the everyday lives of Lum Edwards and Abner Peabody, the naive owners of the Jot 'Em Down Store in Pine Ridge, Arkansas. The program is simply an exchange of dialogue between Lum and Abner as they discuss life, attend to business and mingle with friends and customers. *Other regular characters:* Mose Muich, the barber; Grandpappy Spears; Dick Huddleston, the postmaster; Cedric Wehunt, the chap who cares for the store when Lum and Abner are away. Lum and Abner are members of the Golden Era Club and the store phone rings two shorts and one long. Abner mentioned his wife's name as Lisabeth and his daughter as Pearl (who was away at nursing school). Lum was single. (On 11/2/49, CBS-TV aired a *Lum and Abner* pilot featuring the radio cast that failed to generate a series). For information on the 30-minute version of the series, see *The New Lum and Abner Show*.

Cast: Chester Lauck (*Lum Edwards/Grandpappy Spears/Cedric Wehunt*); Norris Goff (*Abner Peabody/Dick Huddleston*); Andy Devine (*Mose Muich*). ***Announcers:*** Gene

Baker, Lou Crosby, Gene Hamilton, Roger Krupp. ***Organists:*** Sylvia Bock, Elsie Emerson.

OPENING

SOUND: Phone rings.

LUM: The phone's ringing, Abner. I believe that's our ring.

ABNER: I believe you're right, let's see [picks up phone]. Hello, Jot 'Em Down Store. This is Lum and Abner.

ANNOUNCER: Now let's see what's going on in Pine Ridge...

946. LUNCHEON AT SARDI'S. Interview, 15 min., Mutual, 1954–1955.

A daily program of interviews from Sardi's Restaurant in New York City by Bill Slater and Tom Slater.

947. LUNCHEON AT THE WALDORF. Variety, 30 min., NBC Blue, 1940–1941.

Music and songs set against the background of the Empire Room of the Waldorf-Astoria Hotel in New York City. Ilka Chase was the host; vocalist Frank Luther provided the songs; Bert Parks did the announcing; and music was by Paul Baron and his orchestra.

LUX PRESENTS HOLLYWOOD *see* **THE LUX RADIO THEATER**

948. THE LUX RADIO THEATER. Anthology, 60 min., NBC, 1934–1935; CBS, 1935–1954.

Top name guest stars in radio adaptations of Broadway plays and Hollywood feature films. The program, sponsored by Lever Brothers, the makers of Lux soap, is also known as *Lux Presents Hollywood* and served as the basis for *The Lux Video Theater* television series. *Stories include:*

Swanee River. A biographical drama based on the life of composer Stephen Foster starring Al Jolson, Dennis Morgan and Frances Gifford.

Burlesque. Al Jolson, Ruby Keeler, Lou Merrill, Frank Nelson and Wally Maher in a musical drama about a group of burlesque performers.

All About Eve. Bette Davis, Anne Baxter and Gary Merrill in a story about an ambitious actress who will stop at nothing to reach the top.

Wuthering Heights. Ida Lupino and Basil Rathbone in an adaptation of the Emily Bronte novel about a tragic love affair in 18th-century England.

The Farmer's Daughter. A beautiful and ingenious farm girl (Loretta Young) changes the life of a congressman (Joseph Cotten).

Hosts: Cecil B. De Mille, William Keighley, Irving Cummings. (From January to December 1945, guests served as the host.) ***Announcers:*** Ken Carpenter, John Milton Kennedy, Melvin Ruick. ***Music:*** Louis Silvers.

OPENING (from 1945;
Hal Wallis was the guest host)

ANNOUNCER: Lux Presents Hollywood. *The Lux Radio Theater* brings you Margaret O'Brien, Charles Laughton and Tom Drake in "The Canterville Ghost." Ladies and gentlemen, your guest, producer Hal Wallis [who greets the audience, then introduces the play].

CLOSING

ANNOUNCER: Our stars, Charles Laughton, Margaret O'Brien and Tom Drake return for their curtain calls in just a moment. [Commercial airs.] Back to our footlights come Margaret O'Brien, Tom Drake and Charles Laughton. [Each chats briefly with the host, Hal Wallis, about the play.]

HOST: Next Monday, we bring you one of the most talked-about dramas of the year, "The Woman in the Window" starring Edward G. Robinson, Joan Bennett and Dan Duryea. If you never felt sympathy for a murderer, you will in this gripping story of a man who is trapped to kill in self-defense and teams with a woman to conceal their crime from the police. Our sponsor, the makers of Lux Flakes, join me in inviting you to be with us again next Monday night when *The Lux Radio Theater* presents Edward G. Robinson, Joan Bennett and Dan Duryea in "The Woman in the Window." This is Hal Wallis saying good night from Hollywood.

ANNOUNCER: "The Canterville Ghost" was presented through the courtesy of Metro-Goldwyn-Mayer, producer of the Technicolor musical, *Anchors Aweigh*. The next Hal Wallis production for Paramount is *You Came Along* starring Robert Cummings, Lisabeth Scott and Don DeFore. And this is your announcer, John Milton Kennedy, reminding you to tune in next Monday night to hear "A Woman in the Window" with Edward G. Robinson, Joan Bennett and Dan Duryea.

Rita Ascott (left) and Virginia Payne starred in *Ma Perkins*.

This is CBS, the Columbia Broadcasting System.

949. Lyrics by Liza. Variety, 25 min., NBC, 1943.

A program of music and songs with singer-composer Liza Morrow as the host. Music was provided by Jimmy Lytell and his orchestra.

950. Ma and Pa. Comedy, 15 min., CBS, 1936.

An exchange of comic dialogue between an elderly married couple played by Margaret Dee (Ma) and Parker Fennelly (Pa).

951. Ma Perkins. Serial, 15 min., NBC, then CBS, 12/4/33 to 11/25/60.

Events in the life of Ma Perkins, the owner of a lumberyard in the town of Rushville Center. She operated the business with Shuffle Shober, was the mother of three children (John, Evey and Fay) and a guiding light to her neighbors, the Herringbones (Phineas, Flossie, Jessica and Tweetsie). Though the stories were set in a small town, Ma managed to travel widely, mend broken hearts and counsel her family and loved ones. Sponsored by Procter and Gamble, the makers of Oxydol soap flakes. Also known as *Oxydol's Own Ma Perkins*.

Cast: Virginia Payne (*Ma Perkins*); Rita Ascott, Marjorie Hannan, Cheer Brentson, Laurette Fillbrandt, Margaret Draper (*Fay Perkins Henderson*); Dora Johnson, Laurette Fillbrandt, Kay Campbell (*Evey Perkins Fitz*); Gilbert Faust (*John Perkins*); Charles Eggleston, Edwin Wolfe (*Shuffle Shober*); Murray Forbes (*Willie Fitz*); Cecil Roy, Arthur Young, Bobby Ellis (*Junior Fitz*); Herb Butterfield (*Phineas Herringbone*); Angeline Orr (*Flossie Herringbone*); Beryl Vaughn (*Jessica Herringbone*); Elmira Roessler (*Tweetsie Herringbone*); Jonathan Hole (*Paul Henderson*); Nanette Sargent, Judith Lockser (*Paulette Henderson*). ***Announcers:*** Jack Brinkley, Dan Donaldson, Marvin Miller, Dick Wells. ***Music:*** Doc Whipple. ***Producers:*** Anne Hummert, Frank Hummert.

Note: Due to conflicts, both Marvin Miller and Dan Donaldson used the pseudonym "Charlie Warren" when announcing.

OPENING

ANNOUNCER: Now, everybody ready for Oxydol's own *Ma Perkins*, America's mother of the air. Brought to you by Proctor and Gamble, makers of Oxydol.

CLOSING (from the last broadcast)

ANNOUNCER: And now, here's Ma again.

MA: Thank you Dan. This is our broadcast number 7,065. I first came here on December 4, 1933. Thank you for being so loyal to us these 27 years... If you care to write to me, Ma Perkins, I'll try to answer you. Good-bye and may God bless you.

952. THE MCCOY. Crime Drama, 30 min., NBC, 1950–1951.

"I'm a criminal investigator. I'm hired to protect people. Sometimes I don't make it," says Mike McCoy, a private detective who lives in a cheap hotel room in Las Palmas and who rents a Hollywood office previously used by a Persian rug salesman. Stories follow Mike's step-by-step attempts to solve crimes. "I got a crummy license and I'm in a crummy business. People sneak up alleys, people hate, people rob, people strangle. But that's where my money comes from—from people who do all those things." *Other regular characters:* Judy, Mike's answering service girl at the Preston Call Service; Police Sgt. Koska of the L.A.P.D. Mike's favorite hangout is the Chez Maison on Sunset Strip.

Cast: Howard Duff (*Mike McCoy*); Joan Banks (*Judy*); Sheldon Leonard (*Sgt. Koska*). ***Music:*** Walter Schumann. ***Producers:*** Milton Fine, David Friedkin.

OPENING

MIKE: This is *The McCoy*.

ANNOUNCER: The National Broadcasting Company presents *The McCoy* starring Howard Duff.

MIKE (typing): For the file, Mike McCoy, Criminal Investigator. File Number 354, the twenty-second of April 1951, Los Angeles, California—where else? Case: "The Three Wayward Girls." [As Mike typed, the story would unfold.]

CLOSING

ANNOUNCER: *The McCoy* starring Howard Duff has been an NBC Hollywood Program Department presentation. Listen in again next week, same time, same station for Howard Duff as *The McCoy*. This is NBC, the National Broadcasting Company.

953. MCGARRY AND HIS MOUSE. Comedy, 30 min., NBC, 6/26/46 to 9/25/46; Mutual, 1/6/47 to 3/31/47.

Dan McGarry is a rookie detective with the New York City Police Department. Kitty Archer, who works in an airline office, is his girlfriend, whom he calls "Mouse." Wherever Dan goes, his "Mouse" goes—not only to share his company, but to watch out for him, as Dan has an uncanny knack for attracting trouble. Stories follow Dan and Kitty as they try to resolve the various situations they encounter (Kitty is the brains and always devises the means by which to exonerate themselves). Kitty's phone number is REgent 7-4599; her address was 37 Forstaff Avenue. Dan and Kitty's favorite eatery is Charlie's Tavern. *Other regular characters:* Inspector Matthew "Matt" McGarry, Dan's uncle (and supervisor at headquarters); Margaret Archer, Kitty's mother; Joe and Bernice, Kitty's friends.

Cast: Roger Pryor, Wendell Corey, Ted de Corsia (*Dan McGarry*); Shirley Mitchell, Peggy Conklin, Patsy Campbell (*Kitty Archer*); Betty Garde (*Margaret Archer*); Jerry Macy, Jack Hartley (*Matthew McGarry*); Carl Eastman (*Joe*); Thelma Ritter (*Bernice*). ***Announcer:*** Bert Parks. ***Music:*** Peter Van Steeden.

OPENING

VOICE: Calling all cars. Calling all cars. Has anybody seen Detective McGarry?

DAN: Yes, Sarge, I have.

SARGE: Who are you?

DAN: Detective McGarry.

ANNOUNCER: Yes, friends, it's *McGarry and His Mouse* starring Wendell Corey with Peggy Conklin. The misadventures of rookie detective McGarry have been made famous by Matt Taylor in the pages of *This Week* magazine. And now here he is, Dan McGarry himself. Handsome as ever, brave as ever, and confused as ever.

954. MAD MASTERS. Variety, 30 min., NBC, 7/12/47 to 8/31/47.

Monte Masters and his wife Natalie as the hosts of a program of music, songs and comedy skits. Helen Kleeb, Henry Leff and Paul Walter were the regulars and Tony Freeman and his orchestra provided the music.

955. MADELINE MASSEY AND THE CONCERT ORCHESTRA. Variety, 30 min., CBS, 1929.

Soprano Madeline Massey as the host of a program of music and songs featuring the CBS Concert Orchestra (conducted by Howard Barlow).

956. MAGGI'S PRIVATE WIRE. Women, 15 min., NBC, 7/10/44 to 6/20/47; ABC, 30 min., 6/23/47 to 4/1/49.

Maggi McNellis as the host of a program of celebrity interviews, human interest accounts, fashion news and gossip. Served as the basis for the 1948–52 television series of the same title.

THE MAGIC DETECTIVE *see* **BLACKSTONE, THE MAGIC DETECTIVE**

957. THE MAGIC KEY. Variety, 60 min., NBC Blue, 1935–1939.

A program of music and songs sponsored by RCA and featuring guest singers, musicians and orchestras. Milton Cross was the host; Ben Grauer did the announcing; John B. Kennedy handled the commentary; and Frank Black conducted the NBC Symphony Orchestra. Also known as *The Magic Key of R.C.A.*

958. MAGIC RHYTHM. Variety, 30 min., Mutual, 1948.

Betty Dorsey as the host of a weekly program of music and songs featuring the vocal group the Debonaires. Jack Block did the announcing.

959. THE MAGNIFICENT MONTAGUE. Comedy, 30 min., NBC, 1950–1951.

In 1926, theater critic Burton Smantle called *King Lear* star Edwin Montague "The Magnificent Montague." Montague is a brilliant Shakespearean actor. He believes he is the world's greatest actor. In the last eight years, he has refused to work in any play in which he did not have the starring role. In the last eight years, he has refused to be in any drama in which he could not rewrite and direct. In the last eight years, he hasn't worked. He believes there will be a return of that golden era of the New York stage and Shakespeare. Edwin is married to Lily Boheme, a former stage star, who takes it upon herself to get Edwin a job—as "Uncle Goodheart" on the radio.

Edwin believes "digging ditches is better than working on radio" (he believes that radio killed the stage) and is reluctant until he learns they need the money and that his identity will be kept secret (he fears that his fellow actors will find out and disassociate themselves from him). So, begrudgingly, Edwin begins work on the daily serial *Uncle Goodheart*. His efforts to adjust to radio (playing it like the theater stage and causing problems for all concerned) is the focal point of the stories. Also detailed are Lily's efforts to keep Edwin in radio despite his various efforts to get the show canceled (everything he does that is bad turns out good for the show).

Edwin is a member of the Proscenium Club (of retired actors). The soap opera *Aunt Agatha* is *Uncle Goodheart*'s competition. Edwin makes $200 a week and his show is sponsored by the Shalamar Soap Company (Uncle Goodheart is an all-around problem-solver who waits for the weary traveler in a vine-covered cottage). Edwin first met Lily when she was the star of *The Naughty Little Princess* (it was at this time that Edwin was known as "the worst scene stealer in America"). Lily is secretary to a local club called the Bird Watchers of America. Edwin's favorite breakfast is raw eggs with worcestershire sauce; kippered herring; two mutton chops (rare); and au gratin potatoes. Edwin awakens at eight each morning and proceeds to do his vocal exercises. Edwin believes he is "the foundation of America; the Sinatra of the Twenties." Agnes, their wisecracking maid, believes he is "the Great Windbag."

Cast: Monty Woolley (*Edwin Montague*); Anne Seymour (*Lily Montague*); Pert Kelton (*Agnes*). ***Announcer:*** Don Pardo. ***Music:*** Jack Ward.

OPENING

ANNOUNCER: *The Magnificent Montague* starring Monty Woolley as Edwin Montague. The Magnificent Montague, or, as he modestly puts it himself, the greatest living Shakespearean actor on the stage, is today a broken man. This paragon of the legitimate theater, this thespian rock who sneered at anything not connected with the theater; this man today is in radio, thanks to his wife Lily Boheme, his one-time leading lady. Montague, the King Lear, the Macbeth of yesteryear, is today *Uncle Goodheart*, hero of an afternoon radio serial.

CLOSING

ANNOUNCER: Tune in next week to find out what happens when the Magnificent Montague and radio meet head on. Remember next week, same time, same station, it's *The Magnificent Montague* starring Monty Woolley, created and written by Nat Hiken.

960. The Mahalia Jackson Show. Variety, 30 min., CBS, 1954.

Songstress Mahalia Jackson as the host of a program of music and songs. Hal Stark did the announcing and the Jack Halloran Quartet provided the music.

961. Main Street Music Hall. Variety, 15 min., CBS, 1949.

A weekly program of music and songs with hosts Russ Emery and Earl Wrightson. Nancy Evans was the featured vocalist and Alfredo Antonini and his orchestra provided the music.

Maisie *see* **The Adventures of Maisie**

962. The Majestic Radio Hour. Variety, 60 and 30 min. versions, CBS, 1927–1932.

A program of music, songs and comedy sponsored by Majestic Radios. Charles Mack and George Moran, billed as "The Two Black Crows," were the hosts; vocalists Ruth Etting and Arthur Croft were regulars; and music was provided by the Majestic Orchestra. Also known as *The Majestic Hour* and *The Majestic Theater of the Air*.

963. Major Bowes and the Original Amateur Hour. Variety, 60 min., NBC, 1935–1936; CBS, 1936–1946.

Promising but undiscovered amateur talent received the opportunity to perform. About 20 hopefuls appeared on each broadcast and received $10 for performing. See also *The Original Amateur Hour* for the ABC version (1948–1952) and the following title.

Host: Major Edward Bowes. ***Announcers:*** Norman Brokenshire, Ralph Edwards, Don Hancock, Graham McNamee, Tony Marvin, Dan Seymour, Warren Sweeney, Jimmy Wallington. ***Music:*** Lloyd Marx.

Note: The program began on local New York radio station WHN in 1934 and moved to NBC in 1935. Jay C. Flippen hosted the local version while Major Bowes did the network broadcast.

OPENING

ANNOUNCER: Chase and Sanborn presents *Major Bowes and the Original Amateur Hour.*

MAJOR: Good evening, friends, welcome to our weekly wheel of fortune. Around and around she goes, where she stops, nobody knows.

964. Major Bowes' Shower of Stars. Variety, 30 min., CBS, 1945–1946.

An extension series based on the prior title that continues to showcase talented amateurs as well as return performances by *Amateur Hour* winners who found success as a result of their appearance on the earlier show.

Host: Major Edward Bowes. ***Regulars:*** Larry Elliott, Regina Resnick. ***Orchestra:*** Morton Gould.

965. Major Hoople. Comedy, 30 min., NBC Blue, 6/22/42 to 4/26/43.

Major Amos Hoople and his wife Martha run the Hoople Boarding House. Amos is a military man and claims to be a descendant of British aristocracy. He considers himself a philosopher and takes credit for winning just about every other battle that was ever won by the British. Martha, patient and understanding, puts up with his fibs, and boarder Tiffany Twiggs keeps him in check. Stories, which are based on the comic strip *Our Boarding House* by Gene Ahern, relate the comic situations that occur as the Hooples struggle to run their establishment. *Other regular characters:* Alvin Hoople, Amos's nephew.

Cast: Arthur Q. Bryan (*Major Amos Hoople*); Patsy Moran (*Martha Hoople*); Mel Blanc (*Tiffany Twiggs*); Franklin Bresee (*Alvin Hoople*). ***Music:*** Lou Bring, Walter Greene.

OPENING

ANNOUNCER: He's not a sergeant, he's not a lieutenant; he's not a captain; he's a major. Yes, ladies and gentlemen, it's *Major Hoople.*

From out of the comic strip and into your homes we bring you that overstuffed philosopher Major Amos Hoople, his ever-loving but not-too-trusting wife Martha, his precocious nephew Little Alvin and his star boarder and number one complainer, Tiffany Twiggs.

CLOSING

ANNOUNCER: *Major Hoople* comes to you each week at this time over most of these same stations. This program comes to you from Hollywood. This is the Blue Network.

966. MAJOR NORTH, ARMY INTELLIGENCE. Drama, 30 min., ABC, 1945–1946.

A World War II action series about Major Hugh North, a U.S. Army intelligence agent battling Nazi-fascist plots against international security. Also known as *The Man from G-2*.

Cast: Staats Cotsworth (*Major Hugh North*); Joan Alexander (*His assistant*). ***Music:*** Bernard Green.

967. MAKE BELIEVE TOWN. Anthology, 30 min., CBS, 1949–1950.

Dramatizations set against the background of Hollywood. Virginia Bruce was the host and Johnny Jacobs did the announcing.

968. MAKE MINE MUSIC. Variety, 30 min., CBS, 1948.

A weekly program of music and songs with vocalists Connie Russell and Bill Leach. Caesar Petrillo and his orchestra provided the music.

969. THE MALCOLM LAPRODE SHOW. Variety, 15 min., NBC, 1924.

An early program of music and songs with singer Malcolm LaProde as the host. Organist Lew White provided the music.

970. MAN ABOUT HOLLYWOOD. Variety, 30 min., CBS, 1939.

A weekly program of music, talk and celebrity interviews. George McCall was the host; Maxine Beach, Sara Berner, Willie Desmond, Linda Ware and Steve White were the regulars; and Wilbur Hatch and his orchestra provided the music.

971. MAN AGAINST CRIME. Crime Drama, 30 min., CBS, 1949–1951.

Mike Barnett is a tough private detective based in New York City. He doesn't believe a gun is necessary and takes an unarmed approach to dealing with criminals. Stories follow Mike's exploits as he becomes involved with a wide variety of characters while attempting to help his clients. Premiered on both radio and television on 10/7/49 with the video version running until 1956.

Cast: Ralph Bellamy (Mike Barnett). ***Producers:*** Edward J. Montagne, Paul Nickell.

Note: Robert Preston replaced Ralph Bellamy as Mike for three months in 1951. When the radio series ended, Bellamy, who also played the role on television, was replaced by Frank Lovejoy for the remainder of the video run.

972. THE MAN BEHIND THE GUN. Anthology, 30 min., CBS, 1942–1944.

Dramatizations based on the actual experiences of servicemen in the various branches of the U.S. Armed Forces.

Narrator: Jackson Beck. ***Music:*** Nathan Van Cleave. ***Producer:*** William N. Robson.

OPENING

ANNOUNCER: Tonight the Man Behind the Gun is a woman. The Columbia Broadcasting System presents *The Man Behind the Gun*, dedicated to the fighting men and women of the United States and the United Nations and broadcast in the hope that these authentic accounts of men and women at war will bring you a better understanding of the job being done by our fighting forces everywhere in the world and the job we have to do to keep them fighting.

NARRATOR: This is something for the girls. This story is for the girls who swoon at the sight of blood as readily as they swoon at the sight of a crooner. This is for the girls to whom war's greatest tragedy is no nylons. This is for those American girls not yet in uniform, blue jeans, khaki or war worker slacks. This is "Something for the Girls."

CLOSING

NARRATOR: Well, girls, how about it? The invasion is being prepared. When it comes, and it will be soon, the action you just heard will be multiplied a thousandfold. To be ready for this vast task of healing, which will follow the break in the walls of the fortress of Europe, the Army Medical Corps needs nurses; it needs 2,000 nurses a month. Registered Nurses are urgently requested to apply for commission to the Surgeon General of the United States Army at Washington, D.C., or the Red Cross chapter in your city. This is indeed a matter of life and death. Women without previous nurse's training are wanted as volunteer nurses' aides to fill in the gaps this war has made on nursing facilities here at home. Your local Red Cross will tell you how you can serve at home and help release a registered nurse for duty at the front.

ANNOUNCER: All the incidents broadcast were based on fact; the names used, however, are fictitious and any similarity to actual individuals in our armed forces is purely coincidental. Tune in again next week at this same time when *The Man Behind the Gun* brings you another report of history in the making. And remember, you'll listen with clearer conscience if you've already bought that extra war bond. *The Man Behind the Gun* is a Robson Production. This is CBS, the Columbia Broadcasting System.

973. THE MAN CALLED X. Adventure, 30 min., CBS, 7/10/44 to 8/28/44; NBC Blue/ ABC, 9/9/44 to 3/3/45; NBC, 6/12/45 to 9/4/ 45; NBC, 6/18/46 to 9/17/46; CBS, 4/3/47 to 9/26/48; NBC, 10/13/50 to 5/20/52.

Ken Thurston is an American Intelligence Agent who operates under the code name "X." He is "the man who crosses the ocean as readily as you and I cross town. He is the man who fights today's war in his unique fashion so that tomorrow's peace will make the world a safe neighborhood for all of us." His partner, Pagan Zeldschmidt, has a streak of larceny but always manages to stay on the right side of the law no matter how badly he is tempted. Stories follow their exploits as they battle evil throughout the world.

Cast: Herbert Marshall (*Ken Thurston*); Leon Belasco (*Pagan Zeldschmidt*). ***Announcers:*** Jack Latham, Wendell Niles. ***Music:*** Milton Charles, Johnny Green, Felix Mills.

OPENING (from 10/1/51)

ANNOUNCER: Listen to Herbert Marshall as *The Man Called X.* Wherever there is mystery, intrigue, romance in all the strange, dangerous places of the world, there you will find *The Man Called X.*

CLOSING

ANNOUNCER: Now here is our star, Herbert Marshall.

MARSHALL: Join us, won't you, when next I return as *The Man Called X.* Good night.

ANNOUNCER: *The Man Called X* starring Herbert Marshall is a J. Richard Kennedy production. All characters and incidents in this program are fictitious and any resemblance of incidents is purely coincidental. So until next week, please consult your local papers for time and station. This is Jack Latham saying good night for *The Man Called X.*

THE MAN FROM G-2 *see* **MAJOR NORTH, ARMY INTELLIGENCE**

974. THE MAN I MARRIED. Serial, 15 min., NBC, 1939–1941; CBS, 1941–1942.

Dramatic incidents in the life of Adam Waring, the disinherited son of a millionaire, and his wife Evelyn as they struggle to make a life for themselves in a small town.

Cast: Vicki Vola, Gertrude Warner, Lesley Woods, Betty Winkler, Barbara Lee (*Evelyn Waring*); Van Heflin, Clayton "Bud" Collyer (*Adam Waring*); Santos Ortega (*Phineas Grant*); Frances Carden (*Ella Hunt*); Spencer Bentley (*Shelly*); Jack Grimes (*Ted Hunt*); Arnold Moss (*Frank*); Betty Worth (*Florence*); Raymond Edward Johnson (*Edward Spaulding*). ***Announcers:*** Del Sharbutt, Howard Petrie. ***Music:*** Don Becker. ***Producers:*** Anne Hummert, Frank Hummert.

975. A MAN NAMED JORDAN. Adventure, 15 min., CBS, 1945–1947.

Rocky Jordan is the proprietor of the Cafe Tambourine in Cairo, Egypt. He is tough but has a soft spot for a beautiful damsel in distress. Stories relate his efforts to help people in trouble. See also *Rocky Jordan.*

Cast: Jack Moyles (*Rocky Jordan*). ***Music:*** Milton Charles. ***Producer:*** Cliff Powell.

OPENING

ANNOUNCER: Again we bring you a story of adventure with *A Man Named Jordan*, proprietor of the Cafe Tambourine in Cairo.

976. THE MAN OF MAGIC. Variety, 30 min., Mutual, 1944.

Demonstrations on the art of mind reading with master mentalist Felix Greenfield. Wendy Barrie was his assistant and the program was sponsored by Eichler's Beer.

977. Mandrake the Magician. Adventure, 15 min., Mutual, 1940–1942.

In a mysterious Tibetan valley where the ancient secrets of Egypt and the magic of China have been preserved over the centuries, a young boy (Mandrake) is taught the secrets by Theron, the Master of Magic. Ten years later, Mandrake becomes greater than his master. Upon his release from the College of Magic, he teams with his servant Lothar, and together they set out to battle evil. Stories relate their efforts to help people in trouble. Based on the comic strip by Lee Falk and Phil Davis. *Other regular character:* Narda, the beautiful princess who assists them.

Cast: Raymond Edward Johnson (*Mandrake*); Juano Hernandez (*Lothar*); Francesca Lenni (*Princess Narda*). ***Producer:*** Henry Souvaine.

978. Manhattan Merry-Go-Round. Variety, 30 min., NBC, 1933–1949.

Music and songs from imaginary nightclubs in New York City. Each week a different club was chosen to present guest singers and a cast of regulars performing the top songs of the day (based on record and sheet music sales) and "sung so clearly you can understand every word."

Host-Announcers: Ford Bond, Roger Krupp. ***Regulars:*** Rachel Carley, Glenn Cross, Marian McManus, Lucy Marlowe, Dick O'Connor, Dennis Ryan, Conrad Thibault, Thomas L. Thomas, the Jerry Mann Singers, the Men About Town. ***Orchestra:*** Victor Arden, Andy Sanella. ***Producer:*** Frank Hummert.

OPENING

Song: Jump on the Manhattan Merry-Go-Round, we're touring alluring old New York town ... we're serving music, fun and laughter ... and we'd like to have you all with us on the Manhattan Merry-Go-Round.

Announcer: Here's the *Manhattan Merry-Go-Round* that brings you the bright side of life, that whirls you in the music to all the big night spots of New York town to hear the top songs of the week sung so clearly that you can understand every word and sing them yourself.

979. Manhattan Mother. Serial, 15 min., CBS, 1939–1940.

Patricia and Tony Locke are a married couple whose happiness ends suddenly when Tony estranges himself from her and her daughter to make a career for himself in New York City. Stories relate events in their lives as Patricia struggles to make her life complete again.

Cast: Margaret Hillias, Kay Brinker (*Patricia Locke*); Dan Sutter (*Tony Locke*); Louise Fitch (*Their daughter*).

OPENING

Announcer: Cities are made of steel and stone, but human hearts are of a different stuff. We give you *Manhattan Mother*.

980. Manhunt. Crime Drama, 15 min., Syndicated, 1945.

Bill Morton is a detective with the Homicide Department. He is high-strung, easily excitable and is anxious to solve crimes as fast as possible. Drew Stevens is a police lab scientist who is eager to investigate crimes and accompanies Bill on cases. He is laid back, patient and feels it is necessary to take time and examine every aspect of a case. When a baffling crime occurs (for example, a man shot in a locked room), Bill and Drew are on the case. Stories follow their joint efforts to solve the crime—Bill through his questioning, Drew through science. Pat, Drew's secretary and love interest, assists Bill—much to Drew's dissatisfaction (he fears she will get hurt).

Cast: Maurice Tarplin (*Bill Morton*); Larry Haines (*Drew Stevens*); Vicki Vola (*Pat*).

OPENING

Announcer: *Manhunt*. "The Story of the Strange Strangler" whose deadly work led to *Manhunt* [clash of cymbals is heard]. No crime has been committed—yet. No murder has been done—yet. No manhunt has begun—yet.

Effect: A crime is then heard [for the above story, that of a girl being strangled].

Announcer: Very clever murderer. No gun that can be traced, no knife; just your two hands. And no fingerprints either, you've seen to that. Who will know where or how to look for you? Who will start the *Manhunt* [clash of cymbals]. *Manhunt* and "The Case of the Strange Strangler" begins [clash of cymbals].

981. The March of Games. Game, 30 min., CBS, 1939.

The program was designed to test knowledge and involved five children as contestants. Each competed in a series of question-and-answer rounds. The highest scoring child received $5; the second place winner won $3.

Host: Arthur Ross. ***Assistant:*** Sybil Trent. ***Producer:*** Nila Mack.

982. THE MARCH OF TIME. Documentary, 30 min., CBS, 1931–1937; NBC Blue, 1937–1942; NBC Red, 1943–1944; ABC, 1944–1945.

The program, sponsored by *Time* magazine, presented dramatizations of news events and interviews with news-making people. The series, also known as *The March of Time Through the Years*, sounded like a Movietone newsreel and painted a vivid picture of the current events of the day (for example, the rise of Hitler, the kidnapping of the Lindbergh baby). Over 300 reporters were on call for the radio editors (who could rewrite the script for fast-breaking stories).

Host-Narrators: Ted Husing, Harry Von Zell, Westbrook Van Voorhis. ***Recurring Cast:*** Ed Jerome (as Josef Stalin); Ted de Corsia (as Benito Mussolini); Bill Adams, Art Carney, Staats Cotsworth (as Franklin D. Roosevelt); Agnes Moorehead, Nancy Kelly, Jeanette Nolan (as Eleanor Roosevelt); Maurice Tarplin (as Winston Churchill). ***Music:*** Howard Barlow, Donald Voorhees. ***Producers:*** Arthur Pryor, Jr., Tom Harrington.

OPENING

ANNOUNCER: *The March of Time*! *Time*, the weekly news magazine, takes you to the warfront and the homefront bringing you news in the making, people who make the news and the men and women of *Time* magazine who report the news.

HOST: This is Westbrook Van Voorhis speaking for the editors of *Time* magazine. Tonight...

983. THE MARGARET DAUM PROGRAM. Variety, 30 min., CBS, 1937–1938.

A weekly program of music and songs with Metropolitan soprano Margaret Daum and the music of the CBS Concert Orchestra conducted by Howard Barlow.

984. MARIE, THE LITTLE FRENCH PRINCESS. Serial, 15 min., CBS, 1933–1935.

CBS radio's first daytime serial: the dramatic story of Marie, a princess from a mythical country who fled to the United States to find love and happiness as an ordinary American girl.

Cast: Ruth Yorke (*Marie*); James Meighan (*Richard*). ***Announcer:*** Andre Baruch. ***Producers:*** Anne Hummert, Frank Hummert.

985. THE MARIO LANZA SHOW. Variety, 30 min., NBC, 1951–1952.

A weekly program of music and songs with tenor Mario Lanza as the host. Giselle MacKenzie was the featured vocalist and Bill Baldwin did the announcing. Ray Sinatra and his orchestra provided the music.

MARK SABRE *see* **INSPECTOR MARK SABRE**

986. MARK TRAIL. Adventure, 30 min., Mutual, 1950–1951; ABC, 1951–1953.

Mark Trail is an outdoorsman and conservationist who is dedicated to protecting nature from the evils of man. He lives in the Lost Forest and has a St. Bernard named Andy. Stories follow Mark's exploits as he and his young friends Scotty and Cherry risk their lives to battle the enemies of the wilderness. The program, based on the comic strip by Ed Dodd, stressed the importance of protecting forests and wildlife.

Cast: Matt Crowley, John Larkin, Staats Cotsworth (*Mark Trail*); Ben Cooper, Ronald Liss (*Scotty*); Joyce Gordon, Amy Sidell (*Cherry*). ***Announcers:*** Jackson Beck, Glenn Riggs. ***Music:*** John Gart.

OPENING

ANNOUNCER: For more punch till lunch, it's Kellogg's Corn Flakes, and for more thrilling adventures in the great outdoors, it's *Mark Trail*. Battling the raging elements, fighting the savage wilderness, striking at the enemies of man and nature, one man's name resounds from snow-capped mountains down across the sun-baked plains—Mark Trail.

987. THE MARK WARNOW SHOW. Variety, 45 min., CBS, 1939.

Music and songs with orchestra leader Mark Warnow as the host. The program was sponsored by Lucky Strike cigarettes and featured Lanny Ross and the Raymond Scott Quintet. Andre Baruch was the announcer and Speed

Riggs did the commercial spots. Mark Warnow's orchestra provided the music.

988. THE MARLIN HURT AND BEULAH SHOW. Comedy, 30 min., CBS, 1945–1946.

A spinoff from *Fibber McGee and Molly* that placed their black maid Beulah in the household of Marlin Hurt, a busy businessman who lived with his Aunt Alice. Beulah, played by a white man, was easily excitable and meddling, and her efforts to resolve domestic crises were the focal point of stories. *Other regular character:* Bill Jackson, Beulah's boyfriend. See also *Beulah* for the revamped version of this series.

Cast: Marlin Hurt (*Beulah/Marlin Hurt/Bill Jackson*); Kathryn Carnes (*Aunt Alice*). ***Announcer:*** Ken Niles. ***Vocalists:*** Penny Piper, Carol Stewart, Eileen Wilson. ***Music:*** Albert Stack. ***Producer:*** Helen Mack.

OPENING

ANNOUNCER: Tums, famous quick relief for acid indigestion, presents *The Marlin Hurt and Beulah Show* with lovely Carol Stewart, the music of Albert Stack and his orchestra and starring Marlin Hurt and—

BEULAH (singing): Got the world in a jug, Lord, got the stopper in my hand.

ANNOUNCER: Yes, sir, it's Beulah. Every week at this time, the makers of Tums present *The Marlin Hurt and Beulah Show* written by Phil Leslie.

CLOSING

ANNOUNCER: Don't forget to be with us again next week at this same time for another half-hour with Marlin Hurt and Beulah, produced and directed by Helen Mack. And this is Ken Niles reminding you night and day, at home or away, always carry Tums. T-u-m-s. This is CBS, the Columbia Broadcasting System.

989. THE MARRIAGE. Comedy, 30 min., NBC, 10/4/53 to 3/28/54.

Domestic incidents in the lives of the Marriot family: Ben, his wife Liz and their children Emily and Pete. Ben is a lawyer and worries about bills (especially how much money his family spends on electricity); Liz is the devoted, problem-solving housewife. Emily, a pretty 15-year-old girl, is just starting to date—which worries Ben, who feels she is not ready for such endeavors. Liz contends that she can handle it because "girls are older than boys at the same age." Pete is an adolescent who is curious and somewhat mischievous and likes to build model cars. Each episode begins with Liz recalling an event from her family's past; through flashbacks, the incident is presented for the listener with Liz narrating. The Marriots live in an apartment in New York City, bank at the Center Trust Company and shop at Hunt's Department Store. Served as the basis for the television series of the same title.

Cast: Hume Cronyn (*Ben Marriot*); Jessica Tandy (*Liz Marriot*); Denise Alexander (*Emily Marriot*); David Pfeffer (*Pete Marriot*). ***Announcer:*** Bob Denton.

OPENING

ANNOUNCER: Jessica Tandy and Hume Cronyn in *The Marriage*. With a conviction that marriage remains the most popular domestic arrangement between friendly people, NBC takes pleasure in presenting one of the most distinguished couples in the American theater, Jessica Tandy and Hume Cronyn, transcribed, as Liz and Ben Marriot in the love and laughter of *The Marriage*.

CLOSING

ANNOUNCER: Ben and Liz Marriot will be back in a moment. In the meantime, let us extend this invitation to all of you to drop by next week at this time for another half-hour observation of *The Marriage*, written by Ernest Kinoy. *The Marriage* is an NBC Radio Network production directed by Edward King. This program came to you from our Radio City Studios in New York. Let a kitchen radio fill your day with the wonderful music on the NBC Radio Network.

990. MARRIAGE CLUB, INC. Interview, 30 min., NBC, 1939–1940; CBS, 1940–1941.

The format called for married couples to discuss their domestic problems in return for merchandise prizes. Haven MacQuarrie served as the host and Nelson Case did the announcing.

991. MARRIAGE FOR TWO. Serial, 15 min., NBC, 1949–1950; ABC, 1951–1952.

A daily drama about Vikki Adams, a romantic but level-headed young woman who marries Roger Hoyt, an affectionate but irresponsible young man, and their efforts to make their marriage work despite the difficulties that arise through Roger's foolishness.

Cast: Fran Lafferty (*Vikki Adams*), Staats Cotsworth (*Roger Hoyt*); Evelyn Varden (*Vikki's mother*). ***Also:*** Marian Barney, Gertrude Warner. ***Announcer:*** John Tillman. ***Music:*** Fred Feibel.

992. MARRIED FOR LIFE. Human Interest, 30 min., Mutual, 1946.

Couples who were about to wed were interviewed. A short dramatization followed, relating how the couple met and fell in love. Following this, the couple was again interviewed, along with friends and relatives. Merchandise prizes were awarded to the participants.

Host: Bill Slater. ***Cast:*** Bryna Raeburn, Eleanor Shernon, Johnny Sylvester, Lawson Zerbe. ***Announcer:*** Don Fredericks.

MARTHA WEBSTER *see* **LIFE BEGINS**

993. THE MARTIN AND LEWIS SHOW. Variety, 30 min., NBC, 1949–1952.

A weekly program of music, songs and comedy skits involving the handsome "straight man" (Dean Martin) in wacky situations created by his not-too-bright foil (Jerry Lewis).

Hosts: Dean Martin and Jerry Lewis. ***Regulars:*** Florence MacMichael, the Skylarks. ***Announcers:*** Ben Alexander, Ed Herlihy, Johnny Jacobs, Jimmy Wallington. ***Orchestra:*** Dick Stabile.

OPENING

ANNOUNCER: It's *The Martin and Lewis Show.* The National Broadcasting Company brings you transcribed from New York *The Martin and Lewis Show.* Our guest tonight, John Garfield, and featuring Florence MacMichael, Dick Stabile and his orchestra and starring Dean Martin and Jerry Lewis.

994. MARTIN KANE, PRIVATE EYE. Crime Drama, 30 min., Mutual, 1949–1951; NBC, 1951–1952.

Martin Kane is a rugged private detective who uses determination and force of character to achieve results. He is based in New York City (he has offices in the Wood Building in Manhattan) and goes where the work is. He also charges a fee that he believes is appropriate to the case at hand (as much as $500). Stories relate his exploits as he goes about dispensing his own brand of justice. *Other regular characters:* Tucker "Hap" McMann, Kane's

Dean Martin (left) and Jerry Lewis hosted *The Martin and Lewis Show.*

friend, the owner of McMann's Tobacco Shop (Kane's favorite hangout); Police Sgt. Ross; Captain Burke. Served as the basis for the television series of the same title.

Cast: William Gargan, Lloyd Nolan (*Martin Kane*); Walter Kinsella (*Tucker "Hap" McMann*); Nicholas Saunders (*Sgt. Ross*); Frank M. Thomas (*Capt. Burke*). ***Announcer:*** Fred Uttal. **Music:** *Charles Paul.* **Producer:** *Edward L. Kahan.*

995. MARVIN MILLER, STORYTELLER. Anthology, 5 min., Syndicated, 1948–1949; CBS, 1957–1958.

Capsule dramatizations of famous people who faced a crisis in their lives. Marvin Miller provided voices for all characters and also served as the host and narrator.

996. THE MARX BROTHERS SHOW. Comedy, 30 min., CBS, 1937–1938.

The Square Deal Amusement Company is a theatrical agency in Hollywood. Groucho Marx and his brother Chico are its owners—"representatives of talent of the screen; sellers of sensational stars." "It's also the headquarters for slot machines, pinball games, turkey raffles and marked cards," says Groucho. Groucho and Chico claim, "We're Hollywood agents, we get people jobs in pictures. We get ten percent of their salaries." And what do their clients get? "Nothing" says Groucho, "we're agents." (They are so bad that even Chico couldn't get himself a job. He tried for a role in a film called *The Human Race* and was told, [You're] not the type"). They have a fine office but Groucho contends, "With the type of people we're getting in here, our main entrance must be in an alley." Stories, which are basically an exchange of conversation between Groucho and Chico, relate their efforts to find clients and how they deal with the strange people who come in off the street seeking to become stars.

Cast: Groucho Marx (*Groucho Marx*); Chico Marx (*Chico Marx*). ***Vocalist:*** Hollis Shore. ***Orchestra:*** Raymond Paige.

OPENING

ANNOUNCER: From Hollywood, California, the Hotchkins Packing Company presents *The Marx Brothers Show*.

GROUCHO: Good evening, ladies and gentlemen. This is Groucho Marx speaking and already it's not such a good evening. Tonight, Chico and myself, with the help of that grand musical director, Raymond Paige, bring you a slice of life in that crazy world they call Hollywood. As we drop into your home every Friday night, we're going to try to show you the unsung heroes of the motion picture business—the Hollywood agents.

CLOSING

GROUCHO: Ladies and gentlemen, this is Groucho Marx hoping that you liked the program... And so, my friends, for Raymond Paige and myself, I say good night. Say good night, Chico.

CHICO: Good night, Chico.

GROUCHO: Remember that the Hotchkins Packing Company will not be responsible for any comedians left over 30 days.

ANNOUNCER: This is the Columbia Broadcasting System.

997. MARY AND BOB'S TRUE STORIES. Anthology, 30 min., CBS, 1928–1932; NBC Red, 1932; NBC Blue, 1938–1939.

Light dramas adapted from *True Story* magazine with Mary and Bob as the hosts and frequent stars (backed by weekly guests).

Cast: Nora Stirling, Elizabeth Wragge (*Mary*); William Brenton, Cecil Secrest, David Ross, Eddie Wragge (*Bob*). ***Announcers:*** Paul Douglas, Ted Husing. ***Music:*** Howard Barlow.

998. MARY FOSTER, THE EDITOR'S DAUGHTER. Serial, 15 min., Mutual, 1941–1948.

Dramatic events in the life of Mary Foster, a reporter for the *Sentinel*, a small town newspaper owned by her father, Henry Foster. Also known as *The Editor's Daughter*.

Cast: Joan Banks (*Mary Foster*); Parker Fennelly (*Henry Foster*); Effie Palmer (*Amelia*); Harry Elders (*Dan Hanson*); Hugh Studebaker (*Bill Nelson*).

OPENING (from 11/1/48)

ANNOUNCER: Kroger, the store that gives you better value, better baked foods, presents *Mary Foster, the Editor's Daughter*, transcribed.

SONG: Kroger's, Kroger's, everything from bread to cake is better if it's Kroger-baked. Money-saving value too, Kroger is the store for you, Kroger's, Kroger's.

ANNOUNCER: Yes, friends, Kroger's is famous for fine baked foods, better baked foods. You'll agree when you taste Kroger bread... yes, lady, if you want a bread that's velvet smooth, that stays fresh longer, then you want Kroger bread. Try it. Enjoy the best bread Kroger ever made... And now, *Mary Foster, the Editor's Daughter*. As we visit the Fosters today, we find Mary and her father with Dr. Bill Nelson after dinner...

CLOSING

ANNOUNCER: Is Henry right? Is it that Boothby House is burning? We'll hear more about this on Monday. And now, in just a moment, Henry Foster will return with another of his shrewd comments. But first... you'll find the value of the week at your Kroger store, and this week it's Kroger Pineapple Fudge Golden Layer Cake, another oven pleasure from the famous Kroger bakery... It's the cake of the week, the value of the week for only 59 cents. And now, Henry Foster.

HENRY: Well, sir, I've been reading where a professor said that man was just as intelligent 10,000 years ago as he is today. I'm kind of wondering how much of a tribute that is for our prehistoric ancestors. Well, see you soon.

ANNOUNCER: Tune in again Monday at this same time for another dramatic, transcribed chapter of *Mary Foster, the Editor's Daughter*.

999. The Mary Mercer Show. Variety, 5 min., CBS, 1943.

A filler program of songs with vocalist Mary Mercer as the host and featuring the music of Charles Paul and his orchestra.

Master Radio Canaries *see* **The Canary Pet Show**

1000. Matinee at Meadowbrook. Variety, 60 min., CBS, 1941.

A weekly program of music and songs with John Tillman as the host. Chris Adams, Art Carney, Frank Dailey, Bernie Gould, Kay Little, Helen Lewis, Teddy Norman, Jerry Wayne and Jackson Wheeler were the regulars. The Bobby Byrne and Ray McKinley orchestras provided the music.

1001. Matinee in Rhythm. Variety, 15 min., NBC, 1939.

Music and songs with vocalist Ruth Norcross as the host. Vera Holly, Tiny Schwartz and the Men of Note were the regulars. Ed Reimers did the announcing, and Bob Armstrong and his orchestra provided the music.

Matinee with Bob and Ray *see* **The Bob and Ray Show**

1002. Maude and Cousin Bill. Comedy, 15 min., NBC Blue, 1932–1933.

An exchange of comedy dialogue between a young woman named Maude (played by Maude Ricketts) and her Uncle Bill (Bill Ricketts).

1003. Maudie's Diary. Comedy, 30 min., CBS, 8/14/41 to 9/24/42.

Events in the life of Maudie Mason, a fun-loving teenage girl who records the day's activities in her diary (hence the title). *Other regular characters:* Davey Dillon, Maudie's boyfriend; Pauley, Maudie's girlfriend; Sylvia Mason, Maudie's sister; Maudie's parents.

Cast: Mary Mason, Charita Bauer, Carol Smith (*Maudie Mason*); William Johnstone (*Maudie's father*); Betty Garde (*Maudie's mother*); Marjorie Davis (*Sylvia Mason*); Robert Walker (*Davey Dillon*); Carol Smith (*Pauley*). ***Announcer:*** W. Arthur Millet. ***Music:*** Elliott Jacoby.

Maverick Jim *see* **Appendix**

Maxwell House Coffee Time *see* **The George Burns and Gracie Allen Show**

1004. Maxwell House Coffee Time. Variety, 30 min., NBC, 1940–1944.

A program of music and songs coupled with the comedy of Frank Morgan and the antics of Baby Snooks and her Daddy. Sponsored by Maxwell House Coffee. See also *The George Burns and Gracie Allen Show*.

Host: John Conte. ***Cast:*** Frank Morgan (*Himself*); Fanny Brice (*Baby Snooks*); Hanley Stafford (*Daddy*); Arlene Harris (*Mommy*); Leone Ledoux (*Robespierre, Snooks' brother*). ***Announcer:*** John Conte. ***Music:*** Meredith Willson.

Maxwell House Showboat *see* **Showboat**

1005. Mayor of the Town. Comedy, 30 min., NBC, 1941–1942; CBS, 1942–1947; ABC, 1947–1948; Mutual, 1949.

The old-fashioned house on Elm Street in Springdale is the residence of the mayor, his ward Roscoe Gardner (nicknamed Butch) and their housekeeper, the talkative, advice-giving Marilly. Stories are simple in nature, focusing on the situations that try the mayor's patience and his efforts to solve them through his warm and understanding philosophy. The mayor enjoys sitting in his easy chair by the fireplace reading the town newspaper, the *Morning Chronicle*. Butch is a mischievous youngster whom Marilly says "can do more damage doing nothing than 20 people doing something." Their pet cat is named Sweet Alice and they have two goldfish named Mr. and Mrs. Weissmuller. Capitol City is 60 miles away and is the nearest major metropolis to Springdale.

Cast: Lionel Barrymore (*The mayor*); Agnes Moorehead (*Marilly*); Conrad Binyon (*Roscoe "Butch" Gardner*). ***Announcers:*** Frank Martin, Carlton KaDell, Harlow Wilcox. ***Commercial Spokeswoman*** (for Rinso): Veola Vonn. ***Music:*** Bernard Katz, Frank Worth.

OPENING

ANNOUNCER: Noxcema presents *Mayor of the*

Town starring Lionel Barrymore with Agnes Moorehead as Marilly and Conrad Binyon as Butch. And now *Mayor of the Town* starring Lionel Barrymore.

CLOSING

ANNOUNCER: Be sure to be with us next week at this same time when the makers of Noxcema present the *Mayor of the Town* in a chapter called "I Dreamt I Dwelt in a Marble House." The original *Mayor of the Town* theme was composed by Mr. Barrymore. Mr. Barrymore appeared by arrangement with Metro-Goldwyn-Mayer. And now this is Frank Martin wishing you all a very pleasant good night from Noxcema. This was transcribed. This is ABC, the American Broadcasting Company.

1006. ME AND JANIE. Comedy, 30 min., NBC, 7/12/49 to 10/4/49.

Events in the day-to-day lives of the O'Hanlons—George, his wife Janie and their son Tommy. George is employed by Mr. Lamb (of the Lamb Paper Box Company) and has a habit of always being late for work. George is simply a nice guy who gets the short end of the stick. He is always helping others and always manages to foul things up. But George is persistent and vows to set things right—"Your troubles are over, George O'Hanlon is on the job"—and through much fumbling, situations always work out for the best. The O'Hanlons have a dog named Midnight; Mr. Lamb's dog Tweetlers is nearsighted and wears glasses.

Cast: George O'Hanlon (*George O'Hanlon*); Lurene Tuttle (*Janie O'Hanlon*); Jeffrey Silver (*Tommy O'Hanlon*); Willard Waterman (*Mr. Lamb*). ***Announcer:*** Don Wilson. ***Music:*** Johnny Duffy.

OPENING

ANNOUNCER: Yes, friends, it's the Tums show, *Me and Janie*, starring George O'Hanlon, the guy next door who is always trying to get under the eight ball. And this is Don Wilson, ladies and gentlemen, to tell you that if your favorite foods ... give you heartburn or acid indigestion ... it's Tums for the tummy. Only ten cents a roll ... at all drug stores. And now, *Me and Janie*, another adventure in the lives of George and Janie O'Hanlon.

1007. MEET CORLISS ARCHER. Comedy, 30 min., CBS, 1943–1952; ABC, 1952–1953; CBS, 1954–1956.

Sixteen-year-old Corliss Archer, the daughter of Harry and Janet Archer, lives at 32 Oak Street in a small American town. Corliss is a pretty high school sophomore with a penchant for getting herself into trouble. She has a weekly allowance of one dollar ("Gee, I wish I could get my father to increase my allowance. A dollar doesn't go far these days") and a steady boyfriend named Dexter Franklin—who also complains about his dollar-a-week allowance ("I have an allowance that rattles. I wish I had one that rustles"). Dexter is the innocent victim of Corliss's endless efforts to improve him (she feels he needs to be more mature). Her efforts often backfire. "Golly," she says, "how do I manage to mess things up?" Her father sums it all up: "I'll admit it takes talent," and he often remedies the situation at the end of the episode. Harry is a private practice attorney and has been married to Janet for 18 years. "Janet," he says, "is a remarkable woman. She is not only attractive and intelligent, but she is also a wonderful housekeeper and an extremely talented cook." *Other regular characters:* Mildred, Corliss's girlfriend. Corliss has a dog named Merocia; the after-school hangout is Schroeder's Drug Store. Served as the basis for the television series of the same title.

Cast: Janet Waldo, Priscilla Lyon, Lugene Sanders (*Corliss Archer*); Fred Shields, Frank Martin, Bob Bailey (*Harry Archer*); Irene Tedrow, Mary Jane Croft, Helen Mack (*Janet Archer*); Sam Edwards, David Hughes, Irving Lee, Bill Christy (*Dexter Franklin*); Barbara Whiting (*Mildred*). ***Announcers:*** Ken Carpenter, Jack Hartz, John Heistand, Del Sharbutt. ***Music:*** Charles "Bud" Dant, Wilbur Hatch, Felix Mills.

OPENING

ANNOUNCER: And now, transcribed from Hollywood, we invite you to *Meet Corliss Archer*, America's teenage sweetheart, featuring Sam Edwards, Fred Shields, Mary Jane Croft and starring Janet Waldo.

CLOSING

ANNOUNCER: *Meet Corliss Archer* starring Janet Waldo is based on characters created by F. Hugh Herbert. It is a James L. Sasser Production directed by Steven Hayden.

1008. MEET ME AT PARKY'S. Comedy, 30 min., NBC, 1945–1947; Mutual, 1947–1948.

Parky's is a restaurant known for delicious food and good, wholesome dishes (beef stew is the specialty of the house). It is run by Nicholas "Nick" Parkyakarkas, an advice-giving Greek known to all as Parky. Stories focus on Parky as he attempts to run the restaurant and becomes involved with staff and clientele problems—all of which he solves quite by accident. *Other regular characters:* Betty, the restaurant vocalist; Opie, the orchestra leader; Orville Sharp, the owner of Orville Sharp's Cooking School; Joan, the cashier, Prudence Rockbottom, a fussy customer.

Cast: Harry Einstein (*Nick "Parky" Parkyakarkas*); Betty Jane Rhodes (*Betty*); Opie Cates (*Opie*); Sheldon Leonard (*Orville Sharp*); Joan Barton (*Joan*); Ruth Perrott (*Prudence Rockbottom*). ***Vocalists:*** Patty Bolton, Peggy Lee, David Street. ***Announcer:*** Art Gilmore. ***Orchestra:*** Opie Cates.

OPENING

ANNOUNCER: *Meet Me at Parky's*. Well, come along to Parky's Restaurant and say hello to Betty Rhodes, Sheldon Leonard, Wally Maher, Opie Cates, his clarinet and his orchestra, and our genial host, the star of our show, Parkyakarkas.

1009. MEET ME IN ST. LOUIS. Comedy, 30 min., NBC, 9/17/50 to 11/5/50.

Events in the lives of the Smiths, a family of five living in St. Louis, Missouri, at the turn of the century. Particular focus is on Esther Smith, a young woman with a knack for finding trouble. Based on the *New Yorker* magazine stories by Russell Beggs. *Other regular characters:* Alonzo and Anne, Esther's parents; Tootie, her sister; Glenn, her brother; John Truitt, her boyfriend; Katie, their housekeeper.

Cast: Peggy Ann Garner (*Esther Smith*); Vinton Hayworth (*Alonzo Smith*); Agnes Young (*Anne Smith*); Brook Byron (*Tootie Smith*); Jack Edwards (*Glenn Smith*); Billy Redfield (*John Truitt*); Ethel Wilson (*Katie*). ***Music:*** Vladimir Selinsky.

1010. MEET MILLIE. Comedy, 30 min., CBS, 7/2/51 to 9/23/53.

Millie Bronson is a secretary who works for Johnny Boone, Sr., an investment counselor. She lives at home (Apartment 3B at 137 West 41st Street in Manhattan) with her mother "Mama" Bertha, and is longing for a relationship with Johnny Boone, Jr., her boss's son. Mama wants Millie and Johnny to marry so she can have a grandchild ("to bounce on my knee while I still have a little bounce in me"). Mama is a widow and her efforts to spark a romance between Millie and Johnny is the focal point of stories. A major comedy aspect of the program is Millie's friend, Alfred E. Printzmetal, who longs to be a poet and an artist but until that happens, he works for Schercases Delicatessen. Women think that Alfred is handsome "in an eerie sort of way" and Mr. Boone, Sr., believes Alfred is strange and bad luck (he has begun a collection to get him carfare back to Mars). Despite the fact Alfred gives the elder Mr. Boone the willies, he is very sensitive and when the opportunity arises, Alfred will recite his awful poems—for example, "Ode to a Wristwatch":

Hail to you, old faithful 17-jewel,
Automatic-winding, shockproof time
piece with the pigskin band.
You're so hard for me to understand
Tick tock, tick tock, do you feel hurt?
Do you think life is shoddy,
Because you have a face and hands,
But you ain't got no body?

Served as the basis for the television series of the same title.

Cast: Audrey Totter, Elena Verdugo (*Millie Bronson*); Bea Benaderet, Florence Halop (*Mama Bronson*); Marvin Kaplan (*Alfred Printzmetal*); John Tracy, Rye Billsbury (*Johnny Boone, Jr.*); Earle Ross (*Johnny Boone, Sr.*). ***Announcer:*** Bob Lemond. ***Music:*** Irving Miller. ***Producer:*** Frank Galen.

OPENING

ANNOUNCER: And now, *Meet Millie*, created and transcribed by Frank Galen and starring Audrey Totter. Yes, we're about to say hello to Mama, played by Bea Benaderet, and Alfred, played by Marvin Kaplan, as once again we *Meet Millie*.

CLOSING

ANNOUNCER: Don't forget next week at this same time when you have another date to *Meet Millie* starring Audrey Totter. This is CBS, the Columbia Broadcasting System.

1011. MEET MISS JULIA. Serial, 15 min., Mutual, 1940.

A daily drama about Miss Julia, a 70-years-young, all-wise motherly housekeeper at a boarding house on Gramercy Park in New York City. Josephine Hull played the role of Miss Julia.

1012. Meet Miss Sherlock. Crime Drama, 30 min., CBS, 7/3/46 to 10/26/47.

Jane Sherlock is an exuberant buyer for the Blossom Department Store. She is engaged to Peter Blossom, an attorney and the son of the store's owner, and loves to meddle in other people's business—*so* much so that she believes she would make a great detective. Although only an amateur, she goes about poking her nose in all the wrong places and constantly winds up in trouble. She recruits Peter (by getting him clients he doesn't want) and involves the police (especially Capt. Dingle of the N.Y.P.D.); stories follow Jane as she helps Peter and Capt. Dingle solve crimes. (Jane often calls Capt. Dingle "Dingie." He always responds with, "Don't call me Dingie.")

Cast: Sandra Gair, Betty Moran, Monte Margetts (*Jane Sherlock*); Dave Vale (*Peter Blossom*); William Conrad (*Capt. Dingle*). ***Announcer:*** Murray Wagner. ***Music:*** Luther Charles. ***Producer:*** Dave Vale.

OPENING

PETER: Oh, ah, Jane.
JANE: Yes, Peter?
PETER: Now.
JANE: Now *what*, Peter?
PETER: Will you marry me now, tonight?
JANE: Oh, Peter, I'm so sorry, I can't tonight. Tonight I have to solve the case of "Wilmer and the Widow."
PETER: Ohhhh!
ANNOUNCER: Well, it's about time, about time to *Meet Miss Sherlock*, a smart little gal who has stumbled across a real live clue.

CLOSING

ANNOUNCER: Next week, Jane and Peter become involved with a big game hunter who says he's being hunted in "The Case of the Pink Elephant." So be with us next week at this same time when you *Meet Miss Sherlock*, presented from Columbia Square in Hollywood. This is CBS, the Columbia Broadcasting System.

1013. Meet Mr. McNultey. Comedy, 30 min., CBS, 1953–1954.

Ray McNultey is a professor of English at the Lynhaven College for Women in the town of Lynhaven. He lives at 187 Maple Terrace with his wife Peggy, and stories relate the problems that befall Ray at work and at home. *Other regular characters:* Pete "Petey" Thompson, their friend, a real estate salesman; Ruth, Pete's wife; Josephine Bradley, the college dean. Basically a rebroadcast of the television soundtrack of first season episodes. When the series locale switched to California, the radio version was dropped. Sponsored by General Electric.

Cast: Ray Milland (*Ray McNultey*); Phyllis Avery (*Peggy McNultey*); Gordon Jones (*Pete Thompson*); Jacqueline deWit (*Ruth Thompson*); Minerva Urecal (*Josephine Bradley*). ***Announcer:*** Del Sharbutt.

OPENING

ANNOUNCER: Time now for another visit to Lynhaven College and its favorite professor, Ray McNultey, as we *Meet Mr. McNultey* starring Ray Milland with Phyllis Avery as Peggy.

1014. Meet Mr. Meek. Comedy, 30 min., CBS, 1940–1942.

Events in the lives of the Meek family: Mortimer, the henpecked head of the family; Agatha, his understanding, problem-solving wife; Peggy, their teenage daughter; and Agatha's brother Louie, a loafer who lives with them. *Other regular characters:* Walter Barker, Mortimer's boss; Birdie Barker, Walter's wife. Also known as *The Adventures of Mr. Meek* and *Meet the Meeks*. See also *Meet the Meeks*.

Cast: Wilbur "Budd" Hulick, Frank Readick (*Mortimer Meek*); Adelaide Klein (*Agatha Meek*); Doris Dudley (*Peggy Meek*); Jack Smart (*Uncle Louie*); Agnes Moorehead (*Their first maid*); Ann Thomas (*Lily, their second maid*); Charles Cantor (*Walter Barker*); Jeanette Nolan (*Birdie Barker*). ***Announcer:*** Dan Seymour.

1015. Meet the Dixons. Serial, 15 min., CBS, 1939.

A daily drama about newspaperman Wesley Dixon, his wife Joan and their struggles to survive on a scanty income.

Cast: Richard Widmark (*Wesley Dixon*); Barbara Weeks (*Joan Dixon*); Charles Dingle (*Wesley's employer*).

1016. Meet the Meeks. Comedy, 30 min., NBC, 9/6/47 to 4/30/49.

A revised version of *Meet Mr. Meek*. The little white house with green shutters on Elm Street in the town of Civil Center is the setting for a weekly visit to the Meek family: Mortimer, a somewhat timid and henpecked husband who works for Walter Barker and Company (a merchandising outfit), his wife Agatha, an overall problem solver who enjoys canning her own fruits and vegetables; Peggy, their pretty, head-in-the-clouds daughter, "a girl who wouldn't get anyone in trouble" (on purpose, that is), and Louie, Agatha's brother, a loafer who lives with them (he seeks to avoid work and belongs to the Three Cushions Club).

Cast: Forrest Lewis (*Mortimer Meek*); Beryl Vaughn (*Agatha Meek*); Fran Allison (*Peggy Meek*); Cliff Soubier (*Uncle Louie*), Ian McAllister (*Walter Barker*). ***Announcer:*** John Weigel. ***Producer:*** Len Weinrod.

OPENING

ANNOUNCER: Say, it's time for—

WOMAN: All Sweet.

MAN: Did you hear what the lady said?

WOMAN: I said All Sweet. All Sweet is the margarine with the delicate, natural flavor.

ANNOUNCER: Yes, friends, that's what all the ladies are saying. All Sweet, the margarine with the delicate, natural flavor. Swift's All Sweet margarine invites you to *Meet the Meeks*.

CLOSING

ANNOUNCER: *Meet the Meeks* stars Forrest Lewis and Beryl Vaughn. Today's script was written by Sherman Marks and produced and directed by Les Weinrod. Be sure to join us over these same stations next Saturday when All Sweet, the margarine with the delicate, natural flavor, again invites you to *Meet the Meeks*. This is John Weigel speaking. This is NBC, the National Broadcasting Company.

1017. MEET YOUR LUCKY PARTNERS. Game, 30 min., Mutual, 1948.

A question-and-answer session in which a studio audience player is teamed with a home listener (who is heard over the telephone). Each question that is answered correctly earns the team one point. If the team can answer three questions correctly within a specified time limit, they each win a merchandise prize.

Host: Paul Brenner.

1018. MEET YOUR MATCH. Game, 30 min., Mutual, 1949–1950; NBC, 1952–1953.

Two contestants chosen from the studio audience competed. The winner of a question-and-answer session received money and the opportunity to select another player from the audience as his opponent. The one player who remained until a bell sounded the end of the competition was the overall winner and received a chance to earn additional money by answering the jackpot question, related by a masked character called the Baron. Served as the basis for a short-lived television version of the same title.

Host: Tom Moore, Jan Murray.

1019. THE MEL BLANC SHOW. Comedy, 30 min., CBS, 1946–1947.

Mel Blanc's Fix-It-Shop is a small business run by Mel Blanc, a confused young man who is plagued by life's endless mishaps (namely those caused by his stuttering, dim-witted assistant, Zookie). Stories follow Mel's efforts to run the shop and his attempts to impress Betty Colby, a girl whose father wants nothing to do with him. Mel belongs to a lodge called the Loyal Order of the Benevolent Zebras (Mr. Cushing is the head of the lodge and the secret password is "ugga-ugga boo, ugga boo-boo ugga"). Betty's father owns the town's supermarket; Mel's hangout is Blum's Candy Shop; and he lives on Elm Street. The show is also known as *Mel Blanc's Fix-It-Shop* and *The Fix-It-Shop*.

Cast: Mel Blanc (*Mel Blanc/Zookie*); Mary Jane Croft (*Betty Colby*); Joseph Kearns (*Betty's father*); Jill Walker, Bea Benaderet (*Betty's mother*); Hans Conried (*Mr. Cushing*). ***Announcer:*** Bud Easton. ***Music:*** Victor Miller. ***Producer:*** Joe Rines.

OPENING

ANNOUNCER: From Hollywood, Colgate Tooth Powder presents *The Mel Blanc Show*, written by Max Benoff, with Mary Jane Croft, Joseph Kearns, Hans Conried, Earle Ross, Jill Walker, Victor Miller and his orchestra and starring the creator of the voice of Bugs Bunny—

MEL: Ahhh, what's up Doc?

ANNOUNCER: Starring himself in person, Mel Blanc.

MEL: Hi folks. Ugga-ugga boo, ugga boo-boo ugga.

CLOSING

MEL: This is Mel Blanc saying thanks for listening tonight and tha-tha-tha-tha-tha-that's all, folks!

ANNOUNCER: This is Bud Easton reminding you that Colgate Tooth Powder for breath that's sweet and teeth that sparkle brings you *The Mel Blanc Show* every Tuesday night at this time. Be sure to join us next Tuesday night for more fun with Mel and the people you'll meet in *Mel Blanc's Fix-It-Shop*. This is CBS, the Columbia Broadcasting System.

1020. THE MEL TORME SHOW. Variety, 15 min., NBC, 1947–1948; 30 min., NBC, 1948.

The program began as a quarter-hour series of music and songs with singer Mel Torme as the host. He was backed by the Mel-Tones vocal group and the music of the Walter Gross Quartet. When the series switched to a half hour in 1948, a comedy skit was added with Mel as a college student and John Brown as the Dean of Fairmont University. Janet Waldo, then Barbara Eiler played Mel's girlfriend, and Sidney Miller was Mel's sidekick. Dean Elliott and his orchestra provided the music. John Reed King did the announcing in both versions.

1021. MELACHRINO MUSICALE. Variety, 15 min., Syndicated, 1954.

Music and songs with orchestra leader George Melachrino. Veryle Mills did the announcing and music was supplied by the George Melachrino Orchestra. Weekly guests provided the songs.

1022. MELODY AND MADNESS. Variety, 30 min., CBS, 1939.

A weekly program of music and songs with Robert Benchley as the host. The program, sponsored by Old Gold cigarettes, featured vocalists Helen Forrest and Dick Todd. Artie Shaw and his orchestra provided the music.

1023. MELODY HIGHWAY. Variety, 30 min., ABC, 1952–1953.

Music and songs with Milton Cross as the host. Stuart Foster and Earl Wild were the regulars and Bernard Green and his orchestra provided the music.

1024. MELODY LANE WITH JERRY WAYNE. Variety, 30 min., Mutual, 1942–1945.

Piano and organ solos, songs and performances by guests with singer Jerry Wayne as the host. Peter Donald was the announcer and Patti Clayton provided the songs. Jeff Alexander and his orchestra supplied the music. See also *The Jerry Wayne Show*.

1025. MELODY MASTERPIECES. Variety, 30 min., CBS, 1934–1935.

A program of classical music with baritone Evan Evans, soprano Mary Eastman and the music and Howard Barlow and his orchestra.

1026. MELODY MATINEE. Variety, 30 min., NBC, 1936–1937.

A Sunday afternoon program of concert music with Muriel Dickson as the host and the music of Victor Arden and his orchestra.

1027. MELODY PUZZLES. Game, 30 min., NBC Blue, 1937–1938.

A dramatic skit, which contained clues to the identity of a song, was performed on stage. If a player could guess the song, he won a merchandise prize.

Host: Fred Uttal. ***Vocalists:*** Buddy Clark, Georgia Gibbs. ***Announcer:*** Ed Herlihy. ***Orchestra:*** Harry Salter.

MELODY RANCH *see* **GENE AUTRY'S MELODY RANCH**

1028. MELODY ROUNDUP. Variety, 30 min., Syndicated, 1942–1946.

Country and western music and songs with Andy Devine as the host. The regulars were Jim Doyle, Henry Russell, Sonny Spencer, Bob Nolan and the Sons of the Pioneers and the Range Singers. Perry Botkin and his orchestra provided the music.

1029. THE MERCURY SUMMER THEATER OF THE AIR. Anthology, 30 min., CBS, 6/7/46 to 9/13/46.

A revised version of *The Mercury Theater on the Air* (see next entry) that continued to present original dramatic productions as well as adaptations of motion pictures, plays and books.

Host: Orson Welles. ***Regular Performers:*** Mercedes McCambridge, Orson Welles. ***Announcer:*** Ernest Chappell. ***Music:*** Bernard Herrmann. ***Producer:*** Orson Welles.

OPENING (from 6/12/46)

ORSON: Good evening, this is Orson Welles,

your producer of a special series of broadcasts presented by the makers of Pabst Blue Ribbon—*The Mercury Summer Theater of the Air*.

ANNOUNCER: Tonight and every Friday night, blended splendid Pabst Blue Ribbon presents you with a front row seat at one of the greatest plays ever produced. And now, here is America's most famous producer, writer and director, Orson Welles.

ORSON: Our story tonight, ladies and gentlemen, is an original for radio by that most original of radio writers, Miss Lucille Fletcher. Its title, "The Search for Andy LeFeve."

ANNOUNCER: And now Orson Welles and his own Mercury production of "The Search for Andy LeFeve."

CLOSING

ANNOUNCER: You have just heard Orson Welles' Mercury production of "The Search for Andy LeFeve," a radio play by Lucille Fletcher. And now Mr. Welles.

ORSON: Next week, ladies and gentlemen, we will be bringing you "Treasure Island." So join us next week, please, same time, same station. Until then, speaking for my sponsor, the makers of Pabst Blue Ribbon Beer, and for the whole Mercury Theater, I remain obediently yours.

Orson Welles hosted and starred in *The Mercury Theater on the Air*.

1030. THE MERCURY THEATER ON THE AIR. Anthology, 60 min., CBS, 7/11/38 to 9/10/39.

Quality adaptations of stories by famous authors featuring Orson Welles and a group of talented performers. The program of 10/30/38, "The War of the Worlds," is perhaps the most famous radio broadcast of all time. The adaptation of the H.G. Wells story was done so realistically that it caused a nationwide panic when many people actually believed the Earth was being invaded by Martians. A listener favorite was "The Hitchhiker," which was repeated several times by popular demand. It told the story of a man whose cross-country motor trip turns to terror when he keeps seeing the same hitchhiker—a man who is always one step ahead of him. The story was adapted by Rod Serling to television as "The Hitchhiker" episode of *The Twilight Zone* with Inger Stevens as the motorist. See also *The Campbell Playhouse*.

Host-Star: Orson Welles. ***Dramatic Cast:*** William Alland, Edgar Barrier, Ray Collins, Joseph Cotten, Helen Hayes (frequently cast), John Houseman, Burgess Meredith, Agnes Moorehead, Frank Readick, Everett Sloane, Richard Wilson. ***Announcers:*** Ernest Chappell, Dan Seymour. ***Music:*** Bernard Herrmann. ***Producer:*** Orson Welles.

OPENING (Typical)

ANNOUNCER: The Columbia Network takes pride in presenting Orson Welles and the *Mercury Theater on the Air*, dramatizing famous narratives by great authors. This is the first time a complete theatrical producing company has been brought to radio. Every week, Orson Welles invites our listeners to suggest their favorite stories. Tonight, *The Mercury Theater on the Air* presents "The Hitchhiker." Ladies and gentlemen, the director of the Mercury Theater and our star of these broadcasts, Orson Welles. [Welles would then introduce the story and the drama would begin.]

1031. THE MEREDITH WILLSON–JOHN NESBITT SHOW. Variety, 30 min., NBC, 6/30/42 to 9/22/42.

The 1942 summer replacement for *Fibber McGee and Molly*. Music from Meredith Willson and his orchestra coupled with stories from John Nesbitt and his "Passing Parade" (a look back at historic events).

1032. THE MERRY LIFE OF MARY CHRISTMAS. Comedy, 30 min., CBS, 1945.

Hectic events in the life of Mary Christmas, a Hollywood gossip columnist. Mary Astor played Mary Christmas and Paul Marlon was her husband. Also in the cast were Howard Dinsdale, Jerry Epstein and Frank Martin.

1033. THE MERRY MACS. Variety, 15 min., NBC Blue, 1933–1936.

A program of light music with Joe, Judd and Ted McMichael (a musical group known as the Merry Macs), Helen Carroll and Cheri McKay.

1034. THE METROPOLITAN OPERA AUDITIONS OF THE AIR. Variety, 30 min., NBC, then ABC, 1935–1958.

Milton Cross was the host of a program of concert music that also featured operatic hopefuls competing for cash and prizes and a performance at the Metropolitan Opera. Wilfred Pelletier conducted the Met Orchestra. Howard Claney did the announcing.

1035. THE MEYER DAVIS ORCHESTRA. Variety, 30 min., Mutual, 1954.

A weekly program of popular music featuring Meyer Davis and his orchestra. Larry Higgin was the host and announcer.

1036. THE M-G-M SCREEN TEST. Variety, 15 min., Syndicated, 1942.

The program showcased promising but undiscovered talent performing a scene with an established star (who appeared as a guest). Dean Murphy was the host and vocalist Charlotte Manson was a regular. Ted Steele and his orchestra provided the music.

1037. THE M-G-M THEATER OF THE AIR. Anthology, 60 min., Mutual, 1952.

Radio adaptations of M-G-M film scripts and featuring top name performers as guests. Howard Dietz was the host and Joel Herron and his orchestra provided the music.

1038. MICHAEL AND KITTY. Mystery, 30 min., NBC Blue, 1941.

Light comedy is mixed with mystery in the adventures of Michael and Kitty, a husband-and-wife detective team. John Gibson played Michael and Elizabeth Reller was Kitty.

1039. MICHAEL SHAYNE, PRIVATE DETECTIVE. Crime Drama, 30 min., Mutual, 1944–1946.

Michael Shayne is a clever, hard-boiled private detective who is somewhat enthusiastic, but also a bit rough around the edges. He has an eye for detail, is relentless and a bit too persistent for some people. Phyllis Knight is his assistant and girlfriend (he calls her "Sugar," "Honey" and "Baby"). Phyllis attended Huxley College, has a sense of humor (moreso than Michael), is charming (a bit *too* charming, Michael believes—especially when other men come on to her) and can usually calm Michael down when he flies off the handle. She always says, "I like you just like you are and I wouldn't change you if I could." Although Michael likes to work alone, Phyllis always tags along. Stories follow their investigations as they attempt to solve crimes—mostly murders. See also *The Adventures of Michael Shayne* and *The New Adventures of Michael Shayne*.

Cast: Wally Maher, Louis Arthur (*Michael Shayne*); Cathy Lewis (*Phyllis Knight*).

OPENING

(from "Death Goes to College")

ANNOUNCER: *Michael Shayne, Private Detective* starring Wally Maher and Cathy Lewis. A detective without a murder case is like flapjacks without syrup. Yet that is just the predicament for our friend Michael Shayne. In fact, things are so dull we find Michael and his blonde assistant, Phyllis Knight, not at the office, not at the police headquarters, but squirming uncomfortably in the seat of higher learning, in other words, the office of the president of Huxley College...

1040. THE MICKEY MOUSE THEATER OF THE AIR. Children, 30 min., NBC, 1937–1938.

A mix of music (featuring Donald Duck's Swing Band), songs (by the Minnie Mouse Woodland Choir) and comedy with the antics of Mickey Mouse and his girlfriend Minnie Mouse; the easily exasperated Donald Duck; the not-too-bright Goofy; and the sensible Clarabell Cow. Based on characters created by Walt Disney.

Cast: Walt Disney (*Mickey Mouse*); Thelma Boardman (*Minnie Mouse*); Clarence Nash (*Donald Duck*); Stuart Buchanan (*Goofy*); Florence Gill (*Clarabell Cow*). ***Music:*** Felix Mills. ***Producer:*** Walt Disney.

Mickey of the Circus *see* **Appendix**

1041. Midstream. Serial, 15 min., NBC, 1939–1940.

The dramatic story of Julia and Charles Meredith, a middle-aged couple seeking a life of their own after devoting most of their lives to their children, now raising families of their own.

Cast: Betty Lou Gerson, Fern Parsons (*Julia Meredith*); Hugh Studebaker, Russell Thorson, Sidney Ellstrom (*Charles Meredith*); Mercedes McCambridge, Laurette Fillbrandt, Sharon Grainger (*Midge Meredith*); William Farnum (*David Meredith*); Connie Osgood, Annette Harper, Sylvia Jacobs (*Ruth Andrews*); Josephine Gilbert (*Amy Bartlett*), Lesley Woods (*Meredith Conway*); Bob Jellison (*Sandy*); William Bouchey (*Stanley Bartlett*); Nina Klowden, Lenore Kingston (*Jimmie Storey*); Olan Soule, Pat Murphy (*Timothy Storey*). ***Announcer:*** Gene Baker.

OPENING

Announcer: Teel Tooth Liquid presents *Midstream*, the eventful story of a man and woman who have reached the halfway point in their journey across the river of life. The story of Julia and Charles Meredith.

Mike Hammer *see* **That Hammer Guy**

Mike Molloy, Private Eye *see* **Appendix**

1042. The Mildred Bailey Revue. Variety, 30 min., CBS, 1944.

A program of music and songs with vocalist Mildred Bailey as the host. Red Norvo and Teddy Wilson were the regulars and music was by Paul Baron and his orchestra.

1043. The Milt Herth Trio. Variety, 15 min., NBC, then CBS, 1938–1945; Syndicated, 1946.

A program of light music with Ed Cooper, Marty Jacoby, King Johnson and the music of the Milt Herth Trio.

1044. The Milton Berle Show. Variety, 30 min., NBC, 9/22/48 to 6/15/49.

A Saturday evening program of music, songs and outlandish comedy skits with Milton Berle heading a talented cast of regulars. The program, sponsored by Texaco Gasoline, served as the basis for Berle's pioneering television series *The Texaco Star Theater*, which ran on NBC from 1948 until 1953. See also *Kiss and Make Up*, *Let Yourself Go* and *Stop Me If You've Heard This One*.

Host: Milton Berle. ***Regulars:*** Jack Albertson, Jackson Beck, Ed Begley, Arthur Q. Bryan, Jack Gilford, Bert Gordon, Charles Irving, Arnold Stang, Roland Winters. ***Vocalist:*** Eileen Burton. ***Announcer:*** Frank Gallop. ***Orchestra:*** Ray Bloch.

OPENING

Announcer: Texaco presents *The Milton Berle Show* with your host, Milton Berle, Jack Albertson, Arnold Stang, Eileen Burton, the music of Ray Bloch and his orchestra, yours truly, Frank Gallop, and now here's the star of our show, Milton Berle.

1045. The Mindy Carson Show. Variety, 15 min., NBC, 1949–1950; CBS, 1952– 1953.

A program of music and songs with vocalist Mindy Carson as the host. Don Pardo did the announcing and Norman Cloutier and Russ Case and their orchestras supplied the music.

1046. Mirth and Madness. Variety, 30 min., NBC, 1943–1944.

A daily morning show that combined vaudeville routines with satirical skits—all of which were set at the Madhouse Little Theater. See also *The Jack Kirkwood Show* for a revised version of this series.

Host: Jack Kirkwood. ***Regulars:*** Lee Brodie, Billy Grey, Tom Harris, Lillian Leigh, Jean McKean, Don Reid, Ransom Sherman, Herb Sheldon. ***Announcer:*** Jimmy Wallington. ***Orchestra:*** Jerry Jerome, Irving Miller.

1047. Miss Hattie. Serial, 30 min., ABC, 1944–1945.

Dramatic events in the lives of the Thompsons, a typical American family facing normal, everyday problems. Ethel Barrymore played Hattie Thompson; Eric Dressler was her husband; and Dick Van Patten and Lois Wilson were their children. Also in the cast were John Gibson, Warren Parker and Andree Wallace. Roland Winters did the announcing and Doc Whipple and his orchestra provided the music.

1048. Miss Meade's Children. Serial, 15 min., Mutual, 1942.

Dramatic events in the lives of three children who are sent to live with their aunt (Miss Meade). Margaret Ryan played Miss Meade and Arlene Brock, Joan Barrett and Lemond Scherer portrayed the children. Dave Cheskin and his orchestra provided the music.

1049. Miss Pinkerton, Inc. Crime Drama, 30 min., NBC, 1941.

Mary Vance is studying law at Cornell University in Ithaca, New York. She is five feet, three inches tall, 118 pounds, "smokes occasionally and drinks occasionally even less." One day she receives word that her Uncle Mike, the owner of the Vance Detective Agency in New York City, has died and that she has inherited the business. Mary travels to Manhattan to settle her uncle's estate with plans to sell the agency. However, when she meets up with Mr. Parker, the agency manager, and discovers that they are shorthanded and need a girl to attend a lavish party to guard the Bentley Emeralds, Mary volunteers. This whets her appetite for adventure, especially when she meets the handsome Dennis Murray, an N.Y.P.D. detective sergeant assigned to guard the emeralds. Mary and Dennis become fast friends, but Mary gets on the wrong side of Dennis when she stops a robbery and ruins a police sting to catch a notorious jewel thief. Despite the harsh words from the police department, Mary decides to keep the agency to prove a woman can be just as effective as a man when it comes to crime solving ("I had intended to sell [the agency] but you men who think all women are helpless nitwits give me 12 kinds of a pain. Not only am I going to keep the agency, but I'm going to show you [Dennis] that I can outsleuth you in every direction.") As Mary leaves the office, Dennis turns to Parker and says, "So she's going to be Miss Pinkerton, Inc. ... One of these days she's going to poke that pretty nose of hers into something and get it caught. And I won't be around to unlock it—or will I?" Stories follow Mary's efforts to run her agency, her love-hate relationship with Dennis, and the occasions when Mary does poke her pretty nose into criminal cases and complicates matters for the police. The Pinkerton in the title refers to the famous Pinkerton Detective Agency and is used here as a play on words as female detectives on radio were somewhat rare at the time.

Cast: Joan Blondell (*Mary Vance*); Dick Powell (*Dennis Murray*); Hanley Stafford (*Mr. Parker*); Ed Max (*Bingo Doherty, Mary's assistant*). ***Announcer:*** Art Gilmore. ***Music:*** Lenny Conn. ***Producer:*** J. Donald Wilson.

OPENING

Sound: Police whistles and sirens, then music.

Announcer: *Miss Pinkerton, Inc.*, starring Joan Blondell and Dick Powell. We present the first in a new series of half-hour comedy detective dramas complete in each episode, yet featuring the same principal characters in situations of adventure, thrills and romance.

CLOSING

Announcer: Listen in next week to *Miss Pinkerton, Inc.*, for the story of a man who becomes obsessed with the urge to kill, starring Joan Blondell and Dick Powell. This is NBC, the National Broadcasting Company.

1050. Miss Switch the Witch. Children, 15 min., Syndicated, 1957.

A daily comedy about the mishaps of a bumbling witch named Miss Switch (played by Miriam Wolfe).

1051. The Missus Goes-a-Shopping. Game, 30 min., CBS, 1944.

The format mixes stunts, gimmicks and audience participation. Selected members of the studio audience go on quests involving shopping (in return for prizes). John Reed King served as the host; Paul Mowry, who produced, also assisted King.

1052. Mr. Ace and Jane. Comedy, 30 min., CBS, 2/14/48 to 12/31/48.

Jane and Goodman Ace are a typical American couple living in a typical American town ("New York City, a city of 7,000,000, give or take one"). Goodman works as an advertising executive for Dutton, Sutton, Muttin and Norris and says, "It's a pretty fair job and I make a pretty fair salary" (Jane thinks Goodman is much more important than he thinks he is and tells everybody, "He's a big cog in the machinery"). Goodman is level-headed, has been married to Jane for 15 years, and loves her very much despite her sometimes harebrained antics. While Goodman can contend with Jane, he has a hard time putting up with Paul, Jane's deadbeat brother who refuses to work ("The dollar isn't worth as much as it used to be and until it is, I can't force myself to look for a job"). If a job opportunity arises, Paul catches a case of the flu—"intentional flu," says Jane. Paul is always in need of money—and he sees Goodman as the perfect patsy, but Goodman refuses to give in—"It's not the principle, it's the money." With no other choice, Paul asks for Jane's help—and like the blind leading the blind, Jane and Paul manage to involve Goodman in their antics. His efforts to resolve the situations they cause is the focal point of stories. Living next door to the Aces is Ken Roberts, a radio announcer who has a tendency to spell things out as he speaks (for example, "It's produced by the Krobber Company. That's the Krobber Company, spelled C-O-M-P-A-N-Y"). Ken is the only celebrity Jane knows and she asks for his autograph each time she sees him. *Other regular characters:* J.K. Norris, Goodman's employer; Miss Anderson, Goodman's secretary.

Cast: Goodman Ace (*Goodman Ace*); Jane Ace (*Jane Ace*); Ken Roberts (*Ken Roberts*); Leon Janney (*Paul Sherwood*); Eric Dressler (*J.K. Norris*); Florence Butler (*Miss Anderson*).

OPENING

ANNOUNCER: From New York City comes now the new *Mr. Ace and Jane* program, a weekly half-hour comedy series starring radio's comedy couple, the Aces. Once again the strains of *Manhattan Serenade* introduce the story of Mr. Ace and his wife Jane. Tonight, Chapter One, entitled, "Jane's brother Paul, who hasn't worked in 12 years, tries to borrow $200 from Mr. Ace and Mr. Ace says 'Why don't you go to work?' and Paul says, 'Don't use that four-letter word in front of my sister.'"

CLOSING

ANNOUNCER: Next week, Chapter Two, entitled, "Jane gets a summons to serve on a jury but she doesn't like the case being tried so she goes upstairs and gets on another jury hearing a spicy divorce case, making it 11 on one jury and 13 on another. And Mr. Ace gets fined $50 for contempt of court."

GOODMAN: Or is there no justice. Good night Jane.

JANE: Good night.

ANNOUNCER: This is CBS, the Columbia Broadcasting System.

1053. MR. ADAMS AND EVE. Game, 30 min., CBS, 1942.

Two teams of four (male vs. female) competed in a question-and-answer session wherein the highest-scoring team received $50; the runners-up won $25. Frank Crumit was the host and Julia Sanderson assisted him.

1054. MR. ALADDIN. Crime Drama, 30 min., CBS, 7/7/51 to 9/8/51.

Robert Aladdin is a private detective who advertises himself as "the man who can do anything"—a situation that presents him with an array of unusual clients and cases. Stories follow Mr. Aladdin as he tries to resolve the strange cases that come his way (for example, trying to find a home for a jealous poodle). *Other regular characters:* Jeannie Mobley, his secretary; Sam, bartender at the Taj Mahal, his favorite bar/hangout.

Cast: Paul Frees (*Robert Aladdin*); Sylvia Sims (*Jeannie Mobley*); Sidney Miller (*Sam*). ***Announcer:*** Bill Anders. ***Music:*** Marlin Skiles. ***Producer:*** Elliott Lewis.

OPENING

ANNOUNCER: Once upon a time, the year being 1951, a young man walked down the streets of an island, the island called Manhattan, and if some of the feats he performed have the feeling of magic, is that surprising? His name was Aladdin. *Mr. Aladdin*, a wonderful new adventure series starring Paul Frees. Tonight, Mr. Aladdin performs, transcribed, "The Miracle of the Four-Legged Husband."

1055. MR. AND MRS. Comedy, 30 min., CBS, 1929–1931; NBC, summer of 1946.

Humorous events based on the lives of a married couple. The CBS version, based on the comic strip by Clare Briggs, starred Jack Smart as Joe and Jane Houston as Vi. The NBC series, which was not based on the comic, featured Eddie Albert as Jimmie and Georgia Field as Jane.

1056. MR. AND MRS. BLANDINGS. Comedy, 30 min., NBC, 1951.

With a dream to provide a decent life for their children Susan and Joan, Jim and Muriel Blandings leave the congestion of Manhattan and move to Connecticut where they have purchased some land and contract to have their dream house built. The headaches soon begin when construction costs more than they can actually afford—"But this is what we dreamed about," says Jim. "Mr. Blandings' dream house," exclaims Muriel. Jim and Muriel are in debt and their efforts to live their dream life (despite numerous obstacles) is the focal point of stories. *Other regular characters:* Bill Cole, their lawyer and best friend; Janette, their housekeeper (in later episodes she is called Maude); Margaret, Jim's secretary. Jim is an advertising executive who works in Manhattan and whose commute is 45 minutes each way. The Blandings' phone number is 431 Ring 2; Bill's phone number is Whiteside 6-4893. Joan and Susan have a sheep dog named Rover.

Cast: Cary Grant (*Jim Blandings*); Betsy Drake (*Muriel Blandings*); Gale Gordon (*Bill Cole*); Anne Whitfield (*Susan Blandings*); Patricia Ianola (*Joan Blandings*); Gail Bonney (*Janette/Maude*); Jeanne Bates (*Margaret*). ***Announcers:*** Wendell Niles, Don Stanley. ***Music:*** Bernard Katz. ***Producers:*** Warren Lewis, Nat Wolfe.

OPENING

ANNOUNCER: Flying's the way to travel and the way to fly is TWA, Trans World Airlines. Presenting Cary Grant and Betsy Drake as Mr. and Mrs. Blandings in a new series based on Eric Hodgins' best-selling novels *Mr. Blandings Builds His Dream House* and *Blandings Way*. Did you that TWA offers the only one airline service from coast to coast in the United States and all the way to Europe, Africa and Asia?

SONG: You love to fly high in the sky; you ride the airways to starry stairways. Smoother and quicker find the way; and the best way to fly is TWA.

ANNOUNCER: *Mr. and Mrs. Blandings* starring Cary Grant and Betsy Drake with Gale Gordon as Bill Cole.

CLOSING

ANNOUNCER: Tune in next week, same time, same station for *Mr. and Mrs. Blandings* starring Cary Grant and Betsy Drake, brought to you by Trans World Airlines. Across the U.S. and overseas, you can depend on TWA. Betsy Drake appeared through the courtesy of RKO Radio Pictures and David O. Selznick. [Over the NBC chimes:] Three chimes means good times on NBC.

1057. MR. AND MRS. NORTH. Comedy, 30 min., CBS, 1941–1942.

Pamela and Jerry North are a comfy couple whose amusing domestic adventures provide the basis for a weekly look at their lives. Peggy Conklin was Pamela North and Carl Eastman played Jerry North in this series based on the stories by Richard and Frances Lockridge. See the following title for the better-known detective version of the series.

1058. MR. AND MRS. NORTH. Crime Drama, 30 and 15 min. versions, NBC, 1942–1950; CBS, 1950–1955.

Whether they're attending a dinner party, a play, or planning to spend an enjoyable evening at a friend's apartment, something will always happen to Jerry North, a prominent New York book editor or Pamela North, his pretty, level-headed wife. Pamela doesn't mean to find trouble; it just seems to find her—and her and Jerry's efforts to resolve the situation (usually murders) are the focal point of stories. Jerry often complains that Pamela's adventures often leave him little time to actually do his job, but confesses, "Since I married you, disrupted plans in life are the one thing I can count on." The Norths live at 24 Saint Anne's Place in Greenwich Village; Pamela loves cats, talks in riddles and uses her feminine intuition to solve crimes before the police. *Other regular characters:* Detective Bill Weingand; Sgt. Mullins; Susan, Pamela's niece; Mahatma McGloin, the cab driver. Based on the stories by Richard and Frances Lockridge. On 7/4/49, NBC aired a television test film with Joseph Allen and Mary Lou Taylor as Jerry and Pamela North that failed to generate a series. A video series with Barbara Britton and Richard Denning ran from 1952 to 1954.

Cast: Joseph Curtin, Richard Denning (*Jerry North*); Alice Frost, Barbara Britton (*Pamela North*); Staats Cotsworth, Frank Lovejoy, Francis De Sales (*Bill Weingand*); Walter Kinsella (*Sgt. Mullins*); Betty Jane Tyler (*Susan*); Mandel Kramer (*Mahatma McGloin*).

OPENING

EFFECT: Pamela and Jerry at their apartment door. Pamela opens the door.

PAM: Jerry!

JERRY: The lights.

PAM (flicking light switch): A fuse must have blown.

JERRY: Or someone pulled the master switch. In that case, the murderer is still in the house.

ANNOUNCER: *Mr. and Mrs. North*, transcribed, starring Richard Denning and Barbara Britton. Listen as Pam and Jerry solve the mystery, "Deadly Innocent."

CLOSING

ANNOUNCER: Pam and Jerry are sure to have more exciting adventures next week. Listen in, won't you? There's always mystery well-sprinkled with humor on *Mr. and Mrs. North*.

1059. MR. BROADWAY. Drama, 30 min., ABC, 1952.

The format had a Broadway columnist with a penchant for spinning yarns about the Great White Way tell his story to a nightclub chanteuse, who interrupted the story four times for a song.

Cast: Anthony Ross (*Broadway Columnist*); Irene Manning (*Singer*). ***Music:*** Glenn Osser.

1060. MR. CHAMELEON. Crime Drama, 30 min., CBS, 1948–1952.

Stories open to establish a group of characters (who will become suspects) and a crime involving them. When the police are called, famed detective Mr. Chameleon and his assistant, Detective Dave Arnold (of Central Police Headquarters in New York City), appear on the scene to investigate. The program then follows the various subjects as they are questioned by Mr. Chameleon. Twist in the series is Mr. Chameleon's use of various disguises to get the proof he needs to bring the culprit to justice (the disguise is always known to the listener but not the suspects). When a suspect is accused, Mr. Chameleon recaps the evidence he gathered to make a conviction.

Cast: Karl Swenson (*Mr. Chameleon*); Frank Butler (*Dave Arnold*); Richard Keith (*Police Commissioner*). ***Announcers:*** George Bryon, Howard Claney, Roger Krupp. ***Music:*** Victor Arden. ***Producers:*** Anne Hummert, Frank Hummert.

OPENING

ANNOUNCER: Tonight, we again present the famous Mr. Chameleon of Central Police Headquarters in another of his celebrated cases of crime and murder. Mr. Chameleon, as you know, is the dreaded detective who frequently uses a disguise to track down the killer—a disguise which at all times is easily recognized by the audience. Tonight we give you *Mr. Chameleon* in "The Case of Murder and the Million Dollar Smile."

CLOSING

ANNOUNCER: Listen next Friday evening at this same time for *Mr. Chameleon*, the man of many faces, in "The Custody of the Child Murder Case." And remember, *Gangbusters* goes into action on Saturday nights on the CBS Radio Network.

1061. MR. DISTRICT ATTORNEY. Crime Drama, 30 min., NBC Red, 1939; NBC Blue, 1939–1940; NBC Red, 1940–1951; ABC, 1951–1952; Syndicated, 1952–1953.

Dramatizations based on the files of various state district attorney offices. When the series first began, stories were based on the files of Thomas E. Dewey, a crime-busting New York D.A. At this time (episodes broadcast from 1939 to 1952), the producers could not obtain the right to use Mr. Dewey's name, so the D.A. remained nameless (usually called "Boss" or "Chief" by his coworkers and "Mr. District Attorney" by the people he served). In 1952, when the syndicated version began, the D.A. was given the name of Paul Garrett. *Other regular characters:* Edith Miller, the D.A.'s secretary; Harrington, his investigator; Miss Rand, the receptionist.

Cast: Dwight Weist, Raymond Edward Johnson, Jay Jostyn (*Mr. District Attorney*); David Brian (*Paul Garrett*); Vicki Vola (*Edith Miller*); Jay Jostyn, Walter Kinsella (*Harrington*); Eleanor Silver, Arlene Francis (*Miss Rand*). ***Voice of the Law:*** Maurice Franklin, Jay Jostyn, David Brian. ***Announcers:*** Ed Herlihy, Mark Hawley, Fred Uttal. ***Music:*** Gil Markel, Harry Salter, Peter Van Steeden. ***Producer:*** Phillips H. Lord.

OPENING

ANNOUNCER: Mr. District Attorney, champion of the people, defender of truth, guardian of our fundamental rights to life, liberty and the pursuit of happiness.

MR. D.A.: And it shall be my duty as District Attorney not only to prosecute to the limit of the law all persons accused of crimes perpetrated within this county but to defend with equal vigor the rights and privileges of all its citizens.

(Left to right) Jay Jostyn, Len Doyle, Vicki Vola and Jerry Deuthe during a broadcast of *Mr. District Attorney*.

CLOSING

DAVID BRIAN: This is David Brian. I hope you enjoyed this case from the files of Mr. District Attorney... Join us when we present our next case based on the facts of crime from the files of Mr. District Attorney.

1062. MISTER FEATHERS. Comedy, 30 min., Mutual, 1949–1951.

Mister Feathers is the elderly owner of the Pike City Pharmacy in the town of Pike City. He is the inventor of the All-Purpose Ointment, a cure-all salve (it grows hair and can fix clogged printing presses) and is prone to telling yarns and dispensing friendly advice. Stories follow incidents in the life of Mister Feathers as he goes about helping people in need. Mister Feathers has no first name. When someone asks, "What do your friends call you?" he responds, "Mister Feathers" (even his wife calls him Mister Feathers). The large economy size jar of the All-Purpose Ointment, Improved 950 Formula, sells for 49 cents. *Other regular characters:* Bunny Feathers, his wife; Norbert Corbett, his part-time delivery boy (he attends Pike City High School); Emma Klause, Norbert's girlfriend; Doc Bellows, Mister Feathers' friend.

Cast: Parker Fennelly (*Mister Feathers*); Elinor Phelps (*Bunny Feathers*); Mert Coplin (*Norbert Corbett*); Lee True Hill (*Emma Klause*); Wendell Holmes (*Doc Bellows*). ***Announcer:*** Bob Emerick. ***Music:*** Ben Ludlow. ***Producer:*** Herbert Rice.

OPENING

ANNOUNCER: Mutual presents Parker Fennelly as *Mister Feathers*.

MR. FEATHERS (gives an opinion for each episode): Yes, I believe that when any gentleman sees a poor defenseless female in distress, he should notify the police.

ANNOUNCER: It's *Mister Feathers* and "The Woman in the Case." *Mister Feathers*, written by Gerald Holland and starring Parker Fennelly. Mister Feathers, a man not quite like any next door neighbor you've ever had.

Mister Feathers at grips with life in the untroubled and quiet untypical town of Pike City.

CLOSING

ANNOUNCER: You've been visiting with *Mister Feathers* starring Parker Fennelly. Join us next week at this time for another visit with *Mister Feathers*, heard in Canada through the facilities of the Canadian Broadcasting Corporation. This is the Mutual Broadcasting System.

1063. MR. FIX-IT. Advice, 15 min., Mutual, 6/5/49 to 4/1/50.

A typical married couple (played by Art Van Horn and Loretta Ellis) face a home repair or maintenance problem at the beginning of each episode. After failing to remedy the situation, Mr. Fix-It (played by Jim Boles) comes to the rescue by dispensing advice on how to correctly remedy the dramatized problem.

1064. MR. KEEN, TRACER OF LOST PERSONS. Crime Drama, 15 and 30 min. versions, NBC Blue, 1937–1942; CBS, 1942–1943; CBS, 1943–1951; NBC Red, 1951–1952; CBS, 1952–1955.

"What kindness, what understanding!" is what clients say about Mr. Keen, a gray-haired gentleman detective when he helps them overcome their troubles. Mr. Keen and his assistant Mike Clancy specialize in locating missing people; stories follow their step-by-step investigations as they become involved in murder and mayhem while helping their clients. The program began as a thrice-weekly quarter-hour serial. In 1942, when the half-hour format was adapted, the concept changed to focus on Mr. Keen as a homicide detective even though the "Tracer of Lost Persons" remained in the title. Mr. Keen (no first name given) was kind with a benevolent charm and soft persuasion. Mike Clancy was his complete opposite—a big, not-too-bright Irishman who was as nimble as a bull in a china shop; his catch-phrase was, "Saints preserve us, Mr. Keen." Mike called Mr. Keen "Boss." For the final year of the series, a 15-minute serialized version ran alongside the half-hour edition. *Other regular characters:* Maisie Ellis, Mr. Keen's secretary.

Cast: Bennett Kilpack, Phil Clarke, Arthur Hughes (*Mr. Keen*); Jim Kelly (*Mike Clancy*); Florence Malone (*Maisie Ellis*). ***Announcers:*** Larry Elliott, James Fleming. ***Music:*** John Winters, Al Rickey. ***Producers:*** Anne Hummert, Frank Hummert.

OPENING

ANNOUNCER: *Mr. Keen, Tracer of Lost Persons* is on the air. [Over theme, "Someday I'll Find You":] Mr. Keen, Tracer of Lost Persons is one of the most famous characters of American fiction and one of radio's most thrilling dramas. Tonight and every Thursday night from 7:30 to eight, Eastern War Time, the famous old investigator will take from his files and bring to us one of his most celebrated missing persons cases. Now, *Mr. Keen, Tracer of Lost Persons*.

CLOSING

ANNOUNCER: You've been listening to *Mr. Keen, Tracer of Lost Persons*, now on the air at a new time, every Thursday night at 7:30 to eight, Eastern War Time, over this network. Don't miss *Mr. Keen* next Thursday night when the kindly old tracer turns to "The Case of Murder in the Air." This is Larry Elliott saying good night.

1065. MR. MERCURY. Adventure, 30 min., ABC, 1951.

Mr. Mercury is a circus acrobat who moonlights as a private investigator. Stories follow his exploits as he uses his expertise as a circus performer to solve crimes.

Cast: John Larkin (*Mr. Mercury*). ***Music:*** John Gart.

1066. MR. MOTO. Crime Drama, 30 min., NBC, 5/20/51 to 10/20/51.

I.A. Moto is a Japanese-born American citizen. He has an eye for the ladies and a talent for solving crimes. He is a world-famous detective and is dedicated to battling the enemies of the U.S. government. Mr. Moto works for Major Grant and stories follow his global assignments as he tries not to lose face while battling the bad guys (and girls). When Mr. Moto does make a mistake (outwitted by the enemy), he exclaims, "I must not lose face" and becomes even more determined to complete his assignment. Based on the character created by J.P. Marquand.

Cast: James Monks (*Mr. I.A. Moto*); John Larkin (*Major Grant*). ***Producer:*** Harry W. Junkin.

OPENING

MR. MOTO: This is Mr. Moto.

ANNOUNCER: NBC presents the world's greatest international detective-philosopher. Mr. I.A. Moto, a man of mystery, of culture and sensitivity, a man who, while hating violence, fights Communism ruthlessly both at home and abroad with his courage, his brains and his fabulous knowledge of international persons, places and things.

1067. MR. PRESIDENT. Anthology, 30 min., ABC, 6/26/47 to 9/23/53.

Weekly dramatizations based on little-known incidents in the lives of U.S. presidents. The subject of each story was not revealed until the end of the broadcast. Edward Arnold portrayed the presidents and William Conrad and Betty Lou Gerson appeared in supporting roles. Ted deCorsia did the narrating and Ted Doyle, Richard Jennings and Richard Woollen were the producers.

OPENING

ANNOUNCER: *Mr. President* starring Edward Arnold. Mr. President, the man in the White House chosen by his fellow citizens as the first citizen. We invite you now to become better acquainted with one of America's greatest men. These are transcribed stories of the men who have lived in the White House. Dramatic, exciting, but little-known events in their lives which you and I so rarely hear. True, human stories of Mr. President.

NARRATOR: Perhaps you do not believe in the kind of ghosts that are supposed to haunt houses; but there are other kinds. There are ghosts of words once spoken, ideas once held, personalities once present. Take, for instance, a tour of our nation's capitol. Here, you think, Lincoln once stood as he pondered the problems of a country at war. Even as you look, your fancy conjures up a picture of that tall, gaunt figure stooped in thought. There you knew Washington, Jefferson and Monroe discussing the future of the newborn nation. And, as imagination takes hold, the powdered wigs and lace cuffs seem more real than reality itself. These are the memories, the all-pervasive ghosts of Washington. But for those of us who are unable to visit the capitol, this same warm familiarity with the heroes of America's past is possible through this program. *Mr. President* stars Edward Arnold. So listen now and see if you can name the president on whom this episode is based.

1068. MRS. ELEANOR ROOSEVELT. Talk, 15 min., NBC, 1932.

Informal conversation on topics of special interest to American women with Eleanor Roosevelt as the host. Lee Wiley provided the vocals and Leo Reisman and his orchestra supplied the music.

1069. MRS. MINIVER. Drama, 30 min., CBS, 1943–1944.

The series, which begins where the film and book *Mrs. Miniver* (by Jan Struther) ended, follows the Miniver family's move from war-torn England to America, where their struggles to begin a new life were dramatized. *Regular characters:* Kay and Clem Miniver, the parents; Judy and Vin, their children; Carl Bixby, their friend.

Cast: Judith Evelyn, Gertrude Warner (*Kay Miniver*); Karl Swenson, John Moore (*Clem Miniver*); Betty Jane Tyler (*Judy Miniver*); Alister Kay (*Vin Miniver*); Carl Eastman (*Carl Bixby*); Sarah Burton (*Carl's wife*). ***Narrator:*** Arnold Moss. ***Music:*** Nathan Van Cleave. ***Producer:*** Nila Mack.

1070. MRS. WIGGS OF THE CABBAGE PATCH. Serial, 15 min., CBS, 1935–1936; NBC, 1936–1938.

A Cabbage Patch is a polite term for a slum-like area outside a fashionable city or town of the early 1900s. The Wiggs are one such family who live in a Cabbage Patch. Serialized stories relate their day-to-day struggles as they seek to better their lives. Based on the novel by Alice Caldwell Rice. *Regular characters:* Elvira and Hiram Wiggs, the parents of Billy; Tabitha Hazy, their neighbor; Lucy Alcott, the rich girl who befriends them; Bob Redding, Lucy's beau.

Cast: Betty Garde, Eva Condon (*Elvira Wiggs*); Robert Strauss (*Hiram Wiggs*); Andy Donnelly (*Billy Wiggs*); Agnes Young, Alice Frost (*Tabitha Hazy*); Marjorie Anderson (*Lucy Alcott*); Frank Provo, Bill Johnstone (*Bob Redding*). ***Announcer:*** George Ansbro. ***Producers:*** Anne Hummert, Frank Hummert.

1071. THE MOBIL OIL CONCERT. Variety, 30 min., NBC, 1929–1932.

A weekly program of light concert music sponsored by the Mobil Oil Corporation. Singer James Melton was the host and Erno Rapee and his orchestra provided the music.

1072. Model Minstrels. Comedy, 30 min., CBS, 1939–1940.

The program, sponsored by the Model Tobacco Company, featured the hijinks of the comedy team of Tom Howard and George Shelton.

1073. The Modern Adventures of Casanova. Adventure, 30 min., Mutual, 1951–1952.

Christopher Casanova, modern-day charmer, is a direct descendant of the famous Italian lover. Also an agent for the World Criminal Police Commission, he assumes the role of an international playboy to perform his assignments—always, like his namesake, encountering women who are not only gorgeous, but treacherous as well.

Cast: Errol Flynn (*Christopher Casanova*). ***Music:*** Walter Schumann.

OPENING

Girl: Darling, why darling, no one has made me feel this way before. But darling, I don't even know your name.

Man: My name, oh, didn't I tell you, darling? It's Casanova.

Announcer: *The Modern Adventures of Casanova*, starring Errol Flynn as Christopher Casanova, direct descendant of the fabulous Italian diplomat, artist and soldier of fortune, a brave spirit and a free one, whose sensible fault was not that he kissed, but that he told. Today's Casanova is often embarrassed at the implications of his name, though he carries it proudly through the drawing rooms of international society and few know that this modern Casanova has another identity—agent for the World Criminal Police Commission. It is from his experiences we bring you *The Modern Adventures of Casanova*. And now, *The Modern Adventures of Casanova* starring Errol Flynn.

CLOSING

Announcer: You have just heard *The Modern Adventures of Casanova* based upon an idea by and starring Errol Flynn. Be with us again when we return with Errol Flynn in *The Modern Adventures of Casanova*. This is the Mutual Broadcasting System.

1074. Modern Cinderella. Serial, 30 min., CBS, 1936–1937.

A daily drama about Hope Carter, a young woman who is desperately trying to improve her social status in life and find the man of her dreams.

Cast: Rosemary Dillon, Laine Barklie (*Hope Carter*); Ben Gage (*Jim Gale*); Eddie Dean (*Larry Burton*). ***Announcer:*** Roger Krupp.

1075. Modern Romances. Anthology, 30 min., NBC Blue, 1936–1937.

Dramatizations based on stories appearing in *Modern Romances* magazine. Each program was narrated by Gertrude Warner as Helen Gregory, the magazine's editor. Bob Sabin did the announcing and George Henninger provided the organ music.

1076. Modern Romances. Anthology, 15 min., ABC, 1949–1955.

A daily, revised version of the prior title that continued to feature stories from *Modern Romances* magazine. This time, however, the adaptations were presented in a serialized form. Kathi Norris and later Eloise McElhone hosted and narrated.

1077. The Mohawk Treasure Chest. Variety, 15 min., NBC, 1934–1935.

Ralph Kirkberry, billed as "The Dream Singer," served as the host of a weekly program of music and songs sponsored by Mohawk Carpets. Harold Levy and his orchestra provided the music.

1078. The Molle Mystery Theater. Anthology, 30 min., NBC, 1943–1948; CBS, 1948–1951; ABC, 1952–1954.

A weekly program of mystery and detective fiction yarns sponsored by Molle Shaving Cream. In 1948, when Molle dropped sponsorship, the title changed to simply *Mystery Theater*. In 1951, it became *Hearthstone of the Death Squad* and in 1952, when the series switched to ABC, the title became *Inspector Mark Sabre*. The latter series are listed separately.

Host: Bernard Lenrow (as mystery expert Geoffrey Barnes). ***Announcer:*** Dan Seymour. ***Music:*** Jack Miller.

OPENING

Announcer: And now *The Molle Mystery Theater* presented by M-o-l-l-e. Molle, the heavier brushless shaving cream for tough whiskers or tender skin.

HOST: Good evening, this is Geoffrey Barnes welcoming you to *The Molle Mystery Theater*, the program that presents the best in mystery and detective fiction. Tonight our story by Robert Mitchell and Gene Levitt is entitled "Make No Mistake" and star Alan Baxter, well-known young actor of stage, screen and radio, currently appearing in the hit motion picture *Close-Up*, will play the leading role of Dave. Dave is one of two people, neither very good or very bad, who finds that one mistake can put into action a series of events that leads inevitably to disaster. And now act one of tonight's Molle mystery, "Make No Mistake" starring Alan Baxter.

CLOSING

ANNOUNCER: Be with us next week when the *Mystery Theater* will present "The Inescapable Corpse" starring Henry Morgan. This is NBC, the National Broadcasting Company.

1079. MOMMIE AND THE MEN. Serial, 15 min., CBS, 1945–1946.

The story of a woman (played by Elspeth Eric) and the four men in her life: her husband (Lon Clark) and her three children (Charles Mullen, Dolores Gillen and Jackie Grimes). Richard Keith and Sid Ward were also cast. Ron Rawson did the announcing and Dick Liebert provided the music.

1080. MONDAY MERRY-GO-ROUND. Variety, 30 min., NBC Blue, 1941–1942.

A program of music and songs with vocalist Phil Duay as the host. The regulars were Alan Holt, Marian McManus, Evelyn McGregor, Bea Wain and the Myer Rapport Chorus. Ford Bond did the announcing and Victor Arden and his orchestra provided the music.

1081. MONEY-GO-ROUND. Game, 30 min., NBC Blue, 1944.

Selected members of the studio audience were awarded cash prizes if they could answer questions based on vocal clues given by the Larry and Ginger Duo. Benay Venuta was the host and Fred Uttal was her assistant and the announcer.

1082. MOON DREAMS. Variety, 15 min., Syndicated, 1946–1947.

A daily series of music and poetry readings with Marvin Miller as the host and narrator. Vocalist Warren White provided the songs and the Del Castillo and Ivan Eppinoff orchestras supplied the music. Carl Kraazt was the producer.

1083. MOON RIVER. Variety, 15 min., Syndicated, 1946.

A daily program of music and poetry similar to *Moon Dreams*. There were no regulars and a guest served as the narrator for each episode. The program was created and produced by Edward Byron.

OPENING

NARRATOR (guest Charles Woods): Moon River, a lazy stream of dreams where vain desires forget themselves in the loneliness of sleep.

CLOSING

NARRATOR: Down the valley of a thousand yesterdays flow the bright waters of Moon River, on and down, forever flowing, forever waiting to carry you down to the land of forgetfulness, to the knowledge of sleep, to the realm of *Moon River*.

1084. MOONSHINE AND HONEYSUCKLE. Drama, 30 min., NBC, 1930–1933.

Serialized stories about incidents in the lives of a group of mountain people who inhabit the small Southern town of Lonesome Hollow.

Cast: Louis Mason (*Clem Betts*); Clyde Cooper (*Peg Leg Gaddis*); Anne Elstner (*Cracker Gaddis*). ***Also:*** Jeanie Begg, Sara Haden, John Milton, Virginia Morgan.

MORTIMER GOOCH *see* **APPENDIX**

1085. THE MORTON DOWNEY SHOW. Variety, 30 min., NBC, 1939–1943.

Music and songs with Irish tenor Morton Downey as the host. Joe King did the announcing and music was provided by the Eddy Duchin and Carmen Mastren orchestras. See also *The Coke Club* and *Songs by Morton Downey*.

1086. MOTHER AND DAD. Variety, 15 min., CBS, 1943–1944; 1947–1948.

Comedy dialogue, quotations, poems and songs delivered by an elderly couple to the friends and neighbors who visited their home.

Cast: Charme Allen, Effie Palmer (*Mother*); Parker Fennelly (*Dad*). ***Organist:*** Tiny Renier.

1087. MOTHER KNOWS BEST. Variety, 30 min., CBS, 1947–1948.

A daily program of music, songs and quizzes geared to female listeners. Aired on the East Coast only on WCBS, New York; in California over the Columbia Pacific Network. Warren Hull was the host, Isabelle Beach his assistant, and Ralph Paul the announcer.

1088. MOTHER OF MINE. Serial, 15 min., NBC Blue, 1940.

Following the death of her husband, who left her in serious debt, a woman (called Mother Morrison) regretfully sold her home and moved in with her married son (John), the owner of a farm. Stories focused on the struggles of Mother Morrison and the trials and tribulations of John, his wife Helen and their children, Anne and Peter.

Cast: Agnes Young (*Mother Morrison*); Donald Cook (*John Morrison*); Ruth Yorke (*Helen Morrison*); Patte Chapman (*Anne Morrison*); Jackie Kelk (*Peter Morrison*). ***Also:*** Arthur Allen, Paul Nugent, Betty Jane Tyler. ***Announcer:*** Charles Stark.

1089. MOTOR CITY MELODY. Variety, 30 min., CBS, 1940.

A weekly program of music and songs with Cyril Wezemael as the host. Bill McCullough and Orrin Kelly were the announcers; the Don Large Choir provided the songs; and Samuel Benavie and his orchestra supplied the music.

1090. MOUQUIN INC., PRESENTS.... Variety, 15 min., Syndicated, 1932.

Music and songs with orchestra leader Louis F. Mouquin as the host. The Mouquin Salon Orchestra provided the music.

1091. MOVIETOWN RADIO THEATER. Anthology, 30 min., Syndicated, 1949.

A weekly series of dramatic presentations featuring a different cast and story each week. *Stories included:*

1. To Love Again. Virginia Bruce in a strange love story about a woman who dreams of a man whose every trait and feature she can visualize. As the dream becomes clearer, she meets the man of her dreams—a man who tells her that he has dreamed of her for years also.

2. Mulligan the Mighty. During the American Revolution, a diminutive tailor (Jimmy Gleason) risks his life to smuggle vital secrets to George Washington.

3. Schizo-Schizo. A reporter (Jeanne Cagney) attempts to interview a psychiatrist and is mistaken for—and treated like—a mental patient.

Host: Les Tremayne.

OPENING

HOST: From time to time, we introduce new ideas which have been received quite well by our radio audience. And this week we'd like to present two new stars. First, I'd like you to meet the young man who made such a great impression on nightclub and theater audiences all over America, Mr. Bill Shirley.

BILL: Thank you very much, Les. I listen to your show very often and I think I've mastered your technique. So maybe you'll let me introduce my co-star.

LES: Okay, go ahead.

BILL: And now we'd like you to meet the beautiful red-haired creature you've seen in such pictures as *The Barkleys of Broadway* and *Oh, You Beautiful Doll*, Miss Gale Robbins.

GALE: Why, thank you, Bill. Hello, Les.

LES: Hello, welcome to our radio theater. [Les would chat briefly, a commercial would air and the play would begin.]

1092. THE MOYLAN SISTERS SHOW. Variety, 15 min., NBC Blue, 1939–1942.

The program, sponsored by Thrivo Dog Food, featured songs and music by Joan, Marianne and Peggy Moylan, three sisters billed as "The Angels of the Airwaves." Don Lowe did the announcing and pianist Morry Howard provided the music. Isaac Clements was the producer and the sisters' dog Rascal was also a part of the show.

1093. MULLIGAN'S TRAVELS. Audition (Comedy), 30 min., performed on 6/8/47.

Milton Mulligan, an educated New York City cab driver, is constantly trying to improve himself. He has "a fleet of one cab" and is attending night classes at Metropolitan College. The proposed series was to relate the incidents that befall Mulligan as he tries to put his best foot forward—"But every time I do, someone gets kicked in the face. I guess I'm a square block in a round hole." *Other regular characters:* Eloise, the waitress at Mandelbaum's Cafe, his favorite hangout "on 46th Street just west of Broadway"; his friends Stitch and Fingers. In the audition episode, Milton faces numerous setbacks as he struggles to study for an exam on *Romeo and Juliet.*

Cast: Sheldon Leonard (*Milton Mulligan*); Bea Benaderet (*Eloise*); Ed Max (*Stitch*); Arthur Q. Bryan (*Fingers*). ***Guest Cast:*** Verna Felton (*Mrs. Oberdorf*); Sarah Selby (*Miss Wimbly*); Eric Snowden (*Prof. Beemish*). ***Announcer:*** Ken Niles. ***Music:*** Al Harris. ***Producer:*** Cal Coon. ***Writer:*** Jerome Epstein.

OPENING

ANNOUNCER: *Mulligan's Travels.* The makers of this audition record present *Mulligan's Travels* starring Sheldon Leonard.

MULLIGAN: For inspiration with your transportation, travel with Mulligan.

ANNOUNCER: That's right, that's Mulligan. *Mulligan's Travels*, the story about Milton Mulligan, taxi driver, ex–G.I., scholar and solid guy. Do you want to get from Times Square to the Bowery? Do you want the inside dope on the Dodgers? Do you want to know what's with *Romeo and Juliet*? Well then, travel with—

MULLIGAN: Taxi, folks.

ANNOUNCER: Mulligan!

MULLIGAN: Hop in, folks. Where to? [A passenger would give a destination and the episode would begin.]

1094. THE MUNROS. Comedy, 15 min., NBC Blue, 1941.

Serialized events in the life of a young married couple: Gordon Munro, an obituary writer for a local newspaper, and his wife Margaret, who found housework more of a chore than she bargained for. Neal Keehan played Gordon Munro and Margaret Heckle portrayed Margaret Munro.

1095. MURDER AND MR. MALONE. Crime Drama, 30 min., ABC, 1947–1948.

The program begins by establishing the suspects in a forthcoming crime. When the dastardly deed is committed and the police arrest a suspect, "the best mouthpiece in Chicago," criminal lawyer John J. Malone, is hired. Malone then turns detective and questions all the suspects in the case, making people very nervous. Using tact as opposed to violence, Malone formulates a plan to trap the real culprit. The scheme doesn't always work as Malone had planned, but it eventually produces results—exposure of the guilty party. "I don't know how you did it Malone," is the final verdict. The program became *The Amazing Mr. Malone* in 1948 (see entry for additional information).

Cast: Frank Lovejoy (*John J. Malone*); Larry Haines (*Lt. Brooks*). ***Announcer:*** Dresser Dahlstead. ***Music:*** Rex Koury. ***Producer:*** Bernard L. Schubert.

OPENING

ANNOUNCER: The American Broadcasting Company presents *Murder and Mr. Malone*, an exciting half-hour of mystery created by Craig Rice and starring Frank Lovejoy. Our locale is the city of Chicago. The time is the present and the hero of these weekly adventures is the amazing Mr. Malone.

CLOSING

MALONE: Ever hear the story of the blasé character who thought nothing could surprise him until he tried murder? Then he was shot to death. I'll fill you in next week, so why not pick me up at my office at this same time. I'll be waiting for you. Good night.

ANNOUNCER: Frank Lovejoy was starred as John J. Malone. This is Dresser Dahlstead inviting you to tune in next week. This is ABC, the American Broadcasting Company.

1096. MURDER AT MIDNIGHT. Anthology, 30 min., Syndicated, 1946–1947.

Spine-tingling dramatizations featuring top name performers. Raymond Morgan was the host and announcer and organist Charles Paul provided the music.

OPENING

ANNOUNCER: *Murder at Midnight*! Midnight, when the graves gape open and death strikes. How? You'll learn the answers in just a moment in tonight's story, "The Man with the Black Beard."

1097. MURDER BY EXPERTS. Anthology, 30 min., Mutual, 1949–1951.

Stories of murder and mayhem chosen by leading writers of mystery fiction.

Hosts: John Dickson Carr, Alfred Hitchcock, Brett Halliday. ***Announcer:*** Phil Tonkin.

Music: Emerson Buckley. ***Producers:*** Robert Arthur, David Cogan.

OPENING (from 6/13/49)

ANNOUNCER: *Murder by Experts.* The Mutual Broadcasting System presents *Murder by Experts* with your host and narrator, Mr. John Dickson Carr, world-famous mystery novelist and author of the recently published best-seller *The Life of Sir Arthur Conan Doyle.*

HOST: This is John Dickson Carr. Each evening at this time, *Murder by Experts* brings you a story of crime and mystery which has been chosen for your approval by one of the world's leading detective writers. Those experts who are themselves masters of the art of murder, and can hold tensity at its highest. Tonight's guest expert is Mr. Hugh Pentecost, author of many memorable thrillers, who has selected a story by a young newcomer you'll do well to watch—Andrew Evans… And now we present "Summer Heat" [the story of a college prank that turns a naive student into a madman].

CLOSING

HOST: And so the curtain falls on "Summer Heat." Next week at this time, *Murder by Experts* brings you the story of a woman who pitted her wits against death, a story selected for your approval by Brett Halliday, creator of the rough, tough detective known as Michael Shayne. This is your host, John Dickson Carr, saying good night.

1098. MURDER CLINIC. Anthology, 30 min., Mutual, 1942–1946.

A series of mysteries featuring a different cast and story each week. Each episode begins by establishing the characters who are to be involved in a murder. After the crime is committed, the evening's guest detective steps in and investigates. The story then follows his efforts to solve the crime. In the episode "Gulf Stream Green," for example, Deputy Chief Paar of the Homicide Squad, the detective with "a nose for murder," investigates the death of a young girl who was mistaken for a famous opera star and killed by her anonymous admirer (the title referred to the color of her dress). In another example, "Death in the Dressing Room," Henry H.M. Merrivale, an inspector with Scotland Yard's Department of Queer Complaints, becomes involved with a nightclub owner with a problem—a mistress and a dead wife.

Host-Announcer: Frank Knight. ***Cast*** (examples listed): Mark Smith (*Deputy Paar*); Roland Winters (*H.M. Merrivale*). ***Music Composed By:*** Ralph Barnhart. ***Music Conducted By:*** Bob Stanley. ***Producer:*** Alvin Flanigan.

OPENING

ANNOUNCER: *Murder Clinic.* Stories of the world's greatest detectives—men against murder. Each week at this time, WOR-Mutual turns the spotlight on one of the world's great detectives of fiction and invites you to listen to the story of his most exciting case. Tonight we meet Sir Henry Merrivale, known to all his friends as H.M., in a story, "Death in the Dressing Room."

CLOSING

ANNOUNCER: You have been listening to *Murder Clinic. Murder Clinic,* the WOR-Mutual series which brings you each week one exciting case; one member from the select branch of the world's great detectives. Next week, *Murder Clinic* will bring you one of the best-known and best-beloved figures of all crime fiction, Agatha Christie's Hercule Poirot. Tales told on *Murder Clinic* are adapted by authors Lee Wright and John A. Blanton. This is the Mutual Broadcasting System.

1099. MURDER IS MY HOBBY. Crime Drama, 30 min., Mutual, 1945–1946.

Barton Drake is a police inspector who is also the author of *Mystery Is My Hobby* books. Stories follow Drake's investigations as he solves crimes to acquire story material. See also *Mystery Is My Hobby* for information on the revised version of this series.

Cast: Glenn Langan (*Barton Drake*). ***Announcer:*** Rod O'Connor.

1100. MURDER WILL OUT. Game, 30 min., NBC, 1945–1946.

Selected members of the studio audience compete. A real-life criminal case is dramatized and stopped prior to its conclusion. Each contestant is asked to solve the crime. Prizes are awarded to players who correctly guessed the solution.

Host-Announcer: Larry Keating. ***Dramatic Cast:*** William Gargan (*Inspector Burke*);

Eddie Marr (*Detective Nolan*). ***Producer:*** Lew Lansworth.

1101. Music America Loves Best. Variety, 30 min., ABC, 1944.

A weekly program of music and songs with Louise Calhern, Jan Peerce, Sigmund Romberg and Martha Stewart. Jay Blackton and his orchestra supplied the music.

1102. Music and Manners. Variety, 30 min., Mutual, 1949–1950.

Music, songs and comedy with Wilbur "Budd" Hulick, Henry Morgan and Jimmy Shields. Ernie Fiorito and his orchestra provided the music.

1103. Music by Camarata. Variety, 30 min., ABC, 1954.

A weekly program of music and songs (by guest vocalists) with the music of Tutti Camarata (as the host) and his orchestra.

1104. Music by Gershwin. Variety, 15 min., NBC Blue, 1934–1935.

A program of music and songs featuring the work of composer George Gershwin, who served as the host. Don Wilson did the announcing.

1105. Music for Moderns. Variety, 30 min., NBC, 1940.

Orchestra leader Clarence Fuhrman as the host of a weekly program of popular standards. The Clarence Fuhrman orchestra supplied the music and the announcing was done by a man identified only as Gulliver.

1106. Music for You. Variety, 30 min., CBS, 1948–1953.

Vocalist Earl Nightingale as the host of a weekly program of music and songs featuring Billy Leach, Elaine Rodgers and Joe Rumoro. Caesar Petrillo and his orchestra supplied the music.

1107. Music in the Moonlight. Variety, 25 min., NBC, 1941.

Singer Jane Grant as the host of an evening program of romantic music and songs. Lionel Reiger and the Moonlighters were the regulars. Beasley Smith and his orchestra provided the music.

1108. The Music of Andre Kostelanetz. Variety, 30 min., CBS, 1945.

A weekly program of popular music and songs with orchestra leader Andre Kostelanetz as the host. Alexander Scott was the narrator; Larry Elliott did the announcing and the Andre Kostelanetz Orchestra provided the music.

1109. Music of Manhattan. Variety, 30 min., NBC, 1945.

Vocalist Louise Carlyle as the host of a weekly program of music and songs broadcast from New York City. William Young did the announcing and Norm Cloutier and his orchestra provided the music.

1110. Music Tent. Variety, 25 min., ABC, 1955.

A weekly program of popular music and songs with Dirk Fredericks as the host. The regulars were Robert K. Adams, Barbara Buchanan, Clarence Day, Jr., Joyce Krause, Vincent Lopez and Elaine Spaulding. Doug Browning did the announcing and Glenn Osser and his orchestra provided the music.

1111. Music That Satisfies. Variety, 15 min., CBS, 1932–1934; NBC, 1934–1936.

Singer Ruth Etting as the host of a program of music and songs sponsored by Chesterfield Cigarettes. Arthur Tracy, "The Street Singer," and the Boswell Sisters (Connie, Martha and Vet) were the regulars. Norman Brokenshire did the announcing and Nat Shilkret and his orchestra supplied the music. Also known as *The Ruth Etting Show*.

1112. Music That Satisfies. Variety, 30 min., CBS, 1944–1945.

A revised version of the prior title (also sponsored by Chesterfield Cigarettes) featuring singers Monica Lewis and Harry Prime and the music of Paul Baron and his orchestra.

1113. Music with the Hormel Girls. Variety, 30 min., CBS, 1950.

A weekly program of music and songs sponsored by Hormel food products and featuring the Hormel Girls Orchestra and Chorus. Betty Dougherty and Elina Hart were the hosts and Marilyn Wilson did the announcing.

1114. Musical Album. Variety, 60 min., CBS, 1927–1936.

A mix of classical, popular, jazz and ballet music with Howard Barlow and the Columbia Symphony Orchestra. Soprano Mary Eastman was featured and Andre Kostelanetz became the orchestra conductor in 1932.

1115. Musical Autographs. Variety, 30 min., ABC, 1944–1945.

A weekly program of music and songs with orchestra leader Guy Lombardo as the host. Kenny Gardner, Carmen Lombardo, Lebert Lombardo, Rosemarie Lombardo and Victor Lombardo were the regulars. Z.A. Riggs did the announcing and Guy Lombardo's orchestra provided the music. See also *Guy Lombardo Time* and *Lombardo Land, U.S.A.*

1116. Musical Bouquet. Variety, 30 min., ABC, 1945.

A Sunday program of romantic music and songs with Bret Morrison as the host. Vocalists Paul Frent and Louise Marlow were the regulars; Earl Sheldon and his orchestra provided the music.

1117. Musical Gems by Ray Pearl. Variety, 30 min., CBS, 1955.

Performances by guest vocalists were featured in a program of easy listening music with the orchestra of Ray Pearl (who also served as the host).

1118. Musical Millwheel. Variety, 30 min., NBC, 1941.

Walter Paterson as the host of a program of popular standards music and songs sponsored by Pillsbury. Dan Donaldson was the announcer and music was provided by the Pillsbury Besters.

1119. Musical Mock Trial. Game, 30 min., CBS, 1940.

Six players, chosen from the studio audience, were designated as jurors; musical tunes were the plaintiff and the defendant. A mystery musical selection was played followed by a judge's reading of a short story about it. The jurors had to determine if the defendant (the mystery song) was guilty or innocent (whether or not the song related to the story). If the jurors found the song innocent (belonged with the story), they received one dollar; if they found the song guilty and were correct, they won ten dollars to be split among them. No matter what the decision, jurors received three dollars per minute of jury duty.

Host-Judge: Ben Bernie. ***Regulars:*** Lew Lehr, Dinah Shore, the Bailey Sisters. ***Announcer:*** Frank Chappell.

1120. Musical Steelmakers. Variety, 30 min., Mutual, 1938–1941; NBC Blue, 1941–1944; ABC, 1944.

A program of music and songs with Lois Mae Nolte and John Winchell (who portrayed "the Old Timer") as the hosts. The regulars were Regina Colbert, Dorothy Anne Crowe, Carolyn Lee, Lois MacNoble, Earl Summers, the Evans Sisters, the Singing Millmen and the Steele Sisters. Thomas Whitney did the announcing. The Lew Davis orchestra and the Steelmakers Orchestra provided the music. The program was sponsored by the Wheeling Steel Corporation.

1121. Musical Story Lady. Children, 10 min., NBC Blue, 1937–1941.

A Sunday morning program of musical stories for the small fry with Alice Remsen as the host (the Musical Story Lady).

1122. Musical Toast. Variety, 15 and 30 min. versions, CBS, then NBC, 1935–1937.

Music and songs with vocalists Buddy Clark, Jerry Cooper and Sally Singer. Ray Bloch and his orchestra provided the music.

1123. Musical Treasure Chest. Game, 30 min., NBC, 1940.

The format called for selected studio audience members to answer musically oriented questions in return for merchandise prizes. Horace Heidt was the host and his orchestra provided the music.

1124. Musical Vignettes. Variety, 15 and 30 min. versions, CBS, 1929.

The music of various countries was showcased featuring Howard Barlow and the Columbia Concert Orchestra.

1125. Musicomedy. Variety, 30 min., CBS, 1948.

Singer Johnny Desmond as the host of a

weekly program of music and songs. The regulars were Don Appell, Kenny Bowen, Julie Conway and the Escorts Quartet. Dan Seymour did the announcing and Raymond Paige and his orchestra supplied the music.

1126. My Best Girls. Comedy, 30 min., NBC Blue, 1944; ABC, 1944–1945.

Events in the lives of the Bartletts, a family of four living in Chicago: Russell, the father, a widower, and his three daughters: Linda (17), Penny (14) and Jill (9).

Cast: John Griggs, Roland Winters (*Russell Bartlett*); Mary Shipp (*Penny Bartlett*); Mary Mason (*Penny Bartlett*); Lorna Lynn (*Jill Bartlett*). ***Announcer:*** Dan Seymour. ***Music:*** Don Baker.

1127. My Children. Serial, 15 min., Syndicated, 1939.

A daily drama about incidents in the lives of the Gilman family: parents George and Eileen and their daughters, Deborah and Mary.

Cast: Sydney Rogers (*George Gilman*); Mary Parker (*Eileen Gilman*); Grace Holtby (*Deborah Gilman*); Lelah McNair (*Mary Gilman*); Max West (*Mr. Singleton, George's boss*). ***Music:*** Dick Aurandt.

1128. My Favorite Husband. Comedy, 30 min., CBS, 10/2/48 to 3/31/51.

George and Liz Cooper are a happily married couple who live at 321 Bundy Drive in the town of Sheridan Falls. George is a level-headed fifth executive vice-president of the Sunset State Bank. Liz is attractive but scatterbrained and determined to help other people solve their problems. Stories relate the mishaps that occur when Liz's well-intentioned efforts backfire and involve a reluctant George in various dilemmas. *Other regular characters:* Rudolph Atterbury, George's employer; Iris Atterbury, Rudolph's wife; Katie, the Coopers' maid. Served as the basis for the 1953–1955 television series of the same title.

Cast: Lee Bowman, Richard Denning (*George Cooper*); Lucille Ball (*Liz Cooper*); Ruth Perrott (*Katie*); Gale Gordon (*Rudolph Atterbury*); Bea Benaderet (*Iris Atterbury*). ***Announcer:*** Bob Lemond. ***Music:*** Wilbur Hatch.

Note: In July of 1948, an episode of *My Favorite Husband* was produced to fill a void when *Our Miss Brooks* could not air as scheduled. The program starred Lee Bowman and Lucille Ball as George and Liz Cugat, with John Heistand as their friend Corey Cartwright. The show proved to be so popular that it was made into a series beginning on 10/2/48. George and Liz acquired the new last name of Cooper and the character of Corey was rewritten as Rudolph Atterbury.

OPENING

Announcer: It's time for *My Favorite Husband* starring Lucille Ball. Yes, the gay family series starring Lucille Ball with Richard Denning, transcribed, and brought to you by the Jell-O family of red letter desserts.

Song: Oh, the big red letters stand for the Jell-O family, that's Jell-O, yum, yum, yum, Jell-O puddings, yum, yum, Jell-O tapioca puddings, yes sir-reeeee.

Announcer: And now Lucille Ball and Richard Denning as Liz and George Cooper.

My Favorite Story *see* **Favorite Story**

1129. My Friend Irma. Comedy, 30 min., CBS, 4/11/47 to 8/23/54.

Irma Peterson is a beautiful but dumb blonde who works as a legal secretary to Milton J. Clyde; Jane Stacy is her roommate, a level-headed girl who is constantly plagued by Irma's scatterbrained antics. The girls met on the street: Jane was looking for a place to live; Irma ran into her and offered to let her share her Manhattan apartment, "a one-room furnished basement Irma called home" at 185 West 73rd Street. (The residence is known as Mrs. O'Reilly's Boarding House.) Stories also focus on the men in the girls' lives: Al, Irma's jobless and impoverished boyfriend (who calls her "Chicken"); and Richard Rhinelander III, Jane's boss, an investment counselor she is struggling to impress and hopefully one day marry. (Jane, who lived in Connecticut, came to New York to find a rich husband; Irma, whose family owned a farm in Minnesota, just came to New York.) *Other regular characters:* Mrs. Kathleen O'Reilly, Irma's landlady; Prof. Kropotkin, Irma's downstairs neighbor, a musician the girls call "Maestro." (He calls the girls his "musical masterpieces"—Jane, a Strauss waltz; Irma, the Nutcracker Suite. Jane calls Irma "Cookie.") Served as the basis for the movie and television series of the same title.

Lucille Ball and Richard Denning starred in the comedy series *My Favorite Husband*.

Cast: Marie Wilson (*Irma Peterson*); Cathy Lewis, Joan Banks (*Jane Stacy*); Leif Erickson (*Richard Rhinelander III*); John Brown (*Al*); Gloria Gordon (*Mrs. Kathleen O'Reilly*); Hans Conried, Benny Rubin (*Prof. Kropotkin*); Alan Reed (*Milton J. Clyde*); Myra Marsh (*Richard's mother*). ***Announcers:*** Frank Bingham, Johnny Jacobs, Wendell Niles. ***Vocalists:*** The Sportsman Quartet. ***Music:*** Lud Gluskin. ***Producer:*** Cy Howard.

OPENING

ANNOUNCER: The Columbia Broadcasting System presents a new comedy.

JANE: *My Friend Irma.*

ANNOUNCER: Starring Marie Wilson as Irma, Cathy Lewis as Jane, with John Brown as Al.

SONG: Friendship, friendship, just the perfect blendship. When other friendships have been forgot, theirs will still be hot.

JANE: Sure, it's something to sing about and they can sing about it maybe because they haven't got any friends. But I'm singing the blues about it because I've got a friend, *My Friend Irma.* Now, don't get me wrong, I love that girl; most people do. It's just that Mother Nature gave some girls brains, intelligence and cleverness, but with Irma, well, Mother Nature slipped her a Mickey. [Jane would then talk about the episode to follow.]

MY GOOD WIFE *see* **APPENDIX**

Marie Wilson portrayed Irma Peterson in *My Friend Irma.*

1130. MY LITTLE MARGIE. Comedy, 30 min., CBS, 12/7/52 to 6/26/55; Mutual, 1953–1954.

Marjorie "Margie" Albright and her widowed father Vernon "Vern" live at 792 Park Avenue in New York City. Margie is a beautiful 21-year-old girl with a problem—her father, a 50-year-old ladies' man who just won't settle down ("I want a nice old comfortable father. I try to look after him, but he just won't settle down. Between you and me, I've got a problem"). Vern, an investment counselor for Honeywell Industries, also has a problem—Margie ("I've been both mother and father to her since she was born. When she was little, I had control over her; I could make her mind me. But what do you do when a girl reaches this age? She's completely out of hand. I've got a problem, believe me, I've got a problem"). Stories relate incidents in Margie and Vern's lives as they attempt to resolve their respective problems. Margie loves to meddle in Vern's business and private affairs. When Margie does something and Vern finds out, he decides to teach her a lesson. However, as Vern tries to teach Margie a lesson, she finds out and turns the tables by trying to teach him a lesson for trying to teach her a lesson (the basic subplot of virtually every episode). Margie appears to have no job (she says her first job was assistant beauty consultant at Stacey's Department Store; she actually handed out samples of cosmetics). Margie cares for the apartment while Vern is at work and is always being hit on by men. She uses her beauty to get men to do what she wants. *Other regular characters:* Freddie Wilson, Margie's impoverished boyfriend, sees her as "a beautiful, ravishingly delicious creature." Margie contends, "I don't have anything other girls don't have." "Yes," Freddie says, "I know, but what you have is better organized." Freddie appears to be permanently suited for unemployment and it is only love that keeps him and Margie together. (Vern thinks Freddie is a "droop" and will never amount to anything.) Mrs. Clarissa Odetts, Margie's elderly neighbor, is always eavesdropping on her and Vern. She is 82 years old and has been married a number of times. She finds pure delight in helping Margie turn the tables on Vern. *Other regulars:* Roberta Townsend, Vern's steady girlfriend in later episodes; George Honeywell, Vern's employer; Connie, Margie's girlfriend. Served as the basis for the television series of the same title.

Cast: Gale Storm (*Margie Albright*); Charles Farrell (*Vern Albright*); Gil Stratton, Jr. (*Freddie Wilson*); Doris Singleton (*Roberta Townsend*); Will Wright (*George Honeywell*); Verna Felton (*Mrs. Clarissa Odetts*); Shirley Mitchell (*Connie*). ***Announcer:*** Roy Rowan. ***Music:*** Lud Gluskin. ***Producer:*** Gordon D. Hughes.

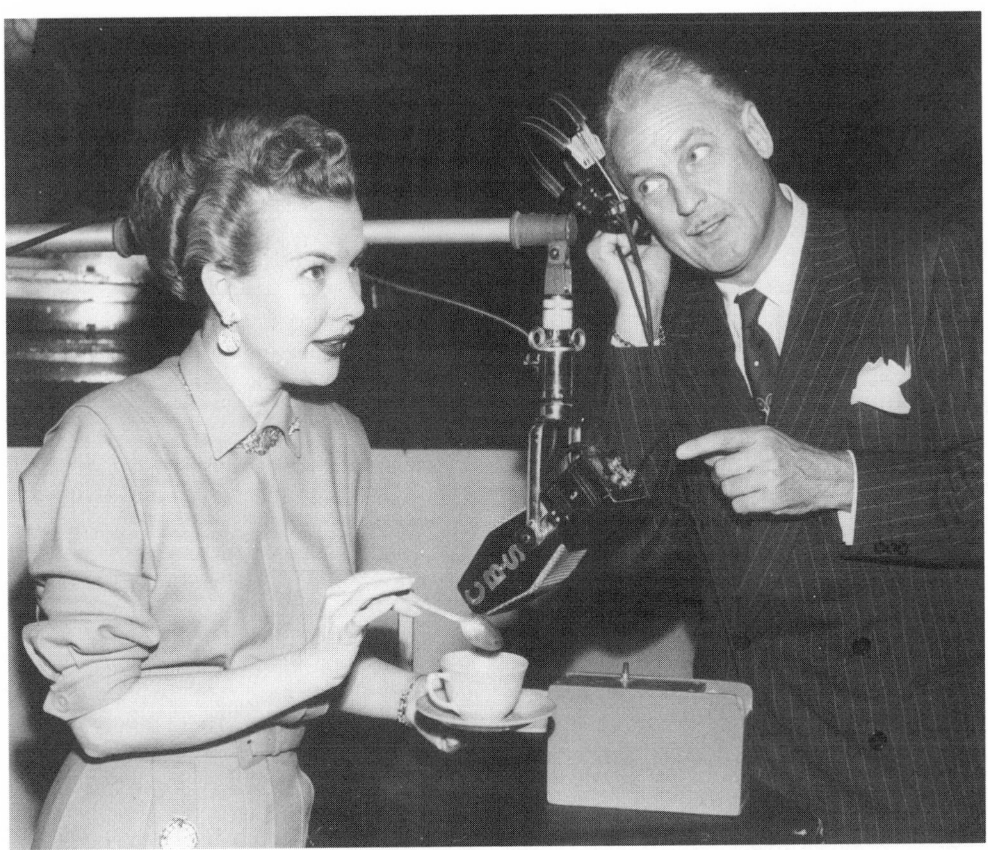

Gale Storm and Charles Farrell costarred in *My Little Margie*.

OPENING

ANNOUNCER: *My Little Margie* starring Gale Storm and Charles Farrell, transcribed in Hollywood. Margie Albright is a well-adjusted, normal person, but like many other normal people, she has certain little peculiarities and one of those peculiarities is a tendency to be slightly superstitious [the episode would then begin].

CLOSING

VERN: Well, that's *My Little Margie*.

ANNOUNCER: *My Little Margie* starring Gale Storm and Charles Farrell is based on characters created by Frank Fox. Be with us next week for another episode of *My Little Margie*. This is CBS, the Columbia Broadcasting System.

1131. MY MOTHER'S HUSBAND. Comedy, 30 min., NBC, 7/2/50 to 7/16/50.

St. Louis at the turn of the century is the setting for a look at life in simpler times as seen through the eyes of Virginia Brickel, the 18-year-old daughter of Harvey and Dorothy Brickel. Harvey is a dedicated Republican and president of the St. Louis and Northern Railroad. He is also very old-fashioned and refuses to accept the progress that is rapidly changing the world (he drives a horse and buggy and is not impressed by automobiles). Dorothy puts up with him; and Virginia, the "boy" Harvey waited nine months for (he is not overly fond of females "because they cut down the Republican vote"), tries to understand. The Brickels live on Vander Veller Place in an 18-room mansion that resembles the Taj Mahal. *Other regular characters:* Uncle Willie, Dorothy's brother and Harvey's live-in headache; Ella Mae, their cook.

Cast: William Powell (*Harvey Jefferson Brickel*); Sarah Selby (*Dorothy Brickel*); Sharon Douglas (*Virginia Brickel*); Lillian Randolph (*Ella Mae*); Tom Tully (*Uncle Willie*). ***Announcer:*** Jack McCoy. ***Orchestra and Chorus:*** Jeff Alexander. ***Producer:*** Joe Rines.

OPENING

ANNOUNCER: William Powell in *My Mother's Husband.*

CHORUS: Oh backward, turn backward, oh time in thy flight, when a bike built for two was a courtship divine.

ANNOUNCER: Ladies and gentlemen, we introduce *My Mother's Husband* starring William Powell.

CHORUS: When ladies wore blushes and gents the moustache; and an actress in tights was a barbershop smash.

ANNOUNCER: A new program about a gentleman of the old school in those grand and fabulous days when we and the century were very young.

CHORUS: Oh days that we treasure with memories a-glow, when we sat on the front porch and sang soft and low.

VIRGINIA: Visitors to St. Louis will tell you that the most awe-inspiring sights in this growing metropolis are the great Union Station, the gigantic Gage Bridge and *My Mother's Husband*, Harvey Jefferson Brickel. Yes, and proud tourists often boast that they not only witnessed the four o'clock feeding of the man-eating lion at the Forest Park Zoo, but they also saw the six o'clock homecoming of *My Mother's Husband* to Vander Veller Place for supper…

CLOSING

CHORUS: Good night, ladies, good night, ladies…

ANNOUNCER: This program was created and written by Charles Tazwell. The entire production was under the direction of Joe Rines. The star of *My Mother's Husband* was William Powell.

CHORUS: Good night, ladies.

HARVEY: Good night, Dorothy, good night, Virginia, good night, everyone.

CHORUS: Good night, ladies, we're going to sleep tonight.

1132. MY SECRET STORY. Anthology, 30 min., NBC, 1952–1954.

Anne Seymour as the host of a weekly series of dramatizations that stressed human emotion.

1133. MY SILENT PARTNER. Comedy, 30 min., NBC, 6/23/49 to 8/18/49.

The story of a small-town girl who establishes herself in business in New York City as a trouble consultant. Faye Emerson played the girl; Lyle Sudrow was her romantic interest, a lawyer; Cameron Andrews was the janitor; Harold Stone the soda fountain counterman; and Ruth Gilbert the public stenographer. Dick Dudley did the announcing.

1134. MY SON AND I. Serial, 15 min., CBS, 1939–1940.

Connie Watson is a vaudeville entertainer who works under the stage name Connie Vance. Following the death of her husband, Connie loses a court case to retain custody of her son Buddy, who was reared in the wings. The court feels theater life is unsuitable for the child and assigns him to the custody of Addy Owens, Connie's husband's aunt. Stories follow Connie's attempts to appeal the decision and prove to the court that she can provide a decent life for Buddy.

Cast: Betty Garde (*Connie Watson*); Kingsley Colton (*Buddy Watson*); Agnes Young (*Addy Owens*). ***Also:*** Alan Hewitt, Gladys Thornton. ***Announcer:*** Andre Baruch.

1135. MY SON JEEP. Comedy, 30 min., NBC, 1/53 to 6/53; CBS, 15 min., 10/55 to 11/56.

Robert Allison is a physician (affectionately called "Doc") in the small town of Grove Falls. He is a widower and the father of two children, Peggy and Jeep. Stories focus on Robert's efforts to reconstruct his life after the death of his wife, and on Jeep, a very mischievous ten-year-old boy. *Other regular characters:* Barbara Miller, Robert's receptionist; Mrs. Bixby, the housekeeper. Based on the television series of the same title.

Cast: Donald Foster, Paul McGrath (*Robert Allison*); Martin Houston, Bobby Alford (*Jeep Allison*); Joan Lazer (*Peggy Allison*); Lynne Allen, Joyce Gordon (*Barbara Miller*); Leona Powers (*Mrs. Bixby*). ***Announcers:*** Gaylord Avery, Fred Collins. ***Music:*** John Geller.

OPENING

ANNOUNCER: Yes, it's *My Son Jeep*, the bright and warm-hearted adventures of the Allison family of Grove Falls, transcribed by the National Broadcasting Company and starring Donald Foster as Doc, with young Martin Houston as the irrepressible, unpredictable ten-year-old Jeep Allison.

DOC: Some of the nicest moments around our

house take place after supper. We all gather in the living room to talk over the events of the day and plan the events for the days coming up. This is also when I usually get no inkling whatsoever of what's in store for me…

1136. My True Story. Anthology, 30 min., ABC, 1943–1961; Mutual, 1961–1962.

Dramatic adaptations of stories from *My True Story* magazine. Glenn Riggs did the announcing and organist Rosa Rio provided the music.

1137. Myrt and Marge. Serial, 15 min., CBS, 1931–1947.

The dramatic story of Myrt Spear and Marge Minter, show business girls, and the problems each faced while making a career for herself. Myrt was the experienced showgirl, and Marge was a newcomer whom Myrt made it her business to protect.

Cast: Myrtle Vail, Alice Yourman (*Myrt Spear*); Donna Damerel Fick, Helen Mack, Alice Goodkin (*Marge Minter*); Vinton Hayworth, Santos Ortega (*Jack Arnold*); Jackson Beck (*Pat Hargate*); Eleanor Rella (*Billie*); Lucy Gilman (*Edna Seymour*); Michael Fitzmaurice (*Jimmy Kent*); Joe Latham (*Pop*); Lucille Fenton (*Paula Kirby*); Dorothy Day (*Phyllis Rogers*); Marie Nelson (*Maggie*); Violet LeClair (*Agatha Folsom*); Matt Crowley (*Anthony Link*); Cliff Arquette (*Thaddeus*); Arthur Elmer (*Bill Boyle*). ***Announcers:*** Andre Baruch, David Ross, Tom Shirley. ***Organists:*** Rosa Rio, John Winters. ***Producer:*** Robert Brown.

OPENING

Announcer: The story of Myrt and Marge. *Myrt and Marge* is a story of Broadway, a story that goes beyond the lights of the Great White Way into the lives of two chorus girls; two girls from the cast of that most glittering of all Broadway extravaganzas, *Hayfield's Pleasures*. The house lights go down; the floodlights go on. In a moment, the curtain will go up on the first chapter in the story of Myrt and Marge.

1138. The Mysterious Traveler. Anthology, 30 min., Mutual, 1943–1952.

A weekly series of supernatural-based stories hosted by a man (a doctor by profession) who rode a train and invited listeners to join him for the evening's story (some of which involve patients of his).

Cast: Maurice Tarplin (*The Mysterious Traveler*). ***Announcer:*** Jimmy Wallington. ***Music:*** Henry Sylvern, Doc Whipple. ***Producers:*** Robert A. Arthur, David Logan, Jock MacGregor.

OPENING

Announcer: Mutual presents *The Mysterious Traveler*.

Traveler (over train sounds): This is the Mysterious Traveler inviting you to join me for another journey into the realm of the strange and terrifying. I hope you will enjoy the trip and it will thrill you a little and chill you a little. So, settle back, get a good grip on your nerves and be comfortable, if you can. Where are we going? We're going to join Charles Foster as he takes an excursion into crime. I call the story "The Case of Charles Foster."

CLOSING

Traveler (over train sounds): This is the Mysterious Traveler again. Did you enjoy our little trip? Too bad about Charles Foster, wasn't it? As he was strapped into the electric chair, there was an ironic smile on his face, for he was being executed for something he had not done… I knew another man who thought it would be a simple thing to dispose of his wife; unfortunately he—oh, oh, you're getting off here, sorry, but perhaps we'll meet again soon. I take this same train every week at this time.

Announcer: You have just heard Chapter 64 of *The Mysterious Traveler*, a series of dramas of the strange and terrifying. In tonight's story, "The Case of Charles Foster," Humphrey Davis played Charles Foster, Nancy Sheridan played Julie and Joan Shea played Agatha. The entire production is under the supervision of Jock MacGregor. This is Mutual.

1139. Mystery Chef. Cooking, 30 min., NBC Blue, 1931–1932; CBS, 1932–1934; NBC Blue, 1934; NBC Red, 1932–1938; NBC Red, 1941; ABC, 1942–1945.

Culinary tips, advice and recipes with John MacPherson as the host (he was originally not identified, hence the title). Organist Rosa Rio provided the music. The program appeared on both the NBC Red and Blue networks at one point.

1140. Mystery File. Game, 30 min., ABC, 1950–1951.

A criminal case was reenacted and stopped prior to the conclusion. Players had to determine the culprit on the basis of the clues presented in the case. Players with correct responses won a cash prize. Walter Kiernan was the host and Charles Wood the announcer.

1141. Mystery House. Anthology, 30 min., Syndicated, 1946.

Mystery House is a publishing company owned by Barbara and Dan Glenn. They will not publish any book until it is performed as a play by their staff (guests). Stories are the weekly manuscripts being considered for publication.

Cast: Nanette Sargent (*Barbara Glenn*); Forrest Lewis (*Dan Glenn*).

OPENING

ANNOUNCER: *Mystery House*. Mystery House, that strange publishing firm run by Dan and Barbara Glenn, where each new novel is acted out by the Mystery House staff before it is accepted for publication. *Mystery House*.

DAN: Well, Barbie, I understand we all get into the cowboy mood tonight; well, pardner.

BARBARA: That's right, pardner, we're going to act out a story about the wild and woolly west where men are men and murders are plum serious...

1142. Mystery House. Anthology, 30 min., Mutual, 1951.

A weekly series of horror, suspense and tales of the supernatural with film star Bela Lugosi as the host and frequent star.

1143. Mystery in the Air. Crime Drama, 30 min., NBC, 7/5/45 to 9/27/45.

Stonewall Scott is a private detective who has a special talent for solving baffling crimes. Dr. Alison is a beautiful pathologist who assists him. Scott uses deductive reasoning and Dr. Alison scientific methods to apprehend criminals.

Cast: Stephen Courtleigh (*Stonewall Scott*); Joan Vitez (*Dr. Alison*).

1144. Mystery in the Air. Anthology, 30 min., NBC, 7/3/47 to 9/25/47.

Dramatizations of great crime classics with actor Peter Lorre as the central figure in each tale. *Stories include:*

1. The Black Cat. While intoxicated, a man (Peter Lorre) sees the reincarnation of his pet cat, which he strangled long ago. In a fit of rage, he kills his wife, then finds his life haunted by both her spirit and the cat's.

2. The Lodger. Peter Lorre and Agnes Moorehead in a retelling of London's notorious Jack the Ripper—the true story of a mysterious killer of young women.

3. Challenge to Listeners. An unusual story in which one of the two leads (Richard Widmark, Everett Sloane) is murdered, but his identity is not revealed. The program challenged listeners to guess which one it was.

4. The Horla. A Frenchman (Peter Lorre) is haunted by an evil invisible spirit known as the Horla.

Host: Peter Lorre. ***Announcers:*** Harry Morgan, Michael Roy. ***Music:*** Paul Baron.

OPENING

ANNOUNCER: *Mystery in the Air* starring Peter Lorre, presented by Camel Cigarettes. Each week at this hour, Peter Lorre brings up the excitement of the great stories of the strange and unusual, of dark and compelling masterpieces culled from the four corners of world literature. Tonight, Edgar Allan Poe's immortal American classic, "The Black Cat."

CLOSING

ANNOUNCER: Next week, *Mystery in the Air* starring Peter Lorre brings you an adaptation of one of our star's greatest motion pictures, *Crime and Punishment*. This is Harry Morgan inviting you to be with us next week for another *Mystery in the Air*. This is NBC, the National Broadcasting Company.

1145. Mystery Is My Hobby. Crime Drama, 30 min., Syndicated, 1947–1949.

A revised version of *Murder Is My Hobby* (see entry). Barton Drake is a wealthy mystery writer (author of *Mystery Is My Hobby* books) who works with the police, especially Inspector Danton, to get story material. In a twist on normal situations, here Inspector Danton invites Barton to accompany him to a crime scene (as opposed to the reporter following the police). Stories follow Drake's investigations as he and Danton solve crimes. When Drake does solve a crime, Danton exclaims, "I could have solved this if I wasn't thrown a curve." "Sure, Inspector," replies Drake, "but *Mystery Is My Hobby*." *Other regular characters:* Mike, Barton's houseboy.

Cast: Glenn Langan (*Barton Drake*); Ken Christy, Norman Field (*Inspector Danton*); Charles Lung (*Mike*). ***Announcer:*** Bruce Buell. ***Music:*** Len Salvo. ***Producer:*** Dave Titus.

OPENING

DRAKE: *Mystery Is My Hobby*. Ladies and gentlemen, Barton Drake speaking. For tonight's drama, I've selected case history number 126 from my book, *Mystery Is My Hobby*. I call it "Death Asks Questions."

ANNOUNCER: And now to Glenn Langan as Barton Drake for the first act of—

DRAKE: *Mystery Is My Hobby*.

CLOSING

ANNOUNCER: And now here's Glenn Langan with a word about next week's story.

GLENN: Thank you Bruce Buell. Next week plan to be with us when I bring you case history number 127; it's the story of a woman's greed. I call it "Death Buys Diamonds." Until then, this is Glenn Langan saying good night.

1146. THE MYSTERY MAN. Anthology, 15 min., NBC, 1941–1942.

Jay Jostyn as the Mystery Man, the host for a daily series of dramas based on popular novels. Guests appeared in the serialized stories.

MYSTERY THEATER *see* **THE MOLLE MYSTERY THEATER**

1147. MYSTERY WITHOUT MURDER. Crime Drama, 30 min., NBC, 1947.

Peter Gentle is a private detective who is opposed to violence. These crime dramas do not involve murders; in Peter's investigations, he uses brains, not brawn, to solve mysteries.

Cast: Luther Adler (*Peter Gentle*); Teri Keane (*His secretary*).

1148. NAME THAT TUNE. Game, 30 min., NBC, 12/20/52 to 4/10/53.

Two contestants compete in a game designed to test musical knowledge. Brief musical selections are played, after which contestants try to name them. Five such rounds are played, worth $5, $10, $30, $40 and $50. The winner receives a chance to play the jackpot round and win $500 by identifying three mystery tunes. Served as the basis for the television series of the same title.

Host: Red Benson. ***Announcer:*** Wayne Howell. ***Vocalist:*** June Valli. ***Orchestra:*** Harry Salter.

1149. NAME THE MOVIE. Game, 30 min., Mutual, 5/12/49 to 11/3/49.

In return for merchandise prizes, players had to identify film titles from several lines of dialogue that were read to them by a celebrity guest.

Emcee: Marvin Miller. ***Singing Host:*** Clark Dennis. ***Vocalist:*** Peggy Mann, the Starlighters. ***Announcer:*** Marvin Miller. ***Orchestra:*** Edward Gilbert.

1150. NAME THE PLACE. Game, 30 min., NBC, 2/12/39 to 7/16/39.

The format called for players to identify locales (cities, states or countries) from brief descriptions read to them by the host (Ben Grauer). Charles O'Connor did the announcing.

1151. NATIONAL AMATEUR NIGHT. Variety, 30 min., CBS, 1934–1936.

Promising amateur talent performed with the hope of receiving a radio contract and a gold medal. Ray Perkins was the host and a panel of five guests judged the performances. Arnold Jackson and his orchestra provided the music.

1152. THE NATIONAL BARN DANCE. Variety, 60 and 30 min. versions, NBC Blue, 1933–1940; NBC Red, 1940–1946; ABC, 1949–1959.

A Saturday night program of country and western music, songs and comedy set at "The Old Hayloft." The program was broadcast from Chicago and began locally on WLS in 1924.

Host: Joe Kelly (as "The Man in Overalls"). ***Cast:*** Pat Barrett (*Uncle Ezra*); Luther Ossiebrink (*Arkie, the Arkansas Woodchopper*); Myrtle Cooper (*Lulu Belle*); Scotty Weisman (*Scotty*); Hoyt Allen (*Pokey Martin*); Malcolm Claire (*Spare Ribs*); Linda Parker (*The Sun-*

bonnet Girl); Sally Foster (*Little blue-eyed Sally*); Bob Hastings (*The 12-year-old boy soprano*). ***Regulars:*** Pat Buttram, "Little" Georgie Gobel, the Cumberland Ridge Runners, the Dinning Sisters, the Hoosier Hot Shots, Louise Massey and the Westerners. ***Announcer:*** Jack Holden. ***Orchestra:*** Glenn Welty. ***Producers:*** Jack Frost, Peter Lund.

OPENING

HOST: Hello, hello, hello, everybody everywhere. Yes, fellas and gals, wherever you might be tonight, *The National Barn Dance* invites you to join with your friends and neighbors back home who drop in at the Old Hayloft for the evening's festivities.

1153. THE NATIONAL FARM AND HOME HOUR. Variety, 60 min., NBC Blue/ABC, then CBS, 1929–1958.

A daily afternoon program of humor, country and western music and news commentary. Everett Mitchell was the host. Don Ameche (and later Raymond Edward Johnson) played the Forest Ranger (when sponsored by the U.S. Department of Agriculture). Hilmer Baukage did the news portion of the program; Jack Baus and the Cornbusters provided the songs and Harry Kogen and the Homesteaders provided the music.

1154. THE NATIONAL LAMPOON RADIO HOUR. Satire, 30 min., Syndicated, 1972–1973.

If it could be made fun of, it was; outrageous spoofs of anything—from radio and television programs to people and their customs. Sponsored by *National Lampoon Magazine*.

Cast: Polly Beard, Anne Beatts, John Belushi, Richard Belzer, Judy Chafman, Chevy Chase, Billy Crystal, Bob Dryden, Andrew Duncan, Christopher Guest, Janet Hirsch, Lou Holtzman, Paul Jacobs, Shawn Kelly, Bruce McCall, Bob Michaelson, Bill Murray, Michael O'Donoghue, Bob Perry, Emily Praeger, Gilda Radner, Sam Sawyer, Tony Shearin, Sidney Taft, Vernon Taft, Bob Tishler, John Wald, Ed Zubinski.

OPENING (each episode had its own unique signature, such as this spoof of television's *The Outer Limits*)

ANNOUNCER (over tuning frequency noises): There is nothing wrong with your radio; do not attempt to change the station. We are controlling the transmission. We control the volume. We can change the tone to a fuzzy bass, or focus it to a tinny treble. We can speed things up so fast that you can hardly understand what is being said; or we can make things so s-l-o-w y-o-u d-o-n-'t c--a--r--e. We control the content. We can make it boring or hilarious. We can make it stupid or moronic. It's our show, we can do anything we want because this is *The National Lampoon Radio Hour*.

1155. THE NAVY HOUR. Variety, 30 min., NBC, 1945.

A program of big band music with actor Robert Taylor as the host and the music of the U.S. Navy Symphony Orchestra. Sponsored and produced by the U.S. Navy.

1156. THE NBC RADIO THEATER. Anthology, 30 min., NBC, 1959.

A daily series of dramatic presentations featuring a rotating cast of four stars (who played the lead; guests appeared in supporting roles).

Host: Lee Bowman. ***Cast:*** Lee Bowman, Madeleine Carroll, Gloria DeHaven, Celeste Holm. ***Producer:*** Himan Brown.

1157. THE NBC STAR PLAYHOUSE. Anthology, 60 min., NBC, 1953.

John Chapman as the host to a series of dramatic presentations featuring a different cast and story each week.

1158. THE NBC STORY SHOP. Anthology, 30 min., NBC, 1947.

Fictional characters from books, cartoons, mythology and comic strips come to life to visit the Story Shop and relate an experience from their "lives" to the children of the listening audience.

Story Teller: Craig McDonnell. ***Announcer:*** Charles F. McCarthy. ***Producer:*** Art Richards.

OPENING

ANNOUNCER: Presenting *The NBC Story Shop* with stories for young people as told by Craig McDonnell and our special guest for today, in person, Donald Duck (voice of Clarence Nash) in "Donald Duck's Vacation Adventures."

CLOSING

CRAIG: And now, fellows and girls, my story

for next week is a famous one. It's a story of a famous sailor of the Arabian Knights, "The Story of Sinbad the Sailor." Listen next week at this very same time. Until then, this is your Story Teller Craig McDonnell saying good-bye until next time, fellows and girls.

ANNOUNCER: "Donald Duck's Vacation Adventures" was an original story written for radio by Richard E. Davis. *The Story Shop* was produced in Radio City, New York, by Art Richards, and as always, your Story Teller was Craig McDonnell. And don't forget, boys and girls, next week Craig McDonnell will tell another wonderful story, "The Adventures of Sinbad the Sailor." That's next Saturday at this very same time over this very same station on *The Story Shop*. This is NBC, the National Broadcasting Company.

1159. THE NBC SYMPHONY ORCHESTRA. Variety, 60 and 90 min. versions, NBC, 1937–1954.

A weekly program of classical music hosted by Ben Grauer (who also did the announcing). Frank Black, Pierre Monteaux and Arturo Toscanini conducted the NBC Symphony Orchestra.

1160. THE NEBBS. Comedy, 30 min., Mutual, 1945–1946.

Rudy Nebb sometimes believes that he has a counterfeit rabbit's foot as the simplest of situations always emerge into major dilemmas. These not only involve him, but his wife (Fanny) and their son (Junior). Stories follow Rudy's mishaps as he struggles to overcome the various situations that develop. *Other regular characters:* Obie Slider, the mayor; Buck and Donna, Junior's friends; Herb, the barber; Sylvia Appleby, the town gossip.

Cast: Gene Lockhart (*Rudy Nebb*); Kathleen Lockhart (*Fanny Nebb*); Conrad Binyon (*Junior Nebb*); Francis "Dink" Trout (*Obie Slider*); Dick Ryan (*Buck*); Patricia Dunlap (*Donna*); Billy Roy (*Herb*); Ruth Perrott (*Sylvia Appleby*). ***Announcer:*** Tom Dixon. ***Music:*** Bud Carlton. ***Producer:*** Wally Lansing.

OPENING

ANNOUNCER: Cystex presents *The Nebbs* starring Gene Lockhart and Kathleen Lockhart as Rudy and Fanny Nebb. *The Nebbs*, straight from America's famous comic strip with Junior, Obie Slider and all the others you laughed and adventured with for 22 years. [Cystex was a medicine that "helped eliminate acids through the bloodstream to make you feel more vitality."]

CLOSING

ANNOUNCER: Join us next Sunday at this same time when Cystex again presents Gene Lockhart and Kathleen Lockhart as *The Nebbs*. If you would like to attend one of our broadcasts to see Gene and Kathleen Lockhart in person, write to radio station KHJ, Los Angeles, 38, for tickets. This is Tom Dixon saying good night for Cystex. This is the Mutual Broadcasting System.

1161. NED JORDAN, SECRET AGENT. Adventure, 30 min., Mutual, 1940–1942.

Ned Jordan is a U.S. government agent who works undercover as an insurance investigator for the Consolidated American Railroad. While pretending to settle claims, he is actually battling "the crackpots who try to overthrow America." His experiences as he attempts to prevent ill will between the United States and friendly nations is the focal point of stories. Ned's true missions are known only to J.B. Medwick, president of the railroad, and Agent Proctor of the Federal Department. Judy Medwick, Ned's girlfriend, is also J.B.'s beautiful daughter and his assistant (Judy loves adventure and helps Ned in secret—"My father would be furious if he knew what I was doing"). Ned constantly worries about Judy—"too much," she says, but she also remarks, "I wonder if I'm a valued ally or a fool dame who sticks out her neck too far?"

Cast: Jack McCarthy (*Ned Jordan*); Shirley Squires (*Judy Medwick*); Dick Osgood (*Agent Proctor*). ***Announcer:*** Bob Hite. ***Producer:*** George W. Trendle.

OPENING

EFFECT: Sound of a train roaring down the tracks.

ANNOUNCER: Speeding from coast to coast, the Federal Express thunders through the night. Adventure, thrills, romance; ride the rails with *Ned Jordan, Secret Agent*.

CLOSING

CONDUCTOR'S VOICE: All aboard! All aboard for Atlanta.

ANNOUNCER (over train pulling out of station): You have just heard the adventure of "The

True Light Cult." These exciting dramas originate in the studios of WXYZ, Detroit, and are sent to you each Tuesday night at this same time. Bob Hite speaking. This is the Mutual Broadcasting System.

1162. THE NELSON EDDY SHOW. Variety, 30 min., CBS, 1942; NBC, 1943.

A weekly program of music and songs with baritone Nelson Eddy as the host. Choral backing was provided by the Robert Armbruster Singers and music by the Robert Armbruster Orchestra.

NERO WOLFE *see* **THE ADVENTURES OF NERO WOLFE** and **THE NEW ADVENTURES OF NERO WOLFE**

1163. THE NEW ADVENTURES OF MICHAEL SHAYNE. Crime Drama, 30 min., ABC, 1948–1950.

A revised version of *Michael Shayne* (see entry, and also *The Adventures of Michael Shayne*) that finds the tough, hard-boiled private detective now based in his old neighborhood in New Orleans. He is as brash and abrasive as ever, and this time he works alone (his prior series secretary Phyllis Knight is not part of the new series). If Shayne believes a client is innocent, he will take the case and do what it takes to clear him. Stories follow Shayne's investigations into the cases that he takes but sometimes wishes he hadn't ("Of all the private eyes in New Orleans, you had to pick me. I should have my head examined for taking this case").

Cast: Jeff Chandler (*Michael Shayne*). ***Announcer:*** Bill Russo. ***Music:*** John Duffy.

OPENING (from "The Case of the Phantom Neighbor")

MICHAEL: There I was, squinting down the gun barrel at my throat. I wish I had taken LeFeve's advice and kept out of the whole deal. Then I saw his finger start to tighten on the trigger and all I could do is stand there, helpless, knowing in one more second death would be flying my way.

ANNOUNCER (over theme music): *The New Adventures of Michael Shayne* starring Jeff Chandler. Michael Shayne, back in his old haunts in New Orleans. This is your director, Bill Russo, inviting you to listen to another transcribed episode we call "The Case of the Phantom Neighbor."

1164. THE NEW ADVENTURES OF NERO WOLFE. Crime Drama, 30 min., NBC, 1950–1951.

A revised version of *The Adventures of Nero Wolfe* (see entry). Nero Wolfe is a world-famous private detective known for his ability to solve the most baffling crimes. He is also a gourmet, a horticulturalist, and very reluctant to stray from his home at 601 West 35th Street in Manhattan (he appears to be somewhat overweight and feels uncomfortable outside his world of food and flowers). Nero has a keen attention to detail and can solve virtually any crime while his associate, Archie Goodwin, does the actual legwork for him. Archie is a ladies' man ("a bit psychotic," Nero believes) who investigates for Nero, brings him the facts—and even suggests who the culprit might be (to which Nero responds, "You don't solve crimes by imagination"). When Nero feels he has sufficient evidence to make a conviction, he gathers all the suspects in the case at his home. He recaps the crime, reveals the guilty party and turns him (or her) over to Inspector Cramer of the N.Y.P.D. Nero charges as much as $1000 a case and Archie calls him "Boss." Based on the character created by Rex Stout.

Cast: Sydney Greenstreet (*Nero Wolfe*); Wally Maher, Lamont Johnson, Larry Dobkin, Harry Bartell (*Archie Goodwin*); Bill Johnstone (*Inspector Cramer*). ***Announcer:*** Don Stanley.

OPENING

SOUND: Phone ringing.

ANNOUNCER: Ladies and gentlemen, the ringing of that phone bell brings you mystery, adventure.

ARCHIE (picking up phone): Nero Wolfe's office, Archie Goodwin speaking.

ANNOUNCER: Ladies and gentlemen, it's that renowned genius, the most brilliant detective in the world, yes, none other than that chair-borne mass of unpredictable intellect, Nero Wolfe, created by Rex Stout and brought to you in a new series of adventures over this NBC station in the person of Mr. Sydney Greenstreet.

CLOSING

ANNOUNCER: You have been listening to *The New Adventures of Nero Wolfe* starring Sydney Greenstreet. Tonight's transcribed story was based on the character created by Rex Stout. Next week at this same time, Nero Wolfe and Archie will bring you "The Case of the Telltale Ribbon." Don Stanley speaking. This is NBC, the National Broadcasting Company.

THE NEW ADVENTURES OF THE THIN MAN *see* **THE ADVENTURES OF THE THIN MAN**

THE NEW EDGAR BERGEN HOUR *see* **THE EDGAR BERGEN HOUR**

THE NEW JIMMY DURANTE SHOW *see* **THE JIMMY DURANTE SHOW**

1165. THE NEW JUNIOR JUNCTION. Variety, 30 min., ABC, 1950.

A weekly program of music, songs, games and quizzes for children. Jack Lester was the host and Peggy Murdock and Bill Snary were the regulars. Bruce Case and his orchestra provided the music.

1166. THE NEW LUM AND ABNER SHOW. Comedy, 30 min., CBS, 1947–1950; ABC, 1950–1954.

A revised, half-hour version of the quarter-hour *Lum and Abner* (see entry) that continues to relate events in the simple lives of Lum Edwards and Abner Peabody, naive country bumpkins who run the Jot 'Em Down General Store in Pine Ridge, Arkansas. *Other regular characters:* Ben Withers, their friend; Cedric Wehunt, the chap who minds the store when Lum and Abner are away; Andy Devine, a friend of Lum and Abner; Miss Pitts, the town's do-gooder (who is in love with Lum); Cliff Arquette, the town's busy-body (preys into everyone's business); Opie, the not-too-bright friend of Lum and Abner.

Cast: Chester Lauck (*Lum Edwards*); Norris Goff (*Abner Peabody*); Francis "Dink" Trout (*Cedric Wehunt*); Clarence Hartzell (*Ben Withers*); Andy Devine (*Andy Devine*); ZaSu Pitts (*Miss Pitts*); Cliff Arquette (*Cliff Arquette*); Opie Cates (*Opie*); Jim Backus (*Various roles*). ***Announcer:*** Wendell Niles. ***Music:*** Opie Cates, Felix Mills.

OPENING (from 12/18/48)

EFFECT: Phone ringing.

LUM: By grannie's, Abner, I believe that's our ring.

ANNOUNCER: Frigidaire presents *The New Lum and Abner Show*. Tonight, Frigidaire, a division of General Motors, brings you a brand new kind of visit with those old characters down in Pine Ridge, Arkansas, with Clarence Hartzell as Ben Withers, the music of Felix Mills and starring your old favorites, Lum and Abner. America's number one refrigerator is Frigidaire ... number one in popularity ... number one in dependability... So when it comes to a new refrigerator for your home, remember ... Frigidaire, America's number one refrigerator. As we look in on the little community of Pine Ridge we find the old fellas in their Jot 'Em Down Store...

CLOSING

ANNOUNCER: *The New Lum and Abner Show* is brought to you each week with the best wishes of your Frigidaire dealer, a division of General Motors, manufacturers of a complete line of appliances, air conditioners and commercial refrigeration equipment. And until next Sunday night, same time, same station, this is Wendell Niles saying good night for Frigidaire, America's number one refrigerator.

1167. NEWS AND RHYTHM. Variety, 30 min., CBS, 1939.

Music and songs coupled with news reports with Todd Hunter as the host and reporter. Dave Bacal assisted; Tommy Bartlett did the announcing; and Carl Hohengarten and his orchestra supplied the music.

1168. NEWS GAME. Game, 30 min., NBC, 1954.

Kenneth Banghart was the host of a program wherein guest news experts answered questions against a ticking clock. Their cash prizes (determined by the number of correct responses) were awarded to a hospitalized G.I.

1169. NEWSSTAND THEATER. Anthology, 30 min., ABC, 1951–1952.

A different cast appeared each week in dramatizations of stories from the Crowell-Collier Publishing Syndicate (which included *Collier's* magazine).

NEXT, DAVE GARROWAY *see* **THE DAVE GARROWAY SHOW**

1170. NICK CARTER, MASTER DETECTIVE. Crime Drama, 30 min., Mutual, 4/11/43 to 9/25/55.

Nick Carter is a private detective who is a master of deductive reasoning. He prefers to use his wits, rather than guns, to capture criminals. Stories relate his case investigations, almost all of which team him with "Matty" Mathison, a tough police sergeant who is forever being outwitted by Nick. *Other regular characters:* Patsy Bowen, Nick's secretary; Scubby Wilson, a newspaper reporter. See also *Chick Carter, Boy Detective*, the spinoff series.

Cast: Lon Clark (*Nick Carter*); Helen Choate, Charlotte Manson (*Patsy Bowen*); Ed Latimer (*Matty Mathison*); John Kane (*Scubby Wilson*). ***Announcers:*** Michael Fitzmaurice, Ken Powell. ***Music:*** Hank Sylvern, Lew White. ***Producer:*** Jock McGregor.

OPENING

EFFECT: Knocks and bangs at a door.

WOMAN: What's the matter? What is it?

MAN: Another case for Nick Carter, Master Detective!

ANNOUNCER: Yes, it's another case for that most famous of all manhunters, the detective whose ability at solving crime is unequaled in the history of detective fiction, *Nick Carter, Master Detective*. Today's curious adventure, "An Eye for an Eye."

CLOSING

ANNOUNCER: Join us again next week for "The Mystery of the Upstate Murder," another intriguing adventure with *Nick Carter, Master Detective*. This program came to you from New York. This is the Mutual Broadcasting System.

1171. NIGHT BEAT. Crime Drama, 30 min., NBC, 1950–1952.

When the sun goes down, Randy Stone, topnotch reporter for the *Chicago Star*, goes to work. His is the world of the night beat and stories follow his exploits as he searches through the city for the strange stories waiting for him in the darkness (from human interest accounts to the seedy criminals who thrive at night). Randy's phone number was given as Butterfield 13-003 and he ended each story by calling, "Copy boy."

Cast: Frank Lovejoy (*Randy Stone*); Edmond O'Brien (*Randy Stone, audition episode*). ***Announcer:*** Donald Rickles. ***Music:*** Frank Worth. ***Producer:*** Warren Lewis.

OPENING

ANNOUNCER: *Night Beat.*

RANDY: Hi, this is Randy Stone. I cover the night beat for the *Chicago Star*. Stories start in many different ways; this one began in a nightclub with jazz music and laughter and ended in a church with organ music and death.

ANNOUNCER: *Night Beat* starring Frank Lovejoy as Randy Stone.

CLOSING

RANDY (summing up the episode): It's all about laws that made criminals and laws that made them not criminals. It's kind of a wandering piece of copy that never really gets anywhere or solves anything. Copy boy.

ANNOUNCER: You have been listening to *Night Beat* starring Frank Lovejoy as Randy Stone. Join us again next week, same time, same station for *Night Beat*. This is NBC, the National Broadcasting Company.

1172. NIGHT EDITOR. Anthology, 15 min., NBC Blue, 1943–1944; ABC, 1944–1945.

A weekly program of dramatizations based on actual newspaper accounts. Sponsored by Edwards' Coffee and featuring a different cast for each story. Hal Burdick played the newspaperman (narrator).

1173. NIGHT LIFE. Variety, 30 min., CBS, 1946.

An evening program of music and songs with Willie Brandt as the host. Pete Johnson, Maxine Sullivan and the Lamuel Morgan Trio were the regulars. Bob Hite did the announcing and Teddy Wilson and his orchestra provided the music.

1174. NIGHT LIFE. Variety, 30 min., NBC, 1955.

A weekly program of jazz music with Ken Nordine as the host. Singer Bobby Gibson was the featured regular and Fred Kaz and his trio provided the music.

1175. NIGHT WATCH. Reality, 30 min., CBS, 1954–1955.

Don Reed is a police reporter who calls himself a "police recorder" due to the fact that he carries a portable audio tape recorder and rides with the officers of the Culver City, California,

Police Department. The program uses no script, no actors and no music; the sounds captured by Reed's recorder as he accompanies officers to crime scenes are heard as Don narrates each episode. Don Reed portrays himself.

OPENING

DON: This is Don Reed; I'm a police recorder. The sounds you are listening to are real. This is a police car reporting in service for night duty. You will actually ride with this detective unit and follow the activities of the police officers in this car. You'll watch and listen to me as the cases unfold. And, as you listen, remember the people you hear are not actors and all the voices and sounds are authentic. For this is *Night Watch*.

ANNOUNCER: *Night Watch*. For the first time through the medium of network radio, the actual on-the-scene report of your police force in action. There are no actors; there is no script. The investigations are recorded as they actually occurred. *Night Watch*, presented with the cooperation of the police department of Culver City, California, W.N. Hildebrand, Chief. We switch you to Car 54, now on patrol and police recorder Don Reed...

1176. NIGHTMARE. Anthology, 30 min., Mutual, 1953–1954.

Peter Lorre as the host and narrator of a weekly series of horror stories designed to send chills up and down the listener's spine.

OPENING

ANNOUNCER: In the dark of night, from the shadows of the senses comes fits of fantasy and fear—*Nightmare*, starring as your exciting guide to terror, Peter Lorre.

1177. NINETY-NINE MEN AND A GIRL. Variety, 30 min., CBS, 1939.

A weekly program of music and songs featuring Hildegarde Loretta Sell ("The Incomparable Hildegarde") and the 99-piece Raymond Paige Orchestra.

1178. NITWIT COURT. Comedy, 30 min., NBC Blue/ABC, 1944.

The program is set against the background of a courtroom. A problem was read by the bailiff (host) to a trio of jurors: Hornblower, a fumbling motorboatist; Bubbles Lowbridge, a less-than-intelligent woman; and Willow, a lisping man. Each provided comic responses.

Cast: Ransom Sherman (*Host*); Arthur Q. Bryan (*Willow*); Mel Blanc (*Hornblower*); Sara Berner (*Bubbles Lowbridge*). ***Vocalists:*** Jimmie Dodd, Johnny "Scat" Davis. ***Orchestra:*** Jack Rose.

NO SCHOOL TODAY *see* **BIG JON AND SPARKIE**

1179. NOAH WEBSTER SAYS. Game, 30 min., NBC, 1942–1951.

Listeners sent in a list of five difficult words. A member of the studio audience was chosen and asked to define each word. The player received money for each correct definition (beginning at $2, then increasing to $10 in later years). The listener also received money—$2 for each word the player failed to define. All definitions were based on *Webster's Dictionary*.

Host: Haven MacQuarrie. ***Judge:*** Dr. Charles F. Lindsley. ***Announcers:*** John Frazer, Doug Gourlay, John Storm.

1180. NOBODY'S CHILDREN. Human Interest, 30 min., Mutual, 1939–1941.

Dramatizations intended to make listeners aware of the plight of orphans. The orphans, who appeared with guest celebrities, were from the Children's Home Society of Los Angeles. Top name guests appeared in the dramas (for example, Jack Benny, James Cagney, Bob Hope and Barbara Stanwyck).

Cast: Georgia Fifield (*Matron*); Walter White, Jr. (*Host-Narrator*). ***Announcer:*** Bill Kennedy.

1181. NONA FROM NOWHERE. Serial, 15 min., CBS, 1950.

The story, set against the background of Hollywood, followed the career of Nona Dutell, a 23-year-old actress with one ambition—to find her real parents (she was adopted as a young girl and feels she has no real past).

Cast: Toni Darnay (*Nona Dutell*); Karl Weber (*Vernon Dutell*); James Kelly (*Patrick Brady*); Florence Robinson (*Gwen Parker*); Mitzi Gould (*Thelma Powell*). ***Announcer:*** Ford Bond. ***Producers:*** Anne Hummert, Frank Hummert.

1182. THE NORMAN BROKENSHIRE SHOW. Variety, 30 min., ABC, 1945.

A program of music and songs sponsored by

Nehi Beverages. Norman Brokenshire was the host and singers Martha Lou Harp and Bob Huston were the regulars. Bernie Green and his orchestra provided the music.

1183. The Notorious Tarique. Crime Drama, 30 min., ABC, 1947.

Francois Tarique is a suave and sophisticated Frenchman with a most unusual job. He punches no time clock, has no regular office hours and has no boss. He collects things—objects that are rare and valuable. Women find him attractive, but the unscrupulous call him "one of the most dangerous men in the world." In the world's most exotic locales, Tarique seeks the unusual and battles the diabolical characters who come along with the job.

Cast: Turhan Bey (*Francois Tarique*). ***Music:*** Basil Adlam. ***Producer:*** Milton Merlin.

OPENING

ANNOUNCER: The American Broadcasting Company presents *The Notorious Tarique*.

TARIQUE: Mine is a strange business. No time clocks, no office, no title. My work may take an hour or a year. It may lead me across the street or around the world. You see, I find and collect things. Things of great rarity and value. And wherever there are such things, wherever stakes are high, there are sure to be scoundrels who search and plunder and often it seems, for one reason or another, there also am I. Oh, yes, my name is Francois Tarique.

ANNOUNCER: And who is the Notorious Tarique? He is many things to many men—and women. To some his name strikes terror, to others it spells enchantment, to you it means adventure, intrigue and romance. Ladies and gentlemen, the American Broadcasting Company is proud to present *The Notorious Tarique* starring that celebrated actor, Turhan Bey.

CLOSING

ANNOUNCER: You have just heard the first in a new series of romantic adventures starring Turhan Bey as *The Notorious Tarique*. This is a presentation of the American Broadcasting Company.

1184. N.T.G. and His Girls. Variety, 30 min., NBC, 1935–1936.

Broadway producer Nils Thor Granlund as the host of a weekly series that featured performances by talented chorus girls (who appeared as guests). Harry Salter and his orchestra provided the music and special guests (former chorus girls who made it on Broadway) were also part of the program.

1185. Official Detective. Crime Drama, 30 min., Mutual, 1946–1957.

A behind-the-scenes look at the work of a police department as depicted through the cases of Dan Britt, a hard-boiled detective lieutenant assisted by Sgt. Al Bowen. Stories are culled from the pages of *Official Detective Stories* magazine. Served as the basis for the television series of the same title.

Cast: Ed Begley, Craig McDonnell (*Dan Britt*); Louis Nye, Tom Evans (*Al Bowen*). ***Announcer:*** Jack Irish. ***Music:*** Sylvan Levin.

OPENING

ANNOUNCER: *Official Detective*, dedicated to the men who guard your safety and protect your home, your police department. *Official Detective*, presented by the Mutual Broadcasting System in cooperation with *Official Detective Stories* magazine and starring Craig McDonnell as Detective Lt. Dan Britt.

1186. O'Hara. Crime Drama, 30 min., CBS, 1951.

Robert "Bob" O'Hara is a freelance journalist "in the far places of the world." He is a reporter who does more than just write the stories—he becomes personally involved with them, and his efforts to help the people he encounters is the focal point of each episode. *Other regular:* Commissioner Phelps, his friend in Hong Kong. O'Hara works for Trans World News.

Cast: Jack Moyles (*Bob O'Hara*); Byron Kane (*Commissioner Phelps*). ***Announcer:*** Art Gilmore. ***Producers:*** Tommy Tomlinson, Sterling Tracy.

OPENING

ANNOUNCER: *O'Hara*!

O'HARA: O'Hara, Hong Kong, to Trans World News, San Francisco. I'm forwarding herewith the most unusual story I've run across in 15 years of reports. You may think it belongs in the Sunday supplement; I think it deserves the front page. Details to follow. Signed, O'Hara.

ANNOUNCER: CBS brings you *O'Hara* starring

Jack Moyles, the adventures of a freelance correspondent in the far places of the world. Tonight O'Hara cables from Hong Kong in a story entitled "The Judas Vase."

1187. Oklahoma Roundup. Variety, 30 min., CBS, 1946–1947.

A program of country and western music with Hiram Higsby as the host. Ann Bond, Lem Hawkins, Mary Lou and Dick Reinhart were the regulars and Alan Page did the announcing.

1188. The Old Gold Program.

A series of 30-minute comedy and variety programs sponsored by Old Gold cigarettes.

1. The Old Gold Program, NBC Blue, 1933–1938. Dick Powell was the host and Ted Fiorito and his orchestra provided the music.

2. The Old Gold Comedy Theater, NBC Blue, 1938–1939. Robert Benchley as the host with the music of Artie Shaw and his orchestra.

3. The Old Gold Program, CBS, 1942–1943. Singer Nelson Eddy as the host with the music of the Robert Armbruster Orchestra.

4. The Old Gold Show, CBS, 1944–1947. Allan Jones as the host with regulars Frankie Carle, Woody Herman and Sammy Kaye. Red Barber was the announcer.

5. The Old Gold Show, CBS, 1947–1948. Don Ameche and Frances Langford (as John and Blanche Bickerson) sharing the spotlight with Frank Morgan and Marvin Miller (Morgan related monologues full of exaggerations; Miller was his foil). Miller also did the announcing and Carmen Dragon and his orchestra provided the music. See also *The Bickersons.*

1189. Olivio Santoro. Variety, 15 min., NBC Blue, 1940–1942.

Olivio Santoro, billed as "The Boy Yodeler," as the host of a Sunday afternoon program of music and songs (Olivio also played the guitar and sang). Glenn Riggs did the announcing.

1190. Olmsted and Company. Variety, 30 min., NBC, 1948.

Music and songs with Nelson Olmsted as the host. Tom Scott did the announcing and Norman Cloutier and his orchestra provided the music. The "company" in the title referred to the guest entertainers who appeared on the program.

1191. The Olsen and Johnson Show. Comedy, 30 min., CBS, 1933–1934.

Vaudeville comics and motion picture stars John "Ole" Olsen and Harold "Chic" Johnson host a weekly program of skits, music and songs (provided by guests). Harry Sosnik and his orchestra provided the music.

1192. On a Sunday Afternoon. Variety, 30 min., CBS, 1955–1957.

A Sunday afternoon program of music and songs with Byron Palmer as the host; vocalist Joan Weldon and the Pied Pipers were the regulars and music was provided by Wilbur Hatch and his orchestra.

1193. On Stage. Anthology, 30 min., CBS, 1953–1954.

A weekly series of comedy and drama productions featuring Cathy Lewis and Elliott Lewis as the female and male leads in stories. Lud Gluskin and his orchestra provided the music; Elliott Lewis also produced.

1194. On Stage America. Variety, 30 min., ABC, 1945.

A weekly program of performances by established performers and non-professional talent (who were seeking their big break). Paul Whiteman was the host and his orchestra provided the music.

1195. On the Town. Variety, 15 min., Mutual, 1940.

Music, songs and skits with comedian Eddie Mayehoff as the host. Tommy Dorsey and his orchestra provided the music.

1196. The Ona Munson Show. Variety, 30 min., CBS, 1944–1945.

Actress Ona Munson as the host of a program that combined celebrity interviews (conducted by Munson), songs (by vocalist Anita Ellis) and music (by the Lud Gluskin Orchestra).

1197. One Foot in Heaven. Serial, 30 min., ABC, 1945.

Events in the life of Reverend Spence

***One Man's Family* featured (left to right) Dawn Bender, J. Anthony Smythe, Minetta Ellen and Bernice Berwin.**

(Philip Merivale) and the problems faced by a small community during World War II. Also in the cast were Peggy Allenby, Edwin Cooper, Doris Dalton, Peter Fernandez, Raymond Ives, Muriel Kirkland, John McGovern, Bobby Raedick and Evelyn Varden. Joseph Stopak and his orchestra provided the music.

1198. One Man's Family. Serial, 30 min., NBC, 5/17/33 to 6/4/50; 15 min., NBC, 6/5/50 to 5/8/59.

The dramatic story of the Barbour family, residents of the swank Sea Cliff section of Bay City in San Francisco. *Regular characters:* Henry Barbour, the father, a stockbroker; Frances, his wife; their children Paul, Hazel, Clifford and Claudia (twins) and Jack; Bill Herbert, Hazel's first husband; Dan Murray, Hazel's second husband; Hank and Pinky Herbert, Hazel's twin sons; Teddy, Paul's adopted daughter; Nicholas Lacey, Claudia's husband; Betty Barbour, Jack's wife; Abigail, Elizabeth, Mary Lou, Jane, Deborah and Constance Barbour, Jack and Betty's six daughters; Margaret Herbert, Hazel's daughter; Irene, Cliff's wife; Penny Lacey, Claudia's daughter by Bill. Served as the basis for the television series of the same title.

Cast: J. Anthony Smythe (*Henry Barbour*); Minetta Ellen, Mary Adams (*Frances "Fanny" Barbour*); Michael Raffeto, Russell Thorson (*Paul Barbour*); Bernice Berwin (*Hazel Barbour*); Kathleen Wilson, Floy Margaret Hughes, Barbara Fuller, Laurette Fillbrandt (*Claudia Barbour*); Barton Yarborough (*Clifford Barbour*); Page Gilman (*Jack Barbour*); Wally Maher, Russell Thorson, Bill Bouchey, Ken Peters (*Dan Murray*); Richard Svihus, Dix Davis, Billy Idelson, Eddie Firestone, Jr., Tommy Bernard, George Perrone (*William Herbert "Pinky" Murray*); Conrad Binyon, Dick Meyers, Billy Idelson (*Henry Herbert "Hank" Murray*); Winifred Wolfe, Jeanne Bates (*Teddy Barbour*); Walter Paterson, Tom Collins, Dan O'Herlihy, Ben Wright (*Nicholas Lacey*); Jean Rouverol, Virginia Gregg (*Betty Barbour*); Bert Horton (*Bill Herbert*); Mary Lansing, Jill Oppenheim, Susan Luckey, Marilyn Steiner, Susan Odin (*Elizabeth Barbour*); Mary Lansing, Mary McGovern (*Mary Lou Barbour*); Jana Leff, Susan Luckey, Susan Odin (*Jane Barbour*); Leone Ledoux (*Abigail Barbour/Deborah Barbour/Constance Barbour*); Dawn Bender, Margaret Herbert, Naomi Stevens, Janet Waldo (*Irene Barbour*); Anne Whitfield (*Penny Lacey*). ***Announcers:*** William Andrews, Frank Barton, Ken Carpenter. ***Organists:*** Paul Carson, Sybil Chism, Martha Green.

OPENING

ANNOUNCER: This is *One Man's Family. One Man's Family* is dedicated to the mothers and fathers of the younger generation and to their bewildering offspring. Today, transcribed, we present Chapter 12, Book 72, entitled "A Touch of Christmas Spirit."

1199. $1,000 REWARD. Game, 30 min., NBC, 6/25/50 to 10/29/50.

A whodunit drama was enacted and stopped prior to its conclusion. A telephone call was placed to a listener (postcard selection) who could win $1000 by identifying the culprit.

Host: John Sylvester. ***Dramatic Cast:*** Ralph Bell, Ethel Everett, Ken Lynch, Bill Smith. ***Announcer:*** Ken Roberts.

1200. THE O'NEILLS. Serial, 15 min., Mutual, 1934; CBS, 1934–1935; NBC, 1935–1941; CBS, 1941–1942; NBC, 1942–1943.

Mrs. O'Neill is a widow and the mother of two children (Peggy and Danny). She is also the adoptive mother of Janice and Eddie Collins, whom she took in after the death of their parents in a car accident. Stories, set in the town of Royalton, relate events in the lives of the individual family members. *Other regular characters:* Trudy Bailey, a friend; Monte Kayden, Peggy's husband.

Cast: Kate McComb, Luise Barclay (*Mrs. O'Neill*); Jimmy Donnelly, Nick Dawson (*Eddie O'Neill*); Betty Caine, Violet Dunn, Claire Niesen, Betty Winkler (*Peggy O'Neill Kayden*); Janice Gilbert (*Janice Collins*); James Tansey (*Danny Collins*); Jane West (*Trudy Bailey*); Chester Stratton (*Monte Kayden*). ***Announcers:*** Ed Herlihy, Craig McDonnell. ***Organist:*** Herbert Little.

1201. ONLY YESTERDAY. Variety, 30 min., CBS, 1943.

Mary Small and Benny Rubin as the hosts of a program recapturing the music, songs and comedy of the 1920s. Van Alexander and his orchestra provided the music.

1202. THE OPEN DOOR. Drama, 15 min., CBS, 6/21/43 to 6/30/44.

"Dean Hansen, you've helped so many people, please help me," is a familiar tune to Erik Hansen, Dean of Students at fictitious Vernon University in the town of Jefferson. While students find comfort in consulting Dean Hansen, the townspeople also seek his advice and comfort. Stories, which are basically a dialogue, show how Erik's advice helps those who come through his *Open Door*. Erik's secretary Cory Lohman lives in Residence Hall.

Cast: Dr. Alfred T. Dorf (*Erik Hansen*); Charlotte Holland (*Cory Lohman*). ***Announcer-Narrator:*** Arnold Moss. ***Commercial Spokeswoman*** (for Royal Puddings): Mary Woods.

OPENING (from 6/6/44)

ANNOUNCER: Welcome, friends, you've come to *The Open Door* and the makers of Royal Puddings and Royal Gelatin invite you to enter and meet Dr. Hansen.

HANSEN: Come in, come in, the door is open...

CLOSING

ANNOUNCER: Be sure to listen tomorrow to *The Open Door*. Your narrator for *The Open Door*, Arnold Moss. This is CBS, the Columbia Broadcasting System.

1203. OPEN HOUSE. Variety, 30 min., NBC, 7/19/41 to 8/30/41.

Torch singer Helen Morgan as the host of a weekly program of music and songs. Frank Barton, Charles Bernard, Helen Kleeb, Monty Mohn, Sam Moore and Gladys Simpson were the regulars; the Ruordo Orchestra provided the music.

1204. THE OPIE CATES SHOW. Comedy, 30 min., ABC, 1947–1948.

Opie Cates is a likable young man who resides at Ma Bushkirk's Boarding House in Clinton, Arkansas. He is eager but a bit trouble-prone, and stories relate events in his life as he seeks to better himself. *Other regular characters:* Cathy, his girlfriend; Ma and Pa Bushkirk, the boarding house owners.

Cast: Opie Cates (*Opie Cates*); Noreen Gommill (*Cathy*); Barbara Fuller (*Ma Bushkirk*); Fred Howard (*Pa Bushkirk*). ***Music:*** Basil Adlam.

1205. OPRY HOUSE MATINEE. Variety, 60 min., Mutual, 1945–1946.

A Saturday afternoon program of country and western music with singer Eddy Arnold as the host. The program featured performances by guests as well as entertainment from its regular cast: Jack Baker, Becky Barfield, Lorue Buck, Jud Collins, Mack McGarr, the Old

Hickory Singers, Owen Bradley and His Tennessians, Rod Bradfield and His Sweetheart Susie, the Short Brothers, the Tennessee Playboys and the Troubadours.

1206. The Orange Lantern. Adventure, 30 min., NBC Blue, 1932–1933.

Richard Norris is a district attorney who has devoted his life to bringing criminals to justice, especially Batnik, the evil and cunning head of a notorious gang of jewel thieves. Norris is assisted by his girlfriend Olga Nesheim, and stories relate their efforts to end Batnik's reign.

Cast: William Shelley (*Richard Norris*); Georgia Backus (*Olga Nesheim*); Arthur Hughes (*Batnik*). ***Also:*** Peggy Allenby, Agnes Moorehead. ***Music:*** Sven Hallberg.

1207. The Original Amateur Hour. Variety, 30 min., ABC, 1948–1952.

A revised version of *Major Bowes and the Original Amateur Hour* (see entry) that continued to spotlight promising but undiscovered talent. This version, sponsored by Old Gold cigarettes, served as the basis for the television series *Ted Mack and the Original Amateur Hour*.

Host: Ted Mack. ***Announcer:*** Roy Greece. ***Music:*** Lloyd Marx.

1208. Orson Welles' Almanac. Variety, 30 min., CBS, 1/26/44 to 7/19/44.

A weekly program of music, songs and comedy with Orson Welles as the host. Arthur Q. Bryan, Ray Collins, Groucho Marx, Agnes Moorehead and Martha Stewart were the regulars; Lud Gluskin and his orchestra provided the music.

The Orson Welles Theater *see* **Campbell Playhouse**

1209. Our Gal Sunday. Serial, 15 min., CBS, 3/29/37 to 1/2/59.

Henry Brinthrope is a titled English lord and owner of a manor called Black Swan Hall in Virginia. He is married to a girl named Sunday, an orphan who was raised by two prospectors (Jackie and Lively) when they found her as an infant, abandoned on the steps of their cabin in Silver Creek, Colorado. Stories follow events in Sunday's life as she attempts to find happiness. Sunday's best friend Irene Galway and Irene's husband Peter own Bow Ridge, the mansion next to Black Swan Hall.

Cast: Dorothy Lowell, Vivian Smolen (*Sunday*); Karl Swenson, Alistair Duncan (*Henry Brinthrope*); Fran Carlon (*Irene Galway*); Joseph Curtin (*Peter Galway*); Jay Jostyn (*Jackie*); Robert Strauss, Roy Fant (*Lively*); Vicki Vola (*Elaine*); Kay Brinker (*Barbara*); Van Heflin (*Slim Delaney*); Elaine Kent (*Charlotte*); Florence Robinson (*Rose Hunt*); Charita Bauer (*Lanette*); Joan Tompkins (*Madeline Travers*); Anne Seymour (*Prudence Graham*); John McQuade (*Steve Lansing*). ***Announcers:*** Ed Fleming, John Reed King, Art Millet, Bert Parks, Charles Stark, John A. Wolfe. ***Producers:*** Anne Hummert, Frank Hummert.

OPENING (from 1/29/46)

Announcer: Once again we present *Our Gal Sunday*, the story of an orphan girl named Sunday from the little mining town of Silver Creek, Colorado, who in young womanhood married England's richest, most handsome lord, Lord Henry Brinthrope. The story that asks the question, "Can this girl, from a little mining town in the west, find happiness as the wife of a titled Englishman?" And now *Our Gal Sunday*. Last night, a chance remark made by Sunday's close friend Irene Galway gave Sunday a jolt. All night she has lain awake with one thought spinning through her mind.

Sunday: Yesterday, Dr. Abbott told me I was all right, nothing wrong with me. Why then did Irene see Henry coming out of Dr. Abbott's office... I must find out. What is Henry keeping from me...

1210. Our Miss Brooks. Comedy, 30 min., CBS, 7/19/48 to 7/7/57.

Constance "Connie" Brooks is an English teacher at Madison High School in the small town of Madison. She lives at Mrs. Davis's Boarding House on Carroll Avenue, and tomato juice and pancakes are her favorite breakfast. After a hard day at school, Connie has what she calls "School Teacher's B and B"—a bath and then bed. Connie also has frequent dreams about her boyfriend Philip Boynton, the bashful biology teacher. And, as usual, Connie says about her dreams, "Nothing happens."

Philip is shy and Connie wishes he would take "brave shots." Philip is just not romantic. He treats Connie with respect (*too* much, Connie believes), and Connie's efforts to make him more romantic is the subplot of stories that focus on Connie's misadventures at home and at work. *Other regular characters:* Osgood Conklin, Madison's always yelling, easily upset and stern principal; Walter Denton, a student who is friends with Connie but considered "a lamebrain dunce" by Osgood; Harriet Conklin, Osgood's daughter (and Walter's girlfriend); Mrs. Margaret Davis, Connie's landlady; Fabian "Stretch" Snodgrass, the not-too-bright student. Philip has a pet lab frog named McDougall; Mrs. Davis's cat is named Minerva; Walter's nickname for Mr. Conklin is "Old Marble Head"; Connie is the faculty adviser for the school newspaper, the *Madison Monitor*. Served as the basis for the television series of the same title.

Cast: Eve Arden (*Connie Brooks*); Jeff Chandler, Robert Rockwell (*Philip Boynton*); Joe Forte, Gale Gordon (*Osgood Conklin*); Richard Crenna (*Walter Denton*); Gloria McMillan (*Harriet Conklin*); Jane Morgan (*Margaret Davis*); Leonard Smith (*Stretch Snodgrass*). ***Announcers:*** Johnny Jacobs, Bob Lemond, Verne Smith, Jimmy Matthews, Roy Rowan. ***Music:*** Wilbur Hatch, Lud Gluskin. ***Producer:*** Larry Berns.

OPENING

ANNOUNCER: Palmolive Soap, your beauty hope, and Lustre Creme Shampoo, for soft, glamorous, caressable hair, bring you *Our Miss Brooks* starring Eve Arden.

CLOSING

ANNOUNCER: Next week tune in to another *Our Miss Brooks* show, brought to you by Palmolive Soap, your beauty hope, and Lustre Creme Shampoo for soft, glamorous, caressable hair. *Our Miss Brooks* starring Eve Arden is produced by Larry Berns, written and directed by Al Lewis, with music by Wilbur Hatch. America listens most to the CBS Radio Network.

1211. Our Secret World. Serial, 30 min., Mutual, 1942–1943.

Michael and Irene are young marrieds separated by the outbreak of war. Michael has been assigned to duty in England; Irene remains at home in America. At a fixed time each evening, Michael and Irene think of each other. Through "soliloquies by telepathy," each relates daily happenings. Irene speaks first, assuring Michael of her love for him, of the sense of his presence, and of her sustained hope and faith that they will soon be together again. As Irene finishes telling Michael about how her previously meaningless daily activities have suddenly taken on a new meaning, Michael speaks from England. He relates the bitterness of war, his thoughts of her, his loneliness, his anxiety and his one desire—to return home to her. The program, with its sketchy backgrounds and characterizations, was designed to let the listener identify with its sentimental or romantic nature through personal daydreaming.

Cast: Milton Stanley (*Michael*); Ann Starrett (*Irene*).

1212. Out of the Deep. Adventure, 30 min., NBC, 1945–1946.

The *Blue Falcon* is a cargo ship whose men call the docks of Santa Monica, California, home. The ship is captained by Gunnar Carlisle, a noted deep sea diver and soldier of fortune. He will go anywhere the work is—"as long as I know what the job is and what the money will be." Stories, which are based on the true-life experiences of Gunnar Carlisle, relate his exploits as he becomes involved with shady characters in all ports of the world. *Other regular characters:* Charlie Bartlett, Gunnar's first mate; Lo Wing, the cook. Gunnar's favorite watering hole is the Anchor Cafe.

Cast: Wally Maher, Ted Maxwell (*Gunnar Carlisle*); Ed Max (*Charlie Bartlett*); Charlie Lung (*Lo Wing*). ***Announcers:*** Robert Campbell, Don Stanley. ***Music:*** Joe Enos. ***Producer:*** Warren Lewis.

OPENING

VOICE: All hands, stand by for adventure.

ANNOUNCER: *Out of the Deep*, strange stories based on the true-life adventures of Capt. Gunnar Carlisle, noted deep sea diver and soldier of fortune. Tonight's story, "The Amazon Episode."

CLOSING

ANNOUNCER: From *Out of the Deep* has come "The Amazon Episode," another strange story based on the true-life adventures of Capt. Gunnar Carlisle, noted deep sea diver and soldier of fortune. Wally Maher played Capt. Carlisle. This is a presentation of the NBC Hollywood Program Department.

1213. Ozark Jubilee. Variety, 30 min., ABC, 1954–1955.

A Saturday evening program of country and western music with Red Foley as the host and the music of Grady Martin's Crossroads Gang.

The Ozzie Nelson–Harriet Hilliard Show *see* **The Adventures of Ozzie and Harriet**

The Pabst Blue Ribbon Show *see* **The Ben Bernie Show**

1214. The Packard Show.

A series of variety programs sponsored by Packard Motors:

1. The Packard Show, 30 min., NBC Blue, then CBS, 1934–1936. A program of concert music with baritone Lawrence Tibbett as the host.

2. The Packard Show, 30 min., NBC, 1936–1937. Fred Astaire as the host with the music of Johnny Green and his orchestra; the comedy of Charlie Butterworth; and songs by vocalist Trudy Wood.

3. The Packard Hour, 60 min., NBC, 1937–1938. Lanny Ross as the host with regulars Cliff Arquette, Charlie Butterworth, Florence George, Walter O'Keefe and Trudy Wood. Don Wilson did the announcing and Raymond Paige and his orchestra provided the music.

1215. Packham Inn. Variety, 30 min., NBC, 1946.

A weekly program of music, comedy and songs with Bill Packham as the host. Fred Caspter, Ilene Woods and the Four Vagabonds were the regulars and Rex Maupin and his orchestra supplied the music.

1216. Paducah Plantation. Variety, 30 min., NBC, 1936.

Country and western music and songs set at the fictitious Paducah Plantation in Kentucky. Irwin S. Cobb was the host (as the Old Southern Colonel). Gayne Whitman was the announcer and regulars included Norman Field, John Mather, Clarence Muse, Dorothy Page, the Four Blackbirds and the Hall Johnson Choir.

1217. Paging Mike McNally. Comedy, 30 min., Mutual, 1945.

Events in the life of Mike McNally, a harassed department store manager. Walter Kinsella played the role of Mike McNally. Also in the cast were Joan Alexander, Alan Bunce and Hope Emerson.

1218. Paging the Judge. Game, 15 min., ABC, 1953.

Selected studio audience members were placed in prearranged situations that tested their ability to solve problems. Winners, determined by a panel of guest judges, received merchandise prizes.

Host: Robert Paige.

1219. The Palmolive Beauty Box Theater. Variety, 30 min., NBC, 1934–1936; CBS, 1936–1937.

Originally (on NBC) a program of music, songs and comedy sponsored by Palmolive Soap. The comedy segment featured Fanny Brice and Hanley Stafford (as Baby Snooks and Daddy); the musical segment starred John Barclay, Jane Froman and Gladys Swarthout. When the series switched to CBS, it became more of an anthology wherein half-hour versions of famous operettas were presented. Jessica Dragonette was the host and occasional performer. Charles Kuhlman appeared in leading male roles and Richard Kollmar narrated. Benny Fields provided comic relief and Al Goodman and his orchestra supplied the music.

1220. The Palmolive Hour. Variety, 60 min., NBC, 1927–1931.

A weekly program of concert music sponsored by Palmolive Soap. Frank Munn and Virginia Rea were the lead singers and music was under the direction of Gus Haenschen. Performances by guests were spotlighted as were the regular cast: Frank Black, Wilfred Glenn, Lewis James, Elizabeth Lennox, James Melton, Elliot Shaw and the Revelers Quartet.

1221. Panorama Time. Variety, 25 min., Mutual, 1955.

A short-lived program with singer Johnny Desmond hosting a weekly series of recorded music and songs.

1222. The Park Avenue Penners. Comedy, 30 min., CBS, 1936–1940.

The antics of Joe Penner, the black sheep member of a prestigious New York family who live on Park Avenue.

Cast: Joe Penner (*Joe Penner*); Martha Wentworth (*Joe's mother*); Gay Seabrook (*Susabelle*); Margaret Brayton (*Gertrude*). ***Vocalists:*** Gene Austin, Joy Hodges. ***Music:*** Jimmy Grier.

OPENING

ANNOUNCER: Cocoa-Malt presents *The Park Avenue Penners* starring the black sheep of the family, Joe Penner, with Gene Austin and the music of Jimmy Grier.

1223. The Parker Family. Comedy, 15 min., NBC Blue, 1939–1944.

Events in the lives of the Parkers, a not-so-typical American family consisting of the parents, their children Nancy, Richard and Elly and their grandfather.

Cast: Jay Jostyn (*Mark Parker*); Linda Carlon-Reid, Marjorie Anderson (*Mrs. Parker*); Mitzi Gould (*Nancy Parker*); Leon Janney, Michael O'Day (*Richard Parker*); Patricia Ryan (*Elly Parker*); Roy Fant (*Grandfather Parker*). ***Announcer:*** Hugh James. ***Producer:*** Don Becker.

Note: on 5/9/41, NBC adapted the format to television in an experiment that failed to produce a series. Taylor Holmes played Mark Parker; Violent Henning portrayed his wife; Leon Janney played Richard; and Mitzi Gould played daughter Nancy. Also in the cast were Helen Claire (as Mrs. Jennings) and William Lynn (as Dr. Dennison). Warren Wade was the producer.

1224. The Passing Parade. Documentary, 15 and 30 min. versions, Mutual, 1937; NBC, 1937; CBS, 1938–1939; NBC, 1939; NBC Blue, 1940–1941; NBC Red, 1943; CBS, 1944; NBC, 1948–1949.

Strange but true stories of unusual happenings hosted and narrated by John Nesbitt. Ken Carpenter and Harlow Wilcox did the announcing and the orchestras of Carmen Dragon, Meredith Willson and Victor Young provided the music.

OPENING

ANNOUNCER: *The Passing Parade.* Your favorite stories as told by your favorite storyteller, John Nesbitt.

CLOSING

ANNOUNCER: You have been listening to your favorite stories as told by America's favorite storyteller, John Nesbitt. Be with us the next time we move to the reviewing stand for yet another glimpse of *The Passing Parade.*

1225. Passport for Adams. Drama, 30 min., CBS, 8/17/43 to 10/12/43.

Douglas "Doug" Adams was the editor of a small-town newspaper in the town of Centerville. He is married and the father of two children. Perry "Quiz" Quisinberry was a New York photographer. Together they are now a photojournalist team assigned by the Consolidated Syndicate to report on the principal allies of the United States during World War II. Doug is level-headed and inquisitive and deeply interested in the people and cultures of the places they visit. Quiz, who speaks three languages ("English, American and double talk") is a Romeo, constantly thinking of beautiful women and constantly getting himself and Doug into trouble. Stories, which are semi-documentary in presentation, follow their adventures as they learn about the people of the countries they visit.

Cast: Robert Young, Myron McCormick (*Doug Adams*); Dane Clark, Paul Mann (*Perry Quisinberry*). ***Music:*** Lud Gluskin.

OPENING

ANNOUNCER: Columbia presents *Passport for Adams,* the sixth of a series of programs starring Robert Young as Doug Adams, the country editor who has been sent on a trip around the world to visit the cities and talk to the people of the United Nations. Tonight's program, written and directed by Norman Corwin, takes Adams to the important war city of Tel Aviv, Palestine.

CLOSING

ANNOUNCER: You have been listening to *Passport for Adams* starring Metro-Goldwyn-Mayer's distinguished Robert Young. Tonight's *Passport* was written, directed and produced by Norman Corwin. Next week at this time, Columbia's *Passport for Adams* takes war correspondent Doug Adams to Moscow, the capital city of our great fighting ally, the Union of Soviet Socialist Republics. This is CBS, the Columbia Broadcasting System.

1226. Passport to Romance. Variety, 30 min., Mutual, 1946.

A musical comedy about two singing stewards (played by Mitzi Green and Larry Brooks) aboard a ship called the S.S. *Harmonia*.

1227. Pat Novak for Hire. Crime Drama, 30 min., ABC, 1949–1950.

Pat Novak is a private detective who is independent of everyone and everything. He does what it takes to make money, including renting boats on the San Francisco waterfront. He has a nasty disposition and a best friend, Jocko Madigan, a hard-drinking ex-doctor who is now a wharf bum ("Jocko was a good man until he got to figure the last drink in a bottle is just as easy to get as the first"). Pat also has an enemy—Inspector Hellman of the S.F.P.D., a cop who dislikes Novak and would like to see him in jail. Pat is tough. If somebody steers him wrong, watch out—"If anything goes wrong, I'll look you up and it won't be pretty. I'll dirty you up like a locker room towel." Stories follow Pat's exploits as he goes about making a buck "any way I can." Jocko calls Pat "Patsy" and says, when Pat requires his help, "Risking my life is one of the bravest things you do." And, of Hellman's investigations, Pat claims, "Hellman couldn't find a brass ring in a dead man's nose." The program began locally in San Francisco on station KGO in 1946 and was billed as "the network's most unusual crime detective series." Jack Webb and later Ben Morris played Pat in the local version.

Cast: Jack Webb (*Pat Novak*); Tudor Owen (*Jocko Madigan*); Raymond Burr, John Galbraith (*Inspector Hellman*). ***Announcers:*** Franklyn Evans, George Fenneman. ***Music:*** Basil Adlam. ***Producer:*** William Russo.

OPENING

ANNOUNCER: Gallan Kamps presents *Pat Novak for Hire*.

SONG: Cinderella lost a shoe and so she got a mate. With lovely shoes, a girl can't lose—in Gallan Kamps shoes she'll rate.

ANNOUNCER: More miles to a Gallan Kamps. Yes, Gallan Kamps, the family shoe stores with the yellow front, the largest store chain in the west, with stores from Canada to Mexico… Gallan Kamps presents *Pat Novak for Hire*.

PAT: Sure, I'm Pat Novak for hire. That's what the sign out in front of my office says, *Pat Novak for Hire*. Down on the waterfront in San Francisco, you always bite off more than you can chew. It's tough on your windpipe but you don't go hungry. Down here a lot of people figure it's better to be a fat guy in a graveyard than a thin guy in a stew—that way you can be sure of a tight fit. I rent boats and do anything else that makes a sound like money.

CLOSING

ANNOUNCER: Be sure to join us next Sunday evening and every Sunday at this same time, same station for radio's newest show, *Pat Novak for Hire*. And don't forget the store with the yellow front, the Gallan Kamps store. Gallan Kamps shoes are good shoes, there's something about them you'll like. This is ABC, the American Broadcasting Company.

1228. The Patti Clayton Show. Variety, 15 min., CBS, 1945.

Vocalist Patti Clayton as the host of a program of music and songs with the music of Archie Bleyer and his orchestra. Bill Cullen did the announcing.

1229. The Paul Whiteman Hour. Variety, 60 min., ABC, 1946.

Orchestra leader Paul Whiteman as the host of a weekly program of big band music and songs. Eugene Baird, Johnny Thompson, Duffy's Swinging Strings Choir and the Joe Mooney Quartet were the regulars. Paul Whiteman's orchestra provided the music.

1230. Paul Whiteman Presents. Variety, 30 min., NBC, 1943.

A weekly program that combined performances by established personalities with those of undiscovered and promising talent. Glenn Osser served as the host; Dinah Shore and the Modernaires were the regulars; and Paul Whiteman and his orchestra provided the music. Also known as *Paul Whiteman's Teen Club*.

1231. The Paul Winchell–Jerry Mahoney Show. Variety, 30 min., Mutual, 11/29/43 to 7/10/44.

Music, songs and comedy sketches that center on Jerry Mahoney, the mischievous wooden dummy of ventriloquist Paul Winchell. Jerry is in sixth grade, not the best of students and calls Paul "Winch."

Host: Paul Winchell (with Jerry Mahoney). ***Vocalist:*** Vera Barton. ***Orchestra:*** Bob Stanley. ***Producer:*** Roger Bower.

OPENING (from 7/10/44)

ANNOUNCER: Yes, it's *The Paul Winchell–Jerry Mahoney Show* featuring that lovely young singing star, Vera Barton, and Bob Stanley and his orchestra. And here he is, that talented young ventriloquist, Paul Winchell and his little wooden dummy pal, Jerry Mahoney.

CLOSING

ANNOUNCER: Well, folks, that's our show for tonight. And with it we bid good-bye to Paul and Jerry for the summer. We hope you'll be with us again next week at 9:30 P.M. Eastern War Time when we'll be inaugurating a new program. So, for the time being at least, here is Paul Winchell to say—

PAUL: So long, folks; have a nice vacation and don't get too much of a sunburn.

ANNOUNCER: And here's Jerry to say—

JERRY: Ouch!

PAUL: What's the trouble, Jerry?

JERRY: I'm already burned to a charcoal.

PAUL: Oh, never mind. Well, good night, folks. Hope to see you again in the fall.

JERRY: Good night.

ANNOUNCER: *The Paul Winchell–Jerry Mahoney Show* was produced at the Mutual Theater in New York. This is Mutual.

1232. THE PAULA STONE–PHIL BRITO SHOW. Variety, 15 min., NBC, 1944.

Music, songs and comedy with child star Paula Stone and her assistant, Phil Brito. Tom Shirley did the announcing and Doc Whipple and his orchestra supplied the music.

1233. THE PAUSE THAT REFRESHES. Variety.

A Coca-Cola–sponsored program of music and songs that is also known as *The Coca-Cola Program*.

1. The Pause That Refreshes on the Air, 30 min., NBC, 1934–1935. Frank Black and his orchestra were featured.

2. The Coca-Cola Program, 30 min., CBS, 1940–1944. Songs by John Charles Thomas and music by Albert Spalding (a violinist who also narrated) and Andre Kostelanetz and his orchestra.

3. The Pause That Refreshes, 30 min., CBS, 1947–1948. Roger Pryor was the host; Ginny Simms and Jane Froman provided the songs; and the Andre Kostelanetz and Percy Faith orchestras provided the music.

1234. PAYROLL PARTY. Game, 25 min., ABC, 1952.

Nicholas Girrard as the host of a game show wherein housewives, selected from the studio audience, competed in various stunts for fun and cash prizes.

1235. THE PEABODYS. Comedy, 15 min., Syndicated, 1946–1947.

Events in the life of Harvey Peabody, a not-so-bright businessman, his wife Helen and their daughter Harriet.

Cast: Norman Gottschalk (*Harvey Peabody*); Fran Allison (*Helen Peabody*); Joan Alt (*Harriet Peabody*); Elmira Roessler (*Sister-in-law*). ***Announcer:*** Bob Cunningham. ***Organist:*** Dave Bacall.

1236. PEEWEE AND WINDY. Comedy, 30 min., NBC, 1930s.

After months at sea, two happy-go-lucky sailors (Peewee and Windy) receive shore leave and go about enjoying what free time they have. Jack MacBryde played Peewee and Walter Kinsella was Windy. Joe Rines provided the music.

1237. THE PEG LACENTRA SHOW. Variety, 15 min., NBC, 1938.

Vocalist Peg LaCentra as the host of a program of music and songs with the music of organist John Gart and the group the Jesters.

1238. THE PEGGY LEE SHOW. Variety, 15 min., CBS, 1951–1952.

A twice-weekly program of music and songs with singer Peggy Lee as the host. Bill Adams did the announcing and Russ Case and his orchestra provided the music.

1239. THE PENNY SINGLETON SHOW. Comedy, 30 min., NBC, 1950.

Penny Williamson is a young widow and the mother of Sue and Dorothy, better known as "D.G." Penny lives in the town of Middleton and is partners with Horace Wiggins in the real estate firm of Williamson and Wiggins. Stories relate Penny's efforts to provide a decent life for herself and her family. Sue is the younger of the two daughters, likes boys, sports and has pet frogs, toads and lizards. Dorothy, more down to earth, is intensely interested in reading and a bit amazed by her tomboyish sister. *Other regular characters:* Margaret, the Williamsons' cook; Judge Beshomer Grundell, a suitor for Penny's hand (as is Horace—and both devise elaborate schemes to impress her); Ida, Penny's neighbor.

Cast: Penny Singleton (*Penny Williamson*); Sheila James (*Sue Williamson*); Marylee Robb (*Dorothy "D.G." Williamson*); Bea Benaderet (*Margaret*); Jim Backus (*Horace Wiggins*); Gale Gordon (*Judge Beshomer Grundell*); Sara Selby (*Ida*). ***Announcer:*** Frank Martin. ***Music:*** Von Dexter.

OPENING

ANNOUNCER: On stage tonight from Hollywood, another of NBC's outstanding half-hour presentations, *The Penny Singleton Show*.

PENNY: Hello, happy you're listening.

CLOSING

ANNOUNCER: *The Penny Singleton Show*, written and produced by Robert Sotoberg, stars Penny Singleton.

PENNY: Good night, keep well.

ANNOUNCER: This is NBC, the National Broadcasting Company.

1240. PENTHOUSE BLUES. Variety, 15 min., CBS, 1939.

A program of music and songs with Judith Arlen as the host.

1241. PENTHOUSE PARTY. Variety, 30 min., NBC Blue, 1934–1935.

Music and conversation with Ilka Chase and Gladys Glad. Music was provided by Mark Hellinger and his orchestra.

1242. PEOPLE ARE FUNNY. Game, 30 min., NBC, 1942–1960.

Selected members of the studio audience performed specific stunts designed to test their willingness to make fools of themselves in return for money. Served as the basis for the 1954–1961 television series of the same title.

Hosts: Art Baker, Art Linkletter. ***Announcers:*** Herb Allen, Ed Herlihy, Ted Myers, Rod O'Connor. ***Producer:*** John Guedel.

Note: On 6/11/46, NBC adapted the radio program to television in a test that failed to generate a series. Art Linkletter was the host and Ed Herlihy did the announcing.

1243. PEPPER YOUNG'S FAMILY. Serial, 15 min., NBC Blue, then Mutual and CBS, 1936–1959.

Events in the lives of the Young family, in particular Larry, nicknamed "Pepper," an oil field worker in the town of Elmwood.

Cast: Curtis Arnall, Lawson Zerbe, Mason Adams, Peter Fernandez (*Larry "Pepper" Young*); Jack Roseleigh, Bill Adams, Thomas Chalmers, Bill Johnstone (*Sam Young*); Elizabeth Wraggle (*Peggy Young*); Marion Barney (*Mary Young*); Eunice Howard (*Linda Young*); Maureen McManus (*Sally Young*); Greta Kvalden (*Hattie, the maid*). ***Announcers:*** Martin Block, Alan Kent, Richard Stark. ***Music:*** William Meader.

OPENING

ANNOUNCER: *Pepper Young's Family*. The story of your friends the Peppers is brought to you by Camay, the mild beauty soap for a smoother, softer complexion... And now, *Pepper Young's Family*.

THE PEPSODENT SHOW *see* **THE BOB HOPE PEPSODENT SHOW**

1244. THE PERCY FAITH ORCHESTRA. Variety, 30 min., Mutual, 1939.

Orchestra leader Percy Faith as the host of a program of big band music and songs featuring weekly guest stars. The Percy Faith orchestra provided the music.

1245. THE PERRY COMO SHOW. Variety, 15 min., CBS, 1943–1944.

Singer Perry Como as the host of a program of music and songs featuring the Three Sisters vocal group and the music of Paul Baron and his orchestra.

1246. THE PERRY COMO SHOW. Variety, 15 min., CBS, 1954–1955.

A simulcast of the last season episodes of *The Perry Como Show* television series on CBS. Singer Perry Como was the host. He was assisted by the Fontaine Sisters (Bea, Geri and Margie) and the Ray Charles Singers. Dick

Stark did the announcing and Mitchell Ayres and his orchestra provided the music. Lee Cooley was the producer.

1247. Perry Mason. Crime Drama, 15 min., CBS, 1943–1955.

A daily crime serial based on the characters created by Erle Stanley Gardner featuring the activities of Perry Mason, a brilliant criminal attorney, as he defends clients. *Other regular characters:* Della Street, his secretary; Paul Drake, his investigator; Lt. Arthur Tragg; Sgt. Dorsett.

Cast: Bartlett Robinson, Santos Ortega, Donald Briggs, John Larkin (*Perry Mason*); Gertrude Warner, Jan Miner, Joan Alexander (*Della Street*); Matt Crowley, Charles Webster (*Paul Drake*); Mandel Kramer, Frank Kane (*Arthur Tragg*); Arthur Vinton (*Sgt. Dorsett*). ***Announcers:*** Bob Dixon, Alan Kent, Richard Stark. ***Organist:*** William Meader. ***Musical Director:*** Paul Taubman. ***Producers:*** Leslie Harris, Tom McDermott.

1248. The Pet Milk Show. Variety, 30 min., NBC, 1948–1950.

A weekly program of music and songs sponsored by Pet Milk and starring singer Vic Damone. Warren Sweeney served as the host and announcer. Singer Kay Armen and the Emily Coty Singers were the regulars and the Pet Milk Orchestra was conducted by Bob Crosby and Gus Haenschen.

OPENING

Vic (singing): You and the night and the music fill me with flaming desire, setting my being completely on fire.

Announcer: Pet Milk, the original evaporated milk, presents *The Pet Milk Show* with Kay Armen, the Emily Coty Singers, Gus Haenschen and the Pet Milk Orchestra and starring Vic Damone.

CLOSING

Announcer: This is Warren Sweeney, your host for Pet Milk, the original evaporated milk, wishing you good luck and good night. This is NBC, the National Broadcasting Company.

1249. The Pet Milk Show. Variety, 30 min., NBC, 1950.

A revised version of the prior title that combined comedy with music and songs. Comedian Jack Pearl was the host and Mimi Benzell, Cliff Hall and Russ Emery were the regulars. Ed Herlihy did the announcing and Gus Haenschen conducted the Pet Milk Orchestra.

1250. Pete Kelly's Blues. Drama, 30 min., NBC, 7/4/51 to 9/19/51.

Kansas City, Missouri, during the 1920s, was the setting for a music-oriented series about Pete Kelly, a cornet player and leader of the Big Seven, a jazz band that plays regularly at Lupo's, a speakeasy at 417 Cherry Street. Pete is laid back, but tough when he has to be (especially when he's roughed up). People with problems turn to him for help. Though somewhat reluctant, he rallies to assist. Stories relate his exploits as he becomes involved with the shady characters who inhabit the music world. *Other regular characters:* Maggie Jackson, Pete's friend, the singer at Fat Annie's, the speakeasy on the Kansas side of the border; George Lupo, the club owner. Served as the basis for a feature film and television series of the same title.

Cast: Jack Webb (*Pete Kelly*); Meredith Howard (*Maggie Jackson*); Jack Kruschen (*George Lupo*). ***Big Seven Band:*** Dick Cathcart (cornet), Judd DeMotto (bass), Nick Fatoo (drums), Matty Matlock (clarinet), Mac Schneider (trombone), Ray Sherman (piano), George Van Eps (guitar). ***Regulars*** (Various roles): Herb Butterfield, Whitfield Connor, William Conrad, Vic Perrin, Peggy Webber. ***Music:*** Dick Cathcart. ***Scoring:*** Matty Matlock.

OPENING

Announcer: This one's about Pete Kelly. It's about the world he goes around in; it's about the big music, the big trouble and the big twenties. So when they ask you, tell them this one's about the blues—*Pete Kelly's Blues. Pete Kelly's Blues* starring Jack Webb with story by Jo Esinger and music by Dick Cathcart.

Pete: My name's Pete Kelly; I play cornet. You'll find us at 417 Cherry Street, Kansas City, on the Missouri side; just wide enough to frame a suspicious eye and the bottom of shot glasses aren't quite thick enough to reach the top. It's a well-run, orderly crib, the kind of place the local prohibition agents can bring their wives to. The lease is owned by George Lupo; he's a fat, friendly little guy who always has his hand in his pocket. We start grinding every night about ten and we play until Lupo runs out of inventory—but that's all right with us; he lets us play the kind of music we like. [The story would then begin as Pete tells of the evening's adventure.]

1251. The Peter Lind Hayes Show. Variety, 30 min., CBS, 1954–1955.

A weekly program of music, songs and comedy skits with Peter Lind Hayes as the host. He was assisted by his wife Mary Healey, and the regulars were Harry Snow, Leslie Uggams, Jerry Vale, the Mariners and the Toppers. George Bryan and Jack Haskell did the announcing and music was provided by the Norman Leyden Orchestra and the Norman Paris Trio.

1252. Peter Quill. Mystery, 30 min., Mutual, 1940–1941.

Peter Quill is a detective who uses scientific technology to outwit criminals. Stories relate to his exploits as he and his assistant Gail Carson battle saboteurs, traitors and spies.

Cast: Marvin Miller (*Peter Quill*); Alice Hill (*Gail Carson*); Ken Griffin (*Police Capt. Roger Dorn*).

1253. The Phil Baker Show. Variety, 30 min., NBC Blue, then CBS, 1933–1939.

Music and songs coupled with comedy skits that revolve around Phil Baker, a vaudeville headliner (comedian and accordionist), his butler Bottle and a heckling ghost named Beetle. Also appearing was Mrs. Sarah Heartburn, the advice columnist for the *Gazette*. The program is also known as *The Armor Jester*, *The Gulf Headliner* and *Honolulu Bound* (when sponsored by Dole pineapple).

Cast: Phil Baker (*Phil Baker*); Harry McNaughton (*Bottle*); Hank Ladd, Ward Wilson, Sid Silvers (*Beetle*); Agnes Moorehead (*Sarah Heartburn*). ***Regulars:*** Mabel Albertson, Artie Auerbach, Oscar Bradley, the Seven G's vocal group. ***Announcer:*** Harry Von Zell. ***Orchestra:*** Eddie deLange, Hal Kemp, Frank Shields.

1254. The Phil Harris–Alice Faye Show. Comedy, 30 min., NBC, 1948–1954.

Humorous incidents in the home life of Phil Harris, orchestra leader on *The Jack Benny Program*. Phil is married to singer Alice Faye and is the father of two daughters, Phyllis and Little Alice. *Other regular characters:* Willie Faye, Alice's wimpy brother (he lives with Phil and drives him crazy; his catch-phrase is "Good morning, Philip"); Frankie Remley, Phil's left-handed guitar player and friend; Julius Abbruzio, "the little brat" who annoys Phil and Frankie (Julius is a delivery boy with a thick Brooklyn accent who usually turned up in the latter part of the show to get Phil and Frankie into more hot water than they were already in); Mr. Scott, an officer of the Rexall Drug Company (the show's sponsor).

Cast: Phil Harris (*Phil Harris*); Alice Faye (*Alice Faye Harris*); Jeanine Roos (*Little Alice Harris*); Anne Whitfield (*Phyllis Harris*); Elliott Lewis (*Frankie Remley*); Walter Tetley (*Julius Abbruzio*); Robert North (*Willie Harris*); Gale Gordon (*Mr. Scott*). ***Announcer:*** Bill Forman. ***Orchestra:*** Walter Scharf.

OPENING

Announcer: Good health to all from Rexall. It's *The Phil Harris–Alice Faye Show*, presented by the makers of Rexall Drug products and 10,000 independent family druggists. And now your Rexall family druggist brings you *The Phil Harris–Alice Faye Show* written by Dick Singer and Ray Chevillat, with Elliott Lewis, Walter Tetley, Robert North, Jeanine Roos, Anne Whitfield, Walter Scharf and his music, and our special guest, Jack Benny, and starring Phil Harris and Alice Faye.

The Phil Harris Orchestra *see* **Let's Listen to Harris**

1255. The Phil Silvers Show. Variety, 30 min., ABC, 1947.

Comedian Phil Silvers as the host of a program of music, songs and comedy sketches. The regulars were Lee Brady, Beryl Davis, Roger deKoven, Betty Garde, Jean Gillespie, Jack Hartley, William Keane and Danny Ocko. Ralph Norman and his orchestra provided the music.

1256. The Phil Spitalny Show. Variety, 30 min., NBC, 1936.

A weekly program of music and songs with orchestra leader Phil Spitalny as the host. John

Little Words (vocal group) were the regulars. Del Sharbutt did the announcing and Phil Spitalny and His All-Girl Orchestra provided the music.

1257. The Philco Radio Playhouse. Anthology, 30 min., ABC, 1953–1954.

Radio adaptations of plays originally broadcast over *The Philco Television Playhouse*. Joseph Cotten served as the host and the program was sponsored by Philco appliances.

1258. Philco Radio Time. Variety, 30 min., ABC, 1946–1949.

A weekly program of music and songs that devoted most of its air time to performances by weekly guests. Sponsored by Philco appliances.

Host: Bing Crosby. ***Regulars:*** Al Jolson, Connie Russell, John Charles Thomas, Skitch Henderson. ***Announcer:*** Glenn Riggs. ***Orchestra:*** John Scott Trotter.

OPENING

BING (singing): When the blue of the night meets the gold of the day, someone waits for me.

ANNOUNCER: This is Glenn Riggs welcoming you to *Philco Radio Time*, produced and transcribed in New York with John Scott Trotter and his orchestra, Skitch Henderson and Bing's guests, Fred Allen and Connee Boswell. And here is the star of the show, Bing Crosby.

Philip Marlowe *see* **The Adventures of Philip Marlowe**

1259. The Philip Morris Follies of 1946. Variety, 30 min., NBC, 1946.

Singer Johnny Desmond as the host of a weekly program of music and songs sponsored by Philip Morris Cigarettes. Herb Shriner and Margaret Whiting were the regulars; Ken Roberts did the announcing; and the Jerry Gray Orchestra and Chorus provided the music and additional songs.

1260. The Philip Morris Playhouse. Anthology, 30 min., CBS, 1939–1943; 1948–1949.

Tales of crime, murder and suspense sponsored by Philip Morris Cigarettes, represented by a bellboy named Johnny. At the end of each broadcast, Johnny presented the guest cast with a carton of cigarettes.

Host: Charles Martin. ***Announcers:*** Art Ballinger, Clayton "Bud" Collyer, Joe King, Ken Roberts. ***Commercial Spokesman (Johnny):*** Johnny Roventini. ***Music:*** Ray Bloch, Lud Gluskin, Johnny Green, Russ Morgan.

OPENING

ANNOUNCER: Johnny presents *The Philip Morris Playhouse*. Produced, edited and directed by William Spier. Tonight's star—Howard Duff.

JOHNNY: Call for Philip Mor-rees, call for Philip Mor-rees!

ANNOUNCER: It's a wonderful, wonderful feeling to wake up fresh with no cigarette hangover. Yes, you'll be glad tomorrow if you smoke Philip Morris today.

JOHNNY: Call for Philip Mor-rees!

ANNOUNCER: And now, with Howard Duff as our star, we bring you "Four Hours to Kill," tonight's production transcribed on *The Philip Morris Playhouse*.

CLOSING

HOWARD DUFF: What have you lined up for next week, Johnny?

JOHNNY: Next week, *The Philip Morris Playhouse* will present Chester Morris in an exciting script called "Papa Turns Green." But before you go, may I present you with this carton of Philip Morris cigarettes and thank you for being with us.

HOWARD: Thank you, Johnny. Good night.

JOHNNY: Good night, Mr. Duff.

ANNOUNCER: And now good-bye Johnny, see you next Friday, same time, same station when once again we will present transcribed, *The Philip Morris Playhouse* starring Chester Morris. Until then—

JOHNNY: Call for Philip Mor-rees!

ANNOUNCER: Tonight's original radio play was by Howard Swanton. Music for *The Philip Morris Playhouse* is under the direction of Lud Gluskin. All names and characters used on this program are fictitious. Any similarity to persons living or dead is purely coincidental. This is Art Balliner saying good night for Philip Morris.

1261. Philo Vance. Crime Drama, 30 min., NBC, 1945; Syndicated, 1948–1950.

"Somewhere along the line, a murderer

makes a mistake; it's my job to find that mistake," says Philo Vance, a shrewd private detective who possesses a knack for solving complex cases. When the police are baffled, District Attorney Frank "F.X." Markham calls on Vance; when ordinary people suddenly find their lives in turmoil and require confidential help, they seek Philo Vance. *Other regular characters:* Ellen Deering, Philo's secretary and girlfriend (she insists that during working hours, Philo address her as Miss Deering and that she call him Mr. Vance); Police Sgt. Ernest Heath, who is jealous of Vance (for solving the cases that he can't).

Cast: Jose Ferrer, Jackson Beck (*Philo Vance*); Joan Alexander, Frances Farras (*Ellen Deering*); George Petrie (*Frank "F.X." Markham*); Humphrey Davis (*Ernest Heath*). ***Music:*** Henry Sylvern. ***Producer:*** Frederic W. Ziv.

1262. Phone Again Finnegan. Comedy, 30 min., NBC, 1946; CBS, 1946–1947.

Events in the life of Fairchild Finnegan, the well-meaning but inept manager of the Welcome Arms Apartments. Stories relate his efforts to solve the various problems he encounters while attempting to help guests. *Other regular characters:* Miss Smith, the switchboard operator; Longfellow Larson, the Swedish janitor.

Cast: Stu Erwin, Frank McHugh (*Fairchild Finnegan*); Florence Lake (*Miss Smith*); Harry Stewart (*Longfellow Larson*). ***Announcer:*** Ken Niles. ***Music:*** Lou Kosloff.

1263. The Phrase That Pays. Game, 15 min., NBC, 1953–1955.

A contestant chosen from the studio audience was presented with three clues to the identity of a well-known phrase. Prizes were awarded based on which clue led to the identification; if the player failed to identify the phrase, the listener who submitted it won a prize.

Hosts: Red Benson, Ted Brown.

1264. The Piano Playhouse. Variety, 30 min., ABC, 1945–1953.

An afternoon program that featured the music of guest pianists. Milton Cross served as the host and Stan Freeman, Cy Walter and Earl Wild were the regulars.

1265. Pick a Date. Game, 30 min., ABC, 9/19/49 to 9/15/50.

A woman selected from the studio audience was asked to name a memorable year in her life. She stated the reason for its selection and answered questions based on incidents that occurred during that year in return for merchandise prizes. Buddy Rogers served as the host.

1266. Pick and Pat Time. Variety, 30 min., Mutual, 1944–1945; ABC, 1945.

Music, songs and comedy with Pick Malone and Pat Padgett (comedians who were known for their blackface routine called Molasses and January) as the hosts. Diane Courtney, Bruce Hayes, Mary Small and the Jesters were the regulars. Paul Douglas and Tiny Ruffner did the announcing and Vincent Lopez and his orchestra supplied the music.

1267. Pick and Play with Bob and Ray. Game, 30 min., NBC, 1953.

The comedy of Bob and Ray (see *The Bob and Ray Show*) coupled with a game show format that found selected members of the studio audience first choosing a number, then answering a question associated with it. A contestant remained at play for as long as he could answer questions correctly, seeking to win a jackpot of merchandise gifts. Players who failed to give a correct response were also awarded a prize.

Hosts: Bob Elliott, Ray Goulding. ***Announcer:*** Jack Costello. ***Music:*** The Paul Taubman Trio.

Pickens' Party *see* **The Jane Pickens Show**

1268. Pipe Dreams. Comedy, 5 min., NBC, 1939.

A daily comedy sketch of tall tales with Alan Reed as Willoughby Fibbe, M.P. (Master Prevaricator).

1269. Pipe Smoking Time. Variety, 30 min., CBS, 12/30/40 to 2/17/41.

A program of music and songs sponsored by Model pipe tobacco that invited male listeners "to light up, lean back and listen." Arthur Fields served as the host and Woody Guthrie, Fred Hall and Edmund C. Roecker were the regulars. Ray Bloch and his orchestra provided the music.

1270. Pitching Horseshoes. Anthology, 5 min., Mutual, 1941.

Capsule dramatizations of stories that appeared in Billy Rose's "Pitching Horseshoes" newspaper column. Billy Rose served as the host and Frank Waldecker did the announcing.

1271. Plantation Jubilee. Variety, 30 min., Mutual, 1949.

Curt Massey as the host of a weekly program of country and western music, songs and comedy. George Beatty, Allen Massey and the Robbins Sisters were the regulars. Charles Lyon did the announcing and the Westerners provided the music.

1272. Plantation Party. Variety, 30 min., NBC, 1936–1943.

A program of country and western music with Whitey Ford (as the Grand Ole Opry's "Duke of Paducah") as the host. Irvin S. Cobb, Dolly Good, Milly Good, Michael Stewart, Louise Massey and the Westerners, the Doring Sisters, the Plantation Choir and the vocal group Tom Dick and Harry were the regulars. Charles Lyon did the announcing and music was by the Range Riders.

1273. Play Broadcast. Game, 30 min., Mutual, 1940–1941.

The format called for selected members of the studio audience to locate clues hidden in comedy skits performed by Marvin Miller. June Baker assisted and Guy Savage did the announcing. Harold Stokes and his orchestra provided the music.

1274. The Player. Anthology, 15 min., Syndicated, 1948–1949.

Dramatizations of various stories with Paul Frees, billed as "America's most versatile actor," playing all the roles. Gary Goodwin was the announcer. The program is also known as *Studio X*.

1275. Pleasure Parade. Variety, 15 min., Syndicated, 1945–1947.

Vocalist Lillian Carroll as the host of a weekly program of music and songs. Dick Brown and Paula Kelly and the Modernaires were the regulars. Vincent Lopez and his orchestra supplied the music.

1276. The Poet Prince. Human Interest, 15 min., NBC, 1930s.

A program of poetry readings with Abraham Feinberg as Anthony Frome, "The Poet Prince."

1277. Poetic Madness. Human Interest, 15 min., NBC Blue, then NBC Red and CBS, 1932–1938.

Tenor Jack Fulton as the host and reader of an evening program of poetry. Billy Mills and his orchestra provided the background music.

1278. Poet's Gold. Human Interest, 15 min., CBS, 1938.

Poetry readings by David Ross and music by Victor Bey and his orchestra.

1279. Point Sublime. Comedy, 30 min., ABC, 10/6/47 to 5/31/48.

Point Sublime is a fictional village somewhere on the Pacific Coast. It has one newspaper, a golf course, a general store, 750 people and a way of life that is all but forgotten in twentieth-century America. Stories follow comical events in the life of Ben Willett, town mayor, storekeeper, hotel owner, town philosopher and a man of great curiosity who is the hero of Point Sublime. *Other regular characters:* August Moon, the stuttering railroad clerk who doubled as Ben's helper in the store; Evelyn "Evie" Hanover, Ben's girlfriend, a widow who came to the town to work for a paleontologist; Howie MacBrayer, the retired Texas cattleman who also seeks Evie's affections.

Cast: Cliff Arquette (*Ben Willett*); Mel Blanc (*August Moon*); Jane Morgan, Verna Felton (*Evelyn Hanover*); Earle Ross (*Howie MacBrayer*). ***Music:*** Charles "Bud" Dante.

1280. Police Headquarters. Anthology, 15 min., NBC, 1931–1932.

Dramatizations of police law enforcement in action. Varying presentations and casts.

1281. Police Woman. Crime Drama, 15 min., ABC, 1946–1947.

Dramatizations based on actual incidents in the life of Mary Sullivan, a New York City policewoman for 35 years and the former director of the Police Woman's Bureau.

Cast: Mary Sullivan (*Host-Narrator*); Betty

Garde (*Mary Sullivan*). ***Announcers:*** Dick Dunham, Walter Herlihy. ***Music:*** Jessie Crawford.

The Pond's Program *see* **Mrs. Eleanor Roosevelt**

1282. Popeye the Sailor. Comedy, 15 min., NBC, 1935–1936; CBS, 1936–1938.

"Friendship is the strongest and the best thing what a man has," says Popeye, a tough sailor who finds that protecting his friends from harm is a full-time job. Popeye, the adoptive father of the orphaned newspaper boy Matey, is in love with Olive Oyl, a forever-in-distress damsel who runs a lunch wagon. Popeye is also friends with J. Wellington Wimpy, who loves hamburgers and is afraid of his own shadow (but claims, "A Wimpy knows no fear"). Popeye's enemies are Bluto, the sailor who is also fond of the fickle Olive Oyl; and Sinbad, the hulking, unkempt brute. When a situation arises that requires Popeye to perform extraordinary feats to save his friends, he relies on the strength he derives from his sponsor's product—Wheatena cereal (not spinach). Each situation requires a different amount of Wheatena; for example, three bowls to stop a runaway trolley car. After eating the cereal, Popeye exclaims, "Wheatena, do your stuff." As it works, he says, "Now looks at me muscules." *Other regular characters:* Swee'pea, the foundling left on Olive's doorstep. Based on the characters created by E.C. Segar.

Cast: Det Poppen, Floyd Buckley, Jack Mercer (*Popeye*); Olive LaMoy, Mae Questel (*Olive Oyl*); Jackson Beck (*Bluto*); Charles Lawrence (*J. Wellington Wimpy*); Jim Donnelly (*Matey*); Mae Questel (*Swee'pea*); Jackson Beck (*Sinbad*). ***Announcer:*** Kelvin Keech. ***Music:*** Victor Erwin.

OPENING

ANNOUNCER: All hands on deck, here's Popeye.

SOUND: Ship's bells ringing.

POPEYE (singing): I'm Popeye the sailor man, I'm Popeye the sailor man. I am what I am, because I am what I am, I'm Popeye the sailor man.

ANNOUNCER: Wheatena's his diet, he asks you to try it, with Popeye the sailor man.

1283. Port of Missing Hits. Variety, 30 min., NBC, 1945.

Vocalist Edna Phillips as the host of a program that features performances of lesser-known songs. The Thomas Haywood Chorus provided the vocal backing and Milton Katims and his orchestra supplied the music.

1284. Portia Faces Life. Serial, 15 min., CBS, 1940–1941; NBC, 1941–1944; CBS, 1944; NBC, 1944–1951.

Portia Blake, a widowed attorney and the mother of a young son (Dickie), lives on Beach Street in Parkerstown. Stories relate events as she struggles to raise her son. Later in the series, she marries Walter Manning. Served as the basis for the television series of the same title.

Cast: Lucille Wall (*Portia Blake*); Raymond Ives, Larry Robinson, Edwin Bruce (*Dickie Blake*); Myron McCormick, Bartlett Robinson (*Walter Manning*); Joan Banks (*Arline Manning*); Frances Woodbury (*Portia's aunt*); Carleton Young (*Kirk Roder*); Donald Briggs (*Dr. Holton*); Marjorie Anderson, Esther Ralston, Selena Royale, Rosaline Greene, Anne Seymour (*Kathy Marsh*); Ginger Jones (*Joan*); Richard Kendrick, Les Damon (*Bill Baker*); Luise Barclay (*Leslie Palmer*). ***Announcers:*** George Putnam, Ron Rawson. ***Producers:*** Don Cope, Tom McDermott.

OPENING

ANNOUNCER: We present *Portia Faces Life*, a story reflecting the courage, spirit and integrity of American women everywhere.

1285. Postcard Serenade. Variety, 15 min., Mutual, 1945.

Vocalist Judy Lang, who accompanied herself on the piano, sang songs requested on postcards sent in by listeners. Frank Waldecker did the announcing.

1286. Pot o' Gold. Game, 30 min., NBC, 1939–1940.

The program began with a spin of the Wheel of Fortune to determine a state phone book. A second spin of the wheel designated the page number. A final spin pinpointed a specific line. A telephone call was then placed to the person chosen by the Wheel of Fortune. If a connection was made, the host yelled "Stop, Horace" (a cue to Horace Heidt and His Musical Knights to stop playing music) and the listener was asked a question. A correct response won the listener $1000. If the listener was not at home, $100 was awarded for being selected. The program created such a rage that movie theaters began to see a decline in business when people stayed at home to be near their phones. To combat radio, some movie houses resorted to bribes, offering their patrons $1000 if *Pot o' Gold* called while they were at the theater. See also the following title.

Host: Ben Grauer. ***Vocalists:*** Amy Arnell, Don Brown. ***Announcer:*** Bob Shepherd. ***Orchestra:*** Horace Heidt, Tommy Tucker. ***Producer:*** Edward Byron.

1287. Pot o' Gold. Game, 30 min., ABC, 1946–1947.

A revised version of the prior title that continued to offer listeners the opportunity to win $1000 by correctly answering a question when telephoned by the host.

Host: Happy Felton. ***Vocalists:*** Jimmy Carroll, Vera Holly. ***Announcer:*** Len Sterling. ***Orchestra:*** Harry Salter.

1288. Powers Charm School. Women, 25 min., ABC, 1946.

Beauty tips and advice hosted by modeling executive John Robert Powers. Peggy Allenby, Pat Hosley and Ken Lynch were the regulars and Walter Herlihy did the announcing.

1289. Prairie Folks. Serial, 15 min., NBC, 1940.

Minnesota during the 1800s was the setting for a daily drama about the struggles of three pioneering families: the Nielsens, Bassetts and Anders.

Cast: Erik Rolf (*Thor Nielsen*); Helen Warren (*Anna Nielsen*); Kingsley Colton (*Hancey Nielsen*); Morris Carnovsky (*Adam Bassett*); Cliff Carpenter (*Curtis Bassett*); Josephine Fox (*Anne Anders*); Joe Helgeson (*Arnie Anders*); Parker Fennelly (*Smiley*).

1290. Prescott Presents. Variety, 30 min., NBC Blue, 1941.

Household hints, music, songs and chatter with Allen Prescott as the host. Joan Brooks, Diane Courtney and the group Hi, Lo, Jack and a Dame provided the songs. Music was by Jimmy Lytell and his orchestra.

Presenting Charles Boyer *see* **The Charles Boyer Show**

1291. Press Club. Drama, 30 min., CBS, 1939–1940.

The work of newspapermen as seen through the experiences of Mark Brandon, a reporter who is representative of the men and women who risk their lives to cover the news. Marvin Miller played Mark Brandon and was supported by a different cast each week.

1292. Pretty Kitty Kelly. Serial, 15 min., CBS, 1937–1946.

Events in the life of Kitty Kelly, a spirited Irish girl living in New York City.

Cast: Arline Blackburn (*Kitty Kelly*); Clayton "Bud" Collyer (*Inspector Michael Conway*); Helen Choate (*Bunny Wilson*); Bartlett Robinson (*Byron Welby*); Ethel Intropidi (*Phyllis Welby*); Dennis Hoey (*Edward Welby*). ***Announcer-Narrator:*** Matt Crowley.

1293. The Private Files of Matthew Bell. Crime Drama, 30 min., Mutual, 1952.

Matthew Bell is a police surgeon who encounters the worst and the best of society—from the violent offenders to the rich and famous to the innocent victims of crime. Stories relate his investigations as he uses compassion and understanding to solve crimes.

Cast: Joseph Cotten (*Matthew Bell*). ***Announcer:*** Phil Tonken.

1294. The Private Files of Rex Saunders. Crime Drama, 30 min., NBC, 5/2/51 to 8/1/51.

Rex Saunders is a suave and sophisticated British private detective who is now based in New York City. Each week he relates the details of one of his cases and stories follow his investigations as he and his assistant Alec do whatever is necessary to help their clients. Rex lives at 643 West 69th Street.

Cast: Rex Harrison (*Rex Saunders*); Leon Janney (*Alec*). ***Announcer:*** Kenneth Banghart. ***Producer:*** Himan Brown.

OPENING

Announcer: RCA Victor and its thousands of dealers present Rex Harrison starring in another intriguing adventure, transcribed from *The Private Files of Rex Saunders*.

Rex: "Concerning Murder" [episode title]. I've learned that you can readily protect yourself against the lady with danger in her eyes, the one who baffles you; however, beware the lady with hate in her heart.

ANNOUNCER: And now *The Private Files of Rex Saunders*. RCA Victor, world leader in radio, first in recorded music and first in television, brings you a new series of exciting detective adventures with Rex Harrison, a brilliant international star of stage and screen [the story would then begin].

CLOSING

ANNOUNCER: Rex Harrison will return in a moment to tell you about next week's adventure. In the meantime, remember, whether you're buying a television set, a radio, a Victrola phonograph or records, put your faith in the cornerstone of American home entertainment for three generations, RCA Victor. And now here is Rex Harrison to tell you about next week's adventure from *The Private Files of Rex Saunders*.

REX: Next week it's "Concerning Art" [episode title]. The value of a portrait does not always depend on the artist. There is a model to be considered—especially when the model turns out to be a shocking still life.

ANNOUNCER: RCA and its dealers have brought you *The Private Files of Rex Saunders*, written by Ed Adamson. This is Kenneth Banghart speaking for RCA Victor. This is NBC, the National Broadcasting Company.

THE PRIVATE LIVES OF ETHEL AND ALBERT *see* **ETHEL AND ALBERT**

1295. THE PRIVATE PRACTICE OF DR. DANA. Drama, 30 min., CBS, 1947–1948.

Steve Dana is a caring private practice doctor who also works part-time at Hayes General Hospital. Stories relate his experiences as he takes a personal interest in the lives of his patients. *Other regular characters:* Dr. Carol Tracy, his girlfriend. She works at Pershing Heights Hospital and is called "Trace" by Steve; Nurse Gorcey, Steve's office assistant (Steve is a bit forgetful and Gorcey, as she is called, looks out for him—from reminding him of appointments to letting him know when it is time for a haircut).

Cast: Jeff Chandler (*Dr. Steve Dana*); Betty Lou Gerson (*Dr. Carol Tracy*); Mary Lansing (*Nurse Gorcey*). ***Music:*** Eddie Dunstedter. ***Producer:*** Sterling Tracy.

OPENING (from Christmas episode of 1947; Marlene Ames guests as Sophia)

STEVE: Patient's name: Sophia Howard. Age: 10. Remarks: If there is anything wrong with this patient, I hope it's contagious; it would be one epidemic the world could really stand [Christmas cheer].

ANNOUNCER: It's *The Private Practice of Dr. Dana* starring Jeff Chandler and brought to you each Sunday afternoon at five, Pacific Standard Time. And now another story from the colorful career of the private practice of Steve Dana, M.D.

STEVE: That's right, I'm Steve Dana, and you never know how things are going to turn out... It all started two days before Christmas...

CLOSING

ANNOUNCER: And there you have *The Private Practice of Dr. Dana* starring Jeff Chandler. This is CBS, the Columbia Broadcasting System.

1296. PRIVATE SHOWING. Anthology, 30 min., Mutual, 1946–1947.

Dramatizations suggested by famous paintings—for example, "Rehearsal on Stage," based on a Degas painting, told a story of murder in the French ballet; "Poor House on a Hill," a story of greed, was suggested by a Cezanne painting. Walter Hampden, the host, also performed the leading roles (assisted by a different supporting cast each week).

1297. PROFESSOR QUIZ. Game, 30 min., CBS, 1936–1941; ABC, 1946–1948.

The program, billed as "The Battle of Wits," had five studio audience members compete in a series of question-and-answer rounds in return for cash awards.

Hosts: Craig Earl, Gene Hamilton. ***Announcers:*** Gene Hamilton, Robert Trout.

1298. PROUDLY WE HAIL. Anthology, 30 min., Syndicated, 1947–1957.

Dramatizations depicting the American spirit with host and frequent star Conrad Nagel. Kenneth Banghart was the announcer and the program was sponsored by the U.S. Army and Air Force.

1299. THE PRUDENTIAL FAMILY HOUR. Variety, 45 and 60 min. versions, CBS, 1941– 1948.

A program of music and songs sponsored by the Prudential Life Insurance Company.

***Professor Quiz* host Gene Hamilton with his son, Geoffrey.**

Hosts: Deems Taylor, Jose Ferrer. ***Regulars:*** Eileen Farrell, Ross Graham, Patrice Munsel, "Smiling" Jack Smith, Rise Stevens, Gladys Swarthout. ***Announcer:*** Frank Gallop. ***Orchestra:*** Al Goodman.

1300. THE PRUDENTIAL HOUR OF STARS. Anthology, 30 min., CBS, 1948–1949.

The program, sponsored by the Prudential Life Insurance Company, featured top name stars in original radio productions (both comedy and drama). The star of the particular episode served as the host. Truman Bradley did the announcing and Carmen Dragon and his orchestra supplied the music.

1301. PURSUIT. Crime Drama, 30 min., CBS, 1949–1952.

Peter Black is a tough British police inspector with Scotland Yard whose exploits are detailed as he relentlessly pursues criminals.

Cast: Ted de Corsia, Ben Wright (*Peter Black*). ***Announcer:*** Don Baker, Bob Stevenson. ***Music:*** Eddie Dundstedter, Marlin Skiles, Leith Stevens. ***Producer:*** Elliott Lewis.

OPENING

ANNOUNCER: And now, *Pursuit*. A criminal strikes and fades quickly back into the shadows of his own dark world. And then the man from Scotland Yard, the famous Inspector Peter Black and the dangerous, relentless *Pursuit*—when man hunts man. Now, with Ben Wright starred as the famous Peter Black of Scotland Yard, we bring you tonight's story of *Pursuit* and "The Ladies of Farthing Street."

1302. THE PURSUIT OF HAPPINESS. Anthology, 30 min., CBS, 1939–1940.

Dramatizations stressing American democracy and featuring name guest stars. Burgess Meredith served as the host and Mark Warnow and his orchestra provided the music.

1303. QUEEN FOR A DAY. Game, 30 min., Mutual, 1945–1957.

Pre-selected women were interviewed and asked to explain why they were in need of one specific item. One woman, whose response most impressed a panel of studio audience judges, was crowned "Queen for a Day" and received not only the prize she sought, but several others: nightclub reservation, a Fifth Avenue beauty parlor appointment and a shopping spree in a New York department store. Served as the basis for a television series of the same title.

Hosts: Dud Williamson, Jack Bailey. ***Announcers:*** Gene Baker, Bob Bunce, Mark Houston. ***Producer:*** Bud Ernst.

1304. QUICK AS A FLASH. Game, 30 min., Mutual, 1944–1949; ABC, 1949–1951.

Six members of the studio audience competed. Each was assigned a specific light color. Clues to the answer of a question based on history, music, news or show business were either read or dramatized on stage. At any point, a player could press a button, flash his light and stop the clue-giving process. If a correct answer was given, he won a prize; if not, he was disqualified and the game continued. The highlight of the series was a mystery play performed by top stars in character (for example, Lon Clark as "Nick Carter, Master Detective," John Archer as "The Shadow," Santos Ortega as "Nero Wolfe," Hugh Marlowe as "Ellery Queen" and Ed Begley as "Charlie Chan"). Served as the basis for the television series of the same title.

Hosts: Ken Roberts, Win Elliot, Bill Cullen. ***Announcers:*** Frank Gallop, Cy Harrice. ***Music:*** Ray Bloch.

1305. QUICKSILVER. Game, 30 min., NBC Blue, 1939–1940.

A microphone was concealed somewhere at a busy locale. A passerby was approached and asked to answer a riddle that had been submitted by a listener (who received $5). The participant received $5 also if he correctly answered the riddle; if not, he received one silver dollar.

Hosts: Ransom Sherman, Bob Brown.

1306. QUIET PLEASE. Anthology, 30 min., Mutual, 1947–1948; ABC, 1948–1949.

Imaginative mystery stories that went beyond the limits of reality and focused on a hazy dreamworld where things were not always as they seemed.

Host-Narrator: Ernest Chappell. ***Announcer:*** Ed Michael. ***Music:*** Albert Buhrmann, Gene Perrazzo. ***Producer:*** Wyllis Cooper.

OPENING

ANNOUNCER: Quiet please. Quiet please. The Mutual Broadcasting System presents *Quiet Please*, which is written and directed by Wyllis Cooper and which features Ernest Chappell. *Quiet Please* for tonight is called "Some People Don't Die."

CLOSING

ANNOUNCER: You have listened to *Quiet Please*, which is written and directed by Wyllis Cooper. The man who spoke to you was Ernest Chappell. Now for a word about next week's *Quiet Please*, here is our writer-director, my good friend, Wyllis Cooper.

COOPER: For next week, I've written a story about a man who wasn't satisfied with his modern wife who tried to change him; it's called "Little Fellow."

HOST: And so, until next week at this time, I am quietly yours, Ernest Chappell. *Quiet Please* came to you from New York. This is the Mutual Broadcasting System.

1307. Quixie Doodle. Game, 30 min., Mutual, 1938–1941.

Two teams competed, the Submitters vs. the Answerers. The Submitters were given ten questions and posed them to the Answerers, one at a time. Each correct response awarded the Answerers $10; an incorrect response scored $10 for the Submitters. Originally titled *Bob Hawk's Quixie Doodle Quiz.*

Hosts: Bob Hawk, Frederick Chase Taylor. ***Announcer:*** Alan Reed.

1308. The Quiz Kids. Game, 30 min., NBC Red, 1940; NBC Blue, 1940–1944; ABC, 1944–1946; NBC, 1946–1951; CBS, 1952–1953.

A panel of five exceptionally bright children answered questions either submitted by listeners or posed to them by studio audience members.

Host: Joe Kelly. ***Announcers:*** Roger Krupp, Bob Murphy, Fort Pearson, Ed Scott. ***Producer:*** Louis G. Cowan.

Note: The program spawned a television series (1949–1956) and also an experimental video version (DuMont, 3/6/45). The program was set in a schoolroom with the host dressed in a cap and gown and posing questions to four very bright children. Joe Kelly served as the host. Pat Conlon, Harve Fishman, Joel Kupperman and Richard Williams were the children.

1309. Quizzer's Baseball. Game, 30 min., CBS, 1941.

Two three-member teams competed in a question-and-answer session patterned after the game of baseball. Answers were scored from a base hit to a home run, depending on the rapidity with which a player answered. The team scoring the most runs received $100.

Host: Harry Von Zell. ***Team One Captain:*** Glenda Farrell. ***Team Two Captain:*** Wilbur "Budd" Hulick. ***Announcer:*** Harry Von Zell. ***Music:*** Peter Van Steeden.

1310. Radio City Playhouse. Anthology, 30 min., NBC, 1948–1950.

A weekly series of original stories and adaptations of works by noted authors that tended to be sentimental in nature or to involve people in life and death situations. Each production was referred to as an "Attraction."

Narrator: Harry W. Junkin. ***Leading Roles:*** John Larkin, Jan Miner. ***Announcers:*** Fred Collins, Robert Warren. ***Music:*** Roy Shields. ***Producer:*** Richard P. MacDonnell.

OPENING (from 7/10/48)

Announcer: The National Broadcasting Company presents *Radio City Playhouse*, Attraction Two. Before we raise our curtain, we would like to take time for a small speech. It amounts to this. Thanks. Thanks very much for many, many wonderful letters and praise of our opening play, "Long Distance." Bowing to your wishes, we promise we'll repeat it later on in this series. Tonight's play is titled "Ground Floor Window." It was written by an extremely talented young author, Ernest Kinoy, with Bill Redfield starring as Danny and directed by Harry W. Junkin. Here is *Radio City Playhouse*, Attraction Two: "Ground Floor Window."

CLOSING

Announcer: That was "Ground Floor Window," Attraction Two, *Radio City Playhouse* as written by Ernest Kinoy and directed by Harry W. Junkin. Next week, the *Radio City Playhouse* presents "Of Unsound Mind," written by our director, Harry W. Junkin. It is the story of Myra, beautiful, gracious, charming—and without a soul. We sincerely hope you will be with us next Saturday when we bring you "Of Unsound Mind" by Harry W. Junkin, Attraction Three, *Radio City Playhouse*. Robert Warren speaking, this is NBC, the National Broadcasting Company.

1311. The Radio Hall of Fame. Variety, 60 min., NBC Blue, 1943–1944; ABC, 1944–1946.

The program, sponsored by Philco appliances and produced by *Variety* magazine, featured performances by radio entertainers and celebrities in other fields. Deems Taylor was the host; vocalist Martha Tilton a regular; and music was by Paul Weston and his orchestra.

1312. Radio Reader's Digest. Anthology, 30 min., CBS, 1942–1948.

Adaptations of stories from *Reader's Digest* magazine. Also known as *Reader's Digest: Radio Edition.*

Host-Narrators: Conrad Nagel, Richard Killmar, Les Tremayne. ***Music:*** Nathan Van Cleave. ***Producers:*** Anton M. Leader, Carl Schullinger.

1313–14. Radio Theater of Famous Classics. Anthology, 30 min., Syndicated, 1946.

Adaptations of classic stories featuring a different cast each week. Organist Eddie Baker provided the music.

1315. Raffles. Crime Drama, 30 min., Syndicated, 1942–1945.

When someone needs help and has no place to turn, they seek an Englishman named A.J. Raffles, a gourmet, gentleman and reformed burglar turned sometimes private detective ("Now and then for my amusement"). Raffles' favorite hangout appears to be his office—Felipo's Restaurant. Raffles will help a damsel in distress—as long as he can avoid the police ("They fail to believe my intentions are no longer dishonorable")—for a price. Stories follow Raffles as he involves himself in other people's lives to help his clients.

Cast: Horace Braham (*A.J. Raffles*). ***Producer:*** Jock MacGregor.

OPENING

Announcer: There's danger; there's mystery; there's action on the way with *Raffles*. Raffles, formerly gentleman cracksman, gentleman adventurer, ace of knaves. Raffles, now reformed, matches wits with the underworld; devotes his time and talent to upholding law and order, even though his methods are highly unconventional and would never be found in the police manual. Tonight's story, "Murder Signs Its Name."

CLOSING

Announcer: The radio mysteries of *Raffles* are heard over this station every week at this same time. Be with us again next week when there's danger, there's mystery, there's action on the way with *Raffles*.

1316. The Railroad Hour. Anthology, 45 and 30 min. versions, ABC, 1948–1949; NBC, 1949–1954.

The program, sponsored by the American Association of Railroads, featured musical dramas based on the lives of famous musicians, the works of prominent writers, Broadway plays and light operas. *Stories include:*

1. The Merry Widow. A prince (Gordon MacRae) must court and wed a rich widow (Dorothy Kirsten) to save his country from financial ruin. Jack Kirkwood also appeared.

2. New Moon. A pirate (Gordon MacRae) falls in love with a lady of nobility (Mimi Benzell).

3. Showboat. The story of a riverboat gambler (Gordon MacRae) and his lady love (Margaret Truman).

4. Sari. A famed Gypsy violinist, his daughter, and a would-be fiddler seek fame and fortune. Gordon MacRae and Margaret Truman star.

Host-Male Lead: Gordon MacRae. ***Regulars:*** Billie Burke, Lurelle Norman, the Sportsman, the Norman Luboff Choir. ***Announcer:*** Marvin Miller. ***Orchestra:*** Carmen Dragon, John Rarig.

1317. Rainbow House. Children, 60 min., Mutual, 1940–1944; 30 min., Mutual, 1944–1946.

Music, songs and stories for the small fry with "Big Brother" Bob Emery as the host. Music was by a children's choir called the Dolphe Martin Orchestra.

The Raleigh and Kool Cigarette Show *see* **The Tommy Dorsey Show**

1318. The Raleigh Room. Variety, 30 min., NBC, 1944–1946.

A program of music, songs and light comedy sponsored by Raleigh cigarettes. Hildegarde Loretta Sell, a singer-pianist known as "The Incomparable Hildegarde," served as the host. Comic pianist Oscar Levant was a regular and Harry Sosnik and his orchestra provided the music.

OPENING (from 10/17/44)

Announcer: Does your cigarette taste different lately? Not if you smoke Raleigh. They're blended with fully aged, fully mellowed tobacco. Raleigh cigarettes invites you to the beautiful *Raleigh Room*; to the music of Harry Sosnik and his orchestra and our guest tonight, Patsy Kelly. There goes the spotlight and here she comes, our vivacious star, the Incomparable Hildegarde [who would first sing a song, then greet her home and studio audience].

The Ralph Edwards Show *see* **Truth or Consequences**

1319. The Ralph Flanagan Orchestra. Variety, 30 min., ABC, 1950–1955.

A weekly program of music and songs with the Ralph Flanagan orchestra. Robert Q. Lewis was the host; guest vocalists also entertained.

1320. The Ransom Sherman Show. Variety, 30 min., NBC Blue, 1939; CBS, 1942.

Comedian Ransom Sherman as the host of a weekly program of music, songs and sketches. Fran Allison, Bill Thompson and Wayne Van Dine were the regulars; Rex Maupin and his orchestra provided the music.

1321. Rate Your Mate. Game, 30 min., CBS, 1950–1951.

Married couples competed. While one mate was isolated in a soundproof booth, the other had to predict whether or not his or her spouse could answer a specific question. A cash prize (up to $100) was awarded on the accuracy of the prediction. Joey Adams was the host and Hal Simms did the announcing.

1322. The Ray Bolger Show. Variety, 30 min., CBS, 1945.

Singer-dancer Ray Bolger as the host of a weekly program of music, songs and comedy sketches. Elvia Allman, Verna Felton, Harry Lang and Jeri Sullivan were the regulars. Howard Petrie did the announcing and Roy Bargy and his orchestra provided the music.

1323. The Ray Noble Orchestra. Variety, 30 min., CBS, 1935–1936.

The music of the Ray Noble orchestra with Ray Noble as the host and Connee Boswell as the featured vocalist.

1324. The Raymond Paige Orchestra. Variety, 30 min., NBC, 1940.

Music and songs with host Milton Cross; the commentary of Deems Taylor; songs by the Mixed Choir; and music by Raymond Paige and his orchestra.

1325. The Raymond Scott Show. Variety, 15 min., CBS, 1939–1945.

Orchestra leader Raymond Scott as the host of a program of music and songs with vocalists Dorothy Collins, Nan Wynn and the Raymond Scott Chorus, and music by the Raymond Scott Orchestra.

RCA Radio Radiotrons *see* **Appendix**

The RCA Victor Hour *see* **Appendix**

1326. The RCA Victor Show. Variety, 30 min., NBC, 1945.

A program of music and songs sponsored by RCA Victor. Leonardo Feather, Robert Merrill and Deems Taylor were the regulars; Kenny Delmar did the announcing; and music was by the Raymond Paige Orchestra (later by Arthur Fiedler and the Boston Pops Orchestra).

Reader's Digest: Radio Edition *see* **Radio Reader's Digest**

1327. Real Stories from Real Life. Anthology, 15 min., Mutual, 1944–1947.

Short dramatizations that focus on a central character, telling his or her own story (presented in a series of flashbacks). A different cast appeared each week; the program was produced by Anne Hummert and Frank Hummert.

1328. The Realsilk Program. Variety, 30 min., NBC Blue, 1936–1937.

The program, sponsored by the Indianapolis-based Realsilk Hosiery Mills, featured music and short dramatizations. Edwin Miller was the host and Harry Sosnik and his orchestra provided the music.

1329. Red Benson's Movie Matinee. Game, 30 min., Mutual, 1949.

The format called for contestants to answer questions based on film titles in return for prizes. Red Benson served as the host and Carl Warren did the announcing.

1330. Red Hook 31. Chatter, 15 min., Mutual, 1947–1948.

The exchange of conversation between Woody Klose, a radio scriptwriter, and his wife Virginia as they discussed their life, in particular their move from the city to the 102-acre

Echo Valley Farm in Dutchess County, New York. Red Hook 31 was their telephone number. Woody Klose and Virginia Klose portrayed themselves.

1331. Red Horse Tavern. Variety, 30 min., CBS, 1935–1936.

The Red Horse Tavern was a mythical music hall and the advertising logo of the show's sponsor, Socony Oil. Eleanor Powell and Osgood Perkins served as the hosts; guests performed and Harry Sosnik and his orchestra provided the music.

1332. Red Ryder. Western, 30 min., Mutual, 1942–1949.

The Painted Valley in the Colorado Rockies is home to Red Ryder, a cattle rancher and unofficial lawman, and his partner Buckskin, the owners of the Red Ryder Ranch. Red is also friends with Little Beaver, a Navajo Indian, and stories follow their adventure as they battle desperadoes. Based on the comic strip by Fred Harman. Red's horse was named Thunder; Little Beaver's horse was Papoose.

Cast: Reed Hadley, Carlton KaDell, Brooke Temple (*Red Ryder*); Tommy Cook, Henry Blair (*Little Beaver*); Horace Murphy (*Buckskin*). ***Regulars*** (Various roles): Charles Lung, Lurene Tuttle, Fred Shields. ***Announcer:*** Ben Alexander. ***Music:*** Robert Armbruster. ***Producer:*** Paul Franklin.

OPENING

Announcer: From out of the West comes America's famous fighting cowboy, *Red Ryder*.

1333. The Red Skelton Show. Variety, 30 min., NBC, 1941–1952.

The program, also known as *Red Skelton's Scrapbook*, featured monologues, musical numbers, songs and skits that revolved around comedian Red Skelton's array of wacky characters: Clem Kadiddlehopper, Junior, "The Mean Widdle Kid," Sheriff Deadeye, Willy Lump Lump, Bolivar Shagnasty and J. Newton Numbskull. Served as the basis for the television series of the same title.

Cast: Red Skelton (*Host/Star*); Harriet Hilliard, Lurene Tuttle (*Junior's mother*); Harriet Hilliard, Gee Gee Pearson (*Mrs. Willy Lump Lump*); Harriet Hilliard, Lurene Tuttle (*Daisy June*); Harriet Hilliard (*Calamity Jane*); Gee Gee Pearson (*Sara Dew/Mrs. Bolivar Shagnasty/Mrs. J. Newton Numbskull*); Verna Felton (*Junior's grandmother*); Marlin Hurt (*Mademoiselle Levy*). ***Vocalists:*** Anita Ellis, Harriet Hilliard, Ozzie Nelson, the Four Knights. ***Regulars:*** Arthur Q. Bryan, Tommy Mack, "Wonderful" Smith. ***Announcers:*** Truman Bradley, John Holbrook, Pat McGeehan, Marvin Miller, Rod O'Connor. ***Orchestra:*** Dave Forrester, Ozzie Nelson, David Rose. ***Producer:*** Jack Simpson.

OPENING

Announcer: *The Red Skelton Show*. Here's the David Rose orchestra, Anita Ellis, Verna Felton, Lurene Tuttle, Pat McGeehan, Rod O'-Connor and your star, Red Skelton.

1334. The Redhead. Comedy, 30 min., ABC, 1952.

Events in the life of a brash, wise-cracking young girl from a small town in Nebraska as she struggles to achieve fame and fortune as a model in New York City. Mary McCarty played the girl and Dick Van Patten was her romantic interest.

1335. Refreshment Time. Variety, 30 min., CBS, 1950.

A program of music, songs and comedy sponsored by Coca-Cola and featuring singer Morton Downey as the host. Stan Freeman and Kitty Kallen were the regulars; Ray Morgan did the announcing; and Carmen Mastren and his orchestra provided the music.

1336. Reg'lar Fellers. Children, 30 min., NBC, 6/8/41 to 8/31/41.

The comical escapades of two brothers (Jimmie and Dinky Dugan) who seek fun but find only misadventure. *Other regular characters:* Their friends, Puddinhead Duffy, Washington Jones, Aggie, Daisy and Victor. Based on the comic strip by Gene Byrnes.

Cast: Dick Van Patten (*Jimmie Dugan*); Dickie Monahan (*Dinky Dugan*); Ray Ives (*Puddinhead Duffy*); Orville Phillips (*Washington Jones*); Patsy O'Shea (*Aggie Riley*); Joyce Van Patten (*Daisy*); Skip Homeier (*Victor*).

1337. Relaxation in Music. Variety, 15 min., Mutual, 1944.

Music and songs with Bob Bary and Jean

Tighe as the hosts and the music of Dick Adams and his orchestra.

1338. The Remarkable Miss Tuttle. Drama, 30 min., NBC, 1942.

One person's efforts to help others as seen through the eyes of Miss Tuttle, a well-meaning spinster who involved herself in the lives of troubled people.

Cast: Edna Mae Oliver (*Miss Tuttle*); Arnold Stang (*Her nephew*); Lillian Randolph (*Her maid*); Cy Kendall (*Judge Carter*). ***Also:*** Martin Gosch, Howard Harris. ***Announcer:*** Murray Boler.

1339. Reminiscin' with Singin' Sam. Variety, 15 min., Syndicated, 1946.

A program of musical memories with Harry "Singin' Sam" Frankel as the host. The Mullin Sisters provided additional songs and Charles Magnoule and his orchestra provided the music.

1340. Rendezvous with Romance. Variety, 30 min., ABC, 1946.

A program of music and songs with Bess Myerson as the host and the music of Al D'Artega and His All-Girl Orchestra. Guest vocalists assisted each week.

1341. Renfrew of the Mounted. Adventure, 30 min., CBS, 1936–1937; NBC Blue, 1937–1940.

A modern-day version of *Sergeant Preston of the Yukon* that related the exploits of Douglas Renfrew, an inspector with the Royal Canadian Mounted Police, as he battled evildoers in the wilds of Canada. *Other regular characters:* Carol Girard, his romantic interest.

Cast: House Jameson (*Douglas Renfrew*); Joan Baker (*Carol Girard*); Brad Barker (*Animal sounds*). ***Announcer:*** Bert Parks.

OPENING

Voice (over howling winds): Renfrew, Renfrew of the Mounted!

Renfrew: Renfrew reporting, ready for action.

Announcer: Once again we bring you *Renfrew of the Mounted*, in another story of the famous inspector of the Royal Canadian Mounted Police. Known to thousands of admirers through the books and stories of Laurie Yorke Erskine and adapted to radio by George Ludlum.

1342. Request Performance. Variety, 30 min., CBS, 1945–1946.

Listener requests were honored with guests either performing songs or dramatic skits. Del Sharbutt served as the host and announcer; Leith Stevens and his orchestra provided the music; and William N. Robson was the producer-director.

Reserved for Garroway *see* **The Dave Garroway Show**

1343. Results, Inc. Mystery, 30 min., Mutual, 10/7/44 to 12/30/44.

Johnny Strange and Terry Travers are lovers who are also co-owners of Results, Inc., a detective agency that will take any case for money. Johnny is the laid-back and easygoing president; Teresa "Terry" Travers is the adventurous vice-president and secretary. She is anxious for work and often takes cases Johnny is hesitant to investigate—until he becomes involved and finds adventure. Still, he has to remind Terry, "You are only the vice-president of this company, not the chief." But he adds, "We're a pretty happy combination with a good president and a swell vice-president. I'm the luckiest guy in the world to have you." Stories follow their various investigations as they try to deliver what they promise—results.

Cast: Lloyd Nolan (*Johnny Strange*); Claire Trevor (*Terry Travers*). ***Announcer:*** Bob O'Connor. ***Music:*** Russ Trump.

OPENING

Announcer: Presenting Lloyd Nolan and Claire Trevor in another adventure of *Results, Inc.*

CLOSING

Announcer: The mystery-comedy series *Results, Inc.* has starred Lloyd Nolan as Johnny Strange and Claire Trevor as the irrepressible Teresa Travers. Miss Trevor has appeared through the courtesy of RKO Studios and Mr. Nolan through the courtesy of 20th Century–Fox. This is Mutual.

1344. Reveille Round-Up. Variety, 15 min., NBC, 1941–1945.

A program of country and western music and songs hosted by Charles Kirby and Tom Wallace. Louise Massey and the Westerners (Allen Massey, Curt Massey, Milt Mobie and Larry Wellington) were the regulars.

1345. Revere All-Star Revue. Variety, 15 min., Mutual, 1948.

Vocalist Andy Russell as the host of a program of music and songs. Marion Hutton and the Pied Pipers were the regulars; Toby Reed did the announcing; Ray Sinatra and his orchestra provided the music. Revere Cameras sponsored the program.

The Rexall Show *see* **The Jimmy Durante Show**

1346. The Rexall Summer Show. Variety, 30 min., NBC, 1948.

Francis X. Bushman, Virginia Bruce and Pat O'Brien as the stars of a weekly program of music and songs sponsored by Rexall Drugs. Bill Forman and Barbara Eiler served as the announcers and Roy Bargy and his orchestra provided the music.

1347. Rhapsody in Rhythm. Variety, 30 min., NBC, 1946–1947; CBS, 1947.

A program of music and songs with Connie Haines (1946) and Peggy Lee and Johnny Johnston (1947) as the hosts. Skitch Henderson, the Golden Gate Quartet and the Pied Pipers were the regulars. Art Gilmore did the announcing and Jan Savitt and his orchestra provided the music.

1348. Rhythm on the Road. Variety, 60 min., CBS, 1955.

Bob Dixon as the host (and announcer) of a weekly program of music and songs with the Honeydreamers vocal group and the music of Elliott Lawrence and his orchestra.

1349. Rhythm Road. Variety, 30 min., CBS, 1943.

Vocalist Johnny Morgan as the host of a weekly program of music and songs. Victoria Cordova, Sidney Fields and Alastair and Ann Thomas were the regulars; Glenn Riggs did the announcing; Jimmy Lytell and his orchestra provided the music.

1350. Richard Diamond, Private Detective. Crime Drama, 30 min., NBC, 1949–1950; ABC, 1951–1952; ABC, 1953 (repeats).

"If trouble is around, yours truly will most likely get a chunk of it," says Richard Diamond, a former cop with the Fifth Precinct who is now a private detective (he carries a .38 in a shoulder holster). Diamond operates out of an office at 51st Street and Broadway in New York City and likes to be called Rick. Stories follow his efforts to solve the crimes he becomes involved with (when someone calls him from a phone, Diamond says, "You spend a dime, you name the crime"). *Other regular characters:* Lt. Walt Levinson, Homicide Division, Fifth Precinct; Helen Asher, Diamond's girlfriend; Otis Ludlum, the desk sergeant; Francis, Helen's butler.,

Cast: Dick Powell (*Richard Diamond*); Ed Begley (*Walt Levinson*); Virginia Gregg (*Helen Asher*); Wilms Herbert (*Otis Ludlum/Francis*). ***Music:*** David Baskerville, Frank Worth.

OPENING

Sound: Richard Diamond whistling.

Announcer: Here's Dick Powell as *Richard Diamond, Private Detective*.

1351. Richard Lawless. Adventure, 30 min., CBS, 1946.

Seventeenth-century England was the setting for a series about Richard Lawless, a crusader who battled the injustices during the reign of Charles II.

Cast: Kevin McCarthy (*Richard Lawless*). ***Also:*** Peter Bayne, Neil Fitzgerald, Kathleen Fordell. ***Music:*** John Gart.

1352. The Richard Maxwell Show. Variety, 15 min., CBS, 1938–1940.

Tenor Richard Maxwell as the host of a program of hymns coupled with talk. John Harper did the announcing.

1353. The Right to Happiness. Serial, 15 min., NBC Blue, 1939–1940; CBS, 1940–1941; NBC Red, 1941–1960.

Dramatic events in the lives of the Kramers, a family that moves from the slums to a respectable neighborhood, as they attempt to find happiness.

Cast: Eloise Kummer, Claudia Morgan (*Carolyn Kramer*); Leora Thatcher (*Carolyn's mother*); Julian Noa (*Carolyn's father*); Selena Royle, Constance Crowder, Irene Hubbard (*Doris Cameron*); Ruth Bailey (*Rose Kransky*); Charles Webster, Art Kohn (*Fred Minturn*); Les Damon, Alexander Scourby (*Richard Camp-*

bell); Anne Starrett (*Ginny*); Violet Heming, Luise Barclay (*Constance Wakefield*); Charita Bauer (*Susan Wakefield*); Reese Taylor (*Bill Walker*); Jimmy Dobson, Billy Redfield (*Ted Wakefield*); Staats Cotsworth (*Alex*); Ginger Jones (*Jane*); Peter Fernandez (*Skip*). ***Narrator:*** Marvin Miller. ***Announcers:*** Hugh Conover, Michael Fitzmaurice, Ron Rawson. ***Music:*** William Meeder. ***Producers:*** Fayette Krum, Kathleen Lane, Paul Martin, Carl Webster.

OPENING

ANNOUNCER: This is *The Right to Happiness*, brought to you by CBS radio. Happiness is the sum total of many things—of health, security, friends and loved ones. But most important is a desire to be happy and the will to help others find their right to happiness as well.

1354. RIN TIN TIN. Adventure, 15 min., NBC Blue, 1930–1934.

Stories of a dog's courage as witnessed by Francis X. Bushman (playing himself) as the owner of Rin Tin Tin, "The Wonder Dog" (star of silent movies). Rin Tin Tin was actually owned by Lee Duncan. See also *The Adventures of Rin Tin Tin*.

1355. RIPPLING RHYTHM REVUE. Variety, 30 min., NBC Blue, 1936–1937.

Music, songs and comedy skits coupled with monologues. Bob Hope was the host, Frank Parker (tenor) and the country and western singing team of Anne, Judy and Zeke Canova were the regulars. Music was by an orchestra billed as "The Rippling Rhythm of Shep Fields."

1356. THE RISE STEVENS SHOW. Variety, 30 min., NBC, 1945.

Opera star Rise Stevens as the host of a program of music and songs that featured a guest orchestra conductor each week. Lou Crosby did the announcing.

1357. RIVER BOAT REVELS. Variety, 30 min., NBC, 1941.

Kay Carlisle as the host of a program of music and songs with David Cobb, Joseph MacPherson, Frank Marlowe, Minnie Pearl and the Old Timers Quartet as the regulars. Pietro Brescia and his orchestra provided the music.

1358. THE RKO HOUR. Variety, 60 min., NBC, 1929–1930.

A weekly program of music and songs with vocalist Irene Bordoni as the host and the music of Leo Reisman and his orchestra.

1359. THE RKO THEATER. Variety, 30 min., NBC, 1930–1932.

Songs with singer-comedian Phil Cook and music with David Applon and his orchestra.

1360. THE ROAD OF LIFE. Serial, 15 min., NBC, 1937–1954; CBS, 1952–1959 (it appeared on both NBC and CBS from 1952 until 1954).

Dramatic events in the life of Jim Brent, an intern (later doctor) in the town of Merrimack. Stories, although focusing on doctors and nurses, strayed from the office to relate personal incidents in the lives of the people known by Dr. Brent. Served as the basis for the television series of the same title.

Cast: Ken Griffin, Matt Crowley, Don MacLaughlin, David Ellis, Howard Teichmann (*Dr. Jim Brent*); Lesley Woods, Barbara Luddy, Louise Fitch, Marion Shockley (*Carol Evans Martin*); Elizabeth Lawrence, Eileen Palmer, Evelyn Varden (*Frances Brent*); Donald Katz, Roland Butterfield, Lawson Zerbe, David Ellis, Bill Lipton (*Butch Brent*); Sarajane Wells (*Claudia Wilson*); Vicki Vola, Beryl Vaughn (*Faith Richards*); Peggy Allenby, Betty Lou Gerson, Muriel Bremner, Janet Logan (*Helen Stephenson*); Reese Taylor (*Dr. Reginald Parsons*); Lyle Sudrow (*Frank Dana*); Julie Stevens, Helen Lewis (*Maggie Lowell*); Dick Post, Willard Waterman, Robert Duane (*Dr. Grant Frasier*); Sidney Breese (*Dr. Ralph Thompson*); Jeanette Dowling, Angel Casey (*Nurse paging Jim in the opening theme*). ***Announcers:*** George Bryan, Clayton "Bud" Collyer, Ron Rawson. ***Music:*** Charles Paul. ***Producers:*** Fayette Krum, Kay Lane, Carl Webster.

1361. THE ROAD TO DANGER. Adventure, 30 min., NBC, 11/6/42 to 3/4/45.

Stumpy and Cottonseed are World War II U.S. Army truckers who have been through the mill—bombs, torpedoes, "the whole works." They go where anything can happen and there is no telling what might pop up. "Saboteurs, spies, Lord knows what," says Stumpy. "And take it from me, folks, this ain't no joy ride," exclaims Cottonseed. Stumpy worries about everything; Cottonseed is cool and calm and believes everything will turn out for the best. They have been assigned to the European theater of war and stories relate their exploits as they travel the road of danger transporting supplies to the front lines.

Cast: Curley Bradley (*Stumpy*); Clarence Hartzell (*Cottonseed*). ***Organist:*** Romelle Fay.

OPENING

ANNOUNCER: The National Broadcasting Company presents *The Road to Danger*, the story of two American truck drivers on the unmarked highways of the world. Today we find Stumpy and Cottonseed at an American post not many miles behind the front lines in Italy. Their truck has just been loaded with shells and they are ready to head to an ammunition depot at the front. Right this minute they're ready to shake, rattle and roll up to the lines where the air is filled with flying steel; they're set for another long haul along the highway that is *The Road to Danger*.

CLOSING

ANNOUNCER: You have just heard another in NBC's series *The Road to Danger*, based on an original story by James Street and directed by Jack Simpson. Next week, same time, same station, be sure to join us again on *The Road to Danger* when you'll hear—

COTTONSEED: Stumpy, what are we waitin' on?

STUMPY: Not a darn thing, Cottonseed, let's go [truck is heard speeding off].

ANNOUNCER: This is the National Broadcasting Company.

1362. THE ROBERT BENCHLEY SHOW. Variety, 30 min., NBC, 1939.

A weekly program of music and songs with radio critic Robert Benchley as the host. Del Sharbutt did the announcing and Artie Shaw and his orchestra provided the music.

1363. THE ROBERT BURNS PANATELA SHOW. Comedy, 30 min., CBS, 2/22/32 to 5/17/33.

Various comedy routines with the husband-and-wife team of George Burns and Gracie Allen, here playing single friends with the absent-minded Gracie involving George in various comical situations. Sponsored by the General Cigar Company, makers of Robert Burns Panatela Cigars. See also *The White Owl Program*.

Hosts: George Burns, Gracie Allen. ***Vocalists:*** Carmen Lombardo, Phil Regan. ***Announcers:*** Frank Knight, Santos Ortega. ***Orchestra:*** Guy Lombardo and His Royal Canadians.

1364. THE ROBERT MERRILL SHOW. Variety, 30 min., NBC, 1945.

Singer Robert Merrill as the host of a weekly program of music and songs. Robert Denton did the announcing and Leopold Spitalny and his orchestra provided the music.

1365. THE ROBERT Q. LEWIS SHOW. Variety, 15, 30 and 60 min. versions, NBC, 1945; CBS, 1947–1950; ABC, summer of 1950; CBS, 1951–1953; CBS, 1954–1959.

A weekly program of music, songs and light comedy. The program is also known as *The ABC's of Music* and *Robert Q's Waxworks*.

Host: Robert Q. Lewis. ***Regulars:*** Jan Arden, Eugene Baird, Jackson Beck, Toby David, Richard Hayes, Lois Hunt, Judy Johnson, William Keene, Phil Kramer, Jaye P. Morgan, Kathy Norman, Florence Robinson, Herb Sheldon, Billy Williams, Earl Wrightson, Bill Wyatt, the Ames Brothers, the Chordettes, the Mixed Choir. ***Announcers:*** Kenneth Banghart, Warren Sweeney, Lee Vines. ***Orchestra:*** Ray Bloch, Dave Grupp, Lee Irwin, Milton Kaye, Howard Smith, George Wright.

1366. ROBINSON CRUSOE, JR. Children, 15 min., CBS, 1934–1935.

A mythical island was the setting for a daily adventure serial about Robinson Brown, Jr., a rich child, and his friends (Julie and Jinky) who were marooned with Brown's butler Friday and maid Katie.

Cast: Lester Jay (*Robinson Brown, Jr.*); Toni Gilman (*Julie*); Michael O'Day (*Jinky*); Arthur Hughes (*Friday*); Jean Sothern (*Katie*).

1367. ROCK 'N' ROLL DANCE PARTY. Variety, 30 min., CBS, 1956.

A weekly program of music and songs with Joe Williams as the host. Bern Bennett did the announcing and the Count Basie Band supplied the music.

1368. ROCKING HORSE RHYTHM. Variety, 15 min., Mutual, 1943–1944.

The program began at 10:45 P.M. and consisted of jokes, celebrity interviews and songs—all of which were performed by Bobby Hookey, a five-year-old boy who conducted the show from a wooden rocking horse with a microphone attached to its head. *Newsweek* reported that Bobby "was the youngest star ever to host his own weekly network radio program." Mort Howard provided the music. The program is also known as "Hookey Hall."

1369. Rocky Fortune. Crime Drama, 30 min., NBC, 1/10/53 to 3/30/54.

Rocky Fortune (real name: Rocco Fortunato) is a footloose and frequently unemployed young man who takes whatever work he can find to support himself. Stories follow Rocky's adventures when his jobs land him in deep trouble. The Gridley Employment Agency in New York City tries to find Rocky work. When there are no jobs, he lives off his unemployment insurance. *Other regular characters:* Hamilton J. Finger, the N.Y.P.D. sergeant who believes Rocky is always guilty of something—and is determined to prove it one day.

Cast: Frank Sinatra (*Rocky Fortune*); Barney Phillips (*Hamilton J. Finger*). ***Announcer:*** Eddie King.

OPENING

Announcer: Now Frank Sinatra, transcribed, as *Rocky Fortune*. NBC presents Frank Sinatra starring as that footloose and fancy free young gentleman, Rocky Fortune.

Rocky: Did I ever tell you about the time I got mixed up in a plan to murder Santa Claus? Yeah, it all started when I answered a Christmas ad for a department store...

CLOSING

Announcer: NBC has presented Frank Sinatra as that footloose and fancy free young gentleman, *Rocky Fortune*. Now, to tell you about next week's adventure, here's Frank Sinatra as Rocky Fortune.

Rocky: Did I ever tell you about the time I conducted a sightseeing tour of the museum? Man, they got dead people in sarcophagi laying all over the place. Not that I'm squeamish about a bunch of mummies, believe me. But when they try to embalm me, that's where I drew the line. I'll tell you about it next week. See you around.

Announcer: This is NBC, the National Broadcasting Company.

1370. Rocky Jordan. Adventure, 30 min., CBS, 10/31/48 to 9/10/50.

A revised version of *A Man Called Jordan* (see entry). The Cafe Tambourine is a Cairo, Egypt, bar owned by Rocky Jordan, a man who would like nothing else than to mind his own business and run his establishment. But the cafe is an open door for everyone from "dames in trouble to lost souls seeking help." "I gotta help, I like it here in Cairo," says Rocky; his various adventures as he turns private detective are the focal point of stories. *Other regular characters:* Sam Sabaaya, captain of the Cairo Police Department. See also the following title.

Cast: Jack Moyles (*Rocky Jordan*); Jay Novello (*Capt. Sam Sabaaya*). ***Announcer:*** Larry Dobkin. ***Music:*** Milton Charles. ***Producer:*** Cliff Powell.

OPENING (from "The Battered Bride Groom")

Announcer: Time now for *Rocky Jordan*.

Rocky: It was a hot afternoon in Cairo when she walked into the Cafe Tambourine. She was beautiful but there was something else, something so wrong with the picture that I couldn't take my eyes off her. It wasn't the blonde hair piled on the top of her head or the dress that clung to her like a football player covering a fumble, not even the set expression on her face. But when she stopped in front of me, I knew what it was. She was all woman, but not an inch under six-foot-four.

Announcer: Again we bring you a story of adventure with a man named Rocky Jordan, proprietor of the Cafe Tambourine in Cairo. Cairo, gateway to the ancient East where modern life unfolds against the backdrop of antiquity. Tonight's story, "The Battered Bride Groom."

Rocky: We've had a pretty fair assortment of customers here at the Tambourine, almost anything on feet, but when I looked up into the icy face of six-foot-four of blonde female, I knew we had our first Amazon...

CLOSING

Announcer: And now a note for you listeners. *Rocky Jordan* has joined one of the most outstanding mystery lineups in radio over your CBS station every Sunday night. You'll hear not only *Rocky Jordan*, but *Sam Spade*, Dashiell Hammett's great private eye, and *The Whistler*, one of the most popular shows on the air. Remember this same time each

Sunday night for *Rocky Jordan*. *Rocky Jordan* is produced from Columbia Square in Hollywood and stars Jack Moyles in the title role. This is CBS, the Columbia Broadcasting System.

1371. Rocky Jordan. Adventure, 30 min., CBS, 6/27/51 to 8/22/51.

A revised version of the prior title. Rocky Jordan is just an ordinary guy trying to run an ordinary business—the Cafe Tambourine in Cairo, Egypt—but nothing is ordinary about Cairo. Rocky seems to have a knack for meeting people in trouble and murder is almost always an outcome of his encounters. His efforts to clear himself or a friend are the focal point of stories. When the revised version began, Rocky was the owner of a cafe called the Grand Bazaar in Istanbul. The change in locale didn't appear to work and Rocky returned to his second home in Cairo and the Cafe Tambourine. In addition to Capt. Sam Sabaaya of the Cairo Police Department, Chris the bartender was added to the series. Chris, who called Rocky "The Rock," narrated the stories. See also *A Man Called Jordan*.

Cast: George Raft (*Rocky Jordan*); Anthony Barrett (*Chris*); Jay Novello (*Capt. Sam Sabaaya*). ***Announcer:*** Joe Walters. ***Music:*** Richard Aurandt.

OPENING

Announcer: Now starring George Raft, we bring you a world of adventure with *Rocky Jordan*.

Rocky: I'm Rocky Jordan, I run the Cafe Tambourine in Cairo.

Announcer: The Cafe Tambourine, crowded with tourists, camel drivers, women, sheiks, forgotten men down on their luck, the lonely and the lost. For this is Cairo, gateway to the ancient East where modern adventure and intrigue unfold against the backdrop of antiquity. Tonight's transcribed story, "The Man in the Nile."

CLOSING

Rocky: Hope to see you in the Cafe Tambourine next week. Until then, *sieta* (good-bye).

Announcer: This transcribed program came to you over the CBS Radio Network.

1372. Roger Kilgore, Public Defender. Crime Drama, 30 min., Mutual, 4/27/48 to 10/12/48.

Roger Kilgore is a public defender of indigent clients. He works closely with the police and the D.A. to resolve a case before a trial begins. Stories, which are presented in the flashback technique, relate Roger's step-by-step investigations. *Other regular characters:* Miss Carpenter, Roger's secretary; Sam Howard, the district attorney.

Cast: Raymond Edward Johnson, Santos Ortega (*Roger Kilgore*); Bryna Raeburn (*Miss Carpenter*); Staats Cotsworth (*Sam Howard*). ***Music:*** Milton Kane, Sylvan Levin. ***Producer:*** Jock MacGregor.

OPENING

Announcer: The Mutual Broadcasting System presents *Roger Kilgore, Public Defender*.

Voice: We hold these truths to be self-evident that all men are created equal. That they are endowed by their creator with certain inalienable rights. That among these are life, liberty and the pursuit of happiness.

Roger: I'm Roger Kilgore, Public Defender, a paid servant of the public. It's my duty to defend any person accused of a crime who is unable to pay for his own defense.

Announcer: Tonight, "The Case of Eddie Lewis."

CLOSING

Announcer: All names, places and dates used in this program were, for obvious reasons, fictitious. Remember that justice, equal justice, is the sacred right of all people in a democracy. This is the Mutual Broadcasting System.

1373. Rogers of the Gazette. Comedy, 30 min., CBS, 1953–1954.

Events in the lives of the citizens of the small town of Olearia as seen through the eyes of Will Rogers, Jr., the editor of the town's only newspaper, the *Gazette*. Rogers not only reports the stories but involves himself in the problems of others. Olearia hasn't changed much in over a century: "People with the same names live in the same houses and for the most part, they have pretty much the same ideas as the generations which went before. The town just doesn't want to change and the people here like things just the way they are." *Other regular characters:* Maggie Button, Will's assistant; Doc, Will's friend; Ed Miller, the police officer.

Cast: Will Rogers, Jr. (*Will Rogers, Jr.*);

Georgia Ellis (*Maggie Button*); Parley Baer (*Doc*); Harry Bartell (*Officer Ed Miller*). ***Announcer:*** Bob Lemond. ***Music:*** Lud Gluskin, Wilbur Hatch. ***Producer:*** Norman McDonnell.

OPENING

MAGGIE: Ladies and gentlemen, the editor of the Olearia *Weekly Gazette*, Mr. Will Rogers, Jr.

WILL: Thank you. You know, some newspapers claim they print all the news that's fit to print and some others, who won't admit it, just print the news that fits.

ANNOUNCER: *Rogers of the Gazette*, offering you again, tonight, transcribed, another heart-warming story of a country newspaper and its friendly editor and starring Will Rogers, Jr.

1374. ROGUE'S GALLERY. Crime Drama, 30 min., Mutual, 6/23/45 to 6/20/46; NBC, 6/23/46 to 9/28/47; ABC, 11/29/50 to 11/21/51.

Richard Rogue is a slick private detective who pays his bills by trailing luscious blondes, protecting witnesses, spying on unfaithful husbands, solving murders—basically, whatever he can do to make money. When the trouble-seeking Rogue is knocked out, his consciousness drifts to Cloud Eight, where he meets his alter ego, Eugor (Rogue spelled backward), "a nasty little spook" who consoles him before he regains his senses and returns to earth—to find additional trouble.

Cast: Dick Powell, Barry Sullivan, Paul Stewart (*Richard Rogue*); Peter Leeds (*Eugor*). ***Announcer:*** Jim Doyle. ***Music:*** Leith Stevens.

OPENING

ANNOUNCER: The F.W. Fitch Company presents Dick Powell as private investigator Richard Rogue in *Rogue's Gallery*.

1375. ROMANCE. Anthology, 30 min., CBS, 4/19/43 to 12/11/46; 4/23/47 to 2/5/49; 6/2/50 to 8/8/50; 1/6/51 to 1/5/57.

Tales of romance and adventure featuring females in leading roles (including prominent and dangerous situations). The program is also known as *Theater of Romance* and *Jergens Hollywood Playhouse* (when sponsored by Jergens in 1952 and 1953).

Host-Narrators ("The Voice of Romance"): Doris Dalton, Kay Brinker. ***Announcers:*** Dan Cubberly, Roy Rowan. ***Music:*** Jerry Goldsmith, Charles Paul.

OPENING (from 3/31/56)

ANNOUNCER: Now, from Hollywood, *Romance*. *Romance*, transcribed stories of love and adventure, of comedy and crisis, of conflict and human emotion. Today, an adventure on the high seas, a fierce and lusty pirate tale from the pen of Anthony Ellis, with Ray Lawrence as Capt. Blackton and starring Paula Winslow as "Bloodthirsty Kate."

CLOSING

ANNOUNCER: *Romance* is produced and directed by William Froug. "Bloodthirsty Kate" was written by Anthony Ellis and featured Paula Winslow with Ray Lawrence... Musical supervision by Jerry Goldsmith. This is Dan Cubberly inviting you to hear *Romance*, transcribed, next week at this same time. This is the Columbia Broadcasting System.

1376. THE ROMANCE OF HELEN TRENT. Serial, 15 min., CBS, 1933–1960.

The dramatic story of Helen Trent, a 35-year-old fashion designer, and her struggles to find a true love. Her most lasting romance was with Gil Whitney, a married lawyer whose wife refused to give him up.

Cast: Virginia Clark, Betty Ruth Smith, Julie Stevens (*Helen Trent*); Marvin Miller, David Gothard (*Gil Whitney*); Audrey McGrath (*Monica Smith*); Bernice Silverman, Bernice Martin, Florence Robinson (*Ginger Leroy*); David Gothard (*Philip King*); Marilyn Erskine (*Cherry Martin*); Mary Jane Higby (*Cynthia Carter*); Lucy Gilman (*Toni Griffin*); Marie Nelson, Katherine Emmet, Bess McCammon (*Agatha Anthony*); Reese Taylor (*Drew Sinclair*); Ginger Jones (*Alice Carroll*); Bret Morrison (*Jonathan Howard*); John Larkin (*Roy Gabler*); Alan Hewitt (*Karl Dorn*); Olan Soule (*Eric Stowell*); Patricia Dunlap (*Nina Mason*). ***Announcers:*** Pierre Andre, Fielden Farrington, Don Hancock. ***Theme:*** "Juanita" (hummed by Stanley Davis; later Lawrence Salerno). ***Producers:*** Anne Hummert, Frank Hummert.

OPENING

ANNOUNCER: *The Romance of Helen Trent*. The real-life drama of Helen Trent who, when life mocks her, breaks her hopes, dashes her against the rocks of despair, fights back bravely, successfully, to prove what so many women long to prove in their own lives: that because a woman is 35 or more, romance in

Virginia Clark gave voice to the title character in *The Romance of Helen Trent.*

life need not be over; that romance can begin at 35.

1377. ROMANCE, RHYTHM AND RIPLEY. Variety, 30 min., CBS, 1945.

A short-lived program of music, songs and strange facts from the "Ripley's Believe It or Not" newspaper column. Dick Haymes was the variety segment host; Robert L. Ripley emceed the "Believe It or Not" segment. Vocalist Martha Tilton sang; Jim Ameche did the announcing; Ray Bloch and his orchestra provided the music.

1378. THE ROOKIES. Comedy, 30 min., Mutual, 1941.

The bickering relationship between an Army training camp sergeant (played by Jay C. Flippen) and a bumbling boot camp trainee (Joey Faye). Loulie Jean portrayed the camp hostess and Bob Stanley and his orchestra supplied the music.

1379. ROOSTY OF THE AAF. Drama, 30 min., Mutual, 4/9/44 to 1/20/45.

A program of music and drama with William Tracy as Roosty, the host and star of adventure stories based on his exploits in the Army Air Force. Bob Carroll provided the vocals and Felix Slatkin and his orchestra supplied the music.

1380. ROSE OF MY DREAMS. Serial, 15 min., CBS, 1946.

The dramatic story of two sisters (Rose, who is sweet and kind, and Sarah, who is devious and scheming) and their attempts to win the heart of an Englishman—a man who toys with both of them.

Cast: Mary Rolfe (*Rose*); Charita Bauer (*Sarah*); Joseph Curtin (*Englishman*); James Burke (*Producer*).

Announcer: Larry Elliott.

1381. ROSEMARY. Serial, 15 min., NBC, 1944–1945; CBS, 1945–1955.

Dramatic events in the life of Rosemary Dawson, a stenographer who lives with her mother and sister (Patty) in the small town of Springdale.

Cast: Betty Winkler (*Rosemary Dawson*); Jone Allison, Patsy Campbell (*Patty Dawson*); Marion Barney (*Mrs. Dawson*); Sydney Smith (*Peter Harvey*); James Van Dyke (*Dick Phillips*); Lesley Woods, Joan Alexander (*Audrey Roberts*); George Keane (*Bill Roberts*); Jackie Kelk (*Tommy Taylor*); Helen Choate (*Joyce Miller*). ***Announcers:*** Fran Barber, Bob Dixon, Ed Herlihy, Joe O'Brien. ***Music:*** Paul Taubman. ***Producer:*** Tom McDermott.

1382. THE ROSEMARY CLOONEY SHOW. Variety, 15 min., CBS, 1954–1955.

Vocalist Rosemary Clooney as the host of a program of music and songs. Johnny Jacobs did the announcing and Buddy Cole and his orchestra provided the music.

1383. ROXY'S GANG. Variety, 30 min., NBC Blue, 1927–1931.

A program of music, songs and comedy that was broadcast from the Capitol Theater, then the Roxy Theater and finally Radio City Music Hall (making it the first radio series to be broadcast from a theater).

Host: Samuel Lionel Rotafel. ***Regulars:*** Caroline Andrews, Betsy Ayres, Beatrice Belkin, Alvy Bomberger, Julia Glass, Peter Hanover, James Melton, Jan Peerce, Gladys Rice, Douglas Stanbury, the Roxy Male Quartet. ***Announcers:*** Phil Carlin, Milton Cross. ***Music Arranger:*** Leo Russotto.

Vocalist Rosemary Clooney hosted her own variety show.

1384. The Roy Rogers Radio Show. Western, 30 min., NBC, 1951–1955.

A revised version of *The Roy Rogers Show* (see next entry). Stories of the modern West as told by Roy Rogers, "King of the Cowboys," as he and his wife Dale Evans, "Queen of the West," solved crimes as unofficial law enforcers. Roy and Dale owned the Double R Bar Ranch and their best friend, Pat Brady, was the ranch foreman. Each program began with Roy and Dale singing a song that reminded them of a specific incident. The flashback technique was used to relate the story to the listener. At the conclusion of the story, Roy and Dale performed the entire song (for example, the song "Sierra Sue" reminded Roy of an incident in which a blackmailer threatened to tell a man's daughter that she was adopted). Roy's dog was Bullet; his horse, Trigger; Dale's horse was Buttermilk. Served as the basis for the television series *The Roy Rogers Show*.

Cast: Roy Rogers (*Roy Rogers*); Dale Evans (*Dale Evans*); Pat Brady (*Pat Brady*). ***Regulars:*** The Mello Men. ***Announcer:*** Lou Crosby. ***Orchestra:*** Frank Smith.

OPENING

ANNOUNCER: *The Roy Rogers Radio Show.* Yes, folks, it's *The Roy Rogers Radio Show* for the whole family. Adventure! Suspense! Mystery! And music! starring Roy Rogers, "King of the Cowboys," and Dale Evans, "Queen of the West," with Pat Brady, the Mello Men and an all-star cast. And now, to greet you with a song and story, here are Roy and Dale.

CLOSING

ROY: That's all for now, folks. This is Roy Rogers saying to all of you from all of us, good-bye, good luck and may the good Lord take a liking to you. See you next week.

1385. THE ROY ROGERS SHOW. Variety, 30 min., Mutual, 1944–1945; NBC, 1946–1947; Mutual, 1948–1950.

Country and western music and songs coupled with skits featuring the adventures of Roy Rogers, "King of the Cowboys," his wife Dale Evans, "Queen of the West," and Roy's sidekick Gabby Hayes. See also *The Roy Rogers Radio Show*.

Hosts: Roy Rogers, Dale Evans. ***Regulars:*** Pat Friday, Gabby Hayes, Forrest Lewis, Bob Nolan and the Sons of the Pioneers, Foy Willing and the Riders of the Purple Sage, the Whippoorwills. ***Narrator:*** Frank Hemingway. ***Announcers:*** Lou Crosby, Verne Smith. ***Orchestra:*** Perry Botkin, Frank Smith.

THE ROYAL GELATIN HOUR *see* **THE RUDY VALLEE SHOW**

1386. ROYAL THEATER. Anthology, 30 min., CBS, 10/4/53 to 5/30/54.

A weekly series of dramatic presentations broadcast from England. Laurence Olivier served as the host and Sidney Torch and his orchestra provided the music. Also known as *Theater Royal*.

1387. THE RUDY VALLEE SHOW. Variety, 60 min., NBC, 8/6/36 to 9/28/39; 30 min., NBC, 3/7/40 to 3/4/47.

A weekly program of music, songs, comedy and dramatic skits with orchestra leader Rudy Vallee. Also known as *The Royal Gelatin Hour* (1936–1939) and *Vallee Varieties* (1940–1943). See also *The Fleischmann Yeast Hour* for information on Vallee's 1929–1936 series.

Host: Rudy Vallee. ***Regulars:*** John Barrymore, Sara Berner, Frank Case, Mary Boland, Billie Burke, Andy Devine, Virginia Gregg, Abe Reynolds. ***Announcers:*** Truman Bradley, Frank Graham, Carol Hurst, Graham MacNamee, Marvin Miller, Jimmy Wallington. ***Orchestra:*** Xavier Cugat, Ken Darby, Benny Krueger. ***Chorus:*** Elliot Daniel, Benny Krueger. ***Producer:*** Ed Gardner.

OPENING (from 6/17/37)

ANNOUNCER: Rudy Vallee requests your attention for *The Royal Gelatin Hour* with guests Fanny Brice, Tallulah Bankhead and Joe Laurie, Jr.

RUDY: Hi ho, everybody, this is Rudy Vallee and company. Tonight, Fanny Brice brings her little hellcat, Baby Snooks, to an eastern microphone for the last time before leaving for Hollywood in a new screen contract. Tallulah Bankhead will be heard in a new play by Dorothy Parker; and Joe Laurie, Jr., continues on his novel way for the fourth consecutive week.

CLOSING

RUDY (singing): Good-bye, girls, it's through; each girl that I have met, I say good-bye to you without the least regret…

RUDY (speaking): This is Rudy Vallee saying good night.

ANNOUNCER: This is NBC, the National Broadcasting Company.

1388. RUMPUS ROOM. Variety, 30 min., ABC, 6/29/46 to 9/14/46.

A weekly program of music, songs, chatter, skits and audience participation segments wherein selected members won prizes for performing a stunt or answering a question.

Host: Johnny Olsen. ***Regulars:*** Kay Armen, Gene Kirby, Hal McIntyre. ***Music:*** The Buddy Weed Trio, the Hank D'Amico Orchestra.

1389. The Russ Brown Show. Variety, 15 min., Syndicated, 1945.

Singer Russ Brown as the host of a program of music and songs with the Cadets and the Bennett Sisters vocal groups. Eddie Ballantine and His Rhythm Makers supplied the music.

The Ruth Etting Show *see* **Music That Satisfies**

1390. The Sad Sack. Comedy, 30 min., CBS, 6/12/46 to 9/4/46.

In the 1940s, George Baker created a comic strip for *Yank* magazine called "The Sad Sack," a comical look at Army life as seen through the eyes of the Sad Sack, a disorganized buck private. The strip was adapted to radio and begins with the Sad Sack's discharge from the service and his endless attempts to cope with civilian life. *Other regular characters:* Lucy Twitchell, his girlfriend; Chester Fenwick, his friend.

Cast: Herb Vigran (*Sad Sack*); Jim Backus (*Chester Fenwick*); Sandra Gould (*Lucy Twitchell*). ***Announcer:*** Dick Joy. ***Music:*** Lou Kosloff.

1391. The Saint. Adventure, 30 min., NBC, 1945; CBS, 1945; 1947–1948; Mutual, 1949–1950; NBC, 1950–1951.

Simon Templar, alias "The Saint," is a wealthy, swashbuckling, devil-may-care, modern-day Robin Hood who helps people in trouble—despite the fact that the police believe he is a criminal and are out to nail him. Stories follow Simon's adventures as he tries to remain just one step ahead of the police in his quest to help others. Based on the character created by Leslie Charteris. *Other regular characters:* Happy, Simon's houseboy (for his New York City apartment); Patricia Holmes, Simon's girlfriend; Louie, Simon's cab driver; Police Inspector Fernak.

Cast: Edgar Barrier, Brian Aherne, Vincent Price, Tom Conway, Barry Sullivan (*Simon Templar*); Ken Christy (*Happy*); Louise Arthur (*Patricia Holmes*); Lawrence Dobkin (*Louie*); Ken Christy, John Brown, Theodore von Eltz (*Inspector Fernak*). ***Announcers:*** Doug Gorlay, Dick Joy, Carlton KaDell, Harold Ross, Don Stanley. ***Music:*** Louis Adrian, Von Dexter, Harry Zimmerman.

OPENING

Announcer: The adventures of *The Saint*, starring Vincent Price. The Saint, based on characters created by Leslie Charteris and known to millions from books, magazines and motion pictures. The Robin Hood of modern crime now comes to radio starring Hollywood's brilliant and talented actor, Vincent Price, *The Saint*.

CLOSING

Announcer: You have been listening to another transcribed adventure of *The Saint*, the Robin Hood of modern crime. And now here is our star, Vincent Price.

Price: This is Vincent Price inviting you to join us again next week at this same time for another exciting adventure of *The Saint*. Good night.

The Sal Hepatica Revue *see* **The Fred Allen Show**

The Salad Bowl Revue *see* **The Fred Allen Show**

Sally of the Talkies *see* **Appendix**

1392. Salute to Youth. Anthology, 30 min., NBC, 1943–1944.

A weekly series that recounts the achievements of young Americans. Berry Kroeger was the narrator; Nadine Cantor provided the songs; William L. White related "The Service Story of the Week" and Raymond Paige conducted the National Youth Orchestra.

Sam Spade *see* **The Adventures of Sam Spade**

1393. The Sammy Kaye Show. Variety, 30 min., NBC, 1937–1949; ABC, 1949–1954; Mutual, 1954–1956.

A weekly program of music and songs with orchestra leader Sammy Kaye ("Swing and Sway with Sammy Kaye").

Host: Sammy Kaye. ***Regulars:*** Tony Alamo, Red Barber, Barbara Benson, Jimmy Bram,

Clyde Burke, Don Connell, Laura Leslie, Don Rogers, Tony Russo, Tommy Ryan, Sally Stewart, Billy Williams, Arthur Wright, the Kay Choir, the Kaydettes, the Vass Family. ***Announcer:*** Gene Hamilton. ***Orchestra:*** Sammy Kaye.

Note: The program is also known as *Sammy Kaye's Showroom* (1949) and *Sammy Kaye's Sunday Serenade* (1954).

1394. Sara's Private Caper. Comedy, 30 min., NBC, 6/15/50 to 8/24/50.

Sara Berner, a secretary at an unnamed police station, has "a crush on crime," but all her boss (the lieutenant) wants her to do is "type reports, answer the telephone, sharpen pencils and leave the crime-solving to my detectives." But Sara believes those detectives are incapable of solving a crime and makes their cases her private capers by doing what they should do—thoroughly investigate. Stories follow Sara as she dons various disguises and goes undercover. *Other regular characters:* Melvin, Sara's boyfriend (and unwitting accomplice), a clerk at a grocery store called the United Tea Company; Mr. Sacks, Melvin's employer.

Cast: Sara Berner (*Sara Berner*); Bob Sweeney (*Melvin*); Frank Nelson (*Mr. Sacks*); Donald Morrison (*Lieutenant*). ***Announcer:*** Frank Martin. ***Music:*** Robert Armbruster. ***Producer:*** Joe Parker.

OPENING (FROM 6/15/50)

Announcer: Wheaties presents Sara Berner in *Sara's Private Caper*. On stage tonight from Hollywood, another in the Wheaties big parade of half-hour presentations. Tonight, the premiere performance, starring Sara Berner in *Sara's Private Caper*.

Satan's Waitin' *see* **Appendix**

1395. The Saturday Morning Vaudeville Theater. Variety, 30 min., NBC, 7/12/41 to 1/3/42.

Jim Ameche as the host of a weekly program that recreated the music, song and comedy of vaudeville. Anita Boyer, Charles Kemper, Jess Mack, Joan Shea, Dick Todd, the Polka Dots and the Symphonettes were the regulars. Al D'Artega and his orchestra provided the music.

1396. Saturday Night Party. Variety, 30 min., NBC, 1936–1937.

A weekly program of music and songs hosted by James Melton and featuring singer Don Dickson and the comedy team of Howard and Shelton. Robert Dolan conducted the orchestra.

1397. The Saturday Night Revue. Variety, 30 min., CBS, 1946.

Music, songs and light comedy with Robert Q. Lewis as the host. Bill Harrington, Vera Holly, Elsa Mirande, Art Tatum and Henny Youngman were the regulars; Ted Brown did the announcing; and John Gart and his orchestra provided the music.

1398. Saturday Night Serenade. Variety, 30 min., CBS, 1936–1948.

A long-running program of music and songs with the orchestras of Howard Barlow, Gus Haenschen and Sammy Kaye. Jessica Dragonette, Mary Eastman, Billy Perry and Horace Shaw were the vocalists.

1399. Saturday Night Swing Club. Variety, 30 min., CBS, 1936–1938.

A program of swing music with Leith Stevens and his orchestra. Paul Douglas (and later Ted Husing) hosted.

1400. Saturday Party. Variety, 60 min., NBC, 1933–1934.

Robert L. Ripley as the host of a program of music coupled with tales from the "Ripley's Believe It or Not" newspaper column. Guest vocalists provided the songs and B.A. Rolfe and his orchestra supplied the music.

1401. The Saturday Senior Swing. Variety, 30 min., NBC, 1945–1946.

A post-war program of music and songs geared to selling war bonds. Vocalist Jill Warren served as the host with Patsy Garrett and Jack Manning as the regulars. Music was by the Hank D'Amico Quintet and the Bill Dornell Orchestra under the direction of Ray Carter.

1402. The Saturday Showcase. Variety, 30 min., NBC, 1946.

Singer Snooky Lanson as the host of a weekly program of music and songs with Bradley Kincaid, Evelyn Parker and the Varieteers as regulars. Owen Bradley and his orchestra provided the music.

Vera Holly lent her singing talents to *The Saturday Night Revue*.

1403. SATURDAY SHOWDOWN. Variety, 30 min., NBC, 1943.

Actor John Gibson as host of a weekly program of music and songs. Ted de Corsia, Tommy Taylor and the Murtok Sisters were the regulars. The orchestra and chorus of Irving Miller provided additional songs and the musical backing.

1404. SATURDAY THEATER. Anthology, 30 min., CBS, 1954.

A Saturday evening program of dramatic presentations featuring well-known radio and film stars. George Walsh was the host and announcer.

1405. The Scarlet Pimpernel. Adventure, 30 min., NBC, 1952–1953.

England during the 1790s was the setting for a weekly series about Sir Percy Blakeney, a man of wealth and social status who adopts the guise of the Scarlet Pimpernel, a mysterious crusader who battles injustice wherever he finds it. Sir Percy was assisted by Lord Tony Dewhurst and derived his alias from a small red flower common to the English countryside.

Cast: Marius Goring (*Sir Percy Blakeney*); David Jacobs (*Lord Tony Dewhurst*). ***Music:*** Sidney Torch.

The Scarlet Queen *see* **Voyage of the Scarlet Queen**

1406. Scattergood Baines. Serial, 15 min., CBS, 2/22/37 to 6/12/42.

Dramatic stories of the people of the small town of Cold River as seen through the eyes of Scattergood Baines, a warm and friendly hardware store owner. Scattergood is married to Mirandy and they are the adoptive parents of Jimmy, the boy they raised after the death of their son. See also the following title.

Cast: Jess Pugh (*Scattergood Baines*); Viola Berwick (*Mirandy Baines*); Chuck Grant (*Jimmy Baines*); John Heaine (*Hippocrates Brown*); Francis "Dink" Trout (*Pinky Pickett*); Arnold Robertson (*Ed Potts*); Caroline McCune (*Clara Potts*); Forrest Lewis (*J. Wellington Keats*); Louise Fitch (*Eloise Comstock*); Norma Jean Ross (*Beth Reed*). ***Announcers:*** Roger Krupp, George Walsh.

1407. Scattergood Baines. Drama, 30 min., Mutual, 2/10/49 to 10/26/49.

A revised version of the prior title. The town of Cold River is home to Scattergood Baines, the kind, philosophical owner of the local hardware store. Scattergood is married to Mandy and is a leader in the community. Stories revolve around that fact as Scattergood attempts to help where he can. *Other regular characters:* Hannibal Gibbey, Scattergood's friend (Hannibal works in the feed and grain store); Matilda "Tildy" Gibbey, Hannibal's wife; Fern, Scattergood's assistant; Chief Workley, head of the police department. Scattergood's phone number is 4494; the town newspaper is the *Clarion*; the town has three police squad cars and 12 uniformed officers.

Cast: Wendell Holmes (*Scattergood Baines*); Leora Thatcher (*Mandy Baines*); Parker Fennelly (*Hannibal Gibbey*); Eleanor Phelps (*Matilda Gibbey*); Don Douglas (*Chief Jake Workley*); Bryna Raeburn (*Fern*). ***Announcer:*** Bob Emerick. ***Music:*** Ben Ludlow. ***Producer:*** Herbert Rice.

OPENING

Announcer: Mutual brings you your old friend, *Scattergood Baines*. Yes, it's Clarence Buddington Kelland's famous character Scattergood Baines, brought to life in a new series of fast-moving adventures. But he's the same old Scattergood you all know—the shrewd and jovial hardware merchant who usually finds himself drawn into just about everything that happens around him. Scattergood Baines, the best-loved, most cussed-at and by all the fattest man in the bustling town of Cold River.

CLOSING

Announcer: This has been another adventure of *Scattergood Baines*, Mutual's new dramatic series based on the famous character created by Clarence Buddington Kelland. Be with us next week at this time for another adventure of *Scattergood Baines* titled "Scattergood vs. Father Time." This is the Mutual Broadcasting System.

1408. Scotland Yard. Crime Drama, 30 min., Mutual, 1/27/47 to 12/29/47.

Inspector Burke is a brilliant detective with the London-based Scotland Yard. Burke is opposed to violence and encompasses deductive reasoning to capture criminals. Stories relate his experiences as he and his assistant, Sgt. Abernathy, struggle to solve bizarre and baffling crimes. Also known as *Scotland Yard's Inspector Burke*.

Cast: Basil Rathbone (*Inspector Burke*); Alfred Shirley (*Sgt. Abernathy*). ***Announcer:*** Phil Tompkins. ***Music:*** Sylvan Levin.

1409. Scout About Town. Variety, 15 min., Mutual, 1946.

Anna May Dickey and Hunt Stromberg, Jr., as co-hosts of a weekly program that showcased promising but undiscovered talent. Ralph Paul did the announcing and the orchestra of Sylvan Levin provided the music.

1410. Scramby Amby. Game, 30 min., NBC Blue, 1944; ABC, 1944–1945; Mutual, 1946–1947.

Selected studio audience members were presented with a series of scrambled words and three clues: a musical and/or vocal selection, a daffy rhyme, and the dictionary definitions of the words. The first player to unscramble the words (for example, "batles" should be "stable"), received a cash prize.

Host: Perry Ward. ***Vocalists:*** Lynn Martin, Anne Nagel. ***Announcer:*** Larry Keating. ***Orchestra:*** Charles "Bud" Dant, Paul Martin.

1411. Screen Director's Playhouse. Anthology, 30 min., NBC, 1949–1950; 60 min., NBC, 1950–1951.

Radio adaptations of feature films that are introduced by their directors and often starring the principals of the film. Also known as *Screen Director's Assignment. Stories include:*

1. The Uninvited. Two spirits seeking revenge on the granddaughter of the original owner of the mansion they now haunt. Ray Milland stars.

2. Appointment for Love. After marrying, a girl (Gale Storm) insists that she and her husband (Charles Boyer) retain their individuality.

3. Miracle on 34th Street. Edmund Gwen in the classic story of a man who believes he is the real Santa Claus.

4. Criss Cross. Burt Lancaster as an armored car guard who plans to rob his company so he can finance the life he longs to live with his fiancée.

OPENING

ANNOUNCER: From Hollywood, the NBC Theater presents—

VOICE: Screen Director's Assignment. Production: "The Ghost Breakers." Director: George Marshall. Star: Bob Hope.

ANNOUNCER: The Hollywood Screen Directors present a comedy of terrors—"Ghost Breakers," starring Bob Hope in his original role, and introducing the director of the film, George Marshall [he would then talk about the production].

CLOSING

ANNOUNCER: Next week, NBC Theater brings you a motion picture romance set against the background of memorable music. The story is "Music for Millions," and our star will be June Allyson. Good night, Bob Hope and George Marshall. This is NBC, the National Broadcasting Company.

1412. The Screen Guild Show. Variety, 90 min., CBS, 1939.

A program of music and songs that was a benefit for the Motion Picture Relief Fund (guests donated their earnings to the charitable organization that provided help to aging movie stars in need). George Murphy was the host; John Conte did the announcing; and Oscar Bradley and his orchestra provided the music.

1413. The Screen Guild Theater. Anthology, 30 min., CBS, 1939–1948; NBC, 1948–1949; ABC, 1950–1951.

A weekly series of motion picture adaptations often featuring the stars of the film in the radio presentation. The stars who appeared donated their earnings to the Motion Picture Relief Fund, a charitable organization for aging movie stars. The program is also known as *The Gulf Screen Guild Theater* (when sponsored by Gulf Oil) and *The Lady Esther Screen Guild Playhouse* (under the sponsorship of Lady Esther Cosmetics). *Stories include:*

1. High Sierra. Humphrey Bogart and Ida Lupino in a story about an escaped convict who decides to pull one last job.

2. Arsenic and Old Lace. Boris Karloff and Eddie Albert in a tale about two elderly women who find pleasure in poisoning their male boarders.

3. The Paleface. Bob Hope and Jane Russell in a comedy about Painless Potter, a dentist who travels west to find new patients—and becomes involved with Indians and outlaws.

4. The Bells of St. Mary's. Bing Crosby and Ingrid Bergman in the heartwarming story of Father O'Malley and his efforts to acquire financial help for St. Mary's school.

Host: Roger Pryor. ***Announcer:*** Truman Bradley. ***Music:*** Wilbur Hatch.

OPENING

(from "My Client Curley," 2/4/46; about a boy with a dancing caterpillar)

ANNOUNCER: Good evening, ladies and gentlemen. Tonight, Lady Esther presents the Screen Guild Players in one of the most delightful stories it has ever been our pleasure to bring you. It is "My Client Curley" by Norman Corwin, based on the short story by Lucille Fletcher. It stars Robert Montgomery as the agent and Ted Donaldson as Stinky.

CLOSING

ANNOUNCER: On behalf of the Motion Picture

Relief Fund, thank you Robert Montgomery and Ted Donaldson for your delightful performances in tonight's play. Next week, the Lady Esther Screen Guild Players will present "Don Quan Quilligan." It will star Phil Silvers and William Bendix. Be sure to listen in. "My Client Curley" was presented through the courtesy of Norman Corwin and Lucille Fletcher. Robert Montgomery appeared through the courtesy of Metro-Goldwyn-Mayer, producers of the Technicolor musical *The Harvey Girls*; Ted Donaldson can be seen in the 20th Century–Fox production *A Tree Grows in Brooklyn*. This is Truman Bradley speaking for Lady Esther. Thank you and good night. This is CBS, the Columbia Broadcasting System.

1414. Screen Test. Variety, 15 min., Mutual, 1944.

Aspiring actors and actresses appeared with established stars in short dramatizations designed to act as screen tests. Sponsored by MGM. John Conte served as the host; Ted Steele and his orchestra provided the music.

1415. The Sea Has a Story. Anthology, 30 min., CBS, 1945.

Weekly dramatizations depicting man's struggles against the sea. Pat O'Brien served as the host and narrator; Lud Gluskin and his orchestra provided the music.

1416. The Sea Hound. Children, 15 min., ABC, 1942–1944; Mutual, 1946–1947; 30 min., ABC, 1948; ABC, 1951.

Adventurers on the high seas with Capt. Silver, owner of the ship the *Sea Hound*, his first mate Jerry and his Oriental sidekick Kai.

Cast: Ken Daigneau, Barry Thompson (*Capt. Silver*); Bob Hastings (*Jerry*); Alan Devitt (*Kai*). ***Announcer:*** Doug Browning.

1417. The Sealed Book. Anthology, 30 min., Mutual, 3/18/45 to 9/9/45.

Eerie tales of murder and madness as told by the Keeper of the Sealed Book, a mysterious volume of twisted tales. Stories do not actually conclude; the listener must provide his own conclusions—"You'll have to decide for yourself, the answer is not here."

Cast: Philip Clarke (*Keeper of the Sealed Book*). ***Announcer:*** Jimmy Wallington. ***Producer:*** Jock MacGregor.

OPENING

SOUND: Sinister laughing.

KEEPER: *The Sealed Book.*

SOUND: A large gong.

ANNOUNCER: Once again, the Keeper of the Book is ready to unlock the ponderous volume in which are recorded all the secrets and mysteries of mankind through the ages. All the lore and learning of the ancients, all the strange and mystifying stories of the past, the present and the future.

SOUND: A large gong.

ANNOUNCER: Keeper of the book, what tale will you tell us this time?

KEEPER: First I must unlock the great padlock which keeps the Sealed Book safe from prying eyes. Now [after opening the book], what story shall I tell you? I have here tales of every kind, tales of murder, tales of madness, of dark deeds and events strange beyond all belief. Let me see [flipping pages]. Yes, here's a tale for you, a dark story of two brothers. One of them killed because he could not help himself. The other was interested in murder too—but in a very different way. The title of the tale is "The Hand of Death." Here is the tale as it is written in *The Sealed Book*. It began in San Francisco on a night of thick, suffocating fog...

CLOSING

SOUND: A large gong.

KEEPER: The sound of the Great Gong tells me I must lock the Book once again.

ANNOUNCER: One moment, Keeper of the Book. What story from *The Sealed Book* will you tell us next time?

KEEPER: Next time? Are you sure you want to know? Perhaps my next story will be about you. For I have here all the stories that ever happened and many that have yet come to pass, but I'll find one for you in just a moment [commercial airs].

ANNOUNCER: And now, Keeper of the Book, have you found the story you will tell us next time?

KEEPER: Yes, I've found one. It's a story about a man who found the secret of immortality, of life everlasting. The title of the tale is "The King of the World."

ANNOUNCER: Be sure to be with us next time when the Great Gong heralds another strange and exciting story from—

KEEPER: *The Sealed Book.*

The Sealtest Hour *see* **The Rudy Vallee Show**

The Sealtest Variety Show *see* **The Dorothy Lamour Show**

1418. The Sealtest Village Store. Comedy, 30 min., NBC, 1943–1948.

The program, set against the background of the Sealtest Village Store (named for the sponsor), dealt with the situations that develop as its owners, Joan Davis (1943–1945), Jack Haley (1945–1947) and Jack Carson (1947–1948), deal with staff and clientele problems. When Joan Davis left for her own series (see *The Joan Davis Show*), Jack Haley became the store owner (he previously assisted Joan) and Eve Arden was brought on to assist him. David Street provided the songs and the regulars were Penny Cartwright, Verna Felton, Gil Lamb and Shirley Mitchell. Hy Averback and John Laing did the announcing; music was by the Frank DeVol and Eddie Paul orchestras. Also known as *The Village Store*.

1419. The Sears Radio Theater. Anthology, 60 min., Syndicated, 1979.

A program of varying presentations (including gothic chillers, comedies, Westerns, dramas and adventures) sponsored by Sears, Roebuck and Company.

Hosts: Lorne Greene, Andy Griffith, Vincent Price, Cicely Tyson, Richard Widmark. ***Announcer:*** Art Gilmore. ***Music:*** Nelson Riddle. ***Producer:*** Elliott Lewis.

1420. Second Honeymoon. Game, 30 min., ABC, 1948–1949.

Seven housewives appeared to relate a story as to why she would like a second honeymoon. A panel of five judges chose the wife who they believed told the best story. The winner received that second honeymoon plus a new wardrobe.

Host: Bert Parks. ***Announcer:*** Ed Michael. ***Organist:*** Rosa Rio.

1421. Second Husband. Serial, 15 min., CBS, 1937–1948.

The dramatic story of Brenda Cummings and the problems that arise within her family when she marries Grant Cummings, her second husband.

Cast: Helen Menken, Cathleen Cordell (*Brenda Cummings*); Joseph Curtin, Richard Waring (*Grant Cummings*); Carleton Young, Ralph Lee Robertson (*Bill Cummings*); Janice Gilbert, Charita Bauer, Mercer McCloud (*Fran*); Tom Donnelly, Jackie Grimes (*Dick Cummings*); Arlene Francis, Madeline Belgrad (*Marion Jennings*); Jay Jostyn (*Ben Porter*); Ethel Wilson (*Louise*); Joy Hathaway (*Irma*); William Podmore (*Butler*); Jacqueline DeWit (*Valerie*); Judy Blake (*Marsha*); Lois Hall (*Linda*); Virginia Dwyer (*Elsa King*). ***Announcer:*** Andre Baruch. ***Producers:*** Anne Hummert, Frank Hummert.

OPENING (from 6/6/44)

Announcer: Now, *Second Husband*, starring Helen Menken as Brenda Cummings. *Second Husband* is presented by the makers of Dr. Lyons Tooth Powder. Linda has just delivered an ultimatum to her 16-year-old daughter Fran and to Elsa King that Fran is to leave Elsa's house and come home by the next day...

CLOSING

Announcer: *Second Husband* starring Helen Menken as Brenda Cummings will be on the air this same time tomorrow. This is CBS, the Columbia Broadcasting System.

1422. The Second Mrs. Burton. Serial, 15 min., CBS, 1946–1960.

Dramatic incidents in the lives of marrieds Terry and Stan Burton. The title refers to Terry; the first Mrs. Burton was Stan's mother—a "bad mother-in-law" who always caused Terry trouble.

Cast: Sharon Douglas, Claire Niesen, Patsy Campbell, Teri Keane (*Terry Burton*); Dwight Weist (*Stan Burton*); Dix Davis, Karl Weber, Ben Cooper, Larry Robinson (*Brad Burton*); Evelyn Varden, Ethel Owen (*Stan's mother*); Joan Alexander, Cathleen Cordell (*Marion Sullivan*); King Calder (*James Anderson*); Elspeth Eric (*Lillian Anderson*); Alexander Scourby (*Greg Martin*); Staats Cotsworth, Les Tremayne (*Jack Mason*); Madaline Lee (*Wendy Burton*); Lois Holmes (*Jane Waters*). ***Announcers:*** Hugh James, Harry Clark. ***Organists:*** Chet Kingsbury, Richard Leibert. ***Producers:*** Ira Ashley, Lindsay MacHarrie.

OPENING

Announcer: CBS Radio brings you *The Second Mrs. Burton* featuring Terry Burton and her struggle to find happiness.

1423. Secret City. Mystery, 15 min., NBC Blue, 1941–1942.

The cases of private detective Ben Clark and his friend and assistant Jeff Wilson, a mechanic.

Cast: Bill Idelson (*Ben Clark*); Jerry Spellman (*Jeff Wilson*); Franklin Adams (*Mayor*).

1424. SECRET MISSIONS. Anthology, 30 min., Mutual, 1948–1949.

Dramatizations based on the files of Ellis M. Zacharias, World War II deputy chief of the Office of Naval Operations.

Cast: Edward Arnold (*Ellis M. Zacharias*). ***Host-Narrator:*** Admiral Ellis M. Zacharias. ***Announcer:*** Bill Hightower. ***Music:*** Elliot Jacoby.

1425. SERENADE TO LOVELINESS. Variety, 30 min., NBC, 1940.

Romantic music and songs for the female listener sponsored by Chamberlain Lotion. John Stanton served as the host; Andrew Gainey provided the vocals; Gil Berkley did the announcing and Milton Sherdnick and his orchestra provided the music.

1426. SERGEANT PRESTON OF THE YUKON. Adventure, 30 min., Mutual, 1951–1955.

The retitled version of *Challenge of the Yukon* (see for original information) that continues to relate the exploits of William Preston, a sergeant with the Northwest Mounted Police, as he and his fearless dog Yukon King struggle to maintain law and order in Canada during the Gold Rush days of the Yukon (1890s). *Other regular characters:* Inspector Conrad, Preston's superior at Dawson City.

Cast: Paul Sutton, Jay Michael, Brace Beemer (*William Preston*); John Todd (*Inspector Conrad*). ***Commentators:*** Jay Michael, John Slagle. ***Announcers:*** Fred Foy, Bob Hite, Jay Michael. ***Music:*** Benny Kyte's Band. ***Theme:*** "The Donna Diana Overture" by Von Rezicek.

OPENING

ANNOUNCER: Now, as howling winds echo across the snow-covered reaches of the wild Northwest, the Quaker Oats Company, makers of Quaker Puffed Wheat and Quaker Puffed Rice, the delicious cereal shot from guns, presents *Sergeant Preston of the Yukon.* [Over dog barks:] It's Yukon King, swiftest and strongest lead dog of the Northwest, breaking the trail for Sgt. Preston of the Northwest Mounted Police in his relentless pursuit of lawbreakers. And now, the adventures of Sgt. Preston and his wonder dog Yukon King as they meet the challenge of the Yukon.

CLOSING

ANNOUNCER: These *Sergeant Preston of the Yukon* adventures are brought to you Monday through Friday at this time by the Quaker Oats Company by special recording in cooperation with the Mutual Broadcasting System. They are a copyright feature of Sergeant Preston of the Yukon, Inc. Created by George W. Trendle, produced by Trendle-Campbell-Muir, Inc., and directed by Fred Flowerday. The part of Sgt. Preston is played by Paul Sutton. This is Jay Michael wishing you good luck and good health for Quaker Puffed Wheat and Quaker Puffed Rice. So long. This is Mutual, radio network for all America.

1427. SERVICE WITH A SMILE. Variety, 30 min., NBC, 1941.

The program, broadcast from various army camps, featured performances by servicemen. Garry Moore served as the host and Ben Grauer did the announcing.

1428. SETH PARKER. Variety, 30 min., NBC, 1929–1935.

Music, songs (mostly hymns), comedy and serial-like vignettes set in the small town of Jonesport, Maine. Phillips H. Lord, who created the series, played Seth Parker, a philosopher, and his wife "Ma" Parker was portrayed by Effie Palmer (later by Barbara Bruce). *Other regular characters:* Sophia M. Lord (Phillips' wife; as Lizzie Peters), Joy Hathaway and Eva Giles (as Jane), Raymond Hunter, Bennet Kilpack, Richard Maxwell, Agnes Moorehead.

1429. SEVEN FRONT STREET. Anthology, 30 min., Syndicated, 1947.

Mystery presentations set against the background of a waterfront bar located at Seven Front Street. Kenneth King, who played a mythical author, served as the host and narrator. Ralph Paul did the announcing.

OPENING

ANNOUNCER: Are you bored? Do you have that want-to-get-away-from-it-all feeling? Then why not get up and go as you are to *Seven Front Street*. If you hurry, there is still time to join that popular author Kenneth King on his weekly visit to this famous waterfront night spot. If you like romance, highly seasoned with the unexpected, then start right now, make a beeline for *Seven Front Street*.

1430. The Shadow. Mystery, 30 min., CBS, 1930–1932; NBC, 1932–1935; Mutual, 1937–1954.

A character called "The Shadow" first appeared as the narrator of a show about conventional detectives called *The Detective Story Hour* in 1930. "The Shadow" became the hit of the show and in 1931, Walter Gibson was asked to write a "Shadow" novel under the pen name of Maxwell Grant. His first novel *The Living Shadow* created a new cult hero (he went on to write 283 "Shadow" novels). On 9/26/37, Street and Smith Publications brought the pulp fiction character back to radio with Orson Welles as Lamont Cranston, a wealthy man-about-town and amateur criminologist who was actually the Shadow, a mysterious figure who aids the forces of law and order. Years ago, while in the Orient, Cranston had learned the secret of a hypnotic power to cloud men's minds so they could not see him. Margot Lane, his lovely friend and companion, was the only other person who knew of Cranston's secret ability to turn himself into the Shadow. Stories follow Lamont's efforts to help Police Commissioner Weston solve baffling crimes as the Shadow. *Other regular characters:* Shrevie, Lamont's friend, a cab driver; the Blue Coal Heating Expert (Blue Coal Heating sponsored the program).

Cast (1930–1935): James LaCurto, Frank Readick, Robert Hardy Andrews (*The Shadow*). ***Cast*** (1937–1954): Orson Welles, Bill Johnstone, Steven Courtleigh, Bret Morrison (*Lamont Cranston/The Shadow*); Agnes Moorehead, Margo Stevenson, Marjorie Anderson, Gertrude Warner, Grace Matthews, Lesley Woods (*Margot Lane*); Dwight Weist, Ken Roberts, Arthur Vinton, Kenny Delmar, Santos Ortega, Ted de Corsia (*Commissioner Weston*); Keenan Wynn, Alan Reed, Mandel Kramer (*Shrevie*); John Barclay (*Blue Coal's Heating Expert*). ***Announcers:*** Andre Baruch, Sandy Becker, Carl Caruso, Don Hancock, Frank McCarthy, Ken Roberts. ***Organists:*** Charles Paul, Rosa Rio, Elsie Thompson.

OPENING

Shadow: Who knows what evil lurks in the hearts of men? The Shadow knows [laughs menacingly, followed by a terrifying musical rendition of Saint-Saëns' "Omphale's Spinning Wheel"].

Announcer: The Shadow, Lamont Cranston, a man of wealth, a student of science and a master of other people's minds, devotes his life to righting wrongs, protecting the innocent and punishing the guilty. Using advanced methods that may ultimately become available to all law enforcement agencies, Cranston is known to the underworld as the Shadow—never seen, only heard. Haunting to superstitious minds as a ghost, as inevitable as a guilty conscience, the Shadow's true identity is known only to his constant friend and aide Margot Lane. The thrilling adventures of *The Shadow* are on the air, brought to you each week by the Blue Coal dealers of America. These dramatizations are designed to demonstrate to the old and young alike that crime does not pay. Today's adventure of *The Shadow*, "The Ghost in the Silver Slipper."

CLOSING

Announcer: You have been listening to a dramatized version of one of the many copyrighted stories which appear in *The Shadow* magazines.

Shadow: The weed of crime bears bitter fruit. Crime does not pay. The Shadow knows [laughs menacingly].

Announcer: Next week, same time, same station, the Blue Coal dealers of America will bring you an adventure of *The Shadow* that is astoundingly thrilling and truly amazing.

1431. The Shadow of Fu Manchu. Adventure, 30 min., CBS, 1932–1933; 15 min., Syndicated, 1939–1940.

Dr. Fu Manchu was a brilliant Chinese physician who turned to a life of crime when his wife and son were inadvertently killed by James Petrie, a British officer, during the Boxer Rebellion. Bitter, he has vowed to avenge their deaths by destroying the world. Seeking to stop him are Dr. Petrie and Sir Dennis Nayland Smith, a Scotland Yard inspector. Stories, which are based on the characters created by Sax Rohmer, follow the evil doctor as he uses diabolical weapons—from killer fungi to the Paralyzing Flowers of Silence—to defeat his pursuers and achieve his goal. Also known as *Fu Manchu.*

Cast: John C. Daly, Harold Huber (*Dr. Fu Manchu*); Bob White (*Dr. James Petrie*); Charles Warburton, Hanley Stafford, Gale Gordon (*Sir Dennis Nayland Smith*); Sunda Love, Charlotte Manson (*Karameneh, the Slave Girl*).

1432. Sheaffer Parade. Variety, 30 min., NBC, 1947.

A program of music and songs sponsored by the Sheaffer pen company. Fort Pearson was the host and Eddy Howard and his orchestra provided the music. Guests were featured in vocal segments.

1433. Shell Chateau. Variety, 60 min., NBC, 1935–1937.

The program, sponsored by Shell Oil, featured music and songs with hosts (in order) Al Jolson, Wallace Beery, Smith Ballew, Edward Everett Horton and Joe Cook. Vocalist Nadine Conner provided the songs; Victor Young and his orchestra supplied the music.

The Sheriff *see* **Death Valley Sheriff**

1434. Sherlock Holmes. Mystery, 30 min., NBC Red, 1930–1931; NBC Blue, 1931–1932; NBC Red, 1932; NBC Blue, 1932–1933; NBC Red, 1934–1935; Mutual, 1936; NBC Blue, 1939–1941; NBC Red, 1941–1942; Mutual, 1943–1946; ABC, 1946–1950; NBC, 1955; ABC, 1956.

The apartment at 221-B Baker Street in London is the home of Sherlock Holmes and his friend and biographer, Dr. John H. Watson (who is also known as Dr. James Watson). Holmes is a brilliant consulting detective who will help people in deep trouble and work with the police to solve baffling crimes. Holmes is deeply interested in crime detection, plays the violin to relax and considers solving crimes a game—"I play the game for the game's sake and for only that reason." Stories follow Holmes and Watson as they use deductive reasoning to solve crimes. Based on the character created by Sir Arthur Conan Doyle. Also known as *The Adventures of Sherlock Holmes.*

Cast: William Gillette, Richard Gordon, Louis Hector, Basil Rathbone, Tom Conway, Ben Wright, John Stanley, Morry Powell, Carlton Hobbs, Sir John Gielgud (*Sherlock Holmes*); Leigh Powell, Nigel Bruce, Eric Snowden, Alfred Shirley, Ian Martin, Peter Barthurst, Norman Sheary, Sir Ralph Richardson (*Dr. John H. Watson*). ***Announcers:*** Herb Allen, Owen Babbe, Harry Bartell, Joseph Bell, Cy Harrice, Knox Manning. ***Organist:*** Albert Buhrmann. ***Orchestra:*** Graham Harris, Lou Kosloff, Sidney Torch.

OPENING (typical)

Announcer: *The Adventures of Sherlock Holmes*, the original, immortal stories of Sir Arthur Conan Doyle, dramatized anew with Sir Ralph Richardson as Dr. Watson and Sir John Gielgud in the role of Sherlock Holmes. And now *The Adventures of Sherlock Holmes* with Sir John Gielgud as Sherlock Holmes and Sir Ralph Richardson as our storyteller, Dr. James Watson.

1435. Shirley Temple Time. Variety, 30 min., CBS, 12/5/39 to 12/26/39.

A three-episode series that combines music and songs with dramatic sketches. Child actress Shirley Temple served as the host and top name guests appeared in the sketches. Shirley Temple returned to the airwaves via CBS in 1941 for a four-episode music and song fest called *The Shirley Temple Variety Show* (12/5– 12/26/41). Truman Bradley did the announcing and the program was sponsored by Elgin Watches.

1436. Short, Short Story. Anthology, 15 min., CBS, 1/22/40 to 1/17/41.

Capsule dramatic presentations with George Putnam as the host and announcer. A different cast appeared in each episode.

1437. Shorty Bell. Comedy, 30 min., CBS, 3/28/48 to 6/27/48.

John Marshall Bell, Jr., nicknamed "Shorty," is an eager-beaver cub reporter (obituary column) for the *Daily Times*, a crusading newspaper in Capital City (population 100,000). Shorty's late father, John Marshall Bell, Sr., was the paper's publisher, and Shorty hopes to follow in his footsteps. Stories follow Shorty's comical adventures as he seeks to become a full-fledged reporter by using his street contacts to acquire headline-making stories. *Other regular characters:* Joan, Shorty's girlfriend (the paper's receptionist); Packrat, Shorty's snitch.

Cast: Mickey Rooney (*Shorty Bell*); Jeanne Bates (*Joan*); Parley Baer (*Packrat*). ***Music:*** Cy Feuer. ***Producer:*** William N. Robson.

OPENING (from 3/28/48)

ANNOUNCER: The Columbia Broadcasting System proudly presents *Shorty Bell*, the first in a new radio series written by Samuel W. Taylor with music by Cy Feuer. Produced and directed by William N. Robson, and in the title role, the great Metro-Goldwyn-Mayer star, Mickey Rooney.

CLOSING

ANNOUNCER: Next week, Mickey Rooney returns in the role of Shorty Bell, cub reporter, young man about town and thorn in the side of Smear Inc.* Until this same time next week then, good night. Mickey Rooney appears through the courtesy of Metro-Goldwyn-Mayer and may be seen soon in *Killer McCoy*. This is CBS, the Columbia Broadcasting System.

1438. THE SHOW SHOP. Variety, 30 min., NBC Blue, 1942.

Vocalist Gertrude Niesen as the host of a weekly program of music and songs. Ray Nelson and his orchestra provided the music.

1439. SHOWBOAT. Variety, 60 min., NBC, 1932–1937; NBC, 1940.

The program, based on the Broadway and movie musical *Showboat*, is set on a showboat traveling down river and featuring performances by top variety stars. Also known as *The Maxwell House Showboat*.

Hosts (1932–1937): Charles Winninger, Frank McIntire (*Capt. Henry*); Lanny Ross (*Himself*); Jack Haley (*Himself*). ***Host*** (1940): Hugh Studebaker. ***Cast:*** Carlton Brickert (*Capt. Barney Barnett*); Irene Hubbard (*Aunt Maria*); Hattie McDaniel (*Mammy*); Marlin Hurt (*Beulah*); Pick Malone (*Molasses*); Pat Padgett (*January*). ***Regulars:*** Sonny Childs, Ross Graham, Annette Hanshaw, Bob Hope, Mary Lou, Willie Morris, Lanny Ross, Conrad Thibault, Dick Todd, Virginia Verrill, Louise Massey and the Westerners, the Maxwell House Singers. ***Frequent Guest:*** Jessica Dragonette. ***Announcers:*** Tiny Ruffner, John Stephenson. ***Orchestra:*** Al Goodman, Gus Haenschen, Donald Voorhees.

OPENING

SOUND: People on shore awaiting the arrival of the showboat.

ANNOUNCER: Ladies and gentlemen, here she comes, *The Maxwell House Showboat*. Here you are, one solid hour of entertainment with Frank McIntire as Capt. Henry, Louise Massey and the Westerners, Bob Hope, Sonny Childs, Ross Graham, the famous Maxwell House Singers, Gus Haenschen and the Showboat Band. The Mississippi's favorite showboat is puffing right down into Casco Bay tonight.

SONG: Here comes the Showboat. Here comes the Showboat, puff, puff, puff, puffing along.

ANNOUNCER: And there on the bridge waving is Capt. Henry himself.

CAPTAIN: Howdy, howdy, folks. Come up the gangplank, everybody is welcome. Your ticket of admission is just your enjoyment of Maxwell House Coffee...

1440. THE SILENT MEN. Anthology, 30 min., NBC, 10/14/51 to 5/28/52.

Dramatizations based on the investigations of various U.S. agents. The program's host, Douglas Fairbanks, Jr., portrays the central agent in each story.

OPENING (from "Visas for Sale")

ANNOUNCER: Douglas Fairbanks, Jr., in *The Silent Men*. The National Broadcasting Company proudly presents Douglas Fairbanks' production of *The Silent Men*, transcribed stories of the undercover operations of the special agents of every branch of our Federal government and their relentless fight against crime. Now, here is Douglas Fairbanks.

DOUGLAS: The international boundaries dividing the United States from Canada and Mexico are eternal monuments to the truth that nations can live side by side in peace and brotherhood. But there are people who mistake trust and good will for weakness and who for profit and with criminal intent would violate the immigration laws governing our borders. Of special concern to the Department of Labor in Washington was the existence of a group of criminals whose specialty was the smuggling of aliens ... into this country. To help smash this ring, an undercover agent was assigned to the Los An-

**In a continuing storyline, Shorty's efforts to uncover the culprits behind a smear campaign were depicted.*

geles division. In tonight's story, I will assume his identity—Special Agent Peter Bradford in file case entitled "Visas for Sale."

1441. Silver Eagle. Adventure, 30 min., ABC, 7/5/51 to 3/10/55.

Jim West is a Canadian Northwest Mounted Policeman whose exploits have earned him the name Silver Eagle. An eagle feather arrow is his trademark and he is assisted by Joe Bideaux, a tall French-Canadian. Stories follow their exploits as they risk their lives to uphold the law. Also known as *Silver Eagle Mountie*.

Cast: Jim Ameche (*Jim West*); Jack Lester, Mike Romano (*Joe Bideaux*); John Barclay, Jess Pugh (*Inspector Argyle*); Clarence Hartzell (*Doc*). ***Narrators:*** Bill O'Connor, Ed Prentiss. ***Announcers:*** Ed Cooper, Ken Nordine. ***Music:*** Richard Dix. ***Producer:*** James Jewell.

OPENING

Announcer: The *Silver Eagle*! A cry of the wild, a trail of danger, a scarlet rider of the Northwest Mounted, serving justice with the swiftness of an arrow—the *Silver Eagle*.

1442. Silver Theater. Anthology, 30 min., CBS, 10/3/37 to 8/17/47.

Dramatic presentations sponsored by the International Silver Company.

Hosts: Conrad Nagel, John Loder. ***Announcers:*** Henry Charles, John Conte, Dick Joy, Roger Krupp.

OPENING

Announcer: International Silver Company presents the *Silver Theater* starring Orson Welles in "One Step Ahead," directed by Conrad Nagel. Brought to you this week on behalf of International Sterling, world-famous solid silver. We present the twenty-sixth program in our current *Silver Theater* series and here, ladies and gentlemen, with a word for you is our director, Conrad Nagel.

Conrad: Thank you, Henry Charles, and to you in our audience, welcome to *Silver Theater*. The house lights dim, the silver curtain rises and here is "One Step Ahead," starring Orson Welles as Timothy Wheeler with Lurene Tuttle as Alice and Mary Shipp as Stella.

1443. Sincerely, Kenny Baker. Variety, 15 min., Syndicated, 1945.

Vocalist Kenny Baker as the host of a program of music and songs. Donna Dae was the featured singer; Jimmy Wallington did the announcing; and the Buddy Cole Trio provided the music.

1444. The Sinclair Minstrel Show. Variety, 30 min., NBC Blue, 1932–1936.

A program of music and songs sponsored by the Sinclair Oil Company. Gene Arnold was the original host; he was replaced by Gus Van. Malcolm Claire and the Sinclair Minstrel Men were the regulars; music was by the Sinclair Quartet (Art Jones, Fritz Meissner, Pat Patterson, Al Rice) and the Harry Kogan Orchestra.

1445. Sing Along. Variety, 15 min., CBS, 1942.

A program of familiar songs that enabled listeners to sing along. Ken Roberts was the host and announcer and the Landt Trio provided the music.

1446. Sing for Your Dough. Game, 30 min., NBC Blue, 1942–1943.

Before the broadcast, microphones were placed before selected members of the studio audience. Once on the air, the host led the audience in a community sing. After a given time, the host cued the audience to stop. If the person (or persons) stationed near a microphone continued the song, they received two dollars.

Host: Lew Valentine. ***Organist:*** Don Baker.

1447. Sing for Your Supper. Game, 30 min., Mutual, 5/5/49 to 9/15/49.

Four contestants, chosen from the studio audience, had to sing a song while performing a stunt. The player who was judged the best at performing and singing won a merchandise prize.

Host: Tommy Tucker. ***Regulars:*** Nancy Donovin, Tom Mahoney, the Ray Charles Quartet. ***Announcer:*** Phil Tonkin. ***Orchestra:*** Tommy Tucker.

1448. Sing It Again. Variety, 60 min., CBS, 1948–1951.

The first half of the program was devoted to amateur songwriters who appeared to perform rearrangements of popular songs. The second half-hour was a quiz segment wherein contestants had to identify a recorded phantom voice through a series of rhyming clues.

Host: Dan Seymour. ***Regulars:*** Patti Clayton, Alan Dale, Bob Howard, the Riddlers. ***Orchestra:*** Ray Bloch.

1449. Singin' Sam the Barbasol Man. Variety, 15 min., CBS, 1930–1939.

New and old ballads with Harry Frankel, a baritone known as Singin' Sam; the program was sponsored by Barbasol Shave Cream.

1450. The Singing Lady. Children, 15 min., NBC Blue, 1932–1941; ABC, 30 min., 1945.

Actress-singer Ireene Wicker as the host of a program of music, songs and stories for children. Bob Brown did the announcing and Milton Rettenberg provided the music. Also known as *The Singing Story Lady* and *Stories for Children*.

Note: Three attempts were made to turn the radio program into a television series:

1. Ireene Wicker Sings, 15 min., NBC, 7/28/39. An adult version of the show wherein Ireene Wicker sang the top songs of the day.

2. Tele-Tales for Children, 20 min., ABC, 9/21/45. One of ABC-TV's first experiments. Ireene Wicker told the story of "The Three Little Pigs" to a studio audience of children.

3. The Ireene Wicker Show, 15 min., ABC, 8/15/46. Ireene Wicker in a program of songs, music and stories for children that again failed to become a series. Two television series did eventually air: *The Singing Lady* (ABC, 1948–1950) and *Ireene Wicker Story Time* (ABC, 1953–1954).

1451. Sisters of the Skillet. Comedy, 15 min., NBC Blue, 1930–1934.

A parody on "how to" and advice programs with host Ralph Dumke and Ed East dispensing absurd solutions to everyday problems.

1452. The Six Shooter. Western, 30 min., NBC, 9/20/53 to 10/11/54.

The West of a century ago was the setting for an above-average series about Britt Poncett, an easygoing gentleman cowboy with a fast gun who lent a helping hand to people in need. Britt hailed from Texas, rode a horse named Scar and carried the nickname "The Six Shooter" (although he never shot to kill). Despite his legend, Britt says, "I'm just an old cowpoke and don't even know if I'm going to have a job tomorrow" (he works what jobs he can get, usually a ranch hand). Britt rode the length and breadth of Texas and knew a lot of people; his efforts to help where needed was the focal point of stories.

Cast: James Stewart (*Britt Poncett*). ***Announcers:*** Hal Gibney, John Wald. ***Music:*** Basil Adlam. ***Producer:*** Jack Johnstone.

OPENING

Announcer: *The Six Shooter* starring James Stewart. The man in the saddle is angular and long-legged. His skin is sun-dyed brown; the gun in his holster is gray steel and Rainbow Mother of Pearl; its handle, unmarked. People call them both the Six Shooter. James Stewart as *The Six Shooter*, the transcribed series of radio dramas based on the life of Britt Poncett, the Texas plainsman who wandered through the western territories leaving behind a trail of still-remembered legends.

The $64.00 Question *see* **Take It or Leave It**

1453. The $64,000 Question. Game, 30 min., CBS, 1955.

A simulcast of the television series. Players first choose a subject category, then answer related questions beginning at the one dollar level. Each correct response doubles a question's value from one dollar to $64,000. Players have the option to continue, risking a loss of their winnings if an incorrect response is given, or stop and leave with what they have earned. Based on the radio series *Take It or Leave It* (also known as *The $64.00 Question*).

Host: Hal March. ***Assistant:*** Lynn Dollar. ***Announcer:*** Wayne Howell. ***Music:*** Norman Leyden.

1454. The Skip Farrell Show. Variety, 15 min., ABC, 1947.

Vocalist Skip Farrell as the host of a program of music and songs. The Honeydreamers vocal group provided additional songs; Jack Lester did the announcing; and the George Barnes Trio provided the music.

1455. Skippy. Comedy, 15 min., NBC, 1/11/32 to 7/9/32; CBS, 7/11/32 to 3/29/35.

A radio adaptation of the Percy Crosby comic strip about the innocent misadventures of Skippy Skinner and his friends (Sooky Wayne and Carol), adolescents with a knack for finding trouble.

Cast: Franklin Adams, Jr. (*Skippy Skinner*); Francis Smith (*Sooky Wayne*); Patricia Ryan (*Carol*). ***Producers:*** Anne Hummert, Frank Hummert.

1456. THE SKIPPY HOLLYWOOD THEATER. Anthology, 30 min., Syndicated, 1941–1949; CBS, 1949–1950.

A weekly series of dramatizations sponsored by Skippy Peanut Butter. When the program first began, a regular cast performed the different stories; major guest stars later appeared in the productions.

Cast: Robert Clarke, Howard Cowan, Tyler McVey, Rosemary Reddins, Charles Starrett. ***Announcer:*** Van Resautel. ***Music:*** Del Castillo, Mahlon Merrick.

1457. SKY BLAZERS. Anthology, 30 min., CBS, 1939–1940.

Dramatizations based on the real-life exploits of aviators (who appeared as a guest on the show). Col. Roscoe Turner, a renowned pilot, served as the host; Phillips H. Lord was the producer.

1458. SKY KING. Adventure, 15 min., ABC, 1946–1947; 30 min., ABC, 1947–1950; Mutual, 1950–1954.

Skyler "Sky" King is an ex–FBI agent and Navy pilot turned owner of the Flying Crown Ranch. He lives with his niece Penny and nephew Clipper. Stories, set in the modern West, relate their exploits as they battle evil. Sky flew several planes, including the *Song Bird* and the *Flying Arrow*, and was often assisted by his ranch foreman, Jim Bell. Early, 15-minute episodes are serial-like presentations detailing Sky, Penny, Clipper and Jim's exploits in various areas of the world as they battle international criminals (in these episodes, Sky flew a DC-3). Served as the basis for the television series of the same title.

Cast: Roy Engel, Earl Nightingale, Jack Lester (*Sky King*); Beryl Vaughn (*Penny*); Johnny Coons, Jack Bivens (*Clipper*); Cliff Soubier (*Jim Bell*). ***Announcer:*** Mike Wallace.

OPENING

ANNOUNCER: Sky King.

SOUND: Thunder cracking followed by the sound of a plane roaring by.

ANNOUNCER: Now, the adventures of *Sky King*!

1459. SKYLINE ROOF. Variety, 15 min., CBS, 1946.

Singer Gordon MacRae as the host of a program of music and songs. Harry Clark did the announcing and Archie Bleyer and his orchestra provided the music.

1460. THE SLAPSIE MAXIE SHOW. Comedy, 30 min., NBC, 1948–1949.

A somewhat exaggerated attempt to show the problems faced by a real-life ex-prizefighter (Slapsie Maxie Rosenbloom) as he attempts to become a radio star. Maxie Rosenbloom played himself; Patricia Bright played his girlfriend. Also in the cast were Betty Harris, Phil Kramer, Florence MacMichael and Bernie West. Norman Cloutier and his orchestra provided the music.

1461. SLEEP NO MORE. Anthology, 15 min., ABC, 1952–1957.

A daily series of horror stories presented in serialized form. Nelson Olmsted was the host and narrator; Ben Grauer did the announcing.

OPENING

HOST: This is Nelson Olmsted. Sleep no more. Sleep no more. Turn down the lights, sink back into your chair and don't look into the shadows. In the shadows, there may be moving things. Tonight it may be that you will sleep no more.

1462. SLEEPY JOE. Children, 15 min., ABC, 1949–1951.

The program, also known as *Sleepy Joe Time*, features Jimmy Scriber as Sleepy Joe, a lovable character who spins yarns for the small fry. Jimmy also provided all the voices.

1463. A SLIGHT CASE OF IVORY. Variety, 30 min., CBS, 1941.

Orchestra leader Walter Gross as the host of a weekly program of big band music with vocalists Anita Boyer and Bob Hanna. The Walter Gross Orchestra provided the music.

1464. THE SLOAN SIMPSON SHOW. Variety, 30 min., Mutual, 1954–1955.

Celebrity interviews, gossip and chatter with Sloan Simpson as the host.

1465. The Slumber Hour. Music, 60 min., NBC, 1927.

A late-night program of music that ran from 11 P.M. to midnight. Milton Cross introduced the music as conducted by Ludwig Laurier, Hugo Mariani, Harold Sanford and Cesare Sodero.

1466. The Smile Parade. Variety, 30 min., NBC, 1938–1939.

A weekly program of music and songs with Ransom Sherman as the host. Fran Allison, Lillian Carroll, Paul Paige and Wayne Van Dine were the regulars and the Vagabonds supplied the music.

1467. Smile Time. Variety, 30 min., Mutual, 1940–1942.

A daytime program of music, songs and comedy skits with Steve Allen as the host and June Foray and Wendell Noble as the regulars. Skitch Henderson provided the music; Steve Allen and Wendell Noble were the producers.

1468. The Smiley Burnette Show. Variety, 15 min., Syndicated, 1947–1952.

Country and western music and songs with film comedian Smiley Burnette as the host. Georgia Brown and the Rancheros were the regulars and the Whippoorwills provided the music.

1469. Smilin' Ed and His Buster Brown Gang. Children, 30 min., NBC, 9/2/44 to 4/11/53.

Stories, songs and comedy sketches that were set in a clubhouse and featured such characters as Froggie the Gremlin, Midnight the Cat, Squeaky the Mouse and Grandie, the Talking Piano, Stories were read by the host (Smilin' Ed); as he spoke, the stories were dramatized. Squeaky played the Magic Music Box and guests were annoyed by Froggie the Gremlin, a frog who became visible when Smilin' Ed spoke the words, "Plunk your magic twanger, Froggie." Kids participated at home via "The Brown Jug Jingle Box": A jingle, sent in by a child, was sung by Ed on the air; for example, Geraldine Atkins of Greenfield, Ohio, sent in this one: "Oh, you should see my brother Bert, he spills his breakfast on his shirt. I guess his eyesight must be dim and when he eats eggs, the yolk's on him." Smilin' Ed called his club members "My Buddies." The program was sponsored by Buster Brown Shoes (represented by Buster Brown and his dog Tige) and served as the basis for the television series of the same title. Also known as *The Buster Brown Gang* and *The Buster Brown Gang Starring Smilin' Ed McConnell.*

Cast: Ed McConnell (*Smilin' Ed/Froggie the Gremlin*); June Foray (*Midnight the Cat/ Grandie*); Jerry Maren (*Buster Brown*); Bud Tollefson (*Tige*). ***Announcer:*** Arch Presby. ***Music:*** Ken Cameron.

OPENING

ED: Hi, kids, you better come running, it's old Smilin' Ed and His Buster Brown Gang.

SONG: The happy gang of Buster Brown is on the air, the happy gang of Buster Brown is on the air, we frolic, we sing and play, come on and shout hooray, Buster Brown is on the air.

ED: Hello, kids, hello, mother, hello, daddy, hello, grandmother, hello, granddad, this is your buddy Smilin' Ed and all his Buster Brown gang here in Hollywood for a good old Saturday hoop-'em-up.

CLOSING

ED: Now, kids, don't forget to be on hand next Saturday at this same time. Don't forget church and Sunday School and be listening next Saturday for our little tune from Hollywood. When you hear it, come a-running. [Singing:] The happy gang of Buster Brown now leaves the air, the happy gang of Buster Brown now leaves the air, so watch us buddies next Saturday when we return with a bang, hip-hooray, Buster Brown is on the air.

1470. Smilin' Jack. Adventure, 15 min., Mutual, 1939.

Aviation adventures based on the comic strip by Zack Mosley. Frank Readick starred as Smilin' Jack, a pilot who sought adventure wherever he could find it.

1471. The Smiths of Hollywood. Comedy, 30 min., Mutual, 1947.

When a financial setback forces him to relocate, Sir Cecil Smythe decides to leave England and visit his nephew Bill Smith, in Hollywood. (When Cecil became a Sir, he changed Smith to Smythe.) Bill, a lawyer, is married to Nancy and they are the parents of ten-year-old Shirley, who is nicknamed Bumps. Their lives are turned upside down when Cecil arrives and announces his intentions to remain with the family for "a short spell." Stories relate the misadventures that befall Uncle Cecil as he attempts to adjust to America and the Smiths' efforts to adjust to Uncle Cecil (whom Bumps calls "Uncle Ceese"). Bumps' hobby is photography and she hopes to become the editor of *Look* magazine. Her favorite radio show is *The Lonesome Stranger*. See also the following title for information on the audition version of this show.

Cast: Harry Von Zell (*Bill Smith*); Brenda Marshall (*Nancy Smith*); Jan Ford (*Shirley "Bumps" Smith*); Arthur Treacher (*Uncle Cecil Smythe*). ***Announcer:*** Tyler McVey. ***Music:*** Carl Hoff, Charles Hathaway. ***Producer:*** Andrew Hickox.

OPENING

HARRY VON ZELL: From Hollywood, California, we bring you *The Smiths of Hollywood*. Bill Smith, that's me, Harry Von Zell. Nancy Smith—

BRENDA MARSHALL: That's me, Brenda Marshall.

HARRY: Our charming little daughter, Bumps Smith—

JAN FORD: That's me, Jan Ford.

HARRY: And our uncle, Sir Cecil Smythe—

ARTHUR TREACHER: That is I, Arthur Treacher.

HARRY: *The Smiths of Hollywood*.

ANNOUNCER: Yes, ladies and gentlemen, it's *The Smiths of Hollywood*, with Arthur Treacher, Brenda Marshall, Harry Von Zell, Carl Hoff's orchestra and a distinguished supporting cast from screen and radio. And now, here's Bill Smith.

BILL: Hello. Hollywood is the home of many moving picture stars. It's also the home of Bill and Nancy Smith. You never heard of them? Well, let's get acquainted.

CLOSING

ANNOUNCER: Well, the Smiths had a hard day; let's leave now so they can turn off the lights. But be back for our next show, same time, same station. This is Mutual.

1472. THE SMITHS OF SAN FERNANDO. Audition (Comedy), 30 min., NBC, 9/20/46.

The original concept for *The Smiths of Hollywood* (see prior title). Bill and Brenda Smith are residents of Sherman Oaks, California. They are the parents of Shirley (nicknamed Bumps) and respected residents of the community. Bill is a lawyer and also living with them is Bill's titled but poor uncle, Sir Cecil Smythe—a snooty Englishman who is a confirmed bachelor, not very fond of children and very self-centered. The proposed series was to relate incidents in the lives of the Smiths of San Fernando. In the audition episode, Uncle Cecil arrives in America and promptly becomes involved in an automobile accident with one of Bill's important clients (Cynthia LaMore). *Other regular characters:* Jimmy, Bumps' friend.

Cast: William Holden (*Bill Smith*); Brenda Marshall (*Brenda Smith*); Barbara Jean Wong (*Shirley "Bumps" Smith*); Arthur Treacher (*Uncle Cecil Smythe*); Ruth Perrott (*Cynthia LaMore*); Billy Roy (*Jimmy*). ***Announcer:*** Tyler McVey. ***Music:*** Carl Hoff. ***Producer-Director:*** Robert Presnell, Jr. ***Writers:*** Dick Gossaman, Franklin Phillips.

OPENING

ANNOUNCER: Ladies and gentlemen, put away your knitting, huddle the children and listen to open madhouse at *The Smiths of San Fernando*, with Arthur Treacher, Brenda Marshall, William Holden and a distinguished supporting cast from screen and radio, with music by Carl Hoff and his orchestra. Ever been to Sherman Oaks, a suburb of Hollywood? It's also the home of Bill and Brenda Smith. Ever heard of them? Then get acquainted...

CLOSING

ANNOUNCER: *The Smiths of San Fernando* Valley with Arthur Treacher, Brenda Marshall and William Holden have open madhouse every week at this time. You're invited back. This is Ty McVey speaking. Cheerio. This is the National Broadcasting Company.

1473. SMOKE DREAMS. Variety, 30 min., ABC, 9/2/45 to 2/24/46.

The format had the listener visualize a man (The Dreamer) seated in his easy chair in the living room. As he blew smoke rings, he reminisced about the past, which was presented in musical numbers. The program was sponsored by Chesterfield cigarettes (which had the theme "Smoke dreams from smoke rings as a Chesterfield burns").

Host: Tom Moore (as the Dreamer). ***Regulars:*** Virginia Speaker, Wayne Van Dine. ***Orchestra:*** Frank Worth.

1474. Snow Village Sketches. Comedy, 30 min., NBC, 1936–1937; NBC, 1942–1943; Mutual, 1946.

Humorous incidents in the lives of the people of a rural town (Snow Village, New Hampshire) as seen through the simple pleasures and trying times of Dan'l Dickey and his friend Hiram Neville, farmers who often performed other chores around the town. *Other regular characters:* Hattie, Hiram's wife; townspeople Wilbur, Marge, Carrie and Grammie.

Cast: Arthur Allen (*Dan'l Dickey*); Parker Fennelly (*Hiram Neville*); Agnes Young, Kate McComb (*Hattie Neville*); John Thomas (*Wilbur*); Katherine Raht (*Carrie*); Elsie Mae Gordon (*Grammie*).

1475. So the Story Goes. Anthology, 15 min., Syndicated, 1945–1946.

Supposedly true dramas based on little-known incidents that changed the destinies of famous men and women. John Nesbitt and Knox Manning served as the hosts and narrators. Organist Dick Platt provided the music.

1476. So You Think You Know Music. Game, 30 min., CBS, 1939; Mutual, 1945.

The format called for contestants to answer questions based on music and composers in return for merchandise prizes.

Host: Ted Cott. ***Regulars:*** Kitty Carlisle, Alan Dinehart, Richard Dyer-Bennett, Percy Grainger, Felix Knight, Leonard Lieblin. ***Announcers:*** Jack Barry, John Reed King. ***Orchestra:*** Allen Roth, Henry Sylvern.

1477. So You Want to Lead a Band. Game, 30 min., ABC, 1946–1948.

Sammy Kaye and his orchestra were the stars of this program wherein selected members of the studio audience were given the opportunity to conduct the orchestra in the performance of a familiar tune. A studio audience applause meter selected the best performer, who received a merchandise gift, the baton he used to conduct the orchestra and the opportunity to compete at a later date in a bandleading contest.

1478. Solitaire Time. Variety, 15 min., ABC, 1946.

A program of music to relax by with Warde Donovan as the host. Tex Antoine did the announcing and Ving Merlin and his orchestra provided the music.

1479. Somebody Knows. Anthology, 30 min., CBS, 1950.

Dramatizations of actual, unsolved murder cases. Following the broadcast, a description of the killer was given to the radio audience in the hopes that someone might possess knowledge and contact the police. A $5,000 reward was offered for knowledge that led to the arrest of the culprit.

1480. The Somerset Maugham Theater. Anthology, 30 min., CBS, 1950–1952.

Dramatizations of stories by William Somerset Maugham (who served as the host and narrator). Served as the basis for the *Teller of Tales* television series.

1481. Something New. Variety, 30 min., NBC, 1945–1946.

A weekly program of music, songs and comedy with popular standards composer Hoagy Carmichael as the host. Comedian Pinky Lee and the team of Hal March and Bob Sweeney were the regulars. Jimmie Higson conducted the orchestra.

1482. The Song of Your Life. Variety, 30 min., NBC Blue, 1940.

Orchestra leader Harry Salter as the host of a program of music and songs. Jack Arthur, Clark Dennis and Gwen Williams were the regulars and music was provided by the Harry Salter Orchestra.

1483. The Song Shop. Variety, 30 min., CBS, 1938.

Music and songs with vocalists Kitty Carlisle and Alice Cornett with the music of Frank Crumit and His Band.

1484. Songs by Eddie Fisher. Variety, 15 min., NBC, 1950.

A program of music and songs with singer Eddie Fisher as the host. The orchestra of Alvy West provided the music.

1485. Songs by George Bryan. Variety, 15 min., Syndicated, 1946.

A program of music and songs with singer-composer George Bryan as the host. Dan Seymour did the announcing and Jeff Alexander and his orchestra provided the music.

1486. Songs by Marcia Neil. Variety, 15 min., NBC, 1942.

Vocalist Marcia Neil as the host of a program of music and songs. Irving Miller and his orchestra provided the music.

1487. Songs by Morton Downey. Variety, 15 min., CBS, 1948.

A daily program of light music and songs featuring tenor Morton Downey and sponsored by Coca-Cola beverages. Joe King did the announcing and Carmen Mastren and his orchestra provided the music. See also *The Coke Club* and *The Morton Downey Show*.

1488. Songs by Sinatra. Variety, 15 min., CBS, 1943–1945; 30 min., CBS, 1945–1947.

Music and songs coupled with short dramatic and comedy skits. Sponsored by Old Gold cigarettes.

Host: Frank Sinatra. ***Regulars:*** June Hutton, Peggy Mann, Jane Powell, Lina Romay, the Bobby Tucker Chorus, the Page Cavanaugh Trio, the Pied Pipers. ***Announcers:*** Jerry Lawrence, Marvin Miller. ***Orchestra:*** Axel Stordahl.

OPENING

Announcer: *Songs by Sinatra*. Columbia invites you to another informal session in which there'll be songs by Sinatra and the Bobby Tucker Chorus, and the music of Axel Stordahl.

1489. Songs for Sale. Variety, 60 min., CBS, 1950–1952.

The material of amateur songwriters was performed, then judged and evaluated by a professional panel. After the verdict, the songs were offered for sale. A simulcast of the television series.

Hosts: Richard Hayes, Jan Murray. ***Vocalists:*** Toni Arden, Tony Bennett, Eileen Burton, Bob Carroll, Don Cherry, Betty Clooney, Rosemary Clooney, Joan Edwards, Helen Forrest, Johnny Johnston, Martha Stewart, Margaret Whiting, the Four Aces. ***Judges:*** Morey Amsterdam, Martin Block, Duke Ellington, Bob Hilliard, Dorothy Loudon, Mitch Miller. ***Orchestra:*** Ray Bloch.

1490. Songs of a Dreamer. Variety, 15 min., Syndicated, 1940.

A program of romantic music and songs with Doris Moore as the host. Gene Baker provided additional vocals and Larry Larsen and his orchestra supplied the music.

1491. Sonny Skylar's Serenade. Variety, 15 min., Mutual, 1943–1945.

Vocalist Sonny Skylar as the host of a program of music and songs. Henry Sylvern and his orchestra provided the music.

1492. The Space Adventures of Super Noodle. Science Fiction, 15 min., CBS, 10/11/52 to 4/4/53.

Super Noodle is a futuristic space hero named for the show's sponsor, the I.J. Grass Noodle Company. Super Noodle and his friend Rik lived 500 years in the future and their battle against the evils of the era were depicted.

Cast: Charles Flynn (*Super Noodle*); Robert Englund (*Rik*). ***Also:*** Everett Clarke, Tomi Thurston.

1493. Space Patrol. Science Fiction, 30 min., ABC, 9/18/50 to 3/19/55.

The Space Patrol is a thirtieth century police-like organization responsible for protecting the United Planets (Earth, Mars, Venus, Jupiter and Mercury) from evil. Space Patrol is based on the manmade city of Terra and is headed by Buzz Corey, its commander-in-chief. Stories follow Buzz's exploits as he and his assistant Cadet Happy safeguard the United Planets. *Other regular characters:* Carol Carlisle, daughter of the Secretary General of the United Planets; Major "Robbie" Robertson, the security chief; Tonga, a former alien villain turned Space Patrol ally; Dr. Van Meter, the scientist; the evil Prince Bacarrati, Agent X and Mr. Proteus. Based on the television series of the same title. Buzz's first ship was the *Battle Cruiser 100*; he then piloted the *Terra IV* and finally the *Terra V*.

Cast: Ed Kemmer (*Buzz Corey*); Lyn Osborn (*Cadet Happy*); Virginia Hewitt (*Carol Carlisle*); Rudolph Anders (*Dr. Von Meter*); Nina Bara (*Tonga*); Ken Mayer (*Major Robertson*); Bela Kovacs (*Prince Bacarrati*); Norman Jolley (*Agent X*); Marvin Miller (*Mr. Proteus*). ***Announcer:*** Dick Tufeld.

OPENING

Announcer: High adventure in the wild, vast

regions of space. Missions of daring in the name of interplanetary justice. Travel into the future with Buzz Corey, commander-in-chief of the *Space Patrol*.

1494. Spade Cooley and His Dance Group. Variety, 15 min., Syndicated, 1946.

Music to dance by with orchestra leader Spade Cooley as the host. Precious Price and Tex Williams were the regulars and the Spade Cooley Orchestra provided the music.

1495. The Spade Cooley Show. Variety, 60 min., CBS, 1951.

Orchestra leader Spade Cooley as the host of a weekly program of music and songs with Phil Gray, Ginny Jackson, Freddie Love, Hank Penny and Wally Ruth as the regulars. Bob Lemond did the announcing and Spade Cooley's orchestra provided the music.

1496. Sparkle Time. Variety, 30 min., CBS, 1946.

A weekly program of music and songs with Ben Gage as the host. Annette Warren provided the vocals and the Vivian Gray Trio supplied the music.

1497. The Sparrow and the Hawk. Adventure, 15 min., CBS, 1945–1946.

Spencer Mallory, nicknamed "The Hawk," is a former lieutenant colonel with the Army Air Corps (discharged due to combat injuries). Barney Malloy, his nephew, is a flying enthusiast who is called "The Sparrow" by his friends. Together they share a love of flying, and stories follow their adventures in exotic locales (always helping people in need along the way). *Other regular characters:* Laura Weatherby, Spencer's romantic interest; Tony, Spencer's friend; Mrs. Mallory, Barney's mother.

Cast: Michael Fitzmaurice (*Spencer Mallory*); Donald Buka (*Barney Mallory*); Susan Douglas (*Laura Weatherby*); Joseph Julian (*Tony*); Mary Hunter (*Mrs. Mallory*). ***Announcer:*** Tony Marvin

Special Agent *see* **Gentleman Adventurer**

1498. Special Assignment. Audition (Adventure), 30 min., produced on 11/7/37.

A proposed radio series that relates the work of the newsreel cameramen who risk their lives to record the news as it happens. These cameramen are represented by Richard Arlen, special assignment man for Jeff Haggerty, head of the International Newsreel Service. Haggerty would like Arlen to take simple pictures, but Arlen prefers to go where the action is and take daring moving pictures, not the tame ones Haggerty wants. Haggerty feels the public doesn't want action shots and fears such a waste of film will bankrupt him. Arlen's slogan: "Where you find me, you'll find action." In the audition program, Arlen is assigned to cover a society wedding, a dull affair until the groom is shot while walking down the aisle. *Other regular characters:* Linda Hayes, the radio broadcaster.

Cast: Richard Arlen (*Richard Arlen*); Linda Hayes (*Linda Hayes*); Jeff Haggerty (*Jeff Haggerty*).

OPENING

Announcer: The makers of Klean Soap present—

Voice: *Special Assignment.*

Announcer: Floods, war, disaster. Every day, every moment, somewhere on the Earth, there is news in the making, electrifying events that change the destinies of men and nations. Wherever and whenever news is made, there are too the men behind the cameras, the newsreel men of the world, dauntless, unfearing men, ofttimes sacrificing life itself to bring to the silver screen the shadows of major events. To these men of the cameras and to their courage do we humbly dedicate *Special Assignment* starring Richard Arlen with Linda Hayes.

CLOSING

Announcer: Flash! Mr. Jeff Haggerty, editor-in-chief of the International Newsreel Service, announces that next week he is assigning Richard Arlen to a special assignment that promises to be the most exciting of Arlen's career. Listen to this station, same time next week for all the details.

1499. Speed Gibson of the International Secret Police. Adventure, 15 min., Syndicated, 1937–1938.

The International Secret Police is an organization dedicated to battling evil wherever it exists. Its most diabolical enemy is the Octopus, an evil criminal who manages to stay one step ahead of authorities. Assigned to capture the Octopus are agents Speed Gibson, a 15-year-old pilot, and his uncle, Clint Barlow. Stories, which were set in exotic locales, follow Speed and Clint as they battle the Octopus. Speed and Clint flew a plane called the *Flying Clipper. Other regular characters:* Barney Dunlap, the pilot who assists Speed and Clint.

Cast: Howard McNear (*Speed Gibson*); John Gibson (*Clint Barlow/The Octopus*); Elliott Lewis (*Barney Dunlap*).

1500. Spend a Million. Game, 30 min., NBC, 1954–1955.

Contestants, chosen from the studio audience, each received $1,000. The first player to correctly answer a question received the opportunity to purchase merchandise at varying prices. The first player to spend all his money won what he purchased.

Host: Joey Adams. ***Announcer:*** Fred Collins.

1501. The Spike Jones Show. Variety, 30 min., NBC, 1945; CBS, 1947–1949.

A weekly series of music, comedy and performances by guest stars. Much of the comedy revolved around the songs played by orchestra leader Spike Jones and his band, the City Slickers (who did novelty versions of songs).

Host: Spike Jones. ***Regulars:*** Jack Dolly, Sir Fredric Gass, Dick Morgan, Freddy Morgan, Dorothy Shay, Doodles Weaver (as Prof. Feedlebaum), the City Slickers. ***Announcer:*** Michael Roy. ***Music Conductor:*** Henizi Rene.

OPENING

Announcer: Coca-Cola presents *The Spike Jones Show* with Spike and the City Slickers, including Doodles Weaver as Prof. Feedlebaum, George Roth, Dick and Freddy Morgan, Sir Fredric Gass, Jack Dolly and our special guest, Don Ameche.

1502. Spin to Win. Game, 45 min., CBS, 1949.

After a recorded song was played, a telephone call was placed to a listener who was asked to name the title and type of song (dance, jazz, ballad, etc.). If the listener answered correctly, he won a prize and the opportunity to win the $15,000 jackpot by identifying the title of a song played backwards.

Host: Warren Hull.

1503. Spotlight on Paris. Variety, 30 min., NBC, 1954.

The program, also known as *Stars from Paris* and produced in cooperation with the French Broadcasting System, featured various European entertainment acts. Gregoire Aslan was the host.

1504. Spotlight Revue. Variety, 30 min., CBS, 1948.

Cabaret singer Margaret Whiting as the host of a program of music and songs with Jimmy Castle, Al Galante and the Joe Mooney Quartet as the regulars. Joe King did the announcing and Dick Jurgens and his orchestra provided the music.

1505. Squad Car. Anthology, 15 min., Syndicated, 1954.

Dramatizations of cases from the files of the Louisville, Kentucky, Police Department. Peter French served as the host and narrator; James Van Sickle did the announcing.

The Squeaking Door *see* **Inner Sanctum Mysteries**

1506. S.R.O. Game, 30 min., ABC, 1953.

The format called for four panelists to answer questions submitted by listeners. Those whose questions stumped the panel received their choice of theater tickets or a savings bond as a prize.

Host: Betty Furness. ***Panelists:*** Whitney Bolton, Jimmy Cannon, Eloise McElhone, Jean Meegan. ***Announcer:*** Douglas Browning.

1507. Stag Party. Variety, 30 min., NBC, 1942.

A mix of comedy and music with Alan Young as the host. Bill Herbert and Freddy Hill were the regulars and Harry Price and his orchestra provided the music.

1508. Stage Door Canteen. Variety, 30 min., CBS, 1942–1945.

The program, set against the background of a World War II canteen, presented performances by top name entertainers.

Host: Bert Lytell. ***Announcer:*** Clayton "Bud" Collyer. ***Orchestra:*** Raymond Paige.

OPENING

ANNOUNCER: Corn Products presents *Stage Door Canteen*, starring tonight Louella Parsons, Connee Boswell, Bob Benchley, Benny Goodman, Eddie Green and Raymond Paige and the Canteen Orchestra. Stand by—curtain up for victory!

1509. STAIRWAY TO THE STARS. Variety, 30 min., ABC, 5/5/46 to 6/30/46.

Vocalist Martha Tilton as the host of a weekly program of music and songs. Glenn Riggs did the announcing and Paul Whiteman and his orchestra provided the music.

1510. THE STAN FREBERG SHOW. Satire, 30 min., 7/14/57 to 10/20/57.

A 15-episode series of satirical comedy skits, music, songs and interviews with unusual people (for example, Big Foot, a margarine sculptor).

Host: Stan Freberg. ***Regulars:*** Daws Butler, June Foray, Peter Leeds, Peggy Taylor, Jud Conlon's Rhythmaires. ***Announcer:*** Peter Leeds. ***Orchestra:*** Billy May. ***Producers:*** Peter Barnum, Stan Freberg.

OPENING

CHORUS: This is the seventh show of the series, of a brand new radio series.

ANNOUNCER: From Hollywood, we present *The Stan Freberg Show*.

CHORUS: With the music of Billy May.

ANNOUNCER: With Daws Butler, June Foray, Peter Leeds and Jud Conlan and the Rhythmaires.

CHORUS: You may not find us on your TV because, in case you did not know, we're being brought to you on R-A-D-I-O.

CLOSING

STAN: Until next week, this is Stan Freberg saying thanks for listening. God bless you and good night.

1511. THE STAR AND THE STORY. Anthology, 30 min., CBS, 1944.

Dramatic presentations that featured major film stars in stories they personally selected. Walter Pidgeon served as the host; Toby Reed did the announcing.

1512. STAR FOR A NIGHT. Game, 30 min., NBC Blue/ABC, 1943–1944.

The format called for contestants to perform in comedy skits for merchandise prizes.

Host: Paul Douglas. ***Assistant:*** Wendy Barrie. ***Announcer:*** Hugh James.

1513. STAR WARS. Science Fiction, 30 min., National Public Radio, 1/80 to 4/80.

A 13-episode radio adaptation of the first two-hour feature film about Luke Skywalker, a young moisture farmer on the planet Tatooine, who joins the Rebel Alliance to battle the ruthless Empire and rescue the kidnapped Rebel Princess Leia from the evil Darth Vader, the malevolent Dark Lord of Sith. Luke is joined by Ben Kenobi, the last of the Jedi Knights (who were once the guardians of peace and justice in the old world); Han Solo, the cynical captain of the millenium *Falcon* (a Corellian pirate ship); and the robots C-3P0 and R2-D2.

Cast: Mark Hamill (*Luke Skywalker*); Ann Sacs (*Princess Leia Organa*); Brock Peters (*Darth Vader*); Anthony Daniel (*C-3P0)*; Bernard Barons (*Ben Kenobi*); Perry King (*Capt. Han Solo*); Ben Burt (*R2-D2*); David Ackroyd (*Antilles*); Stephen Elliott (*Prestor*). ***Announcer:*** Bob Aaronson. ***Music:*** John Williams. ***Producer:*** Richard Toskin. ***Writer:*** Brian Daley. ***Director:*** John Madden.

OPENING

ANNOUNCER: A long, long time ago, in a galaxy far away, there came a time of revolution when rebels united to challenge a tyrannical empire. High among the Rebel Council stood the Royal House of the planet Alderaan, which have long been supporters of the old republic before it was overthrown by the Empire. The dedication of the Royal House to the return of peace and justice was total and fierce. Ordinary individuals swept along by the fervor of rebels like the Princess Leia found themselves immersed in critical events... [The story would then begin with a recap of the prior episode.]

1514. STARLIGHT CONCERT. Variety, 30 min., CBS, 1950.

A weekly program of music and songs with Eloise Dragon as the host. Don Wilson did the announcing; the Norman Luboff Choir were the regulars and Carmen Dragon and his orchestra provided the music.

1515. Starlight Serenade. Variety, 30 min., Mutual, 1944.

A weekly program of music and songs with Nestor Chayres, Victoria Cordova, Bernard Dudley, Harrison Knox and Bea Wain. Del Sharbutt did the announcing and Alfredo Antonini and his orchestra supplied the music.

1516. Starr of Space. Science Fiction, 30 min., ABC, 1953–1954.

The program, also known as *Captain Starr of Space*, is set in the futuristic world of Nova City and relates the exploits of Capt. Rocky Starr as he and his assistants, Gail Archer and Cadet Sgt. Stripes, battle evil throughout the universe.

Cast: John Larch (*Rocky Starr*); Jane Harlan (*Gail Archer*); Tom Hubbard (*Cadet Stripes*). ***Announcer:*** Lou Cook.

1517. Starring Boris Karloff. Anthology, 30 min., ABC, 1949.

A weekly series of mystery and suspense presentations frequently starring Boris Karloff (who also served as the host). George Gunn did the announcing and music was by organist George Henninger. The program served as the basis for the television series of the same title.

1518. Stars and Starters. Variety, 30 min., NBC, 1950.

Promising but undiscovered talent acts received the opportunity to showcase their skills when they were teamed with an established star to perform a song or act in a dramatic skit.

Host: Jack Barry. ***Orchestra:*** Norman Cloutier.

1519. Stars in Khaki 'n' Blue. Variety, 30 min., NBC, 1952.

A weekly program that featured performances by members of the armed services. Arlene Francis served as the host; Jack Costello did the announcing; and Bernie Leighton and his orchestra provided the music.

1520. Stars in the Air. Anthology, 30 min., CBS, 1951–1952.

Top name stars in condensed adaptations of famous motion pictures. Johnny Jacobs did the announcing and Alexander Courage and his orchestra provided the music.

1521. Stars Over Hollywood. Anthology, 30 min., CBS, 1941–1954.

A weekly series of dramatizations, including comedies and romances, that featured top name performers.

Host: Knox Manning. ***Announcers:*** Jim Bannon, Art Gilmore, Frank Goss, Marvin Miller. ***Music:*** Del Castillo, Ivan Ditmars.

Station EZRA *see* **Uncle Ezra's Radio Station**

1522. Stay Tuned for Terror. Anthology, 15 min., Syndicated, 1945.

Varied mystery and suspense presentations enacted by a regular cast and adapted to radio by Robert Bloch (later the author of *Psycho*).

Cast: Craig Dennis, Din Doolittle, Frances Spencer. ***Organist:*** Romelle Fay.

1523. Stella Dallas. Serial, 15 min., CBS, 1938–1955.

Dramatic events in the life of Stella Dallas, a seamstress in a small shop in Boston, her husband Stephen and her daughter Laurel. Presented as a sequel to the novel by Olive Higgins Prouty.

Cast: Anne Elstner (*Stella Dallas*); Frederick Tozere (*Stephen Dallas*); Joy Hathaway, Vivian Smolen (*Laurel Dallas*); Carleton Young, Macdonald Carey, Spencer Bentley, George Lambert (*Dick Grosvenor*); Julie Benell (*Helen Dallas*); Jane Houston (*Mrs. Grosvenor*); Mary Jane Higby (*Bea Martin*); Frank Lovejoy, Tom Tully (*Charles Martin*); Helen Claire (*Ada Dexter*); Grace Valentine (*Minnie Grady*); Raymond Bramley (*Lewis Johnson*); Helen Carew (*Vera Johnson*); Barbara Barton (*Nellie Ellis*); Mandel Kramer (*Sam Ellis*). ***Announcers:*** Ford Bond, Howard Claney, Jack Costello, Frank Gallop, Roger Krupp, Jimmy Wallington. ***Organist:*** Richard Leibert. ***Producers:*** Anne Hummert, Frank Hummert.

OPENING

Song: Memories, memories, dream of love so true.

Announcer: And now, *Stella Dallas*, the true-to-life sequel as written by us, to the world-famous drama of mother love and sacrifice.

Song: In my beautiful memories.

Announcer: And now for our sequel to *Stella Dallas*, in which Stella saw her own beloved daughter Laurel marry into wealth and society and, realizing the differences in their worlds, went out of Laurel's life. These episodes in the life of Stella Dallas are based on the novel by Olive Higgins Prouty. Today, Stella Dallas is in New York with her daughter Laurel cleaning up the mystery surrounding the theft of an Egyptian mummy...

STEPMOTHER *see* **KAY FAIRCHILD, STEPMOTHER**

1524. STEPPING OUT. Variety, 15 min., CBS, 1950.

Vocalist Rosemary Clooney hosted this program of music and songs with Tony Bennett and the music of Johnny Guarneri and his orchestra. Sandy Becker did the announcing.

1525. THE STEVE ALLEN SHOW. Variety, 30 min., CBS, 1950–1953.

Actor-composer-singer Steve Allen as the host of a weekly program of music, songs and comedy with vocalist Ilene Woods as a regular. Johnny Jacobs and Hal Simms did the announcing and music was by the Jerry Shard Trio and the Bobby Sherwood Trio.

1526. STEVE CANYON. Adventure, 30 min., CBS, 1948.

During World War II, Stevenson "Steve" Canyon was a pilot with the Army Air Transport Corps. When the war ended, Steve continued as an air cargo pilot by purchasing a surplus C-54 and charging four dollars a mile ("That includes flying, feeding and fighting"). Steve is assisted by his co-pilot Breck Manzeer, a man who has an eye for the ladies and "who gets into more saloon fights than a bouncer." Steve is always in need of money, and hauling cargo (and passengers) "is what we do—lugging some load from some place to some other" (and helping people in trouble along the way). Stories open with Steve's friend Col. Philip G. "Flip" Cochran reading the latest letter from Steve to listeners. The incidents are then dramatized "with Steve eventually finding trouble." Based on the comic strip by Milton Caniff.

Cast: Barry Sullivan (*Steve Canyon*); Tony Barrett (*Breck Manzeer*); Col. Philip G. Cochran (*Phil Cochran*); Wendell Corey (*Steve Canyon, audition episode*). ***Music:*** Richard Aurandt. ***Producers:*** Paul Dudley, Gil Dowd.

OPENING

ANNOUNCER: Take off time for *Steve Canyon*, colorful hero of Milton Caniff's exciting newspaper adventure strip, brought to the air by Canyon's wartime flying buddy, the gallant leader of America's first flying commando unit in Burma, the original Phil Cochran himself, Col. Philip G. Cochran.

PHIL: This is Phil Cochran. You know, a guy doesn't bring many good things out of a war; the one good thing I was lucky to hang onto was the friendship of a lean, rangy rascal named Steve Canyon—pardon me, Capt. Steve Canyon of the Air Transport Command. When the powers-that-be stopped World War II, somehow they just plum forgot to turn off old Steve; he's still out there, flying all over the place in a big surplus C-54; destination, the nearest available dollar. And the dollars have been coming in few and far between. Maybe he's not the best businessman, but he's sure a good correspondent; he loves to write. I get a letter from him every week, and this being another week, here's another letter postmarked August 27th, Rangoon, Burma. It starts "Dear Phil"...

CLOSING

PHIL (reading the end of Steve's letter): "...I didn't make up a word of it, Honor Bright. Pass this letter to any of my friends you might bump into and I'll be shooting you another one next week. As usual, Steve Canyon." Well, that's it, there's no telling what postmark next week's letter from Steve will be wearing. One thing we do know, it will be a half-hour long. Rendezvous point for next week is this same time, this same station. Until then, this is Phil Cochran saying good night to you and to Steve Canyon out there wherever you are. Long runways and happy landings.

ANNOUNCER: This is CBS, the Columbia Broadcasting System.

1527. STOOPNAGLE AND BUDD. Comedy, 15 and 30 min. versions, CBS, 1931–1932; 1932–1937; 1943–1944; Mutual, 1948.

Col. Lemuel Q. Stoopnagle is a fast-talking, scatterbrained inventor. He constantly gives advice but takes little himself. His exchange of conversation with his straight man, Budd, is the focal point of the program. Also known as *The Gloom Chasers* and *The Colonel Stoopnagle Show*.

F. Chase Taylor (left) and Wilbur "Budd" Hulick starred in *Stoopnagle and Budd*.

Cast: F. Chase Taylor (*Col. Lemuel Q. Stoopnagle*); Wilbur "Budd" Hulick (*Budd*); Louis Sain (*Erasmus Bumfildorfer*); John Gibson (*Quackenbush*). ***Regulars:*** Margaret Arlen, Joan Banks, Harry Clark, Hope Emerson, Alice Frost, Eddie Green, Florence Halop, Elaine Howard, Amanda Randolph, Jeri Sullivan, Mary Wickes. ***Announcer:*** Harry Von Zell. ***Chorus:*** Bobby Tucker. ***Orchestra:*** Paul Baron, Archie Bleyer, Peter Van Steeden, Donald Voohrees.

1528. Stop and Go. Game, 30 min., CBS, 1943–1944; ABC, 1944–1945.

Servicemen were assigned a category in which to answer questions that take the form of a mythical journey, and a cash prize of two dollars. (If an incorrect response was given, the player remained stationary.) The first player to acquire eight dollars completed his journey and won the game.

Host: Joe E. Brown. ***Orchestra:*** Matty Malneck.

1529. Stop Me If You've Heard This One. Comedy, 30 min., NBC, 1939–1940; Mutual, 1947–1948.

The host read a joke submitted by a listener (who received five dollars). If a member of a comedy panel believed he knew the punchline, he stopped the host from reading and supplied the ending. If he failed the give the correct ending, the listener received an additional five dollars.

Hosts: Milton Berle, Roger Bower. ***Panelists:*** Morey Amsterdam, Jay C. Flippen, Harry Hershfield, Lew Lehr. ***Announcers:*** Ted Brown, Dan Seymour. ***Orchestra:*** Horace Heidt, Joe Rines.

1530. Stop the Music. Game, 60 min., ABC, 1948, 1950–1952; CBS, 1954–1955.

As a song played, a telephone call was placed to a listener. When a connection was made, the music stopped. If the listener could identify the song, he won a $1000 savings bond. Served as the basis for the television series of the same title.

Hosts: Bert Parks, Bill Cullen. ***Vocalists:*** Kay Armen, Dick Brown, Jill Corey, Jack Haskell. ***Announcers:*** Doug Browning, Hal Simms. ***Orchestra:*** Ray Bloch, Harry Salter.

1531. Stories by Olmsted. Readings, 15 min., NBC, 1941.

A simple format wherein host Nelson Olmsted read a story to listeners.

1532. Stories of Escape. Anthology, 30 min., NBC, 1943–1944.

Psychological dramas that depict the plight of people who seek escape from their dull existences. Kleve Kirby was the announcer and organist Elwyn Owen provided the music.

1533. Stories of the Black Chamber. Adventure, 15 min., NBC, 1935.

Bradley Drake is head of a sophisticated coding room called the Black Chamber. The agency decodes the secret messages of the enemies of the free world and stories follow Drake as he battles one such enemy, the master spy Paradine. *Other regular characters:* Betty Andrews, Drake's secretary; Joyce Carraway, Paradine's assistant.

Cast: Jack Arthur (*Bradley Drake*); Gale Gordon (*Paradine*); Helen Claire (*Betty Andrews*); Rosaline Greene (*Joyce Carraway*).

1534. The Story of Bess Johnson. Serial, 15 min., CBS, 1941.

A spinoff from *Hilltop House* that continued to follow events in the life of Bess Johnson, a former matron of the Hilltop House Orphanage, turned superintendent of a boarding school.

Cast: Bess Johnson (*Bess Johnson*); Joseph Curtin (*Mr. Jordan*); Irene Winston (*Mrs. Jordan*); Mitzi Gould (*Barbara Bartlett*); Nancy Marshall (*Natalie Holt*); Adrienne Marden (*Patricia Jordan*); Agnes Moorehead (*Mrs. Townsend*).

1535. The Story of Bud Barton. Serial, 15 min., NBC, 1939–1942.

Dramatic and sometimes humorous events in the life of Bud Barton, an adventurous youth who lives with his parents (Ma and Pa) and grandmother in a small American town. Also known as *The Bartons*, *The Barton Family* and *Those Bartons*.

Cast: Dick Holland (*Bud Barton*); Bill Bouchey (*Pa Barton*); Fern Parsons (*Ma Barton*); Kathryn Card (*Grandma Barton*).

1536. The Story of Dr. Kildare. Drama, 30 min., Syndicated, 1950–1952.

A radio adaptation of the motion picture series *Dr. Kildare* that details the work of James Kildare, a young physician, and his mentor, the wise and elderly diagnostician, Leonard Gillespie. The doctors work at Blair General Hospital, "one of the great citadels of American medicine; a clump of gray-white buildings planted deep in the heart of New York; a nerve center of medical progress where great minds and skilled hands wage man's everlasting battle against death and disease. Blair General Hospital where life begins, where life ends, where life goes on." Also known as "Dr. Kildare."

Cast: Lew Ayres (*Dr. James Kildare*); Lionel Barrymore (*Dr. Leonard Gillespie*); Ted

Osborne (*Dr. Walter Carew*); Lurene Tuttle (*Nurse Molly Bird*); Virginia Gregg (*Nurse Parker*). ***Announcer:*** Dick Joy. ***Music:*** Joey Harmon, Walter Schumann.

OPENING

ANNOUNCER: *The Story of Dr. Kildare.*

KILDARE: Whatsoever house I enter, there I will go for the benefit of the sick. And whatsoever things I see and hear concerning the life of men, I will keep silence thereon, counting such things to be held in sacred trusts.

ANNOUNCER: *The Story of Dr. Kildare* starring Lew Ayres and Lionel Barrymore. Metro-Goldwyn-Mayer brought you those famous motion pictures; now this exciting, heart-warming series is heard on radio. In just a moment, *The Story of Dr. Kildare.*

CLOSING

ANNOUNCER: You have just heard *The Story of Dr. Kildare* starring Lew Ayres and Lionel Barrymore. *Dr. Kildare* is presented by arrangement with Metro-Goldwyn-Mayer, producers of *Key to the City* starring Clark Gable, Loretta Young, Frank Morgan and Marilyn Maxwell. Original music was composed and conducted by Walter Schumann. Dick Joy speaking.

THE STORY OF ELLEN RANDOLPH *see* **ELLEN RANDOLPH**

THE STORY OF KATE HOPKINS *see* **KATE HOPKINS, ANGEL OF MERCY**

1537. THE STORY OF MARY MARLIN. Serial, 15 min., NBC, 1934–1943; CBS, 1943–1945; ABC, 1951–1952.

Dramatic incidents in the life of Mary Marlin, the wife of a U.S. Senator (Joe), as she struggled to cope with the world of politics (Mary was a small-town Iowa girl). The Marlins lived on Main Street in Cedar Springs.

Cast: Joan Blaine, Anne Seymour, Betty Lou Gerson, Muriel Kirkland, Eloise Kummer, Linda Carlon (*Mary Marlin*); Bob Griffin (*Joe Marlin*); Phillips H. Lord, Fred Sullivan (*Frazier Mitchell*); Fran Carlon, Templeton Fox (*Bunny Mitchell*); Francis X. Bushman (*Michael Dorne*); Arnold Moss (*Giles*); Loretta Poynton (*Cynthia Adams*); Elinor Harriot (*Sally Gibbons*); Raymond Edward Johnson (*Henry Matthews*); Frank Dane, William Lee (*"Never Fail" Hendricks*); Bess Johnson (*Frances Matthews*); Arthur Kohl, Robert White (*Arnold*); Helen Behmiller, Charme Allen (*Sara Jane Kane*); Eddie Firestone, Jr., Bill Lipton (*Dennis McKenzie*); DeWitt McBride, Bob Fiske (*Arthur Adams*); Constance Crowder, Isabel Randolph (*Marge Adams*). ***Announcers:*** Truman Bradley, Nelson Caes, Les Griffith, John Tillman. ***Music:*** Allan Grant, Joseph Kahn.

1538. THE STORY OF RUBY VALENTINE. Serial, 15 min., CBS, 1955–1956.

A spinoff from *As the Twig Is Bent* that featured an all-black cast. Harlem was the setting for a story about Ruby Valentine, the owner of a beauty parlor. Juanita Hall played the part of Ruby Valentine. Ruby Dee, Viola Dean and Earl Hyman were also in the cast. Luther Henderson provided the music.

1539. THE STRADIVARI ORCHESTRA. Variety, 30 min., NBC, 1943.

A weekly program of music and songs featuring the Stradivari Orchestra. Paul LaValle was the host and Jacques Gasselen and Harrison Knox were the regulars. Jack Costello did the announcing.

1540. STRAIGHT ARROW. Western, 30 min., Mutual, 5/6/48 to 6/21/51.

The West of a century ago is the setting. Steve Adams is the owner of the Broken Bow Ranch. As a child, he was raised by and taught the ways of the Comanche Indians. Steve is also Straight Arrow, a mysterious figure for justice who appears whenever evil threatens good people. Stories relate Steve's exploits when he dons Comanche war paint to become Straight Arrow. Steve rides a golden Palamino named Fury.

Cast: Howard Culver (*Steve Adams/Straight Arrow*). ***Announcers:*** Frank Bingham, Fred Cole.

OPENING

SONG: N-A-B-I-S-C-O, Nabisco is the name to know. For a breakfast you can't beat, try Nabisco Shredded Wheat.

ANNOUNCER: Keen eyes fixed on a flying target. A gleaming arrow set against a rawhide string. A strong bow bent almost to the breaking point. And then [arrow is set loose] Straight Arrow. Nabisco Shredded Wheat presents *Straight Arrow*, a new, thrilling adventure story from the exciting days of the Old West. To friends and neighbors alike, Steve Adams appeared to be nothing more than the young owner of the Broken Bow cattle spread. But when danger threatened innocent people and when evildoers plotted against justice, then Steve Adams, rancher, disappeared, and in his place came a mysterious stalwart Indian wearing the dress of war paint of a Comanche; riding the great golden Palomino, Fury. Galloping out of the darkness to take up the cause of law and order throughout the West comes the legendary figure of *Straight Arrow*.

1541. Strange. Anthology, 15 min., ABC, 5/30/55 to 10/28/55.

Stories of the supernatural with Charles Woods as the host and announcer. Walter Gibson provided the narration.

1542. Strange As It Seems. Anthology, 15 min., CBS, 1939–1940.

Dramatizations based on the newspaper strip "Strange As It Seems" by John Hix. Also known as *Strange Adventure*. Patrick McGeehan (and later Gayne Whitman) served as the host and narrator.

1543. The Strange Dr. Karnac. Mystery, 30 min., NBC Blue, 2/20/43 to 4/3/43.

Dr. Karnac is a physician and amateur sleuth. His romantic interest, Dr. Watson, is also his assistant, and stories relate their efforts to solve crimes with supernatural overtones.

Cast: James Van Dyke (*Dr. Karnac*); Jean Ellyn (*Dr. Watson*). ***Announcer:*** Fred Cole. ***Organist:*** Bob Hamilton.

1544. The Strange Dr. Weird. Anthology, 15 min., Mutual, 1944–1945.

Chilling and sometimes grisly fantasies that were actually a mini-version of *The Mysterious Traveler* and which compressed stories into a 15-minute format. The program was hosted by Dr. Weird, who beckoned listeners to join him in his house "on the other side of the cemetery."

Host: Maurice Tarplin (as Dr. Weird). ***Announcer:*** Dick Willard. ***Producers:*** Robert Arthur, David Cogan.

OPENING

ANNOUNCER: Adam Hats presents [over thunderstorm effects] *The Strange Dr. Weird.*

DR. WEIRD (opening his front door): Good evening. Come in, won't you? Well, what's the matter? You seem to be pale. Have you been working too hard? Possibly a story might help relax you; a story, say, about a man who could read other men's minds. I call this story "The Man Who Knew Everything."

CLOSING

DR. WEIRD (after summing up the story): Oh, you have to go. Perhaps you'll drop in again soon. Just look for the house on the other side of the cemetery, the house of Dr. Weird.

ANNOUNCER: Be with us again next week when Adam Hats presents *The Strange Dr. Weird.* This is Mutual.

1545. The Strange Romance of Evelyn Winters. Serial, 15 min., CBS, 11/20/44 to 11/12/48.

Following his medical discharge from the service during World War II, Gary Bennett, a successful Broadway playwright, found that he had been named guardian of Evelyn Winters, the attractive, 23-year-old daughter of his former colonel (who was killed in action). Stories relate events in their lives and the strange romance that develops between them.

Cast: Toni Darnay (*Evelyn Winters*); Karl Weber, Martin Blaine (*Gary Bennett*); Flora Campbell (*Janice King*); Ralph Bell (*Charles Gleason*); Kate McComb (*Maggie*); Helen Claire (*Edith Winters*); Mary Mason (*Ginny Roberts*); Stacy Harris (*Ted Blades*). ***Announcer:*** Larry Elliott. ***Producers:*** Anne Hummert, Frank Hummert.

OPENING (from 2/28/45)

ANNOUNCER: We now present *The Strange Romance of Evelyn Winters*, the story of Gary Bennett, playwright, who suddenly and unexpectedly finds himself the guardian of lovely Evelyn Winters. It's thrillingly new, Sweetheart Soap's actual guarantee of loveliness to every woman who will change from inadequate care with wrong soap to more thorough beauty care with Sweetheart, the soap that agrees with your skin... And here's our guarantee. Get Sweetheart Soap today, try it in place of wrong soap... Then, either you look lovelier or mail us the wrapper and get your money back... And now, *The Strange Romance of Evelyn Winters*. To Evelyn's distress, her little friend, Ginny Roberts, has been told she has a hidden talent as an actress and it's Willard Hughes who told her, despite Evelyn's warning…

CLOSING

ANNOUNCER: Will Hughes really try to force Gary to put Ginny in his play? And will Evelyn react to that knowing if she does, she is the real backer? Be sure to listen tomorrow to the following chapter of *The Strange Romance of Evelyn Winters*. Till then, this is Larry Elliott saying good-bye for Sweetheart Soap, the soap that agrees with your skin. This is CBS, the Columbia Broadcasting System.

1546. STRANGE WILLS. Anthology, 30 min., Syndicated, 1946.

Dramatizations of cases in which missing heirs were sought. Warren William played the Investigator (the host); Marvin Miller did the announcing and Del Castillo and his orchestra provided the music. Carl Kraatz was the producer.

OPENING

VOICE: *Strange Wills.*

ANNOUNCER: Starring the distinguished Hollywood actor Warren William and featuring Lurene Tuttle with Howard Culver and an all-star Hollywood cast.

HOST: Dead men's wills are often strange. We do not attempt to understand them, or try to find the answers; we can but tell the story. This is Warren William to tell you the story of "The Girl in Cell 13."

1547. STREAMLINE JOURNAL. Variety, 30 min., NBC, 1940.

A program of music and songs with Alma Kitchell as the host. Irving Miller and his orchestra provided the music.

1548. STRICTLY BUSINESS. Drama, 30 min., NBC, 5/31/40 to 8/23/40.

A weekly drama about a sophisticated press agent (played by Lawson Zerbe) and his slightly wacky assistant (portrayed by Shirley Booth). Paul LaValle provided the music.

1549. STRICTLY FROM DIXIE. Variety, 30 min., NBC, 1941; ABC, 1954.

Dixieland music with Helena Horne as the host. She was assisted by John Hicks; guests appeared with regular vocalist Elizabeth Council. Henry Levine and his orchestra provided the music.

1550. STRIKE IT RICH. Game, 30 min., CBS, 1947–1950; NBC, 1950–1957.

Four contestants related their hardships, stating their single most-needed possession. Home listeners were then invited to call in and donate money to a Heartline. The person with the saddest story, as determined by studio audience applause, received the money in the Heartline. At one point in the series, it was also a quiz wherein players tried to win $800 by correctly answering five straight questions. The first format description served as the basis for the television series of the same title.

Hosts: Todd Russell, Warren Hull. ***Announcers:*** Don Baker, Ralph Paul. ***Organist:*** Hank Sylvern.

1551. STROKE OF FATE. Anthology, 30 min., NBC, 1953.

Dramatizations that depict the effects the Hand of Fate has on the lives of ordinary people. Walter Kiernan served as the host and narrator; Allan Nevin provided the commentary.

1552. THE STU ERWIN SHOW. Variety, 30 min., CBS, 6/11/45 to 9/24/45.

A weekly program of music, songs and comedy sketches with actor Stu Erwin as the host. Cameron Andrews, Peggy Conklin and Pert Kelton were the regulars. Milena Miller provided the songs; John Reed King did the announcing; Jay Blackton and his orchestra supplied the music.

1553. STUDIO ONE. Anthology, 60 min., CBS, 1947–1948.

Stylish adaptations of well-known stories and plays and featuring top name film and radio performers. Fletcher Markle served as the host and Alexander Semmler provided the music. Served as the basis for the television series of the same title.

STUDIO X *see* **THE PLAYER**

1554. SUMMER CRUISE. Variety, 30 min., ABC, summer of 1952.

Vocalist Johnny Andrews as the host of a warm weather program of music and songs. Marilyn Ross was the featured vocalist (she was assisted by a weekly guest) and Ralph Norman and his orchestra provided the music.

1555. Summerfield Bandstand. Variety, 30 min., NBC, 6/11/47 to 9/3/47.

The summer replacement for *The Great Gildersleeve* that featured cast members from the series in various sketches. The title was derived from the series locale, the small town of Summerfield.

Cast: Ken Carson, Richard Legrand, Earle Ross, Walter Tetley. ***Announcer:*** John Wald. ***Orchestra:*** Jack Meakin.

1556. The Sunbrite Smile Parade. Variety, 30 min., NBC Blue, 1938–1939; NBC Red, 1939.

Music, songs and comedy skits with Ransom Sherman as the host. Fran Allison, Sylvia Clark, Bill Thompson, Wayne Van Dine and the Cadets were the regulars; music was by Rex Maupin and his orchestra.

1557. Sunday at Home. Variety, 30 min., NBC, 1953–1954.

Comedian Jan Murray as the host of a weekly program of music, songs and comedy sketches with Vic Marsallo, Pat O'Day, Frank Stevens and the Toppers. Elliott Lawrence and his orchestra provided the music.

1558. Sunday Dinner at Aunt Fanny's. Variety, 30 min., NBC, 1938–1939.

The program featured Fran Allison in her "Breakfast Club" role of Aunt Fanny, hosting a Sunday dinner party with guests from the program. Durward Kirby did the announcing and Harry Kogen and his orchestra supplied the music.

1559. Sunday Evening Party. Variety, 30 min., ABC, 1945–1947.

Vocalist Louise Carlyle as the host of a weekly program of music and songs. Donald Dane was featured; Charles Stark did the announcing and Phil Davis and his orchestra provided the music.

1560. Sunday Night Serenade. Variety, 30 min., CBS, 1940.

A weekly program of music and songs with Cecil Bailey, Kitty Kallen and Snooky Lanson. Francis Craig and his orchestra provided the music.

1561. Sunday on the N.K. Ranch. Variety, 30 min., ABC, 1945.

A program of country and western music and songs sponsored by Nash-Kelvinator Home Appliances. Carol Bruce served as the host; Curt Massey, the Charles Doucet Mixed Choir and the N.K. Ranch Hands were the regulars. Harry Sosnik and his orchestra provided the music.

Sunday with Garroway *see* **The Dave Garroway Show**

Superman *see* **The Adventures of Superman**

1562. Superstition. Anthology, 30 min., ABC, 1948–1949.

Dramatizations based on familiar fetishes with Ralph Bell as "The Voice of Superstition" (the host-narrator-advisor-confidante). Jimmy Blaine did the announcing and Bernie Green and his orchestra supplied the music.

1563. Surprise Package. Game, 30 min., ABC, 1950.

Selected members of the studio audience competed in various stunt contests in return for prizes. Jay Stewart served as the host.

1564. Surprise Serenade. Variety, 30 min., NBC, 1949.

A weekly program of music and songs with Ed Davies and Don Gordon as the hosts. Hugh Downs did the announcing; Joseph Gallichio and his orchestra provided the music.

1565. Suspense. Anthology, 30 min., CBS, 6/17/42 to 9/30/62.

Mystery and suspense presentations "that were well-calculated to keep you in suspense." The program was originally hosted by a character called the Man in Black (and later by the directors of the various episodes). *Stories include:*

1. Commuter's Ticket. Jim Backus, Howard Duff and J. Carrol Naish in the story of a frustrated husband who murders his philan-

Agnes Moorehead in a scene from the *Suspense* episode "Sorry, Wrong Number" (sound man Berne Surrey is in the background).

dering wife then seeks to arrange the perfect alibi.

2. The Man Who Thought He Was Edward G. Robinson. To escape his nagging wife and friends, a meek man (Edward G. Robinson) adopts the tough guy characterization of Edward G. Robinson.

3. Love's Lovely Counterfeit. James Cagney and Robert Montgomery in a story about a hoodlum who, after a brief bout with decency, reverts to his past criminal activities.

4. Star Over Hong Kong. A young movie star (Marie Wilson) is kidnapped while on a publicity tour of the Orient in this light-hearted installment.

5. The Jolly Death Riders. A San Francisco police commissioner (William Holden) attempts to apprehend a woman's murderer.

Cast: Joseph Kearns, Ted Osborne (*The Man in Black*). ***Announcers:*** Truman Bradley, Bob Stevenson, Larry Thor, Harlow Wilcox. ***Music:*** Lud Gluskin. ***Producers:*** Elliott Lewis, Norman McDonnell, William Spier.

OPENING (Early Episodes)

ANNOUNCER: *Suspense.*

MAN IN BLACK: This is the Man in Black here again to introduce Columbia's program, *Suspense*. If you have been with us on these Tuesday nights, you well know that *Suspense* is compounded of mystery and suspicion, of dangerous adventure. In this series are tales calculated to intrigue you, stir your nerves, to offer you a precarious situation and then withhold the solution until the last possible moment. At so it is with "Sorry, Wrong Number" and the performance of Agnes Moorehead. We again hope to keep you in *Suspense*.

OPENING (Later Episodes)

ANNOUNCER: Now Roma Wines, R-O-M-A, made in California for enjoyment throughout the world, Roma Wines presents *Suspense*. Tonight, Roma Wines brings you Mr. Sheldon Leonard and Mr. Elliott Reed in "Feast of the Furies," a suspense play produced, edited and directed for Roma Wines by William Spier. *Suspense*, radio's outstanding theater of thrills, is presented for your enjoyment by Roma Wines, those excellent California wines that can add so much pleasantness to the way you live... Yes, right now a full glass would be very pleasant as Roma Wines brings you Sheldon Leonard and Elliott Reed in a remarkable tale of *Suspense*.

CLOSING

ANNOUNCER: *Suspense*, presented by Roma Wines, R-O-M-A, made in California for enjoyment throughout the world. Sheldon Leonard will soon be seen in the Frank Capra production, *It's a Wonderful Life*; Elliott Reed appeared through the courtesy of Paramount Pictures, producers of *To Each His Own*. Next Thursday, same time, Roma Wines will bring you Mr. Michael O'Shea as star of *Suspense*, radio's outstanding theater of thrills, produced by William Spier for the Roma Wine Company of Fresno, California. This is CBS, the Columbia Broadcasting System.

1566. THE SWAN SOAP SHOW. Comedy, 30 min., NBC, 10/7/41 to 6/25/45.

The program first portrays George Burns and Gracie Allen as a married couple (their prior radio series had them as single friends; see *The George Burns and Gracie Allen Show* for titles) and focused on the home and working lives of the show business couple. Gracie's harebrained antics were the focal point of each story with George, the recipient, trying to resolve the chaos before the program ended. The series, sponsored by the Lever Brothers Company, makers of Swan Soap, also featured music and songs.

Stars: George Burns and Gracie Allen. ***Regulars:*** Elvia Allman, Bea Benaderet, Mel Blanc (as the postman), Hans Conried (as Cueball, the schemer), Edith Evanson, Richard Haydn, Hal March, Clarence Nash, Dick Ryan. ***Vocalists:*** Jimmy Cash, the Swandets. ***Orchestra:*** Felix Mills, Paul Whiteman. ***Announcer:*** Bill Goodwin.

OPENING

SOUND: Doorbell rings; door is opened.

GRACIE: Well, hello, come right in. Oh, George, we've got company.

ANNOUNCER: Lever Brothers, makers of Swan Soap, your best wartime buy, presents *The Swan Soap Show* with George Burns, Gracie Allen, Jimmy Cash, the Swandets and Felix Mills and his orchestra. And now meet the people who live in the Burns house, George and Gracie...

CLOSING

ANNOUNCER: This is Bill Goodwin for Swan Soap inviting you to join us again next week when we will have as our guest star, Brian Donlevy. And now, until next week, this is Bill Goodwin saying try Swan. Good night.

1567. THE SWEENEY AND MARCH PROGRAM. Comedy, 30 min., CBS, 7/5/46 to 10/1/48.

Hal March and Bob Sweeney are promising comedians who host their own radio series (*The Sweeney and March Program*). Hal is the sensible one, Bob is the silly one, and stories relate their mishaps as they plan their weekly show.

Starring: Hal March, Bob Sweeney. ***Vocalists:*** Patsy Bolton, the Sweeney and March Choral Society. ***Announcers:*** George Ansbro, Bob Lemond. ***Orchestra:*** Wilbur Hatch, Lud Gluskin, Irving Miller.

OPENING

ANNOUNCER: *The Sweeney and March Program.* The Columbia Broadcasting System and its affiliated stations present *The Sweeney and March Program*, starring the young comedy stylists, Bob Sweeney and Hal March, and featuring the music of Lud Gluskin and his orchestra and the songs of the Sweeney and March Choral Society.

CLOSING

ANNOUNCER: Next week, same time, same station, CBS will present *The Sweeney and March Program* with Lud Gluskin and his orchestra and the Sweeney and March Choral Society. This is CBS, the Columbia Broadcasting System.

1568. SWEET RIVER. Serial, 15 min., NBC Blue, 10/4/43 to 7/21/44.

A daily drama about a minister and his wife in the small town of Sweet River. Ed Prentiss and Betty Arnold played the couple. Also in the cast were Kay Campbell, Carl Kroenke, Dick Turner and Helen Van Tuyl. Howard Hoffman was the narrator.

1569. SWINGTIME AT THE SAVOY. Variety, 30 min., NBC, 1948.

A weekly program of music and songs set against the background of a Harlem nightclub. Noble Sissle was the host; the regulars were Paul Breckinridge, Jackie "Moms" Mabley, Lucky Millinder, Miller and Lee and the Hall Sisters. The King Adum Quartet provided the music.

1570. TAILSPIN TOMMY. Adventure, 30 min., CBS, 1941–1942.

Thomas "Tommy" Tompkins, nicknamed "Tailspin Tommy," and his friends Betty Lou Barnes and Skeets Milligan live in the town of Three Point, Texas. Tommy is an air ace and stories follow his various adventures as he becomes involved in crimes associated with the world of aviation. Tommy's plane is the *Silver Streak*.

Cast: Mark Williams (*Tailspin Tommy*); Marjorie Reynolds (*Betty Lou Barnes*); Milburn Stone (*Skeets Milligan*).

OPENING

ANNOUNCER: *Tailspin Tommy* is on the air. Here he is again, ladies and gentlemen, come to tell you another thrilling story, that likable, exciting aviation hero, Tailspin Tommy and his flying pals, Skeets and Betty Lou. Stepping out of newspapers from coast to coast and jumping down from the motion picture screen, Tailspin visits you each week over radio. So join us for another exciting half-hour with that ace hero of the skies, *Tailspin Tommy.*

TOMMY: Good afternoon, folks; well, it's nice to be here again with Skeets and Betty Lou to tell you about another of our adventures...

CLOSING

TOMMY: I'll be with you again next Sunday afternoon to tell you another thrilling story. So until then, good afternoon, all.

ANNOUNCER: Be with us again next week at this same time when Tailspin Tommy will be heard in the story, "The Ghost Room," another in the adventures of *Tailspin Tommy.* Tune in every week at this time for that daring hero of the skies and his pals Skeets and Betty Lou straight from pictures and newspapers, created by Hal Forrest, *Tailspin Tommy.* This is the Columbia Broadcasting System.

1571. TAKE A CARD. Game, 30 min., Mutual, 1943–1944.

Four studio audience members competed. Each in turn drew four cards from a deck of 52 playing cards. The host related a question pertaining to one of the chosen cards. The player who possessed that card and was able to correctly answer the question received money according to the face value of the card.

Host: Wally Butterworth. ***Assistant:*** Margaret Johnson.

1572. TAKE A NUMBER. Game, 30 min., Mutual, 1948–1955.

Questions submitted by listeners were put to selected members of the studio audience. If a player answered correctly, he won five dollars; if not, the listener received the money. The player with the most correct answers competed in the jackpot by choosing a number from a board. If he answered the rather difficult question associated with the number, he won the money that had been accumulated through the defeats of the other players.

Hosts: Red Benson, Bob Shepherd. ***Announcer:*** Jack Irish.

1573. TAKE IT EASY. Variety, 30 min., CBS, 1940.

Orchestra leader Ed Drew as the host of a program of music and song. Harmon Hyde was the featured vocalist, Ed Pearson did the announcing and the Ed Drew Orchestra provided the music.

1574. TAKE IT EASY TIME. Variety, 15 min., Mutual, 1945.

Dick Willard as the host of a program of music and songs. The Song Chiefs provided the vocals and Frank Novak and his orchestra supplied the music.

1575. TAKE IT OR LEAVE IT. Game, 30 min., CBS, 1940–1947; NBC, 1947–1950.

One player at a time competed in a series of question-and-answer rounds—each worth from one dollar doubled to $64. At any point in the game, the player could take what he had already earned, or leave it and attempt to double his winnings by answering another question (risking the loss of everything if he should fail). Became *The $64.00 Question* in 1950 and served as the basis for television's *The $64,000 Question*.

Hosts: Phil Baker, Bob Hawk, Garry Moore, Jack Paar, Eddie Cantor. ***Announcers:*** Ken Niles, Ken Roberts, Jay Stewart. ***Orchestra:*** Ray Bloch.

1576. TALENT SEARCH, COUNTRY STYLE. Variety, 30 min., NBC, 1951.

Performances by undiscovered country and western entertainers. Tom George served as the host and Ray Barrett did the announcing.

1577. TALES OF FATIMA. Crime Drama, 30 min., CBS, 1/8/49 to 10/1/49.

Basil Rathbone, a renowned stage actor famous for playing Sherlock Holmes, portrays himself as an actor with a keen interest in detective fiction who moonlights as a private investigator ("I'm nosy by nature"). Rathbone smokes Fatima cigarettes (the show's sponsor) and draws his inspiration by dreaming of the fabulous Princess Fatima, a sultry woman who speaks to him and provides inspiration. Stories follow Rathbone as he and his assistant, his wardrobe woman Lavender, attempt to solve intriguing crimes.

Cast: Basil Rathbone (*Basil Rathbone*); Agnes Young (*Lavender*); Francis DeSales (*Lt. Dennis Farrell*). ***Music:*** Carl Hoff, Jack Miller. ***Producer:*** Harry Ingram.

OPENING (from 5/21/49)

BASIL: Hello there, this is Basil Rathbone. I'm so glad you can be with me and Fatima tonight. She helps me solve an uncanny tale that begins when a poison drink was poured and reached its climax when a dead man came to life.

ANNOUNCER: The *Tales of Fatima*, a new series of exciting mystery stories starring that distinguished actor, Mr. Basil Rathbone.

BASIL: Before we begin tonight's tale, I've got something to say to you. If you smoke a long cigarette, smoke the new long Fatima. You see, the name Fatima has stood for the best quality for 30 years, and now the new Fatima is the best of the long cigarettes. Ladies and gentlemen, if you smoke a long cigarette, smoke the best of the long cigarettes, smoke Fatima. Our author for tonight, Gail Ingram, has written an astonishing mystery especially for me. I didn't know the solution until I recalled the words of Fatima.

FATIMA: In the words of Fatima, habit is law; we are, all of us, slaves to a habit.

BASIL: Those words are the key to tonight's *Tale of Fatima*. And here it is, "A Much Expected Murder."

CLOSING

ANNOUNCER: Join us again next week when we'll have another exciting *Tale of Fatima*. Right, Mr. Rathbone?

BASIL: Yes indeed. Fatima helps me solve an amazing tale that started on a darkened street with a chase and reached its climax in a darkened room with a shot. See you then, everyone. Good night.

1578. TALES OF THE TEXAS RANGERS. Western, 30 min., NBC, 1950–1952.

Dramatizations based on the actual files of the Texas Rangers as seen through the investigations of Jace Pearson, a Ranger who assisted various law enforcement agencies when outside help was needed. Capt. Stinson was his superior; Jace rode a horse called Charcoal.

Cast: Joel McCrea (*Jace Pearson*); Tony Barrett (*Capt. Stinson*). ***Announcer:*** Hal Gibney.

OPENING

ANNOUNCER: NBC presents *Tales of the Texas*

Rangers starring Joel McCrea as Ranger Jace Pearson. Texas, more than 260,000 square miles and 50 men who make up the most famous and oldest law enforcement body in North America. Now, from the files of the Texas Rangers, come these stories based on fact. Only names, dates and places are fictitious for obvious reasons; the events themselves are a matter of record. Case for tonight, "Paid in Full."

CLOSING

ANNOUNCER: Next week, hear Joel McCrea in another authentic reenactment of a thrilling case from the files of the Texas Rangers.

1579. TALES OF TOMORROW. Anthology, 30 min., ABC, 1/1/53 to 2/26/53; CBS, 3/5/53 to 4/9/53.

Adaptations of stories appearing in *Galaxy Science Fiction* magazine. Based on the television series of the same title and hosted by Raymond Edward Johnson.

OPENING

ANNOUNCER: *Tales of Tomorrow*. Tales beyond human imagination—until they happen. *Tales of Tomorrow*, story number four, "The Other Now," by Murray Leinster.

HOST: This is your host saying hello for ABC. Look at your watch. But don't take it too seriously. If it's a few seconds after nine P.M., Eastern Standard Time, in California, it's three hours earlier; in London, it's 12 o'clock tomorrow morning; and in Japan it's almost tomorrow afternoon. What time is it right now on the planet Saturn? Silly question? I wonder. The point is, time is a clock with many faces, but your time is not necessarily anyone else's, and what we think of the present is only relative. Let's prove that thesis with a remarkable tale from *Galaxy*, the science fiction magazine and a most timely story titled "The Other Now."

TALES OF WILLIE PIPER *see* **WILLIE PIPER**

1580. TANGEE VARIETIES. Variety, 30 min., Mutual, 1944.

A program of music, songs and comedy sponsored by Tangee Cosmetics. Ventriloquist Paul Winchell (assisted by his dummy friend Jerry Mahoney) were the hosts and Sammy Kaye and his orchestra provided the music.

1581. TARZAN. Adventure.

Lord John Greystoke and his wife Alice are aboard a ship bound for England when a mutinous crew spares their lives by putting them ashore on the coast of Africa. When all attempts to escape fail, John builds a small shack near the sea. One year later, a son is born to them. Shortly after, their hut is attacked by a tribe of bull apes. John and Alice are savagely slaughtered and little Lord Greystoke is taken by Kalah, a young female ape who raises him as Tarzan, Lord of the Jungle. Twenty years later, a young girl named Jane Parker strays from a safari and is suddenly propelled into a web of impending death: a rampaging elephant and savage pygmies. She is rescued by Tarzan, whom she befriends, teaches to speak, and decides to remain with in the jungle. Stories relate Tarzan's efforts to protect his adopted homeland from evildoers. Based on the stories by Edgar Rice Burroughs.

Four different series were produced. In the first one, *Tarzan of the Apes* (Syndicated, 1932–1934), James Pierce played Tarzan and Joan Burroughs was Jane. In 1934, a 39-episode serial called *Tarzan and the Diamonds of Asher* starred Carlton KaDell as the Lord of the Jungle. KaDell repeated his role as Tarzan in a second syndicated, 39-episode serial entitled *Tarzan and the Fires of Tohr* in 1936. The final version, called *Tarzan*, appeared on CBS (1952–1953) and starred Lamont Johnson as Tarzan. Charles Arlington did the narrating and Albert Glasser provided the music.

OPENING

VOICE: Tarzan's jungle call.

ANNOUNCER: From the heart of the jungle comes a savage cry of victory. This is Tarzan, Lord of the Jungle. From the black core of dark Africa, land of enchantment, mystery and violence comes one of the most colorful figures of all time. Transcribed from the immortal pen of Edgar Rice Burroughs, Tarzan, the bronzed light son of the jungle.

1582. TEA TIME AT MORRELL'S. Variety, 30 min., NBC, 1936–1937.

A program of music and songs sponsored by the John Morell Company, makers of Red Heart Dog Food. Don McNeill was the host; Gale Page and Charles Sears were the regulars; Joseph Gallichio and his orchestra provided the music.

1583. Ted Drake, Guardian of the Big Top. Adventure, 30 min., Mutual, 1949.

The story of Ted Drake, a circus detective for a traveling tent show. Vince Harding played the role of Ted Drake and Fred Rains was his sidekick. Bob Larrimore did the announcing.

1584. The Ted Lewis Show. Variety, 30 min., Syndicated, 1934–1935; 1947–1948.

A weekly series of music and songs featuring singer and orchestra leader Ted Lewis as the host. Geraldine DuBois was the featured vocalist (1947 version) and the orchestras of Ted Lewis (1934) and Paul Arnold (1947) provided the music.

OPENING

Theme: "When My Baby Smiles at Me."

Announcer: "When My Baby Smiles at Me." What a familiar, tuneful radio signature and need I tell you, ladies and gentlemen, this melody heralds the approach to the microphone of that lovable high-rated tragedian of song, Ted Lewis.

Ted: Good evening, ladies and gentlemen, Yes sir, is everybody happy? [He would then begin the show.]

1585. The Ted Mack Family Hour. Variety, 30 min., ABC, 1/7/51 to 12/2/51.

An extension series based on *The Original Amateur Hour* with Ted Mack hosting a series of performances by guests. Andy Roberts was the featured vocalist; Dennis James did the announcing; and Lloyd Marx and his orchestra provided the music. A simulcast of the television series of the same title.

1586. The Ted Steele Show. Variety, 30 min., NBC, 1942.

Orchestra leader Ted Steele as the host of a weekly program of music and songs with vocalists Rita Grande and the Five Marshalls. Paul LaValle and his orchestra provided the music.

1587. Ted Steele's Novatones. Variety, 15 min., NBC, 1939.

A program of music and songs featuring host Ted Steele (on novachord), Doc Whipple (electric organ) and Howard Smith (drums).

1588. The Teen-Timers Club. Variety, 30 min., NBC, 1945–1947.

Singer Johnny Desmond as the host of a weekly program of music and songs geared to teenage listeners. Susan Douglas, Hope Emerson, Ray Ives, Phil Kramer, Jr., and J. Scott Smart were the regulars; Tom Hudson did the announcing and Johnny Long and his orchestra provided the music.

1589. Teen Town. Variety, 30 min., ABC, 1946.

A weekly program that showcased teenage performers. Dick York served as the host and vocalists Jackie Dvorak and Tony Frantina were the regulars. Mary Hartline and her orchestra provided the music.

1590. Tell It Again. Anthology, 30 min., CBS, 1948–1949.

Marvin Miller as the host, narrator and all voices for a series of dramatizations of classic novels geared for children. Organist Del Castillo provided the music.

1591. Ten-Two-Four Ranch. Variety, 30 min., Mutual, 1941–1945.

A program of country and western music sponsored by Dr. Pepper soda (its slogan at the time was "Ten-Two-Four"). The Tune Twisters and the Ivan Ditmars Orchestra provided the music; Don Forbes did the announcing and the program featured the vocal talents of Martha Mears and Bob Nolan and the Sons of the Pioneers.

1592. Tena and Tim. Comedy, 15 min., CBS, 1944–1946.

Humorous incidents in the lives of Tena, a Swedish maid (for Mr. and Mrs. Hutchinson), and her devoted friend and admirer Tim, an Irish janitor.

Cast: Peggy Beckmark (*Tena*); James Gardner, George Cisar (*Tim*); John Goldsworthy (*Mr. Hutchinson*); Gladys Heen (*Mrs. Hutchinson*). ***Also:*** Claire Baum, Arthur Young.

1593. The Tennessee Ernie Ford Show. Variety, 15 min., CBS, 1954.

A daily program of music, songs and homespun chatter with singer Tennessee Ernie Ford as the host. Jack Narz did the announcing; Cliff Stone and his orchestra provided the music.

1594. Tennessee Jed. Adventure, 15 min., ABC, 5/14/45 to 11/7/47.

The program is set in the post–Civil War

West and first told of the exploits of Tennessee Jed Sloan, a sharpshooter who used his guns to help people threatened by evil. In later episodes, Jed's exploits as an undercover agent to President Grant were depicted. Jed is a squirrel gun marksman, has an eye like a hawk, was taught by the Comanche Indians how to follow a trail and rides a horse named Smokey.

Cast: Johnny Thomas, Don McLaughlin (*Tennessee Jed Sloan*); Humphrey Davis (*Sheriff Jackson*); Raymond Edward Johnson (*Masters, the gambler*); Juano Hernandez (*Various Indian Chiefs*). ***Announcer-Narrator:*** Court Benson. ***Producer:*** Paul DeFur.

OPENING

VOICE: There he goes, Tennessee, get him. [Gun shot is heard.] Got him, dead center.

ANNOUNCER: That's Jed Sloan, Tennessee Jed, deadliest man ever to ride the western plains. Brought to you transcribed by the makers of Tip Top Bread.

1595. TERKEL TIME. Variety, 30 min., NBC, 1950.

Restaurant owner Studs Terkel as the host of a program of music and songs with John Conrad, Jack Haskell and Connie Russell as the regulars. The Art Van Damme Quintet provided the music.

1596. TERRY ALLEN AND THE THREE SISTERS. Variety, 15 min., CBS, 1944.

A program of music and songs with Terry Allen as the host and featuring the vocal group the Three Sisters (Bea, Geri and Margie Ross). Music was by a group called the Captivators.

1597. TERRY AND TED. Children, 15 min., NBC Red, 1937–1938; NBC Blue, 1938–1939; ABC, 1943–1948.

Nine-year-old Terry and 11-year-old Ted are the guardians of Major Campbell, an ingenious inventor who created an all-terrain vehicle called the Land Cruiser. Stories relate their adventures as they use the Land Cruiser to battle evildoers.

Cast: Lester Jay (*Terry*); Jerry Macy (*Ted*). ***Narrator:*** Don Carney.

1598. TERRY AND THE PIRATES. Adventure, 15 min., NBC, 1937–1939; ABC, 1943–1948.

An adaptation of the comic strip by Milton Caniff that begins when Terry Lee, a U.S. Air Corps colonel, inherits an abandoned gold mine in the Orient. Soon after Terry begins a search for the mine, he and his friends, Patrick Ryan and Hot Shot Charlie, are captured by Lai Choi San, an evil Eurasian known as the Dragon Lady. Terry and his friends eventually escape, but decide to remain in the Orient to battle her as well as other sinister villains, with the additional assistance of Connie and Burma. During World War II episodes, Terry and the Dragon Lady teamed to battle the Japanese, but the audience was never quite sure whose side she was actually on—or whether or not she would stab Terry in the back. After the war, they became enemies again.

Cast: Jackie Kelk, Cliff Carpenter, Owen Jordan (*Terry Lee*); Clayton "Bud" Collyer, Lawrence Alexander, Warren Anderson, Bob Griffin (*Patrick Ryan*); Agnes Moorehead, Adelaide Klein, Marion Sweet (*Dragon Lady*); Cameron Andrews (*Hot Shot Charlie*); Cliff Norton, Peter Donald, John Gibson (*Connie*); Frances Chaney (*Burma*). ***Announcer:*** Douglas Browning. ***Music:*** Kelvin Keech.

OPENING

VOICES: Nonsense mumbo-jumbo that sounded like Chinese.

SOUND: A large gong.

ANNOUNCER: *Terry and the Pirates.* Quaker Puff Wheat presents *Terry and the Pirates.* [The gong sounds again and the story begins.]

1599. TERRY'S HOUSE PARTY. Variety, 30 min., NBC Blue, 1944.

Terry Pepin as the host of a weekly program of music and songs with Ted Cole and the Bobby Norris Orchestra.

1600. TEX AND JINX. Variety, 30 min., NBC, 7/2/47 to 9/24/47; 6/30/48 to 9/29/48.

A daily program of topical conversation, music and songs with the husband-and-wife team of Tex McCrary and Jinx Falkenburg. Mary Martin, Billy Rose and Helen Carroll and the Escorts were the regulars. Dan Seymour did the announcing and Johnny Guarneri and his orchestra provided the music.

1601. THE TEXACO STAR THEATER. Variety, 60 min., CBS, 1938–1939; 30 min., CBS, 1942–1948.

The program, sponsored by Texaco Gasoline, was divided into two 30-minute segments: a variety session from Hollywood and dramatizations of Broadway plays from New York. The variety segment featured guest hosts (for example, Kenny Baker, Jane Froman, Adolphe Menjou) and a cast of regular performers—Kay Armen, John Gibson, Bob Hanna, Al Kelly, Pert Kelton, Frances Langford, Arnold Stang, Edward Trevor and the Mixed Chorus. Frank Gallop and Jimmy Wallington did the announcing and music was by the David Broekman, Al Goodman and Allen Roth orchestras. The drama segment featured a different cast and story each week. In 1942, the program returned after a three-year absence as a 30-minute variety outing with James Melton as the host and the music of David Broekman and his orchestra. The final version of the show aired in 1947–48 with host Gordon MacRae, vocalist Evelyn Knight and comedian Alan Young. John Reed King did the announcing and Victor Young and his orchestra provided the music. See also *The Fred Allen Show*, which was sponsored by Texaco in 1940.

1602. That Brewster Boy. Comedy, 30 min., NBC, 1941–1942; CBS, 1942–1945.

Life in a small town as experienced by Joey Brewster, the mischievous son of Jim and Jane Brewster, prominent residents of the community. Also residing with the family is Nancy, Joey's teenage sister (who has a steady relationship with Phil Hayworth, a medical student). Joey's "cohort in crime" is his best friend Chuck, an all-talk, no-action kid who always gets Joey into more trouble than he is already in—and who always manages to disappear when things get hot, leaving Joey to face the music alone. When Joey thought he could make millions selling door-to-door, he went into business selling Begonia Butter Cutters (cuts butter into the shape of flowers). Jim calls Jane "Mother"; Jane calls him "Dad." Phil calls Joey "Small Fry" and "Sprout." Joey believes Phil is a loser and doesn't want him for a brother-in-law. *Other regular characters:* Herbert Clark, a man who is also fond of Nancy (Phil believes he is a threat to his and Nancy's relationship); Miss Edmond, Joey's English teacher.

Cast: Eddie Firestone, Jr., Arnold Stang, Dick York (*Joey Brewster*); Hugh Studebaker (*Jim Brewster*); Constance Crowder (*Jane Brewster*); Louise Fitch, Patricia Dunlap (*Nancy Brewster*); Bob Bailey (*Phil Hayworth*); Bob Jellison (*Herbert Clark*); Billy Idelson (*Chuck*); Ruth Perrott (*Miss Edmond*). ***Announcer:*** Marvin Miller. ***Music:*** Glenn Welty.

OPENING

JOEY: Nancy's dating Herbert again, so it's up to me to do something. I don't want that drip for a brother-in-law.

MOTHER: Oh, that boy.

FATHER: That boy.

ANNOUNCER: *That Brewster Boy*. Quaker Oats, truly America's super breakfast, brings you *That Brewster Boy* starring Eddie Firestone, Jr. Did you have your Quaker Oats today? In 1942, I resolve to give my family the benefits of a hot breakfast ... delicious, healthful Quaker Oats... Quaker Oats is super-economical, it still costs less than half a cent a serving... So tomorrow ask your grocer for Mother's Oats or Quaker Oats... This is the story of an average American family, the Brewsters. Of course, I don't care what I say when I call all the Brewsters average. That may be true of Mom and Dad and Nancy, but Joey's as unaverage a young sprout as you're likely to know in some time...

CLOSING

ANNOUNCER: Next week, Joey gets himself into a situation that has serious but funny consequences. And we'll probably hear him talking to Chuck on the phone saying—

JOEY: Hello, Chuck. Hey, look, if I'm going to be appointed traffic court judge on Safety Day, I gotta have a campaign slogan. Yes, something sharp. Yes, something that'll make 'em realize I'm a pretty rugged gent; something that'll make 'em see how smart I am, how honest, how trustworthy. You what, you got a slogan for me, Chuck? Yeah, what is it? Oh. "Joey for Judge."

ANNOUNCER: Be sure to tune in again next Monday at this same time for another enjoyable evening with *That Brewster Boy*. Meanwhile, be sure to ask your grocer for Quaker Oats, truly America's super breakfast. This is the Red Network of the National Broadcasting Company.

1603. That Hammer Guy. Crime Drama, 30 min., Mutual, 1952–1953.

Mike Hammer is a New York–based private detective who is tough but has a live-and-let-live philosophy—until it comes to the lowlifes he encounters. "What a crummy joint!" refers to Mike's fleabag of an apartment—cold in winter, sweltering in the summer, "but I call it home." Mike doesn't like being used for target practice, "but it's part of my profession." Mike also likes women—"blondes, brunettes and redheads who look like they just stepped out of a pool." He also has a daily date with someone's fist ("I get beaten up every day of the week") and is always involved with some sort of criminal—from "a beautiful dame in distress to a hood who's aiming for strike three." Hard-hitting, gritty stories relate Mike's experiences as he becomes involved with unscrupulous characters "and lousy jobs. But when I get paid for a job, I do the job." Based on the character created by Mickey Spillane. Also known as *Mike Hammer*.

Cast: Ted deCorsia, Larry Haines (*Mike Hammer*).

OPENING

ANNOUNCER: Here is Larry Haines in the Mickey Spillane mystery *That Hammer Guy*.

MIKE: Like the song says, there's nothing like a dame. And there isn't, you know. You've met all kinds—from the obvious barroom fright who'll stop at nothing to sell a drink to the Park Avenue smoothie who'll stop at nothing to get their Grecian profile on the society page. Yeah, that's what you know about dames, so naturally you're suspicious... [The episode "Laura Fenton" then began with Laura, "105 pounds of platinum topped with curves," entering Mike's office.]

1604. THAT'S A GOOD IDEA. Anthology, 30 min., CBS, 1945.

Dramatizations based on proposals for inventions (submitted by listeners) that could benefit mankind. Dave Vaille was the host and narrator; Jay Stewart did the announcing; Del Castillo and his orchestra provided the music.

1605. THAT'S A GOOD ONE. Comedy, 15 min., NBC Blue, 1943.

A weekly joke-telling session in which guest comedians exchanged humorous stories with a cats of regular comics.

Host: Faye Emerson. ***Regulars:*** Art Elmer, Al Lee Reiser, Ward Wilson. ***Announcer:*** Ed Herlihy. ***Organist:*** John Gart.

1606. THAT'S LIFE. Human Interest, 30 min., CBS, 1946.

The format allowed anyone who wanted to get on the air to do so. Microphones were turned over to eager performers, people with gripes, and to people with a story to tell.

Host: Jay C. Flippen. ***Announcer:*** Jay Stewart. ***Music:*** Ivan Ditmars.

1607. THAT'S MY POP. Comedy, 30 min., CBS, 1945.

Events in the life of a lovable but lazy head of a household—a man whose last means of employment was selling sunglasses during the 1929 eclipse.

Cast: Hugh Herbert (*Father*); Mary Wickes (*Wife*); Peggy Conklin (*Daughter*); Ronald Liss (*Son*). ***Also:*** Jack Albertson, Tony David, Walter Kinsella, Ethel Owen.

1608. THAT'S RICH. Comedy, 30 min., CBS, 1/8/54 to 9/23/54.

Richard "Rich" E. Wilk is a hopeful actor and songwriter struggling to make his mark in Hollywood. He resides at the Baltimore Bigelow Courts with his uncle/business manager Jonathan Wilk (who sold Rich's first song, a love ballad called "When It's Pickle Picking Time in Dixie, Dixie Picked a Pickle for Me"). Rich is down on his luck and feels that he is as low as one can get and still be at the bottom of the barrel. Jonathan is also out of work and is constantly seeking employment—for Rich—and stories relate the mishaps that occur as Rich goes about seeking jobs. *Other regular characters:* Susie Elwood, Rich's girlfriend; Hugh McHugh and Mrs. Carlson, Rich's neighbors; Freckles, the giggly girl with a crush on Rich; Mrs. Elwood, Susie's mother (who dislikes Rich and wants Susie "to have champagne, not warm beer"). Other songs written by Rich include "Ode to a Highway" and "Come to Me, My Mellonhead Baby."

Cast: Stan Freberg (*Richard E. Wilk*); Alan Reed (*Jonathan Wilk*); Daws Butler (*Hugh McHugh*); Patte Chapman (*Susie/Freckles*); Myra Marsh (*Mrs. Elwood*); Jeanne Bates (*Mrs. Carlson*). ***Regulars*** (Various roles): Hans Conried, Patricia Dunlap, Peter Lind Hayes. ***Announcer:*** Bill Anders. ***Music:*** George Fields. ***Producer:*** Al Schwartz.

OPENING

ANNOUNCER: From Hollywood, transcribed,

CBS brings you a gay new comedy show, *That's Rich*, starring Stan Freberg as Rich. Last year in Hollywood, California, there were 356 feature films produced. This multibillion dollar industry employs tens of thousands of people, uses untold quantities of raw material and its products are seen in the four corners of the globe. But no one has summed up the cinema's contribution to the world as well as Richard E. Wilk, when he said it with great sincerity—

RICH: Why can't I get work? I can't seem to get anywhere with my career. Other men have gotten somewhere, got to the top. There must be room at the top because it's so crowded down at the bottom where I am.

ANNOUNCER: That's our hero, Richard E. Wilk. Let's join him now...

THE THEATER GUILD ON THE AIR *see* **THE U.S. STEEL HOUR**

1609. THERE WAS A WOMAN. Anthology, 30 min., NBC, 1937–1938; Mutual, 1945–1946.

Dramatizations of various situations in which a woman played an integral part. Also known as *There's Always a Woman*.

Regular Performers (NBC): Betty Caine, Raymond Edward Johnson. ***Regular Performer (Mutual):*** Arlene Francis. ***Announcers:*** Les Griffith (NBC), Ted McNally (Mutual). ***Music:*** Bob Monroe and Hank Sylvern (Mutual).

1610. THERE'S MUSIC IN THE AIR. Variety, 30 min., CBS, 1953.

A weekly program of music and songs with Donald Richards as the host. Clark Dennis, Nancy Evans and Frances Greer were the regulars; Olin Tice did the announcing and Alfredo Antonini and his orchestra provided the music.

THE THIN MAN *see* **THE ADVENTURES OF THE THIN MAN**

1611. THINK. Anthology, 30 min., ABC, 1953.

Stories designed to make the listener *think*: Suspense tales in which people propelled into unexpected situations use positive thinking. Stories conclude with the resolutions to be determined by the listener.

Host: Dave Ballard (as "The Voice of Think"). ***Announcer:*** Bill Essen. ***Producer:*** Steve Martin.

OPENING

ANNOUNCER: To make you think ... think ... think ... think.

HOST: You live in a world made by you, a world of fact and fantasy. But where does fact end and fantasy begin? This is a program designed to make you think ... think ... think.

CLOSING

HOST: Next week, a study in psychological behavior, John Edward Kingsley's "The Man Who Murdered Stalin." This is a program designed to make you think ... think ... think ... think. Bill Essen speaking. America is sold on ABC, the American Broadcasting Company.

1612. THINK FAST. Game, 30 min., ABC, 1949–1950.

Mason Gross as the host of a weekly program wherein a panel (David Broekman, George Combs, Leon Janney and Eloise McElhone) responded to questions submitted by listeners.

THE THIRD MAN *see* **THE LIVES OF HARRY LIME**

1613. THIRTY MINUTES IN HOLLYWOOD. Variety, 30 min., Mutual, 1937.

A program of music and songs with host George Jessel, a former vaudeville comic, and his wife, film star Norma Talmadge, as the hosts. Sam Carlson, Ernest Chappell and Mary Small were the regulars. Dick Himber and his orchestra provided the music.

1614. THIS DAY IS OURS. Serial, 15 min., CBS, 1938–1940; NBC Blue, 1940–1941.

The dramatic story of Eleanor MacDoanld, the daughter of a missionary, as she struggled to help people in war-torn China. *Other regular characters:* Curtis, a missionary; Paul, the clerical worker; Pat Curtis, Curtis's wife; Wong, Eleanor's friend.

Cast: Templeton Fox, Joan Banks (*Eleanor MacDonald*); Jay Jostyn (*Curtis*); Frank Lovejoy (*Paul*); Alan Devitt (*Wong*); Patricia Dunlap (*Pat Curtis*). ***Announcer:*** Mel Allen. ***Organist:*** Don Becker.

1615. This Is Broadway. Variety, 60 min., CBS, 1949.

A recreation of the music and songs from the Great White Way.

Host: Clifton Fadiman. ***Regulars:*** Adele Clark, Phil Foster, Nancy Franklin, Helen Hayes, George S. Kaufman, Mary McCarty, Frank Parker, Artie Shaw. ***Orchestra:*** Ray Bloch.

1616. This Is Helen Hayes. Anthology, 15 min., Mutual, 1945.

Actress Helen Hayes as the host and narrator of a series of dramatizations depicting the work and sacrifices of Army and Navy nurses. Hal Lansing did the announcing.

1617. This Is Life. Human Interest, 15 min., Mutual, 1941–1943.

A three-times-weekly program in which host Vincent Pelletier read letters submitted by listeners that were meant to help locate missing friends, relatives or possessions. Victor Powell and Marvin Miller did the announcing.

1618. This Is My Best. Anthology, 30 min., Syndicated, 1944–1946.

A weekly series of prestigious dramas featuring top name guests. Edward Arnold, Orson Welles and Don Clark served as the hosts; John McIntire did the announcing.

OPENING

ORSON: Good evening, this is Orson Welles inviting you to listen to Walt Disney's "Snow White and the Seven Dwarfs" on Cresta Blanca's *This Is My Best*.

ANNOUNCER: *This Is My Best*. America's greatest stars in the world in the world's best stories, presented each week by Cresta Blanca, wine of a friendly nature ... symbol of hospitality, compliments to honored guests, a wine to serve proudly saying *This Is My Best*, this is Cresta Blanca. Our guest tonight is Jane Powell, who appears through the courtesy of Metro-Goldwyn-Mayer, producers of *The Picture of Dorian Gray*.

1619. This Is Nora Drake. Serial, 15 min., NBC, 1947–1959.

Dramatic incidents in the life of Nora Drake, a nurse in a large metropolitan hospital.

Cast: Charlotte Holland, Joan Tompkins, Mary Jane Higby (*Nora Drake*); Joseph Conway, Everett Sloane, Ralph Bell (*Arthur Drake*); Evelyn Varden, Elspeth Eric (*Dorothy Stewart*); Arnold Robertson (*Dr. Jensen*); Lesley Woods, Joan Alexander, Mercedes McCambridge (*Peggy Martinson*); Joan Lorring (*Suzanne*); Grant Richards (*Charles Dobbs*); Charlotte Manson (*Gillian Gray*); Alan Hewitt (*Dr. Ken Martinson*). ***Announcers:*** Bill Cullen, Ken Roberts. ***Organist:*** Charles Paul.

OPENING

ANNOUNCER: Toni, Toni, Toni Home Permanents presents—

WOMAN: *This Is Nora Drake*.

ANNOUNCER: *This Is Nora Drake*, a modern story seen through the window of a woman's heart.

1620. This Is Paris. Variety, 30 min., Mutual, 3/1/49 to 9/22/49.

A program of romantic music and songs broadcast from Paris. Maurice Chevalier served as the host and the regulars were Claude Dauphin, Marjorie Dunton, Gaumont Lanvin, Yves Montand and Line Renaud. Paul Baron and his orchestra supplied the music.

1621. This Is the Story. Anthology, 30 min., Mutual, 1944.

Madeleine Carroll as the host of a weekly series that dramatized famous novels.

1622. This Is Your FBI. Anthology, 30 min., ABC, 4/6/45 to 1/30/53.

Harsh dramatizations based on the files of the Federal Bureau of Investigation as seen through the assignments of Jim Taylor, the agency's top operative.

Cast: Stacy Harris (*Jim Taylor*). ***Narrators:*** Dean Carlton, Frank Lovejoy, William Woodson. ***Announcers:*** Milton Cross, Carl Frank, Larry Keating. ***Producer:*** Jerry Devine.

OPENING

ANNOUNCER: *This Is Your FBI*, the official broadcast from the files of the Federal Bureau of Investigation. Tonight, the subject of our FBI file is armed robbery; it's titled "The Larceny Express."

CLOSING

ANNOUNCER: The incidents used in tonight's broadcast are adapted from the files of the Federal Bureau of Investigation. However, all names used are fictitious and any similarity thereof, to the names of persons or places, living or dead, is accidental. *This Is Your FBI* is a Jerry Devine production. This is ABC, the American Broadcasting Company.

1623. This Is Your Life. Variety, 30 min., NBC, 11/9/48 to 5/30/50.

Unsuspecting celebrities were surprised with a capsule history of their lives by host Ralph Edwards. As incidents from a celebrity's life were given, family members and friends were brought on as guests. John Hollbrook did the announcing. Served as the basis for the television series of the same title.

1624. This Life Is Mine. Serial, 15 min., CBS, 1943–1945.

The dramatic story of the Channing family: Eden, the mother, a schoolteacher estranged from her husband, actor Edwin Lorimer; her children, David and Joe; and her younger sister, Jane.

Cast: Betty Winkler (*Eden Channing*); Paul McGrath (*Edwin Lorimer*); Henry M. Neeley (*David Channing*); Raymond Ives, Jr. (*Joe Channing*); Ruth McDevitt (*Jane*). ***Also:*** Bert Burnham, Philip Gordon, Jay Meredith. ***Announcer:*** Tony Marvin. ***Organist:*** John Gart.

1625. This Small Town. Serial, 15 min., NBC, 1940.

Dramatic incidents in the lives of Carrie and Russ Willard, young marrieds who live in a small New England town.

Cast: Joan Banks (*Carrie Willard*); Jay Jostyn (*Russ Willard*). ***Also:*** Eleanor Audley, Carl Eastman. ***Announcer:*** Ed Herlihy.

Those Bartons *see* **The Story of Bud Barton**

1626. Those Good Old Days. Variety, 30 min., NBC Blue, 1942.

A musical revue that revives the music, song and comedy of the early 1900s.

Host: Pat Barnes. ***Regulars:*** Lulu Bates, Ethel Gilbert, Aileen Stanley, Hal Willard. ***Orchestra:*** Joe Rines.

1627. Those We Love. Serial, 30 min., NBC Blue, 1938–1939; NBC Red, 1939–1940; CBS, 1940–1941; NBC Red 1941–1942; CBS, 1942–1943; NBC Red, 1943–1945.

Dramatic events in the life of John Marshall, a lawyer and the widowed father of two children, Kathy and Kit. Emily Mayfield, the children's aunt, helps raise them and the family is cared for by their housekeeper, Martha Newbury. The Marshalls live in Westbridge, Connecticut.

Cast: Hugh Sothern, Oscar O'Shea, Francis X. Bushman (*John Marshall*); Nan Grey (*Kathy Marshall*); Richard Cromwell, Bill Henry (*Kit Marshall*); Virginia Sale (*Martha Newbury*); Alma Kruger (*Emily Mayfield*). ***Announcer:*** Dick Joy.

1628. Those Websters. Comedy, 30 min., CBS, 1945–1946; Mutual, 1946–1948.

The house at 46 River Road in Spring City is home to the Webster family: parents George and Jane and their children Elizabeth (Liz) and William (Billy). George is a grocer and head of the family, but it is the level-headed Jane who guides the family through its trying times (situations caused by George as he tries to help others or by the antics of their mischievous but well-meaning children). *Other regular characters:* Emil Stooler, Bill's friend, a motherless boy who just loves to eat and eat and eat—at the Websters'; and Stewie Stooler, Emil's father.

Cast: Willard Waterman (*George Webster*); Constance Crowder (*Jane Webster*); Joan Alt (*Elizabeth Webster*); Gil Stratton, Jr. (*Billy Webster*); Jerry Spellman (*Emil Stooler*). ***Announcers:*** Charles Irving, Charles Lyon. ***Producers:*** Joe Ainley, Les Weinrot.

OPENING

Sound: Phone ringing.

Woman (picking up receiver): Hello.

Voice: Are you listening to your radio, ma'am?

Woman: Yes.

Voice: To what program are you listening, please?

Woman: *Those Websters*.

Voice: Can you tell me what's advertised?

Woman: Of course, everybody knows that. Delicious Quaker Oats.

Announcer: *Those Websters*, the Quaker Oats program, each week reminds you that families are fun. Now, in just a moment, we'll take you to 46 River Road to see what's doing at the home of *Those Websters*. But first, now let Quaker Oats cut breakfast costs... This delicious growth and energy food costs less than one cent a serving... It's one of the world's finest foods yet it costs less than one cent a serving. We take you now to *Those Websters* for our weekly reminder that families are fun.

1629. THREE CITY BYLINE. Commentary, 15 min., ABC, 1953–1955.

A three-city hookup featuring the commentary of Hy Gardner (New York), Sheilah Graham (Hollywood) and Irv Kupcinet (Chicago).

THE THREE FLATS *see* **JUST NEIGHBORS**

1630. THREE FOR THE MONEY. Game, 60 min., Mutual, 6/26/48 to 9/25/48.

Three players compete in a question-and-answer session that determines one winner. This contestant can win $300 by predicting how three songs to be played by the orchestra will score in popularity with the studio audience (registered by applause). The player could win additional money ($500) by predicting a second bracket of three tunes. A third level existed for players who managed to correctly predict the prior six songs. Here $5,000 could be won if the player could predict an additional grouping of songs.

Host: Clayton "Bud" Collyer.

Vocalists: Russ Emery, Mary Small, the Stardusters Quartet. ***Orchestra:*** Mark Warnow.

1631. THREE RING TIME. Variety, 30 min., CBS, 3/8/43 to 12/20/43.

A program of music, songs and comedy sponsored by Ballantine Beer (the title refers to the sponsor's logo of three interlocking rings). Milton Berle was the host. Charles Laughton and Shirley Ross were the regulars and Bob Crosby and his orchestra provided the music.

1632. THREE SHEETS TO THE WIND. Serial, 30 min., NBC, 2/15/42 to 7/5/42.

The setting is a luxury liner, the *Empress*, which has embarked on a 180-day world cruise. Two of its passengers are not who they seem: Joan Lockwood, in the guise of a high society woman, is actually a master spy for British Intelligence, and Dan O'Brien, who appears to be an intoxicated American playboy, is a government intelligence agent. Their missions, working independently of the other (at first), were to uncover a mysterious killer linked with the theft of a set of fabulous jewels and its associated "Sultan's Curse." The 26-episode adventure follows their efforts to uncover the source behind the curse as the ship visits "the bizarre ports of the Seven Seas." *Three Sheets to the Wind* was a radio rarity; it was actually the audition for a motion picture (to be called *Three Sheets to the Wind*) that appears to have never been made. The series was conceived under the title *World Cruise*. Dan resides in cabin E-28; Joan in cabin D-47.

Cast: Brian Donlevy, John Wayne (*Dan O'Brien*); Helga Moray (*Joan Lockwood*). ***Announcer:*** Ray Garrett. ***Music:*** Edward Ward. ***Producer:*** Tay Garnett.

OPENING

ANNOUNCER: From Hollywood, California, Tay Garnett, veteran film director, offers his colorful radio creation, *Three Sheets to the Wind*, starring Brian Donlevy with Helga Moray. I know you'll all be happy to meet the man who has been responsible for many of your favorite films in the past, Hollywood's foremost adventure director. He wants to tell you about his latest experiment, startling, exciting and new. Ladies and gentlemen, this is Tay Garnett.

TAY: Thank you. Good evening. You have all heard radio plays adapted from motion pictures. Now, I believe for the first time, we bring you a story on the air from which the picture will later be made. The screenplay *Three Sheets to the Wind* bounces from the prolific pen of Ken England, author of many of Hollywood's greatest comedies. It was originally titled *World Cruise*. To add realism to the film, I circled the globe in a small boat, photographing in many colorful countries that are no longer accessible to the people of the free world. Of course, that was for the movie. Now we're ready to make that movie and we need your help. We want to bring you this picture before we make it. Won't you write us your opinion? Yours will be the voices that will ultimately guide us in the production of our motion picture. And now with your kind indulgence, we'll shove off on the first leg of our adventure.

CLOSING

ANNOUNCER: And so the curtain descends on

the first episode of *Three Sheets to the Wind*. And now a final word from our producer-director, Tay Garnett.

TAY: Ladies and gentlemen, you have just heard reel one of *Three Sheets to the Wind* in what is believed to be the first sneak preview of a picture ever given before the picture was made. Won't you let us hear from you, tell us how you liked it? You can help us greatly. Thank you.

1633. THUNDER OVER PARADISE. Serial, 15 min., NBC Blue, 1939–1940.

Dramatic events in the life of a woman rancher (Barbara) living in Central America. The program begins with Barbara facing a crisis: the outbreak of a revolution.

Cast: Laurette Fillbrandt, Elizabeth Day (*Barbara*); Sid Ellstrom, Luis Van Rooten (*Gen. Durango*); Mike Romano (*Ranch hand*); Bill Crawford (*Aviator*).

1634. THURSTON THE MAGICIAN. Adventure, 15 min., NBC Blue, 1932–1933.

Dramatic skits that explore acts of magic as told by Howard Thurston, a master magician. Cliff Soubier portrayed Thurston and his assistant was played by Carlton Brickert. William Kephart did the announcing.

1635. TILLIE THE TOILER. Comedy, 30 min., CBS, 4/11/42 to 10/10/42.

A radio adaptation of the comic strip by Russ Westover that follows events in the life of Tillie Jones, a hard-working woman who feels it is her duty to help people in trouble. *Other regular characters:* Mac, Tillie's boyfriend; Simpkins, the absent-minded gentleman; Mrs. Jones, Tillie's mother.

Cast: Caryl Smith (*Tillie Jones*); John Brown (*Simpkins*); Billy Lynn (*Mac*); Margaret Burlen (*Mrs. Jones*). ***Music:*** Alexander Semmler.

1636. TIM AND IRENE. Variety, 30 min., NBC Blue, 1934–1935; NBC Red, 6/28/36 to 9/27/36.

A weekly program of music, songs and comedy with Tim Ryan and Irene Ryan as the hosts. Teddy Bergman (later to become Alan Reed) and Martin Boles were the regulars. Don Wilson did the announcing and Donald Voorhees and his orchestra provided the music.

1637. TIME FOR LOVE. Drama, 30 min., CBS, 1/15/53 to 5/27/54.

Dianne La Volte is a mysterious international figure for law and order. Stories relate her adventures as she helps people threatened by evil.

Cast: Marlene Dietrich (*Dianne La Volte*); Robert Readick (*Reporter*). ***Announcer:*** Lee Vines. ***Music:*** Alec Wilder. ***Producer:*** Marlene Dietrich.

TIME TO SHINE *see* **HAL KEMP IS ON THE AIR FOR GRIFFIN**

1638. TIME TO SMILE. Variety, 30 min., NBC, 1944.

Eddie Cantor as the host of a weekly program of musical numbers and comedy skits. John Brown, Arthur Q. Bryan, Joan Davis, Bert Gordon and Nora Martin were the regulars. Harry Von Zell did the announcing and Leonard Sues and his orchestra provided the music.

1639. TIME'S A-WASTIN'. Game, 30 min., CBS, 1948.

Selected members of the studio audience competed in a series of question-and-answer sessions designed to be played in ten-second intervals. Each correct answer to a question earned a player a merchandise prize, the value of which began at $1,000 and decreased by $100 with each second the player used to answer.

Host: Clayton "Bud" Collyer.

1640. THE TIMID SOUL. Comedy, 30 min., Mutual, 1941–1942.

A radio adaptation of the comic strip by H.T. Webster that relates the mishaps of Casper Milquetoast, a timid soul whose main goal in life was to become more assertive.

Cast: Billy Lynn (*Casper Milquetoast*); Cecil Roy (*Madge Milquetoast, his wife*). ***Also:*** Jackson Beck, Mona Moray, Katherine Renwick.

1641. TITLE TALES. Game, 30 min., Mutual, 1940.

The format called for a cast to relate a story based on five song titles that were submitted by a listener. Their failure to relate a satisfactory story earned the listener $50.

Host: Sylvia Rhodes. ***Cast:*** Bert Farber, Paul

Jones, the Devere Sisters, the Marathon Melody Men. ***Announcer:*** Bill Frost. ***Orchestra:*** Jimmy James.

1642. T-MAN. Anthology, 30 min., CBS, 7/1/50 to 9/2/50.

Dramatizations based on the files of the U.S. Treasury Department. Dennis O'Keefe appeared as Treasury Agent Steve Larsen and Bob Lemond did the announcing.

OPENING

ANNOUNCER: *T-Man*, starring Dennis O'Keefe. T-Man, the law enforcement agent of the Treasury Department, skilled fighter against crime, relentless enemy of the underworld. T-Man Steve Larsen, played by Dennis O'Keefe, in tonight's transcribed treasury case, "The Big Mexican Dope."

1643. TO BE PERFECTLY FRANK. Variety, 15 min., NBC, 1953–1954.

A twice-weekly entertainment session in which host Frank Sinatra introduced his own records, sang one live tune with a small combo and played the records of popular singers (for example, Ella Fitzgerald and Eddie Fisher).

1644. TODAY AT THE DUNCANS. Comedy, 15 min., CBS, 1942–1943.

A daily series that related humorous incidents in the life of the Duncan family. Frank Nelson played the father; Mary Lansing was his wife; Dix Davis played their son.

1645. TOM CORBETT, SPACE CADET. Science Fiction, 30 min., ABC, 1/1/52 to 7/3/52.

Tom Corbett is a cadet at Space Academy, an Earth-based West Point where young men and women train to become Solar Guards, the agents of a celestial police force established to protect Earth, Mars, Venus and Jupiter (the planets that comprise a universal council of peace known as the Solar Alliance). Stories, which are set in the year 2350, follow Tom as he and his assistant, Astro, the Venusian, battle the sinister forces of evil throughout the universe. *Other regular characters:* Cadet Roger Manning; Capt. Larry Strong; Dr. Joan Dale. Based on the television series of the same title.

Cast: Frankie Thomas (*Tom Corbett*); Al Markim (*Astro*); Jan Merlin (*Roger Manning*); Edward Bryce (*Larry Strong*); Patricia Ferris (*Dr. Joan Dale*). ***Announcer:*** Jackson Beck.

OPENING

VOICE: Stand by to raise ship. Blast off minus five ... four... three ... two ... one ... zero.

SOUND: Ship heard blasting off.

ANNOUNCER: Kellogg's Pep, the build-up wheat cereal, invites you to rocket into the future with *Tom Corbett, Space Cadet.* As roaring rockets blast off to distant planets and far-flung stars, we take you to the age of the conquest of space with *Tom Corbett, Space Cadet.*

1646. THE TOM MIX RALSTON STRAIGHTSHOOTERS. Western, 15 min., NBC Red, 1933–1937; NBC Blue, 1937–1942; Mutual, 1944–1951.

A series of Old West adventures with Tom Mix, a daring crusader for justice and owner of the TM-Bar Ranch near Dobie, Texas. He lived on the ranch with his wards Jane and Jimmy, and was assisted by Pecos Williams and a character called Wrangler. (When the series returned in 1944 after a two-year absence, Sheriff Mike Shaw became Tom's new sidekick; Curley Bradley, who previously played Pecos, became the new Tom Mix.) Although Tom was a rancher, he spent little time doing so. He was "greased lightning on the draw," often worked with the Texas Rangers and devoted his life to battling evil wherever he found it. *Other regular characters:* Lee Loo, the Chinese cook; Amos Q. Snood, the "Scrooge" of Dobie; Calamity, Tom's accident-prone friend; Tony, "The Wonder Horse," Tom's horse. Tom and his friends were called "straightshooters—and straightshooters always win." The program, sponsored by Ralston cereals, is also known as *The Tom Mix Show* and *The Tom Mix Straightshooters*.

Cast: Artells Dickson, Russell Thorson, Jack Holden, Curley Bradley (*Tom Mix*); Curley Bradley (*Pecos Williams*); Percy Hemus (*Wrangler*); Winifred Toomey, Jane Webb (*Jane*); Andy Donnelly, George Gobel, Hugh Rowlands (*Jimmy*); Leo Curley, DeWitt McBride, Harold Peary, Willard Waterman (*Sheriff Mike Shaw*); Sidney Ellstrom, Curley Bradley (*Amos Q. Snood*); Bruno Wick (*Lee Loo*); Bob Jellison (*Calamity*); Patricia Dunlap (*Pat Curtis*); Arthur Peterson (*Judge Parsons*). ***Announcers:*** Frank Ferguson, Don Gordon, Les Griffith.

OPENING

SONG: Shredded Ralston for your breakfast, starts a day off shining bright; gives you lots of cowboy energy with a flavor that's just right. It's delicious and nutritious; bite-size and ready to eat; take a tip from Tom, go tell your Mom, Shredded Ralston can't be beat.

ANNOUNCER: *The Tom Mix Ralston Straight-shooters* bring you action, mystery and mile-a-minute thrills in radio's biggest Western detective program. Tonight, you're about to hear another episode in "Mystery of the Border Smugglers." Tom Mix is working with the Texas Rangers to smash a powerful gang of smugglers. In a moment, we'll learn what happens next. But first, here's Pecos Williams.

PECOS: Howdy, everybody. Hey, these sure are days when it's up to you and me ... to keep in top condition. And the best way I know to do this is to saddle up every morning with a hot dish of good old Ralston ... it packs cowboy energy ... why not tell your maw tonight to get you a red and white checkerboard package of good old Ralston tomorrow?

ANNOUNCER: And now come up to the Rio Grande country. In the light of a full moon, Tom and Pecos are galloping toward the old abandoned ranch house, not realizing they are about to step into a dangerous trap...

CLOSING

ANNOUNCER: What will happen next? For fast action, mystery and thrills, be sure to listen tomorrow—

PECOS: Hold it there, Don, it's round-up time, so let's get going.

TOM (over his horse whinnying): Up Tony, up boy, up [he rides off].

PECOS: This here's Pecos, reminding you to buy Defense Bonds to help Uncle Sam win the war. You can buy them at your bank, post office, or ask your newspaper carrier or retailer for them. Don't forget to tune in to Tom Mix tomorrow at 5:45. Good night.

1647. TOM, TIMMY AND MAE. Variety, 15 min., NBC, 1949.

A program of music, songs, skits and chatter with Tom Glazzer as Tom and Mae Questel as Timmy and Mae.

TOMMY DORSEY AND HIS ORCHESTRA *see* **THE TOMMY DORSEY SHOW**

1648. THE TOMMY DORSEY SHOW. Variety, 30 min., NBC, 1937–1946.

A weekly program of music and songs that is also known as *The Raleigh and Kool Cigarette Program*, *The Tommy Dorsey Variety Show* and *Tommy Dorsey and His Orchestra*.

Host: Tommy Dorsey. ***Regulars:*** Bunny Bergan, Ziggy Elman, Connie Haines, Sy Oliver, Buddy Rich, Frank Sinatra, Jo Stafford. ***Orchestra:*** Tommy Dorsey.

OPENING

ANNOUNCER: The *Raleigh and Kool Cigarette Program* with Tommy Dorsey.

SONG: Two cigarettes on the air.

ANNOUNCER: And here he is, the star of our show, Tommy Dorsey.

1649. TOMMY RIGGS AND BETTY LOU. Variety, 30 min., NBC, 10/1/38 to 9/13/46.

Music and songs coupled with comedy skits about a mischievous seven-year-old girl named Betty Lou. Tommy Riggs played himself and provided the voice for Betty Lou. (In 1943, Betty Lou became Tommy's niece in skits and Wally Maher was added as Wilbur, Betty Lou's dim-witted boyfriend.) Bea Benaderet, Verna Felton, Bill Goodwin and Bea Wain appeared in skits; Jimmy Cash, Anita Kurt and Eileen Woods provided the songs.

Announcers: Bill Goodwin, Jack Mather, Paul Masterson, Dan Seymour, Don Wilson. ***Orchestra:*** Larry Clinton, Frank DeVol, Felix Mills.

1650. TONIGHT AT HOAGY'S. Variety, 30 min., Mutual, 1944–1945.

A program of music and songs set at the home of composer Hoagy Carmichael (who served as the host to a weekly jam session). The regulars were Ruby Dandridge, Opie Cates, Pee Wee Hunt and the Thrasher Sisters. The Hoagy Carmichael Orchestra supplied the music.

1651. TONIGHT ON BROADWAY. Variety, 30 min., CBS, 1946.

Singer Connee Boswell as host of a weekly program of music and songs from the Great White Way. Bob Doyle and Ted Husing were the regulars. Ken Roberts did the announcing; Ray Bloch and his orchestra provided the music.

TONY AND GUS *see* **APPENDIX**

1652. THE TONY MARTIN SHOW. Variety, 30 min., CBS, 1947–1948.

A weekly program of music and songs with Tony Martin as the host. Bill Forman and Jimmy Wallington did the announcing; Jeff Alexander and his chorus provided songs; and Victor Young and his orchestra supplied the music.

1653. TONY WONS' SCRAPBOOK. Variety, 30 min., CBS, 1940.

A weekly program of romantic poetry readings, music and songs with host Tony Wons. Vocalist Shirley Sadley provided the songs; Lewis Rowen did the announcing and Irma Glenn and her orchestra supplied the music.

1654. TOO MANY COOKS. Comedy, 30 min., CBS, 7/3/50 to 8/21/50.

Hal March and Mary Jane Croft as the parents of a family with ten children. George Fenneman, Jerry Hausner, Bob Sweeney and Willard Waterman were also in the cat. Marlin Skiles provided the music.

1655. THE TOP GUY. Crime Drama, 30 min., ABC, 10/17/51 to 5/28/53.

The story of a police commissioner (played by J. Scott Smart) and his battle against crime. Ken Lynch played his assistant.

1656. TOP SECRET. Adventure, 30 min., NBC, 6/12/50 to 10/26/50.

Karen Gaza is a beautiful World War II undercover agent for Central Intelligence. She also works for Britain's MI-2 and has been called "the cleverest operator MI-2 ever had" by her superior, Lord Harland. Without recognition and without fear, Karen fights for the forces of freedom. Stories relate her exploits as she goes behind the lines to defeat the enemy.

Cast: Ilona Massey (*Karen Gaza*); Ian Martin (*Lord Harland*). ***Announcer:*** Fred Collins. ***Music:*** Roy Shields. ***Producer:*** Harry W. Junkin.

OPENING

ANNOUNCER: This story is *Top Secret*. *Top Secret*, starring beautiful Ilona Massey as the Baroness Karen Gaza in transcribed stories of international intrigue and espionage. Brought to you each week at this time by NBC. Tonight, as Assignment Nine, "Disaster in London."

CLOSING

ANNOUNCER: You have just heard Ilona Massey starring in NBC's *Top Secret*, stories of intrigue and espionage brought to you each week at this time. Here is Miss Massey to tell you about next week's show.

ILONA: Next week, the story of Catherine Scotland and the fluttering of a bird started danger. The case of a wounded pigeon, a story until now *Top Secret*. This is NBC, the National Broadcasting Company.

TOPPER *see* **THE ADVENTURES OF TOPPER**

TOWN HALL TONIGHT *see* **THE FRED ALLEN SHOW**

1657. TRANSATLANTIC QUIZ. Game, 15 min., NBC/BBC, 4/15/44 to 9/2/45.

The program is similar in format to *Information Please* and has a panel in the United States and Great Britain attempting to answer some rather difficult questions submitted by listeners.

Host (United States): Alistair Cooke. ***Hosts*** (Great Britain): Lionel Hale, Ronny Waldman. ***U.S. Panel:*** Buck Crouse, Christopher Morley. ***British Panel:*** Prof. Dennis Brazan, Col. David Niven.

1658. TREASURE HOUSE OF SONG. Variety, 30 min., Mutual, 1943.

A weekly program of music and songs with Lucia Albonese, Alois Harille and Francesca Valentino. Alfredo Antonini and his orchestra provided the music.

1659. TREASURE TRAILS OF SONG. Variety, 25 min., NBC, 1941.

Country and western music and songs with Mary Martha Briney, Dick Fulton, Peggy Nelson, Paul Shannon, the Kinder Sisters and the Pioneer Quartet. Aneurin Bodycombe and his orchestra supplied the music.

1660. TREASURY AGENT. Drama, 30 min., ABC, 4/14/47 to 6/6/48.

The work of the U.S. Treasury Department as seen through the assignments of Joe Lincoln, the U.S. Treasury Chief. Based on official files from the Treasury Department.

Cast: Raymond Edward Johnson (*Joe Lincoln*). ***Narrator:*** Elmer Lincoln Drey (retired chief coordinator of all law enforcement agencies within the Treasury Department). ***Music:*** Ralph Norman. ***Producer:*** Phillips H. Lord.

OPENING

ANNOUNCER: The American Broadcasting Company presents *Treasury Agent.*

VOICE: United States Treasury, largest group of law enforcement agencies in the world.

VOICE: The United States Secret Service. We protect the President of the United States at all times. And protect the money of the United States from counterfeiting.

VOICE: United States Revenue Intelligence. Jurisdiction over tax fraud evasion.

VOICE: The United States Bureau of Narcotics.

VOICE: Bureau of Customs, Alcohol Tax Unit.

VOICE: United States Coast Guard—crimes committed on the high seas.

ANNOUNCER: *Treasury Agent*, based on the general modus operandi of the United States Treasury Agents, operating here and all over the world.

1661. TREASURY STAR PARADE. Variety, 15 min., Syndicated, 1942–1944.

A daily program that mixes music and songs with dramatic skits—all performed by guests and sponsored by the U.S. Government.

Host: Carlton KaDell. ***Recurring Guests:*** Carol Bruce, Jessica Dragonette, Patsy Garrett, Georgia Gibbs, Frank Sinatra. ***Orchestra:*** William Artzt, David Broekman and the Treasury Ensemble.

1662. TREASURY VARIETIES. Variety, 30 min., Mutual, 1949–1950.

A program of music and songs featuring Henry Jerome and his orchestra. Frank Walldecker did the announcing and the regulars were Hal Burton, Morrie Allen and the Glee Club, and the Three Jays.

1663. TREAT TIME. Variety, 15 min., CBS, 1941.

The program, sponsored by Armour Meats, presented skits based on composers' lives. Buddy Cole served as the host; Marvin Miller did the announcing; and Caesar Petrillo and his orchestra supplied the music.

1664. A TREE GROWS IN BROOKLYN. Drama, 30 min., NBC, 7/8/49 to 9/30/49.

Events in the lives of the Nolans, a poor but proud family living in a Brooklyn tenement in 1912: Johnny, the father, an alcoholic who struggles to provide for his family by taking whatever jobs he can find; Katie, his strong-willed wife; their daughter Francie, the dreamer who believes better times are coming; and their son Neely, the realist who accepts the life he is living. Based on the book by Betty Smith.

Cast: John Larkin (*Johnny Nolan*); Anne Seymour (*Katie Nolan*); Denise Alexander (*Francie Nolan*); Bernie Raeburn (*Neely Nolan*).

1665. TREMENDOUS TRIFFLES. Drama, 5 min., CBS, 1955.

Capsule stories based on the syndicated newspaper column *Tremendous Triffles*. George Hicks was the host and narrator.

1666. TROMAN HARPER, RUMOR DETECTIVE. Commentary, 15 min., Mutual, 1942–1943.

A wartime anti-propaganda program in which news correspondent Troman Harper set the record straight about various rumors.

OPENING

ANNOUNCER: Here's Troman Harper, the Rumor Detective, with the truth about rumors, presented by Groves Bromo Quinine Cold Tablets.

TROMAN: Good evening. If you believe rumors, you're a sucker; if you repeat rumors, you're one of Hitler's best soldiers. Learn the truth about rumors. The truth is a banner; with it, you can jab and slice a rumor to ribbons.

1667. THE TROUBLE WITH THE TRUITTS. Comedy, 30 min., NBC, 6/11/50 to 9/20/51.

The Truitts are a family of five who live in the town of Hope Springs, U.S.A. Elmer, head of the family, is the owner of the Bit of Cheer Greeting Card Company. Gert, his wife, is an understanding woman who helps guide the family through its trying times. Their children are Gladys, Maggie and Clarence. Also living with them is Elmer's father, lovingly referred to as "Grandpa." Stories relate the comic mishaps that befall the various family members (or, as the announcer says, "A comedy of family based on the proposition that a family may be a lot of trouble, but it's also a lot of fun"). *Other regular characters:* Roscoe, Gladys's boyfriend; Hugo, Clarence's friend. Also known as *The Truitts*.

Cast: John Dehner (*Elmer Truitt*); Constance Crowder (*Gert Truitt*); Barbara DuPar, Jane Webb (*Gladys Truitt*); Dawn Bender (*Maggie Truitt*); Eddie Firestone, Jr., Gil Stratton, Jr. (*Clarence Truitt*); Parley Baer, Ralph Moody (*Gramps*); Charles Woolf (*Roscoe*); Billy Idelson (*Hugo*). ***Announcers:*** Eddie King, Arch Presley. ***Music:*** William Lava. ***Producer:*** Bill Carne.

OPENING

ANNOUNCER: During the next half-hour, we'd like you to meet the Truitts, a delightful American family who are all set to win their way into the hearts of the radio public. The Truitts are real people drawn from the broad canvas of contemporary life. They'll probably remind you of your neighbor down the street, or maybe you'll see reflected in them your own family and some of the fun and trouble you've had together. Radio audiences will be quick to identify themselves with the Truitts and to add them to their list of favorite radio families, a list which now includes the Aldriches, the Fibber McGees and *The Halls of Ivy*. What's trouble for the Truitts can be good news for you. The National Broadcasting Company brings you *The Trouble with the Truitts*. Well, let's see what's troubling the Truitts this time. It's a sweltering hot night in Hope Springs. Hot outside and hotter inside as Elmer and Gert are in the living room...

CLOSING

ANNOUNCER: The National Broadcasting Company invites you to join us next week at this same time for another laugh at *The Trouble with the Truitts*.

1668. TRUE ADVENTURE. Anthology, 30 min., CBS, 1937.

Floyd Gibbons as the host of a weekly series of stories based on suggestions submitted by listeners (who each received a cash prize if their story was selected).

1669. TRUE DETECTIVE MYSTERIES. Anthology, 30 min., CBS, 1929–1938; Mutual, 1938–1958.

Dramatizations based on stories from the pages of *True Detective* magazine. Following each story, the magazine's editor offered a $1,000 reward for information leading to the arrest of a wanted criminal.

Host-Narrators: Richard Keith (as *John Shuttleworth*, the editor of *True Detective* magazine), John Griggs (as the unnamed editor when Shuttleworth's name was dropped). ***Announcers:*** Frank Dunne, Hugh James. ***Music:*** Chet Kingsbury, Paul Taubman.

OPENING

ANNOUNCER: And now *True Detective Mysteries*. In cooperation with the editor of *True Detective* magazine and the Mutual Broadcasting System, we present *True Detective Mysteries*.

1670. TRUE OR FALSE. Game, 30 min., Mutual, 1938; NBC Blue, 1938–1943; Mutual, 1948–1956.

Two six-member teams compete (male vs. female). The format has the teams responding to a series of true or false questions with the highest scoring team winning $30 (the prize was later increased to $5 per correct response).

Hosts: Dr. Harry Hagen, Eddie Dunn, Bill Slater. ***Announcer:*** Glenn Riggs.

1671. THE TRUE STORY HOUR. Anthology, 60 min., CBS, 1928–1932.

Dramatizations based on features in *True Story* magazine. The program was hosted by and sometimes starred the characters of Mary and Bob.

Cast: Nora Stirling (*Mary*); William Brenton, Cecil Secrest, David Ross (*Bob*). ***Announcers:*** Paul Douglas, Ted Husing. ***Music:*** Howard Barlow.

THE TRUITTS *see* **THE TROUBLE WITH THE TRUITTS**

1672. TRUTH OR CONSEQUENCES. Game, 30 min., CBS, 1940; NBC, 1940–1950; CBS, 1950–1951; NBC, 1952–1956.

A contestant, chosen from the studio audience, was asked a question that was nearly impossible to answer. When the player could not provide an answer, he had to pay the consequences by performing a silly stunt in return for prizes.

Host: Ralph Edwards. ***Announcers:*** Mel Allen, Ken Carpenter, Clayton "Bud" Collyer, Milton Cross, Ed Herlihy, Ken Roberts, Verne Smith, Jay Stewart, Harlow Wilcox. ***Music:*** Buddy Cole.

OPENING

CHORUS: D-U-Z, D-U-Z...

GIRL VOCALIST: Put DUZ in your washing machine, take your clothes out bright and clean; when you DUZ your wash, you'll sing "DUZ does everything."

ANNOUNCER: Hello, there, we've been waiting for you; it's time to play *Truth or Consequences*. Yes, *Truth or Consequences*, the show that does everything on the air, is brought to you by DUZ, the soap that does everything in your wash. And here he is, the star of our show, Ralph *Truth or Consequences* Edwards.

Note: While the radio series paved the way for a successful television version (1950–1965), it also produced three early television experiments with Ralph Edwards as the host. The first telecast on 7/1/41 was an adaptation of the radio program with stunts geared for a visual medium (for example, a player performing a hula-hula dance in a grass skirt). May 27, 1944, saw the second attempt, a simulcast of a radio episode. The final test occurred on 1/21/49 and featured stunts designed for video (for example, people taking a pie in the face).

1673. TUNE IN WITH LUCIE ARNAZ. Interview, 5 min., Syndicated, 1978.

A 26-episode series of celebrity interviews with actress Lucie Arnaz as the host and interviewer. Sponsored by S.C. Johnson and Son.

1674. TUNE UP TIME. Variety, 30 min., CBS, 1939–1940.

Singer Tony Martin as the host of a weekly program of music and songs. David Loughlin, Kay Thompson and the Rhythm Singers were the regulars. Dan Seymour did the announcing and Andre Kostelanetz and his orchestra provided the music.

1675. TUNES WITH TRENDLER. Variety, 30 min., Mutual, 1952–1953.

Orchestra leader Robert Trendler as the host of a weekly program of music and songs. Marshall Kent did the announcing and vocalists Tony Fontaine and Paul Raye were the regulars. Robert Trendler's orchestra provided the music.

1676. THE TWENTY-FIRST PRECINCT. Crime Drama, 30 min., CBS, 1953–1956.

Frank Kennelly is the captain in command of the Twenty-First Police Precinct in New York City. The precinct covers nine-tenths of a square mile between Fifth Avenue and the East River and is responsible for protecting the 173,000 people who live there. Through Frank's eyes, "a factual account of the way police work in the world's largest city" is depicted. Each program is devoted to a single crime and the work of detectives as they attempt to solve the crime is presented in a manner similar to *Dragnet*, but without music and in a somber atmosphere.

Cast: Everett Sloane (*Capt. Frank Kennelly*); Ken Lynch (*Lt. Matt King*); Harold J. Stone (*Sgt. Waters*); Jack Orrisa (*Sgt. Collins*). ***Announcers:*** Art Hanna, Bob Hill. ***Producer:*** Stanley Niss.

OPENING (typical; each begins with the reporting of a crime)

SOUND: Switchboard telephone ringing.

VOICE: Twenty-First Precinct, Sgt. Collins. Who's trying to kill her? How old is the girl? Sixteen. Where is this? Yeah, East 75th Street in the basement.

FRANK: You're in the Muster Room of the Twenty-First Precinct, the nerve center. A call is coming through. You will follow, by transcription, the action taken pursuant to that call from this minute until the final report is written in the 124 Room of the Twenty-First Precinct.

ANNOUNCER: *The Twenty-First Precinct*. It's just lines on a map of the city of New York. Most of the 173,000 people wedged into the nine-tenths of a square mile between Fifth Avenue and the East River wouldn't know if you asked them if they lived and worked in the Twenty-First. Whether they know it or not, the security of their homes, their persons and their property is the job of the men of the Twenty-First Precinct.

FRANK: The Twenty-First—160 patrolmen, 11 sergeants and four lieutenants of whom I am the boss. My name is Kennelly, Frank Kennelly, I'm captain in command of the Twenty-First.

CLOSING

FRANK: And so it goes, around the clock, through the week, every day, every year. A police precinct in the city of New York is a flesh-and-blood merry-go-round. Anyone can catch the brass ring—or the brass ring can catch anyone.

ANNOUNCER: *The Twenty-First Precinct*, a transcribed, factual account of the way police work in the world's largest city, is presented with the official cooperation of the Patrolman's Benevolent Association, an organization of more than 20,000 members of the police department, city of New York. This is CBS, the Columbia Broadcasting System.

1677. TWENTY QUESTIONS. Game, 30 min., Mutual, 1946–1954.

Panelists had to identify persons, places or objects within 20 questions. If the panel failed to do so, the listener who submitted the item won a prize. The "Mystery Voice," speaking from an isolation booth, provided descriptions of the objects for the home audience. Served as the basis for the television series of the same title.

Hosts: Bill Slater, Jay Jackson. ***Panel:*** Bobby McGuire, Herb Polesie, Florence Rinard, Fred Van Deventer. ***Mystery Voices:*** Bruce Elliott, Frank Waldecker. ***Commercial Spokeswoman*** (for Ronson lighters): Charlotte Manson. ***Announcer:*** Frank Waldecker.

1678. TWENTY-SIX BY CORWIN. Anthology, 30 min., CBS, 5/4/41 to 11/9/41.

A 26-episode series of stories written or adapted by Norman Corwin. *Stories include:*

1. Murder in Studio One. Minerva Pious, Eddie Mayehoff, Ruth Gordon and Kenny Delmar in the story of a female sleuth and her efforts to find the killer of a radio announcer.

2. Radio Primer. A comical look at the radio industry with Frank Gallop and Everett Sloane.

3. Lip Service. Ted de Corsia, Larry Adler and Frank Lovejoy in a comedy about a hillbilly harmonica player who becomes a government diplomat.

4. Old Salt. June Havoc, Larry Robinson and Everett Sloane in a story about an old sea captain who spins tall tales to his nephew.

5. The Human Angle. Frank Lovejoy, Everett Sloane and Martin Wolfson in a strange tale about a deep sea diver who finds a live man trapped in a sunken ship.

Host: Norman Corwin. ***Regular Performers:*** Frank Lovejoy, Eddie Mayehoff, Everett Sloane, Hester Sondergaard. ***Music:*** Lyn Murray, Mark Warnow. ***Producer:*** Norman Corwin.

OPENING

(from "The People, Yes," 5/17/41)

ANNOUNCER: The Columbia Workshop presents the third of *Twenty-Six by Corwin*, "The People, Yes." Tonight, Columbia is privileged to present a special radio premiere of a section from a new American opera by Earl Robinson and Norman Corwin. This opera, suggested by Carl Sandburg's volume "The People, Yes," is being prepared for Broadway production and tonight's broadcast marks the first public performance to be heard.

CLOSING

ANNOUNCER: You've been listening to the premiere performance of *The People, Yes*, a new American opera by Earl Robinson and Norman Corwin, suggested by Carl Sandburg's volume of that name. Next week at this time, the Columbia Workshop will present the fourth of *Twenty-Six by Corwin*, a new comedy entitled "Lip Service" and starring the great harmonica virtuoso, Larry Adler. This is the Columbia Broadcasting System.

1679. TWENTY THOUSAND YEARS IN SING SING. Anthology, 30 min., NBC Blue, 1933–1939.

Dramatizations from the files of Sing Sing Prison (the title was derived from the total time being served by the inmates). Lewis E. Lawes, the warden of Sing Sing, served as the host and narrator. Joseph Bell interviewed Lawes before and after each dramatization and Kelvin Keech did the announcing.

1680. THE TWO DAFFODILS. Variety, 15 min., Syndicated, 1932.

An early variety series featuring the team of Duke Attenbury and Ken Gillum.

1681. TWO ON A CLUE. Crime Drama, 15 min., CBS, 1944–1946.

The series, which dramatized actual case histories, followed the investigations of Jeff and Debby Spencer, a husband-and-wife private detective team.

Cast: Ned Wever (*Jeff Spencer*); Louise Fitch (*Debby Spencer*); John Gibson (*Police Sgt. Cornelius Trumbull*). ***Announcer:*** Alice Yourman.

1682. Two on a Shoestring. Comedy-Drama, 15 min., Mutual, 10/1/38 to 12/16/38.

The trials and tribulations of two small-town career girls as they struggled to succeed as radio personalities in New York City. Peggy Zinke (as Sally) and Eleanor Phelps were the girls; Dick Keith played the hotel manager.

1683. Two Thousand Plus. Anthology, 30 min., Mutual, 3/15/50 to 1/2/52.

Chilling science fiction tales set in the future—at a time when science can control various aspects of life—and at a time when science can go awry.

Announcer: Ken Marvin. ***Music:*** Emerson Buckley, Milton Kaye. ***Producers:*** Sherman H. Dryer, Robert Weenolsen.

OPENING

Announcer: *Two Thousand Plus*, science fiction adventures from the world of tomorrow, the years beyond 2,000 A.D. Tonight, *Two Thousand Plus* presents "The Insect."

CLOSING

Announcer: Next week a strange drama of a silver rocket and an unseen visitor from space. Be sure to listen to *Two Thousand Plus*, radio's different series. This is the Mutual Broadcasting System.

1684. Uncle Don. Children, 30 min., WOR (N.Y.), 9/28 to 2/49; Mutual, 1938–1939.

An early program for the small fry that set the pace for others to follow. The program was basically a local New York series, broadcast by WOR and appearing briefly on the Mutual network. The host, Uncle Don, entertained kids with music (he played piano), songs, stories, birthday announcements, talent contests and advice.

Host: Don Carney as Uncle Don. ***Announcers:*** Jack Barry, Joe Bolton, Norman Brokenshire, Barry Gray, Arthur Hale, Frank Knight, Henry Morgan, Floyd Neal. ***Producer:*** Don Carney.

OPENING

Don (singing): Hello, nephews, nieces too; mothers, daddies, how are you? This is Uncle Don all set to go with a meeting on the radio.

1685. Uncle Ezra's Radio Station. Variety, 15 min., NBC, 1934–1938; 30 min., NBC, 1940–1941.

A satirization of small-town radio outlets as heard through the antics of the staff of radio station EZRA, "a powerful little five-watter down in Rosedale," that presented country and western music. Also known as *Station EZRA*.

Cast: Pat Barrett (*Uncle Ezra*); Nora Cunneen (*Cecelia*); Fran Allison (*Aunt Fanny*); Cliff Soubier (*Major Boggs*). ***Vocalists:*** The Hoosier Hot Shots, the Rosedale Trio, the Sons of the Pioneers.

1686. Uncle Jim's Question Bee. Game, 15 and 30 min., versions, NBC Blue, 1936–1939; CBS, 1940; NBC Blue, 1940–1941.

The format called for players to answer questions, submitted to them by Uncle Jim, in return for cash prizes.

Host: Jim McWilliams (Uncle Jim), Bill Slater. ***Announcer:*** Dan Seymour.

Note: On 7/1/41, NBC attempted a television series based on the radio program that resulted in a one-time airing. It did, however, set a record: It was the first televised quiz show to be sponsored (in this case by Lever Brothers). Bill Slater was the host.

1687. Uncle Walter's Dog House. Variety, 30 min., NBC, 5/2/39 to 2/6/42.

A weekly series of musical numbers and comedy skits hosted by Tom Wallace as Uncle Walter. Mary Ann Mercer and the Dog House Chorus were the regulars and the orchestras of Phil Davis and Bob Strange provided the music. See also the following title.

1688. Uncle Walter's Dog House. Comedy, 30 min., NBC, 2/11/42 to 7/8/42.

A revised version of the prior title that became more of a situation comedy and related

***Uncle Don* star Don Carney is surrounded by a group of fans.**

events in the life of Walter Wiggins, a down-on-his-luck relative who comes to stay with his nephew and his family. Music and songs were featured between acts.

Cast: Tom Wallace (*Walter Wiggins*); Charles Penman (*Mr. Wiggins*); Kathryn Card (*Mrs. Wiggins*); Beryl Vaughn (*Margie Wiggins*); Betty Arnold (*Mrs. Dramp, the neighbor*). ***Also:*** Fred Brady, Frank Dane, Marvin Miller. ***Vocalist:*** Mary Ann Mercer. ***Announcer:*** Charles Lyon. ***Music:*** Bob Strange.

1689. Under Arrest. Crime Drama, 30 min., Mutual, 7/28/46 to 9/1/46; 6/8/47 to 10/4/54.

A police captain's battle against the criminal element was the focus of stories. Capt. John Drake began in the crusade (1947); when the series returned the following year, Jim Scott had become the captain.

Cast: Craig McDonnell (*Capt. John Drake*); Joe Di Santis, Ned Wever (*Capt. Jim Scott*). ***Announcer:*** Ted Brown. ***Music:*** Al Finelli.

OPENING

ANNOUNCER: Mutual presents *Under Arrest*. Criminals behind bars. *Under Arrest*, the story of Police Capt. Jim Scott's fight against crime.

1690. THE UNEXPECTED. Anthology, 15 min., Syndicated, 1948–1949.

A different radio actor or film star appeared in stories where fate played an intricate part that led to a surprise ending.

Regular Performers: Barry Sullivan, Lyle Talbot, Lurene Tuttle.

OPENING

ANNOUNCER: From Hollywood, Lyle Talbot in *The Unexpected.*

FEMALE: *The Unexpected.*

MALE: *The Unexpected.*

ANNOUNCER: Life is filled with the unexpected; romantic, tragic and mysterious endings to our most ordinary actions. Dreams come true or dreams are shattered by sudden twists of fate in *The Unexpected.* And now Lyle Talbot, outstanding radio, stage and screen star, in "Silver Fox," a drama of *The Unexpected.*

CLOSING

ANNOUNCER: "Silver Fox" starred Lyle Talbot. Listen soon for another of your favorite motion picture stars in a drama of *The Unexpected.* This program was transcribed in Hollywood.

1691. UNITED STATES POSTAL INSPECTOR. Audition (Anthology), 30 min., produced on 2/26/47.

A proposed weekly series of dramas based on the files of the U.S. Postal Service (stories were set to focus on the misuse of the mails and the efforts of the U.S. postal inspectors to stop rackets). In the audition program, Inspector Jefferson Black tries to break up a racket involving a scheme to offer a service without actually providing it.

Cast: Warren William (*Inspector Jefferson Black*). ***Producer-Writer-Director:*** Robert Westerlake.

OPENING

ANNOUNCER: *United States Postal Inspector.* Your company, makers of your product, present the distinguished actor Mr. Warren William in a series of case histories, of authentic cases of United States Postal Inspectors.

VOICE: Nor rain, nor heat, nor gloom of night, stays these couriers from the swift completion of their appointed rounds.

ANNOUNCER: These words, written more than 400 years before Christ, have been the motto of the men of the postal service for generations. They reveal the unshakable determination of U.S. Postal Inspectors with a record as successful and unyielding as any secret service in the world. Postal inspectors handle their cases quietly, with dignity, invariably bringing their quarry to justice. These stories will reveal for the first time true cases of confidence rackets, frauds, robberies and the countless other offenses which constitute crimes against the mails. And now, to introduce you to tonight's case, meet Warren William as Postal Inspector Jefferson Black.

BLACK: Ladies and gentlemen, this case history taken from court records, was an outgrowth of World War II, one of the vilest schemes ever perpetrated. It was directed against the wives, sweethearts and parents of our soldiers who died in battle...

CLOSING

WARREN: Ladies and gentlemen, reporting a fraud or any crime after it has happened is not enough. Try to help by anticipating. If you have reason to suspect any schemes put to you through the mails, see your nearest postal inspector; he wants to help you and he will if you give him a chance.

ANNOUNCER: Names, places and events have all been changed so that no reflection can fall on any person living or dead. Tune in again next week for another authentic story of *United States Postal Inspector.*

1692. THE U.S. STEEL HOUR. Anthology, 60 min., CBS, 1943–1944; ABC, 1945–1949; NBC, 1949–1953.

A weekly series of dramatic presentations culled from books, films and the stage. The program, sponsored by U.S. Steel, is also known as *The Theater Guild on the Air.*

Hosts: Lawrence Langner, Roger Pryor, Elliott Reid. ***Announcers:*** Norman Brokenshire, George Hicks. ***Soloist:*** Bidu Sayo. ***Music:*** The Howard Levy Orchestra; the NBC Symphony Orchestra.

1693. VACATION SERENADE. Variety, 30 min., NBC, 1943–1944.

A weekly program of music and songs with vocalists Dorothy Kirsten (1943) and Rose Bampton (1944) as the hosts. Reed Kennedy was featured; Ben Grauer did the announcing and Wilfred Pelletier and his orchestra provided the music.

1694. VACATION WITH MUSIC. Variety, 30 min., NBC, 1946.

Music and songs with Phil Brete as the host. Ed Herlihy and Liza Morrow were the regulars; Jack Costello did the announcing and Harry Sosnik and his orchestra supplied the music.

1695. VALENTINO. Variety, 10, 15 and 25 min. versions, ABC, 1952–1956.

Radio's answer to television's *The Continental*. The format had Barry Valentino, "The Prisoner of Romance," bring "love and romance to a housewife's dreary afternoon" through songs and poetry.

VALLEE VARIETIES *see* **THE RUDY VALLEE SHOW**

1696. VALIANT LADY. Serial, 15 min., CBS, 1938; NBC, 1938–1942; CBS, 1942–1946; ABC, 1951–1952.

The small community of Pine River was the setting for the dramatic story of Joan Scott, an actress who relinquishes her career to marry Truman Scott, a noted plastic surgeon. Truman was extremely jealous and unstable and Joan's efforts to guide his life was the focal point of stories.

Cast: Joan Blaine, Joan Banks, Florence Freeman (*Joan Scott*); Charles Carroll, Bartlett Robinson, Martin Blaine (*Truman Scott*); Jean Ellyn (*Margie Cook*); Richard Gordon, Bill Johnstone, Gene Leonard (*Jim Barrett*); Linda Carlon (*Agnes Westcott*);Ethel Owen (*Abby Trowbridge*); Shirling Oliver (*Dudley Trowbridge*); Lawson Zerbe (*Jeffrey Clark*); Everett Sloane (*Lester Brennan*); Ned Wever (*Colin Kirby*); Elsie Mae Gordon (*Estelle Cummings*); Elspeth Eric (*Eleanor Richards*); Irene Winston (*Myra Gordon*); Cathleen Cordell (*Monica Brewster*); Frank Lovejoy (*Chris Ellerbe*); Albert Hayes (*Norman Price*); Judith Lowry (*Emma Stevens*); Raymond Edward Johnson (*Paul Morrison*). ***Announcer:*** Dwight Weist. ***Organist:*** Jesse Crawford.

OPENING

ANNOUNCER: Friday, October 3rd, 1941, time for *Valiant Lady*. General Mills' new Bisquick presents Joan Blaine in *Valiant Lady*, the story of a brave woman and her brilliant but unstable husband. The story of her struggle to keep his feet planted firmly upon the pathway to success.

1697. VARIETY FAIR. Variety, 15 min., Syndicated, 1946.

Holland Engle as the host of a program of music and songs with Elmira Roessler and the Spotlighters.

1698. THE VAUGHN DE LEATH SHOW. Variety, 15 min., CBS, 1931–1933; NBC, 1933–1935; CBS, 1935–1936; NBC Red, 1936–1937; NBC Blue, 1938–1939; Mutual, 1939.

A weekly series of music and songs with Vaughn De Leath, said to be the first woman to have sung on radio.

OPENING

VAUGHN (singing): Red sails in the sunset, way out on the sea, please carry my loved one home safely to me.

ANNOUNCER: Ladies and gentlemen, Vaughn De Leath, radio's first song sensation with next year's style in songs, as up to the minute as tomorrow's newspaper.

1699. THE VAUGHN MONROE SHOW. Variety, 30 min., CBS, 1946–1954.

Singer Vaughn Monroe as the host of a weekly program of music and songs. Marilyn Duke and Tom Shirley were the regulars and the Vaughn Monroe Orchestra provided the music.

1700. THE VERA BURTON SHOW. Variety, 15 min., CBS, 1942.

Vocalist Vera Burton as the host of a program of music and songs. Walter Gross and his orchestra provided the music.

1701. The Vera Vague Show. Variety, 15 min., ABC, 1949.

Comedienne Barbara Jo Allen as the daffy "Vera Vague," hosting a weekly program of music and songs featuring guest artists. Owen James did the announcing.

1702. Vi and Velma Vernon. Variety, 15 min., NBC, 1942.

Singers Vi and Velma Vernon as the hosts of a program of music and songs. Pianist Glenn Hurley provided the music.

1703. Vic and Sade. Comedy, 15 and 30 min. versions, NBC Blue, 1931–1941; NBC Red, 1932–1944; CBS, 1938; CBS, 1941–1943; CBS, 1945; Mutual, 1941–1946.

Events in the lives of the eccentric Gook family, "Radio's Home Folks" and residents of the small town of Crooper, Illinois ("40 miles from Peoria" in "the little house halfway up the next block on Virginia Street"). Vic, the father, was a bookkeeper at Plant 14 of the Consolidated Kitchenware Company; Sade, his wife, was naive and a homebody; their adopted son Russell "Rush" Meadows (also known as Rush Gook and Russell Miller) was actually the son of Sade's sister, who couldn't afford to raise him. There was little music, virtually no sound effects and everything unfolded through dialogue. *Other regular characters:* Uncle Fletcher; the Gooks' friends, Chuck and Dottie Brainfeeble. Vic was a member of a lodge called the Sacred Stars of the Milky Way (also called the Sky Brothers Lodge). The program was so popular that it played on CBS, Mutual and NBC at the same time.

Cast: Art Van Harvey (*Vic Gook*); Bernardine Flynn (*Sade Gook*); Billy Idelson, Johnny Coons, Sid Koss (*Rush Meadows*); Clarence Hartzell (*Uncle Fletcher*); Carl Kroenke (*Chuck Brainfeeble*); Ruth Perrott, Dorothy Day (*Dottie Brainfeeble*). ***Announcers:*** Bob Brown, Ralph Edwards, Clarence Hartzell, Ed Herlihy, Charles Irving, Roger Krupp, Glenn Riggs, Ed Roberts. ***Music:*** Walter Blaufuss. ***Crisco Commercial Spokeswomen:*** Isabella Beach, Betty Ruth Smith.

OPENING

Announcer: And now get ready to smile again with radio's home folks *Vic and Sade*, written by Paul Rapf. Yes, here again, folks, your good friends Vic and Sade, brought to you by the makers of Crisco. And with them is Mrs. Beach, your radio neighbor [she would then deliver the commercial]. And now let's see what is going on at the Gook house. Well, it's late afternoon as we approach the small house halfway up on the next block and here on the front porch we find Mrs. Victor Gook all by herself...

CLOSING

Announcer: That concludes another brief interlude at the small house halfway up the next block. And don't forget to listen to Crisco's *Vic and Sade* next time. This is Ed Roberts speaking.

Note: On July 25, 1949, NBC attempted a television series called *The Gook Family* with Frank Dane (*Vic Gook*), Bernardine Flynn (*Sade Gook*) and Dick Conan (*Rush*). The project, produced by Norman Felton, failed to become a weekly series.

1704. The Vic Damone Show. Variety, 15 min., Mutual, 2/18/47 to 7/1/47.

Vocalist Vic Damone as the host of a program of music and songs. Don Fredericks did the announcing and Sylvan Levin and his orchestra provided the music. Also known as *The Voice of Vic Damone*.

1705. The Victor Borge Show. Variety, 30 min., NBC Blue, 1943–1944; ABC, 1944–1945; NBC, 1945–1946.

Comedian-pianist Victor Borge as the host of a weekly program of music and songs. Pat Friday and the Henry Russell Chorus were the regulars; John Reed King, Ken Roberts and Harlow Wilcox did the announcing; and the Benny Goodman and Billy Mills orchestras provided the music.

Victory Tunes *see* **The Fred Waring Show**

The Village Store *see* **The Sealtest Village Store**

The Vintage White Owl Program *see* **The Adventures of Gracie**

1706. The Voice of Broadway. Gossip, 15 min., CBS, 1941.

Inside news about show business personalities with Dorothy Kilgallen as the host. Allan Stuart did the announcing.

The Voice of Vic Damone *see* **The Vic Damone Show**

1707. Vox Pop. Interview, 30 min., NBC, 1935–1939; CBS, 1939–1947; ABC, 1947–1948.

Travelers, passing through New York City, were met, interviewed and awarded a merchandise prize for relating their experiences of the city. Also known as *Sidewalk Interviews*.

Hosts: Parks Johnson, Jerry Belcher, Wallace Butterworth, Warren Hull. ***Announcers:*** Dick Joy, Roger Krupp, Graham McNamee.

1708. The Voyage of the Scarlet Queen. Adventure, 30 min., Mutual, 7/3/47 to 2/25/48.

Philip Carney is captain of a ship called *The Scarlet Queen*. He is assisted by his first mate, Red Gallagher, and stories relate their adventures in the South Pacific. They transport cargo and passengers and often encounter the unexpected—danger—but "*The Scarlet Queen* has never taken us into any place she's never taken us out of."

Cast: Elliott Lewis (*Philip Carney*); Ed Max (*Red Gallagher*); Howard Duff (*Philip Carney, audition episode*). ***Announcer:*** Charles Arlington. ***Music:*** Richard Aurandt. ***Producer:*** James Burton.

OPENING (from 11/13/47, "The Beautiful Girl in the Bargan Basement")

VOICE: Stand by to make sail.

CARNEY: Log entry: The ketch *Scarlet Queen*, Philip Carney, master. Position: 22 minutes, 15 degrees north; 114 degrees, 45 minutes east. Wind: fresh; sky, fair. Remarks: Departed Hong Kong after successfully liquidating business competition. Reason for success: "The Beautiful Girl in the Bargain Basement."

CLOSING

CARNEY: Log entry: Catch *Scarlet Queen*, 5:30 P.M. Wind: fresh, sky fair, carrying full sail. Ship secure for the night. Signed, Philip Carney, Master.

ANNOUNCER: *The Voyage of the Scarlet Queen* stars Elliott Lewis as Phil Carney. This is Mutual.

1709. Wake Up and Smile. Variety, 30 min., ABC, 1946.

A morning program of music, songs and chatter with Hal O'Holloron as the host. Kay Armen, Salty Holme, Patsy Montana and Boyce Smith were the regulars; Rex Maupin and his orchestra supplied the music.

1710. Walk a Mile. Game, 30 min., CBS, 1952–1954.

The program, sponsored by Camel cigarettes, had contestants answering general knowledge questions in return for a carton of cigarettes. The title was derived from the sponsor's slogan—"I'd walk a mile for a Camel."

Hosts: Win Elliot, John Henry Faluk. ***Announcers:*** Joe King, Mort Lawrence, Ralph Paul, Joe Ripley. ***Music:*** Peter Van Steeden.

1711. The Walt Disney Song Parade. Children, 15 min., Mutual, 1941.

Soundtracks from various Disney films linked together with odd bits of chatter by an announcer.

1712. The Walter O'Keefe Show. Variety, 45 min., CBS, 1938.

Vaudeville performer and songwriter Walter O'Keefe as the host of a weekly program of music and songs. Lily Pons and the Kay Thompson Singers were the regulars. Andre Kostelanetz and his orchestra supplied the music.

1713. Walter Winchell's Journal. Commentary, 15 min., CBS, 1931–1932; NBC Blue, 1932–1944; ABC, 1944–1955; Mutual, 1955–1957.

News items, gossip and commentary by Walter Winchell, an ex-vaudevillian-turned-newspaper columnist. Also titled *The Jergens Journal* (when sponsored by Jergens hand lotion) and *The Lucky Strike Magic Carpet* (under the sponsorship of Lucky Strike cigarettes).

Host: Walter Winchell. ***Announcers:*** Jim Bannon, Ben Grauer, Cy Harrice, Hugh James, Richard Stark.

OPENING (1935)

ANNOUNCER: *The Jurgens Journal* featuring Walter Winchell, America's one-man newspaper. His famous column appears in the New York *Daily Mirror* and over 225 other newspapers from New York to Shanghai. Now to the editorial desk of *The Jergens Journal* and Walter Winchell.

WALTER: Good evening, Mr. and Mrs. North and South America and all the ships and clippers at sea, let's go to press...

OPENING (1949)

SOUND: Car horns.

ANNOUNCER: That means Kaiser-Frazier.

SOUND: Telegraph sounds.

ANNOUNCER: That means Walter Winchell. Walter Winchell is brought to you by the men who sell and service Kaiser automobiles and the Frazier. You. You could win one of the 145 prizes in the great new Kaiser-Frazier contest. Every prize winner will receive $1,000 toward the purchase price of a new 1949 Kaiser or Frazier... Go to your nearest Kaiser-Frazier dealer ... ask for your entry blank. On it you will find one simple statement for you to complete in 25 words or less. Then mail your entry as directed. That's all... But now, Kaiser-Frazier, builders of cars that make automobile history, presents the reporter of news that makes world history. So who, what, when, where and why, from the man America listens to most, Walter Winchell.

WALTER: Good evening, Mr. and Mrs. North and South America and all the ships at sea, let's go to press...

1714. WALTZ TIME. Variety, 30 min., NBC, 9/27/33 to 7/16/48.

A program of music and songs with vocalists Evelyn MacGregor and Frank Munn. Abe Lyman and his orchestra provided the music. Anne Hummert and Frank Hummert were the producers.

1715. WANTED. Anthology, 30 min., NBC, 7/7/50 to 9/29/50.

A weekly series of dramatizations based on actual police files. Walter McGraw served as the host; Fred Collins did the announcing; and Morris Mamorsky provided the music.

WATCH THE FORDS GO BY *see* **AL PEARCE AND HIS GANG**

THE WAYFARING STRANGER *see* **BURL IVES COFFEE CLUB**

1716. THE WAYNE AND SHUSTER SHOW. Variety, 30 min., NBC, 1947.

Music and comedy with comedians Johnny Wayne and Frank Shuster. Vocalist Georgia Dey provided the songs; Herb May did the announcing; and Samuel Hersenhoren and his orchestra provided the music.

1717. THE WAYNE KING SHOW. Variety, 30 min., CBS, 1939–1941.

Orchestra leader Wayne King as the host of a weekly program of music and songs. Vocalists Buddy Clarke and Bob Eberle were the regulars and the Wayne King Orchestra provided the music.

WE ARE ALWAYS YOUNG *see* **APPENDIX**

1718. WE ARE FOUR. Serial, 15 min., Mutual, 1937–1938.

Dramatic events in the lives of marrieds Tony and Nancy Webster and their daughters, Lydia and Priscilla.

Cast: Charles Flynn (*Tony Webster*); Marjorie Hanna (*Nancy Webster*); Alice Hill (*Lydia Webster*); Sally Smith (*Priscilla Webster*). ***Announcer:*** Ed Smith.

1719. WE CARE. Anthology, 15 min., ABC, 1948.

A series of dramatizations sponsored by Care, wherein appeals were made for donations to help the needy in Europe. Douglas Fairbanks, Jr., served as host.

1720. WE DELIVER THE GOODS. Variety, 30 min., CBS, 1944.

The program, sponsored by the Merchant Marines, mixed amateur performances by military talent (variety segment) with professional actors (dramatic segment).

Host: Howard Culver. ***Announcer:*** Sam Brandt. ***Music:*** Curt Roberts and the Maritime Service Band.

1721. WE, THE ABBOTTS. Serial, 15 min., CBS, 1940–1941; NBC, 1941–1942.

Dramatic events in the lives of the Abbotts, a family of five: John, the father, a schoolteacher; Emily, his wife; their twin daughters Barbara and Linda; and their son Jack.

Cast: John McIntire (*John Abbott*); Betty Garde, Ethel Everett (*Emily Abbott*); Betty Jane Tyler, Betty Philson (*Linda Abbott*); Audrey Egan (*Barbara Abbott*); Cliff Carpenter (*Jack Abbott*); Adelaide Klein (*Hilda, the maid*). ***Announcer:*** Ted Pearson.

1722. We Who Dream. Anthology, 15 min., CBS, 3/17/44 to 10/13/44.

Dramatizations based on dreams with Claire Niesen as the voice of the Dream Girl. Sponsored by Englender Mattresses.

OPENING

Announcer: This is the Englender program. Englender, for more than 50 years, the name that stands for the most luxurious rests and sleep.

Dream Girl: Sleep. The curtain of day comes down but the play goes on. Behind the veil of sleep, the actors speak and posture and emit the day gone by. They whisper things to come in dreams.

Announcer: The Englender Company, manufacturers of America's most luxurious mattresses, presents *We Who Dream*, a program of plays that deal with the strange recesses of the unconscious mind. For the mind at sleep is not cut off from life. It dreams and lives another life linked with all our waking hours. This is a program about people who dream. For those dreams, however real or fantastic, are somehow, somewhere based on life, as all dreams must be. Our Englender story for tonight is "The Dream of the Gingerbread House."

1723. Wednesday with You. Variety, 30 min., NBC, 6/25/45 to 9/19/45.

A weekly program of music and songs with Nora Martin as the host. Vocalist Freddie Martel provided the songs; Harry Von Zell did the announcing; and Leonard Sues and his orchestra provided the music.

1724. Weekend Whimsy. Variety, 15 min., NBC, 1941.

Loulie Jean, Sylvia Marlowe and Brad Reynolds as the stars of a program of music and song featuring the orchestra of Dick Dinsmore. Red Hall did the announcing.

1725. Welcome Travelers. Interview, 30 min., CBS, 1940–1941; NBC, 1941–1942; ABC, 1947–1954.

Travelers, passing through Chicago, were met at bus, train and airport terminals and brought before a microphone to relate their impressions of the Windy City. Served as the basis for the television series of the same title.

Host: Tommy Bartlett. ***Announcer:*** Jim Ameche.

1726. Wendy Warren and the News. Serial, 15 min., CBS, 1947–1948.

Events in the life of Wendy Warren, a female radio newscaster. The program began with an actual newscast. When it concluded, the airwaves were turned over to Wendy, who summarized news items of interest to women. Following a commercial break, the program became a daily drama focusing on Wendy's trials and tribulations.

Cast: Florence Freeman (*Wendy Warren*); Douglas Edwards (*Newscaster*); Lamont Johnson (*Mark Douglas*); Les Tremayne (*Gil Kendal*); Anne Burr (*Nora Marsh*); Jane Lauren (*Adele Lang*); Horace Brahan (*Charles Lang*); Meg Wyllie (*Jean*); John Raby (*Don Smith*); Hugh James (*Bill Flood, the radio show announcer*); Rod Hendrickson (*Sam Warren*). ***Music:*** Clarke Morgan.

1727. Western Caravan. Anthology, 30 min., NBC, 6/25/50 to 10/29/50.

A weekly series of Western dramatizations with varying casts and stories. Tex Williams was the host; Robert Armbruster supplied the music.

1728. What Makes You Tick? Game, 15 min., CBS, 1948–1950; ABC, 1950–1951.

Two guest psychologists appraised contestants' answers to a series of ten psychological questions that were posed to them by the host.

Hosts: John K.M. McCaffery (1948), Gypsy Rose Lee (1950). ***Announcer:*** George Ansbro.

1729. What Would You Have Done? Game, 30 min., NBC Blue, 1940.

Selected members of the studio audience, posed with a dilemma, had to solve it to the best of their abilities. Winners, determined by studio audience applause, received merchandise prizes.

Host: Ben Grauer. ***Announcer:*** Jack Costello.

1730. What's Cooking? Women, 30 min., NBC Blue, 1944; ABC, 1944–1945.

A program of cooking tips and advice with Beulah Karney as the host. She was assisted by Earl Tanner and Dick Dowd did the announcing. Harry Kogen and his orchestra provided the music.

1731. What's My Line? Game, 30 min., NBC, 5/20/52 to 8/26/52; CBS, 9/3/52 to 7/1/53.

A panel of four regulars had to identify the occupations of guests through a series of questions. Based on the television series of the same title.

Host: John Daly. ***Panelists:*** Hal Brock, Bennett Cerf, Arlene Francis, Dorothy Kilgallen. ***Announcer:*** Don Briggs.

1732. What's My Name? Game, 30 min., Mutual, 3/25/38 to 3/17/39; NBC, 7/5/39 to 6/27/43; ABC, 6/3/48 to 7/30/49.

Selected members of the studio audience competed. Four clues to the identity of a famous person were related. Players received money based on the clue at which the identity was made (first clue, $10; second clue $9; third, $8; fourth, $7). Later formats increased the cash prize to $15, then $100 on the first clue.

Host: Arlene Francis. ***Co-Hosts:*** Carl Frank, Wilbur "Budd" Hulick, Fred Uttal, Ward Wilson. ***Announcers:*** John Reed King, Ken Roberts. ***Orchestra:*** Walter Gross.

1733. What's New? Human Interest, 60 min., NBC Blue, 9/4/43 to 2/26/44.

An update on events that happened one week prior to the evening's broadcast. Don Ameche served as the host.

1734. What's the Name of That Song? Game, 30 min., Mutual, 1944–1948; ABC, 1948–1954.

Selected members of the studio audience competed to identify a tune played by the host on a piano. Correct answers awarded the player $5. If a player could sing the first line, his money was doubled; if he could sing the chorus, his money was tripled.

Hosts: Dud Williamson, Bill Gwinn.

1735. What's with Herbert? Audition (Comedy), 30 min., NBC, 7/22/50.

Herbert Dwindle was born in Brooklyn, New York, on a cool day in August about halfway through the seventh inning of a Brooklyn Giants ball game. As the nurse carried him out to the waiting room, his father jumped up excitedly and shouted, "Brooklyn's leading four to three." The nurse said, "Mr. Dwindle, it's a boy." His father said, "Gee, I hope they knock this one over the fence." And, ever since, Herbert has had a feeling of not being wanted. The proposed series was to follow Herbert as he seeks a way to become wanted—but can't seem to find it. He is 30 years old now, is unable to hold a job (he believes thinking is the best job, but can't find anyone who will pay him for it), and his parents are embarrassed by him and wish he "would run away from home like other boys." In the audition episode, the family tries to trick Herbert into getting a job. *Other regular characters:* Mom and Pop (a plumber); Helen, Herbert's sister; Freddie Needlefoot, Helen's husband, a used car salesman; Mrs. Andrews, the nosy neighbor; Jimmy and George, Herbert's friends.

Cast: Bill Foster (*Herbert Dwindle*); Bob Sweeney (*Freddie Needlefoot*); Florence Halop (*Mrs. Andrews*); Junius Matthews (*Pop Dwindle*); Ruth Perrott (*Mom Dwindle*); Hal March (*George Schneider*); Jerry Hausner (*Jimmy*); Doris Singleton (*Helen Needlefoot*). ***Orchestra:*** Lou Bring. ***Writer-Director:*** Charles Isaacs.

OPENING

Announcer: What's with Herbert? The National Broadcasting Company brings you *What's with Herbert?* starring Bill Foster and featuring Ruth Perrott, Hal March, Bob Sweeney, Florence Halop, Doris Singleton, Junius Matthews and Jerry Hausner with Lou Bring's orchestra. *What's with Herbert?* is the everyday story of a young man's battle to remain anonymous.

Wheatenaville Sketches *see* **Billy Bachelor**

1736. Wheeler and Woolsey. Variety, 30 min., NBC Blue, 1933–1934.

A weekly program mixing the comedy of Bert Wheeler and Robert Woolsey with the performances of guest entertainers. Nat Shilkret and his orchestra provided the music.

1737. When a Girl Marries. Serial, 15 min., CBS, 1939–1941; NBC, 1941–1951; ABC, 1951–1953; ABC, 1954–1957.

Dramatic events in the lives of Joan and Harry Davis, an impoverished lawyer and his wife, who live in the small community of Cedarville.

Cast: Noel Mills, Mary Jane Higby (*Joan Davis*); John Raby, Robert Haag, Whitfield Connor, Lyle Sudrow (*Harry Davis*); Georgia Burke (*Lillie*); Joan Tetzel, Jone Allison, Toni Darnay (*Sylvia Field*); Anne Francis, Rosemary Rice (*Kathy Cameron*); Jeanette Dowling (*Irma Cameron*); Eunice Hall, Helen Dumas (*Betty McDonald*); John Kane (*Chick Norris*); Michael Fitzmaurice, Richard Kollmar, Staats Cotsworth, Karl Weber, Paul McGrath (*Phil Stanley*); Mary Jane Higby, Wynne Gibson (*Angie*); Jack Arthur (*Steve*). ***Announcers:*** Frank Gallop, Hugh James, Wendell Niles, Charles Stark, Richard Stark. ***Organists:*** Richard Liebert, Rosa Rio.

OPENING

ANNOUNCER: *When a Girl Marries*. Maxwell House, that ripe, mellow satisfying coffee that's good to the last drop, presents *When a Girl Marries*, a tender, human story of young married life, dedicated to everyone who has ever been in love. And now, *When a Girl Marries*, the story of Joan and Harry Davis.

CLOSING

ANNOUNCER: Until tomorrow at this same time, we leave the story of *When a Girl Marries* with Mary Jane Higby and written by Elaine Carrington. Your narrator was Charles Stark. This is NBC, the National Broadcasting Company.

1738. WHERE HAVE YOU BEEN? Game, 30 min., NBC, 1954–1955.

A celebrity panel had to guess where (city, country, state) guest contestants had been through a series of indirect question-and-answer rounds. A prize was awarded to the contestant if the panel failed to uncover the locale.

Host: Horace Sutton. ***Panelists:*** Marc Connelly, Ernie Kovacs, Peggy McCay, Harriet Van Horne. ***Announcer:*** Jack Costello.

1739. WHICH IS WHICH? Game, 30 min., CBS, 1944–1945.

Selected members of the studio audience attempted to identify radio and motion picture stars, who appeared as guests, from hearing only their voices. Prizes were awarded to successful players.

Host: Ken Murray. ***Orchestra:*** Richard Himber.

1740. THE WHISPER MEN. Adventure, 30 min., Mutual, 9/8/45 to 2/2/46.

Max Chandler is a radio commentator who travels throughout the world crusading against the Whisper Men, Communist infiltrators of the underworld. Stories follow his exploits as he and his assistant, Rod Buchanan, go beyond the microphones to help people in trouble. *Other regular characters:* Linda Jones, the crusading reporter for *Globe* magazine.

Cast: Karl Swenson, Joseph Curtin (*Max Chandler*); Kermit Murdock (*Rod Buchanan*); Betty Caine (*Linda Jones*). ***Music:*** Chet Kingsbury. ***Producer:*** Dan Seymour.

OPENING

ANNOUNCER: The Mutual Broadcasting System presents the adventures of Max Chandler featuring Karl Swenson in the role of the famous broadcaster-reporter whose assignments bring him into constant contact with—

VOICE (in echo effect): *The Whisper Men*.

CLOSING

ANNOUNCER: Next week at this time, the Mutual Broadcasting System will bring you another in this series, *The Whisper Men*, based on the stories in *Liberty* magazine. This is the Mutual Broadcasting System.

1741. THE WHISPERER. Crime Drama, 30 min., NBC, 7/8/51 to 12/16/51.

Shortly after obtaining his law degree, Philip Gault suffered an accident that nearly destroyed his vocal chords and left him with a whisper of a voice. With a driving ambition to break up an evil organization called the Syndicate, Philip used an alias (not given) and joined the Syndicate where he received the nickname the Whisperer. The Whisperer soon became the finger man for the Syndicate and quickly his name spread throughout the underworld as a man to fear. Just when Gault had given up hope of ever talking again, he met Benjamin Lee, a brilliant doctor based in Central City. The doctor restored Gault's voice and allowed him to begin a normal life as Philip Gault, criminal attorney, while at the same time continuing in his capacity as the Whisperer (Gault sets up a situation with the Syndicate as the Whisperer; then, as Philip Gault, he uses that knowledge to foil their actions). Philip is assisted by Ellen Norris, Dr. Lee's nurse, the only other person who knows his dual identity. Stories follow Philip's activities as "the man who works the thin edge of death living a double identity." When the Whisperer calls the Syndicate, which is based in New York City (Gault is based in Central City), he uses the phone number Circle 1879 (sometimes given as Circle 1798) and begins with "Central City reporting" followed by his instructions to the Syndicate leader, Moran. Gault has never killed for the Syndicate or broken any laws for them. "They obey my voice and I pass along instructions. I never help in their plans for crime."

Cast: Carleton Young (*Philip Gault/The Whisperer*); Betty Moran (*Ellen Norris*); Jack Moyles (*Lt. Denver, Central City P.D.*); Paul Frees (*Moran*). ***Announcer:*** Don Rickles. ***Music:*** Johnny Duffy. ***Producer:*** Bill Karn.

OPENING

GAULT (in rattling whisper): The Whisperer, the Whisperer.

ANNOUNCER: Presenting *The Whisperer* starring Carleton Young. The Whisperer, a brilliant man who, losing his voice in an accident that crushed his vocal chords, worked his way deep within the crime Syndicate to help destroy it from within. To the underworld, his familiar rattling hiss is the voice of authority to be obeyed without question. Then a miracle of surgery performed by Dr. Benjamin Lee restored his natural voice, enabling him to resume his real identity. Now, as Philip Gault, brilliant young attorney, he skirts the edges of death living his dual role—for as the Whisperer, he sets in motion the forces of the Syndicate, then as Philip Gault, uses his knowledge to fight the organized network of crime which seeks to control the fate of millions in cities and towns across the nation.

CLOSING

GAULT: The Whisperer.

ANNOUNCER: *The Whisperer* is based upon stories and characters created by Stetson Humphrey. This is Don Rickles inviting you to listen next week to another exciting adventure with—

GAULT: *The Whisperer.*

ANNOUNCER: This is NBC, the National Broadcasting Company.

1742. WHISPERING JACK SMITH. Variety, 15 min., CBS, 10/31/32 to 4/13/35.

A daily program of music and songs with Jack Smith, a popular baritone of the era who was called "Whispering" Jack Smith. Don Hancock did the announcing.

OPENING

JACK (singing): Hello, dear friends, hello.

ANNOUNCER: Hello, Jack. Here's Whispering Jack Smith and his Whispering Strings once more bringing you his intimate melodies sung as only he can sing them. This electronically transcribed program by the one and only whispering baritone is brought to you by Ironized Yeast, the new yeast vitamin B and iron tablets through which people everywhere who are thin and rundown because they need these vital elements, are gaining new, naturally attractive pounds, new energy and new health. And now, *Whispering Jack Smith.*

1743. WHISPERING STREETS. Anthology, 30 min., ABC, 1952–1959; CBS, 1959–1960.

The program was originally a drama of life as seen through the narration of a female writer named Hope Winslow (played by Gertrude Warner). Stories were complete in themselves until 1954 when it became a daily serial (usually concluding a story within five days). The Hope Winslow character was dropped and the hosts and narrators became Bette Davis, Cathy Lewis and Anne Seymour.

OPENING

VOICES (in echo effect): Whispering, whispering, whispering.

ANNOUNCER: *Whispering Streets.* And here is Bette Davis.

BETTE: Hello [she would then begin the story]. The streets that span a continent whisper continuously as they hurry from ocean to ocean. To Dorothy Hayes and Loretta Cranford, 69 and 67, respectively, they were crowded with incidents and adventure and certain moments of intense fear…

1744. THE WHISTLER. Anthology, 30 min., CBS (West Coast), 1942–1950; CBS (Network), 1947–1948.

Mystery presentations that depict the plight of people who were suddenly caught in a destructive web of their own misdeeds. The Whistler, identified by the mournful whistling of the theme music, never appeared in stories. His observations on the vices and virtues of the individuals were heard throughout each drama. The show's haunting theme was an eerie 13-note whistled tune performed by Dorothy Roberts and Owen James. *Stories include:*

1. Ghost Hunt. A radio disc jockey (Ralph Edwards) agrees to stay in a haunted mansion to gain publicity.

2. The Morrison Affair. Madeleine Carroll and Gerald Mohr in the story about a childless English bride who passes an adopted child off as her own when her husband returns from the war.

3. Mirage. Wally Maher and Gerald Mohr in the story of an underworld attorney who shuns the woman who gave him his start, and of the woman's attempts to seek revenge.

4. The Wages of Sin. A hooker (Barbara Stanwyck) blackmails gangsters after they use her apartment for a murder.

Cast: Joseph Kearns, Bill Forman, Marvin Miller, Everett Clarke (*The Whistler*). ***Announcers:*** Bob Lemond, Marvin Miller, Don Rickles, Bob Venables. ***Music:*** Wilbur Hatch, Hunter Taylor. ***Producer:*** George Allen.

OPENING

ANNOUNCER: And now stay tuned for the mystery program that is unique among all mystery programs because even when you know who's guilty, you always receive a startling surprise at the final curtain in the Signal Oil program, *The Whistler*. Signal, the famous go-farther gasoline, invites you to sit back and enjoy another strange story by *The Whistler*.

WHISTLER (over theme): I am the Whistler and I know many things for I walk by night. I know many strange tales hidden in the hearts of men and women who have stepped into the shadows. Yes, I know the nameless terrors of which they dare not speak.

ANNOUNCER: Yes, friends, it's time for the Signal Oil program *The Whistler*, rated tops in popularity for a longer period of time than any other West Coast program in radio history. And now the Whistler's strange story, "What Makes a Murderer?"

CLOSING

ANNOUNCER (over theme): Let that whistle be your signal for the Signal Oil program *The Whistler*. Each Wednesday night at this same time, brought to you by the Signal Oil Company, marketers of Signal Gasoline and motor oil and fine quality automotive accessories. *The Whistler* was produced by George W. Allen. Next Wednesday, for a full hour of mystery on most of these stations, tune in a half-hour earlier for *The Saint* as well as *The Whistler*. This is Marvin Miller speaking for CBS, the Columbia Broadcasting System.

1745. THE WHITE OWL PROGRAM. Comedy, 30 min., CBS, 5/24/33 to 6/13/34.

A continuation of *The Robert Burns Panatela Program* (see entry) that, while still under the sponsorship of the General Cigar Company, had a title change to reflect their White Owl cigars. The format is basically the same with George Burns and Gracie Allen playing single friends who become involved in various comical situations caused by Gracie's scatter-brained antics.

Hosts: George Burns and Gracie Allen. ***Vocalist:*** Phil Regan. ***Announcers:*** Frank Knight, Santos Ortega. ***Orchestra:*** Guy Lombardo and His Royal Canadians.

1746. WHITEHALL 1212. Anthology, 30 min., NBC, 11/8/51 to 9/28/52.

Dramatizations based on the items of crime found in London's infamous Black Museum. Each item is associated with a specific crime. After relating the basic information about an item, flashback sequences are used to detail the police investigation of the crime. Following the drama, the host returns to sum up the story. See also *The Black Museum*.

Host: Harvey Hayes as James Davidson.

OPENING (from 12/18/51, "The Blitz Murder Case")

VOICE: This is Scotland Yard. For the first time, Scotland Yard opens its secret files to bring you the authentic true stories of some of its most celebrated cases. These are accurate records drawn from these files by special permission of Sir Harold Scott, commissioner of Scotland Yard. They're true in every respect, except for the names of the participants, which, for obvious reasons, have been changed. The research has been done by Mr. Percy Hoskins, chief crime reporter for the London *Daily Express*. The stories for radio are written and directed by Wyllis Cooper.

ANNOUNCER: New Scotland Yard, the London headquarters of the Metropolitan Police, is situated near the embarkment on Whitehall, part by Ten Downing Street and almost in the shadow of Big Ben. Here also is the headquarters of the CID, the Criminal Investigation Department, the body of men whose exploits for more than a hundred years have made the name Scotland Yard synonymous with brilliant detection of crime and unrelenting pursuit of the criminal. On the lower ground floor of New Scotland Yard is the famous Black Museum whose present custodian is Chief Superintendent James Davidson, a Scotland Yard veteran.

DAVIDSON: Good afternoon. This Black Museum of ours is rather unique. Everything in it was at one time connected with the successful solution of a crime. We possess an imposing collection of lethal weapons here. Each carefully documented to indicate its origin [he would then pick an item and begin the story].

CLOSING

ANNOUNCER: You have just heard "The Blitz Murder Case," drawn from the official files of Scotland Yard. All names were changed in this story for obvious reasons, but everything else is true; it occurred. *Whitehall 1212* is written and directed for radio by Wyllis Cooper. Listen for *Tales of the Texas Rangers*, next on NBC.

1747. THE WHITEMAN VARIETIES. Variety, 60 min., ABC, 1954.

Orchestra leader Paul Whiteman as the host of a program that showcased talented newcomers. Shirley Haimer and Bob Manning were the regulars and Paul Whiteman's orchestra provided the music.

1748. WHIZ QUIZ. Game, 30 min., ABC, 9/11/48 to 12/4/48.

The format called for studio audience members to answer general knowledge questions in return for merchandise prizes. Johnny Olsen served as the host and Sidney Walton did the announcing.

1749. WHO-DUN-IT? Game, 30 min., CBS, 1948.

A mystery case was enacted. Selected members of the studio audience who were able to identify the culprit won $100. If the culprit was not uncovered, the money was placed in a jackpot. The player with the most identifications received a chance to crack the jackpot by solving a case based on one musical clue. The mysteries were based on the files of the fictitious Inspector Slade.

Cast: Bob Dixon (*Host*); Santos Ortega (*Inspector Slade*). ***Orchestra:*** Jack Miller.

1750. WHO KNOWS? Anthology, 15 min., Mutual, 1940.

Dr. Hereward Carrington as the host of mystery and suspense presentations that concerned psychic phenomena. Jack Johnstone did the announcing.

1751. WHO SAID THAT? Game, 30 min., NBC, 7/2/48 to 8/22/50.

A panel of experts attempted to answer questions based on current news events. Served as the basis for the television series of the same title.

Host: Robert Trout. ***Panelists:*** H.V. Kaltenborn, John Cameron Swayze (plus guests). ***Announcer:*** Peter Roberts.

1752. THE WIFE SAVER. Comedy, 15 and 30 min. versions, NBC Red, 1931–1939; NBC Blue, 1939–1942; NBC Red, 1942.

A spoof of the helpful hints programs of the day that presented nonsensical advice for housewives. Allen Prescott served as the host; vocals were by Joan Brooks, Diane Courtney and the group Hi, Lo, Jack and the Dame. Also known as *Allen Prescott Presents*.

1753. WILD BILL HICKOK. Western, 30 min., Mutual, 1951–1956.

The West of a century ago was the setting for a radio version of the television series that told of the exploits of Marshal James Butler "Wild Bill" Hickok and his sidekick, Deputy Jingles P. Jones. Bill is agile, fast on the draw and quick with his fists; Jingles is somewhat overweight, easily scared, a bit clumsy, superstitious and an expert marksman. Together they form a unique team of undercover agents for the Federal government. Stories follow their efforts to maintain law and order throughout the Southwest. Bill rode a horse named Buckshot; Jingles had a horse named Joker. Visual scenes were handled by the conversation between Bill and Jingles or by Wild Bill talking to a character in the story.

Cast: Guy Madison (*Wild Bill Hickok*); Andy Devine (*Jingles P. Jones*). ***Announcer:*** Charles Lyon.

OPENING

ANNOUNCER: *Wild Bill Hickok* starring Guy Madison with Andy Devine as Jingles.

SONG (chorus): Wild Bill Hickok, Wild Bill Hickok. Ride on, ride on, Wild Bill. When Wild Bill guided those settlers west, he made those wagons roll; over hills and plains he led the wagon trains to their goal. Ride on, ride on Wild Bill, Wild Bill Hickok, ride on.

CLOSING

BILL (after he and Jingles complete a mission): Let's go, Buckshot.

JINGLES: Hey, Wild Bill, wait for meeeee! [Song from the opening repeats.]

1754. WILDERNESS ROAD. Drama, 15 min., CBS, 1936–1937.

The struggles and hardships of the pioneering Weston family as, led by trail blazer Daniel Boone, they sought a new life in the West of the 1890s.

Cast: Ray Collins (*Daniel Boone*); Vivian Block (*Ann Weston*); Lon Clark (*Sam Weston*); Anne Elstner (*Mary Weston*); Jimmy Donnelly (*Peter Weston*); Chester Stratton (*John Weston*); James McCallion (*James Weston*); William Johnstone (*Simon Weston*).

1755. WILL BRADLEY AND HIS ORCHESTRA. Variety, 30 min., NBC, 1940.

Orchestra leader Will Bradley as the host of a weekly program of music and songs. Carlotta Dale and Ray McKinley provided the songs and Will Bradley's orchestra supplied the music.

1756. THE WILL ROGERS SHOW. Commentary, 3 min., ABC, 1951.

A transcribed series of 130 three-minute capsule episodes featuring the wit of Will Rogers. The programs were made using recordings of various Will Rogers broadcasts. John Cannon did the announcing.

1757. WILLIE PIPER. Comedy, 30 min., ABC, 1946–1947; CBS, 1947–1948.

The story of Willie Piper, a naive, unpredictable young grocery clerk, and his misguided attempts to succeed in the business world. *Other regular characters:* Martha Piper, his wife; Mr. Bissell, their friend. Also known as *Tales of Willie Piper*.

Cast: Billy Redfield, Dick Nelson (*Willie Piper*); Elaine Rost, Jean Gillespie (*Martha Piper*); Stewart McIntosh (*Mr. Bissell*). ***Announcers:*** Win Elliot, Jack McCarthy. ***Music:*** Ralph Norman.

1758. THE WINDY CITY. Variety, 30 min., Mutual, 1949.

Lee Bennett as the host of a program of music and song from Chicago. The Dinning Sisters were the featured vocalists (assisted by guests) and Robert Trendler and his orchestra provided the music.

1759. WINGS OF DESTINY. Adventure, 30 min., NBC, 10/11/40 to 2/6/42.

A weekly series about the flying assignments of Steve Benton, a daring pilot. *Other regular characters:* Peggy Banning, his girlfriend; Brooklyn, his mechanic.

Cast: Carlton KaDell, John Hodiak (*Steve Benton*); Betty Arnold (*Peggy Banning*); Henry Hunter (*Brooklyn*). ***Announcer:*** Marvin Miller.

1760. WINNER TAKE ALL. Game, 30 min., CBS, 1946–1952.

Players competed in a three-match question-and-answer session wherein the contestant with the most correct answers received merchandise prizes.

Hosts: Bill Cullen, Ward Wilson, Clayton "Bud" Collyer. ***Announcers:*** Bern Bennett, Bill Cullen. ***Music:*** Chet Kingsbury.

1761. THE WITCH'S TALE. Anthology, 15 min., Mutual, 10/15/34 to 3/5/37.

Chilling stories narrated by Old Nancy, a 117-year-old witch, and her black cat Satan.

Cast: Alonzo Deen Cole (*Host*); Adelaide Fitz-Allen, Miriam Wolfe, Martha Wentworth (*Old Nancy*). ***Producer:*** Alonzo Deen Cole.

OPENING

ANNOUNCER: *The Witch's Tale*. The fascination for the eerie, weird, blood-chilling tales told by Old Nancy, the witch of Salem, and Satan, the wise black cat. They're waiting, waiting for you now.

1762. The Wizard of Odds. Game, 15 min., NBC, 1949–1953; CBS, 1953–1954.

Selected members of the studio audience were each given $5 bidding money. The highest-bidding player received a chance to answer a question. A correct response added money to his total based on previously announced odds; an incorrect answer deducted the bet amount. Winners were the highest cash scorers.

Host: Walter O'Keefe.

1763. The Wizard of Oz. Serial, 15 min., CBS, 9/25/33 to 3/23/34.

Dorothy Gale is a young girl who lives on a farm in Kansas with her Uncle Henry and Aunt Em. Dorothy is a lonely girl and her best friend is her dog, Toto. One day, without much warning, a cyclone appears. While attempting to save Toto (who has hidden under her bed), Dorothy—and her house—are swept away and carried to the Land of Oz (which is hidden from view by the Magic Desert). The house lands in Munchkin Land and kills the Wicked Witch of the East, who had kept the Munchkins in slavery. When Dorothy exits the house, she is hailed as "Your Mightiness" (for freeing Munchkin Land). Just then, "the noble lady who rules the North" appears to thank "the Little Sorceress." (Dorothy contends, "I'm not a sorceress. I'm just a little girl from Kansas who blew in on a cyclone and I want to get back as soon as possible.") The Magic Lady is Wanda, the Good Witch of the North (she dresses in white and silver). Good magic then takes over and melts the Wicked Witch of the East away. All that remain are her silver shoes—"and they belong to Dorothy," says Wanda. Dorothy refuses to take them until Wanda tells her, "You must, my child. There is a powerful spell within them, but I never knew what it was." Dorothy tries on the shoes—and they are a perfect fit (they make music when she walks). "Now we must figure a way for Dorothy to get home," says Wanda, and she waves her magic wand. It instructs Dorothy to seek out the Wizard of Oz, the ruler of all Oz, who lives in the Emerald City, which is situated in the center of Oz. But she must set out alone and follow roads that will lead her to encounter many shades of magic. "I don't think getting back to Kansas will be an easy matter," exclaims Dorothy as she begins her journey. Wanda assures her that she will be protected ("I'm only a good witch—my magic isn't strong enough to do more than protect Dorothy on her way to Oz"). Wanda then casts a spell on Dorothy's food basket—"You will always have food, no matter how much you take out." So Dorothy begins her journey, encountering the Scarecrow, the Tin Woodsman and the Cowardly Lion. Serialized stories follow her journey to seek the Wizard of Oz and the secret of the way back to Kansas, not knowing that all the time she had the secret with her—the silver shoes. Based on the story by L. Frank Baum. With the exception of Dorothy, the cast is not identified.

Cast: Nancy Kelly (*Dorothy*). ***Music:*** Charles Paul. ***Producer:*** John L. Coon.

OPENING

Announcer: *The Wizard of Oz*. The great gates of Oz swing open. Come one, come all, down the yellow brick road to the Emerald City with the weird and scary creatures of Oz. And now for the Oz story. Dorothy is the first person for you to meet because it is Dorothy who has all the adventures in Oz. She lives on a big farm way out on the prairie in Kansas with her Aunt Em and Uncle Henry...

CLOSING

Announcer: And so Dorothy has started off on her long, adventurous journey to the Wizard of Oz in Emerald City. Strange and wonderful are the sights in Oz and some of its magic is terrible indeed. Dorothy is protected. She has the Good Witch's kiss and the silver shoes and a basket which will always be filled. *The Wizard of Oz* will come to you again tomorrow at this same time. And now, there goes Dorothy and her new friends, marching away to the music of Charles Paul and his Munchkin Music Men. So good night. This is the Columbia Broadcasting System.

Note: All known sources list this program as being on NBC. The announcer clearly says the Columbia Broadcasting System (CBS) as transcribed above (which was taken directly from a tape of the program).

1764. The Woman. Variety, 30 min., Syndicated, 1946.

Songs, sketches and dramatizations based on features appearing in a magazine called *The Woman*.

Host: Lorna Farrell. ***Regulars:*** Rita Ascot,

Harry Elders, Bryna Raeburn, Sylvia Reigh. ***Announcer:*** John Reed King. ***Orchestra:*** Henry Sylvern.

1765. Woman from Nowhere. Serial, 15 min., CBS, 1944.

Dramatic events in the life of Faith Chandler, a beautiful and intelligent woman with a mysterious past. The program was sponsored by Ralston cereals, who proclaimed their "mature" star, Irene Rich, kept her glamorous figure by eating Ry-krisp cereal.

Cast: Irene Rich (*Faith Chandler*); Ray Montgomery (*Noel Chandler*). ***Also:*** Herb Allen, Dean Fossler, Bill Johnstone, Ann Sloane. ***Narrator:*** Gerald Mohr. ***Announcer:*** Marvin Miller.

1766. The Woman in My House. Serial, 15 min., NBC, 1951–1959.

Daily events in the lives of the Carters, a family of three who live on Elm Street in Miami.

Cast: Forrest Lewis (*James Carter*); Janet Scott (*Jesse Carter*); Peggy Webber (*Sandy Carter*). ***Announcer:*** Charles Lyon. ***Music:*** Paul Carson.

1767. Woman in White. Serial, 15 min., NBC, 1938–1940; CBS, 1940–1941; NBC, 1944–1948.

Dramatic events in the life of Karen Adams, a nurse in love with a young surgeon (Dr. Kirk Harding). In 1944, when the series returned after a three-year absence, Eileen Holmes became "the Woman in White" and Dr. Paul Burton her love interest.

Cast: Luise Barclay, Betty Lou Gerson, Betty Ruth Smith, Peggy Knudsen (*Karen Adams*); Karl Weber, Arthur Jacobson (*Dr. Kirk Harding*); Sarajane Wells (*Eileen Holmes*); Ken Griffin (*Dr. Paul Burton*). ***Announcer:*** Marvin Miller. ***Producer:*** Carl Webster.

1768. A Woman of America. Drama, 15 min., NBC, 1/25/43 to 9/24/43.

Events in the life of Prudence Dane, a widow and the mother of three children (Linda, Tommy and Johnny), as she struggled to begin a new life in Kansas following the Civil War. Her wagon train journey from western Pennsylvania to Kansas (led by wagon master Wade Douglas) was narrated by Margaret, the granddaughter of Prudence. See also the following title.

Cast: Anne Seymour (*Prudence Dane/Margaret*); Coletta McMahon (*Linda Dane*); Richard Leone (*Tommy Dane*); Ogden Miles (*Johnny Dane*); James Monks (*Wade Douglas*). ***Announcer:*** Frank Gallop. ***Organist:*** Richard Leibert.

1769. A Woman of America. Drama, 15 min., NBC, 9/27/43 to 6/21/46.

A revised version of the prior title that is set in modern times and relates dramatic incidents in the life of Prudence Dane, the editor of a newspaper. In both versions, the intent was to dramatize the struggles of the American woman.

Cast: Florence Freeman (*Prudence Dane*). ***Announcer:*** Frank Gallop. ***Organist:*** Richard Leibert.

1770. Woman of Courage. Serial, 15 min., CBS, 1940–1942.

Dramatic events in the life of Martha Jackson, her crippled husband Jim and their children Lucy and Tommy, who live in the small town of Farmington.

Cast: Selena Royle, Alice Frost (*Martha Jackson*); Albert Hayes (*Jim Jackson*); Joan Tetzel (*Lucy Jackson*); Larry Robinson (*Tommy Jackson*).

1771. Women's Club. Human Interest, 15 min., CBS, 1946.

A daily program of information for women with Isobel Leighton as the host and George Byron as the announcer.

1772. Wonderful City. Human Interest, 25 min., CBS, 1953.

The format revolved around the theory of New York City's warm heart and presented people with worthy or human causes.

Host: Harry Wismer. ***Vocalists:*** Jimmy Carroll, Lois Hunt. ***Orchestra:*** Nat Brandwynne.

1773. The Woody Herman Show. Variety, 30 min., ABC, 1945–1946.

A weekly program of music and songs sponsored by Wildroot Creme Oil.

Host: Woody Herman. ***Regulars:*** Bill Harris, Chubby Jackson, Joe "Flip" Phillips, Frances Wayne. ***Orchestra:*** Woody Herman.

OPENING

ANNOUNCER: Yes, it's *The Woody Herman Show*, music and fun by America's band number one, brought to you by the makers of Wild Root Creme Oil for the hair.

1774. THE WOOLWORTH HOUR. Variety, 60 min., CBS, 1955–1957.

A weekly program of music and songs sponsored by F.W. Woolworth and Company. Actor Donald Woods was the host. Giselle MacKenzie and Robert Merrill provided the songs and Percy Faith and his orchestra supplied the music.

1775. THE WORLD'S GREATEST SHORT STORIES. Anthology, 15 min., NBC, 1946.

Dramatic presentations based on great short stories with Nelson Olmsted as the host and narrator. John Holten did the announcing.

1776. X MINUS ONE. Anthology, 30 min., NBC, 4/22/55 to 1/19/58.

Science fiction dramas culled from *Galaxy* magazine or written by top name genre authors. A revised version of *Dimension X* (see entry).

Host: Norman Rose. ***Announcers:*** Fred Collins, Don Pardo, Bob Warren.

OPENING

ANNOUNCER: Count down for blast-off: X minus five ... four ... three ... two ... *X Minus One*! Fire! [A rocket is heard blasting off.] From the far horizons of the unknown come transcribed tales of new dimensions in time and space. These are stories of the future; adventures in which you'll live in a million could-be years on a thousand may-be worlds. The National Broadcasting Company in cooperation with *Galaxy* science fiction magazine presents [in echo effect] *X-x-x-x Minus-minus-minus One-one-one*. Tonight, the Mark Clifton story, "Star Bright."

CLOSING

ANNOUNCER: Tonight, by transcription, *X Minus One* has brought you "Star Bright," a story from the pages of *Galaxy* written by Mark Clifton and adapted for radio by George Lefferts. Your announcer, Fred Collins. *X Minus One* is an NBC Network Radio production.

1777. THE XAVIER CUGAT SHOW. Variety, 30 min., NBC, 1941–1943.

A weekly program of rumba music with orchestra leader Xavier Cugat as the host. The regulars were Carmen Castillo, Bob Graham, Yvette Harris, Bert Parks, Lina Romay, Nita Rose, the Art Ballinger Chorus and the Don Rodney Chorus. Xavier Cugat's orchestra supplied the music. Also known as *Casa Cugat* and *Rumba Review*.

1778. YESTERDAY AND TODAY. Variety, 30 min., NBC, 1942.

A weekly program of music and songs with orchestra leader Blue Barron as the host. Clyde Burke, Charlie Fisher, Billy Kover, Alec Templeton and the Blue Barron Glee Club were the regulars. Blue Barron's orchestra supplied the music.

1779. YOU ARE THERE. Anthology, 30 min., CBS, 7/7/47 to 6/12/49.

Recreations of historical events wherein listeners were given eyewitness accounts by CBS news correspondents using modern broadcasting techniques. Originally titled *CBS Is There*; served as the basis for the *You Are There* television series.

Reporters: Ned Calmer, John Daly, Don Hollenbeck, Quincy Howe, Harry Marble, Ken Roberts. ***Announcers:*** Stuart Metz. Ken Roberts.

OPENING (from 12/23/48)

VOICE: March 9th, 1862, Washington, D.C. *You Are There*.

ANNOUNCER: Washington on the dawn of the day that will see the decisive naval battle between the North and the South, between the Federals and the Confederates. CBS takes you back 86 years to the surprise engagement that ushered in the new era of sea warfare. All things are as they were then except for one thing. When CBS is there—

VOICE: *You Are There*.

ANNOUNCER: *You Are There*, produced and directed by Robert Lewis Shayon, is based on authentic historic facts and quotations. And now—

VOICE: CBS news in Washington and Don Hollenbeck [who would then begin reporting "The Story of the *Monitor* and the *Merrimack*"].

CLOSING

VOICE: March 9th, 1862, the *Monitor* stops the *Merrimack* and the Union fleet is saved.

Groucho Marx (right) was introduced on *You Bet Your Life* by George Fenneman.

ANNOUNCER: You have been listening to "The *Monitor* and the *Merrimack*," another broadcast in the series *You Are There*, produced and directed by Robert Lewis Shayon. Next week—

VOICE: July 21, 1891, "The Surrender of Sitting Bull" and *You Are There*.

ANNOUNCER: This is CBS, where 99 million people gather each week, the Columbia Broadcasting System.

1780. YOU BET YOUR LIFE. Game, 30 min., ABC, 1947–1949; CBS, 1949–1950; NBC, 1950–1956.

A couple, chosen from the studio audience, is first interviewed in a comic fashion by the host. Following this, they receive $20 (later increased to $100) to bet on their ability to answer questions in a previously chosen category (which contained questions valued from $10 to $100). The players choose a question by its value and wager all or part of their betting money. A correct response adds the bet amount to their total; an incorrect answer deducts the bet amount from the total. Their total at the end of four questions is calculated. Two additional couples compete in the same manner. The couple with the highest cash score receives the opportunity to answer the bonus question (a general-knowledge question that begins at $500 and increases by that amount with each couple's failure to answer it). Players could also win a merchandise prize (an Apollo 16mm sound projector) if they said "The Secret Word" while being interviewed (a common word that the announcer revealed at the beginning of the program; $100 was later substituted for the projector). Host Groucho Marx wanted to make each program as funny as possible. He taped for an hour; the edited, 30-minute broadcast reflected the best segments of each show. Served as the basis for the television series of the same title.

Host: Groucho Marx. ***Announcers:*** George Fenneman, Jack Slattery. ***Orchestra:*** Jerry Fielding, Billy May, Jack Meakin, Stan Myersand. ***Producer:*** John Guedel.

OPENING (from 4/7/49)

ANNOUNCER: Ladies and gentlemen, the secret word for tonight is head, h-e-a-d.

GROUCHO: Really?

ANNOUNCER: *You Bet Your Life.* Elgin American, creators of America's most beautiful compacts, smartest cigarette cases, and finest dresser sets, presents Groucho Marx in the Elgin American show, *You Bet Your Life*, the comedy-quiz series produced and transcribed in Hollywood. And here's that sterling Elgin American, the one, the only—

AUDIENCE: Groucho!

GROUCHO: Welcome to Elgin American compacts, Mr. Marx. Oh, that's me, Groucho Marx. [Groucho would then begin the show following audience applause with "Thank you, thank you. Tonight we have $1,000 for one of our couples."]

CLOSING

ANNOUNCER: The Elgin American show, *You Bet Your Life*, is a John Guedel production, transcribed from Hollywood, directed by Bob Dwan and Bernie Smith. Music by Jerry Fielding. Remember, next week's big question pays $1,500. Be sure to tune in next Wednesday night at this time for *You Bet Your Life* starring Groucho Marx, presented by the makers of America's most beautiful compacts, smartest cigarette cases and finest dresser sets. This is ABC, the American Broadcasting Company.

1781. YOUNG DR. MALONE. Serial, 15 min., NBC Blue, 1939–1940; CBS, 1940–1942; NBC, 1942–1943; CBS, 1943–1960.

Dramatic events in the life of Dr. Jerry Malone, a physician at the Three Oaks Medical Center. Served as the basis for the television series of the same title.

Cast: Alan Bunce, Carl Frank, Charles Irving, Sandy Becker (*Jerry Malone*); Elizabeth Reller, Barbara Weeks (*Ann Malone*); Bill Lipton (*Dr. David Malone*); Joan Lazer, Rosemary Rice (*Jill Malone*); Nancy Coleman (*Alice Hughes*); Richard Coogan (*Robert Hughes*); James Van Dyk (*Dr. Dunham*); Richard Barrows (*Dr. Harrison*); Ethel Morrison (*Daisy*); Elspeth Eric (*Marsha*); Paul McGrath (*Dr. Crawford*); Betty Pratt (*Christine Taylor*); Joan Banks (*Phyllis*); Jone Allison, Joan Alexander, Gertrude Warner (*Tracy Malone*); Donna Keith (*Lynne*); Isobel Elsom (*Jessie Hughes*); Helene Dumas (*Veronica*); Larry Haines (*Carl Ward*); Jack Manning (*David Crawford*); Janet McGraw (*Lucille Crawford*). ***Announcer:*** Ron Rawson. ***Organist:*** Charles Paul.

OPENING

ANNOUNCER: And now CBS Radio presents *Young Dr. Malone* featuring Sandy Becker.

1782. YOUNG LOVE. Comedy, 30 min., CBS, 1949–1950.

The campus of Midwestern University was the setting for a romantic comedy about Jerry and Janet, students who marry against school regulations, then struggle to keep it a secret (she lived in the dorm; he resided in the frat house). *Other regular characters:* Molly Belle, Janet's roommate; Prof. Mitchell and Dean Ferguson.

Cast: Jimmy Lydon (*Jimmy*); Janet Waldo (*Janet*); Shirley Mitchell (*Molly Belle*); John Heistand (*Professor Mitchell*); Herb Butterfield (*Dean Ferguson*). ***Also:*** Jerry Hausner, Hal March. ***Announcer:*** Roy Rowan.

1783. YOUNG WIDDER BROWN. Serial, 15 min., NBC, 1938–1956.

Dramatic events in the life of Ellen Brown, a widow and the owner of a tea shop in the small town of Simpsonville.

Cast: Florence Freeman, Wendy Drew (*Ellen Brown*); Ned Wever (*Dr. Anthony Lorring*); Toni Gilman (*Marjorie Williams*); Ethel Remey, Riza Joyce (*Victoria Lorring*); Joan Tompkins, Helen Shields (*Joyce Turner*); Clayton "Bud" Collyer (*Peter Turner*); Arline Blackburn (*Barbara Storm*); Tom Donnelley (*Mark Brown*); Marilyn Erskine (*Jane Brown*); House Jameson, Eric Dressler, Alexander Scourby (*Herb Temple*); Bess McCammon (*Olivia*); Dick Van Patten (*Mark*); Eva Parnell (*Alicia*); Agnes Young, Lorene Scott, Alice Yourman (*Maria Hawkins*); Charita Bauer (*Millie Baxter*); Frank Lovejoy (*Roger Power*). ***Announcer:*** George Ansbro. ***Music:*** John Winters. ***Producers:*** Anne Hummert, Frank Hummert.

OPENING

ANNOUNCER: Time now for *Young Widder Brown*, brought to you by the makers of Aerowax. *Young Widder Brown*, the story of the age-old conflict between a mother's duty and a woman's heart.

1784. YOUR AMERICA. Anthology, 30 min., NBC, 1944; Mutual, 1944–1945.

Programs depicting the development of the American West sponsored by the Union Pacific

Railroad. Nelson Olmsted and Elden Westley were the hosts and narrators. Ray Clark conducted an interview segment with railroad officials and Josef Koestner and his orchestra provided the music.

1785. YOUR DREAM HAS COME TRUE. Game, 30 min., NBC, 1940–1941.

Ian Keith served as the host and Verne Smith did the announcing for a game show that offered contestants chances at their heart's desire if their name was chosen from "The Wishing Well."

1786. YOUR FAMILY AND MINE. Serial, 15 min., NBC, 1938–1939; CBS, 1939–1940.

A light dramatic series about an unsuccessful inventor (Matthew Wilbur) and his family (his wife Winifred and their children Judy and Ken).

Cast: Bill Adams (*Matthew Wilbur*); Lucille Ward (*Winifred Wilbur*); Joan Tompkins (*Judy Wilbur*); Bill Lipton (*Ken Wilbur*). ***Announcer:*** Ford Bond. ***Producer:*** Henry Souvaine.

1787. YOUR HIT PARADE. Variety, 30, 45 and 60 min. versions, NBC Red, 1935–1936; NBC Blue, 1936; NBC Red, 1936–1937; CBS, 1936–1947; NBC, 1947–1953.

Various renditions of the top songs of the week as determined by record and sheet music sales and by songs played over the air and in juke boxes. Sponsored by Lucky Strike cigarettes and the basis for the television version of the same title. Guests hosted the series.

Recurring Host: Frank Sinatra (1943–1945; 1947–1949). ***Regulars:*** Bonnie Baker, Buddy Clark, Jeff Clark, Beryl Davis, Doris Day, Gogo DeLys, Joan Edwards, Georgia Gibbs, Marie Green, Johnny Hauser, Kay Lorraine, Margaret McCrea, Lanny Ross, Andy Russell, Dinah Shore, Kay Thompson, Lawrence Tibbett, Bea Wain, Jerry Wayne, Bonnie Lou Williams, Eileen Wilson. ***Chorus:*** Ken Lane, Lyn Murray, Mark Warnow. ***Orchestra:*** Al Goodman, Johnny Green, Lennie Hayton, Richard Himber, Carl Hoff, Leo Reisman, Freddie Rich, Raymond Scott, Harry Sosnik, Axel Stordahl, Orrin Tucker, Mark Warnow. ***Organist:*** Ethel Smith. ***Commercial Pitchman:*** F.E. Boone, Speed Riggs.

OPENING

ANNOUNCER: Men who know tobacco best, it's Lucky Strike, two to one.

VOICE (over telegraph sounds): L.S.M.F.T., L.S.M.F.T.

ANNOUNCER: You said it, Lucky Strike means fine tobacco, so round, so firm, so fully packed, so free and easy on the draw. Lucky Strike presents *Your Hit Parade* starring Frank Sinatra, with Axel Stordahl, the Lucky Strike Orchestra, Beryl Davis, Ken Lane and the Hit Paraders, and starring Frank Sinatra [who would begin the show with a song].

Note: A new version of the series appeared on CBS (1955–1959) with Andre Baruch presenting the top tunes via recordings.

1788. YOUR HIT PARADE ON PARADE. Variety, 30 min., CBS, 1949.

The top tunes previously presented over the 14-year period in which Lucky Strike sponsored *Your Hit Parade* on NBC were showcased.

Host: Russ Case. ***Regulars:*** Stuart Foster, Marjorie Hughes. ***Announcer:*** Basil Reysdael. ***Orchestra:*** Russ Case.

1789. YOUR HOME BEAUTIFUL. Women, 15 min., Mutual, 1950.

Home decorating and furnishing advice with actress Vicki Vola as the host. Johnny Thompson was her assistant; Bob Shepherd did the announcing and Paul Taubman and his orchestra provided the music.

1790. YOUR LUCKY STRIKE. Variety, 30 min., CBS, 1948–1949.

A showcase for undiscovered talent sponsored by Lucky Strike cigarettes. Don Ameche served as the host and Frank Martin did the announcing.

1791. YOUR PARLOR PLAYHOUSE. Variety, 30 min., Mutual, 1937.

A weekly program of music and songs with William Bouchey, Elmore Gailey, Roweena Williams and the Lovely Lady Quartet. Norman Ross did the announcing and music was provided by Robert Trendler and his orchestra.

1792. YOUR RADIO THEATER. Anthology, 55 min., NBC, 1955.

A weekly series of dramatizations hosted by Herbert Marshall. Don Stanley did the announcing.

1793. Your Song and Mine. Variety, 30 min., CBS, 1948.

Thomas L. Thomas as the host of a weekly program of music and songs. Mary Martha Briney, Felix Knight, Charles Meynante and Edward Slattery were the regulars. Andre Baruch did the announcing and Enrico Wahl and his orchestra provided the music.

1794. Your Unseen Friend. Anthology, 30 min., CBS, 1936–1937.

A weekly program of dramatizations that were designed to help solve problems submitted by listeners. Maurice Joachim played "Your Unseen Friend," a narrator who interpreted the stories and gave advice to the listener who submitted the problem.

1795. You're the Expert. Game, 15 min., CBS, 1941.

Six players, chosen from the studio audience, answered a problem (for example, "Should you tell your best friend that her husband is getting involved with another woman?"). The player with the best response, as determined by a guest judge, won $25; $10 was awarded to the player with the second-best response; and $5 to the player with the third.

Host: Fred Uttal. ***Announcer:*** Del Sharbutt.

1796. Yours for a Song. Variety, 25 min., Mutual, 1948–1949.

Vocalist Jane Froman as the host of a weekly program of music and songs. Robert Weede was the featured regular; Bernard Dudley did the announcing; and Alfredo Antonini and his orchestra provided the music.

1797. Yours Truly, Johnny Dollar. Drama, 15 and 30 min. versions, CBS, 2/11/49 to 9/30/62.

Johnny Dollar is a highly priced freelance insurance investigator (although he works most often for the Continental Adjustment Bureau at 418 Elizabeth Street in Hartford, Connecticut). Johnny would go anywhere for a client—if they would pay his expenses. He has a keen, analytical mind, is a confirmed bachelor and has a nose for murder. Stories, first presented as a 30-minute drama, then as a 15-minute daily serial (complete in five episodes), followed Johnny's adventures as he investigated cases, always keeping a detailed accounting of his expenses (he always ended his report to the insurance company with "Yours Truly, Johnny Dollar"). Johnny also worked for the following companies (also located in Hartford): The Trinity Mutual Insurance Company, the Universal Adjustments Company, Amatron Northern Trust Company, the Continental Adjustment Bureau and Ambassador Casualty Life and Insurance.

Cast: Charles Russell, Edmond O'Brien, John Lund, Bob Bailey, Bob Readick, Mandel Kramer (*Johnny Dollar*). ***Announcers:*** Charles Lyon, Roy Rowan, Bob Stevenson. ***Music:*** Eddie Dunstedter, Rick Marino, Leith Stevens. ***Producers:*** Gordon P. Hughes, Jack Johnstone.

OPENING (Charles Russell episodes)

Announcer: This is another adventure of America's fabulous freelance insurance investigator Johnny Dollar, starring Charles Russell. Insurance investigator Johnny Dollar is not only an expert at making out his expense account, he's an absolute genius.

Johnny: Expense account submitted by special investigator Johnny Dollar to home office, Ambassador Life and Insurance Company, Hartford, Connecticut. Attention Franklin Healey, General Manager. The following is an accounting of my expenditures during my assignment as bodyguard to your policyholder, Anne Connelly...

CLOSING

Johnny: Item eight, $55.10 air fare, Milwaukee to Hartford. Expense account total, $845.30. Signed, Yours truly, Johnny Dollar.

Announcer: *Yours Truly, Johnny Dollar* is produced and directed by Gordon P. Hughes and stars Charles Russell. Be sure to be with us at this same time next week when another unusual expense account is handed in by—

Johnny Dollar: Yours truly, Johnny Dollar.

OPENING (Bob Bailey episodes)

Announcer: From Hollywood, it's time now for *Yours Truly, Johnny Dollar*. Tonight and every weekday night, Bob Bailey and the transcribed adventures of the man with the action-packed expense account, America's fabulous freelance insurance investigator—

Johnny: Yours truly, Johnny Dollar. Expense account submitted by special investigator Johnny Dollar to the Continental Adjustment Bureau, 418 Elizabeth Avenue, Hartford, Connecticut. The following is an accounting of my expenditures during my investigation of "The Forbes Matter."

CLOSING

JOHNNY (after summing up a case): What makes a man steal? Everybody's tried to answer that question at one time or another. Tomorrow I'll take a crack at it. Join us, won't you? Yours truly, Johnny Dollar.

ANNOUNCER: Be sure to join us tomorrow night, same time, same station, for the next exciting episode of *Yours Truly, Johnny Dollar*. Roy Rowan speaking.

OPENING (Mandel Kramer episodes)

ANNOUNCER: The CBS Radio Network brings you Mandel Kramer in the exciting adventures of the man with the action-packed expense account, America's fabulous freelance insurance investigator—

JOHNNY: Yours truly, Johnny Dollar. Expense accounts submitted by special investigator Johnny Dollar to the Trinity Mutual Insurance Company, Hartford Connecticut. Following is an account of the expenses incurred during my investigation of "The Phony Phone Matter."

Note: Dick Powell played Johnny Dollar in the audition show for CBS in 1948 but gave up the role to star in NBC's *Richard Diamond, Private Detective*.

1798. YOUTH VS. AGE. Game, 30 min., NBC Blue, 1939–1940.

Two teams competed, the Adult vs. the Juvenile. A question submitted by a listener was read; the first team to press a buzzer signal received a chance to answer. One point was scored for each correct answer. The highest scoring team received a cash prize (one dollar for each point they scored).

Host: Cal Tinney. ***Announcer:*** Hugh McDerevy.

1799. YVETTE. Variety, 15 min., NBC, 1940.

Singer Yvette Harris as the host of a program of music and songs with Ben Grauer as the announcer.

1800. THE ZANE GREY THEATER. Anthology, 30 min., Mutual, 1947–1948.

Western dramatizations hosted by Tex Throne, a pony express rider made famous in stories by writer Zane Grey. Vic Perrin first played Tex; he was replaced by Don McLaughlin a year later.

1801. THE ZERO HOUR. Anthology, 30 min., Syndicated, 1973.

A daily series of mystery and suspense presentations hosted by Rod Serling. Ferrante and Teicher provided the music and Elliott Lewis was the producer-director.

1802. THE ZIEGFELD FOLLIES OF THE AIR. Variety, 60 min., CBS, 4/3/32 to 6/26/32; 2/22/36 to 6/6/36.

Producer Florenz Ziegfeld originally hosted a series of lavish variety acts featuring Fanny Brice, Jack Pearl and Will Rogers. Eddie Dowling did the announcing and Al Goodman and his orchestra provided the music. Four years later, another short-lived version appeared with James Melton as the host and Al Goodman again supplying the music. Top name guests appeared on the program.

Appendix: Some "Lost" Programs

An alphabetical listing of radio series about which little is known.

1803. CARTON OF SMILES (NBC, 1944–1945). Variety with comedian Henny Youngman, vocalist Carol Bruce and the orchestra of Eddy Howard. Tom Shirley did the announcing and Raleigh cigarettes sponsored the show.

1804. THE CROUPIER (ABC, 1949–1950). Suspense stories with Vincent Price as the host and narrator.

1805. DICK DARING'S ADVENTURES (NBC, 1933–1934). Children's program about a resourceful high school boy (Dick Daring, played by Merrill Fugit) and his mentor, Coach Greatguy (Donald Briggs).

1806. THE DICK ROBERTSON SHOW (Mutual, 1949). A variety series with orchestra leader Dick Robertson as the host.

1807. DICK STEELE, BOY REPORTER (NBC, 1934–1935). Revised version of *Dick Daring's Adventures* that found the hero (now Dick Steele) as a juvenile newspaper reporter. Merrill Fugit again played Dick Steele.

1808. ELECTRIC THEATER (CBS, 1948–1949). A weekly anthology series featuring Helen Hayes as the host and star. The Electric Companies of America sponsored the program.

1809. EMPIRE BUILDERS (NBC Blue, 1928–1931). Varying adventure stories sponsored by the Great Northern Railroad. Don Ameche and Harvey Hayes were recurring performers.

1810. FLYWHEEL, SHYSTER AND FLYWHEEL (NBC, 1932–1933). Comedy about a less-than-honorable lawyer named Waldorf T. Flywheel (Groucho Marx) and his fumbling assistant, Emmanuel Ravelli (Chico Marx).

1811. FOLLOW THE MOON (NBC, CBS, 1936–1938). Daily adventure serial about Clay Bannister (Nick Dawson) and Jean Page (Elsie Hitz).

1812. FRANK WATANABE AND THE HONORABLE ARCHIE (NBC, 1930–1933). Comedy with Eddie Holden as Frank Watanabe, the Japanese houseboy to the Honorable Archie Chiselberg (Reginald Sheffield).

1813. GENERAL MOTORS CONCERTS (NBC, 1934–1937). Classical music featuring a guest conductor appearing with the NBC Symphony Orchestra.

1814. GRANDPA BURTON (NBC, 1935–1937). Dramatic skits in which a grandfather relates stories to his grandson. Bill Barr played all the roles.

1815. THE HONEYMOONERS (NBC Blue, 1934–1937). Eddie Albert and his wife Grace in a comedy-drama about a young married couple.

1816. HOTEL FOR PETS (NBC, 1954–1956). Daily serial about a veterinarian (Charlotte Manson) and an ex–postal worker (Frank McHugh) who run an animal shelter.

1817. THE JEDDO HIGHLANDERS (NBC Blue, 1927–1930). Music and songs sponsored by Jeddo Coal and hosted by Milton Cross.

1818. THE JOAN BENOIT SHOW (NBC, 1941). Variety series with vocalist Joan Benoit as the host.

1819. JUNIOR NURSE CORPS (NBC Blue, 1936–1937). Daily children's serial about a teenage nurse named Clara Barton (played by Sunda Love).

1820. KATIE'S DAUGHTER (NBC, 1947–1948). Serial about theatrical life with Kenneth Banghart, Martin Blaine, Grace Cooper and Marie Geyer.

1821. LAZY DAN (CBS, 1933–1936). Music and songs with tenor Irving Kaufman (who was known as "Lazy Dan, the Minstrel Man").

1822. LITTLE JACK LITTLE (NBC, CBS, 1930–1935). Variety with "Little" Jack Little

(Leonard Little), a singer pianist who stood five feet, four inches, and was billed as "Radio's Cheerful Little Earful."

1823. Louisa (NBC, 1950–1951). Comedy with Spring Byington and Edmund Gwenn.

1824. Maverick Jim (Mutual, 1934). Western with Artells Dickson as Maverick Jim.

1825. Mickey of the Circus (CBS, 1935). Life in the circus with Chester Stratton (Mickey), Betty Garde (Mamie) and Gretchen Davidson (Clara).

1826. The Mighty Show (CBS, 1938–1939). Circus life with Agnes Moorehead (Mrs. Hutchinson), Helen Lewis (Sally) and Anne Boley (Ruth).

1827. Mike Malloy, Private Eye (ABC, NBC, 1953–1957). Steve Brodie as a tough private detective named Mike Malloy.

1828. Mortimer Gooch (CBS, 1936–1937). Comedy serial with Bob Bailey as the trouble-prone Mortimer Gooch and Louise Fitch as Betty Lou.

1829. My Good Wife (NBC, 1949). Comical events in the lives of a young married couple played by Arlene Francis and John Conte.

1830. RCA Radiotrons (NBC Blue, 1926–1927). John Charles Thomas as the host of a program of concert music.

1831. The RCA Victor Hour (NBC Blue, 1927–1930). Tenor John McCormack as host to a program of concert music.

1832. Sally of the Talkies (NBC, 1934–1935). Marjorie Hanson as Sally Madison, a young actress struggling to become a star.

1833. Satan's Waitin' (CBS, 1950). Dramas that depict the Devil as the plot manipulator. Frank Graham was the host.

1834. Tony and Gus (NBC, 1935). Serial about two immigrants: Tony (Mario Chamlee), an Italian who yearned to become a singer; and Gus (George Frame Brown), a Swede who wanted to become a boxer.

1835. We Are Always Young (Mutual, 1941). Daily serial about a composer (William Janney) who worked as a cab driver.

Index

References are to entry numbers.